Robert Simpson

Traditions of the Covenanters

Or, gleanings among the mountains

Robert Simpson

Traditions of the Covenanters
Or, gleanings among the mountains

ISBN/EAN: 9783337317362

Printed in Europe, USA, Canada, Australia, Japan

Cover: Foto ©Andreas Hilbeck / pixelio.de

More available books at **www.hansebooks.com**

TRADITIONS

OF

THE COVENANTERS:

OR,

GLEANINGS AMONG THE MOUNTAINS.

BY

THE REV. ROBERT SIMPSON, D.D.,

SANQUHAR.

"They wandered in deserts, and in mountains, and in dens and caves of the earth."

Edinburgh:

GALL AND INGLIS, 6 GEORGE STREET.

PREFACE TO FIRST EDITION.

The collecting of the following anecdotes respecting our persecuted ancestors was at first purely incidental. The editor of the
" Weekly Christian Teacher " having requested of the author a
communication for his miscellany, there was sent to him a paper
containing two or three anecdotes, entitled " Reminiscences of
the Covenanters," and after its transmission no more was con·
templated. At the further solicitation of the conductor of that
periodical, however, a second paper was prepared, and then a
third. At length the idea was entertained that something more
than a few stray notices of the worthies of the Covenant might,
perchance, be gleaned in the neighbourhood of the author's
residence, as the locality is well known to have been the frequent
resort of the suffering wanderers during the dark and protracted
period of the Church's affliction in Scotland. The attempt was
successful, and resembled the striking of the enchanted ground
with the mystic wand, when innumerable *elfins*, formerly invisible, started up all around. The writer, though fully aware
that the memory of not a few incidents which happened in
those trying times was still retained by the peasantry among the
mountains and glens of the district, had yet no idea of the vast
number of traditional stories that really existed. Having been
made aware of the fact, therefore, his object was to collect and
arrange them in the best manner he could, and then to publish
them in a serial form.

The sources from which these Traditions are drawn are chiefly
the descendants of the persons themselves to whom the incidents
refer. They have been retained as heirlooms in the families of
the worthy men who suffered so much in the cause of truth and
righteousness. This circumstance affords a strong guarantee
for the fidelity and correctness of the narratives as a whole,
although some attendant circumstances may probably, in the
lapse of three generations, have varied in the telling. They are
all of them precisely in keeping with the times to which they
refer. In some cases the same anecdote has been communicated
by different persons in places widely separate, and yet the story,
with a slight variation, was exactly the same—a further proof

that the Traditions are, in the main, faithful. It would seem, however, from the complexion of many of them, that the occurrences related took place mostly after the *seventy-nine*, the year of Drumclog and Bothwell, and of the archbishop's death, the consequent severities of which being heightened by the Sanquhar Declaration, and the skirmish at Airmoss.

The locality which it has been attempted to glean, is *that* chiefly in the midst of which Sanquhar is situated, assuming this place as a centre, and stretching out in a radius of twenty or thirty miles in extent on all sides. It was to this locality, as Wodrow informs us, that great numbers of the wanderers from the more level and exposed parts of the country resorted. "Multitudes," says the historian, "were hiding and wandering in mountains and caves, and not a few from other places of the kingdom had retired to the mountainous parts of Galloway and Nithsdale."

It was not the design of the writer to compose *tales* founded on the incidents, but simply to present the Tradition in its native simplicity and truth. It would be an easy matter to invest these anecdotes with imaginative interest; but then that would destroy their character as traditionary realities. It is the design of this collection to preserve the memory of some of those good men in the inferior ranks of society, whose worth and whose sufferings have not hitherto been recorded. Their names, though those of plain, unlettered men, do not deserve to perish ; and their posterity may, by contemplating the virtues of their ancestors, be stimulated to emulate their godliness.

That the work may be the means of exciting those who read it to a special care about their best interests, and to a stedfast and consistent adherence to the cause of the Redeemer, is the sincere prayer of

Their servant in the Gospel,

R. S.

CONTENTS.

GLOSSARY

OF CELTIC NAMES IN THE TRADITIONS.

THE following names are chiefly from the sister dialects of the British and Scoto-Irish speech. Some of these names, perhaps, may not now appear so significant as when first employed eighteen or twenty centuries ago, because the face of the country has since that period undergone a variety of changes. It may also be remarked, that in some instances a whole district is now called by a name which, in remote times, was given to an individual spot within a wide locality ; and, therefore, in such cases, the propriety of the general appellation may not be so plainly discernible. In every instance, however, the name was strikingly appropriate and descriptive when originally imposed by the Celtic people.

Ae, water.
Afton, a stream.
Airdoch, the little height.
Airds, high.
Al, water.
Alwen, the clear stream.
Anwoth, *an* water, *wath* a hawthorn.
Arran, the heights.
Auchen, the little field.
Auchenbraith, the field of barley.
Auchencairn, the field of the cairn.
Auchencloich, the field of stones.
Auchengee, the goose field.
Auchengeith, the windy field.
Auchengower, the field of the goats.
Auchengrouch, the field of curds.
Auchensauch, the field of willows.
Auchentagart, the field of the priest.
Auchlochan, field of the little loch.
Avon, a river.
Ayr, the clear or shallow stream.
Ballachin, the head of the pass.
Ballagan, the dwelling in the hollow.
Balmaclellan, M'Lellan's town.
Baraby, the top of the little cliff.
Barr, an eminence.
Barskimming, great bend of water.
Beith, a birch tree.
Bellopath, *bel* outrage, and *au* water.
Bellybught, bught beside the broom.
Benbeoch, the bee hill.
Benholt, the wooded hill.
Bennet, the church hill.
Biggar, the little clear stream ; or *bogar*, the boggy place.
Binns, the hillocks
Blagannach, the milking field
Blednoch, the smooth hill.
Bodsberry, the gled's hill.
Caerlowrie, Lowrie's fort.
Cairn, a heap of stones.
Cairnsmoor, the great cairn.
Cairntable, the chieftain's cairn.
Calder, the dark stream (*dur* water).
Caldow, the dark forest.
Cambusnethan, *camus* bend of a river
Camlarg, the crooked *larg* or shank.

Carco, or Carcaw, winding hollow.
Carmacoup, Cormac's hope.
Carrick, a rock.
Carron, the winding stream.
Carsphairn, *carse* swamp, *fearn* alder
Cesnock, the dark hill.
Clauchrie, the red stone.
Clyde, the sheltered stream.
Cog, a cuckoo.
Colline, the wooded water.
Colliston, the town in the wood.
Colven, the hazel hill.
Craigdarroch, the rock of the oak.
Craighit, the rocky height.
Craigturrach, the towering rock.
Crawford, the cattle shelter.
Crawick, the habitation of crows.
Cree, the muddy stream.
Crichope, the rocky hope.
Croglin, the rocky stream, or the cross by the stream.
Cronberry, the round hill.
Crossgellioch, the white cross.
Cruffel, the crow height.
Cumberhead, *cummer* water meeting.
Cumnock, the hollow of the hill.
Dalblair, the battle field.
Daleceles, the field of the church.
Dalgarnock, the field abounding in underwood.
Dalhanna, the green or good field.
Daljig, *dal* field, *jig* ditch or marsh.
Dalmellington, the field of the mill, and *ton* a tower.
Dalquhairn, the field of the cairn.
Dalricket, field of king's slaughter
Dalry, the King's dale.
Dalswinton, Swinton's vale.
Dalveen, the white field.
Dalwick, the village in the dale.
Dalyell, the white field.
Dalzien, daisy field, or John's field.
Dar, or Dair, or Deer, an oak.
Darnoid, the oak wood.
Dee, *dhu*, the dark river.
Deuch, the dark stream.
Doon, the dark lake or stream.

Douglas, dark stream, or grey vale.
Dramore, the great ridge.
Dreva, a dwelling.
Drumclog, the ridge of the stone.
Drumcloich, the stony ridge.
Drumlanrig, ridge on bank of river.
Drummelzier, the dwelling on ridge.
Dumbarton, the fort of the Britons.
Dumfries, *dun* hill, *freas* brushwood.
Dunasken, hill at the water head.
Duneaton, the whinny height.
Durisdeer, the door of the forest.
Earnsallach, *ern* sloe, *sallach* willow.
Elliock, the little rock.
Elvan, the clear stream.
Enock, *ae* water, and *knach* a hillock.
Enterkin the head of the pass.
Ettrick, a wilderness.
Evan, a river.
Fenwick, the village in the fens.
Fewchaw, the cold or wooded water.
Fingland, the white glen.
Fordonmullach, fortlet on the hill.
Garrick fell, the rocky height.
Garrion gill, *garrion* a thicket, and *gill* a water-course.
Garple, the rough or short stream.
Glasgow, *glas* dark, *gau* a valley.
Glaspen, the grey hill.
Glenae, the glen of the *ac*.
Glen Aylmer, Aylmer's glen.
Glenblaith, the flowery glen.
Glencrosh, the red glen.
Glendouren, the glen of the oaks.
Glendyne, the deep glen.
Glenglas, the grey glen.
Glengonar, the glen of the gold sand.
Glenim, the butter glen.
Glenkens, the glen of the Ken.
Glenkill, the kirk glen.
Glenluce, the sunny vale.
Glenmaddie, the fox or the wolf glen.
Glenmead, the wooded glen.
Glenmuir, moor glen, or great glen.
Glenquhargen, the crooked glen.
Glenquhary, the sheep glen.
Glenshilloch, the willow glen.
Greenock, the sandy hill.
Iona, the isle of waves.
Irvine, the green margin.
Keir, a fort.
Kello, the wooded water.
Kells, the woods, or the cells.
Ken, the fair stream.
Kenmore, *can* a lake, and *more* great
Killiecrankie, decayed wood.
Kilmarnock, the cell of Marnock.
Kinloch, loch-head.
Kirkmahoe, kirk or field by the river.
Knees, *eneas*, the breast, bosom.
Knockalloch, the cattle l. ●

Knockenhair, the green hill.
Kyle, the forest.
Lag, a hollow.
Lagminnean, the hollow of the kids.
Laight, a grave.
Lanark, a green, bare place in wood.
Lane, a stream.
Largmore, the great shark.
Lee, a stream.
Lennox, *lin* a stream, *knack* a hill.
Lesmahagow, *lis* a habitation, *magh* of field, and *aga* the bottom.
Linfairn, *lin* stream, *fearn* alders.
Lochbruin, loch of boar or rushes.
Lochdoon, the black loch.
Locherben, *ben* hill, *lacher* marshes
Lochgoin, *llwch gwyn*, the white loch.
Lochmaben, loch of the white field.
Logan, a little hollow.
London, *lon* stream, *don* dark.
Lugar, the bursting stream.
Lye, a stream.
Marburn, the great burn.
Mauchline, the field by the stream.
Meaul, a hill.
Mennock, the ore hill.
Morton, *moredun*, the great fort.
Muirdrogat, the great ridge.
Nethan, the little Nith.
Nith, the whirling stream.
Nypes, the heights.
Ochils, the height.
Ochiltree, the high town.
Pamphy linns, *pemfau* great cave.
Peebles, *pybil*, sheilings, huts.
Penbreck, the speckled hill.
Penicuik, the hill of the cuckoo.
Penncil, the head of the wall.
Penpont, *pen* head, *pant* a valley.
Pentland, the hilly land.
Penyvenie, the milky height.
Polgown, the stream of the smiths.
Polkellie, the wooded stream.
Polkemmet, the stream by the crooked field.
Powtrail, the head stream.
Sanquhar, *scan*, *caer*, the old fort.
Scar, the steep rock on the stream.
Shaw, a tuff of stunted trees.
Sorn, a corner.
Spango, the sparkling stream.
Stobo, the stub, how, or hollow.
Thristane, three stones.
Tinto, the hill of fire.
Torthorwald, tower of Thor in wood
Trahenny, the green hill.
Traquair, the hill fort.
Tweed, the border stream.
Wanlock, *wen* white, *loc* hollow.
Wardlaw, the watch hill.
Yochan, or Euchon, the fair stream

TRADITIONS

OF

THE COVENANTERS.

CHAPTER I.

Sanquhar—Howatson—Hair—William Adams.

In no part of our native land, perhaps, did the fires of persecution rage with a fiercer flame than in the south-west of
Scotland. The higher district of Nithsdale, where it joins
the Upper Ward of Lanarkshire, was especially, at certain
periods of the oppressive reign of the second Charles, a scene
of tragical interest. The locality in the midst of which the
ancient burgh of Sanquhar is situated, was the theatre of
many an act of persecuting violence which history has not
recorded, and which tradition has but imperfectly transmitted
to our times. This town, which, in covenanting times, was
famous as the occasional haunt of our Scottish worthies, and
especially for the *Declaration* which the followers of Cameron
published at its cross, stands in an interesting part of the
country. The scenery in its immediate vicinity wears, in
some places, a magnificent aspect, and in others is unrivalled
for its pastoral beauty and sweetness. The silvery streams
of the Mennock and the Crawick present each a scene of
grandeur which can scarcely be equalled, and which have
been deemed worthy of a panoramic exhibition in the first
cities of the nation. The salubrity of its climate, owing to

the purity and freshness of the air which streams down from the lofty and dry mountains by which the town is surrounded, is tested by the great age to which many of the inhabitants live, and by the absence of those epidemical diseases which prevail in other parts of the country. Nor is this burgh without its monuments of antiquity. It is itself one of the oldest towns in the south of Scotland. It is, as its name imports, of Celtic origin, but of a date too remote to be ascertained. Its castle, which, under the corroding hand of time, is fast crumbling to ruins, stands on a low embankment, which once overlooked the classic stream of the Nith before the river assumed its present bed, and was, in the days of our Scottish patriots, Wallace and Bruce, the scene of bloody conflicts; and its British encampment, so ancient that even tradition itself has forgotten it, is situated on a lovely green eminence to the north-west, commanding a full view of the beautiful basin to which Sanquhar gives the name. The old parish church, which a few years ago was demolished to make room for the handsome structure which now occupies its place, was coeval with the High Church of Glasgow, and contained some of the hallowed relics of the olden time, such as the altar of the *haly bluid*, to see which, and to drink of the consecrated waters of the limpid well of the far-famed Saint Bride, many a devout pilgrim came even from distant parts.*

It has often been remarked, that the inhabitants of the district, for a few miles around Sanquhar, are much superior to their neighbours in point of intelligence and general propriety of conduct. This was especially noticed by Sir Walter Scott; and the circumstance may be so far attributed to those sources of information to which they have an easy access—the locality being furnished with no fewer than six libraries, and one of these comprehending nearly two thousand volumes.

This small town has been favoured with a sound Gospel ministry since the Revolution; and prior to that era it was equally favoured. And as it was always in those places where the Gospel was purely preached that the greatest host of witnesses for the Truth arose, consequently, those who drove the car of Persecution over the breadth and length of a bleeding land had most to do in such localities. The solitudes in the upper parts of Nithsdale were the places of refuge to those who, on account of their faithful adherence to the testimony which they held, were driven from the

* Note A.

bosom of their families to seek a home in the desert; and
the imagination can scarcely conceive of solitudes more
dreary and sterile than those which lie on the north-west
borders of the parish of Sanquhar. From the top of any of
the lofty heights in the vicinity of this wilderness, nothing
can be discovered but rugged mountains of brown heath,
and vast wastes of dark moorland, stretching onward for
miles in the distance, with here and there the blue smoke
curling from the chimneys of the lone huts of the shepherds.
It was in the very heart of these solitudes, and in their most
retired and unknown retreats, that the worthy men of another age betook themselves for shelter, braving the fierce
blasts of the desert that they might escape the still fiercer
storms of a relentless persecution. And many a stirring
incident and perilous adventure, unknown to the historic
page, are told of the witnessing remnant, before the shepherd's blazing hearth during the long winter evenings, by
the inhabitants of the wilderness, many of whom are themselves descendants of the men whose memory they so warmly
cherish, and the incidents of whose lives they so feelingly
narrate. In traversing on a fine summer day, with an intelligent shepherd, the wilds which were once the asylum of
men who deserved a better home, it is thrilling to listen to
the anecdotes of varied interest which the features of the
desert recall to the mind of your companion. There is the
identical spot where the venerable Cargill held a conventicle;
yonder the place where Cameron uttered the denunciations
of divine vengeance against a Gospel-proof generation; yonder
the solitary shieling in which a company of God's hidden
ones were surprised and captured by a brutal soldiery; and
yonder the hill where Peden the prophet was screened by a
miraculous mist from the view of his blood-thirsty pursuers.
In this way, almost every hill and streamlet, and moss and
cottage, has its incident, and is endeared by hallowed associations. We shall narrate a few of those anecdotes relative
to the persecuting period, which are still in circulation
among the people of the moorlands. Many of them possess
great interest, and are worthy of preservation, for the sake
of the men to whom they refer.

There was a worthy man of the name of Howatson, who,
on account of his well-known attachment to covenanting
principles, was obliged to keep himself in perpetual concealment among the more remote and unfrequented glens and
mountains. His house was occasionally searched by the
dragoons, sometimes by day, and at other times by night, for

the purpose of surprising him at some unwary hour in the bosom of his family. It happened, on one occasion, that Howatson ventured to spend a night under his own roof at a time when he did not expect a surprisal from his enemies; for it was generally when the snow lay deep on the ground, or when the solitudes were visited with a severe storm, that the good men who dwelt in the dens and caves of the wilderness durst enter their homes without risk. Under the cloud of night, he stole into his lonely hut without being seen by a human eye. He received, as was to be expected, the cordial greeting of his household. A meal was instantly prepared; his affectionate wife changed his dripping clothes, and his shivering frame was warmed and enlivened by a huge fire of peats, the towering flame of which ascended far up the chimney. It was a happy occasion; and the glad family continued to converse on matters of deep and thoughtful interest till a late hour. At length all retired to rest; and it was not long before the husband and the father, worn out with hunger, and fatigue, and watchfulness, sank into a profound sleep. But while this pious household were slumbering in fancied security from the intrusion of their enemies, those very enemies were at the door. They had set out in quest of their victim, having by some means been informed of his hiding-place; and not finding him there as they anticipated, they hoped to capture him in his own house. Accordingly, having reached the solitary dwelling at the dead of night, they stationed six of their number before the door, while four of them entered the house, having softly lifted the latch— the door, by an unaccountable oversight, having been left unlocked. At this juncture the wife of Howatson awoke, and, to her amazement, saw four men standing before the fire attempting to light a candle; and rightly judging who the intruders were, she, without uttering a word, grasped her husband firmly by the arm. He instantly started up and saw the men, and, observing that their backs were towards him, he slipped gently from his bed on the clay floor, and stole softly to the door. It was guarded by the dragoons. He hesitated for a moment, and then darted like an arrow through the midst of them. The waving of his snow-white shirt, like a sheet of lightning, terrified the horses, and threw the party into confusion, and, though they fired several times, he escaped unscathed. He fled with the utmost speed to the house of a friend, where he obtained a lodging for the remainder of the night; and next day his clothing was conveyed to him by his wife, who could not but observe the hand of a special providence stretched out for the protection of her husband.

On another occasion, however, the same individual was not quite so fortunate, though he eventually escaped with his life. His enemies, being constantly in search of him, at length got hold of him; and the laird of Drumlanrig, the leader of the persecuting party in that district, brought him to his castle and confined him in a dungeon called " the pit of Drumlanrig." This prison-house was covered above with strong boards secured with massive bars of iron, so that escape was rendered impossible. In this place was Howatson incarcerated, not knowing the fate that might be awaiting him, whether he should be hanged aloft on the gallows-tree before the castle gate, or shot by the dragoons on the lawn; or, worst of all, be left to perish with hunger in the pit. There lived in the neighbourhood a half-witted man of the name of Hastie, a person of very great bodily strength, and who frequently performed feats that were incredible. To this person the wife of Howatson offered a sum of money to attempt the rescue of her husband. His bodily prowess and his partial insanity amply qualified him for the undertaking; for by the one he could accomplish the work, and by the other he would be screened from punishment, if caught in the attempt. Hastie agreed to the proposal; and, under the cloud of night, succeeded in removing the covering of the pit, and in effecting the release of the prisoner.

This good man lived some time at Locherben; and his piety and nonconformity exposed him to the notice of his enemies. Like the most of those who were friendly to the same cause, he was obliged to consult his safety by withdrawing from his own house, and hiding himself in the dens and caves of the earth. Near his little cottage there was a rocky place in the hill above, to which he frequently betook himself for concealment. Here he found a refuge when the enemy was searching all around for their prey; and he succeeded in keeping himself out of the way of the destroyer till the danger was overpast. It was no trivial advantage to his family that his place of concealment was so near them; for, on account of its contiguity to his house, he could easily visit them by stealth, and could both give and receive that assistance which was needed. A hiding-place so favourable was not always the good fortune of many of those who were placed in similar circumstances. They had often to remain in the heart of the dreariest solitudes, with none to comfort them, and none to tell how it fared with those who were left

behind. Howatson's family, when he durst not venture to his
house, could occasionally meet him in the cave, and bring him
a supply of food and other necessaries.

On one occasion, when Howatson, on account of the strict
search made for him, was obliged to confine himself to his
cave, his wife was delivered of a child. A party of the dragoons arrived at the house in quest of her husband, and, finding the poor woman in this situation, behaved in the most
insolent and brutal manner. They searched every corner of
the dwelling, but without success. They then proceeded to
the bed on which the woman was lying, and stabbed with
their swords all around her, beneath the bed-clothes, if perchance they might find her husband. The annoyance which
this gave the honest woman was peculiarly distressing to a
person in her condition. They threatened her in the most
violent manner, if she did not instantly reveal her husband's
hiding-place. The good woman, whose mind was kept in
comparative composure, and who was fortified with more
than ordinary strength to maintain her ground, and to outbrave her persecutors, answered with firmness and determination, that she would not comply with their request, nor on
any account betray her husband. The rude and unmannerly
assailants were abashed at her fortitude, and, though they
vaunted and threatened all manner of mischief, they were
not permitted to inflict any injury on her person. She upbraided them for their mean and unmannerly conduct in
thus assaulting a helpless and unprotected female, and expressed her confidence in the protection of that God whom
she and her husband served, and who had promised not to
abandon in the day of their distress those who trusted in him.

During the uproar, a little boy, who was standing near his
mother, began to cry bitterly. He was terrified at the appearance of the dragoons; their pistols, their broad-swords,
and their loud and angry voices filled him with terror. He
clung to the bed on which his mother lay—his little heart was
ready to burst, and his screams filled the apartment. The
behaviour of the child arrested the attention of the soldiers,
and one of them, seizing him by the tiny arm, dragged him
from the house, in spite of the entreaties and expostulations
of his mother. They carried him to the brow of the hill, not
far from his father's hiding-place, who was at that moment
concealed in the cave. Their object was to extort from the
boy information regarding his father's retreat, and they expected to find him more communicative on this subject than
his mother. In order the better to succeed in their design,

they resolved to operate on his fears, and accordingly they tied him to a tree, and plainly informed him that they would either stab him with their swords, or shoot him dead on the spot. The timid child, fearing lest the soldiers would fulfil their threatenings, screamed louder than before, and his shrill and agonizing cries reached the inmost recesses of the cavern in which his father lay. The well-known voice of the boy in the utmost distress, roused Howatson, who, looking forth from his concealment, beheld, in consternation, his beloved child tied fast to a tree, and the dragoons standing before him, as if about to put him to instant death. Not a moment was to be lost; he issued from the cave, and sprang between the soldiers and his little son, prepared to save the life of the dear boy at the expense of his own. The stra-'agem planned by the soldiers being thus successful, Howatson was instantly seized, and his child dismissed. The party proceeded with him to Drumlanrig. The road along which they marched passed a place called Closeburn Mill, where a small house of entertainment was kept; and here the troopers halted, for the purpose of regaling themselves with liquor. They continued to drink deep, and Howatson continued to watch his opportunity of escape. In a short time the intoxicating beverage began to operate, and soon rendered them oblivious, both of themselves and of their prisoner. Howatson, who now saw his advantage, stole quietly from the apartment without being observed, and speedily made his escape. When the soldiers awoke from their stupefaction, their captive was gone. Satan caught them in his snare, and while they were held in it, this honest witness for the truth obtained his freedom. This father was ready to sacrifice his life for the sake of his child; and now the Master whom he served rewarded him by giving him his own life for a prey in return. He was restored again to his family, who in the day of their tribulation trusted in the Lord, and he did not forsake them. Howatson, at length, wearied out by a ceaseless persecution, retired with a fellow-sufferer, of the name of Harkness, to Ireland, where he lived in concealment till the Revolution, when he returned to his native land, and died in peace.

Another anecdote is told of a pious man named Hair, who lived in a secluded place called Burncrooks, near Kirkland, in the parish of Kirkconnel, a few miles to the west of Sanquhar. This inoffensive man was seized by his persecutors, and doomed to die. The cruel and brutal conduct of the dragoons was peculiarly displayed in the treatment of this godly person. They rallied him on the subject of his death, and told him that they intended to kill him in a way that would afford them some merriment; that as his name was Hair, they wished to enjoy something of the same sport in putting an end to his life that they used to enjoy in killing the cowering and timid animal that bore a similar name. Instead, therefore, of shooting him before his own door, they placed him on horseback behind a dragoon, and carried him to the top of a neighbouring hill, that in the most conspicuous and insulting manner they might deprive him of his life. The spot where the cavalcade halted happened to be on the very brink of one of the most romantic glens in the west of Scotland. Glen Aylmer forms an immense cleft between two high mountains, and opens obliquely towards the meridian sun. The descent on either side for several hundred feet, is very steep, and in some places is almost perpendicular. The whole valley is clothed with rich verdure, and through its centre flows a gentle stream of many crooks and windings, appearing from the summit of the declivity like a silver thread stretching along the deep bottom of the glen. The breadth of this sweet vale is, generally speaking, not more perhaps than a hundred yards; and the whole scene strongly reminds one of the beautiful Vale of Tempe, so graphically described by Ælian. And though there are here no altars smoking with incense, no thickets overshadowing the path by the side of the stream, to screen the weary traveller from the noon-day sun, no convivial parties regaling themselves in its groves, no musical birds warbling among the leafy branches of the ivy-mantled trees, as in the celebrated defile between Ossa and Olympus; yet Glen Aylmer is a scene which, for simplicity and majesty, cannot easily be rivalled; and he who has seen it once will not grudge to look on it again.

The party of dragoons, then, having reached the spot where they intended to shoot their captive, had made a halt for the purpose of dismounting, and the soldier behind whom our worthy was seated proceeded to unbuckle the belt which, for greater security, we may suppose, bound the prisoner to his person, when Hair, finding himself disengaged, slid from the horse behind, and lighting on the very edge of the steep declivity, glided with great swiftness down the grassy turf, and frequently losing his footing, he rebounded from spot to spot, till at last he regained his feet, and ran at his utmost speed till he reached the bottom. The soldiers looked with amazement, but durst not follow; they fired thick, but missed him, and were left to gnaw their tongues in painful disappointment. What became of this good man tradition does not say; but on this occasion, at least, he had reason to set up his stone of remembrance, and say : " Hitherto hath the Lord helped me."

In connection with this we may notice the following anecdote of a young man of the name of William Adams, who lived in Wellwood, and who, on account of his piety and nonconforming principles, became an object of hostility to the persons who, in those times, sought every opportunity to harass and persecute the people of God. William, who was about to be married to an excellent and amiable young woman in the neighbourhood, had appointed a meeting with her in the moors. On the day specified, he was first at the *trysting*-place; and, in order to pass the time till his friend should arrive, in the most profitable way, he opened his Bible and read the Word of God. He had not long continued at this employment till his eye caught a party of dragoons close upon him; he started to his feet; the enemy rode up to him, and, in an instant, he was shot dead on the spot. The young woman, who was now advancing at a quick pace along the heath, heard the loud and startling report of fire-arms precisely in the direction in which she was going. She walked onward with a throbbing heart and with a faltering step— she feared lest her beloved William had fallen by the savage hand of the foe; and her worst suspicions seemed to be justified, when she saw several horsemen coming over the rising ground, apparently from the very place where she expected to meet with her lover. She met them just as she was passing along a narrow foot-bridge, thrown by the shepherds, for their own convenience, over the mossy streamlet; and as they were crossing the brook, close by the side of the bridge, one of the dragoons drew his sword, and jocularly struck her with its broad-side, under the pretence of pushing her into the water. Her spirit was imbittered, and her courage was roused; and, wrapping her apron closely round her hand, she seized the sword by the blade, wrenched it from the grasp of the warrior, snapped it in two over her knee, and flung the pieces into the stream. With eager impatience she hastened to the meeting-place. All her fears were realized—her William was lying stiff on the ground, and his blood had stained the heather bloom with a deeper dye.

It is worthy of remark, that the annals of the persecuting period do not record the sufferings of almost any one belonging to the *parish* of Sanquhar, notwithstanding the many good men that must have lived in it at that time. Their

exemption from persecution has been supposed to result, in
a great measure, from the leniency of the curate, who was a
good-natured, easy sort of man, whose name was James
Kirkwood, a man of facetious memory, and of whom some
curious anecdotes are related. Tradition says, that instead
of seeking occasion against those of his parishioners who refused to submit to his ministry, he publicly announced that,
if on a given day they would assemble within the churchyard, though they did not enter the church, he would give a
favourable report of the whole parish, and screen the nonconformists from the vengeance of their persecutors. It would
seem that this request was, to a certain extent at least, complied with.   There is an anecdote current among the people
of this neighbourhood, which displays in some measure the
humane disposition of the incumbent. Two of the covenanting brethren from the wilds of Carsphairn, in full flight
before the dragoons, dashed into the River Nith and reached
the opposite bank a few yards below the manse. It happened that a number of individuals, among whom was the
curate, were playing at quoits on the green. " Where shall
we run ?" cried the two men. " Doff your coats," said the
curate, " and play a game with me." They did so. The
dragoons immediately followed; they passed the curate and
rode on in pursuit, and the men, through his generous interference, escaped.

There is on the east bank of the River Crawick, near the
town, and not far from the place where Sir William Douglas,
many a century ago, concealed his men on the evening prior
to the memorable day when he took the castle of Sanquhar
from General Beauford, who commanded the English troops
who occupied its fastness, an old ruined cavern, said to be the
frequent resort of the intercommuned wanderers. This place
had two entrances ; so that when they were assailed at the
one, they escaped at the other. In the immediate neighbourhood of this retreat are the graves of two worthies,
whose names are unknown, and who probably died of disease
occasioned by the hardships to which they were exposed.

CHAPTER II.

Peden in Glendyne—Escape in the Mist—Warning at Elliock—
Woman at Ingleston—Craigdarroch.

ABOUT the commencement of the persecution in Scotland,
nearly "three hundred and fifty ministers were ejected from
their churches, in the severity of winter, and driven with
their families to seek shelter among the peasants. These
ministers were forbidden to preach even in the fields, or to
approach within twenty miles of their former charges; and all
the people, as well as their pastors, who were not prepared
to abjure their dearest rights, and to submit to the most
galling and iniquitous civil and religious despotism, were denounced as traitors." None were allowed in any way to assist
them, or even to supply them with food, or to shelter them
in their houses; and those whose humanity or Christian
principle inclined them to show kindness to those friendless
followers of Christ, exposed their property and their persons
to the rapacity and cruelty of a wicked and injurious policy.
The apostle's description of the destitute condition of the
ancient people of God, in persecuting times, is literally true
of our forefathers : "They wandered in deserts and in mountains, and in dens and in caves of the earth;" but "they
took joyfully the spoiling of their goods, knowing that in
heaven they had a better and an enduring substance." Often
in the moorland solitudes, concealed from the vigilant eye of
their persecutors, did these devoted servants of the Redeemer
open the wells of salvation for the refreshment of God's
weary heritage, who, thirsting for the water of life, resorted
to them in crowds; and many a blessed outpouring of the
gracious Spirit of God was experienced by them, when, in
the hallowed retreat of the wilderness, they congregated at
the risk of all that was dear to them on earth to worship the
God of their fathers—the enemies of God and his holy
Evangel not permitting them to assemble in temples made
with hands. The Saviour, however, bore testimony to the

word of his own grace, and to the worthiness of that cause
for which his people were suffering, in filling the hearts of
his followers with comfort, and in crowning the ministrations
of his servants with success.

The desolation and distress of many a family, after the
standard of the Gospel was reared in the fields, were un-
utterable. The tender-hearted wife knew not how it fared
with her husband traversing the waste, or lodged in the cold
damp cave; and many a disconsolate hour did she spend in
weeping over her helpless children, who had apparently
nothing before them but starvation and scorn; and the affectionate husband, far from his dearly cherished home, was
full of the bitter remembrance of his beloved family, and
picturing to himself their many wants which he could not
now relieve, and their many sorrows which he could not
soothe, and the many insults from which he could not defend
them; but, notwithstanding all this, they had peace—for God
was with them; and, though their hearts sometimes mis-
gave them, yet, through the grace of him with whose cause
they were identified, their faith recovered its proper tone,
and their despondency vanished.

One of the most renowned of those worthies who persisted
in preaching the Gospel in the wilds of his native land, at
the constant hazard of his life, was the venerable Peden,
whose history is familar in almost every cottage in Scotland.
Many incidents in the life of this good man have already
been collected, but something new may be still added.
There are to be found a few stray anecdotes of him here and
there in the remote parts of the country, and which, for his
sake, may be deemed worthy of record. Few persons possessed a more saintly character than did this man of God.
He was full of faith and of the Holy Ghost. Entirely devoted to his Master's service, he counted not his own life
dear unto him, that he might maintain the cause of truth in
the face of the abounding iniquity of a degenerate age. His
solitary wanderings, his destitution, his painful perseverance
in preaching the Gospel, the peril in which he lived, his
prayerful spirit, and the homeliness of his manners, greatly
endeared him to the people among whom he sojourned. He
had no home, and therefore spent much of his time in the
fields. The caves by the mountain stream, the dense hazel
wood in the deep glen, the feathery brackens on the hill,
the green corn when it was tall enough to screen him from
observation, afforded him by turns, when necessary, a retreat
from his pursuers, and a place for communing with his God

Among the many hiding-places to which this man, of whom the world was not worthy, occasionally retreated, was the solitude of Glendyne, about three miles to the east of Sanquhar. A more entire seclusion than this is rarely to be found. Glendyne stretches eastward, winding among the hills for nearly three miles. The width of the glen at the bottom is in many places little more than five or six times the breadth of the brawling torrent that rushes through it. Dark precipitous mountains, frowning on either side, rise from the level of the valley to an immense height. On the eastern extremity of the glen a cluster of hills gathers to a point, and forms an eminence of great altitude, from which a noble prospect of a vast extent of country is obtained. Near the lower end of this defile, which in ancient times was thickly covered with wood, and where it terminates its sinuous course with one majestic sweep, reaching forward to the bleak moorlands beneath, our revered worthy had selected for himself a place of refuge. This spot, concealed by the dark mantling of the forest, was known only to a few who made the cause of these sufferers their own. It happened, on one occasion, that this honoured servant of Christ, having emerged from his covert, stood by the margin of the forest, on the beautiful slope of the mountain above. It was the balmy month of May, and Nature had just put on her loveliest attire. The forest was vocal with the sweetest music. The blackbird and the thrush were piping their richest notes on the "green wood tree;" the gentle cooing of the wood-dove issued with a delicious softness from the grove; and the joyous lark, high in the air, was pouring a flood of melody down upon the wilderness. The wild bees were humming among the honeyed blossoms of the hawthorn; the scented wind, breathing over the fragrant heath, was playing with the rustling foliage; the brook was murmuring in the ravine below; the lambkins were gambolling on the verdant lea, and the sheep were grazing quietly by their side; while on the distant hill the shepherd was seen, wrapped in his plaid, with his sportive dog at his foot, slowly winding his way up the steep ascent. The good man's heart beat high with rapture—his delighted eye roamed over the charming variety of hill and dale—he contemplated the glorious sun, and all the splendid scenery of the sky—he felt as if he were standing on holy ground, in the midst of the great temple of Nature—he experienced an unusual elevation of mind, and all the freshness and buoyancy of youth seemed once more to take possession of his aged frame. Full of

devout sentiments he uncovered his head, the silvery hairs of
which were streaming on his shoulders, and, lifting up his
hands, he "praised, and honoured, and extolled the King of
heaven, all whose works are truth, and whose ways are judgment." He had fixed his eye on a cottage far off in the
waste, in which lived a godly man with whom he had frequent intercourse; and there being nothing within view calculated to excite alarm, he resolved to pay his friend a visit.
With his staff in his hand he wended his way to the low
grounds to gain the track which led to the house. He
reached it in safety, was hospitably entertained by the kind
landlord, and spent the time with the household, in pious
conversation and prayer, till sunset. Not daring to remain
all night, he left them, to return to his dreary cave. As he
was trudging along the soft footpath, and suspecting no
harm, all at once several moss-troopers appeared coming
over the bent, and advancing directly upon him. He fled
across the moor, and when about to pass a mountain stream
let, he accidentally perceived a cavity underneath its bank,
that had been scooped out by the running brook, into which
he instinctively crept, and stretching himself at full length
lay hidden beneath the grassy coverlet, waiting the result
In a short time the dragoons came up, and having followed
close in his track, reached the rill at the very spot where he
was ensconced. As the heavy horses came thundering over
the smooth turf on the edge of the rivulet, the foot of one
of them sank quite through the hollow covering under which
the object of their pursuit lay. The hoof of the animal
grazed his head, and pressed his bonnet deep into the soft
clay at his pillow, and left him entirely uninjured. His persecutors, having no suspicion that the poor fugitive was so
near them, crossed the stream with all speed, and bounded
away in quest of him whom God had thus hidden as in his
pavilion, and in the secret of his tabernacle. A man like
Peden, who read the hand of God in everything, could not
fail to see and to acknowledge that divine goodness which
was so eminently displayed in this instance; and we may
easily conceive with what feelings he would return to his
retreat in the wood, and with what cordiality he would send
up the voice of thanksgiving and praise to the God of his
life.

It is recorded in the "Scots Worthies," that he was favoured
with a memorable deliverance from the enemy, who were
pursuing him and a small company with him, somewhere in
Galloway, after he came out of Ireland. When their hope

of escape was almost cut off, he knelt down among the heather and prayed: "Twine them about the hill, Lord, and cast the lap of thy cloak over old Sandy and thir poor things; and we will keep it in remembrance, and tell it to the commendation of thy goodness, pity, and compassion, what thou didst for us at such a time." Thus he prayed, and his supplication was recorded in heaven; for he had no sooner risen from his knees than dense volumes of snow-white mist came rolling down from the summit of the mountains, and shrouded them from the sight of their pursuers, who, like the men of Sodom, when they were smitten with blindness, could not grope their way after them. Auchengrouch hill, in the vicinity of Glendyne, was the scene of a similar incident. This occurrence is related by old Patrick Walker in the following words: " After this, in Auchengrouch muirs in Nithsdale, Captain John Mathison and others being with him, they were alarmed with a report that the enemy were coming fast upon him; so they designed to put him in some hole, and cover him with heather. But he not being able to run hard by reason of age, he desired them to forbear a little until he prayed, when he said: ' Lord, we are ever needing at thy hand, and if we had not thy command to call upon thee in the day of our trouble, and thy promise of answering us in the day of our distress, we wot not what would become of us. If thou have any more work for us in thy world, allow us the lap of thy cloak this day again; and if this be the day of our going off the stage, let us walk honestly off, and comfortably thorow, and our souls will sing forth thy praises to eternity for what thou hast done for us.' When ended, he ran alone a little, and came quickly back, saying: ' Lads, the bitterest of this blast is over; we will be no more troubled with them this day.' Foot and horse came the length of Andrew Clark's, in Auchengrouch, where they were covered with a dark mist. When they saw it they roared like fleshly devils, as they were crying out: ' There's the confounded mist again!—we cannot get these execrable Whigs pursued for it.' I had these accounts from the said Captain John Mathison." Such is the statement of the incident given by Walker; the local tradition, however, is much more circumstantial.

Castle Gilmour, as its name imports, was an old baronial residence in the moors, about three miles to the east of Sanquhar, and is now a farm-house. The locality must in ancient times have been very dreary and desolate; for even yet its general aspect is anything but interesting. The

mountains, however, by which it is encompassed on the east
and on the north, are of a very different description. Few
scenes, on a narrow scale, present a more agreeable spectacle
than that which meets the view from the northern limits of
Sanquhar town common, between the parallel streams of
Mennock and the Crawick. The uncultivated moorlands
are flanked by hills whose summits rise like lofty colonnades
to the clouds, and remind one of the sublime Scripture
expression: "The pillars of heaven." The beautiful Knockenhair, in the western corner of the circular range, clad in
velvet green, and topped with its ancient warder cairn,
stands a stately cone detached from the neighbouring mountains, and, presenting itself in advance, invites the first glance
of the spectator's eye. In the eastern corner stands the
grey-clothed height of Auchengrouch, the frequent sanctuary
of the worthy Peden, and to which the memory of that venerable saint has imparted a hallowed interest. The traveller in the bleak dale land which stretches from the base of
these mountains to the south, often meets with the plover
and the peesweep, which, in their aërial gyrations, dive
downwards, and flap with their broad wings his head and
shoulders, as a chastisement for intruding on their solitary
retreats. In this way, it is said, they were occasionally unconscious informers to the enemy of the wanderers who, in
the open field, had concealed themselves in the heart of the
bracken bush, or among the green coverts of the spratty
bent. In the stillness of a sweet summer evening, when, in
meditative mood, one surveys the entire scene, and gathers
in all its associations, there is felt a kind of enchantment,
which one is unwilling to dissipate. We think on the incidents of former times; we reflect on the wanderings and the
prayers of our suffering forefathers, who made the solitudes
their home, and who, when furthest from men, were nearest
God. We think on the times of a still more remote ancestry,
and picture the ancient Celtic people who claimed these
mountains and wilds as their own, and who traversed these
territories as free and as light as the fitful breeze that streams
along the heath; and we ruminate on times that are yet to come,
when righteous generations shall arise, for whose sake God
will remove the curse from the barren wilderness; and when,
under the culture of their skilful hands, that same desert,
over which the eye roams, will "rejoice and blossom as the
rose." An age of millennial blessedness shall arrive, in which
changes and improvements shall take place, of which we
have little anticipation. But we who live shall have passed

away with the former generations that are already in the dust, and our eyes shall not behold among the living the goodness which God has provided for those who shall come after, and whom he will render more worthy of its enjoyments than we are. If, however, our hope be in heaven, and if after death our souls have their dwelling there, we shall enjoy a better millennium and a higher blessedness than they of earth can boast. Only be it our care to secure, by faith in the Redeemer, an entrance into that rest which remaineth for the people of God, and then we shall have occasion to sing: "O how great is thy goodness which thou hast laid up for them that fear thee, which thou hast wrought for them that trust in thee before the sons of men!"

It was in the farm-house of Castle Gilmour, in the immediate vicinity of Auchengrouch, where Mr Peden and a few friends had taken refuge. In their wandering in the moors they were overcome with fatigue and hunger; and to this friendly house they came seeking rest and refreshment. Andrew Clark, in Auchengrouch, was a good man, a zealous Covenanter, and one who readily afforded shelter to the outcasts; and it seems that his neighbour in Castle Gilmour was no less attached to the good cause, and no less hospitable to those who were suffering for Christ's sake. On the farm of Castle Gilmour the dwelling-house and offices were so constructed as to form an exact square, with openings at the corners, through which one individual or two could pass at a time. Mr Peden and his friends were partaking of a repast after their long fasting; and, dreading no harm, were discoursing freely on the subjects that were most interesting to them, when, to their surprise, and without the least warning, a company of dragoons rode into the enclosure before the dwelling-house, and drew up at the door. The party within, seeing no way of escape except in the very face of the enemy, made a simultaneous rush to the door, and waving with their bonnets, ran here and there among the horses before the riders got time to dismount, and escaped, every one of them, through the narrow passages at the angles of the square. The troopers were confounded at an occurrence so unexpected; for they, thinking that their prey was sure, were very much at their ease, and were making no great haste to enter the house. The dragoons, when they understood the true position of matters, and having learned that the persons who had just now issued with so much impetuosity and disorder from the dwelling-house, were the very individuals of whom they were in quest, wheeled round, and departing by the way they entered, pursued with all speed. Meanwhile the fugitives had reached Auchengrouch burn, and arrived at the other side in safety. This was a great point gained; for the place at which they passed the stream was so precipitous, that the horsemen could not follow them. By the time, then, that they emerged on the opposite bank, the troopers, in full chase, were close to the brook; but their progress was instantly arrested by the descent, down which the horses could not march. The shot which they fired across the little ravine took no effect; and the covenanting friends pursued their way along the heath, to where Providence might be pleased to guide them. The soldiers, however, were not to be baffled by the obstacles which now crossed their path; and turning in another direction, cleared the bent with all the speed its rugged surface would permit, and were fast gaining ground. The fleeing party now perceived that there was little likelihood of escape. Mr Peden, whose refuge in the midst of his distresses was prayer, and who used to remark that " it was only praying people that would get through the storm," requested the company to halt a little till he prayed, which he did in the words recorded by Walker, and then he added : " Lads, the bitterest of this blast is over, we will be no more troubled with them this day." The occasion of their rescue was the mist which descended from the hills, and screened them from the view of their pursuers.

Some may be inclined to suppose that this incident is put forth as something miraculous, and to say that the admission of a miracle vitiates the entire statement. There is, however, no occasion whatever to suppose a miracle in this, more than in other providential interferences in answer to prayer. Are we to say, that the Divine Being cannot in any case answer our prayers, in reference to external deliverances, without a miracle? The settling of the mist on the tops of these mountains is a very common occurrence, and could not He who "maketh the clouds his chariot, and who walketh upon the wings of the wind," in answer to the prayer of his servant, in the day of his distress, send a stream of air from the mountain side, and spread the misty covering over his people who trusted in him, without the introduction of a miracle? Some, again, may be inclined to consider the thing as a mere coincidence; but the question is, Who appointed the coincidence, or was it merely fortuitous—a thing of chance—and had the great Disposer of events no hand in it? No person will admit this who believes the Scripture doctrine of a providence—of a particular providence exercised over all creatures and all events. "Are not two sparrows sold for a farthing, and one of them shall not fall on the ground without your Father?—but the very hairs of your head are all numbered." Nor will they who believe in the efficacy of prayer be disposed to deny that the incident was really in answer to prayer: "Call upon me in the day of trouble; I will deliver thee, and thou shalt glorify me." An Infidel will no doubt laugh at this, but a serious Christian will rejoice in the fact that the Lord hears prayer, and that he is prompt to answer it. Prayer is a means of attaining an end; and if the end has a place in the divine appointment, so has the means; and the former is not to be obtained without the latter. The people of God believe the Bible doctrine respecting prayer, both as a duty to be performed and as an instrument of obtaining blessings: "Ask, and ye shall receive." How much do they lose who restrain prayer before God; and what a difference in point of success in prayer is there between the man who prays with a weak and faltering confidence and the man who prays in strong faith! The one receives blessings, copious as the showers which descend from the teeming firmament when the windows of heaven are opened; and what the other receives is only like the scanty rain dripping reluctantly from the skirts of a transient cloud. We are bound to believe, that when we ask blessings from God in the name of Christ, we shall receive them : " For this is the confidence that we have in him, that if we ask anything according to his will, he heareth us;" and, " He that cometh unto God, must believe that he is, and that he is the rewarder of them that diligently seek him." Here, then, the secret of success in prayer, is the *confidence* that our prayers shall be heard for Christ's sake; for he that prays and believes, is answered; while he that prays and believes not, is not answered.

The farm-house of Auchentagart, which is in the vicinity of Castle Gilmour, was also, in the days of persecution, a place of refuge to the wanderers. The name of the place is Celtic, and signifies " the field of the priest." From this it would appear that the ancient Celtic people had somewhere in this locality a church, to which the lands of Auchentagart were attached a proof that the Gospel in remote times was introduced into the neighbourhood, and that God was here worshipped by the people of a forgotten age, in a house of which there is not the least trace nor tradition. It is pleasant to think that the ancient inhabitants of this country, long prior

to the times of Romish superstition, enjoyed a pure dispensation of divine grace, and were in those times brought to the
knowledge of the truth.

It happened one day that a few of the covenanting friends
entered the house of Auchentagart, where they were cordially
welcomed by its master, for the sake of Him in whose cause
they were suffering hardship. As there were more households than one in this moorland part who kindly entertained
the houseless wanderers, the dragoons must therefore have
been more frequently seen traversing the waste, and strolling
from one hiding-place to another, for the purpose of seizing,
in cave or shiel, any who might perchance be concealed in
these retreats. In their ramblings from place to place, they
were, on the very day on which the friends had taken refuge
in Auchentagart, observed coming across the moor straight
to the house. It was obvious that a visit was intended; and
that the soldiers, if meeting with no adventure in the way of
their profession, would in all likelihood demand entertainment both for themselves and their horses, and probably
spend the greater part of the day on the premises. On the
first appearance of the party, information was hastily communicated to the few refugees, who were receiving refreshment within. They instantly left the house, and fled in the
direction of the wood of Glendyne. Their flight, however,
was observed by the troopers, who immediately commenced
a pursuit, but were not able to overtake them. It would appear that the dragoons had, in sallying out on this occasion,
a double object in view; they were prepared for sport as well
as for persecution—for hunting the timid hare as well as for
pursuing men—and were accompanied with a pack of powerful
and cruel dogs. These dogs they sent in chase of the fleeing
Covenanters, and they tracked their path with fleetness and
voracity to the mouth of the woody glen, into which the
fugitives plunged and concealed themselves, before their
canine pursuers could overtake them. In this retreat they
were safe, and were left without interruption, to render a
grateful acknowledgment to Him who had once more shielded
them in the time of danger. One is ready to blush for human
nature, when one class of men are seen employing in this
way animals to pursue another, as if they were beasts of
prey, fit only to be torn in pieces by the fangs of the huntsman's dog. To such degradation, however, and even to
worse, have the people of God been subjected in the treatment which they have received from their enemies. They
have been regarded as " the filth of the world, and as the

offscouring of all things;" but while they were thus disesteemed by men, they were honoured of God, and they deemed themselves happy in being counted worthy to be reproached and maltreated for his name.

The beautiful lands of Elliock lie opposite to Castle Gilmour, and about two miles to the south of Sanquhar. Elliock House is erected in the midst of a pleasant wood. It is an edifice part of which boasts a considerable antiquity, being preserved as the birth-place of the admirable Crichton, notwithstanding the claims which another place has laid to this distinguished honour, as seven cities contended for the birth of Homer. In former times it was the property of the Earl of Carnwath, who, in the days of our persecuted ancestors, sided with their oppressors. Elliock House was, therefore, a station for the dragoons, who accompanied the Earl in his movements through the country for the purpose of subduing a "rebellious" peasantry. It was not, however, the only station in this vicinity; for both the town of Sanquhar and its neighbouring castle must have been the receptacles of a soldiery who were employed to murder their countrymen for the offence of yielding an honest obedience to the divine law in preference to the iniquitous impositions of men. The garrison at Elliock, then, were ready at a moment's warning to scour the high lands that lay to the south, and that stretched along the desert moorlands that reached the Scar; and as there was a constant intercourse between the higher parts of Galloway and the Upper Ward of Lanarkshire, by way of Sanquhar, the services of the soldiers would be in perpetual demand. On the north, Elliock commanded a view of all that was in motion along the line of the Nith, and on the green heights that overlook the highway; so that, in this direction, nothing could escape the vigilance of the warders who might be set to give due notice of what was passing. We formerly observed that a number of those who were favourably disposed towards the Covenanters connected themselves with the royal forces for the express purpose of defeating the plans of the enemy, and of giving warning to the persecuted when danger was near; and the following anecdote of one of the dragoons at Elliock House is illustrative of the fact. One evening the commander gave orders to the troopers to hold themselves in readiness for a raid on the morrow, without specifying the particular quarter to which he intended to proceed. Every man was instantly on the alert and saw that his ammunition and his musket, and his sword and his charger, were all in readiness for the intended sally in the morning. On the grounds of Elliock, on the border of the heath, lived a venerable matron, a mother in Israel, whose name tradition has not preserved, but the door of whose house was always open to the helpless wanderer. This woman had often entertained and sheltered those who, for their Master's sake, had suffered the loss of all things. At the peril of her life, and of all she held dear in this world, she ventured to perform what she reckoned a duty to the followers of Christ in the day of their calamity; and she was blessed in her deed—for Providence shielded her from harm, and even prevented suspicion from lighting upon her as one who dared to harbour, or in any way to assist those who were so obnoxious to the ruling powers. This appears the more remarkable, considering her abode was so near the head-quarters of the troopers, who, in their idle hours, must have been constantly strolling about the neighbourhood, and prying, with an impertinent curiosity, into every house and every corner, and that with the full license, in many cases, to act as they pleased. There was one of the soldiers, however, who was acquainted with her house, and who had some knowledge of the kind of persons who often gathered around its hearth. This man, after the orders were issued by his officer, stole unperceived, under the cloud of night, to the cottage in the moor. "Mistress," said he, "I am come to warn you we are to be out to-morrow, and we may perhaps pass your way; if you have any friends about you at present, give you the watchword that they may provide for their safety, and take care of yourself. Good night." Whether there were any under hiding at this time in her house is not said; but the knowledge that, when practicable, she would receive information of approaching danger, must have kept her mind at ease, and rendered her abode a retreat of comparative security; and the soldier, whether he acted from a mere impulse of humanity or from real principle, must have had a peculiar satisfaction, in knowing that he had been the instrument of shielding from danger a company of worthy men, who had by no means merited the severe treatment to which they were subjected. It is impossible to say of how much use one or two of this description, in a troop of dragoons, must have been to the cause of the suffering party; and it is not easy to calculate the amount of mischief which, in the localities where they were stationed, they must have occasionally prevented. "One friend in the enemy's camp is sometimes worth a thousand men in the field." Truly they are a blessed people whose God is the Lord, for in the time of their calamity he is their help and their shield, and " they need not be afraid of ten thousands of people who have set themselves against them round about; for salvation belongeth unto the Lord, and his blessing is upon his people."

There is a story told of a woman who resided at a place called Ingleston, in the parish of Glencairn in Nithsdale, whose remarkable preservation in the very presence of her enemies, who were eagerly seeking her life, is no less illustrative of the watchful providence of God than the anecdote which has now been related, and which confirms the truth of the adage, that " every man is immortal till his day come." This woman, whose name is not mentioned, was a " mother in Israel." Her truly religious character, and her refusal to attend the ministry of the curate, did not escape the notice of the dominant party, who, in those times of oppression, sought " to wear out the saints of the Most High." The name of the Master whom she served was too conspicuously imprinted on her forehead to admit of concealment. A party of horsemen were one day despatched to the place of her residence in search of her. They were near the house before they were observed, and the worthy woman, guessing their errand, ran for refuge to the barn, in which a female servant was busily employed at her work. " The dragoons ! the dragoons !" cried the fugitive; " where shall I hide ?" " Run to that dark corner," said the servant, " and I will cover you with the straw." The soldiers rushed into the barn, expecting instantly to seize their prey ; and seeing nobody but the servant, who refused to give them any satisfactory information, in their rage and disappointment they began to kick among the straw; and, drawing their long swords, they thrust them at full length, with all their force, through the heaps with which the barn floor was covered, stabbing vengefully in every corner where they thought there was any likelihood of concealment. The nook, however, into which the object of their search had crept was either missed by them, or their swords did not hit on the precise spot where she lay ; for, notwithstanding the closeness of the search, she remained undiscovered and unscathed. In this astonishing manner, then, did the Lord preserve another of his saints who trusted in him, throwing over her the shield of his effectual protection in circumstances in which, to human view, there was no probability of escape.

But the rage of persecuting malignity was not confined in its object merely to the humbler orders of the land, who had neither power nor influence to protect them; it vented itself with equal violence on those who occupied a higher and more commanding station in society—like the desolating storm which descends indiscriminately on the lofty mountains and on the lowly valleys. The attachment of the house of Craigdarroch, in Glencairn, to the principles of the Covenanters is well known; and many an outcast in the days of our forefathers, took refuge under its sheltering wings. The master of Craigdarroch was therefore a marked man, and his enemies were determined to show him no favour. It happened on a fine summer morning when, after a heavy rain which fell during the preceding night, the rivers and burns were greatly swollen, that the laird, as he was termed, was under the necessity of travelling a short distance from home. Orders had been issued to a party of dragoons to watch his movements, and to embrace the first opportunity of seizing his person. As he was ambling slowly along on a fine spirited horse, he was all at once confronted with a company of troopers. The place where they met was at the opening of a stone dyke, through which the road passed. The commander of the party, who seemed to know the laird, cried : "Guard the gap." "I'll guard the gap," replied the laird, who, at the same time turning the head of his swift and powerful steed, galloped off at his utmost speed. The horsemen pursued, and Craigdarroch, seeing that there was but little hope of escape, directed his course to the River Cairn, which at the time was in full flood, and dashed into its foaming torrent, choosing rather to risk his life in the tumultuous waters than be captured by a savage soldiery. He reached the opposite bank, upon which the noble animal landed him with a bound. By the sudden spring two of the nine girths by which his saddle is said to have been secured, were ruptured. The dragoons having noticed the circumstance, bawled out that now he was their prisoner. "Not yet," vociferated our hero, now on the safe side of the stream; "for though two of the bands be broken, there yet remain seven stout and firm; and now I dare you to the pursuit. Throw yourselves into that roaring tide and follow me." This, however, was a challenge which none of them were inclined to accept; for the conviction that they are engaged in a bad cause generally makes men cowards. In this way this worthy man, under the conduct of a gracious Providence, was rescued from the ruthless hands of those who would have shown him no mercy. It is reported that the identical saddle on which the honoured ancestor of the house of

Craigdarroch sat on this occasion is still preserved by the family.

It was in Craigdarroch House where John Stevenson, the Ayrshire Covenanter, lodged in secrecy in some of the hottest days of persecution. His wife, who was nurse to Craigdarroch's child, was greatly esteemed by the lady of the mansion, and for her sake the husband was admitted under hiding, into a private apartment of the house. His abode there was known to none, not even to the laird himself; but the household was blessed for his sake, for his prayers were heard for them in the day of their distress. The Lord never allows any to be losers for his people's sake; even "a cup of cold water given to a disciple, in the name of a disciple, shall not lose its reward." And it is worthy of remark, that those who, in the time of the Church's tribulation, aided the suffering followers of Christ in any way, and especially those who did so at the risk of losing their worldly property or their life, were afterwards prosperous in temporal things; for our Lord takes a special notice of every act of kindness done to his people for his sake: "Inasmuch as ye did it unto the least of these my brethren, ye did it unto me."

The brief history of John Stevenson, written by himself, is well worthy of a perusal. It breathes throughout a spirit of genuine piety and zeal, and confidence in God. It records his religious experiences, the remarkable providences that befell him, the particular passages of Scripture that afforded him the subject of sweet meditation and comfort, and his last and best advice to his children. In the veritable history of such a man we have a practical commentary on the promises and providence of God, calculated to put Infidelity to the blush, and to reprove the unbelief of the Lord's own people.

CHAPTER III.

Sanquhar Declaration—Conventicle in Blagannoch Moss —
Galloway Flail.

THE Sanquhar *Declaration* was published by the followers of
Cameron, on the 22d June 1680, exactly one year after the
Battle of Bothwell, and a month prior to his own death at
Airs Moss. This Declaration deserves notice, both on account of the prominence given to it at the time by the persecuted remnant, and also because it was assumed, on the part
of the Malignants, as a ground of criminal prosecution against
those who acknowledged its propriety. "Do you own the
Sanquhar Declaration?" was a query to which an answer in
the affirmative subjected the individual to whatever punishment the caprice of the judges in the council, or the military
in the field, might see proper to inflict. It was regarded as
a manifesto of a highly treasonable nature; for it in plain
terms disowned Charles as the lawful king of these realms;
and thus coming so soon after the affair of Bothwell Bridge,
it was the means of stimulating, to a very high pitch, the
persecuting fury of the times. The attention of the ruling
faction was now more especially directed to that part of the
country where this Declaration was made public; and a hireling soldiery was found the ready instrument of a merciless
execution. As this Declaration, on account of which so
many worthy people of the land were brought into trouble,
is now probably little known, we shall here give a reprint of
it; it is brief, and will not detain the reader long:—

"The Declaration and Testimony of the True Presbyterian, Anti-prelatic, Anti-erastian, persecuted party
in Scotland. Published at Sanquhar, June 22,
1680 :—

"It is not amongst the smallest of the Lord's mercies to
this poor land, that there have been always some who have
given their testimony against every cause of defection that

many are guilty of; which is a token for good, that he doth
not, as yet, intend to cast us off altogether, but that he will
leave a remnant in whom he will be glorious, if they, through
his grace, keep themselves clean still, and walk in his way
and method as it has been walked in, and owned by him in
our predecessors of truly worthy memory; in their carrying
on of our noble work of reformation, in the several steps
thereof, from Popery, Prelacy, and likewise Erastian supremacy—so much usurped by him who, it is true, so far as we
know, is descended from the race of our kings; yet he hath
so far debased from what he ought to have been, by his perjury and usurpation in Church matters, and tyranny in matters civil, as is known by the whole land, that we have just
reason to account it one of the Lord's great controversies
against us, that we have not disowned him, and the men of
his practices, whether inferior magistrates or any other, as
enemies to our Lord and his crown, and the true Protestant
and Presbyterian interest in this land—our Lord's espoused
bride and Church. Therefore, although we be for government and governors, such as the Word of God and our covenant allows; yet we, for ourselves, and all that will adhere
to us as the representative of the true Presbyterian Kirk and
covenanted nation of Scotland, considering the great hazard
of lying under such a sin any longer, do, by these presents,
disown Charles Stuart, that has been reigning, or rather
tyrannizing, as we may say, on the throne of Britain these
years bygone, as having any right, title to, or interest in, the
said crown of Scotland for government, as forfeited, several
years since, by his perjury and breach of covenant both to
God and his Kirk, and usurpation of his crown and royal pre-
rogatives therein, and many other breaches in matters ecclesiastic, and by his tyranny and breach of the very *leges reg-
nandi* in matters civil. For which reason we declare, that
several years since he should have been denuded of being
king, ruler, or magistrate, or of having any power to act or to
be obeyed as such. As also we, being under the standard of
our Lord Jesus Christ, Captain of Salvation, do declare a war
with such a tyrant and usurper, and all the men of his practices, as enemies to our Lord Jesus Christ, and his cause and
covenants; and against all such as have strengthened him,
sided with, or anywise acknowledged him in his tyranny,
civil or ecclesiastic; yea, against all such as shall strengthen,
side with, or anywise acknowledge any other in like usurpation and tyranny—far more against such as would betray or
deliver up our free reformed mother Kirk unto the bondage

of Antichrist, the Pope of Rome. And, by this, we homolo-
gate that testimony given at Rutherglen, the 29th of May
1679, and all the faithful testimonies of those who have gone
before, as also of those who have suffered of late : and we do
disclaim that Declaration published at Hamilton, June 1679,
chiefly because it takes in the king's interest, which we are several years since loosed from, because of the aforesaid reasons,
and others which may, after this, if the Lord will, be published. As also, we disown and by this resent the reception
of the Duke of York, that professed Papist, as repugnant to
our principles and vows to the Most High God, and as that
which is the great, though not alone, just reproach of our
Kirk and nation. We also, by this, protest against his succeeding to the crown, and whatever has been done, or any
are essaying to do in this land, given to the Lord, in prejudice
to our work of reformation. And to conclude, we hope,
after this, none will blame us for, or offend at, our rewarding
those that are against us as they have done to us, as the Lord
gives opportunity. This is not to exclude any that have declined, if they be willing to give satisfaction according to the
degree of their offence."

Such, then, is the famous Declaration which made so much
noise at the time of its publication, and to which so much
importance was attached by its adherents. This, however,
is not the only Declaration which was published at the cross
of Sanquhar. There were five besides this : one by Mr
Renwick about three years before the Revolution, and four
after it, by the parties who were not satisfied with the existing state of things. Of the four Declarations which were
published at Sanquhar after the Revolution, the first was
August 10, 1692; the second, November 6, 1695; the third,
May 21, 1703; and the fourth, 1707. This ancient burgh
seems to have been fruitful in Declarations. It is the central point of a wide district, which, at that time, was the
favourite resort of many of the sufferers, and a place which
was of easy access from every quarter.

The following anecdotes, however, are connected, not with
the first of these Declarations, but with the second, published
by Renwick after the death of Charles II., and the proclamation of the Duke of York, as king, in 1685. "Mr Renwick,"
says one of his biographers, "could not let go this opportunity
of witnessing against the usurpation by a Papist of the
government of the nation, and his design of overthrowing the
covenanted work of reformation, and introducing Popery
Accordingly, he and about two hundred men went to San

quhar, May 28, 1685, and published the Declaration after-wards called the Sanquhar Declaration."

The eighty-five was, perhaps, with the exception of the year in which the Highland host was let loose in the west, the darkest in the annals of the persecuting period. It is termed by Wodrow, " a black year." During this year the blood of the saints was made to run like water on the ground; and many a loud cry did it send up to that holy heaven which witnessed the sufferings of those devoted ones who loved not their lives unto the death. "How long, O Lord, holy and true, dost thou not judge and avenge our blood on them that dwell on the earth ? And white robes were given unto every one of them, and it was said unto them that they should rest yet for a little season, until their fellow-servants also, and their brethren, that should be killed as they were, should be fulfilled." Satan, knowing that his time was but short, seemed to rage with uncommon fury, and vigorously strove " to wear out the saints of the Most High."

A short time after the accession of James II., Mr Renwick held a conventicle in the moor of Evandale. A great company assembled from all quarters to hear the word of truth preached by this youthful and zealous servant of Christ, who, almost single-handed, maintained the standard of the Gospel in the fields. After the day's work was concluded, a meet-ing was held on the spot, for the purpose of deliberating on what, in the present posture of affairs, was best to be done. After much consultation, it was agreed that a full declara-tion of their principles should be published at the cross of Sanquhar on an early day. They were convinced that no re-dress of their grievances was to be obtained : they saw that they could not rectify matters for themselves, and that the only thing left for them to do was to testify publicly and strongly against the evil complained of. Having, therefore, come to this determination, the assembly dispersed, every one being enjoined to observe the strictest secrecy. It was not an easy matter, however, to secure the secrecy necessary in such cases; for it was not possible to hold any meeting, even in the remotest solitudes, without the intrusion of spies and informers, who appeared among them as wolves in sheep's clothing, and who by goodly words and fair speeches, insinuated themselves into the good graces of the simple-minded people, who, practising no deceit themselves, were not so ready to suspect others. The appointed day of meeting at length arrived. Mr Renwick, who, at this time, lodged in a place called Cumberhead, where he was kindly entertained for his Master's sake, had a journey of about twenty miles to accomplish. He was accompanied by a few faithful friends, one of whom, named Laing, a steady adherent of the cause, lived in Blagannach, not far from the place of the proposed meeting. Blagannach is situated in the very heart of the mountains, about half way between Sanquhar and Muirkirk, and near Hyndbottom, the lonely scene of a great conventicle held on one occasion by Cameron. The locality affords a specimen of one of the most perfect solitudes in the south Highlands; and, in former times, when the glens were not opened by roads, nor cleared of their woods, would not be easily accessible. The Laings of Blagannach are a very ancient family, their race having now been resident in that place nearly four hundred years. The road between Cumberhead and the place where the conventicle was to be held was very rough and mountainous, and not easily travelled on horseback. Mr Renwick and his company, therefore, set out on foot the evening before. The nightseason was adopted for the purpose of concealment; and, after many a weary and toilsome step, they reached the spot in the early morning. As they came along, groups of people were seen gathering in from all parts to the secluded glen. The numbers that were assembling showed the deep interest which the populace generally took in the matter. When a goodly number of the people had congregated, and were silently waiting till the services should commence, a man on horseback was descried in the distance, advancing with all the speed that the ruggedness of the ground would permit. The deep murmuring of voices was heard throughout the congregation, like the low muttering of remote thunder. It was obvious to every one that the horseman was the bearer of important tidings : this was indicated by his hurried and impatient movements. Every heart throbbed with solicitude, and the anxiety of the moment was intense. At length the approach of the messenger put an end to suspense. "Ye are betrayed, my friends!" vociferated he, when he was within cry of the company; " ye are betrayed, and the enemy is at hand." This was indeed the case : a traitor had found his way into the camp at the former meeting, and he lost no time in communicating the designs of the party to the enemy. This informer was a man of the name of Sandilands, from Crawfordjohn, who had been seen in company with the commander of the dragoons on the evening preceding. This infamous character was in the pay of the enemy; and he exerted himself in every way to gain the good opinion of his employers, and to retain his lucrative situation.

This information spread consternation throughout the meeting, and it was resolved instantly to abandon the spot, and to retire to a still more secluded place among the mountains; and the neighbourhood of Blagannach was fixed on as the place of retreat. The tent, under the awning of which Mr Renwick was to address the multitude, was erected on the edge of an impassable morass, and was constructed of strong stakes driven deep into the moss, and covered with the plaids of the shepherds. Before the work of the day commenced, it was agreed that Mr Renwick should exchange clothes with some individual present. The design of this was, that in case of the sudden approach of the troopers, he might the more readily effect his escape. There was no small danger attending this experiment to the man who should assume Mr Renwick's dress—as a person in clerical habiliments would, in those times, be easily distinguishable from the rest of the people. Laing, however, was ready to incur all the risk attending the project; and he generously offered to substitute himself in Mr Renwick's stead. He was a stout and intrepid man, and fully prepared for a tough pursuit by the enemy, should they make their appearance. Mr Renwick was forced to comply with the wishes of the company, and to attire himself for the present in a garb different from his own, but not an inappropriate one, for it was the garb of a shepherd. This was done with a most generous intention; for Mr Renwick, possessing a constitution by no means robust, was much exhausted with the toil of the previous night's journey, and therefore incapacitated for much exertion in flight before his pursuers.

When all things were arranged, and the watches stationed at proper distances to give due warning in case of danger, this little Church convened in the wilderness engaged in the solemn worship of God. The words from which Mr Renwick preached were: "He that toucheth you toucheth the apple of his eye." This text, it would appear, was selected for the occasion; and it is expressive of the peculiarity of the Lord's care and sympathy in reference to his people, whose enemies are watching the opportunity of injuring them. The eye is a very delicate and sensitive organ, and there is no part of the body which we are ready to defend with a more instinctive promptitude. Hence he who harms his people touches Christ in the tenderest part, and inflicts an injury which he is prepared to resent. This subject, then, would be employed by the preacher for the purpose of strengthening the faith and the fortitude of the handful that had now met among the mountains to bear witness to the truth. There is something exceedingly soothing and encouraging in the thought that God exercises over us a special guardianship as his people, that the shield of his providential interference is interposed between us and our foes, and that the sympathies of Christ are ever awake in our behalf.

As the company were listening to the discourse, with minds deeply absorbed in the subject, the work was suddenly inter-rupted by the report that the dragoons were advancing. All was confusion, and the congregation was instantly scattered. The greater part fled to the moss, where the dragoons could not so easily follow them. Laing, arrayed in Mr Renwick's clothes, took a different route; and rendered himself as con-spicuous as possible, for the purpose of attracting the notice of the dragoons to himself, singly and alone, as the supposed individual after whom they were chiefly in quest. The stra-tagem succeeded; and the main body of the troopers turned in the direction in which he was fleeing, and this afforded the people and Mr Renwick the opportunity of escaping. Laing, acting as a decoy, led the soldiers into the deepest and most inextricable parts of the morass. He knew every foot of it, and could wend his way with ease through its entire breadth and length. In these morasses there are generally narrow paths that are known only to the shepherds, who can pass and repass with perfect safety, where strangers might probably lose their lives. Laing, and the few men that were with him, endeavoured to preserve a certain distance from the pursuers—not to advance too far, lest they should give up the chase as hopeless, and turn on the others—and not to proceed too tardily, lest their enemies should get within shot of them. The troopers seemed to have no doubt that the person whom they were following was Mr Renwick, both from his appearance, and from the assistance which they saw was occasionally lent him in stepping the deep moss-hags. The individual about whom so much solicitude was mani-fested could be no other than the minister; and therefore they were determined to capture him, come of the rest what might. When the horsemen had advanced a certain way into the moss, the impossibility of proceeding further became instantly apparent; and therefore it was agreed that two or three of the more robust of the party should dismount and pursue on foot. In a short time, however, it was found that this method was equally impracticable; for the tall, heavy men, with their unwieldy accoutrements, leaping and plunging in the moss, sunk to the waist, and could with difficulty extricate themselves. In this attempt one of their number broke his leg, and this incident put an end to their pursuit. They dragged their disabled companion to the firm ground, and conveyed him to Blagannach. The goodwife of Blagannach was the only person who was within when the party arrived; the rest of the family, who were at the conventicle, not having yet returned. The soldiers behaved very rudely, and questioned her closely respecting her sons and her husband. The honest woman, however, seemed to pay very little regard to their inquiries, professing to be greatly distressed at the loss of a good milk cow that had that morning disappeared in the moss. After they refreshed themselves with what provisions they found in the house, and perceiving that they could elicit nothing satisfactory from the old matron, they departed, being themselves the only party who that day had sustained damage. They marched to Crawfordjohn, where they left their comrade with the fractured limb till he should recover. Tradition says that the soldier who met with the accident became an altered man; that during his confinement he began seriously to reflect on the course he had been pursuing; that the iniquity of his conduct became clearly apparent; that he was led to true repentance and faith in the Saviour; and that, after his recovery, he connected himself with the cause he had persecuted, and lived a zealous, devoted Christian. It is exceedingly gratifying to meet with such an instance of a gracious change in an individual whose employment was to shed the blood of the saints. Such conversions, though not numerous, were, nevertheless, of occasional occurrence; the Lord manifesting his graciousness here and there as something noticeable, and as an encouragement to others of the same profession to turn to him, in the certain hope of likewise obtaining mercy. The Gospel extends the offer of salvation to sinners of every description. The greatest as well as the least sinner is welcome to come to Him, who is able to save to the uttermost; for the blood of Christ cleanseth from all sin. Paul the persecutor found mercy—"one who made havoc of the Church of God, entering into every house, and haling men and women, committed them to prison," and the mercy that Paul obtained, others also may obtain. The forgiveness of great and notorious transgressors eminently illustrates the sovereignty and richness of divine grace, and displays the infinite efficacy of the Christian atonement, and shows that there is no sin so

great but God is ready to forgive it for the Redeemer's sake:
" Though your sins be as scarlet, they shall be white as snow;
and though they be red like crimson, they shall be as the
wool." This poor man was the only individual of his party
who met with anything like a serious accident in their
attempt to disperse and kill the worshippers of God in the
desert; and he was, perhaps, the only one of their entire
number who was brought to the knowledge of the truth.
Afflictions are often messengers of mercy, which the Lord
sends to " bring back his banished;" and, though the fracture of the soldier's leg would doubtless be deemed by him
the greatest calamity that could befall him next to the loss
of his life, yet God made it the precursor of his conversion.
It sometimes happens that an occurrence which we regard at
the time as a very great misfortune, turns out in the event to
be a very great blessing. We are short-sighted creatures;
and are therefore ready to draw the most unfavourable conclusions from apparently disastrous incidents, which, nevertheless, embody the greatest good, and issue in our special
benefit. " All these things are against me," exclaimed the
venerable patriarch, when in truth the whole was secretly
working out the temporal salvation of his household. To
bring good out of evil is the prerogative of Him who is
" wonderful in counsel and excellent in working."

Blagannach, when we consider its situation and the Christian character of its occupants, must have been a place of
frequent resort in the times of ecclesiastical oppression. It
is said that in this place Alexander Shiels wrote part of the
" Hind let Loose"—a work which well deserves a perusal,
even in these enlightened times of civil and religious liberty.

The congregation, having fled on the approach of the
dragoons, pursued their way down the rivulet of the Spank,
towards the River Crawick. The Crawick is a pastoral stream
which rises on the borders of Lanarkshire in the Highlands,
and wends its way in a south-westerly direction, till it falls
into the Nith, in the immediate vicinity of Sanquhar. The
course of this stream exhibits a scene of surpassing beauty.
Its mountains, covered with deep verdure, present the appearance of a newly mown meadow; while some of the hills
are so abrupt from the summit to the base, that a person can
scarcely walk with steadiness along the velvet slope. The
hollow valley of the Crawick was, at the time to which these
sketches refer, closely covered with wood, whose thickets
afforded a secure retreat to the fugitives from Blagannach
Moss. Into this place of concealment it was in vain for the

dragoons to penetrate; and therefore they retired, satisfied that they had at least scattered the conventicle, though they had captured none of the " rebels."

The leaders of the dispersed multitude met on the evening of the same day, in a sequestered glade in the dark forest of Crawick, to concert measures anew respecting the Declaration. It was agreed that, though for the present they were disappointed in their object, they would by no means abandon the design; but that, on a future day, they would meet again to fulfil their purpose. The publication of their projected Declaration they considered as an important duty which they owed alike to God and to their country; and a work which, in the present emergency, they were imperiously called on to perform. They therefore appointed a day for a second convention; and, commending one another to the grace of God and to the care of his providence, they dispersed to their several homes, thanking the Lord for the special protection which had that day been vouchsafed to them.

After the noise which the affair at Blagannach made had ceased, those friendly to the covenanting interest convened from the neighbouring parishes, for the purpose of proceeding to the inland burgh of Sanquhar to publish the Declaration agreed on. About two hundred individuals met accordingly, determined to brave every opposition in the performance of a duty so imperative. On the 28th of May 1685, the inhabitants of Sanquhar were surprised at the appearance of so great a company, who, without any signal of their approach, had stationed themselves in the very heart of their town. The men had a warlike aspect, each prepared with weapons of defence in case of an onslaught. In these unsettled times, when rumours of battles and of bloodshed were constantly ringing in people's ears, it is not to be wondered at that the populace of this quiet and secluded town should have felt some degree of alarm at the unceremonious intrusion of so great a band of men. Their purpose, however, was soon divulged. They were not come to pillage the inhabitants, nor to spill one drop of blood, but to testify publicly their adherence to the covenanted cause of reformation, in the only way which was left open for them to do. Having, therefore, read their Declaration aloud in the audience of the people, and then attached it to the market cross as their testimony against the evils of which they virtuously complained, they, in a peaceable and orderly manner left the place with all convenient speed, lest the enemy, to whom

information of their proceedings would instantly be transmitted, should pursue them. This second Declaration, which
was published with much more pomp and circumstance than
the first by Cameron's party, was equally offensive to the
civil authorities, although not so much was said about it at
the time; for, as the one disowned Charles, the other abjured
James as an obnoxious Papist to whom no allegiance was
lawfully due.

With regard to the propriety of the various Declarations
which were published in these times of oppression, different
persons will doubtless entertain different opinions; but, we
would ask, is not the Revolution Settlement founded on the
principles contained in there Declarations? And in 1688,
did not the whole nation do on a larger scale exactly what
the Covenanters in Scotland did on a small scale? Dr Burns,
the pious and talented editor of Wodrow, in his excellent
" Preliminary Dissertation " to that work, makes the following remark :—" The conduct of the actors in the scenes of
Rutherglen, at Sanquhar, and at Torwood, in disowning the
king, and excommunicating him and his adherents, is indeed
justly censurable as rash and unwarranted; but, we beg to
know, wherein did the primary principles avowed and acted
on on those occasions differ from those principles which, in
the course of a very few years thereafter, roused the dormant
spirit of the country, and chased the oppressor from the
throne?" Let those, then, who glory in the Revolution
Settlement, take care how they censure the principles of the
honest Covenanters of the North.

The following anecdote has a relation to the publishing of
the Sanquhar Declaration, by Mr Renwick and his friends,
1685, on the occasion of the accession of the Duke of York
to the throne. It appears that this celebrated Declaration
was countenanced by a convention of Covenanters from all
parts of the west and south. An unusually deep interest
was felt in reference to this manifesto, because it was dreaded
that the land would be overspread, not only with the Prelatic
abominations already complained of and contended against,
but with what was even more to be dreaded, the Popish
idolatry in all its grossness. Among the many who took an
interest in this matter, were the men of Galloway, than whom
sturdier Covenanters existed not in the country. A deputation from this district, then, or else a company of well-wishers,
on their own account, proceeded northwards, to meet Mr
Renwick at Sanquhar. Their route lay along the beautiful
banks of the Ken. As they were proceeding on their journey

with little suspicion, in the heart of a wild and hilly country, they were informed that a spy, lurking in the neighbourhood, was watching their movements. On receiving this notice, they betook themselves to the more mountainous tracks, to escape observation. The name of the spy was Grier. He was formerly one of the Covenanters, and was well acquainted both with them and their hiding-places. He had renounced the covenant for a bribe; and, being well paid by his employers, he was very assiduous in his vocation. These informers were, especially if they were apostates, peculiarly detested. Their employment was a degradation to humanity; and even those in whose service they were engaged could not but despise them. These active agents of evil were always on the alert, for their temporal interests were combined with success in their infamous calling. One of the covenanting brethren, named M'Lurg, happened to be journeying on the west side of the river, not having yet joined his company; and, observing the spy, he hid himself behind a rock. In this situation he had ample opportunity of subjecting the man to his scrutiny, as he happened to be near him. As he passed the hiding-place full in his view, he discovered that he was an old acquaintance, and the very man who had deserted their cause, and become their vengeful and insidious enemy; that he was the informer who was the cause of so much anxiety and distress to the Nonconformists in the neighbourhood; and that he was at that very moment tracing the steps of him and his friends, with a view to do them mischief. It now occurred that he had a fair opportunity of avenging the wrongs which this unhappy man had been the means of inflicting on the distressed remnant, who were subjected to the incessant harassings of their persecutors. He imagined that by shooting him on the spot, he would perform a righteous deed, and be the praiseworthy instrument of ridding the district of an intolerable nuisance. Accordingly, he lifted his musket to a level with his eye; and levelling the fatal tube at the man's breast, he fired. The ball, entering under the left arm, passed through the heart, and he fell dead on the heath. This act, though performed by a zealous Covenanter, is pointedly to be condemned. M'Lurg acted on a mistaken principle, and was, doubtless, influenced by the supposition that he was doing service to the cause of Christ, by removing, in this way, one of the enemies of that cause; but no circumstance can justify assassination—it is foul and flagrant murder, which no person who regards the authority of the divine law, or who holds the blood of his brother sacred, will dare to defend. Had the Covenanters possessed the same views which we now entertain respecting the treatment of the enemies of religion, they would not in any instance have avenged themselves in an objectionable way. It must, however, be noticed, to the honour of the great body of the Covenanters, that occurrences of this description were comparatively rare; and that, when any incident of the kind did take place, it was by no means generally approved of. The rejection of James M'Michael by the Societies for killing the curate of Carsphairn, is a proof of this; and even the murder of Archbishop Sharp, as Wodrow shows, was an act which, by the friends of the persecuted cause, was very generally condemned at the time. But it is very easy for us, who live in days of religious quietude and safety, to moralize. " Oppression makes wise men mad;" and, had we lived in their times, and endured the same sufferings, it is questionable if, on the whole, we would have acted our part so well. It is to be remarked, too, that among the Covenanters there were not a few who bore the character merely of patriots, and the object which these men had chiefly in view was to avenge the political wrongs of their country; and if, on any occasion, they stepped forward from the ranks of their more Christian brethren, and under the waving of their banners committed injudicious and illegal acts, though with a good design, the humane and pious part are not to be implicated.

The slaughter of the informer took place not far from the Holm of Ken—a most delightful spot near the upper extremity of the glen. It is a kind of Eden in the midst of the wilderness, and far removed from the busy haunts of men. When M'Lurg saw that the man was slain, he left his station behind the rock, and proceeded to strip him of his armour—an article of great account in those days. Among other warlike implements, he found in his possession a weapon called the Galloway flail. What is termed the handstaff of this instrument, was made of the tough and durable ash wood, and about five feet in length. The *soople*, or that part which strikes the barn-floor, was formed of iron, and was about three feet long, and had three joints. This flail was doubtless intended for warlike purposes by the man who carried it, and must have been a formidable weapon when wielded by a muscular arm. By means of the joints in its iron *soople*, it was, when vigorously applied, fitted like a thong to infold the body of a man, and in this way was calculated to crush the ribs, after the manner of a boa constrictor. No swordsman could cope with an individual armed with this weapon.

It could keep any aggressor at a distance. One stroke could shiver a sword to pieces, and leave the person of the defenceless antagonist to be subjected to the same treatment as a sheaf of corn on the barn-floor. This instrument, if not new to M'Lurg, was at least novel in its application to the purposes of warfare. Its utility became instantly apparent, and he carried it off with the determination to use it as occasion might require. When M'Lurg joined his party, who were travelling along the heights, all became loud in their praises of the flail, as a most appropriate implement, when swung by a brawny arm, to clear a goodly space around on the field of conflict. But they had little suspicion that the value of their newly acquired weapon was to be so soon tested. A small company of Lag's men, who were traversing the hills in this direction, happened to emerge somewhat suddenly from a narrow glen, right in the face of M'Lurg and his party. Being thus confronted, a battle appeared to be inevitable, and so the strife instantly commenced. The number on both sides was nearly equal, and neither party thought of flight. In the heat of the engagement it occurred to M'Lurg that now was the time for the exhibition of the flail, and to ascertain if its value on the battle-field was equal to its value on the barn-floor. Accordingly, seizing the handstaff, and waving the *soople* over his head, he magnanimously approached the leader of the opposing party, and furiously assailed him. The onslaught was terrific, and M'Lurg, being a powerful and dauntless man, formed with the gyrations of his thrashing instrument an ample circle around his person, within the verge of which neither friend nor foe durst intrude. The soldiers were confounded at this novel mode of warfare, which appeared to be both sportive and serious. In a brief space, however, M'Lurg succeeded in defeating the leader, who received a fracture on the skull, and a broken arm. This done, he turned in the same furious manner on the soldiers in a body, and dealt his blows so unmercifully, that the party betook themselves to flight, and left the Covenanters masters of the field. Thus terminated a conflict which probably might have proved fatal to the wanderers, had it not been for the incident of the flail. The little company were now left at leisure to pursue, without interruption, their way to the meeting at Sanquhar. In those times of peril and bloodshed, the desert was often as dangerous as the well frequented highway, so that in no place could people be considered in perfect safety from the intrusion of their enemies. In their track through the wilderness they passed some points of scenery incomparably fine, especially the view from Shinnel water-head. The result of the meeting at Sanquhar has been detailed in a former part of this chapter, and therefore further notice of it is unnecessary.

The Galloway flail is particularly mentioned as an implement of warfare, in an ancient Gallovidian ballad, entitled "The Battle of Craignilder," published a few years ago by Captain Denniston. In one of the notes appended to that publication, the author makes the following remarks :—" The Galloway flail must have been a formidable weapon when wielded by a muscular arm. It is described, if we mistake not, by Henry the Minstrel, and seems to have been a weapon indigenous to the country, as several old writers mention it by that name. We had the fortune to see one, reported to have been taken out of Dumbarton Castle; it was in a museum collected by the ingenious Mr Burrell in Edinburgh, about twenty-five years ago. In so far as our recollection of it is to be depended on, its staff might have been about five feet in length, the soople about three and a half or four feet, and joined with iron rings, either in one or two places, so that it doubled with resistless force over any interposing object." The lines of the ballad to which this note is appended, are the following :—

> " With vengeful speed fierce Douglas flew,
> Where rang the swinging *flail* man.

CHAPTER IV.

Scar—James M'Michael—Daniel M'Michael—Legend of Morton
Castle.

THE farm-house of Dalzien is situated in the centre of the
valley of the Scar, and is famous as the birth-place of Daniel
M'Michael, who suffered martyrdom, and of James M'Michael,
his brother, the subject of the following sketch. The Scar,
is a pastoral stream, which runs parallel to the Nith on the
south, opposite Sanquhar, and separated by an intervening
ridge of lofty mountains. The valley is adorned with a considerable variety of scenery; the upper part is plain and
uninteresting, but towards the lower extremity it is enchanting. The chief feature of its topography, however, is an
enormous rock, called Glenquhargen Crag, which rises from
the plain of the valley probably to the height of about six
hundred feet. The south of Scotland, perhaps, can boast of
nothing of the same description of equal magnificence. The
height of the naked rock, however, is much less at present
than it must have been in former ages, for its base is now
deeply buried in its own debris. It is one of those bold features of nature which inspire the beholder with the mingled
feelings of delight and awe. This stupendous scene has its
own legends connected with the covenanting times, but
fraught with a superstition too gross to admit of recital.
Dalzien stands at the head of a charming triangular opening
of the valley, as green and level as a velvet lawn, and lined
on the three sides with hills of a moderate elevation, while
the pure stream of the Scar sweeps along its northern edge.
The entire appearance of the scene, at first sight, strongly
reminds one of some of those beautiful Waldensian valleys,
in the secrecy of which the Church of God concealed herself
for ages. Nor was the character of the inhabitants dissi-
milar; for, even to a recent period, the locality was peopled
with a race of eminent Christians, the fame of whose genuine
worth was not confined to their own neighbourhood.

James M'Michael was a man of a bold and hasty temper, and was easily roused to great energy in the defence of what in his conscience he believed to be the right cause. His temper, however, was frequently a source of uneasiness to his friends, as well as of terror to his enemies, and it required no small share of divine grace to subdue it, and to keep it within proper bounds. His irascibility accounts for the impetuous and reprehensible manner in which he sometimes acted, and throws a considerable shade over his otherwise worthy character. The period in which tradition first brings him into notice is, when he was in the service of the Laird of Maxwellton, and when, on account of the discovery of his religious and political principles, he was obliged to flee for his life. He betook himself to the mountains, avowedly embraced the cause of the Covenanters, and resolved to share their fortunes. He assisted at the skirmish in Airs-moss, where Richard Cameron and a number of his followers fell, defending themselves against the horsemen of Bruce of Earlshall. His patriotic feelings were easily kindled; and being informed by some of the refugees from Ayrshire, who came seeking a retreat among the dark mountains in the upper parts of Galloway, that the enemy were making strict search for Cameron and his followers, he forthwith resolved to join them. With this determination he left his hiding-place on the banks of the Ken, and set out to render what assistance he could to those with whom, in their affliction, he deeply sympathized. He traced them, in their wanderings, to Airs-moss, at which place he arrived during the very heat of the engagement. When he approached the desolate and dreary moor, where the combatants were conflicting in deadly strife, he observed a number of persons holding the horses from which the dragoons had dismounted, and guarding their cloaks, which lay in heaps on the edge of the morass. He hastened into the midst of the battle-field, and encountered a gigantic dragoon, who was dealing around many a deadly blow. The fierce dragoon, being little accustomed to meet his compeer in single combat, despised his opponent, and, like the proud and vaunting Philistine of Gath, threatened to make his carcass a banquet to the fowls of the air. They fought with equal skill and courage, and for a considerable time it was doubtful who should obtain the victory. At length, however, owing to the unevenness of the ground, the dragoon stumbled, and M'Michael, embracing the opportunity, pushed him down, and inflicted a mortal wound. The soldier died, uttering the most horrid imprecations, and denouncing the unlucky fate that had brought him to his end by the sword of a detested Covenanter. What a dreadful evil is war! It is one of the most terrible scourges that ever visited this sinful world. In its ravages it has far surpassed famine or pestilence. It has been the means of spreading a wide desolation over the face of the earth, and has sent millions of souls unprepared into eternity. No sooner had M'Michael performed this part, than he saw that his friends had lost the day, and were fleeing in every direction across the trackless moor. It was now his concern to provide for his own safety; and, having gathered up his armour, he made a speedy retreat from the bloody scene, and returned to his native mountains.

It happened, in the course of his wanderings, that on one occasion he paid a visit to his brother Daniel, who informed him of an intended rescue of a number of prisoners who were to be conveyed from Dumfries to Edinburgh, to be tried. The projected rescue, it is said, was planned by an individual of the name of Harkness, who had collected several countrymen, friendly to the covenanting cause, and who were willing to risk their lives in the attempt. For this purpose they dug a deep trench on the hills opposite to the pass called Enterkin Path, along which the dragoons with their prisoners must necessarily proceed, that from this trench, as from a rampart, they might fire suddenly upon the army, and themselves remain in comparative safety. When everything was prepared, Harkness, who was now impatient for their arrival, set out to reconnoitre, and proceeded onward a few miles in the direction in which he expected them to come. At length he observed the soldiers with the prisoners marching slowly along, and being fully satisfied that they were the party waited for, he retraced his steps with all convenient speed. An individual of the party, however, detected him, and suspecting, from his skulking manner, that he was watching their motions, a detachment was sent in pursuit. He succeeded, however, in making his escape, and left his pursuers entangled in the dangerous intricacies of a deep morass. Having reached the trench in the pass long before the dragoons arrived, he informed his friends of the number of the enemy with whom they expected to cope, and made all suitable preparations for their reception. It was easy to distinguish the prisoners from the soldiers, and therefore their aim in firing on them could be taken with perfect precision, and without risk to the former. In a short time the cavalcade was seen winding up the deep and dangerous ravine, dreading no harm, and utterly unconscious of the fatal ambush that was laid for them. When the party had advanced in a long line exactly opposite the embankment, behind which Harkness and M'Michael, with their trusty friends, had ensconced themselves, the commanding officer was chanting aloud a popular song, which happened to be peculiarly offensive to the Covenanters generally. This circumstance roused the spirit of M'Michael, who deemed the song an intolerable insult, and resting his musket on the top of the trench, he deliberately pointed a deadly aim at the head of the officer, who tumbled in an instant to the bottom of the ravine. The incident roused the whole party, and made them fully aware of their position. They commenced a vigorous firing, but without effect. No impression was made on the combatants behind the fortification, while the soldiers were exposed, without a screen, to the incessant shots of their opponents. At length, tired out, it would appear, with the unequal contest, the troopers sought safety in flight, and all the prisoners, with one exception, were set at liberty. This is probably a different rescue from that mentioned by Defoe; for it appears there were more rescues in this pass than one. The straggling village of Dalry, in Galloway, is situated on the north side of the Ken, on a sunny slope, which terminates in a delightful plain, through which the river pursues its course. It was in this village where the scuffle took place between the dragoons and some of the peasantry, in the kitchen of the inn where they accidentally met, and which led to the rising at Pentland in 1666. In its immediate vicinity is a large moat, the finest, perhaps, in the south of Scotland, used by the ancient Saxons as a meeting-place for judicial purposes. Dalry, owing to its situation in a mountainous country, was frequently resorted to by the Covenanters; and formed, like Sanquhar, a kind of central point to the wanderers of the surrounding district. The farm of Stroanpatrick, in the neighbourhood of this village, was, in the times of persecution, tenanted by a person of the name of Roan. This man was professedly a Covenanter, and apparently much attached to the cause. In process of time, however, his fidelity was suspected, and fears were entertained that he was secretly an informer. In reference to this surmise, however, no proof could be distinctly led; but those with whom he was ostensibly connected, resolved to investigate the matter, as far as circumstances would permit. Accordingly, M'Michael and a few friends were deputed by the " societies," or "fellowship meetings," as they were called, to converse with Roan on the subject, with power to suspend him as a member of the associations, if the inquiry proved unsatisfactory. These "associations," or "praying societies," took their rise after the death of Cargill, and were very common during the latter part of the persecuting period. They were of immense advantage in promoting the growth of true religion among the scattered flock of Christ, in the dark and cloudy day of the Church's tribulation. They were pools of water in the desert, of which God's heritage often drank and were refreshed. They formed little conventicles without a preacher, in which the Word of God was read and commented on by the more aged and experienced members, who had the gift of utterance. They were oratories in which prayer, fervent and effectual, was presented to the Father of mercies, for grace to help in time of need, and in which the high praises of God were sung with thankful and adoring hearts. There is no doubt that in these meetings the children of the desert often met with God, and enjoyed a happiness to which their persecutors, who deemed them wretched exiles, were entire strangers. A man's happiness, however, is not to be estimated by external circumstances; for he who outwardly is everything which one would pronounce blessed, may inwardly be the prey of a misery truly pitiable; while he whose external appearance would indicate much discomfort, may have within him a peace which passeth all understanding. The prayer-meetings which originated among our ancestors, in the times when the preaching of the Gospel was rare, have been continued in some of the landward parts till the present day; and have been upheld by a race of men who, for intelligence and piety, have but few equals. If prayer-meetings were more common throughout the land, the Church of God among us would soon appear to " blossom as the rose," and a happy change would, ere long, be experienced through the whole Christian community. And it is cheering to witness the impulse that has recently been given to the spirit of social prayer, and to see the goodly number of young praying societies that have lately sprung up among us, both as the means and as the fruits of a religious revival.

The deputation, then, from the societies, met with Roan, and strictly interrogated him respecting the rumour of his defection, and traitorous correspondence with the enemy. Roan affirmed that the report was false, and that he was as true to the good cause as ever. He admitted that soldiers had frequently come to his house inquiring after Covenanters; but that no information whatever had at any time been im-

parted by him. His averments were not fully credited; for
there appeared something confused and hesitating about his
manner. M'Michael stated that, as they were by no means
satisfied with his attempted exculpation, they were resolved
to exercise the authority conferred on them by the associations—of interdicting his attendance on their meetings, until
he had clearly purged himself of the accusation of being a
spy and an informer; and that, in the meantime, he must
deliver up his arms. The place where this interview was
held was at some distance from Stroanpatrick, at which
place Roan said his arms were deposited; and to this place
he requested them to proceed, that there they might receive
them from his own hand. It had been observed by one of
the party, that, during the unsatisfactory examination of
their suspected associate, their leader's eye was beginning to
kindle, and fearing lest some untoward incident might
befall, he stole to the door where their fire-arms were leaning against the wall, and extracted the shot from M'Michael's
musket. The party then set out for Stroanpatrick. The
road to this place passed through a broad meadow, through
the midst of which flowed a small stream. As they were
proceeding along the meadow, and near the banks of the
streamlet, Roan, watching his opportunity, darted from his
companions, and sprang over the brook, with the evident
intention of deserting the party. Suspicion was roused, and
it appeared plain to every one that their associate was a
traitor. The alarmed fugitive fled with winged speed, and
M'Michael, with his sword drawn, pursued; but when he
found that he was not gaining ground in the pursuit, he flung
after Roan, with all his might, the glittering blade, which
smote him with such force as to inflict a mortal wound, from
which he bled to death on the spot. Thus ended the mission
on which M'Michael and his fellows were sent: it terminated
disastrously for the poor man to whom suspicion attached,
and not very creditably to those who were commissioned to
remonstrate with him on the alleged dishonesty of his conduct. The deed, on the part of M'Michael, was rash and
unwarranted, and deserved the severest reprehension. It
is revolting to a serious mind, and a deed on account of which
its perpetrator would, no doubt, feel some compunctious visit-
ings. It is probable, however, that M'Michael did not intend to kill the man, but only to disable, and to prevent him
from doing the mischief which in all likelihood he intended.
This supposition receives countenance from the fact, that
James M'Michael aimed at the lower part of his body, where

he actually struck the blow which, unintentionally, we hope, issued in his death.

Peter Pierson, the curate of Carsphairn, was, like many of his brethren, an object of special dislike to the neighbourhood in which he resided. He entered fully into the spirit of the party with which he was connected, and was unwearied in his search after Nonconformists in his parish, and punctual in communicating information respecting them. He cherished, as might be expected, a cordial dislike to the Covenanters; and was constantly taking account of those of his parishioners who refused to attend his church. His interference in this way became at length absolutely intolerable, and the people were determined to submit to it no longer. Accordingly a party, of which M'Michael formed one, proceeded to the manse, with a view to remonstrate with the curate, and, if possible, to bring him to a better understanding. They had drawn up a paper, to the requisitions contained in which they desired of him an express and unequivocal agreement. They informed him that the chief thing that they wanted of him was, that he should allow them to live without molestation in reference to religious matters; and that, if this proposition was agreed to, they would give him no more trouble. When the purport of this interview was made known, he became greatly enraged, and would listen to nothing they had to say. On the arrival of the party at the manse, it was agreed that a few of their number should station themselves at the door to keep watch, while the rest entered the house. When the men entered the curate's apartment, and made known their errand, he barred the door, and presented a loaded pistol to shoot the intruders on the spot. The men without, hearing the uproar, and the cries of their friends for assistance, demanded an instant admittance. On entering the room, M'Michael, seeing the perilous circumstances of his companions, and the danger in which he himself was now placed, in the hastiness of his spirit, fired, and the curate fell dead on the floor. His associates, when they first perceived his intention, commanded him to desist; but he heeded them not. This deed, which M'Michael with a reckless hand perpetrated, was highly disapproved of by the Covenanters in the south-west of Scotland. It was not their wish to shed blood, but rather, by all honest means, to prevent its effusion; and the Societies having taken the matter into consideration, resolved on the expulsion of M'Michael from their associations, because the killing of the curate was, in their estimation, an action which could not be justified. It does not appear, however, that M'Michael had any intention of injuring the incumbent, further than what might befall in mere self-defence. His own life, and the life of his companions, was threatened by a vengeful and turbulent man, whose constant work was, by all means, to harass and persecute the people of God, who were willing to live peaceably, and to do injury to no man. That such a man was, on the present occasion, about to shoot some of the party, there can be no doubt; and it was not to be expected that a man of M'Michael's temper would tamely wait the catastrophe. That M'Michael committed a grievous error cannot be questioned, especially when we consider that the number present in the chamber was sufficient to disarm the curate, without offering violence to his person. The unhappy man, however, lost his life, and lost it as the agent of a very sinful faction, and was therefore the less prepared for entering eternity. Incidents of this kind, instead of alleviating, aggravated the sufferings of the Covenanters; and the guilt of what was done privately and by a few, on their own responsibility, was charged on the whole body, and afforded their adversaries a pretext for rendering the persecution still more general and severe. Wodrow mentions the death of Pierson, and his account coincides with more than the general outline of the tradition. The societies, by their expulsion of M'Michael, showed that they were not connected with this deed, and that it was a step which they repudiated. Whether they saw reason afterwards to admit him, tradition does not say; but their sentiments, expressed in this way, were calculated to produce a salutary impression on the mind of one who doubtless meant well, but whose impetuosity of temper carried him occasionally far beyond the bounds of propriety.

Those who are of an irritable disposition have much need to exercise watchfulness, lest Satan take occasion of their infirmity to hurry them into acts of sin which may grieve the Holy Spirit, dishonour their Christian profession, and wring their own hearts with regret till their dying day. Believers should reflect that there is no feature of the Christian character so amiable, and so much in keeping with the Gospel temper, as a meek and quiet spirit. " Learn of me, for I am meek and lowly in heart, and ye shall find rest unto your souls." Peace cannot dwell in a heart that is constantly fretted with angry passions, and in which the least provocation excites wrathful emotions. Anger, frequently indulged, becomes at length a disease of the mind, which nothing but the all-powerful grace of God can cure. Few persons seem to be more unfit for that heaven where all is love, and peace, and serenity, than those who indulge a turbulent and irascible temper. "The fruit of the Spirit is love, joy, peace, *long-suffering, gentleness,* goodness, *meekness.*" There is, however, no evil habit, or passion, which may not be subdued, and which will not be subdued, if by faith we take hold of the strength of Him who is able to crush all our spiritual enemies under our feet. It is a noble display of the real efficacy of divine grace, when it is seen mollifying and sweetening the temper that was formerly rough and indomitable, and changing the wolf into the lamb. Not to speak of the greater mischiefs which the proud and overbearing tempers of men have produced in society at large, let us look to the heart-burnings and the discomfort among neighbours, and in families, of which peevishness and irritability, not religiously counteracted, are the cause. A fretful disposition, like a canker, corrodes the heart, and leaves it solitary and wretched. "He that hath no rule over his own spirit is like a city that is broken down and without walls."

After the death of Pierson the curate, M'Michael, though in the meantime expelled by the societies, still adhered with unflinching constancy to the cause of civil and religious freedom. He was now under the necessity of using greater caution in his movements, and of retiring more frequently to the desolate parts of the country. His enemies now considered him as a person of some consequence, and were therefore determined to apprehend him. Claverhouse, with his troopers, had entered the district where he was suspected to be lurking, and was using every means to get him and his associates into his power. At this time M'Michael and several of his companions were concealed among the hills, near the Water of Dee; and Claverhouse, having received information of the circumstance, surprised them in their hiding-place at a moment when they dreaded no harm. The sudden onslaught threw the party at first into confusion, and two of their number fled unnoticed into a shepherd's hut; but the others, finding no way of escape, were obliged to stand on the defensive. The skirmish was severe; both parties were brave, and fought with courage. Claverhouse advanced on M'Michael, sword in hand, in the full confidence of gaining an easy conquest. That haughty soldier feared no danger, and seldom met with his equal on the battle-field. In the person of M'Michael, however, he found a warrior who, in point of martial dexterity and true heroism, was not inferior

D

to himself; and long and stiffly was the combat maintained,
till Claverhouse, dreading the consequences, called out lustily
for assistance. "You dare not," cried M'Michael, "abide
the issue of a single combat; and had your helmet been like
mine, a soft bonnet, your carcass had ere this found its bed
on the heath!" The dispute, however, was soon terminated,
for a powerful dragoon, approaching cautiously, came behind
M'Michael, and with one stroke of his ponderous blade clave
his head in two. Thus fell a leal-hearted patriot, whose
prowess the most illustrious cavalier of his time feared to
withstand, and whose conduct, where it is culpable, is more
to be attributed to the times than to the man. M'Michael
was both a Christian and a pat⸍ ⸍t; and while tradition has
preserved more of his patriotism than his Christianity—which
can easily be accounted for, owing to the part which he
was called on to act—this does not prove any decided infe-
riority to the worthies of that trying time, nor any remarkable deficiency in what constitutes "the highest style of
man."

Daniel M'Michael, as has already been noticed in the
account given of his brother James, was born at Dalzien, in
the valley of the Scar, in the parish of Penpont. We have
no notice, however, respecting the time and manner in which
his mind was first savingly impressed with the truth. Whether it was in early youth or in riper years that he became the
subject of a gracious change, tradition has not informed us.
The fact, however, is certain, that he was a true believer, a
genuine follower of the Saviour, and that he was honoured
to seal his testimony with his blood. From the circumstance
of his name being inserted in the fugitive roll, it would appear that his principles as a Nonconformist were well known,
and that he was especially marked by his enemies. In the
roll referred to, he is designated "Daniel M'Michael in Lurg-
foot." The place is now called Blairfoot, and belongs to the
farm of Burn, in the parish of Morton, in Nithsdale. In this
locality there was a cave by the margin of a mountain stream,
to which, in those days, the Covenanters often resorted. It
was a hallowed retreat to many, not only as a place of refuge
from their foes, but as a sanctuary for heavenly fellowship.

Daniel M'Michael's house at Blairfoot was something like
the house of the good John Brown of Priesthill; it was a little
church, a meeting-place to all the religious people in the district, who assembled there for the purpose of hallowed fellowship and prayer. The wanderers who had located themselves in the wilds and dens of the neighbouring mountains,

frequently stole to Daniel's cottage, to spend the hours of a cold and stormy winter's evening in spiritual converse; and many a weary outcast found it a Bethel for God's presence and communion with his saints.

The seclusion of Daniel's residence must, in those times have been very dreary. On the north it is fronted with dismal and frowning hills, the sterile aspect of which impresses the mind with the idea of a loneliness unwonted even in those desert parts. The ancient castle of Morton, mouldering into decay, raises its grim turrets in scowling aspect over the weary scene—a fortlet this once possessed by the doughty Douglases, where deeds of terrific interest, as old legends say, were perpetrated by the haughty lords of the domain, who ruled with almost absolute power in those rough times of feudal barbarism.

The house in which Daniel lived at Blairfoot is now razed from its foundation. It was demolished only the other year, when the ploughshare was made to pass over its site, and a solitary tree is left to mark the spot where this honest worthy lived and prayed in the dark times of Zion's troubles.

In the dreary month of January 1685, Daniel was confined to his bed of a fever, caught it is not said how, but in all probability brought on by his frequent exposure to cold and wet, when he was obliged to withdraw himself from the face of his foes to the bleak and inclement deserts. The worthy men who lay in concealment in the vicinity, often visited Daniel in his affliction, and prayed and discoursed like men who were on the wing to a better world. By means of these heavenly communings his spirit was refreshed. One day a company of these pious persons met at Blairfoot, for the purpose of engaging in religious exercises, and they adopted the common precaution of stationing a friend as a warder, to give notice in case of danger. At this time, Dalziel of Kirkmichael and Lieutenant Straiton, with a party of fifty soldiers, were ranging the country in quest of fugitives. Muncie of Durisdeer, the informer, having received notice of the meeting that was being held in Daniel's house, lost no time in communicating information of the circumstance to the commander of the troops, who led his company without delay to Blairfoot. The watchman, however, observed their approach, and hastened to the house with the unwelcome tidings. The party within instantly prepared for flight, but in their haste to be gone they forgot not their sickly brother. They knew that if he were left alone his sickness would procure him no exemption from the ill usage with which the soldiers might

be disposed to treat him, and therefore they determined to
remove him from his bed, and carry him along with them.
Accordingly they wrapped him in the warm bed-clothes, and
conveyed him with all speed, and unobserved, to the cave.

But there was another informer beside Muncie, and one
who pretended to belong to their party, and who, under the
mask of friendship and of piety, had connected himself with
them, with a view to accomplish his own nefarious designs.
This individual (whose name we do not deem it prudent to
mention) left the cave to give certain information to the party
that was in quest of the fugitives. Another of the company
having left the hiding-place shortly after the departure of the
traitor, and having occasion to call at a smithy in the neigh
bourhood, was informed that their nameless associate was a
wolf in sheep's clothing, and that he would to a certainty
conduct the troopers to their place of concealment. On receiving this report, the man hastened back to his companions
in the cave to expedite their retreat before the soldiers should
arrive. The friends in hiding agreed instantly to vacate the
cavern, and to separate themselves into two companies, the
one party conveying Daniel, who was unable to walk, to move
in the direction of Durisdeer; and the other party to flee
towards the dark moss hags of Kirkhope.

It was the design of the latter party to act as a decoy to
the dragoons, and to draw them away from the party that
was conveying their friend Daniel towards Durisdeer. The
dragoons, however, having observed the movement, divided
themselves also into two parties, the one pursuing the fugitives that were hastening to the wilds of Kirkhope, and the
other following in the route of the company that were moving more slowly with their sickly charge.

The company that fled to the moss expected to secure
themselves in its deep trenches from the approach of the soldiers. In some of the mossy parts of the hills and moors
there are deep gullies, worn by the impetuous streams that
descend from the heights after the melting of the winter
snows, or during the gushing of a great thunder *spate.* These
water courses are in some places covered above with the
tufted heather, which, decked with its purple blossoms, waves
on each margin of the narrow ditch. It was into one of these
slippery conduits that an individual of the fleeing party was
endeavouring to creep, when the troopers came in view of
the dark and rugged peat ground. This circumstance was
observed by one of the dragoons only, who, being unwilling,
it would seem, to expose the life of the poor man, fell to the

rear of his party, and allowing them to proceed, advanced cautiously to the mouth of the mossy outlet, and seeing the cowering fugitive stretched at his full length in his murky hiding-place, accosted him in a suppressed and gentle tone, saying: "Friend, I know you are one of the party whom we are pursuing; I have no desire, however, to reveal you; creep farther into the hole, and stir not till the danger be overpast." He then rejoined his companions in the pursuit, but how the affair ended with this branch of the fugitives tradition has not said.

Meanwhile, the party who were carrying Daniel were pushing westward in the direction of Durisdeer. On this company the dragoons easily gained ground, as their motions were necessarily impeded by means of the burden with which they were charged. It was obvious to every one, and to none more than the sick man himself, that escape was nearly impossible, and it was his urgent request that they should leave him, and provide for their own safety. This they were unwilling to do, but finding that their remaining would endanger their own lives, and could not save his, they, at his earnest desire, concealed him in a cave under the projecting brow of a mountain stream, in hopes that the foe would not find his retreat, while the pursuit would be directed chiefly after themselves. How long, and with what success, the troopers pursued the fleeing party is not said, but had anything of a tragic nature occurred, it is likely that tradition would have preserved it.

Daniel, however, was soon discovered. The soldiers, as was common, were accompanied with dogs, which were often found very useful in leading to a discovery of persons in concealment, and these animals scented out the place where he was hid. The dragoons laid hold on their victim, and mercilessly dragged him from his retreat. Their eye was unaccustomed to spare, and their hearts were unused to pity. Without resistance—for it was impossible, and without remonstrance—for it was needless, this holy man, who was ready to seal his testimony with his blood, resigned himself into the hands of his enemies. He did "not think it strange concerning the fiery trial which was to try him, as though some strange thing had happened unto him." No; for he was already in the furnace, and already had he endured much, and by grace he was prepared to endure more. He heard frequent reports of the martyrdom of his dear friends and beloved brethren, who had embarked in the same common cause, and he himself expected to be numbered with those who were daily falling in the wild moorlands around him and his time to be offered was now near. He was carried by the soldiers to Durisdeer, where he was kept a prisoner during the night, in the silent hours of which he experienced much sweet communion with God, preparatory to the bloody death which he was to suffer on the following day.

Next day he was taken from his place of confinement, sickly as he was, and carried off by the soldiers, with a view, it would appear, to convey him to the garrison in Crawford Moor. The feeble state of his body, however, rendered this impossible, and the troopers were obliged to halt with their charge at the entrance of the pass of Dalveen, where his persecutors determined to ease themselves of their burden by putting an end to his life.

Many questions were put to him, which he declined to answer; and many things were laid to his charge, which he denied. He was told, says Wodrow, that unless he owned the king's supremacy in Church and State, and took the oaths that might be put to him, he must die. " Sir," said he to the commander of the party, " that is what, in all things, I cannot do, but very cheerfully I submit to the Lord's disposal as to my life." Dalziel replied : " Do you not know that your life is in my hand?" " No, Sir," answered he, " I know that my life is in the Lord's hand, and if he see good, he can make you the instrument to take it away."

He had been told the night before to prepare for death, for he should die on the morrow. To this he said, with the utmost calmness, " If my life must go for His cause, I am willing; God will prepare me." And his confidence was not disappointed, for He who calls his servants to the endurance of sufferings and death for his sake, did not desert him in the hour of trial. Wodrow says that the night previous to his martyrdom, " he enjoyed a sweet time of communion and fellowship with God, and great outlets of joy and consolation; so that some of the soldiers desired to die his death, and not a few convictions were left in their bosoms." By this means the Lord strengthened his servant, whom he had called forth to witness for his truth, and prepared him with spiritual fortitude and hope and joy for the fiery trial which was before him.

On the green spot where he was doomed to die, he was permitted to kneel, and to engage for a brief space in those devotional exercises which were befitting a person in his situation—a favour not granted to every one. When he had ended his devotions, he addressed himself in a very grave and solemn manner to Dalziel, who lent himself to work wickedness, and to make havoc of the Church. What impression his discourse made on the commander's mind is not said, but he shrank not from the perpetration of the deed which he meditated.

When the napkin was tied about his face, this faithful witness for Christ, who "loved not his life unto the death," lifted up his voice, and said aloud : "Lord, thou broughtest Daniel through many trials, and hast brought me, thy servant, hither to witness for thee and thy cause; into thy hands I commit my spirit, and hope to praise thee through all eternity." The signal was then given, and four soldiers poured the contents of their muskets into his body, and the warm blood flowed from the wounds in purple streams on the grassy sod. The green heights of Dalveen resounded with the startling report, and the echo leapt from hill to hill, as if to announce to those who dwelt afar in the wilderness that another honoured witness for the truth had fallen. His pains were of short continuance, and his happy spirit, emancipated from its frail tenement, and exulting in glorious victory, winged its way to the regions of eternal bliss.

Among the spectators who were present witnessing this atrocious murder, was a boy named John M'Call, from Dalzien, the place of Daniel's nativity. There happened to be lying on the grass, near the bleeding body of the martyr, a small wooden basin, yclept by the peasantry a *luggie*. The captain commanded the boy, who was standing by, to take the vessel and run to the well to fetch him water, to wash from his hands and clothes the blood that had spurted from the wounds of the slaughtered man, whom, in his contemptuous style, he denominated a *dog*. The boy, with the mingled feelings of terror and indignation, seized the luggie, and ra lowards the well; but instead of fetching water, he dashe k into the limpid fountain, and fled to the hills. The insulted commander ordered the troopers to pursue, and fir on the fugitive. They did so, but he was young and agile, and like the fleet roe, he bounded away, and left the dragoons far behind in the hopeless pursuit. This boy was the great-grandfather of the venerable person who at present occupies the Holm of Drumlanrig.

Daniel M'Michael was a man of eminent godliness and simplicity of character. He lived but for one thing, namely, to honour Him who had called him out of darkness into his marvellous light. Having embraced the truth in the love of it, he adhered to it with constancy; and at the hazard of all he held dearest on earth, he followed Christ, his great leader, wherever he conducted him. And He whom he followed through life did not forsake him in death; his faith in the Redeemer, and the consolations of the Holy Spirit, enabled him to triumph over death, and to afford to those who witnessed his tragic end a proof of the reality of that religion in the profession of which he lived and died.

Few names, indeed, in the lowly walks of life, have more graced the annals of martyrdom than that of Daniel M'Michael He was a "man of honesty, full of the Holy Ghost and of wisdom." His memory is to this day warmly cherished by the inhabitants of the locality where he resided. His mangled body was carried by devout men to the churchyard of Durisdeer, where it was interred close by the east wall of the church. A rude grave-stone, with the following inscription, covers his resting-place :—

> " As Daniel cast was into lions' den,
> For praying unto God, and not to men ;
> Thus lions cruelly devoured me,
> For bearing unto truth my testimony.
> I rest in peace till Jesus rend the cloud,
> And judge 'twixt me and those who shed my blood.'

A suitable monument, lately reared at the mouth of the romantic pass of Dalveen, points out the precise spot where he fell.

We have observed that Daniel M'Michael lived at Blair-foot, in the parish of Morton, in Nithsdale; and this Blair-foot is situated in the immediate vicinity of Morton Castle, respecting which the following legend may here be given, as illustrative of the barbarous manners of a rude and oppressive age.

Morton Castle, a stronghold now in ruins, occupied a commanding position in a wild and secluded locality. Built on the projecting brow of a narrow dell, it reared its frowning turrets in the midst of the dark mantling of the surrounding woods. From the top of its massive walls, which seem to have been built "for all time," the warder had the command of an extensive prospect; and the blast of his bugle horn at the dead of night, when danger was near, sounded afar o'er hill and dale, till the echoes of the forest awoke the startled deer that slept securely in its covert, and summoned from their slumbering couches the faithful retainers of the bold baron to aid him in the hour of peril; while the plashing of the heavy stones, as they rolled down the castle steep into the water-fosse beneath, gave ample warning to the assailants that their approach was not unobserved.

The scene around this baronial seat is one of wild grandeur. The mountains on the north, lofty and rugged, present immeasurable tracts of brown heath, and large spaces occupied with grey rocks and scattered stones. Their bosky glens and deep ravines afforded, in times of persecuting violence, places of retreat to the wanderers of the covenant, who were forced to flee to the remotest solitudes to hide themselves from the fury of their oppressors. In surveying the harsher features of the scene, no one could suspect that there were concealed in the bosom of these dreary heights spots of surpassing loveliness, through which meanders the silvery brook, on the margin of which grows the palmy willow, drooping over the murmuring rill, as it leaves the upland wastes to visit the distant ocean.

As deeds of darkness were perpetrated in the vicinity of these feudal halls, stories of frightful import have, no doubt, been common here as well as elsewhere. The gloomy scenery contributes to the fostering of a superstitious dread in the breast of the traveller who, under the cloud of night, is obliged to pursue his way through a lonely glen or a haunted shaw. "When the yellow ray of the wintry moon is unable to penetrate the thick veil of clouds that overshadow her, and when the breath of the coming storm blows aside for a moment her cloudy covering, the yellow glare that falls upon the leafless woods serves only to make the scene more dismal and dreary. There is not a voice to disturb the solitary meditations of the benighted wanderer, saving the howling blast heard at intervals among the hills, and the lonely murmur of the waters, lamenting the decayed beauty of the woods, and the desolation of the stormy winter."

There lived, as tradition informs us, in the castle of Morton, several centuries ago, and when warlike chieftains exercised the power of life and death within their own domains, a young man in the service of the baron. This youth was possessed of a fine person, a beautiful countenance, and agreeable manners. He was attached to his master, and faithful to his interests. He loved a maiden who wonned on the banks of the Carron—a pleasant stream, which winds its way through the ancient parish of Durisdeer, and falls into the Nith opposite the fine pleasure grounds that surround the ducal castle of Drumlanrig. Its course is not lengthy, but it traverses a field of enchanting scenery. The maiden, whose name was Agnes, resided with her parents in a cottage among the woods in the dale. She was the fairest of the daughters of Carron's vale. All who saw Agnes loved her; for none was more handsome, and none more kind and condescending among the circle of her associates. Among the maidens who met on the cottage green, or in the sunny glades of the flowery woods, to chant their favourite lays, none sang so charmingly as she; for her voice rivalled in sweetness the rich melodies of the warblers in her native groves. Agnes was the darling of her parents, whose hearts yearned over her with the tenderest affection; and good cause had they to love her, for never had parents a child more devoted.

Edward, the youth at the castle, had long cherished a love for Agnes—long indeed before he mustered courage to whisper it in her ear; but at length he revealed the secret, and he had the satisfaction to know that its discovery was not unacceptable. From that moment they were a happy pair, and only waited the proper season when they should become man and wife. Edward's sweetest hours were spent with his Agnes, and her image was never long absent from his mind. But there were others who looked lovingly on Edward besides his darling Agnes; and among these was his own mistress. This woman had long cherished a passion for her servant; and one day, in the absence of her lord, she made confession to him of her affection. The declaration was revolting to the mind of the generous youth, and he retreated from her presence, having first informed her that his heart was wholly given to the maid of Carron, and that on no account could he give his love and his honour to another. The lady was filled with disappointment and shame. She was mortified at the repulse; for she felt it to be a severe censure on the baseness of her conduct. Love and fear now struggled in her breast; she loved the youth, and she feared an exposure. At length fear prevailed; and in order to protect her reputation and her safety, she resolved to work the ruin of the virtuous Edward. She ruminated in her solitary chamber on the best mode of accomplishing her object; and, at last, she determined to prefer against him the same accusation which Potiphar's wife preferred against the blameless Joseph. Accordingly, having fixed on her plan of revenge, she waited patiently till the baron's return; Edward, in the meantime, being unconscious of the storm which was gathering over him.

At length the warder on the castle walls announced the coming of the doughty chieftain, with a company of his horsemen, threading their way through the woods, and appearing now and then in full array in the opening glades of the thickets. It was the evening of a lowering day; the sultry atmosphere had permitted vast masses of vapour and ominous clouds to overspread the firmament. The dark heathy mountains, and the grey turrets of the castle, were shrouded in a more than usual gloom; the flocks were gathering on the hills; the songsters were leaving the open sky, and cowering down among the leafy branches of the woods; and the hoarse mutterings of thunder were heard far away among the distant heights. The baron and his train were admitted within the walls of the fort, and the ponderous portcullis was let fall behind them. The gloomy halls were lighted up, and the festive board groaned with viands suited to the taste of men whose appetite had acquired an unwonted keenness from long journeying in the open air. As the feasting and the revelry proceeded, the lady embraced the first opportunity of preferring her cruel accusation against the unsuspecting youth. The baron listened to the statement; and as he listened his wrath arose, till, frantic with rage, he pronounced the doom of the hapless Edward; which was, that he should perish without food in the lowest dungeon of the castle. As he pronounced the sentence, the first peal of thunder burst from the bosom of the clouds with an appalling crash over the battlements of the fortress, and threatened to lay the pile in ruins. The guilty accuser trembled, as when heaven in judgment bears testimony against the deeds of the wicked; and she clung deadly pale to the arm of her lord, whose voice, raised aloft, was heard above the raving of the tempest, as he issued orders that Edward should immediately be immured in the hold. Never was such an evening witnessed within the walls of Morton. The screaming of the lady—the vociferation of the baron—the remonstrances of Edward—the tumultuous voices of the retainers—the terrific roaring of the thunder, accompanied with lightning as vivid as if it would search through every one's heart, and reveal the secrets that lay hidden there. In the midst of the uproar, however, the baron's commands were performed, and poor Edward was hurried to his prison chamber.

The lady, having witnessed the accomplishment of her direful purpose, was now left to her own reflections ; and these were anything but comfortable. If revenge formerly possessed her breast, it was now supplanted by remorse ; and she became the prey of a wretchedness which no tongue can express. She viewed herself as the base and traitorous murderer of an innocent and honourable youth, whose blood had already dyed her hands with a stain too foul ever to be washed out. The torture of her mind became excessive, and all her worldly enjoyments lost their relish. In the night she was haunted by fearful dreams; and the paleness and anxiety of her countenance indicated the tormenting solicitude that preyed within. The cause of her distress was known to none but herself; and every means was employed by her friends and domestics for the purpose of recruiting her wasted spirits. She frequently retired into the woods, and traversed the pleasant lawns in the vicinity of the castle, to breathe the invigorating air, and to listen to the sweet songsters that carolled on the "greenwood tree;" but all was in vain. It happened one day on her return from her solitary walk in the dell, that, on entering the castle, she passed near the cell in which the victim of her cruelty was confined. From the low grated window she heard him uttering many a deep and piteous moan, and, in the agony of his mind, bewailing his wretched fate. She paused for a moment, and then hastened to her chamber. She called a confidential servant, whom she secretly employed to carry food to the hapless prisoner. As the baron was to leave the castle early in the morning, and to be several days from home, she expected, if she could now succeed in preserving the life of Edward, that, on his return, and when his anger was pacified, the release of the injured youth might, with his consent, be obtained. She succeeded in preserving his life in the dungeon, but it was only that he might die a death more terrible.

During the absence of the baron, the lady sought an interview with Agnes in the woods of Carron, near her father's house. It was on one of the finest days of summer, and Agnes had withdrawn from the cottage to enjoy her solitary retreat in the wood. She had seated herself under her favourite tree, which waved on the margin of the sparkling stream; it was a mountain ash—"a bonny rowan tree," richly clustered with downy blossoms, which shed their fragrance on the breeze. Agnes sat on the green turf under the awning of its branches, which screened her from the burning sun; and while she plied her needle, was chanting with her silvery voice, a pleasant air, in unison with the soft humming of the mountain bees, which had congregated in hundreds among the scented branches. The sportive trout leapt from the limpid pool, which spread itself like a polished mirror at her feet, and in which was fully pictured her own lovely person, on which her eye scarcely for a moment rested, for her thoughts were occupied with the form and the features of another. It was here that Edward and she often met; and, being ignorant of his present situation, she was not unwilling to suppose, that even now he might be on his way to pay her a visit. At this moment, the approach of some person was announced by the rustling of the underwood, and the motion of the branches of the forest trees; and how great was her surprise when the lady of Morton stood before her! —but who was the more lady-like—the lowly maiden, in the bloom of innocence and beauty, or the high-born dame, pale and agitated, and conscience-smitten? "Lady, what ails you?" were the words which, after her first surprise was over, Agnes was about to utter, for she saw that grief and care were inmates of her bosom; and all the sympathies of her gentle and confiding heart were awakened. The lady, however, anticipated her, and stated, with an agonizing energy of expression, the purport of her errand, informing her of the imprisonment of her lover, without assigning the cause, and requesting her to visit the castle on a certain day, to beg from the baron the release of Edward. As the timid deer, when stricken to the heart with the huntsman's arrow, bounds into the thicket to bleed and die unseen, welling out the purple stream of life beside the crystal fountain; so Agnes, as if smitten and blighted by a startling apparition, staggered, almost unconscious of her existence, to the lowly hut, there to pour out the full gush of her grief in the bosom of her sympathizing parents. Edward a prisoner in the deepest dungeon of the castle! the gentle and harmless Edward! For what conceivable crime could he be thus rudely treated?

The time passed heavily on, and Agnes waited with tormenting impatience the day appointed. In her best attire she proceeded to the castle, the very form of whose dusky towers, looming in the distance, smote her timid heart with terror. Within its gloomy walls was confined that which was, of all earthly objects, to her the dearest. She was on her way to attempt the rescue of her friend; but how were her gentle hands to tear asunder the strong bars of his prison-house, or how could her plaintive entreaties move the heart of the gruff and surly baron?

On her arrival, the lady found means to introduce her to her lord, in whose presence she left her to do her best in pleading for her Edward. The interview, however, was brief; for no sooner was his name mentioned as being still alive, than the baron's wrath rose to fury, and he swore a solemn oath that he should instantly die, and that his death should not be a common one. The terror of the gentle Agnes was extreme; and she fled with precipitation from the face of the wrathful man, and stayed not till she hid herself in the cottage on the Carron.

The circumstance of Edward's being still alive excited strong suspicions in the breast of the chieftain; for he knew that no person could survive so long without food. He interrogated his domestics, all of whom denied that they knew anything of the matter. Nevertheless, in the plenitude of his lordly arrogance, he put two of them to instant death, as supposed traitors to their master. If two persons, on mere suspicion, were thus unceremoniously despatched, we may easily conceive that the death of Edward was to be accompanied with circumstances of no ordinary cruelty. The particular kind of death which the youth was to undergo soon suggested itself to the fierce mind of the haughty lord —to hang him on the loftiest tree of the lawn, or to shoot him through the heart with barbed arrow, or to hew his head from his shoulders with the glittering glaive, was, any one of them, a mode of execution too lenient and speedy for a criminal so notorious; and it was decreed that he should be drawn to death at the heels of furious horses. For this purpose, the wildest and most untamable animals were to be sought for, that the scene might be rendered as tragic as possible. Two fierce and intractable horses were found grazing in a neighbouring wood, and these were caught for the purpose of accomplishing the deed. This fact is particularly alluded to in the fragment of an ancient ballad, which is said to have contained a history of the entire transaction, and which some of the very old people in the district remember to have heard recited in their youth, but the whole of which seems now to be forgotten except the following stanza :—

> " Gae, fetch to me yon twa wild steeds,
>   Whilk gang on Knockenshaw;
> And ere I either eat or drink,
>   To death I will him draw."

In order to render the spirited animals as furious as possible, a pair of spurs was attached to each by a girth passing round the body, that at every step the sharp rowels, plunging into their sides, might impel them onward with arrowy speed. Edward was brought from his cell, and, being laid on his back on the ground, the strong ropes which were tied to the horses were bound round his neck and shoulders. The animals were then led a short distance from the castle gate, when, being lashed with sharp whips, they bounded fleetly along the fields, dragging at their heels the screaming victim. As they advanced, the spurs, like the flapping of wings on their impatient sides, goaded them to madness. They pursued their way in the direction of the village of Durisdeer, and when within a short distance of the place, the head was torn from the body. Their race, till this catastrophe occurred, was nearly three miles. At this point they made a turn, and sped onward in a southerly direction, to a place where the Kirk-burn joins the Carron; and having entered the mouth of its deep and narrow channel, they were locked in and caught by the country people, who had assembled in sorrowful groups to witness the scene. The shattered body was disentangled from the cords by which it was bound, and carried back to the place where the head was lying, and buried on the spot.

The report of Edward's cruel death smote the heart of Agnes with a deadly stroke, and she instantly expired in the arms of her parents. The cottage was filled with grief; and nothing was heard in the neighbourhood but expressions of sorrow. She was buried on the green beside her lover. The identical spot of interment is pointed out to this day, and receives the name of "The Heads." A rude stone of memorial still marks the place where repose the ashes of the " Martyr Lovers."

When the death of Edward, and all its attendant circumstances, were recounted to the lady, the report fell upon her spirit like the fiery bolt of heaven upon the trees of the forest. It blighted all her heart, and withered all her joy. Pale, emaciated, and horror-struck, she sat solitary in the gloomy halls of the castle. At length the agony of her mind arose to such a pitch that she was forced to make confession of her crime. In the midst of the upbraidings of her friends and the accusations of her conscience, she lost her reason. She was removed to a lonely apartment, in which she at length died in a most pitiable condition.

Thus Divine Providence sometimes, in the present life, measures out to the wicked their just award, by permitting their criminal conduct to work out its natural results. The punishment which the conscience inflicts on the guilty is frequently more intolerable than any punishment inflicted by human laws.

CHAPTER V.

William Swan—Scene in the Barn—Cave at the Crags—Conventicle at Wardlaw—Birsy the Cobbler—Search for Arms—Incident.

THE house of Braehead, in Dalswinton, is situated on a rising ground, commanding an extensive prospect of the country around, and especially of the vale beneath. This place, in the time of the persecution, was tenanted by a worthy person of the name of Swan. William Swan was a person devoted to the covenanting cause, and no less devoted to the cause of godliness. No heart beat with a kindlier feeling to those who were suffering for righteousness' sake than did the heart of this honest man; and no door was opened with a more cordial welcome than his to admit the homeless wanderer. His mind was no less active than his heart was generous; active in devising expedients for the purpose of concealing, without the risk of discovery, those who fled to his friendly mansion for refuge. In his barn he formed a hiding-place for the reception of those who, knowing his readiness to assist the oppressed, flocked to him in considerable numbers. This hiding-place was an open space which was left between the wall and the corn-sheaves or the hay, which was built up from the floor to the roof, with a small entrance at one corner, which was closed so accurately as not to be perceptible. The vacancy behind was sufficiently large to admit a goodly number of persons; and it is said that he sometimes had no fewer than a score of individuals in this receptacle at once, who, under his guardian care, felt themselves as secure as in a castle. These persons he fed at his own expense, as the good Obadiah did the prophets of the Lord in a cave; and William Swan rejoiced in the exercise of an ample hospitality toward those who were subject to hunger and destitution for Christ's sake. And doubtless he experienced the truth of our Lord's saying: "It is more blessed to give than to receive." They who give for the truth's sake give unto the Lord, and he will repay; and he often repays in *kind:* " The liberal soul shall be made fat; and he that watereth shall be watered also himself." This little chamber in the barn was converted into a church, where these devout worshippers of God often refreshed themselves in the performance of religious exercises; and lest, on these occasions, they should be surprised by their enemies when the loud voice of their united praises might perchance escape beyond the walls of their narrow cell, giving intimation to those who were without of what was going on within, he made use of a particular sign by which he cautiously communicated warning when danger was near. In his immediate neighbourhood there lived a dangerous man of the name of Cowan. This man was by trade a turner, and an infamous informer, who received the payment of a pound for every individual he betrayed to the Government. It was the interest of William Swan, for his own sake, and for the sake of those whom he occasionally concealed in his house, to use every means to lull the suspicions of this person, and to gain, as far as possible, his good-will by the liberal bestowment of valuable presents. In this way a kindly feeling was, to a certain degree, wrought in the breast of Cowan, who, in order to show his respect for Swan, presented him with a little table made of oak, and finished according to the best style of his trade, and which is to this day preserved as an heir-loom by the descendants of William Swan. Thus, " when a man's ways please the Lord, he maketh even his enemies to be at peace with him." Cowan had it in his power to do much mischief; but Providence, by the means specified, was pleased to restrain that power, and the bone that was thrown to the dog prevented its barking.

But William Swan, with all his caution, could not prevent an occasional visit of the enemy. He was suspected of harbouring the intercommuned, as they were called, and one day a party of dragoons were sent to search the premises. Their approach was first noticed by his wife, who, in great consternation, communicated the circumstance to her husband, who had at this time about twenty of the sufferers concealed behind the *mow*, for whose safety he was much concerned. His fertile mind, however, instantly suggested an expedient which, in the result, proved successful in accomplishing their deliverance. He had at this time a great quantity of wool piled up in the end of the barn, opposite the place where the friends were concealed behind the hay. He took his wife into the barn, and explained to her, in the

hearing of the company who were in the hiding-place, **the**
manner in which, in the present emergency, he intended to
act. It was his design, he said, to be apparently engaged in
a severe altercation with her when the soldiers arrived, respecting part of the wool which he was to suppose had been
abstracted from the heap, and, under that pretence, to lock
the door in the face of the dragoons to prevent the intrusion
of thieves. The plan having been agreed to, they waited
with no little anxiety the arrival of the horsemen, who were
just at hand. As they turned into the space before the door,
the loud voice of William Swan was heard rising in angry
tones above the clattering of the horses' feet on the pavement
as they rushed forward to the scene of strife within the barn.
" I will not permit you, my wife though you be," vociferated
Swan, " I will not allow you, nor any one else, to set a foot
on the floor of this barn so long as my wool lies here. Take
that," rolling a fleece in his arms and throwing it at her,
" take that, and make what use of it you please, and be gone."
He then drove his wife from the place, as if she had been a
thief, and stepping out after her, closed the door with violence, and locked it, and then, with apparent rage, and firm
determination, exclaimed, " Let me see the person who will
dare to enter this barn without my permission." If the soldiers were astonished, we may conclude they were equally
amused, for a scene of this kind could not fail to afford men
in their situation much merriment. The scheme, however,
was successful, and the dragoons, without making any investigation whatever, marched off, under the impression that the
information respecting Swan was false. With regard to the
propriety of his procedure in this case, that is another matter;
the plan perhaps was neither the most judicious nor the most
praiseworthy. It was, however, a difficult matter for a man
in his situation to know how to act, and he adopted what on
the spur of the moment appeared to him to be the most eligible method.

Near the Water of Æ, between the parishes of Kirkmahoe
and Tinwald, is a place called the Crags, in which there was
a cave which, like many other places of a similar description
in the wilder parts of the country, was resorted to by those
who sought concealment from their enemies. This place
was well known to William Swan, who did not fail to minister to the wants of those who had taken refuge in its cold
and cheerless recesses. The hospitality of this excellent man
was not confined simply to those who sought an asylum in
his own house; it extended to all within his reach, whether

they were hidden in the moss, or in the wood, or in the cave.
There is a largeness of heart, and an expansive generosity of
soul, which characterize some good men, assimilating them
more than others to the image of Him who is goodness itself.
We respect a just man, and we esteem a righteous man, but
we *love* a good man : his affectionate sympathy, and the assiduity of his kindness, bind our hearts to him with the tie of
a particular attachment, and we contemplate his character
with a sweet complacency. One day after dinner, and thanks
returned to Him who fills all his creatures with plenteousness,
William Swan was reposing in his arm-chair, and musing
with a grateful heart on the benignity of that Providence
that had "prepared a table before him in the presence of
his enemies;" he remembered his brethren in affliction, the
sufferers who were in concealment in the cave at the Crags,
and he felt as if the bountiful meal which he had now received would do him little good unless they, too, were made
sharers of the same provision. "My dear family," said he,
" we have participated amply of our heavenly Father's bounty,
and we are strengthened and refreshed ; but how does it fare
with our poor friends at the Crags, who are nobly enduring
hunger and cold, and every privation in the cause of our
common Lord? My heart bleeds for them ; let us therefore instantly send them a portion from our table, that their
hearts, too, may be comforted." To this proposal the worthy
family cordially responded, and it was agreed to despatch
forthwith a young female servant belonging to the household
with what provisions she could carry to the friends in their
lonely concealment at the Crags. The young woman whom
the family wished to perform for them this deed of beneficence, was in all likelihood selected as a person to whom
less suspicion would be attached if she were seized on the
way than to one of themselves. She, however, had her own
fears, and seemed unwilling to proceed, lest she should encounter the troopers on the moorland, and lest, through her
weakness, she should be tempted to reveal her errand, and
consequently the haunt of the worthies. William Swan endeavoured to allay her fears by representing to her the guardian care of Providence, and by showing the praiseworthy
nature of the deed she was called to perform ; assuring her,
if she was interrupted and interrogated by the enemy, that
courage and words would be given her both how to behave
and how to answer. Being therefore induced to comply, and
having mustered all her fortitude for the attempt, she set out
laden with provisions. A moor of some extent lay between

Brachead and the Crags, over the desert tracts of which she
had to pass ere she reached her destination, and it was here
mainly that danger was to be dreaded. As she entered on
this moorland waste, nothing was to be seen calculated to
excite alarm, and she proceeded onward in hope of escaping
interruption. On a sudden, however, her fond expectations
were blasted, for she descried a company of horsemen advancing in the distance, and apparently marching in a straight
line to the place where she was. In a few minutes the dragoons stood before her, and in an imperious tone asked her
what it was she was carrying, and where she was going. She
appeared unwilling to reply; this excited their suspicion, and
they affirmed that she was conveying food to the rebels, and
expressed their determination to know the whole matter before they parted. In her great perplexity, she happened to
observe on the neighbouring hill a number of persons casting
turf, and she immediately resolved to turn aside to them,
hoping that under the pretext of carrying food to the labourers
she would escape further annoyance. This new idea inspired
her with courage, and she began to address the soldiers with
considerable freedom, and asked them to accompany her to
the height, where the whole of the secret which they seemed
so anxious to know might perhaps be fully unfolded. The
people who were employed on the bent were persons whom
she did not know; but as she expected more favour from the
peasants than from the dragoons, she thought it probable that
they would understand the nature of her situation, and receive her as if she were a person well known to them, and
that by this means the suspicion of the troopers would be
allayed. Her plan was successful, for the soldiers, without
more ado, marched off towards Dalswinton; but not before
they received a severe reprimand for their unmannerly interruption. She was now left alone to pursue her way unmolested; and instead of visiting the workmen on the hill,
she went straight to the cave, and performed the truly Christian service on which her master had sent her. Her escape
prevented, perhaps, the ruin of her master's household, and
saved the lives of the worthies in the cave; and was, in all
likelihood, a direct answer to the prayers of William Swan,
whose care for Christ's suffering people induced him to employ every means for their welfare. A number of years
after the termination of the persecution, a large Bible was
found in the cave, which doubtless had been used by the
pious persons who were forced to take refuge there. A
leaden pitcher was also discovered, which probably belonged

to the hospitable tenant of Braehead. Both the Bible and the pitcher would, no doubt, be preserved as valuable relics by those into whose possession they came.

Shortly after this, one of the outed ministers having visited the neighbourhood, it was agreed that a conventicle should be held at a place called Wardlaw, at some distance from Braehead. These zealous servants of Christ embraced every opportunity of preaching the Gospel, even at the imminent risk of their lives. It was for this end they lived, and in this good work they were ready to die. The visits of such men were occasions of much spiritual refreshment to the people of God, who flocked in great numbers from all parts to hear from their lips the precious words of life. On the day of the meeting a large company assembled from the surrounding district, in the expectation of spending one Sabbath in the worship of God, without disturbance. There was a person of the name of Smith, who resided within the farm of Braehead, a low, selfish character, who expected to reap some worldly advantage at the expense of the meeting at Wardlaw. After the worship was begun, and when the minister in the tent, which was reared in the field, was preaching to the people, who were listening with all earnestness to his discourse, Smith, who was watching his opportunity, came running in great haste to the outskirts of the crowd, crying that a company of dragoons were speedily approaching. This report, which was entirely false, at once threw the multitude into confusion, and occasioned the dispersion of the congregation—the very thing which Smith wanted. In the disorder of the moment, when the people were running to and fro, not knowing which hand to turn to, the temporary tent was overturned with the minister in it, but without any injury to his person; and one man, who had tethered his horse in an adjoining field, that it might graze at leisure during the service, vaulted the animal, forgetting, in his haste and trepidation, to untie the cord by which he was bound, so that, spurring furiously, both the horse and his rider were nearly, if not actually, overturned by the sudden check which the rope, when drawn with violence to its full stretch, occasioned. When the congregation had vacated the spot, and not an individual remained in the field, Smith, at his leisure, gathered the bonnets, and plaids, and Bibles, and other articles which the people, in the scene of confusion that ensued, had left behind them. Having collected the spoil, he returned to his house like a person loaded with the plunder of the slain from the field of battle. This man, actuated by a principle of sordid avarice, was guilty of a base falsehood and of a disgraceful theft, and deprived a great company of hearing the Gospel on one of those occasions which was but rarely enjoyed in those days of tribulation and hazard. Covetousness is one of the worst of those vile affections which have a place in our depraved nature: it was this which prompted Judas to betray our Lord, and it has caused the ruin of innumerable souls. There are perhaps few vices which lurk more insidiously in the heart than this; for men may be under its reigning power without being aware of it; and no evidence is more decisive against a man's Christianity than the dominant love of the world: " Love not the world, neither the things that are in the world. If any man love the world, the love of the Father is not in him."

Smith was a cobbler, and was employed, according to the custom of the times, in the farm-houses and cottages through-out the district, in making or mending shoes. From the trade which he followed, he received the nickname of Birsy, which stuck to him as pertinaciously as the bur clings to the coat of the shepherd boy, when once it has obtained an acci dental adhesion. Birsy was not the most respected man in the world, as the notices already given of him plainly show, and he was, withal, a notorious coward. His timidity amounted to the timorousness of a child; and so oppressive was this weakness, that he durst not travel alone in the dark. Everything he heard or saw, after the shadows of the night closed in, excited terror, and made his hair stand on end. Ghosts and bogles, and fairies and witches, were everywhere. The dusky whin bush, the nodding thistle, the hare started from her lair, and the wild duck plashing in the lake, were sufficient to lift poor Birsy's bonnet from his head, and possessed a magic enough to cause the pearly drops of perspiration to start from his brow. No penance more se-vere could be inflicted on Birsy than to oblige him to walk in the dark; and hence his journeys were uniformly per-formed in broad daylight. William Swan contrived to live on as good terms with his neighbour the cobbler as possible, and as he was a person easily overawed, the honest tenant of Braehead may probably have employed means to keep him in a little subjection, and to prevent him from acting the part of an informer, at least against himself, as he had occasion frequently to harbour in his barn the outcast remnant who drew to him for refuge from the hot pursuit of the foe.

Birsy was a good tradesman, and therefore his services were in great request in the district, and more especially in the winter season, when the feet of the moorland peasantry required to be more firmly and tightly shod. In this way he made a good livelihood, and was well entertained in the different houses where he plied his occupation. Some time prior to the disgraceful affair of the conventicle at Wardlaw, and when he sustained a somewhat less objectionable reputation than he subsequently did, he happened to be invited by the farmer of Auchengeith to come to his house on a Monday morning by break of day, as he had a whole week's employment in store for him. Birsy gladly accepted the invitation. There was, however, a difficulty in his way, and one of rather a serious nature. It was winter, and as Auchengeith was at some distance, he durst not travel in the dark of the morning, in order to reach the place in time to begin his work at the proper hour. To obviate this, however, he determined to take his journey on Sabbath afternoon, and to creep into the house in the dusk unperceived, as he was unwilling to show himself to the family, lest he should be rallied on a point he did not much relish, namely his superstitious cowardice. Birsy performed his journey, and succeeded in entering the house by stealth, and in secreting himself in the loft immediately above the kitchen. The fireplace in the kitchen was in the middle of the floor, and the smoke ascended through a wide opening in the roof, from which it escaped in eddying volumes into the open air. In the centre of the loft was a wide square aperture, which looked down on the fire-place beneath, and from which the persons sitting round the hearth could easily be seen. On entering this place Birsy stretched himself on the boards, along the edge of the opening, to enjoy the heat, and just so far back as to avoid the smoke. Here he lay very composedly, and listened to the conversation that was carried on below, and this spot he intended to make his dormitory for the night.

The gudeman of Auchengeith was a religious person, and one who instructed his family in the fear of God. In the olden time, among the pious part of the peasantry of Scotland, the Sabbath evening was spent in instructing the household from the catechism, and in devotional exercises. The Lord's day was kept with great solemnity; it was a religious festival, and a season of much spiritual refreshment. It is to their devout observance of the Sabbath that the proficiency of our forefathers in divine knowledge and in grace is mainly to be attributed. Theirs was very different from the loose notions now entertained by some respecting the

sanctity of the Lord's-day; for they were truly conscientious
in their adherence to the divine injunction, " Remember the
Sabbath-day, to keep it holy."

The household of Auchengeith were, on the evening on
which Birsy arrived, arranged round the blazing pile of
peats on the hearth, and employed in the exercises befitting
the day of holy rest. In the interval between catechising
and family worship, some of the domestics alluded to Birsy's
coming in the morning, and to the necessity of having things
in readiness on his arrival; and some remarks were made
respecting his want of religion, and other things that were
unbecoming in his character. This conversation, however,
he did not hear; for by this time he was in a profound sleep.
" Let Birsy alone," said the gudeman, "and let all of us look
to ourselves, and see that our profession and behaviour be as
they ought." He then proceeded, with patriarchal grace, to
make worship; a duty which, in the houses of many professed
Christians, is now as much neglected as is the sacred observance of the Sabbath. That household, surely, cannot lay
claim to a religious character, whatever professions it may
otherwise make, in which there is no family recognition of
God. How greatly responsible are parents for the neglect
of this service ! Their children are not trained to worship
God in the domestic circle; and who can tell how much of
the confusion and insubordination which exist in certain
households is to be traced to the neglect of this plain, and
simple, and pleasant duty ! and with how much prosperity
God may bless those families who thus acknowledge him, we
cannot say; but "wherever we have a tent, there should
God have an altar." " Them that honour me, I will honour."

When the household were gathered in a circle round
the fire, and were singing the psalms of David in worship,
they were startled by the descent of a cobbler's awl, which
fell with a *birle* on the hearth. Those that sat near the
place looked with astonishment at one another, and the in-
explicable circumstance produced a momentary cessation in
their singing. How an *elshin*, as it was termed in their
dialect, could drop from the loft in this ominous manner, on
the Sabbath evening, and in the time of worship, was more
than they could divine. They began to feel *eery*, and to
withdraw in a wider circle from the *unsonsy* spot. The gudeman noticed the movement, and the whispering beyond the
fire, but made no remarks, not wishing to interrupt the worship. He next proceeded to read a portion of Scripture,
and during the exercise a broad-bladed knife, firmly ingrafted

in a thick wooden heft, fell with a rebound on the hearth-stone, and lay sharp and glittering before the fire-place. The consternation was now extreme, and they rushed to the opposite side of the apartment. The venerable master of the house, who held the Bible on his knee, paused, and eagerly inquired into the cause of the disturbance. He was informed that first an awl and then a large knife had fallen from the loft on the floor. The worthy man, who was not altogether free of the superstitious notions of the times, considered the incidents as a sort of miraculous reproof for their profaning the Sabbath in talking of Birsy's character, which should not once be named on the Lord's-day. He considered that his interpretation of the incidents was correct, seeing the awl and the knife were the implements of a shoemaker. In this manner he read a lecture to his household on the propriety of speaking evil of no man, and on the duty of abstaining from our own words on the Sabbath-day.

The disturbance in the kitchen below awoke Birsy from his sound sleep on the edge of the loft that overlooked the fire-place. The poor man, forgetting where he was, an being overcome with drowsiness and the sound which was ringing in his ears, began to bestir himself, and, in the act of turning, fell plump down bodily into the fire among the smoking peats. All was now uproar, and every one fled as for his life. Here was the very embodiment of all evil himself that had appeared in the midst of them, and none had the confidence to outface so ominous a visitation. Not one was found possessed of fortitude sufficient to inquire into the matter, save the head of the household himself, who, having mustered up all his firmness, laid hold on the object before him, and dragged it from the burning pile. On examination it was found to be the veritable Birsy himself, who, in dust and smoke, had made his descent into the kitchen of Anchengeith, on the quiet Sabbath evening, when the peaceful family were engaged in the appropriate exercises of the day of rest.

The mystery was now unfolded. The family were called in, and the hapless cobbler narrated the circumstances of the case. Their consternation now gave place to very different feelings, which, had it been on another day of the week, would have found vent in bursts of merriment and raillery.

After the affair of the conventicle, Smith fell into a state of great mental distress. A sense of the impiety of his conduct in this instance, combined with a conviction of the general irreligiousness of his character in other respects, drove him to distraction. He lived despised by others, and despising himself, till his life became an insupportable burden, and, like Judas, he hanged himself. He was found by his own sister, suspended in one of the out-houses belonging to William Swan, and the circumstance created the deepest sensation in the neighbourhood. As soon as the news of the painful occurrence spread abroad, every person seemed horror-struck; for he was regarded as a very wicked man, and his end was viewed as the natural consequence of his nefarious life. This poor man, instead of fleeing to the Saviour for the forgiveness of his sins, yielded to despair, not understanding that all sins, the greatest and the least alike, may be pardoned on the ground of the glorious propitiation of our great High Priest, who " is able to save to the uttermost." Despair of divine mercy originates in a great measure in the powerful legal bias of the unrenewed heart, which prompts us to entertain the supposition, that according to the degree of a man's criminality his pardon is difficult or easy; that God is more ready to forgive a less sin than a greater; and that if we were more worthy, we might with the greater confidence come to Him. All this, however, is obviously unsound; for the Gospel of the grace of God offers salvation to all men without difference, be their sins many or few, because the infinitely efficacious blood of Christ cleanseth from *all* sin.

In former times, and even till a very recent period, public opinion respecting acts of suicide was peculiar, and so peculiar as to forbid the sepulture in the common burying-ground, of all persons who terminated their lives by their own hands. Happily, this opinion is, in our times, greatly modified, if not altogether changed. In the days of William Swan, however, the feeling against such persons ran to the highest extreme, and the body of Smith was not allowed interment in the churchyard. In such cases, the custom was to bury on neutral land, either on the march between two counties, or between two gentlemen's estates, that the dust of such unhappy persons might not find a resting-place on any claimable property. There is a spot on the Lowther hills, exactly on the borders of Nithsdale and Lanarkshire, which, for many generations, was employed as the burial-place of the victims of suicide. It was with great difficulty that any individual could be found to remove the body of Smith, and to prepare it for burial; even his own nearest kindred refused to touch him, and he might have remained

suspended till the flesh fell from his bones, had not the laird
of Dalswinton induced a person to convey the corpse in a
car to a place at Auchengeith, on the march between the
lands of Closeburn and Queensberry, where he was buried.
Smith's conduct at the conventicle, and his character generally,
were so detested, that honest William Swan could not endure
even to see the house standing in which he ended his life;
and he forthwith demolished it, not leaving one stone upon
another, that he might obliterate the scene of so vile an action, and testify his disapprobation of a character so infamous.

"Upon the 8th of May 1679," says Wodrow, "the council
emit a proclamation against travelling with arms without license.   It is founded upon the atrocious acts committed
by persons who go to field conventicles; and discharges all
subjects to travel with arms without license, and appoints
all magistrates to seize such, except noblemen, landed gentlemen, and their children, and servants in company with
them, if they be found with arms; and the soldiers are likewise ordered to apprehend such."   After the passing of this
act a strict search was made for arms, especially in thos
parts of the country where the greatest dissatisfaction wa
known to exist.   The terror lest the peasantry would defend themselves in case of aggression, or perhaps execute
vengeance on those who oppressed them whenever an opportunity should present itself, dictated, no doubt, this measure.   In the general search for arms, then, a party of
dragoons visited Brachead for the purpose of securing what
warlike implements they might find in the possession of the
tenant.   William Swan, however, was beforehand with them;
for having heard of the act, and knowing the uncompromising
rigour with which the search would be made, carried his
arms to the roof of the house and concealed them carefully
among the thatch.   In this place they were as secure as on
the top of a mountain, and the honest man rested satisfied
that search would be fruitless.   When the soldiers arrived
they explored every corner, but found nothing.   There was
a poor widow who lived on the same farm, whose house also
they had received orders to search, and to her residence they
now proceeded.   This woman's husband and his brother had
been Covenanters, but at this time they were in their graves.
They died not by the immediate hand of persecution, but
rather in consequence of the hardships to which they were
subjected; and thus, though they were not slain with the
sword, nor shot with the musket, nor hanged on the gibbet,
for their adherence to the cause of truth, still they were truly

martyrs, for their death was the result of self-denial, and
privation, and suffering for Christ's sake. It was on account,
therefore, of the well-known nonconformity of her husband
that this poor woman's dwelling was to undergo a search.
William Swan, knowing that she was a worthy person, and
that she preserved the arms of her deceased husband with a
superstitious care—often burnishing them, and then deposit-
ing them in a place where they might not receive the slightest
tarnish—was solicitous on her account, and requested her to
conceal them among the thatch, as he had done. To this,
however, she would not consent, but determined still to keep
them below the bed-clothes—the place where she had hitherto retained them. When the soldiers left Braehead, Swan
accompanied them to the widow's house, anxious to witness
the result, and ready to intercede in case of a discovery.
The widow had that same morning gone to the moss to prepare peats for her winter's fuel, and had locked the door behind her ; but previous to her departure, she had made ready
a large *cog* of sowens for her children's breakfast, which she
had placed below the bed-clothes, to keep them warm.
Strachan, who is said to have been the commander of the
party, without ceremony burst open the door, and entering,
immediately commenced the search for the arms under the
bed-clothes—a circumstance which proves that he had received due information of the place where he would find
them. In his haste to seize the weapons, however, he thrust
his hand to the wrist into the scalding sowens; the effect of
which, like a sudden and powerful shock of electricity, made
him spring back to the middle of the floor, while the warm
viscous substance was dripping like clotted blood from his
ruddy hand, the pain of which was intolerable. "Run to
the brook, Captain Strachan," cried William Swan, who
scarcely understood the state of things till the matter was
more fully investigated. The affair afforded the soldiers
unspeakable merriment, especially when they saw their magnanimous leader rinsing his hand and arm in the cleansing
and cooling stream. The circumstance, however, put an end
to the search for arms; and William Swan was gratified to
think that neither he nor the poor woman was likely to be
put to any further trouble for the present.

The persons attached to the covenanting interest, who
lived in the parishes of indulged ministers, were much more
favoured than those who were resident in the parishes of the
curates. Much of the distress of the country arose from information lodged against the Nonconformists, and the curates

were the individuals who were mainly active in this way.
They hated the Presbyterians, and they were especially mortified at the dislike which the people showed to their minis
try, and hence non-attendance at their churches was visited
with their heaviest displeasure. It is true that some of the
Prelatic incumbents, on account of their leniency or indol-
ence, gave comparatively little annoyance to the Covenanters within their bounds; but then these cases were rare.
The indulged ministers, eighty of whom were, in 1672, located
by pairs in parishes, though they were guilty of defection and
foul compliance, operated as a sort of gourd, under which not
a few of the people sat down and screened themselves from
the scorching heat of the persecution. This accounts for
the exemption of persons from trouble, on whom we might
naturally think that the heavy hand of oppression would
have otherwise been laid. Complaints were not lodged, and
the interference of the military was not called for by the incumbents. This gourd, however, under the awning of which
he people in many parishes gladly sheltered themselves, was
often hastily removed. The indulged ministers were very
precariously dealt with; they were expelled at the pleasure
of the council for any reason, or for no reason. They were
hated by the ruling party, although, for certain political
purposes, they were tolerated, and partially countenanced.
If they were detested by the rulers, they were despised by
the more strict and consistent class of the Covenanters, who
stood aloof from them, and sought the enjoyment of the ordinances of religion in a less objectionable connection, although at the risk of their lives.

William Swan sat, in all likelihood, under the ministrations
of an indulged preacher; for though he was known to be a
Presbyterian even by the military, and by some of the most
active agents in the persecution, yet he was left in a great
measure undisturbed. This honest man, as we have shown,
exerted himself to the utmost to shelter and save the helpless wanderers who were driven from place to place at the
point of the sword. He had a retreat in his barn, in which
he concealed them, and fed them with a truly Christian
hospitality. Had this been discovered by the troopers,
neither the leniency of a curate nor the toleration of an
indulged minister would have saved him from his fate.

Claverhouse having, on one occasion, received information
that a number of rebels, as they were denominated, were
concealed in the moors of Dalswinton, proceeded with a
company of his horsemen to search them out. On his way

he called at Brachead, the residence of William Swan; and
as some of the horses of the troopers had become lame, and
therefore utterly unfit to traverse the uneven surface of the
moorland, he pressed into his service all the horses which
honest William Swan could spare, and one from the widow
referred to, who lived at Braefoot, on the same farm. No
ceremony was employed by the military in those days, in
making their demands for the king's service or their own, as
it best suited them; and no remonstrance was available on
the part of those on whom the exaction was made. Not
only were the horses of William Swan pressed into the service, but himself also. Claverhouse demanded his assistance
in the search, and in guiding their way through the wild.
Among the persons who were hiding in the moor were some
near relations of the widow of Braefoot, and she was greatly
concerned for their safety; and under pretence of bringing
back her horse when they had completed the search, she determined to accompany the party.

Claverhouse, it seems, trusted much to William Swan for
the success of this expedition; but William, like all the
guides of his description in similar circumstances, was the
worst he could have chosen. If he knew the retreats of the
wanderers, it was not likely that he would reveal them.
Accordingly, in moving along, William took the very opposite direction from that in which the Covenanters were to
be found; and many a weary and needless step did he lead
them, for he took advantage of every circuitous path to pro-
long the journey, and to render their object fruitless. At
the different places to which they came they received information of the route of the fugitives, who, it seems, amounted
to a considerable number; for it is likely that a conventicle
had been held. This information imparted many useful hints
to William, who, knowing the localities, drew his own conclusions respecting the likelihood of their retreats, and the
speed with which, from the nature of the ground, they were
making their flight. When at any time he feared they were
approaching their lurking-places, he attempted to divert the
soldiers by soliciting them to remain for a little in the place,
and institute a strict search in the vicinity, if peradventure
they might light upon the fugitives. In these cases no one
was more active than William Swan, in running to and fro,
and prying with all apparent eagerness into every place of
conceivable concealment. Expert as the soldiers generally
were at this work, their guide seemed far to outstrip them,
and to be much more zealous in the matter than even the

most ardent among themselves. William knew that minutes were worth hours in this case, and that a very brief space spent in this way might accomplish the deliverance of the helpless persons who were fleeing for their lives. And admirably did they succeed; for a breathing-time was afforded to the fugitives, and an opportunity of retiring to a greater, distance. The promptitude which he displayed on this occasion attracted the notice of Claverhouse, and he formed a very high opinion of him. He was at this time in all the prime and activity of manhood; and he appeared to the leader of the party, from his assiduity and bodily prowess, to be a man quite fit for his purpose, and he proposed to enlist him as a trooper, offering him very advantageous terms. William inwardly shrank from such a proposal, his whole nature recoiled from such a service; and he declined the proffers of the commander, but in such a way, no doubt, as not to excite unnecessary suspicion.

The soldiers continued the pursuit in the direction of Moffat, having swept along the skirts of Tinwald, and passed Parkgate, where inquiries were made respecting the fugitives. When they had gone thus far, they were informed that the persons of whom they were in quest had betaken themselves to Kinnel Water, to seek in the retreats of that locality a hiding-place. Kinnel Water and its neighbourhood had often concealed the wanderers in the day of their destitution. In this direction, then, the soldiers turned in the pursuit, and Swan and the widow were trudging on foot. As a great deal was supposed to depend on Swan's guidance, Claverhouse, not willing to be retarded by one on foot, and the day beginning to decline, commanded him to vault one of the horses, even though a trooper should dismount and walk. The order was speedily obeyed, and William was seated on a horse which happened to be his own. Nor was the poor widow forgotten; for, seeing that she would inevitably be left alone in the moor, he placed her on horseback behind himself. The circumstance, however, displeased Claverhouse; but Swan's entreaties prevailed, and she was allowed to remain.

The fugitives had frequently, during the course of the day been nearly overtaken by the pursuers, but still they had succeeded in eluding them. Their hopes now began to fail, and they feared that there would be no possibility of escape. Their only refuge now was Queensberry Hill, a height which rises conspicuously in the desert, and on whose head the grey mists often rest in lazy volumes. To this eminence they now fled with all speed, and succeeded in their object before the horsemen could reach them. When they reached the mountain it is said that the mantling mist descended from the hovering clouds, and enveloped them. This circumstance often happened, and is of every-day occurrence in mountainous parts of the country. It is, however, probable, that the mist was reposing on the sides of the hill at the very time that the fugitives were in its vicinity; and that this induced them to flee to the height, that, if possible, they might get behind its snowy curtains, and hide themselves from their enemies.

The dragoons, it would appear, had a full view of the fleeing party, and pushed on with all eagerness to overtake them. Their disappointment, therefore, was excessive, when they saw them vanish behind the drapery of the mist that was creeping down the slopes of the hill; and Claverhouse, in an especial manner, gave vent to his rage, in the utterance of profane and blasphemous expressions. "There," he exclaimed, "is the devil's mist again, which has once more prevented us from seizing those rebels, when they were almost within our grasp."

Their search was now fruitless, unless, in the misty atmosphere, they had been pleased to take windle-straws for men. The day was now drawing to a close, and the haze was spreading downwards into the more level parts, threatening to envelop the whole in bewilderment and perplexity. The concern of the soldiers was now extreme; for they feared that if they should leave their way, as the night was approaching, they would perish in the waste. Their eagerness to apprehend the conventiclers was absorbed in solicitude about their own safety; and every consideration was merged in the single one of immediate self-preservation. The bold commander now felt himself helpless as a child; for he could neither extricate himself nor his men from their perilous situation. And what was it? Were they surrounded with innumerable hosts of savage men, with whom they had no power to cope? Were they encompassed with the devouring floods, expecting every moment to be engulfed in their terrible depths? Were they enveloped in the heart of the desolating tempest, when the hot thunderbolts, with destructive energy, were darting their living fires on every side of them? No. They were only infolded in the soft mantling of the dewy mist, which presented no frightful object to their sight, and uttered no terrible sounds in their ears; and yet they were panic-struck, and at their wits' end. Could one have supposed that a thing so simple would have so entirely un manned the redoubted cavalier and his magnanimous troopers? And yet so it was. Claverhouse, in utter consternation, offered William Swan a tempting reward if he would conduct them safely off the hill, and through the moors, to some place of abode during the night. Swan inwardly enjoyed the sport, and rejoiced to see the heroes of the moors so completely *cowed* before the noiseless rolling of the gentle mist; and he determined for once to lead the party at his pleasure, even at the expense of a sleepless night. Claverhouse greatly feared lest, in the murkiness of the evening, he should fall over some precipice, or tumble into some moss-hag, which might prove the grave both of himself and his goodly war-steed. His military skill could not help him here, and his bravery was equally unavailing. He who was so reckless on the field of conflict, and who was rather a savage than a hero, now manifested an excess of concern and timidity that was truly astonishing. But the doughty chieftain found it one thing to face death in the bustle and excitement of the battle-field, and another thing to meet it calmly and ingloriously on the moor.

Swan, though he might be somewhat perplexed by the mist, knew the locality well, and he could, with considerable ease, have conducted them to a regular road, and left them to plod their own way; but this he was resolved not to do, for he was desirous of inflicting some slight chastisement on the troopers, who caused so much distress to the unoffending peasantry. This purpose, however, was defeated; for the party stumbled accidentally on a strolling-shepherd, who was wending his way through the wild. Claverhouse entreated the man to aid them in their difficulty, and threatened him with instant death if he should deceive them. The man, through interest or through fear, did the best he could, and succeeded in conducting them to Mitchelslacks, a farm-house among the hills, where they staid during the night, and then repaired to their garrison in the morning. William Swan and the widow returned home in safety, and, it is said, brought their horses with them—a thing little expected, as Claverhouse seldom parted with such animals when they suited his purpose. Thus terminated the incidents of this day, the morning of which threatened death to the Covenanters—and, the evening, destruction to the troopers.

William Swan of Brachend lived to the great age of ninety-six, and "came to his grave in a full age, like as a shock of corn cometh in his season; an old man and full of years, and was gathered to his people." "The memory of the just shall be blessed ;" and the memorial of this good man is still warmly cherished, not only by his descendants, but by all to whom his good report has reached. His daughter, Helen Swan, was seventy-four years old when she was gathered to her fathers; and his grand-daughter, Helen Fraser, who lives in the village of Minihive in Dumfriesshire, is at present seventy-seven.

CHAPTER VI.

Bellybught—Scene at Auchengrouch—The Pursuit.

THE farm of Bellybught, in the parish of Morton, is situated in a very wild spot among the mountains, and in the times of our suffering ancestors was occasionally resorted to as a place of seclusion from the fury of their persecutors. In this wilderness there was a lonely shieling, which stood in a moor encircled with hills, and in its neighbourhood was a deep and rugged ravine, whose precipitous sides were thickly covered with wood, the dark and unfrequented mazes and recesses of which afforded a sure and safe retreat. On one occasion, a company of wanderers, one of whom was Adam Clark of Glenim, had concealed themselves in this solitary haunt. Adam, on several accounts, was generally regarded as a leader by the party with whom he was connected, and their movements were usually guided by his direction. In this dreary seclusion they held delightful communion on spiritual things, and enjoyed much sweet intercourse with God. It was to preserve unimpaired the full liberty of worshipping according to their conscience the God of their fathers, that they withstood the unrighteous usurpation of those who wished to wreath about their necks the yoke both of a spiritual and a political bondage; and hence they sought, and found, in the remote solitudes, that freedom which could not elsewhere be enjoyed. In this exile, however, they were often in much distress through hunger; and unless when a friend who knew their situation brought them a supply, they were obliged to travel a considerable distance, and in great secrecy, to procure food to preserve their lives. An anecdote is told of a pious man, who had secluded himself in a cave by the Water of Æ, and who was so closely watched by his enemies, that he dared not venture abroad night or day for a considerable time. In this situation, being greatly afflicted with hunger, he observed a large wild-fowl that alighted very near the mouth of his cell, and deposited an egg among the heather. This was done every morning, and on this provision he was sustained during the time of his concealment in the cavern; and in this way, as the Lord preserved the life of his prophet by the brook Cherith, when the ravens brought him bread and flesh in the morning, and bread and flesh in the evening, was this good man, who trusted in God, supported. In the one case the supply was miraculous, and in the other not; still the hand of a guardian Providence was as much concerned in the one case as the other. In ordinary circumstances we are not to expect that the Lord will supply our wants in any other way than in the use of means; and, therefore, while we pray, " Give us this day our daily bread," we are at the same time to labour with our hands to earn an honest subsistence; for the exercise of faith and the diligent use of means are to be combined. In those cases, however, in which we are precluded from using means, we are authorized to trust in God, believing that he will supply our wants in one way or in another; for he will sooner rain bread from the clouds, than suffer the confidence of his people to be defeated.

Adam Clark, who was a robust and active young man, and well acquainted with the locality, issued, with one or two of his companions, from their hiding-place in the night season, for the purpose of providing a meal for the rest who remained in the shieling. He obtained his errand, and returned in safety before the early dawn, congratulating himself and his friends on his success. The party, amounting in all to twenty-eight persons, having with grateful hearts participated of the welcome viands which He who provides for the wants of all his creatures had set before them, were reposing securely within the hut, when Clark, and his brother Andrew, standing near the door, observed a ewe pass with startling haste, and then another, pursued by a swift and powerful dog. " What means this?" exclaimed Andrew. " It is one of Morton's dogs," replied Adam; " our retreat is discovered, and the troopers will be here instantly." The party within were roused to a sense of their danger, and every man had his defensive weapons in readiness. Scarcely had they accoutred themselves when the dragoons in thundering haste surrounded the hiding-place. The friends within rushed simultaneously to the bent, for the purpose, if possible, of making their escape. The leader of the troopers commanded them to seize Clark, come or the rest what might. He was instantly attacked by a powerful dragoon, and Clark, having caught his horse by the bridle reins, pushed him backwards till he stumbled and overthrew his rider. The dragoon was now fully in his power, but he spared his life, resting contented with having come off victorious and unscathed in the perilous scuffle. In the meantime his attention was directed to another quarter, where he saw his brother Andrew prostrated in a moss, and a gigantic dragoon standing over him, and about to hew him in pieces with his ponderous broadsword. Adam sprung to his assistance, and in a moment was at his side. The dragoon turned round to defend himself from the attack of his new opponent, and left Andrew uninjured. In the conflict Adam wrested the sword from the hand of the soldier, and having thrown him on the heath, descended with his companions into the ravine or deep gully, formed by the rushing of the mountain torrent, in the bosky recesses of which they found a retreat from the vengeance of their foes, who dared not venture after them, lest they should receive a fatal shot by the party unseen, from the heart of the dark bushes in which they were hid. Thus did Providence defend this little band of Christian patriots; and while it must have been a matter of thankfulness to them, that no one of their number was missing, nor any of them seriously hurt, it must have been no less satisfactory, that they had left none of their enemies dead on the scene of conflict. Their object was not to destroy the lives of others, but to preserve their own; and if at any time in self-defence they took away life, it was not because they had pleasure in it, but because necessity compelled them.

Many years after this, when the Revolution Settlement had made foes friends again, Adam Clark, now a peaceful store-farmer among the hills of his native district, happened to be in the city of Edinburgh, to which place he had driven a flock of sheep for sale. As he was strolling along the streets he was accosted by a tall and strongly built man, who asked him if he did not recognise him. " No," said Clark, " I do not know you; you seem an entire stranger to me." " I know you, however, having once met with you in circumstances which I shall not easily forget." " To what do you allude?" replied Clark. " Do you not remember," said the man, " the onslaught at Bellybught? Do you not remember the dragoon from whom you wrested the sword, and whom you left prostrate in the moss?" " I do," answered Clark ; " and are you the man?" " I am; and to you I owe my life, for you had me completely in your power. I am beyond measure happy that I now have the opportunity of rendering to you my cor-

dial thanks for your clemency; and I trust that God, in opposition to whose cause I then fought, has in his graciousness
turned my heart to himself. From the moment I escaped
from you with my life, I never lifted a weapon on the side of
persecution, and I most sincerely regret that I ever enlisted
in that cause; but I, like Paul, did it ignorantly and in unbelief." Clark was astonished; he grasped him by the hand,
and hailed him as a brother, and rejoiced that, having left the
path of the destroyer, he had found the way that leads to
peace and everlasting life. "Have you still the sword,"
asked the reclaimed trooper, " which you twisted so rarely
from my grasp ?" " I have," replied Clark, "and I intend to
keep it as an heir-loom in my family." " Keep it, then, you
bravely deserve it; and let it never more be employed, but
in an honest cause." There is something exceedingly agreeable in an occurrence of this kind. Two men who once met
in deadly strife on the battle-field, meeting again in times of
peace, and meeting with hearts united in the same bonds of
Christian fellowship, attached to the cause of the same common Lord, and sharers of the same common salvation, is indeed a circumstance worthy of notice, and delightfully illustrative of the power of the Gospel on the heart.

On another occasion, a company of troopers who were on
their way to the wilds of Crawford Moor, for the purpose of
surprising a conventicle which was to be held in that solitary
retreat, called at Glenim, which lay directly in their route, to
ask a guide to conduct them over the heights. When the
party drew up before the door, Adam Clark went out to meet
them, and in stooping, as the story tells, to draw one of his
shoes more firmly on his foot, being newly roused from his
bed, as it was in the dark of the morning when the soldiers
arrived, he was jostled by one of the horses, and nearly thrown
down. In recovering his position, his temper being a little
heated, he struck the animal a furious blow on the face,
which made him retreat rather hastily and awkwardly for
his rider, who instantly presented a pistol to Clark's breast,
with the apparent intention of shooting him on the spot.
The commander of the party seeing the mischief that might
befall, interfered, and, presenting the broad side of his sword
to the dragoon, prevented him from fulfilling his purpose,
declaring that they had come with no hostile intent, but
simply to request the assistance of a guide. This occurrence.
it is probable, took place prior to the affair of Bellybught.
and near the beginning of the persecution, when the sentiments of the Clarks, both of Auchengrouch and Glenim, in

reference to public matters, were not generally known. When order was restored, and parties had come to a better understanding, Clark consented to conduct them across the wilds. When they came to a place on the west side of the Lowther Hills, not far from the mining village of Wanlockhead, called the Stake Moss, it occurred to Clark that now it was in his power to occasion them some inconvenience, which might probably retard their progress, and prevent them from accomplishing their intended mischief. This moss presents an irregular surface, with here and there deep hags, and some marshy springs. These springs, or cold wells, as the shepherds term them, are, some of them, in the moorland districts in the south-west of Scotland, of great depth, reaching occasionally from six to twelve feet, and in some cases to a much greater depth. Their breadth is sometimes found to be about two or three feet, and their length more than double. The water in these wells rises to a level with the surrounding heath, and its surface is generally covered with long grass and aquatic weeds. A dragoon on horseback stumbling into one of these larger wells, the ordinary springs being much less in dimensions and in depth, would inevitably perish; and this amply accounts for the tradition respecting the occasional and entire disappearance of some of the troopers, man and horse, in the moors. It was in the dusk of the early morning when the party arrived at the Stake Moss, and the obscurity was favourable to Clark's design. They had followed him in safety for several miles; and, having no suspicion of their guide, they rode behind him in perfect confidence. At length, having reached the morass, Clark, being on foot, pressed forward, leaping the mossy ditches with a nimble bound; and the horses plunging after, one after another stuck fast in the sinking peat ground. When Clark saw that the party were fully bemired, and that there was little chance of their getting themselves extricated for a considerable time, he made his escape over the dark heath, and left them to help themselves. It is said that he often regretted his conduct on this occasion; both because he deemed it treacherous, seeing the commander of the party treated him honourably, and because it would tend to exasperate the enemy, and subject all the friends throughout the district to still more rigorous treatment; and his suspicions were not groundless. The more injury the Covenanters, in self-defence, inflicted on their opponents, the more severe did their own sufferings afterwards become; for their enemies delighted in nothing more than in an opportunity of retaliating with seven-fold vengeance. It appears that Adam Clark, from the time that he led the troopers into the moss, was regarded as a dangerous man, and one whom, on the first opportunity, they were determined to apprehend. This determination was amply manifested in the tragic scene which had wellnigh been fully acted on the bent before the house of Auchengrouch. It seems that young Andrew Clark of Auchengrouch bore a striking resemblance to his cousin, Adam of Glenim. One day the dragoons met Andrew in the moors, and believing him to be the identical person who guided them into the moss, apprehended him, and carried him to his father's house. The commander of the party is said to have been Colonel James Douglas, to whom, as Wodrow informs us, an ample commission, with a justiciary power, was granted, for the purpose of harassing the west and south. The poor captive was interrogated respecting his principles, and especially in reference to his conduct at the moss. He declared that he was not the person to whom they alluded, and that, however strong a resemblance there might be between him and the individual who had done them the injury of which they complained, he was entirely innocent. The soldiers, however, positively affirmed that he was the very man who, in the grey of the morning, conducted them along the heights, and left them in the morass, where they sustained no small damage—having, as they asserted, lost some of their best horses, whose legs were broken in the moss. In those days the execution of a man after his impeachment was but the work of a moment; and Andrew was immediately brought out to the field before the house, to be instantly shot. He was allowed time to pray—a favour which, in similar circumstances, was not granted to every one. He knelt down on the bent, and, in the presence of his enemies and of all his father's household, in the presence of angels and before Him for whose truth he was now bearing testimony, and ready to seal that testimony with his blood, he prayed. In the immediate prospect of death, he poured out his soul before the Lord, and made supplication to his Judge. With a melting heart, and in the confidence of faith, he sought acceptance through the great Intercessor, and the remission of all his iniquities through that precious blood which was shed for the sins of the world. He prayed for support in this trying hour: and besought that, as God had brought him to witness publicly for his truth, he would now comfort his heart with the joy of that truth, and enable him to triumph over the fear of death, and submissively, if not exultingly, to surrender his life at

Christ's call. Nor would supplication for his enemies, who were now going to deprive him of life, and for his beloved kindred, from whose dear embraces he was now about to be torn, be omitted. The supplications of this good man, like the powerful and subduing prayer of that great Christian, John Brown of Priesthill, produced a deep impression on the dragoons, who stood around guarding the suppliant as he rested in the attitude of prayer on the heath; and one of the party, more hardened than the rest, perceiving the effect, commanded him to rise from his knees. "No," said the leader, "let the poor man continue in his prayer, we can afford to wait a little; other matters are not pressing; give the man leisure, as his time on earth is but short." There are few hearts so indurated as fairly to outbrave a scene of this nature without some emotion; and James Douglas, though he had witnessed many an act of cruelty, was, in the present instance, scarcely proof against the moving spectacle of a fellow-creature uttering his last prayer, in the presence of weeping and agonizing friends; and, probably, he now wanted only a slight pretext to set the poor victim free, and that pretext was soon found. There lived in the neighbourhood, at a place called Howat's-Burnfoot an aged and worthy woman who had been Andrew Clark's nurse, and for whom, as is common in such cases, she cherished a more than ordinary affection. To this good woman's hut a messenger was instantly despatched to convey the information of what was going on at Auchengrouch. She was a woman of great sagacity, and magnanimity, and piety, who had seen much, both in her native country and in foreign lands; for she had accompanied her husband for sixteen years in the continental wars, and had experienced a variety of fortune. On one occasion, it is said, at the storming of a certain town, when her husband had received a severe wound, she, first having rendered him on the spot what assistance was necessary, next, in order to supply his lack of service, grasped his sword, and pressed forward with the assailants to the attack. Her name—a circumstance to be regretted—has not been preserved; but her worthy character and disinterested actions have found a place in the memory of posterity. This woman lost no time in presenting herself before Colonel Douglas and his company. The sight of soldiers, even in their most terrific array, did not frighten her; for she had been familiar with war. When she arrived at the scene of distress, Andrew had ended his prayer; and the soldiers were prepared, and waiting their commander's orders, to pour the contents of their muskets into the body of the unoffending victim. " Halt, soldiers," cried the matron, whose venerable and commanding aspect inspired the party with something like awe : " Halt, soldiers," cried she, elevating her staff in the attitude of authority, as generals are accustomed to do with the naked blade of their swords on the battle-field, " halt, and listen to me. Let not the brown heath on the moors of Auchengrouch be stained with the blood of an innocent man, lest it cry for vengeance in a voice so loud, and so importunate, as not to be denied." " How now, good mother," said Douglas, " what have you to offer in exculpation of this rebel, who has done what he could to endamage his majesty's interests ? You have heard of the affair of the Stake Moss ?" "I have; but hear me, this man is not he whom you have to blame for that project; he may be like him—he may be his very picture; but he is not the same. Who *he* is that did that deed, it does not befit me to tell, nor shall I. But, Sir, if you be a true soldier, hearken to the wife of one who warred under the banner of your honoured uncle in countries far from this; and, for your uncle's sake, by whose side my husband fought and bled, and for whose sake he would have sacrificed his life, I beg the life of this man, for whom, in his infancy, I acted the part of a mother, and for whom, now in his prime of manhood, I cherish all the warmth of a mother's true affection. I beg on my knees the life of this innocent man." " My good woman," replied the colonel, " his life you shall have. Your appearance is the guarantee for the verity of your statements, and you have mentioned a name that has weight with me. Soldiers ! let him go !"

In this way was the tragical scene at Auchengrouch terminated, and Andrew Clark restored to the arms of his rejoicing friends. Many a blessing would doubtless be poured on the head of the worthy matron by whose intercession his life was spared; and she had her reward in the satisfaction of seeing the life of the guiltless prolonged, and in the consciousness that she had performed a worthy action. There is in goodness, combined with true greatness of mind, a dignity which, when witnessed even in the humblest walks of life, commands respect, and overawes those whose station in life is much superior. How great a blessing must such " a mother in Israel" prove to a whole neighbourhood! She is like a centre, from which emanate goodness, and wisdom, and experience; and the influence of her prudent and godly example must tell with great effect on the entire circle of her acquaintanceship. Such a woman is a crown to her husband, an honour to her kindred, and an ornament to the

Gospel of Christ. The circumstances also in which Andrew Clark was placed brought his Christian character fairly and fully to the test; he was made to look death in the face, and all the realities of eternity were near, but he continued stedfast, and was ready to part with his life for Christ's sake.

Another anecdote is told of two honest men, who, in this same locality, experienced a deliverance from the hands of their persecutors similar to that which Andrew Clark experienced at Auchengrouch. A Covenanter, whose name is not known, had been caught by his enemies, and, under the conduct of two dragoons from Elliock or from Sanquhar, was conveyed through the mountains to be delivered to the custody of a garrison somewhere on the Clyde. As the dragoons were moving slowly along with their solitary charge, they observed in the neighbourhood of Thristane, a place not far from Glenim, a man on the opposite hill clad in a red jacket. "Yonder," exclaimed one of the troopers, "yonder is our deserter; guard the prisoner, and I will pursue." The shepherd on the height observed the movement, and seeing the dragoon advancing with all haste, fled. This circumstance was enough to confirm the suspicions of the soldier, who quickened his pace, thinking him a prize worth the seizing. The shepherd, whose name was Harper, sped his way along the slope of the hill, and took refuge in his own house. When he entered his dwelling he hastily doffed his red vest, justly suspecting that it was the cause of the pursuit, and hid it under the bed-clothes. The dragoon followed and entered the house in breathless haste, thinking that now he was sure of his prey. "Where is the man," demanded he, "where is the man with the red jacket! Deliver him instantly; he is a deserter from our party, and our orders are, to apprehend him, and bring him to punishment. I demand him in the king's name." Harper, who was now arrayed in the ordinary garb of a shepherd, and was sitting with apparent composure by the fire, with a child on his knee, replied that there was no person in his house wearing a dress such as was described. "I saw him enter," vociferated the dragoon, "and he must be here." "You are at liberty to search every corner of this house," said Harper, "and if you find him, you shall be welcome to hold him your prisoner." The trooper, after an unsuccessful search, and after having, as was customary in such cases, stabbed the bed with his sword, departed without his object. When he was gone, the jacket was drawn from the bed perforated in many places by the point of the sharp weapon, but it was never again

used as an article of clothing. During the time that the
zealous dragoon was searching the house of Thristane, his
fellow-soldier was halting with his prisoner till his return.
The place where they stood was on the edge of a precipitous
brow, which descended to a great depth into the valley beneath.
The Covenanter, whose arms were firmly bound together at
the wrists like an infamous felon, thought that now, if he
were unbound, he might easily make his escape. With this
idea, he requested the soldier to untie his hands for a few
minutes, giving as a reason for this request what satisfied
the dragoon. Having obtained his desire, he seated himself
on the grass, on the very brink of the descent, and while his
guard paid no attention to his movements, he seized his
limbs by the ankles, and bending his head forward, threw
his body into something like the shape of a wheel, and
tumbled with great velocity down the steep, and then starting to his feet fled at his utmost speed. The dragoon, taken
by surprise, was confounded at the incident, and hastily
grasping his musket, fired, but without success, as it is always
difficult to secure an effective aim with fire-arms in a sloping direction. He was instantly joined by the trooper from
Thristane, and the two commenced a vigorous pursuit. The
fugitive, however, fled with great speed, and escaped to the
wilds near the source of the Clyde, where he found a shelter
from his deadly foes; the God in whom he trusted having
accomplished his deliverance.

CHAPTER VII.

Muirkirk—John Richard—Thomas Richard—William Moffat of
Hartfell.

THE farm-house in Burnfoot, in times of persecution, stood
on the moorland stream of Greenock Water, at a short distance from the village of Muirkirk, around which, on the
wilds and mountains, many a deed of persecuting cruelty was
perpetrated. It was in the neighbourhood of this village that
John Brown of Priesthill, a man whose saintly character
earned for him the epithet of "*the godly carrier*," fell by the
murderous hand of Claverhouse, on the green turf before his
own door. The solitudes in the vicinity of Muirkirk were
frequently crowded with the scattered flock of Christ, when
they were driven with the rod of violence from those pastures on which they had been formerly nurtured. Muirkirk,
which is now a large and crowded village, was in those more
simple times a small hamlet, with its little church sitting
solitary afar on the waste; but even here, in the lonely wilderness, was the Gospel of our salvation faithfully preached
to the handful of the rural population that weekly convened
in the house of God. The name of Hugh Campbell, the
minister of the parish, is to be found on the roll of the
ejected. This circumstance speaks for his faithfulness as a
servant of Christ, and would authorize us to draw the infer-
ence that he was one of those who maintained the standard
of the truth, when Zion's foes were striving to wrest it from
the hands of her children. The dreary locality in the midst
of which Muirkirk is situated, must have afforded, for a considerable period, a place of refuge to those who were driven
before the storm, and buffeted by the fierce blasts of a relentless persecution. At length, every retreat, however remote,
was carefully searched by those whose delight it was to
drive the ploughshare of ruin through a prostrate land; and

the wilds of Muirkirk afforded a spacious hunting-field to those whose occupation it was to shed on the flowery heath, without a tear, the blood of God's saints. The deep mossy trenches on the mountain's side were often made to flow with the blood of those who, for the truth's sake, jeopardied their lives on the high places of the field, and whose death-groans were heard to mingle with the soft wailings of the gentle lambkins on the moors; but, in the absence of all human condolence, we can believe that the consolations of the Holy Spirit were not wanting, and that the sweet accents of music, uttered, it may be, by the blessed lips of angels, or of sister spirits whose martyred bodies were sleeping in the neighbouring heath, soothed their dying moments, and fortified their hearts in the parting hour. There is, in the desert "flowered with martyrs," presented to the eye of the Christian, a beauty, compared with which the finest and richest scenes on earth are tame and bleak. There is felt by the devout heart a moral interest in the scenery, which stirs all the inner soul, and which binds to the spot his holiest likings.

John Richard, the occupant of the farm of Burnfoot, was a Covenanter. Irvine of Bonshaw, who was at this time ravaging the west, proceeded, with a few dragoons, to Burnfoot, for the purpose of apprehending the worthy tenant. In order the better to accomplish his purpose, he resolved to adopt the night season, when the quiet family would be gathered about the blazing hearth. The night selected for the work of mischief happened to be extremely dark ; and this circumstance gave rise to a proverbial expression, which was long current in the district. When any evening was more than commonly *mirky*, it was said to be " like Bonshaw's night." The obscurity of the night, however, was the safety of the family at Burnfoot. There happened to be in Bonshaw's party, a dragoon of the name of M'Lelland, who was formerly a servant to John Richard; and this individual though a wild and reckless character, entertained a respect for the household in which he had once resided, so that, availing himself of the pitchy darkness of the evening, he stole from his company, and being well acquainted with the locality, proceeded unobserved, and with all speed, to the house of his old master. The family were out of measure astonished when they saw M'Lelland come swaggering into the apartment, in the attire of a rough dragoon. In his vapouring manner he explained the object of his visit ; and having drawn his ponderous blade, struck the *crook* or pendent chain in the chimney thrice, leaving each time a deep notch in the

tron, by which the said Tom M'Lelland would be kept in
memory when his bones were in the dust. The rude kindness of the blunt dragoon was not unappreciated by the honest farmer of Burnfoot and his family, who instantly prepared
for flight. M'Lelland returned and joined his party, without
having been missed, or in any way suspected. As they approached the house, M'Lelland was loudest in his denunciations of vengeance against the Whigs. The party alighted on
a gentle rising ground, on which was reared a huge pyramid
of peats, and prepared to make their attack on the defenceless dwelling. Bonshaw then rushed into the house, expecting to seize its inmates by surprise ; but, to his astonishment,
nobody was within. The search which followed was fruitless,
and the object of the troopers was unexpectedly defeated.
John Richard, being an aged man, and not able to retire far
from his house in the dark, had cowered down at the side of a
stone dyke in the close vicinity of his cottage. The feet of
the horses in moving about in the dark, had nearly trodden
upon him. Perceiving his danger, he, with as little noise and
with as much haste as he could, removed from the spot, and
crept on the wet ground into the midst of some willow bushes
that grew near the place. As he lay here, the horses accidentally approached him again ; and he was not without the
serious apprehension of being crushed to death under their
feet. The boggy ground, however, saved him ; for the heavy
animals sunk to the belly in the marsh, and with difficulty
were extricated. The dragoons finding themselves thus incom-
moded, and seeing that their object could not be gained at
that time, withdrew. Bonshaw, notwithstanding the bewildering darkness of the night, was yet resolved to make further
attempts in another place that lay in his route. Not far
from Burnfoot they stumbled on a weaver's hut, into which
they entered, for the purpose of making inquiries, and of pro-
curing a guide. The weaver had just returned from the
house of one of his customers, to whom he had carried a
newly-wrought web ; and being dressed in his better clothes,
the leader of the party asserted that he had been at a conventicle, or some private meeting of the Covenanters, and
that therefore he must be a Whig. The man endeavoured to
clear himself of the charges, and showed them the true state of
the matter. Bonshaw then declared his readiness to believe
him on the following conditions :— that he should swear
never to lift arms against the king, and that he should conduct them to the farm-house of Netherwood. The weaver,
being no Covenanter, consented to do both. When the party

reached Netherwood, the leader succeeded in obtaining another guide to conduct them to Greenock Mains, at which he expected to apprehend some of the Covenanters. The guide from Netherwood appears to have been the farmer himself, and had no great liking for the business on which he was pressed. He found it in vain to remonstrate, but resolved, if possible, to make the errand of the troopers to Greenock Mains abortive. Near the house of Greenock Mains is a steep brow, down the descent of which Netherwood led the company. It was this honest man's design to convey, by some means or other, a warning to the family of Greenock Mains of the danger that was approaching. Accordingly, when the party reached the top of the brow, Netherwood, in a pretty loud voice, apprised them of the circumstance, and showed the necessity of using great caution in the descent. As they proceeded almost blindfold down the declivity, every little incident or stumbling among the horses or men afforded an occasion to Netherwood to lift his voice still louder—by way of caution to the troopers, on the one hand; and by way of warning to the unsuspecting family, on the other. He seemed to be particularly solicitous about the safety of the commander, whose name he took pleasure in vociferating with great emphasis, and giving him incessantly the high-sounding title of "Your Honour," enjoined him to advance warily in the dark, as life and limbs were both in hazard. Bonshaw, apprehensive lest the noise should alarm the inmates of Greenock Mains, imposed silence; but Netherwood, not appearing to apprehend the import of Bonshaw's advice, seemed intent only on the safety of the party intrusted to his guidance, and cried the louder as he approached the dwelling. Bonshaw threatened—

> " But Netherwood him *honoured* still,
>   Till Greenock Mains sped to the hill."

The result was as Netherwood intended and as Bonshaw feared; for Greenock Mains fled in the dark, and escaped the hands of his enemies, who thirsted for his blood.

The farmer of Greenock Mains, however, did not always thus escape. The very same person, in all likelihood, of whom the worthless Bonshaw was at this time in quest, was afterwards apprehended and shot at Cumnock: his name was Thomas Richard. Tradition mentions that a Covenanter of the name of Richard was in concealment on the heights between Burnfoot and Evan Water, and that he was apprehended by stratagem. The plan taken to circumvent him was the following: A number of individuals, in the guise of Covenanters, came upon him in his hiding-place. They pretended to be very serious persons—each had a Bible; and they requested Richard to read the Scriptures with them, and to pray. The good man, suspecting no deceit, rejoiced to meet with a number of religious friends whom he had never seen before, and gladly complied with their request. As the sky sometimes assumes a very serene and beautiful aspect immediately before the gathering of the storm, so these men assumed a devout and friendly demeanour, which was soon to issue in that of deceivers and murderers. To the blank astonishment of the simple-minded Covenanter, he soon found that he was their prisoner; and that, instead of their being devout worshippers, they were ruthless persecutors. He was carried to Cumnock, where he suffered martyrdom. This anecdote, with some circumstantial variations, is substantially the same with the account of Thomas Richard of Greenock Mains, given by Wodrow. " About this time," says the historian, " a very barbarous murder was committed upon Thomas Richard in Greenock Mains, in the parish of Muirkirk, a godly man, nearly eighty years of age. Peter Inglis, cornet, son to Captain Inglis, with some soldiers, pretended they were friends, and some of the remains of Argyle's men. One of my informations bears that, the better way to carry on the cheat, they had Bibles with them, and pressed and prevailed with Thomas to pray with them; and when at prayer, some of them took notes of some expressions, and afterwards they advised with him upon a designed attack they were about to make upon a neighbouring garrison. Two other narratives before me omit these circumstances, and say, Captain Inglis came into Thomas' house with four or five men pretending to be Whigs; and, after some other discourse, asked him if he knew where any of the honest party were ? The old man, in the innocence of his heart, suspecting no cheat, answered, he knew not of any at present; but that he had lodged some of them some days ago, and was not yet unwilling to give them any entertainment he had. Thus the jest was carried on for a little, till one of them bewrayed himself by an oath, and then they all cast off the mask, and carried the old man to Colonel Douglas, then at Cumnock, who, precisely upon this alleged confession, without jury or trial, next day executed him there. I am well informed, from a reverend minister present, that his case was so favourable, that three ladies of the Episcopal persuasion, upon hearing of it, went to the colonel to beg his life, but were not admitted, only they had a message sent them ' that he could show no favour to these people.'" The anecdote, and the statement of the historian, seem, therefore, to be the same. This venerable saint, like many of his brethren in that treacherous age, lost his life in a cruel and iniquitous manner. It is a pity that nothing but the mere incident of his death has been recorded: it would have been gratifying to know the behaviour of this Christian on the eve of martyrdom. But though nothing respecting this has been handed down to us, there is no doubt that He in whose cause he was called out to suffer before many witnesses, would be with him, to strengthen him to bear honourable testimony to the truth.

Having viewed, then, these scenes and doings in the west, we may now turn round, and for a moment glance at some things which were done in an easterly direction. There lived, says tradition, a man of the name of William Moffat near Hartfell, not far from the beautiful village of Moffat, in Annandale. This man, having experienced the power of the truth in his own heart, was solicitous, it would appear, to impart the knowledge of the same truth to others. For this purpose he formed little conventicles among the hills, and prayed with, and instructed those who resorted to him. The wild locality in the midst of which Providence had fixed his abode, was favourable to the object he had in view, inas-much as there was less danger of meeting with interruption Secluded, however, as this situation was, it was not too secluded from the flying parties of troopers who occasionally scoured moss and mountain in all directions and at all seasons. One day William Moffat had met with a few friends in a retired glen in the vicinity of his dwelling, and was employed with them in religious exercises. While they were engaged in devotion, the large flock of sheep that was quietly grazing on the dark slanting brow of the neighbouring height, was on a sudden observed to be in motion, and then to spread on all sides as if furiously attacked by a pack of ravenous dogs. "We are in danger," cried the honest shepherd; "these sheep are not scattered without a cause." And they were in danger; for a company of dragoons were descending the hill, and the terrified sheep had fled before them, and fled as if to announce to the little flock of worshippers, who were as helpless as themselves, that the enemy was approaching. Whether the troopers were incidentally passing, or had come to make special search, is not said; but they were descending straight on the timid handful who had met in the desert to pray. What was to be done? They could neither fight nor flee, and must therefore inevitably fall a prey to the destroyer. It sometimes happens, however, that

when, in certain perilous circumstances, all hope appears
to be cut off, even then, in our very extremity, a deliverance unexpectedly comes; and so was it with the worshippers in the glen. Those who are acquainted with the mountainous tracts of the country are no strangers to the sudden
falling of the mist on the summits of the lofty heights. Sometimes, instead of descending in a body like a large snowy
cloud spreading itself along the ridges and adown the slopes
of the hills, it comes edgewise trailing along, and like a thin
white veil, extending from the clouds to the earth. On the
present occasion the vapour that had been encircling the
brow of the mountain, and occasionally stretching out in long
defiles into the narrow glens beneath, came like a lofty and
impervious wall between the worshippers and the dragoons.
This covering, which was thus thrown from the clouds,
screened from the view of the soldiers the little conventicle,
and they marched past beyond the misty curtain, not more,
it is said, than a hundred and fifty yards distant. Thus did
this small flock of God's worshippers, that had convened in
the wilderness to gather the manna that might be rained
from his hand, experience his special care, and were protected by him behind a wall of secure defence, when the foe,
like the rushing of the tempest, swept past them on the other
side. We may easily conceive the grateful emotions that
must have stirred within them when they thought on the
kindness that shielded them from so great a danger. It is
said that this and similar deliverances emboldened the shepherd and his friends to persist in holding frequent meetings
for spiritual edification, notwithstanding the hazards to which
they were exposed. Their confidence in God's providential
care was greatly strengthened when, in answer to prayer,
they found protection.

On another occasion William Moffat was surprised by the
dragoons, and narrowly escaped, twice on the same day. He
fled towards Evan Water to hide himself in its woods, or in
some friendly house whose door might perchance be open to
receive him. In his flight he passed near a place called Raccleuch, and in crossing a streamlet in the view of the house,
he observed a hollow place close by the margin of the brook,
in which, like Peden in Glendyne, he resolved to conceal
himself. The dragoons came onward, and passed the stream
without perceiving him, and pursued their course along the
track that led up the Evan. The farmer of Raccleuch had
observed the pursuit, and saw Moffat hide himself in the
hollow among the bushes by the burn; and when the troopers

were past, and the fugitive had crept from his hiding-place,
the honest farmer congratulated him on his escape. The
soldiers, however, perceiving that they had missed their
object, and standing still to look around them, observed
Moffat and the gudeman of Raecleuch conversing together.
They instantly retraced their steps, and commenced the pursuit. Moffat perceiving the movement of the horsemen,
again betook himself to flight; and having passed the Evan,
hied to the heights in the direction of Elvanfoot, in the
neighbourhood of which lived a friend of his own, in whose
house he hoped to find shelter. With this intention he proceeded onward, and far outstripped the troopers, who could
not wend their way through moss and moor with the same
celerity and safety. When he came near Elvanfoot he hid
himself in the hollow places among the dark heather on the
waste, and finally eluded the search of his pursuers. The
brown heath was to him doubtless a sweet and soft bed, after
the long and perilous chase. The feeling of safety is never
so delightfully intense as immediately after escape from imminent danger, nor does the heart ever swell with warmer
emotions of grateful acknowledgments to the Preserver of
our life. And happy must he have been when, prostrate in
concealment and prayer on the bent, he poured out his heart
into "the bosom of his Father and his God." The upland
solitudes, near the source of the Clyde, in the vicinity of the
ancient Roman station at Gadenica—the long sought-for town
of the Damnii—were much frequented in the times of the
Church's tribulation, many a houseless wanderer for conscience' sake seeking there an asylum from the fury of the
oppressor.

CHAPTER VIII.

Durisdeer— Elias Wilson—Adam Clark of Glenim—Muncie the Informer—Mitchelslacks—Michael Smith of Quarrelwood.

THE parish of Durisdeer, in Nithsdale, occupies a very
romantic locality. The name signifies "the door of the
forest," and plainly indicates, what was the fact, that in ancient times it was mostly covered with wood. The hills by
which it is walled in on the east and on the north, present
a scene of indescribable beauty; and in walking along the
margin of the Carron, towards the far-famed pass of Dalveen,
in the balmy softness of a summer's eve, one would almost
imagine that he was transported to the enchanting scenes
of the fabled fairy land. This parish is not without its antiquities—and antiquities, too, of considerable interest. On
the farm of Castlehill there stood an old baronial stronghold,
the residence, no doubt, of some renowned chieftain, whose
name and exploits have long since been forgotten; and the
fields which were anciently the battle-ground of rival clans,
are now subjected to the peaceful hand of agriculture. In
this locality are the remains of an ancient Roman station,
near the church of Durisdeer, and a branch of the Roman
road, which went off to the west, and passed through this
parish. " This road," says the author of the " Caledonia,"
" went up Nithsdale on the east side of the Nith, passing
by the village of Thornhill, and crossing Carron Water, a
little above its influx into the Nith. From this passage the
road continued its course, in a northerly direction, past a
Roman fort, in a remarkable pass above the kirk of Durisdeer; from this pass it pushed through the hill by the defile
called the Wall-path, and went down the east side of Powtrail Water, to its confluence with the Dair." It is interesting to think, that in the days of Lollius Urbicus, above
seventeen centuries ago, and for ages after, a detachment of

Roman soldiers was located in the forest of Durisdeer,
speaking the Latin language, and keeping in subjection to
the power of Rome the ancient Selgovæ, who occupied the
upper part of Nithsdale.

Alexander Strang was minister of Durisdeer at the Restoration, and was one of those worthy men who, because he
would not submit to lordly Prelacy, was banished from his
charge.   This good man, along with Thomas Shields, minister of the neighbouring parish of Kirkbride, took joyfully
the spoiling of his goods, that he might maintain the doctrine of Christ, and a pure conscience.   It is to be regretted
that so little is preserved of those pious men who, for their
nonconformity, were ejected by hundreds from their churches,
by the unrighteous edicts of unprincipled rulers.   Their remembrance, however, is with God, and their labours and their
sufferings have long since terminated in the heavenly rest.   In
more recent times, this upland parish was blessed with the ministrations of an eminently godly man of the name of M'Kill.
The memory of this heavenly man is still warmly cherished
by the older people, who in their youth were under his pastoral care.   His great diligence in his ministerial labours, his
homely and affectionate manners, his fervent and unctuous
preaching, and the great gatherings on sacramental occasions,
are still spoken of with rapture by the worthy inhabitants of
the district.   There is a fragrance in piety which embalms the
memorial of holy men, and which, like odours wafted afar on
the breeze, accompanies their names even to a distant posterity.   Godly men, even in obscure stations, are held in grateful remembrance, while heroes and statesmen, and men of
great earthly renown in their day, are in a short time forgotten.

There lived in a cottage, on the farm of Dalveen, in the
parish of Durisdeer, a Covenanter of the name of Elias
Wilson.   This man, though occupying the humbler walks
of life, was noted for his piety and honesty of principle; and
was therefore an individual who could not long be concealed
from the observant eye of the persecutors.   He was one day
informed, that, being regarded with suspicion, his enemies
at some distance were on their way to apprehend him.   He
communicated the news to his wife, who was a person in all
respects of a kindred spirit with himself, and equally ready
to suffer with him in the cause of righteousness and truth.
They arranged the affairs of their little dwelling the best way
they could, knowing that the unprincipled soldiery would seize
everything they could lay their hands on; and having driven
their cow to the bent, they departed, with their infant child,

to seek a hiding-place in some lonely cave among the mountains. The cave in which they found a refuge was in one of the dark linns of Enterkin, the entrance to which was very difficult and dangerous. The dragoons, as was anticipated, arrived at the cottage at a time when they hoped to capture its inhabitants without much trouble to themselves. In the hut, however, they found matters in a very different situation from what they expected, and being defeated in their object, they were greatly enraged. The cavern, it would appear, to which Wilson and his wife had fled for refuge, was not unknown to some of the dragoons, who proposed to search it, and for this purpose conducted the party to the rocky precipice, in the face of which the dark recess was situated. The approach of the soldiers was perceived by the fugitives, and Wilson accoutred himself for defence. He had brought with him a musket, and with this he was prepared to face his enemies, in case of attack. The passage to the hiding-place being precarious, the troopers did not seem much inclined to force an entrance, but having posted themselves on all sides, they were determined to annoy the inmates by shooting over the rock and into the mouth of the cave. The manly spirit of Wilson was roused, and the strong affection of the husband and the parent took possession of his whole soul, and urged him fearlessly forward in the defence of his wife and child, against a band of armed ruffians and legalized murderers, whom the spirit of evil had let loose on an unoffending peasantry. A dragoon, more audacious than the rest, had approached near the mouth of the retreat, and, leaning over a rock, was peeping into the cave, for the purpose of taking his aim at those who were within. This was observed by Wilson, who instinctively stood on the defensive, and fired on the hostile intruder. The shot reached its victim, and the man tumbled from his station into the deep bottom of the ravine below. The commander of the party, who is said to have been a Captain Greir, when he saw the man fall by the firing which for a moment illuminated the dark interior of the cavern, was transported with rage, and, breathing a fearful oath, threatened ample vengeance on the detestable Covenanter who, in endeavouring to defend himself, had killed one of the king's troopers. In uttering this threat, however, he reckoned without his host, and forgot that, in certain favourable circumstances, one man is as good as ten. The captain, then, with two of the most daring of his followers, attempted to scramble to the mouth of the cave. Wilson observed their movements, and perceived their dreadful determination; his life was in the utmost jeopardy, and a firm and vigorous defence was now imperatively called for. The assailants had reached the entrance, and were about to rush forward with deadly intent, when Wilson firing again, shot a dragoon, who, staggering backwards, fell against his commander, and both were precipitated into the rocky deep beneath; the soldier was killed by the shot, and the officer by the fall. The remainder of the troopers were astonished and appalled at the catastrophe, and not daring to make a second attempt, resolved to keep watch during the night, while one of their party was despatched to the nearest garrison for assistance. Wilson and his wife now plainly saw that, unless they could steal from their hiding-place, their fate would be inevitable. In making their escape, however, a twofold difficulty lay in their way—the dangerous passage from the cave in the dark, and the watchfulness of the soldiers who were stationed around them. They resolved, however, to make the attempt, and accordingly, during the midnight vigils of the dragoons, Wilson and his wife softly and unobserved crept from their prison-house, and left the soldiers in the morning light to wonder at the daring and the dexterity by which their watchfulness had been evaded. The couple, however, got safe away, and sought another hiding-place, where they were sheltered from the vengeance of their enemies. Wilson was obliged for many a day to keep himself in close concealment, and he succeeded in weathering the storm, and lived to see the Revolution. Providence brought him through many trials, and in the end he died in peace.

It was probably in the same cave to which Wilson and his wife fled, that Adam Clark of Glenim, and a company with him, took refuge when they were pursued by the enemy. There lived in Durisdeer a person of the name of Muncie, who bore the character of an infamous informer, and who was constantly prowling about, collecting what information he could regarding the wanderers. By some means or other he found out that Clark and his party were lodged in the cavern, and he hastened to make the discovery to those who were in search of them. The dragoons were instantly in motion, and proceeded with all caution to surprise the fugitives in their place of retreat. It happened, however, that one of the party in concealment observed from the mouth of the cave, where he chanced to be standing at the moment, the approach of the horsemen; and, from the direction in which they were coming, there could be no doubt that they were advancing to assail the niding-place. It was agreed that, instead of standing a siege in the cavity of the rock, they should betake themselves to flight, and seek their safety on the steep sides of the mountains. They issued without delay from the cavern, and as they were scrambling up the rugged face of the acclivity, the troopers came up and fired upon the fugitives, who were in no condition to defend themselves. One of their number was killed, and the rest escaped to the hills. The name of the person who fell is not known, and his dust is doubtless reposing under the grassy turf on the mountain's side, though no one can point out his resting-place. There are probably scores of our Scottish martyrs, whose graves on the heath and on the hills are now entirely unknown. No history has preserved the account of their death, and the narratives, which for a season hung on the lips of tradition, have now dropped into oblivion.

It was understood by Adam Clark and his party, that Muncie, the informer, was the individual who directed the dragoons to the cavern, and who, consequently, was the cause of the death of their friend; and they determined to embrace the first opportunity of administering a suitable chastisement. They accordingly went in a body to Muncie's house one evening, and found him sitting by the fire, with one of his children on his knee. When they entered, he suspected their errand, and instinctively holding up the child as a sort of shield between himself and his visitors, as if he anticipated an immediate assault, he requested them in a fawning and obsequious manner to be seated, and to take supper with him. This they refused, in a manner which plainly indicated the design of their visit. Muncie fled to the door—the assailants pursued, and, with their hands and other weapons, belaboured him in a style befitting his offence, and expressive of their detestation of his infamous vocation. When the party were engaged in punishing the informer, it is said that a person of the name of " The Black M'Michael " struck him with his sword, either accidentally or by design, and killed him. " Evil shall hunt the violent man to overthrow him." The retributions of Divine Providence are sometimes very remarkable, and come with such a precision and distinction on their object, as to point him out with full prominence to the notice of all. A man of Muncie's occupation was detested by all parties, and could never enjoy the approbation of his own mind.

On another occasion, this same Adam Clark and one of his companions met with rather a remarkable deliverance, under the very eye of Claverhouse and a company of his troops. Clark and his friend, it is said, came in their wanderings to the house of Mitchelslacks, in Closeburn, where they were kindly entertained by the family. Claverhouse, who was then in the neighbourhood, was informed of the circumstance, and proceeded with a party of dragoons to the place. When he arrived at the house, he asked if two men of the description which he gave were within? The mistress of the house, who met him at the door, and who saw that it was in vain to attempt concealment, acknowledged that there were at the time two men such as he had mentioned in the dwelling, and that they were at the moment partaking of some food. "Tell them," said the commander, " to come out instantly: they are our prisoners." The men within, hearing what was going on at the door, rose from the table, and hastily girded on their armour to meet their foes at the entrance. Having loaded their muskets, they presented themselves before the dragoons, prepared for a desperate defence. The bold and martial attitude of the two Covenanters, when they showed themselves in the door-way, over-awed the soldiers, ten in number, with Claverhouse at their head; and they retired, drawing their horses backwards, like the mist on the neighbouring hill, when driven by a sudden gust from the mouth of some narrow glen. The horsemen divided and allowed the men, who had assumed so noble a daring, to pass unmolested through their ranks and to escape, without the firing of a single shot. This was certainly a rare occurrence, and might probably be accounted for, if we were acquainted with all the circumstances of the case.

Michael Smith lived in Quarrelwood, not far from Dumfries. He kept a small house of entertainment, which was open to all sorts of persons, and among others, to the Covenanters. Michael had a warm side to the persecuted people, and none were more welcome to his little inn than they. He embraced every opportunity of relieving and sheltering them. It was in his power to do this in the character of an innkeeper, without attaching any suspicion to his conduct, as his house was free to every person. Michael's partiality to the Covenanters, however, became too glaring to pass without notice, and he was complained of as one who harboured the rebels. To ascertain the truth on this point, then, a party of dragoons was despatched to Michael's house. He was asked if he entertained any of the disaffected people, and if he received money from them. Smith replied, "that as he kept an inn, however humble in its pretensions, for the accommodation of travellers—he could not tell who they might be that happened to call at his house, nor was it his business to inquire—that he was in the habit of receiving payment from those who were served either with liquor or with food; but if, on any occasion, it turned out that, when the reckoning was called for, some had nothing wherewith to pay, what could he do but let them go?—that it was a hard thing if the poverty of others should be charged as a crime upon him, or that people should say he harboured the Covenanters, simply because he occasionally received nothing from those who had nothing to give." This statement seemed satisfactory to the party; and, in order to end the matter, it was proposed that he should take the test. The test was administered to suspected persons, and was first imposed in 1681. It has been justly characterized as "a medley of Popery, Prelacy, Erastianism, and self-contradiction." It demanded an acknowledgment of the king's supremacy in all causes, ecclesiastic as well as civil, and a renunciation of the covenants and the Presbyterian Establishment. "For many years," says Wodrow, "it became a handle for persecuting, even to the death, great numbers, and some of them of very considerable rank; and oppressing multitudes of noblemen, gentlemen, and others, who could not comply with it." Honest Michael Smith objected to the test chiefly on the ground of his ignorance of its nature, alleging that it was a hard thing to force a man to take a solemn oath, of which he had no competent understanding; and his reasoning, it seems, prevailed, for the matter was no further insisted on. The dragoons having, no doubt, been entertained in a befitting manner by the innkeeper, who had everything in his possession in the shape of liquors that suited their taste, requested his assistance to enable them to trace their way to the retreat of some Covenanters who were supposed to be lurking in the neighbourhood. It appears that the soldiers frequently forced suspected persons to guide them in their search for the wanderers who were in concealment: this they did, no doubt, on the supposition that they were well acquainted with their hiding-places: but, as we have already seen, it generally happened that they were the worst guides they could have chosen, because they were sure, by some means or other, to defeat the end in view. Michael, on this occasion, accompanied the troopers with no good will to the work on which they were bent. The persons of whom they were in quest were concealed in a wild bosky glen, called the Ballachin Wood, through which murmurs a crystal stream of the same name. As they proceeded along, threading their way among the trees and bushes, Smith happened to be considerably in advance, traversing a narrow foot-path that led across the brook. As he walked onward, and the soldiers following his guidance, he plainly perceived, at a short distance before him, and exactly in the track of his route, a man stretched at his full length on the ground, and fast asleep. He had no doubt whatever that the man was one of the Covenanters in hiding, and, in all likelihood, one of the very party they were seeking. What was to be done? To advance a few yards farther would inevitably lead to a discovery, and to stand still and appear to hesitate would lead to suspicion. In this perplexity Smith had recourse to stratagem; and wheeling round, with his face to the dragoons, cried out, "Do you see that hare?" The soldiers turned to look, and at the moment a hare actually started from the covert near their feet. The circumstance diverted their attention for a while, and afforded the sleeping man time to escape, and to inform his friends of the danger that was approaching. In this way Smith, who became a reluctant guide to the troopers, was the means of saving the persons whom they sought to destroy. Further search of course was fruitless; for the party in concealment hastily removed from the spot, to seek elsewhere a place of retreat. Thus the worthy innkeeper had the satisfaction of having, on one and the same day, both extricated himself from a snare and delivered a company of pious men from death.

On another occasion he was no less successful in saving from their enemies a party of Covenanters in his own house. Three of those men, exhausted with their wanderings, came one evening to his abode, for the purpose of obtaining food and rest. As they were sitting by the fire, after having partaken of a refreshing meal, a detachment of dragoons came galloping to the door. "We are gone," said the men to their landlord; "we shall be captured instantly." "No," replied he; "do as I bid you. Here is a sample of malt which I will spread on the table before you, as if you had been examining it, and lean forward on the board, and appear to be fast asleep." Michael met the dragoons at the door, who asked him if he had any of the Covenanters within? "There are," said he, "three men, who called some time ago: they are in an apartment by themselves, and you can enter and see what you think of them." The dragoons dismounted and followed him to the place where the men were seated, and apparently in a sound sleep, with their heads leaning on the table, and malt spread before them. "You can judge for yourselves," said Smith, "whether these are praying Covenanters, or drunken maltsters; rouse them, and see what they have to say for themselves." The soldiers no sooner saw the state of matters than they turned away, not thinking it worth their while to disturb the repose of the sleeping men after their supposed debauch, and left them to recover themselves at their own convenience. This contrivance was the means of deceiving the troopers, who were withheld from making a particular investigation, which would have doubtless led to a discovery. Thus did Providence throw over these men the shield of protection in the very moment of their imminent danger, and saved them from their enemies, in circumstances in which deliverance appeared almost impossible.

Margaret Smith, a great-granddaughter of Michael Smith, whose memory has supplied these anecdotes of her worthy ancestor, lives at Penpont, and is now an old woman, and full of days.

CHAPTER IX

Thomas Harkness, Andrew Clark, and Samuel M'Ewan--Babe
of Tweedhope-foot—John Hunter.

AFTER the rescue at Enterkin, which took place in the summer of 1684, and of which mention has already been made, the inhabitants of the south and west were subjected to very severe treatment. Orders were issued for assembling all the male population in Nithsdale, above the age of fifteen years, in the different localities appointed, for the purpose of searching the whole county, with a view to apprehend the persons engaged in that enterprise. A meeting was accordingly held in every parish, and a strict search was made in houses, and moors, and woods, but without effect. On the failure of this attempt, it was next agreed on that a public intimation should be made by the curates the next Sabbath, in the ten or twelve parishes nearest the scene of the rescue; —that all above fifteen years should meet at New Dalgerno, to answer, upon oath, what questions might be put to them. A great company met at the appointed place, and the following questions were asked:—" Do you know who rescued the prisoners at Enterkin? Do you know which way they fled? Do you know where they are at present?" The multitude which met at Dalgerno was too numerous to be interrogated in one day, and therefore meetings were appointed to be held in the different parishes, when the above questions were to be put to each individual. Those who failed to appear at those meetings were either imprisoned or obliged to keep the soldiers at free quarters for a specified time. This annoying and vexatious work continued for about six weeks; and it is easy to imagine the trouble and distress to which the district in general was exposed. James Harkness of Locherben, and others with him, who were engaged in the affair of the rescue, were apprehended and carried to Edinburgh. Harkness was tried, and condemned to die, but he happily avoided the execution of the sentence by escaping, along with twenty-five fellow-prisoners, from the Canongate Jail. Thomas Harkness, the brother of James, was not so fortunate. He, along with Andrew Clark of Leadhills, and Samuel M'Ewan of Glencairn, was seized by Claverhouse, when, like a fury, he was roaming through all the places in Nithsdale, where he hoped to apprehend the rebels who had attacked the king's troops. He came upon the three help- less men, as they were sleeping in the fields, in the parish of Closeburn. They were so fast asleep that the soldiers had to rouse them; and when they opened their eyes, and saw their enemies standing over them, like ravenous beasts ready to pounce on their prey, they attempted to flee, but in vain; for the soldiers, who, on account of the defeat at Enterkin, were exceedingly enraged, wounded them, and took them prisoners. Whether any of them were at Enterkin or not does not appear; but the soldiers deponed that they were, and therefore they were conveyed to Edinburgh, and were condemned to die on the same day on which they were tried. " They were," says Wodrow, " brought into Edinburgh about one of the clock, and that same day they were sen- tenced and executed about five of the clock." This evidently shows how eagerly their enemies thirsted for their blood. But though the summons was hasty, they were not unpre- pared; they lived with death constantly before them, and were in hourly expectation of meeting with the last enemy. Their brethren were daily falling on the moors and hills around them, and therefore they held themselves in constant readiness to meet with a similar fate. The interval between the sentence and execution was short; but brief as the period was, they drew up a conjunct testimony to that truth in behalf of which they suffered. This testimony, though expressed in a few words, is worthy of notice, and is as follows:—

> " The joint testimony of Thomas Harkness, Andrew Clark, and Samuel M'Ewan, from the Tolbooth of Edinburgh, August 5 [1684].

" Dear friends and relations whatsomever, we think fit to acquaint you, that we bless the Lord that ever we were ordained to give a publick testimony, who are so great sin- ners. Blessed be he that we were born to bear witness for him, and blessed be the Lord Jesus Christ that ordained the Gospel and the truths of it, which he sealed with his own

blood; and many a worthy Christian gone before us hath
sealed them. We were questioned for not owning the king's
authority. We answered, that we owned all authority that
is allowed by the written Word of God, sealed by Christ's
blood. Now, our dear friends, we entreat you to stand to
the truth, and especially all ye that are our own relations,
and all that love and wait for the coming of Christ. He will
come and not tarry, and reward every one according to their
deeds in the body. We bless the Lord that we are not a
whit discouraged, but content to lay down our life with cheer-
fulness, and boldness, and courage; and if we had a hundred lives, we would willingly quit with them all for the truth
of Christ. Good news! Christ is no worse than he promised.
Now we take our leave of all our friends and acquaintances,
and declare we are heartily content with our lot, and that
he hath brought us hither to witness for him and his truth.
We leave our testimony against Popery, and all other false
doctrine that is not according to the Scriptures of the Old
and New Testaments, which is the only Word of God.
Dear friends, be valiant for God; for he is as good as his promise. Him that overcometh he will make a pillar in his
temple. Our time is short, and we have little to spare, hav-
ng got our sentence at one of the clock this afternoon, and
are to die at five this day; and so we will say no more, but
farewell all friends and relations, and welcome heaven, and
Christ, and the cross for Christ's sake.

" THOMAS HARKNESS.

" ANDREW CLARK.

" SAMUEL M'EWAN."

In this short statement, emitted by these three plain
country men, on the very eve of their death, of which they
were not apprised sooner than four brief hours before it
happened, we perceive no confusion nor perturbation, but an
admirable calmness of spirit, and Christian fortitude, and
confidence in God. The peace and evenness of mind which
they displayed, proves that the experience of the truth on the
heart is a reality, and that the faith of the Gospel is capable of
sustaining the soul in the most trying and appalling circumstances. Had any of their enemies received the sentence of
death themselves as they did, we can easily conceive the
trepidation into which they would have been thrown, and
their blank consternation in the immediate prospect of
death; for the soul without hope in God, and a well-
grounded confidence in his favour, is, at that solemn moment,

like a ship torn from its anchorage, and tossed by the raging winds on the tempestuous bosom of a troubled sea. O how precious is that Gospel which supports the soul amid all the cares, and anxieties, and tribulations of life, and at last, in death, soothes the heart into a sweet and holy serenity— which enables the believer to triumph even in the moment of dissolution!

Andrew Clark, we may add, was a smith in Leadhills, and was brother to Adam Clark of Glenim.

There lived, in this remote and moorland district, a man of the name of Welsh, commonly called "The Babe of Tweedhope-foot." How he acquired this soubriquet it is not easy to say, but he was a man of very great bodily strength; and stories are told of his wonderful feats, that seem to partake more of legend than of sober truth. He was, however, identified with the Covenanters. His house was a home to the ministers, and he had suffered many privations on account of the sympathy which he showed them. Having heard that Colonel James Douglas was in the neighbourhood, and, justly suspecting that he would not leave the district without paying him a visit, he determined to withdraw to the wilds for concealment. He was accompanied by John Hunter, a native of the same place, a good man, and a zealous Covenanter. The place to which they resorted was the solitudes of Corehead, near the source of the Water of Annan. Douglas, however, having got notice of their flight, pursued them with his troop, and soon gained ground on the fugitives. When they saw that there was a likelihood of their being overtaken, they directed their course to a place called the "Straught Steep," which, being difficult of access to the dragoons, they expected would afford them a safe retreat. By this time the horsemen were very near, and began to fire upon them. Hunter, who it seems was fully within the reach of the shot, was struck by a ball which proved fatal. He fell among the stones over which he was scrambling, and his life's blood oozed forth upon the rocks, where he expired. His body was removed, and interred in the churchyard of Tweedsmuir. His death took place in 1685—the "black year." This good man, who was suddenly taken away by a violent death, had no time afforded him to pray, or to compose his mind, before his immediate entrance into eternity; but then he was habitually prepared, and living, it may be, in the constant expectation of a hasty summons into the other world, he was always ready for his departure. "Be ye also ready; for in such an hour as ye think not the Son of Man cometh."

After the death of his companion, Welsh continued his flight across the wilderness, intending, if possible, to reach a place called Carterhope. He arrived at the house without having been seen by the troopers, and placed himself by the fire, to wait the result. The soldiers, though they did not see him enter, had nevertheless followed in the track in which he had fled, and at length came to the place. They entered in their usual uproarious manner, while Welsh was sitting apparently unconcerned before the fire. The soldiers not expecting, perhaps, to find the object of their pursuit in the hut, and having no personal knowledge of him, did not seem to notice him. The mistress of the house, however, fearing lest a discovery should by some means be made, resorted to a kind of stratagem to prevent suspicion. She approached Welsh, who appeared to be carelessly dozing over the fire, and giving him a heavy slap between the shoulders, commanded him to rise and to proceed to his work, chiding him for his slothfulness in sitting all day cowering by the hearth, while his proper business was neglected. He took the hint, and withdrew from the apartment. The soldiers naturally conceived that he was a person belonging to the house, and consequently made no inquiries. He often remarked, that the kindest *cuff* he ever received was from the *gudewife* of Carterhope, whose presence of mind, at that critical moment, was in all likelihood the means of saving his life.

CHAPTER X.

Thomas Hutchison—Marion Cameron.

The farm of Daljig, in the neighbourhood of the village of New Cumnock, in Ayrshire, was, in the times of persecution, occupied by Thomas Hutchison. This locality, as was formerly noticed, was the scene of much suffering on the part of the people of God, and consequently of much oppressive dealing on the part of their enemies. Claverhouse, in his raids through Nithsdale, often visited this quarter, and spread distress among the simple-minded and virtuous inhabitants. From the two garrisons that were placed in Carsphairn, bands of troopers were constantly passing down the romantic defile of the Afton, and across the country by the two Cumnocks, to the different stations in the route to the lower parts of Clydesdale. These military parties, we may easily suppose, never passed the hamlets and cottages of the peasantry without mischief, and many an unwary Covenanter was shot by them in the open fields, or seized in the privacy of their domestic dwellings. The country people that lay on the different tracks between the numerous garrisons with which the south and the west were so thickly studded, could never deem themselves secure for a single day from the intrusion of the strolling companies that were perpetually in motion, and to whose rudeness and insolence there were no bounds. The licentious manner in which the soldiers behaved is scarcely credible. Claverhouse, in making his descent on Dumfriesshire from the west, along the line of the Nith, sometimes, in the mere wantonness of his authority, drove before him indiscriminately the inhabitants on both sides of the river, like a flock of sheep, and then apprehended or dismissed them at his pleasure.

It was when one of these lawless bands was passing through the higher parts of Kyle, that Thomas Hutchison made a narrow escape for his life. He was a very young man, and at an early period of his days became a subject of divine grace. We are not to suppose that those who adhered to the principles of the honest Covenanters were merely aged men, or even persons in the middle stage of life; there were also many youthful persons of both sexes, who valiantly contended for the cause of righteousness and of liberty. Nor were these young witnesses actuated simply by a bigoted preference to the opinions of their fathers, irrespective of the justness of their opinions; they knew and understood the ground on which they stood, and were prepared, at any hazard, to maintain the cause they had espoused. It is a delightful and animating spectacle, to witness those who are in the morning and bloom of their days, seeking the Lord, and devoting themselves to his service. Such a sight is ever stimulating to those who are advanced in the Christian life, and whose years and experience have imparted to them more solidity and strength. The reality of a religious profession was in those days tested to the utmost; for the sufferings and trials to which godly persons were uniformly subjected, operated as a sufficient preventive in hindering those who had only a name to live, from connecting themselves with a party that was environed with so much tribulation.

The youth and simplicity of Thomas Hutchison were no defence against the persecuting spirit of the times in which he lived, and therefore the enemies of that cause which he had espoused determined to show him no favour. The dragoons, in their approach to Daljig, were seen by young Hutchison, who at the time happened to be on the moor, and at a considerable distance from the dwelling-house. He knew the purport of their visit, and he was fully aware of the fate that awaited him if he should fall into their hands, and therefore he determined to secure his safety by flight. Accordingly, he directed his steps to a thicket, in the neighbourhood of which he expected to find a place of concealment from the face of his pursuers. He therefore ran at his utmost speed towards the woody retreat; but there is little likelihood that he would have attained his object, had not Providence placed unexpected help within his reach. As he was hastening with youthful agility and velocity along the bent, he observed before him a young and spirited horse, grazing on the heath, to which, as was customary, he had been driven after the season of labour was past. Hutchison sprang forward, and grasping the horse firmly by the mane, vaulted him at one bound. He had no bridle by which to guide the motions of the animal, but, by slapping with his hand on the head and neck, he succeeded in directing him to the right and left as necessity required. The fleet and willing steed carried him before his pursuers, till he reached the edge of the thicket in which he intended to secrete himself. By this time the troopers were fast approaching. They had commenced the chase the moment they saw him begin to run, for they naturally concluded that none but Covenanters would flee from them; and hence the slightest symptom of timidity, or any attempt at flight, was on every occasion a signal of pursuit. When Hutchison arrived at the covert, he instantly dismounted and plunged into the heart of the densest bushes; but before he had time to conceal himself from their view, the horsemen came up. They did not venture into the thicket, lest they should entangle themselves in the underwood, or otherwise bewilder themselves; but, drawing their pistols from their holsters, they shot after him with vehemence. The leaden bullets went whizzing and booming past his head among the rustling leaves and thick branches of the wood. Not one of the fatal messengers, however, that were sent after him, reached his person, and he escaped unscathed into the heart of the retreat. Providence threw over him a broad shield of safety in the hour of peril, and heard his cry in the day of his distress. The soldiers, when they saw that the prey had escaped them, turned away, baffled and chagrined, and prepared to wreak their vengeance with greater fury on the next suspected person they should meet. Hutchison remained in his hiding-place till the storm for the present had blown over, and he returned to his father's house to receive the congratulations of his friends, and to thank the God in whom he trusted for the special deliverance vouchsafed. Tradition has not retained any other incident respecting this youthful Covenanter, though doubtless many interesting occurrences must have befallen him during the trying times in which his lot was cast. He outlived the persecution for many a long year, and maintained till the end of his days a character consistent with his profession. His religious example was followed by his descendants, who grew up around him in the fear of God, and his posterity have still a name and a place in the Church of Christ.

But though Thomas Hutchison escaped on this occasion the murderous hands of his foes, yet others of the wanderers in the same neighbourhood shared a very different fate. There is a melancholy story related of Marion Cameron, said to be sister to the celebrated Richard Cameron, who fell at

Airs-moss. Marion Cameron, it appears, was a pious young woman, and sincerely attached to the cause of the persecuted. Her brother lost his life in 1680, from which period, onward to the Revolution, the furnace of persecution glowed with a much fiercer heat than formerly. Murders were now common in the fields, and many were shot by the soldiers without trial, and even without warning. It appears that Marion Cameron, with two other individuals, had been surprised by a party of dragoons, and had fled for their lives in the direction of Daljig. They hid themselves in a moss in the vicinity, and, being overpowered with fatigue, they cowered down to rest. In this situation, helpless and exposed, they engaged in prayer, and resigned themselves entirely to the disposal of Him in whose cause they were suffering, and for whose sake they were willing to lay down their lives. Having been refreshed with the consolations of that gracious Spirit by whose influences they were enabled to approach the mercy-seat with the voice of supplication, they rose from their knees, and raised to heaven the serene and melodious sound of praise, by chanting one of the psalms of the sweet singer of Israel, which seemed to be adapted to persons in their situation. And many are the psalms that are suited to God's Church in affliction; for he who wrote them was himself one who suffered persecution, and who had often to betake himself to the dens and caves of the earth for safety. The troopers, who on this occasion followed them, could not fail to be guided by the plaintive and hallowed sound, which issued from the little company of worshippers in the morass, to the very spot where they had hid themselves. On their approach they offered them their lives, on condition, it is said, that they would burn their Bibles. Such a proposal, revolting to their holiest feelings, they rejected with abhorrence, and were willing, far more willing, to part with their lives, than to desecrate the Word of God—that Word of grace by the consolations of which they were supported in their sufferings, and by the faith of which they hoped to be saved. The troopers well knew that this proposal would be rejected, but then it served as an additional pretext, on their part, to proceed to extremities. Accordingly, they avowed their intention to shoot them on the spot, as persons who refused to obey the king's authority in this as well as in other respects. There was no alternative; the defenceless company in the moss could not yield, and they could not escape, and therefore instant death was inevitable. The dragoons, then, without the slightest feeling of compassion, immediately prepared the instruments of death; they fired, and all the three fell prostrate on the heath, and the warm purple stream of life mingled with the dark moss water in the moor, and their redeemed spirits were conveyed by angels from their mangled bodies to the mansion of eternal blessedness. Their enemies appeared to conquer, but they who fell were really the victors; for " they overcame by the blood of the Lamb, and by the word of their testimony; for they loved not their lives unto the death."

They suffered martyrdom in a place where there were no earthly spectators present to sympathize with them, and they were buried in their clothes in the moss where they fell; and as " devout men carried Stephen to his burial, and made great lamentations over him," so the friends of these Christian confessors came, when their enemies had retired from the spot, and dug their graves in the morass, in which they laid their murdered bodies, to rest till the morning of the general resurrection. " Blessed are the dead who die in the Lord from henceforth: yea, saith the Spirit, that they may rest from their labours; and their works do follow them."

The sweet and gentle Marion Cameron, like a delicate and lovely flower, was, in the bloom of her days, despoiled of her life by the rough and pitiless hand of violence. She has a name among the " many daughters who have done virtuously;" and she, with her companions, has obtained the martyr's crown, and now are they with the multitude who have suffered for " the Word of God, and for the testimony of Jesus Christ." How enviable is the situation of the persecuted, even in their greatest affliction, compared with that of their oppressors, even in their greatest prosperity ! The triumph of the wicked is short, while their ruin is endless and irremediable; on the other hand, in the case of the righteous, their " light affliction, which is but for a moment, worketh out for them a far more exceeding and an eternal weight of glory."

About seventy years ago, while some cattle were trampling in the moss exactly over the graves of those worthies, their feet turned up part of the clothes of Marion Cameron, which were then in a tolerably good state of preservation, owing to the antiseptic quality of the moss in which they were imbedded; and a large common yellow pin, which she was accustomed to wear in her raiment, was found and cherished as a precious relic of one whose memory was held so dear. The pin came into the possession of Mrs Gemmel of Catrine, a niece of Thomas Hutchison of Daljig, by whom it was retained all her days, as a precious memorial of the original proprietor. It is now in the possession of a daughter of Mrs Gemmel's, who at present resides in Stranraer, by whom it is preserved with equal care.

The murder of such saintly persons as Marion Cameron, depicts, in colours sufficiently glaring, the dark and revolting barbarity of the times. The sun in the firmament scarcely ever beheld deeds of greater atrocity than those committed by the rude and hardened troopers on the unoffending peasantry of Scotland. But the case of Marion Cameron was not a solitary one; there are other instances of young and timid females who exhibited the greatest firmness and moral heroism, in enduring sufferings for Christ's sake.

Such instances of barbarity show the reckless and unprincipled character of those who were deputed by the equally unprincipled and worthless rulers of the period, to do that work of wickedness to which Satan prompted them. But while such deeds of violence depict the character of those who perpetrated them, and hold them up in a very despicable light to posterity, they who suffered displayed a very different character. Their meekness, their constancy, their blameless deportment, the strength of their faith and hope in God, their confidence in the goodness of their cause, their joy in the Redeemer, and their firmness of purpose in the hour of death, were all displayed in an eminent degree, illustrative of the grace of God, which wrought so powerfully in them, to the entire discomfiture of their foes, who, though they killed the body, could not vanquish their principles.

CHAPTER XI.

Lesmahagow—Thomas Brown of Auchlochan—Smith of Threepod—
John Gill—Stobo.

LESMAHAGOW is a name familiar to all who are in any measure
versant in the times and scenes of Prelatic violence. Few
sections of the country, perhaps, furnished a richer harvest
of godly persons, among whom to thrust the bloody sickle—
persecution; and nobly did these honoured persons maintain
their fidelity, and the credit of that cause to which they were
attached. The moorlands of Lesmahagow, if they could speak,
could tell many a tale of suffering now unknown, and could
also recount many a blessed hour of sacred intercourse with
God, enjoyed by his people in the day of privation and of
peril. The inhabitants of this district seem, in the days of
Zion's affliction, to have been favoured with large communications of divine influence, and with much spiritual fortitude
in the hour of temptation. The Steels of Lesmahagow were
men of renown, and faithful witnesses for Jesus Christ. The
death of David Steel, who was shot at Shellyhill in 1686, in
the thirty-third year of his age, is, in all its circumstances,
equally affecting with the death of John Brown of Priesthill.
He was, after promise of quarter, murdered before his own
door; and Mary Weir, his youthful and truly Christian wife,
who, it is said, cherished an uncommon attachment to her
husband, having bound up his shattered head with a napkin,
and closed down his eyelids with her own hand, looked
on the manly and honest countenance that was now pale in
death, and said, with a sweet and heavenly composure: " The
archers have shot at thee, my husband, but they could not
reach thy soul: it has escaped like a dove far away, and is
at rest." What is it but the reality of religion that can so
fully sustain the hearts of God's people in the day of their

tribulation, and under the pressure of afflictions so over-whelming?

The tale of the martyrs of Lesmahagow has been told by a descendant of one of themselves—the Rev. Charles Thomson of North Shields. In the excellent and heart-stirring narrative which he has given of these worthies, we see, on their part, the display of a genuine godliness, of a patient endurance of trial, and of an unflinching constancy of purpose, even to the death, of a most instructive nature, and which, placed in contrast with the conduct of their heartless oppressors, points them out as the excellent ones of the earth, and as men of whom the world was not worthy.

Of the confessors of Lesmahagow, however, there are yet some gleanings which have not hitherto been made public, one of which shall be given here. Thomas Brown of Auchlochan, in the parish of Lesmahagow, was a good man and a steady Covenanter. He was present at Drumclog, where the fierce Claverhouse sustained a signal defeat by a handful of worshippers, who had been holding a conventicle near the place, on Sabbath the 1st of June 1679. He fought also at Bothwell Bridge, where the power of the Covenanters was lamentably broken, and their army scattered. If, prior to the rising at Bothwell, the furnace of persecution glowed with an intolerable heat, it was now kindled seven times; and the cloud that lowered over the afflicted Church grew darker and more portentous, and threatened to discharge its ominous contents in one full and vengeful tempest on the defenceless heads of those who had hitherto outbraved the fury of the storm, in the support of their civil and religious privileges. At this period, Claverhouse was ravaging the west, and, like a beast of prey, was tearing and devouring on all sides; for that reckless and infatuated Cavalier would not have scrupled to ride, even to the bridle reins, in the blood of the populace, to serve the vindictive purposes of his military employers; and much and precious was the blood which, with unsparing hand, he shed in the fields and moorlands, and loud was the cry which his oppression made to ascend from many a cottage in the land. Two of the troopers under the command of this blood-thirsty adventurer, came suddenly upon Thomas Brown, on the banks of the Nethan, a few yards above the house of Auchlochan. Brown stood on his defence, and, with his sword drawn, warded off for some time the blows of his antagonists. At length, however, he was overpowered, and falling under the heavy strokes of the two powerful troopers, he was left for dead on the field. At this juncture, the appearance of another Covenanter on the opposite side of the stream attracted their notice, and, leaving their victim bleeding on the ground, they crossed the river in pursuit. This man, whose name is not mentioned, was speedily overtaken, and killed on the spot. Thomas Brown, however, though severely wounded, was not dead. He was stupified by the loss of blood, and stunned by the blows he had received; but, by the kind attention of his friends, he gradually recovered. He was at this time in the flower of his age, and he lived till he became an old man. The present proprietor of Auchlochan is his lineal descendant. It is no small honour to be sprung from those who, in their day, were distinguished as Christ's witnesses, and counted worthy to suffer for his sake. The worth of ancestry, however, will not save us; we must ourselves become followers of them who, through faith and patience, are now inheriting the promises.

The following anecdote refers to a striking incident which befell near the village of Galston, in Ayrshire. Ayrshire was at an early period visited with the Gospel. The Culdees and the Lollards of Kyle in different ages overspread this district, and disseminated the principles of religious truth among its population; and the doctrines of the Gospel, thus promulgated in this locality, were never entirely suppressed, either by the superstition of the dark ages, or by the strong arm of persecution. Several years prior to the Reformation, we find that a goodly number of influential individuals in that county had embraced tenets entirely opposed to the Popish creed, and in unison with the pure faith of the Gospel. " We find that, in 1494, Robert Blackatter, the first archbishop of Glasgow, caused to be summoned before the king and his great council held there, about thirty individuals in all, and mostly persons of distinction, accused of Reformation principles. Among these were George Campbell of Cesnock, Adam Reid of Barskimming, John Campbell of New Mills, Andrew Sharp of Polkemmet, Lady Pokellie, and Lady Stair. They were opprobriously called Lollards of Kyle, from Lollard, an eminent preacher among the Waldenses, and were charged, under thirty-four articles, with maintaining that images ought not to be worshipped, that the relics of saints ought not to be adored, and such like obnoxious tenets: but to these accusations they answered with such boldness, constancy, and effect, that the archbishop and his associates were at length constrained to drop the proceedings; and it was judged most prudent to dismiss them, with the simple admonition, to content themselves with the faith of the Church, and to beware of new doctrines."

It was from the lower and more level parts of Ayrshire, that many of the refugees that were found seeking a retreat in the higher and more hilly districts, had come. They sought, among the inhabitants of Nithsdale and Lanarkshire, that repose which could not be obtained in a more exposed and accessible locality.

Threepod is a farm about two miles from the village of Galston. It was, in the time of persecution, occupied by a worthy man of the name of Smith. He was a person, it would appear, of quiet and retired habits, and had cherished secretly, for some time, the principles of the Covenanters. His natural timidity prevented him for a while from making an open and manly avowal of his sentiments. At length he became decided, and firmly took his stand on the side of the oppressed; and resolved on following what appeared to him to be the plain dictates of duty, and to abide the consequences. In Smith's family there was an infant child, which it was the desire of the parents to devote, as soon as an opportunity offered, to the Lord in baptism. There was, it would seem, about the distance of fourteen miles from Threepod, a conventicle meeting, which was held in the night season. To this meeting Smith carried his child to be baptized by the officiating minister. Having obtained his errand, he retraced his steps through the dreary moors in the dark night; and having arrived at his own house before the dawn, he, in order to prevent suspicion, betook himself to the barn, and was thrashing his corn at the early hour at which labourers generally commence that occupation. In spite of all his caution, however, he had been discovered, and information communicated to his enemies. When he saw that the circumstance was known, and that evil was determined against him, he withdrew from his house, and sought a hiding-place in the fields. Here also his retreat was found out, and two soldiers were sent to apprehend him. On their approach, however, he stood to defend himself; and having in his hand a good broadsword, he succeeded in warding off the deadly blows of his ruthless assailants. He was a young and powerful man, and showed himself capable of wielding, with great dexterity, the sword in self-defence; and the soldiers, finding that he was not to be so easily handled as they expected, had recourse to stratagem. The plan, however, which they adopted in order to defeat him, was anything but honourable. When he was engaged in defending himself, and when all his atten-

tion was directed to the opponent with whom he was obliged
to cope face to face, the other soldier stole behind him, and,
approaching with cautious step, threw a cloak over his head,
which both blindfolded him and entangled his sword-arm, so
that on the instant he became an easy prey to his cruel and
wily foes. When the soldiers found that he was now entirely
in their power, they hewed him down without mercy, and
left him lifeless on the field. They gained their object, but
in a way that no noble-minded soldier would choose; they
were, however, base men, and therefore fitted for the perpetration of the base actions in which their unprincipled rulers
so fully employed them. This martyr was buried on the
spot where his blood was shed; a stone, with an inscription,
was laid upon his grave, which is now overgrown with moss;
but a thicket of whins, the prickly guardians of his lonely
sepulchre, marks the place where his ashes rest. Thus fell
an honest patriot and a true Christian, whose constancy of
principle and of purpose exposed him to a cruel death.

John Gill lived in Fife, and was, on account of his attachment to Reformation principles, subjected to the same treatment as his fellow-Covenanters—receiving no favour from
the hand of those who, in that dark and troubled time, made
such fearful havoc of the Church of God. The district of
Fife, generally, was more immediately under the eye of the
Archbishop of St Andrews, the bloody and perfidious James
Sharp, who basely betrayed the cause he was employed to
advocate, and ultimately became Primate of the Episcopal
Church of Scotland. He obtained the object of his ambition,
to be sure, but at the expense of a good conscience. He
scrupled not to shed profusely the blood of the best and the
holiest men the land could boast of; and as he loved to spill
blood, so his own blood was spilt at last, and he was slain on
Magus Moor as he was lolling in his chariot, in the plenitude of his lordly arrogance and pride. His dream, when a
student, as related by Kirkton, which, if real, is curious, and
the coincidence of events in his after-life, of which it seemed
to be indicative, is rather striking. The dream was the following: "That while a student at the college, lying in bed
with his comrade, he fell into a loud laughter in his sleep,
and being awakened by his bed-fellow, who asked him what
he laughed so much for, returned answer, that he had
dreamed that the Earl of Crawford had made him parson of
Crail. Again, in another night, he laughed in his sleep; and
being awaked in like manner, he said he had dreamed he was
in Paradise, as the king had made him Archbishop of St An-

drews. Lastly, he dreamt a third time, and was in great
agony, crying bitterly; when, being awaked as formerly, he
said he was dreaming a very sad dream—that he was driving
in a coach to hell, and that very fast." Such is the dream,
as given by Kirkton. It is certain that he became minister
of Crail, and then Primate of St Andrews; and lastly, that
he met his death, while journeying in his coach on Magus
Moor.

John Gill possessed a small paternal estate in Fife, but
was obliged to abandon it, and all his property, to preserve
his life and a good conscience. He was a good man, and actuated by high principles, and unbending religious integrity.
The harassings which he underwent from the enemy, in
stead of weakening his attachment to the cause of Christ,
served rather to confirm him in his adherence to the truth
—like the oak on the mountain's brow, which, the more it
is exposed to the storms above, strikes its roots more deeply
and firmly into the soil beneath, so that every succeeding
blast leaves it more securely rooted than before. Being
obliged to flee from his native place, he went southward, and
sought refuge somewhere about the Pentland Hills. As
tradition has recorded but little respecting this worthy man,
it is not known whether he suffered death by the hand of his
enemies; but if he outlived the persecution, it is certain that
he never regained the possession of his patrimony. But
what although ?—it is better to lose all than to lose the soul.
" Every one that hath forsaken *houses*, or brethren, or sisters,
or father, or mother, or wife, or children, or *lands*, for my
name's sake, shall receive an hundredfold, and shall inherit
everlasting life."

John Gill had a son of the same name, who was illustrious
for his piety, which, like a blaze of light, shone so clearly
around that it attracted the notice and admiration of all
within the circle of his acquaintanceship. His death-bed
experience was of the most edifying description; and it is
affirmed that he anticipated the very hour of his dissolution,
and expired at the time he mentioned, rejoicing in hope of
the glory of God. He lived after the persecution, and occupied the farm of Loanstane, in the neighbourhood of his
father's place of refuge; and, if report tells right, he was the
first that ploughed the field of Rullion Green, many years
after the battle, and that he raked together into heaps the
bones of the worthies who fell there, and then buried them
deep below the surface. This John Gill, the son, had two
daughters, Catherine and Christian, both of whom walked in

the footsteps of their godly parent. Catherine was good and kind, and being a woman of much affliction, profited under the chastening rod. Christian was a mother in Israel, and had more of an influential and commanding manner. As she grew in years, she advanced in grace. She was married to John Ketchan, overseer to Sir James Montgomery of Stobo, a gentleman of no small note in his time, and who, by his talents and industry, attained both wealth and reputation. John Ketchan was a man of sincere godliness, and of singular integrity in all his dealings, and possessed the unbounded confidence of his master. This worthy man died in 1809, and was interred in the churchyard of Stobo, not far from the more magnificent resting-place of his honoured master, whom for many a long year he had served with unswerving fidelity.

The parish of Stobo is a delightful locality on the Tweed, a few miles above the pleasant town of Peebles. The church of Stobo is an edifice of upwards of five hundred years old. The rectory of Stobo was, more than five centuries ago, converted into a prebend of Glasgow; and of all the prebends in Tweeddale, Stobo was reckoned the most valuable. "Michael de Dunde, the parson of Stubbehou or Stobo, swore fealty to Edward I. at Berwick, on the 2d of August 1296, when the oaths of smaller men were sought for. The rights of the manor of Stobo have been as fiercely contested as the sovereignty of Scotland." The whole parish presents a beautiful aspect. The hills are of a moderate height, and well wooded; the valleys are in the highest state of cultivation, and the centre of the locality is graced with the princely residence of the proprietor. The church is situated near the margin of a silvery stream, which issues from the hills on the background, and pours its limpid waters into the Tweed. The burying-ground contains some few antiquities, and preserves the dust of remote and forgotten generations, having been a place of sepulture for many ages. A more sweetly sequestered spot can scarcely be desired; and the man who would wish to shut himself up in a studious seclusion, could not find a retreat more congenial to his taste.

From the summit of Dramore Hill, in this neighbourhood, from whose bowels there has been disinterred, for sundry ages, the fine blue slate stone, a very magnificent view is obtained, especially toward the west. The spacious plain of Drummelzierhaugh, like the level bottom of a deep basin encircled by green mountains, through which the classic

Tweed holds its majestic course, furnishes an enchanting spectacle. On the upper part of this plain, and near the church of Drummelzier, is the grave of the far-famed Prophet *Merlin*, who flourished in the sixth century. The verdant fields of Altarstone and Dreva occupy the sunny slope, whose base is swept by the flowing stream, and front the frowning heights of ancient Dalwick. This locality, no doubt, could once have furnished incidents of persecuting outrage which are now forgotten. But there can be little dispute that the *nineteen towns* of Stobo contained some whose religious principles subjected them to the treatment common to all who, during that period, maintained the practice of conscientious Nonconformists. Sir William Murray of Stenhope was empowered, in the persecuting times, to exercise a strict supervision over the upper district of Tweeddale; and this power, we may rest assured, was not conferred without a reason. Symptoms of dissatisfaction had shown themselves, which rendered necessary this military oversight—a proof that the spirit of religious liberty and independence was stirring among this secluded population. In the roll of the ministers who were ejected for their nonconformity to Prelacy, we find the names of Patrick Fleming of Stobo, Robert Brown of Lyne, and David Thomson of Dalwick. These parishes, lying together in a cluster, and favoured with a sound Gospel ministry at the time of the Restoration, must have contained many whose principles were akin to those of their ministers; and hence a field was prepared on which the persecutor might exercise his intolerance and oppression. In the fugitive roll we find the name of one man belonging to this parish—"William Forbes, servant to Thomas Weir in Slate-hole." This worthy man, perhaps, was not solitary, though the names of others are not mentioned.

CHAPTER XII.

Martyrdom at Crossgellioch—Hugh Hutchison—Campbell of Dalhanna
—Hair and Corson—Brown and Morice.

"Some time this summer" (1685), says Wodrow, "four men
were coming from Galloway, where they had been hearing
Mr Renwick in the fields, to the shire of Ayr—Joseph Wilson,
John and Alexander Jamison, and John Humphrey. A
party of soldiers overtook them at Knockdon Hill, and upon
their confessing that they had been hearing a sermon, they
immediately shot three of them. What were the reasons
of sparing Alexander Jamison, I know not." Such is the
account given by the historian of the death of these martyrs.
The tradition, however, is much more valuable than the
meagre outline of the historic narrative.

Crossgellioch, and not Knockdon Hill, was the place where
these martyrs fell, and where they lie interred. Knockdon,
however, is in the immediate neighbourhood. Crossgellioch
is an oblong hill on the farm of Daljig, situated on the
western boundary of the upland parish of New Cumnock.
The ascent on three sides is very steep, but on the north the
declivity is gentle. The top of the hill is generally flat, and
interspersed with deep and rugged moss-hags, which were
frequently occupied as hiding-places by the worthies of the
suffering period. It was in the broken morass on the summit of this mountain that the individuals above mentioned
sought, about the time that they were slaughtered by their
enemies, a hiding-place. They had formerly sought a retreat in a place called Tod Fauld, below Benbeoch Craig,
where they lay for some time; but, being informed by one
Paterson, who was himself a refugee, that a reward was
offered for their apprehension, they retired to the more secluded locality of Crossgellioch. It was in this place that
they were ultimately found, after having one day returned

I

from a conventicle at Carsphairn. Claverhouse, it appears, had been in pursuit of the wanderers in that neighbourhood; and they, in order to elude his search, took up their accustomed abode among the dark and shaggy heath on the mountain. In this seclusion they remained for several weeks in comparative safety, because, from their lurking-place, they had a view of all around, and therefore they could easily perceive the approach of the enemy. This shelter became to them a place of encampment, from which they sallied out at convenient times to visit their brethren in the country around. In this way they could occasionally hold intercourse with their fellow-sufferers, and also furnish themselves with provisions, on which to subsist in their solitude. Their hiding-place, it would seem, was known to none in the vicinity, save to one young man of the name of Hugh Hutchison. This youth was their almost daily visitant, and from them he learned the nature of those principles for which they suffered; and he, who formerly sympathized with them from feelings of humanity, in a short time became one with them on religious grounds, and experienced the higher sympathy of Christian brotherhood. His heart being now knit to the sufferers in the bond of a common faith, he made their cause his own; and he conscientiously observed the sacred duty of visiting them in the day of their distress. It was his occupation to attend the horses and cattle that were grazing on the hill; and hence he had ample opportunity of meeting with them without interruption or suspicion. One day, as he was traversing the bent in the way of his calling, he heard the loud report of fire-arms on the top of the hill in the distance; and not knowing what might be the matter, he hastened to the spot. When he reached the summit, and cast his eye along the mossy level, he saw a party of fierce dragoons on the spot where his friends used to conceal themselves; and Alexander Jamison (whom tradition names James Jamison) in full flight along the heath. On observing the scene a little more narrowly, he saw the other three weltering in their blood, shot by the merciless troopers, the firing of whose pistols had drawn him to the place. As he stood gazing in mute astonishment on the tragic scene, he was observed by the soldiers. He instantly fled; and the dragoons called on him to stop, otherwise he should instantly share the fate of those whose lifeless bodies lay stretched on the heath. The youth, however, paid no attention to their commands, but ran at his utmost speed for his life. To gain the heart of the impassable morass before his pursuers on horseback should come up to him he found to be impracticable, and therefore pursued his way adown the steepest part of the hill in the direction of the Nith. He crossed the river by a ford above Daljig, and then pursued his way along Dalricket Moss and endeavoured to reach Daleccles Burn; but finding that his pursuers, in spite of all his efforts, were fast approaching, he changed his purpose, and passing over Auchengeehill, by the farm of Braehead and Rigfoot, he reached what is called the Lane. When he arrived at this place, the softness of the ground obliged him to dismount and flee on foot. The same circumstance, however, which retarded his progress on horseback, retarded that of the dragoons. Having passed over the yielding and sinking ground on foot, he succeeded in hiding himself in the wooded banks of the Lane. The dragoons searched long and eagerly for their fugitive, but without success. The God to whose people he ministered in the day of their distress, and in whose sufferings he sympathized, shielded him from those who thirsted for his blood, and preserved him for further service. He remained in his hiding-place till the soldiers retired; and, with a feeling of security, he observed them marching along the heights of Lane Mark, and moving onwards to the defile of the Afton.

When all fears about his safety for the present were removed, he left his concealment, and returned to Daljig. With a heart full of concern and sorrow, he informed the family of what had happened; and in company with a number of others, he visited the scene of martyrdom, to ascertain the true state of matters. When Hugh and his party arrived at the spot, they found that three out of the four worthies had fallen by the murderous arm of their persecutors. When they were killed, they were left by the savage troopers unburied on the moss. This appears to have been the universal custom; they left the bodies of the slaughtered saints exposed on the face of the open fields, and if others did not choose to inter them, they might, for anything that they cared, become a banquet to the ravens or the eagles of the desert. It is stated in the Book of Revelation, that the murderers of the witnesses would not suffer their dead bodies to be put in graves; and truly those who shed the blood of God's saints so profusely on the moors and mountains of Scotland, acted a part akin to this. The sufferers, however, wanted not friends to perform for them this last office; and there is no doubt, though it is not mentioned, that Hugh Hutchison and his companions dug their graves where they fell, and on the identical spot in the moss that had received their blood from the hands of their persecutors. Their place of sepulture is still conspicuous in the dark morass, where a monument was lately erected over their ashes, for the purpose of keeping in memory the tragical fate of these holy and devoted men, who sealed their testimony with their blood. It is worthy of notice here, that when the monument alluded to was reared, about twelve years ago, the following discovery was made :—In digging down and levelling the place for the foundation, the workmen came upon the bodies of the martyrs, imbedded in the moss. They were lying in their clothes, which were undecayed—the identical apparel in which they were shot. The raiment was a sort of strong home-made cloth of the colour of the moss, and appeared in some parts as if originally dyed with heather. The bodies themselves, in a state of good preservation, were of a dull, sallow appearance. Part of the garments, and a lock of long yellow hair, were preserved as relics by the labourers. The hair was obviously that of a young man—very fine and soft. The bodies of these Christian patriots and martyrs were thus seen, after the lapse of nearly one hundred and sixty years, shrouded in their hosen, in their coats, and in their bonnets, exactly as they fell by the murderous hand of their persecutors. Their resting-place is in the dreary solitude and in the wilderness, where no man dwells; but their souls are in the paradise of God, with Christ their glorious Head, for whose kingly supremacy they suffered the loss of all things, and for whose sake they counted not their lives dear unto them, that they might finish their course with joy. O ye who sought to obtain martial renown by slaying the people of God in multitudes, where now is your fame ? Your names are a dishonour and a reproach among men, and will ere long be forgotten, or remembered only to be despised; while those whom ye vilified as the offscouring of all things, and oppressed and killed, as pestilent and worthless men, are honoured in heaven, and virtuously esteemed on earth. Sleep on, ye bleeding bodies of the saints: sleep in your gory bed; sleep in the martyr's winding-sheet. While ye sleep, ye shall not be unattended; posterity will guard your lonely couch, and point out your dormitory to the inquiring stranger; and He in whose cause ye suffered, and in whose sight the blood of his saints is dear, will at length raise you from your lowly bed to shine among the sons of light in God's own house, and in his own presence throughout a whole eternity.

It is probable that the friends who were killed in the moss

had issued from their concealment, to meet the conventicle convened by Mr Renwick, and that, in returning, they had been followed by the dragoons to the place where they fell. The individual who on this occasion escaped, namely, the brother of John Jamison, was afterwards seized by the enemy, and carried prisoner to Cumnock. No sooner did the report of this reach Hugh Hutchison, than he hastened to Cumnock, to visit his friend. The anxiety and solicitude manifested by him about the fate of Jamison attracted the notice of the persecutors, who began to suspect that he was one of the party. When Hutchison observed that he was noticed by them, he withdrew from the place, and betook himself to flight. This circumstance confirmed the suspicion of the soldiers, who instantly pursued. Hutchison, however, fled with winged speed over moor and moss, and at last succeeded in concealing himself in a cavern in the neighbourhood of Dalmellington, and escaped the breathless pursuit.

But to return to the first pursuit. When Hugh was so keenly chased by the troopers, at the time they shot the three men in the moss, it is said that he observed them from his retreat passing over the heights of Lane Mark, and then descending in a straight line to Dalhanna, a small estate on the remantic banks of the Afton, about two miles above its confluence with the Nith. James Campbell was at this time laird of Dalhanna, and a warm friend to the covenanted cause. The approach of the dragoons was on this occasion observed by the worthy laird, who, suspecting their mission, left his house, to seek a hiding-place in the fields. There was, in the neighbourhood of his dwelling, a rising ground densely covered with broom, among the pliant bushes of which he hid himself. When the party arrived at Dalhanna, they inquired for the master of the house, and not finding him, they left the place, and began to ascend the hill close by the "broomy knowe," and so near his hiding-place, that he expected every moment they would discover him; and discovered he was, but by one who had too much humanity to disclose the secret. When the troopers were marching past the thicket, one of them, who happened to be straggling behind, observed Campbell in the heart of a bush, and, standing still, looked at him for a moment, shook his head, and passed on in silence. This soldier, it would appear, who was less hardened than his fellows, did not think himself obliged to make a discovery, where the party had made none, and left the honest man safe in his hiding-place, where

God had been pleased to conceal him from the eyes of those who sought his hurt.

The dragoons pursued their way over the hills towards the farm of Cairn, beautifully situated on the slope of the range of mountains that line the sweet vale of the Nith on the south. At this place they came upon two men in a hollow among the green and flowery braes, engaged, it is supposed, in devotional exercises. The sound of their voices employed in prayer, or in the singing of psalms, probably attracted the notice of the soldiers, and drew them to the spot. The names of the individuals were Hair and Corson. The circumstances in which they were found were enough to insure their death, and therefore, according to the custom of the times, and the license of the troopers, they were without ceremony shot on the spot. They lie interred on the south side of the great road between Sanquhar and New Cumnock, where a rude stone pillar points out their resting-place.

Hair was one of five brothers who occupied the farm of Glenquhary, in the parish of Kirkconnell, of which they were the proprietors. They were ejected from their patrimony, however, on account of their nonconformity, and forced to wander in the desolate places of the country. One of the five brothers was at the battle of Pentland; which circumstance would doubtless render the whole family more obnoxious to the dominant party. It is probable that Hair of Burncrooks, mentioned in a former chapter, and who effected his escape from the dragoons at Glen Aylmer, was one of the same family; and it is equally probable that Hair of Cleuchfoot, and William Hair of Southmains, were, if not of the household of Glenquhary, at least related. In the old churchyard of Kirkconnell, which is situated at the base of the steep green mountains, and near the mouth of this romantic glen, there are to be seen, in its north-west corner, six *thrugh* stones belonging to this family, indicating the successive generations that, one after another, have been gathered to their fathers. A lineal descendant of this worthy household is at present resident in the farm of Muirfoot, in the parish of New Cumnock, and warmly cherishes, as may be expected, the memory of his witnessing ancestry.

A similar incident to that now related occurred at Craignorth, an abrupt and magnificent mountain near the source of the Crawick, where two Covenanters, named Brown and Morris, were killed by the soldiers. The incident, it is said, befell in 1685—the year in which so many of the worthies were shot in the fields. Two small rivulets descend from the

nill on which they were slaughtered; the name of the one is
Brown's Cleuch, and of the other Morris Cleuch. A more
particular account of their death will be found in Chapter
XV. Near the head of Chapman Cleuch, in the neighbourhood of Nether Cog, lies a martyr; but neither his name
nor the names of those by whom he was killed are known.
More than five hundred persons were shot by the military
in the fields, and therefore it is not to be expected that the
names of all these individuals, or the circumstances of their
death, could be recorded by history, or retained by tradition

CHAPTER XIII.

gh Hutchison—further particulars.

In the last chapter we left Hugh Hutchison in a cave nea Dalmellington, in which he had taken refuge from his pur suers, and in which he continued till the danger was past. These men did not rush on martyrdom, nor needlessly expose their lives, for the honour of having it said that they died as witnesses in the cause of truth. They sought to preserve their lives by all honourable means as long as they could; thus proving that they were not actuated by a blind enthusiasm, but by an enlightened zeal. Life was as sweet to them as it was to other men, and therefore it was their care to preserve it; but then, sweet as it was, they were prepared to yield it up at the bidding of Him from whom they received it. In the neighbourhood of his retreat, Hutchison had the happiness to meet with a fellow-sufferer, with whom he lived in concealment for a season. The name of his new associate was John Paterson. This man occupied the farm of Penyvenie, at the bottom of Benbeach, and the ruins of his dwelling-house are still to be seen on the right hand of the road from Cumnock to Dalmellington. These walls are the venerable remains of a cottage, which, in the suffering period, was a sanctuary to many of the people of God, and a temple consecrated to his worship. Owing to the severity of the times, however, Paterson durst not occupy his dwelling as formerly, but was obliged to seek a hiding-place in the fields. To his retreat in the "Tod Fauld," then, he conducted Hutchison, and here for a considerable time they continued in seclusion and security. Their intercourse in the day of common peril was doubtless such as became witnesses and sufferers in the same cause. Many a sweet hour did the worthies of those times enjoy with God and with one another, in the dreary caves and solitudes of the mountains, when their enemies foolishly imagined that they had despoiled them of all comfort and enjoyment whatever. Their foes might indeed expel them from their homes, and drive them afar to the lonely deserts, but they could not expel them from their rest in God, nor interrupt that spiritual intercourse with Heaven which to them was sweeter far than all earthly comforts, or than even life itself. "Thy loving-kindness is better than life."

From their place of concealment our two worthies descended, as frequently and regularly as circumstances permitted, to the farm-house, by turns, to their meals. One morning, when Paterson had stolen cautiously from his retreat to go to his house to breakfast, leaving his companion in the hiding-place till his return, a circumstance occurred which wellnigh proved fatal to them both. It had been agreed on between Paterson and his friends, that when danger was apprehended, they should cry in his hearing, "The nowt's i' the corn." This watchword was unknown to Hutchison. It happened, on the morning alluded to, when Paterson was in his house at breakfast, that an individual at some distance, who saw three dragoons approaching, hastened to the lurking-place to give the preconcerted warning, not knowing that Paterson was at the moment in the cottage. Hutchison heard the cry, and not being aware that the words implied a sense different from their literal import, sprang from his concealment to drive the cattle from the corn-field. He no sooner issued into the open field than he discovered his mistake, for he saw three troopers marching with all speed towards the dwelling-house. He ran forward, with the intention, no doubt, of giving warning to his friend within, but durst not enter, as the party was close at hand; and going past the end of the house, which intercepted him from the view of the horsemen, he plunged into the heart of a large willow bush, and there secreted himself.

Meanwhile the soldiers drew near, and John Paterson, who was at breakfast, observed their approach. He instantly rose from the table, and grasping his trusty sword, presented himself in the attitude of self-defence at the door. His affectionate wife, whom solicitude for her husband's welfare prompted to expose herself to danger, followed close at his back. The soldiers, in order to overpower their victim, made a simultaneous onset; but Paterson with undaunted breast and powerful arm, brandished his glittering glaive above his head, and dealt his blows so lustily that he disabled two of his opponents, and laid them stunned, but not dead at his feet. The third, a stalwart dragoon, yet unscathed, approached the valiant Covenanter, who so bravely maintained his position before the door, with a view to cut him down, and the more easily, as he was already exhausted by the stiffness of the conflict; but his wife, who, like a guardian angel, was hovering near him, hastily untied her apron, and flung it over the soldier's sword-arm, by means of which the weapon was entangled, so that Paterson made his escape without injury to himself. It was sometime before matters were adjusted on the battle-ground, and before the prostrate soldiers recovered themselves, and by this time the fugitive was beyond their reach. Meanwhile Hutchison was ensconced in the bush, to which the soldiers as they retired approached, and went round it beating it with their swords, as if they expected to start the timid hare from its lair in the interior, or to rouse from their nests the domestic fowls, which in their raids among the peasantry they sometimes did not scruple to destroy or carry off. Hutchison lay trembling and perspiring, expecting every moment to be dragged from his retreat, and murdered by the infuriated soldiers on the spot. No incident, however, occurred; they left the place, and Hutchison remained undiscovered. When they were gone, and no further danger was apprehended, Paterson left his hiding-place, and returned with a throbbing heart to inquire after the state of his household; and having satisfied himself on this point, his next care was to search for Hutchison, whom he found in the heart of the bush. In this seclusion Hutchison chose to remain the whole day, and it was not till evening began to close in that he would consent to leave the covert. This caution, on the part of Hutchison was not without its reason, for the troopers sometimes returned when least expected. It was his intention now to return to Daljig in the evening, considering that his danger with Paterson appeared to be as great as it could be at home. At the earnest entreaty of his friends, however, he remained with them during that night; and on the morrow, as no apprehensions of the speedy return of their enemies were entertained, he agreed to assist his friend in the operations of hay-making. With buoyant spirits, while they inhaled the balmy breath of June, and with arms strong for labour, each with his scythe cleared with ample sweep the space around him, leaving the dewy grass mixed with its "fresh meadow blooms," in long files or *swaithes* of sweetly scented hay behind them. Shortly after high noon, Hutchison had retired to the house to dinner, while Paterson, in case of danger, kept his place

in the meadow, mowing down the soft grass close by the side
of a field of tall standing corn that waved on the margin of
a purling brook, at whose limpid waters the haymakers frequently slaked their thirst.

In these circumstances the startling and warning cry was
again heard—a clear, shrill voice proceeded from a distance
—" The nowt's i' the corn." Paterson rested for a moment
on the staff of his scythe, and then darted into the heart of
the growing corn, and hid himself in a deep furrow. The
dragoons crossed the streamlet exactly at the place where
the mowers had been employed, and perceiving the newly cut
grass, and the scythes lying on the ground, they concluded
that those of whom they were in quest were somewhere in
the vicinity, and instantly proceeded to the search. The
horsemen were accompanied with a few dogs, which they
directed into the corn-field, for the purpose of making a discovery, if perchance any fugitive might be lurking there.
The dogs, at the bidding of their masters, leapt into the corn
and traversed the field in all directions, as if fully aware of
the design of the errand on which they were sent, and seemed
to seek by their scent as keenly for men, as, in other circumstances, they would have done for game. Paterson heard
the rustling of the animals, as they ran hither and thither
among the tall and yielding stalks of corn near his hiding-
place. Doubtless this good man prayed as he lay on the
lowly ground, and besought the Lord to hide him, as in the
hollow of his hand, from the fierce rage of his foes. And
his prayer was heard; for though the dogs came close to him,
and smelt his clothes, going round and round him, yet not
one of them offered to bark, nor to give the least signal of
a discovery, and they retired from the spot as quietly as if
they had found nothing. Wodrow, when mentioning some
very signal deliverances of the Lord's people, when they
were almost in the very hands of their enemies, notices similar occurrences, and remarks that the dogs, as he expresses
it, *snouked* among the stones under which they were lying,
and at the mouths of the caves in which they were concealed,
without making any noise indicative of the presence of the
fugitives. As against the children of Israel, of old, not a
dog in Egypt was permitted to move his tongue, so in these
cases also, they were withheld from acting according to their
natural propensity, when the slightest sound emitted by
them might have proved fatal to the persons in the pursuit
of whom they were sent out.

When the dogs had issued from the corn field, without

having announced, by their barking, the presence of the individuals sought for, the troopers concluded that no person
was there.   Meanwhile Hutchison had taken refuge in his
former retreat—the heart of the willow bush—where he remained without discovery till the soldiers left the place.
Thus were two honest men delivered twice on two successive
days, in circumstances in which deliverance could scarcely
have been expected; but, as was formerly remarked, " every
man is immortal till his day come;" and the Lord can preserve his people in the most perilous situation till their work
be done, and all his gracious purposes respecting them on
earth be accomplished.

This second attack by the soldiers, following the first so
hastily, determined Hutchison instantly to abandon the place
and return to Daljig.   Accordingly next day he took leave
of his kind friends, and proceeded to his home.   On his way,
however, danger beset him still, for in his lonely track he
was encountered by a party of Highland soldiers, who happened to be passing that way.   As nobody escaped the notice
of these marauders, whether on the moor or on the highway,
they instantly stopped, and put to him their usual series of
interrogatives, with the answers to which they seemed to be
satisfied; and they allowed him to pass on.

It appears, notwithstanding what has been said to the
contrary, that after the recall of the Highland host, which
amounted to about ten thousand, and which, like a tempestuous cloud, burst with terrific fury on the west, or like a company of savages and beasts of prey let loose on the helpless
peasantry, and whom even those who employed them were
obliged for their own safety to dismiss, a goodly number of
them were still retained for the iniquitous work to accomplish which they were first brought in.   On this subject
Patrick Walker makes the following remarks :—" There are
many thousands yet alive who can witness, from their
sad experience, that there were one thousand Highlanders, in
the month of March 1685, six years after Bothwell, who
were sent to the south and west of Scotland (it being killing
time) to assist the forces—they being more swift of foot, to
run through bog and moss, hill and glen, to apprehend the
sufferers, than the standing forces, who were turned fat and
lazy with free quartering and strong feeding upon the ruins
of the Lord's people; as also those Highlanders were brought
to the west to rob and plunder, and to frighten people, more
especially women and children, by their strange uncouth
language, not knowing whether they were to kill them or to

save them alive, which is a great aggravation of a judgment. And what great murder and robbery they committed these three months that they were in the south and west of Scotland, there is one instance among many that I could give, which I cannot pass. When they came south through the parish of Morningside, the curate there, Mr Andrew Ure, informed them of worthy Peter Gilles who lived in that parish, who apprehended him, with John Bruce who lived in the parish of West Calder; and when they went through the parish of Carluke, they apprehended William Finneson and Thomas Young who lived there, whom the laird of Lee's footman apprehended, on whom they exercised great cruelty. They carried those four prisoners to Mauchline, and apprehended one John Binning, waiting upon cattle, without either stocking or shoe, and took their Bibles from them, and would suffer none either to sell or lend them Bibles (the first four were my very dear acquaintances), and hanged them all upon one gibbet, without suffering them to pray at their death; and their corpses were buried upon the spot." When the great body of the Highland soldiers were sent home, they returned loaded with booty, as if they had come from the sacking of a city, or from the plundering of a conquered country. Every article that was portable they took with them, although they lost much of it, if not the whole, in passing through the city of Glasgow, on their way to their native mountains.

Hugh Hutchison lived many years after this, and was farmer of a place called Farthing Reoch. His descendants are still resident in the west, and are distinguished for their moral and religious worth. It is pleasant to witness the posterity of the good emulating the piety of a godly ancestry and walking in the truth.

CHAPTER XIV.

John Paterson of Penyvenie.

John Paterson of Penyvenie was born in the year 1650—ten years prior to the Restoration. When he grew up, he embraced the principles of the persecuted people, and followed their preachers in moors and mosses, at the risk of his life. The farm which he rented belonged to Logan of Camlarg, a man who, like the most of the landed proprietors of the period, in order to save his estate, fell in with the ruling party, and submitted to their measures. One day when John Paterson called at Camlarg, for the purpose of paying his rent, the laird remarked that the roads must have been very foul, as his feet were so much besmeared with moss and mud. In his simplicity, John informed him that he had that morning come from Mayfield Hill, from attending a conventicle, which happened to be held there. At this Logan stormed, and severely reprimanded his tenant, pointing out the dangerous consequences that would certainly ensue, if the circumstance were to become known to the authorities. In those days of misrule and oppression, the lairds were made responsible for the behaviour of their tenants, and servants, and cottagers; and Camlarg distinctly saw the danger which threatened himself, if it should be discovered that any of the people on his grounds had transgressed the ecclesiastical law of the times. Logan, therefore, remonstrated with John, and stated, that if he did not desist from the practice of attending field conventicles, he would be obliged, in self-defence, either to inform on him or to eject him from his farm. In Paterson, however, he found a man of unyielding principle, and one who, having counted the cost, was prepared to sacrifice every earthly comfort, and even life itself, in maintaining what he deemed to be the cause of truth and righteousness. When he came home, he informed his wife of what had passed between the laird and him, and intimated his suspicions of what was likely to happen. His wife, who entertained the same views on religious matters with himself, was equally prepared to endure hardship in the cause of Christ. She encouraged her husband, by every virtuous consideration, to maintain an unflinching adherence to the principles which he had espoused. "If it be the will of God," said she, " let us suffer in well-doing; and, at the same time, let us make all necessary preparations for our defence, in case of an attack from the enemy." It was now obvious to John that more than ordinary precautions were necessary. He began to consider how, in case of a surprise, they might be able to conceal themselves from their persecutors in places about the house and out-buildings; and it occurred to him that a small opening might be made in the wall, by which a passage might be secured into the adjoining office-houses, and from thence into the fields. Having, therefore, dug a hole in the gable, through which one person at a time could creep with ease, and all other things being prepared, he, in order to conceal the aperture in the wall, placed before it a large wooden seat, yclept a *lang settle*, a piece of furniture very common in the old farm houses in Scotland. In a day or two, as was anticipated, the soldiers paid them a visit; and Paterson observing their approach, made his way through the opening, and hid himself in a deep trench cut in the moss, not far from the house. The soldiers having, according to their custom, examined every place in which they thought there was any likelihood of his being hid, and not finding him, they became very uproarious, and used very threatening language to his wife. They at last retired, and Paterson returned to his house unscathed.

Some time after this, our worthy attended a conventicle at a place called Fingland, near the source of the Water or Ken; but the meeting having been apprised of the approach of a company of Highland soldiers, broke up, and Paterson pursued his way homeward. As he was proceeding onward, he observed two dragoons on horseback following him; but the ground being very soft and boggy, they made no speed, while he, being on foot, made his way lightly through the moss. It was his intention to conceal himself in some deep hag among the shaggy heath, till his pursuers had passed by. Accordingly, having passed the summit of what is called the " Meikle Hill," he found a mossy furrow, into which he leapt, and lay close in the bottom. The troopers, however, had

dogs with them, which they put on the scent, and directed
them after him. The animals advanced over the broken
surface of the morass, exactly in the line of his hiding-place:
he heard them approaching, and expected every moment
that they would present themselves on the edge of the
trench above him; but just when they were about to spring
forward to the place where he lay, a fox jumped from his
lair, in their very face, and bounded down the hill. The
hunt commenced; the joyous dogs left their former scent,
and stretched themselves out at their full speed after the
fugitive reynard! The soldiers, like the dogs, oblivious of
the principal object of their pursuit, followed in the chase,
and passed Paterson in the moss, a few yards distant from
the place where he lay. Hearing the hubbub, and not knowing what was the matter, he raised himself from his smeary
couch; and peering cautiously over the edge of the deep hag,
he observed the fox, the dogs, and the soldiers, in full
race adown the heathy slope, leaving him far behind in comfortable seclusion. From the place where he had ensconced
himself, he had a full view of the whole track to the door of
his own house. He observed the movement of the party in
the line of their route, till they reached the house, at which
they stopped for a short time, and then moved off in the direction of Dalmellington. He then cautiously left the height,
and came home unobserved. Next day Logan sent for him,
and informed him that he was publicly denounced as a rebel,
and that a reward was offered for his apprehension; and that
now he might consult his safety in the best way he could.

Matters having come to this pass, Paterson resolved to
leave his house, and to take up his residence in Benbeoch
Craigs—a place well adapted for concealment. From this
situation he descended, as frequently as he found it consistent
with his safety, to visit his household. One day, as he was
preparing to go to his house, and had just left his retreat, he
observed a company of dragoons approaching. He instantly
retraced his steps, but was noticed by the troopers, who,
seeing him hastily ascend the hill, as if wishing to avoid
their observation, concluded that he was either the man they
were seeking, or some other equally obnoxious; and accordingly they rode after him. As he was climbing over the
stone-dyke which stood a few hundred yards from the bottom
of the crags, he turned round to see what progress the horsemen were making, and perceiving the speed with which they
advanced, he sprang from the wall, and ran to seek his
hiding-place. In this place there are large masses of coarse

granite, torn from the hill in the vicinity, and tossed to a considerable distance from the parent mountain, obviously by some powerful convulsion of nature. As Paterson in his haste was passing the base of one of these granite heaps, he fell, and tumbled into a deep and dark cavity underneath the rocky pile. Here he found a seclusion altogether unexpected, and much preferable to his usual hiding-place. When he fell into the cavern, he lay in utter astonishment at the incident; and, being partly stunned, could scarcely persuade himself that it was not a dream. As he lay in darkness and silence, he imagined he heard the party, who were in search of him, talking and moving from place to place among the stones. In reflecting on the occurrence, he could not fail to perceive the special hand of Providence, in thus, suddenly and unexpectedly, covering him from the view of those who came to seek his life, and who, if they had found him, would, without ceremony, have shot him on the spot. When he considered the gracious care of that God in whom he trusted, his heart swelled with grateful emotions, and he often looked back to the time he lay under the rock as a season of the purest spiritual enjoyment he ever experienced on earth. It was a Bethel in which he found God; and so delightful was it, as a place of communion with the Saviour, that he did not leave it till next day, when his anxious wife came to seek him, not knowing what had befallen him. John crept from the cavern, and met her in a transport of joy, and recounted his providential deliverance, and the outlettings of divine goodness to his soul; and then the husband and the wife knelt down on the grass and prayed, and gave thanks to the God of their life. The incident at the granite rock was cherished in this good man's memory till his dying day, not simply on account of the temporal safety it afforded him, but more especially on account of that full assurance of his salvation which, during that night, it is said he attained, and of which he made frequent mention on his death-bed.

Paterson was in raptures with his new hiding-place, which had been thus incidentally revealed to him; and he began instantly to arrange the interior, which he found capacious enough to contain several persons at a time, that he might render it a fit habitation for himself, and for any other wanderer who might happen to sojourn with him. It would be easy to make such a place very comfortable, by removing the loose stones, and spreading the earthy floor of the cavity with dry straw, or with soft and scented hay the common carpeting of the floors of the houses of even the nobles of Scotland in ruder times. The entrance to this retreat he contrived so to form that no stranger could easily find it; and thus the place was rendered so secure as to become a very eligible asylum in the time of danger. To this place he conducted the refugees that fell in his way, and it was here that he lodged Hugh Hutchison, the incidents that befell whom, when he sojourned with Paterson, have been already noticed. Though none knew of his particular hiding-place but friends, the people in the neighbourhood, by whom he was greatly respected, were ready to give warning to his family when danger appeared. Among others, the farmer who lived on the side of the valley opposite to Penyvenie, agreed to give notice by crying across the ravine the common watchword, "The nowt's i' the corn;" and by this means he escaped on several occasions the vigilance of his enemies.

Some time after this he was in Galloway, at a place called Irelington, attending a conventicle kept there by Mr Renwick. The meeting was held in the night season, under the serene shining of the bright moon—the night being preferred to the day to avoid discovery. As the company were listening to the preacher, from whose lips the words of eternal life distilled like the refreshing dew on the grass of the field, a sound was heard in the distance, and anon there appeared a huntsman's dog in full chase, but without any apparent object of pursuit. The fleet and hilarious animal bounded several times round the outskirts of the assembly, and then darted in among the crowd. The circumstance attracted the notice of the congregation, and the preacher paused for a moment, and expressed his fears of approaching danger, especially as the dog seemed to have come from a distance, and not to be known to any person present. When they were beginning to deliberate on the propriety of separating, the warder, who had been stationed in the distance to give warning in case of the approach of the enemy, came running in breathless haste, to announce the appearance of a company of Highland soldiers, who were cautiously advancing in the direction of the conventicle. In an instant the meeting was dispersed; for it was now obvious that their gathering was known to the enemy. Paterson, with five of his acquaintances, David Halliday, John Bell, Robert Lennox, Andrew M'Roberts, and James Clymont, took refuge in a barn in Irelington, and hid themselves in the midst of a quantity of wool that was piled up in a corner of the building, and by this means escaped detection

But the danger consequent on his attendance on conventicles did not deter him from meeting with the worshippers in the fields, or in the mosses, whenever an opportunity offered. He again attended a meeting near Little Mill, which gave serious offence to the lairds of Carse and Keir, who complained of him to Logan, who sent for him, and remonstrated with him on the assumed impropriety of his conduct, but without effect. Logan and his fellows did not comprehend the principles on which such men as Paterson acted; they were themselves worldly men, and shifted with the religion of the times from mere expediency, and to retain their earthly possessions—so hard is it for rich men to enter into the kingdom of heaven. The wealthy frequently possess far less independence of mind than the poor; for they have to guard their worldly interests, and to change their opinions and professions to suit these interests; while the poor pious man, finding that the chief things which he has to protect are truth and a good conscience, acts independently of worldly considerations, not seeking to please men, but God. " Buy the truth, and sell it not," was to those worthy men, in the lowly walks of life, an injunction of the most sacred obligation. They indeed sold their lives, but they would not part with the truth. The great men of that time were mean and shuffling characters, compared with the upright and noble-minded peasants, who, reckless of every worldly advantage, stood bravely by the cause of liberty, and high religious principle. They were men, many of them, in whose presence the truckling gentry of the nation were not worthy to stand an hour, and before whom they actually quailed, and from whose face they slunk away, vanquished by an oppressive sense of their own baseness.

Logan probably really wished Paterson well, although, for self-interest, and to ingratiate himself with the ruling party, he was obliged to appear displeased with him. He projected a sort of well-meant, though silly scheme, with a view to bring our Covenanter, in some measure, into the good graces of the neighbouring proprietors, who had conceived a very bad opinion of him. A number of the small lairds, whose grounds lay on the pleasant Water of Doon, had proposed to construct a dam across the stream, either for irrigation or some other purpose; and a day was appointed when they and their dependents should meet for the purpose of executing the plan. Logan, who intended to meet with them, sent for Paterson, and asked him to go with him to assist in the operations, stating, that he hoped his compliance would tend to

produce a favourable impression on the minds of the gentlemen respecting him. John replied, that if his attendance
on that occasion was to be construed into a compliance with
the measures of the times, he would sooner subject himself
to any suffering than move one foot in advance of another
to lend his aid in the work. Logan answered, that all he
wanted was his appearance there as a well-disposed neighbour, ready to assist in any useful undertaking.

Having agreed to accompany the laird, John returned
home, and informed his wife of what had passed, and how
he had promised to go with Logan to help in constructing
the dam on the Doon. His wife, who understood the temper of the men with whom they had to deal, suspected that
a plan was laid to entrap her honest husband, who, in the
simplicity of his heart, had consented to present himself
among the enemies of that cause in which he was a sufferer,
and attempted to dissuade him from carrying the matter
further. John could not deny that his wife had reasons
enough to suspect treachery, but he had promised, and therefore was resolved to perform.

On the day appointed, the party convened on the banks of
the Doon, and Logan appeared with John at his side. They
applied themselves vigorously to the work, and all went on
smoothly and comfortably during the day. Towards night,
however, an incident occurred which broke up the harmony
of the company, and threatened serious consequences.
M'Adam of Waterhead, in lending assistance to the workmen, lifted in his arms a large sod, and, staggering forward
with his burden, flung it with force on the watery embankment, from which it sent a muddy spray, which, reaching in
a shower the place where Logan stood, bespattered his
clothes, and especially his fine white stockings, which so enkindled his ire, that he broke out in furious and profane expressions against the individual who had unintentionally
been the cause of so much annoyance to him. The matter
was beginning to assume a serious aspect, and the wrangling
of parties was likely to issue in more substantial mischief,
had not a peacemaker been at hand. Paterson was distressed at the altercation, and much more so at the profane
language, of which there was no sparing use made by the
parties. His spirit was stirred, and he stood forward, first
as a reprover of sin, and then as a promoter of reconciliation.
He was in the presence of men where danger was to be apprehended, on account of his well-known nonconformity;
and to dare to speak to whom in the language of rebuke

might be regarded as a reason sufficiently strong to deliver him up to the military; but Paterson stood with undaunted breast, and spoke his mind freely, at the risk of incurring the high displeasure of men already exasperated. He had a duty to discharge, and he was not to be deterred from its performance. He addressed himself particularly to Logan, whom he reprimanded, as in the sight of God, for his daring and blasphemous expressions. The whole company stood mute and struck with awe; for there was a solemnity and majesty about his manner that quelled their spirits, and bereft them of power to reply. In the ardour of his address, and when he saw the advantage that he had gained, he drew, it is said, a Bible from his pocket, and read, with great gravity and impressiveness, the parable of the rich man and Lazarus; and, in his own plain way, endeavoured to draw a contrast between rich and wicked persecutors and the pious poor whom they oppressed for conscience' sake. What permanent effect his speech wrought on his auditors at Loch Doon, is not said; but the party separated quietly, and none ventured to assail the honest speaker, nor is it known that any injurious consequences followed. Paterson died so lately as the year 1740, at the great age of ninety, having long outlived the dreary period of persecution. His head was laid in an honoured grave, and his memory is still cherished in the locality where he lived. There were doubtless many interesting incidents in the history of this good man which tradition has not retained, but so many have been preserved as to keep his memorial alive, as a devoted follower of the Redeemer, and as one whom God cared for.

CHAPTER XV.

Capture at Glenshilloch—Rescue—Shooting at Craignorth—Roger
Dun—James Douglas.

In the beginning of the summer of 1685, a year in which the
persecution raged fearfully in the south and west, six men
fled from Douglasdale, namely, David Dun, Simon Paterson,
John Richard, William Brown, Robert Morris, and James
Welsh.   In their wanderings they proceeded southward,
and sought refuge among the more inaccessible heights in
the upper parts of Nithsdale.   They concealed themselves
in a thicket in a place called Glenshilloch, a little to the
west of the mining village of Wanlockhead, in the parish of
Sanquhar, and not far from the ancient farm-house of Cogshead.   This house, now a shepherd's cottage, is situated in a
delightful glen, and surrounded by lofty and green mountains. It stands not far from the edge of a precipitous brow,
the base of which is laved by the limpid brook that traverses
the glen, and pours its slender streamlet into the River Crawick.   In the times of our persecuted forefathers, the place
must have been a desirable retreat, as even now there are
no regular roads that lead to it, except the solitary footpaths
which here and there mark out a track for pedestrians across
the hills.   The family which, at this time, resided in Cogshead,
was related to William Brown, one of the wanderers who had
taken refuge in Glenshilloch; and as the two places were contiguous, Brown made his way stealthily over the intervening
height, and informed his friends of the circumstances in
which he and his companions in suffering were placed.   The
sympathy of this household was easily gained, and an ample
supply of provisions was conveyed to the men in their hiding-
place.   It is not easy to say how long the party might have
continued here among the dense brush-wood during the warm
days of summer, had not a strict search been made for them

in all the glens and hills of the locality in which it was suspected they had taken refuge.

The report had reached Drumlanrig that a company of refugees from Douglas Water had eluded the pursuit of the dragoons, and were somewhere concealed in the wilds between the Mennock and the Crawick. On this information, Drumlanrig collected his troopers for a vigilant search. He formed his party into three divisions, one of which traversed the lonely stream of the Mennock, another the pastoral banks of the Crawick, and the third pursued the middle route by the dark Glendyne. By this means it was confidently expected that the fugitives could not possibly escape, and more especially as no note of warning had been sounded in the district respecting the design of the persecutors. The six men who were lying among the hazel bushes, not anticipating any danger in their solitary retreat, had adopted no precautions in stationing a watch on any of the neighbouring heights to give notice of the approach of the enemy.

Drumlanrig himself conducted the middle division of the troopers; and having led them over the height in the north side of Glendyne, descended on the Water of Cog, and took his station on what is now denominated "The Martyr's Knowe"—a romantic elevation at the lower end of an abrupt ravine, called by the shepherds "The Howken." It happened, while Drumlanrig and his party were on the hillock, that some of the dragoons who were scouring the adjacent hills in search of the reputed rebels, seized a boy who was returning from Glenshilloch to Cogshead, carrying an empty wooden vessel, called by the peasantry a *kit*, in which were several horn spoons—a proof to the soldiers that he had been conveying provisions to some individuals among the hills, and they naturally suspected that the individuals of whom they were in quest were the persons. Under this impression, they carried him to their commander, who strictly interrogated him, but without eliciting anything satisfactory The firmness of the youth enraged Drumlanrig, who drew his sword with the intent to run him through the body, and would have slain him on the spot, had not a second thought occurred, that by using other and gentler means he might eventually succeed in obtaining all the information he desired. With this design he caused him to be bound hand and foot, while he sent out the soldiers in the direction in which he had been seen returning over the hills. It was not long before the troopers, in descending the north side of the mountain, found the men in their hiding-place. They

pounced on them as a falcon on his quarry, and secured
Dun, Paterson, and Richard, while Brown, Morris, and Welsh
made their escape. The troopers having been so far successful in their object, were seen returning triumphantly over the
height; but ere they reached the rendezvous, an unexpected
occurrence befell, which fairly routed the assailants, and accomplished the deliverance of the prisoners. In the hilly
districts, after a clear and chilly night in summer, the incident of a thunder-storm after high noon is not unfrequent.
When the sun has fully evaporated the dew, small dense
clouds with bright edges begin to appear above the tops of
the higher eminences, and, gradually increasing in size, and
approximating each other, form, in a short time, a dark and
lowering mass of vapour, which soon overspreads the whole
sky. An immediate thunder-storm is the consequence, and
so terrific sometimes is the explosion from the clouds, and
the gush of waters from the teeming firmament, as to alarm
the stoutest heart. In these cases the fiery bolts, falling incessantly on the hills, tear up the benty surface for a great
space around; and the tumultuous descent of the waters,
covering the green sides of the hills with a white foam,
gathers into a torrent, which carries moss, and soil, and
rocks promiscuously to the vale beneath, and forms, all at
once, a trench down the steep declivity, which afterwards
becomes the channel of a mountain rivulet. It was with
one of these hasty storms that Drumlanrig and his party
were visited, and which had been gathering over them unperceived. When the dragoons who led the three prisoners
were within a short distance of Drumlanrig's station on the
Martyr's Knowe, the first burst of thunder rattled its startling peal over their heads. The horses snorted, and the sheep
on the neighbouring heath crowded together, as if for mutual
protection. The rapid descent of the hail, the loud roaring
of the thunder, like the simultaneous discharge of a hundred
cannon from the battlements of the hills, and the flashing of
the sheeted lightning in the faces of the animals, rendered
them unmanageable, and they scampered off in every direction,
like the fragments of a fleeing army that has been signally
routed on the battle-field. In the confusion, Drumlanrig
himself panic-struck—as when Heaven bears testimony, by
terrible things in righteousness, against the ungodly when
caught in their deeds of wickedness—fled from the face of
the tempest, reckless both of his men and of his prisoners,
provided he could obtain a place of shelter. It is not said
to what place he fled; but there can be no doubt that it was

to the farm-house of Cogshead, which was scarcely half a mile from the place where he stood. When the soldiers saw their master retreating with such precipitancy from the warring of the elements, they followed his example, and let go the captives. The three worthy men stood undaunted in the storm, because they knew that the God who guided i s fury, was He in whose cause they were suffering; and though it was regarded with consternation by their enemies, it was hailed as a friendly deliverer by them, who were incessantly exposed to the pitiless storms of a wrathful persecution, compared with which the fierce raging of the elements was mildness itself.

When the prisoners found themselves at liberty, and being shrouded in the mantling of the murky tempest, they resolved to embrace the opportunity of instant flight. As they passed the Martyr's Knowe, they observed a person lying on its summit, apparently lifeless. This they found to be the little boy who had brought them provisions in the morning, and whom Drumlanrig, in his haste, had left bound on the spot. They untied him, and found that he was not dead, but only stunned with terror. Having raised him up, and informed him of what had occurred, and directed him to keep himself in concealment till the soldiers should leave the glen, they went westward and sought a retreat among the wilds in the upper parts of Galloway. The other three who escaped at Glenshilloch, namely Brown, Morris, and Welsh, fled northward, and were intercepted by the party who were sent up the vale of the Crawick. Brown and Morris were shot at the back of Craignorth, where they lie interred in the places respectively where they fell, as has already been noticed in a former chapter. Welsh, in the meantime, made his escape, and remained in concealment among the Nithsdale mountains. From the tops of these lofty heights a magnificent view of a great part of the locality in the south and west of Scotland, which was the scene of so much suffering in the persecuting times, is obtained; and hence we feel disposed to survey it with more than ordinary interest. On the south, the range of the Galloway Hills rises to the view; on the west, the dreary solitudes of Kyle; on the east, the heathy mountains of Crawford Moor; and on the north, the majestic Tinto, waving afar his misty mantle, and revealing, through the opening of its folds, the ruddy scars which the angry buffeting of the storms has made on his shaggy and time-worn sides. Its name in the old British speech signifies " the hill of fire,"—an appellation which, in all likelihood, it received either from the red appearance of its soil, or from the fires which the ancient Druids, on May-day, kindled on its summit. The whole of this wide district was traversed in its breadth and length, for many a tedious year, by the holy men who jeopardied their lives on the high places of the field, in support of that cause in which they had honestly embarked; and many a tale, if hills and glens could speak, might perchance be told of those devoted men, which the report of former days has failed to echo to our times.

David Dun, one of the fore-mentioned worthies, was related to Roger Dun, a noted Covenanter, who lived in the higher parts of Ayrshire, and of whom a few notices may here be given. Roger Dun was born in 1659. His father, James Dun, a worthy man, was farmer of Bennet or Benholt, in the parish of Dalmellington, and was, with others, exposed to no small trouble in those trying times. Roger, when he grew up, and was able to judge for himself, resolved to share the fortunes of the Covenanters. It was soon known that Roger Dun had allied himself to the obnoxious party, and therefore his ruin was determined on. A conventicle had been held at Craignew in Carsphairn, and Roger, with two of his brothers, attended the meeting. The report of this circumstance soon spread, and the dragoons were sent to apprehend all they could find returning from the place. They met the three brothers on their way home—Andrew and Allan were made prisoners, and carried back to Carsphairn; but what befell them is not known, for they were never more heard of. Roger, however, by a sudden and unexpected spring, eluded the grasp of the soldier who attempted to seize him; and bounding away, fled to a soft marshy place, into which the horsemen durst not venture, and made his escape.

After this, Dun sought a retreat in Dunasken Glen, a place about two miles from Bennet. One morning, as he was returning home from his hiding-place, he encountered unexpectedly, a party of dragoons who were sent out in search of him. He was so near them that to attempt flight was in vain. In order, therefore, to avoid suspicion, he appeared to be as much at his ease as possible; and walking forward with an undaunted mien, he determined to accost the soldiers in a style that would tend to direct their attention away from himself. " I think I can guess your errand, gentlemen," addressing the troopers in a familiar manner, " I am thinking you are in search of Roger Dun, who is supposed to be in concealment somewhere in this quarter." " It is even so," replied the commander of the party, " he is the very person we are in quest of." " Well," said Roger, " though I hate the name of an informer, yet I think I could direct you to a place in which he is sometimes to be found. See you yon shepherd's hut afar in the waste; bear down directly upon it, and see what you can find." " You are an honest fellow, I opine," answered the leader; " and we will follow your advice." The party then proceeded onward at full speed, and Roger, with all expedition, betook himself to his hiding-place in the glen, which is said to have been beneath the project- ing bank of a mountain streamlet. In this seclusion, where the hallowed voice of prayer often mingled with the soft murmuring of the silvery brook, he found a place of safety from man, and of communion with his God.

On another occasion, when Roger had crept from his con- cealment, and had found his way unperceived to his father's house, he was surprised by the hasty arrival of a company of troopers before the door. He attempted to escape through an aperture in the gable of the house, but which, being partly closed up with rubbish, hindered him from making his way with the speed that was desirable. When the soldiers en tered, Roger was gone, but they found a youth of sixteen years of age, who had not time to follow his friend; him they seized, and how he was disposed of none could tell, for he was never again seen in the country. Dun made his way through a morass, leaving his pursuers behind him, and got with all safety into his retreat in Glenasken.

From the incessant harassings to which he was subjected, Roger Dun found it necessary to leave the district, and to retire to the lower parts of Galloway. When he was in the neighbourhood of Minigaff, residing in the house of a friend who was favourable to that cause in which he suffered hard- ship, he nearly lost his life by the hand of the enemy. The soldiers having made an attack on the house in which he lodged, two of its inmates were killed defending themselves; and Dun, after an ineffectual resistance, fled, and plunging in- to the waters of a neighbouring loch, swam under water, to a shallow place in the middle, where grew several shrubs and willows, at the side of which he emerged, while the soldiers shot into the lake at random. Owing to his immersion in the cold waters he caught a severe fever, which threatened to terminate his life, but from which he ultimately recovered. He lived till after the Revolution, and was at last killed at a place called Woodhead, by an individual who mistook him for another person whom he intended to murder; so that the worthy man, who had so often escaped the sword of the public persecutor, fell by the hand of the private assassin.

The scene of the following anecdote lies in the neighbourhood of the native district of Roger Dun. Near the head of the Afton, which springs from the dark and misty mountains to the south of the village of New Cumnock, was a hiding-place among the brown heath, which was occasionally resorted to by the wanderers of the covenant. The entrance to this retreat is said to have been along one of those deep ruts in the moss which were scooped out by the torrents from the hills, which frequently descend with great impetuosity after the discharge of a heavy thunder-cloud. Some of these trenches are deep and narrow, and the opening at the top is nearly covered over with the purple heather, which, extending itself horizontally from both sides, meets in the centre. In some cases a man can walk at his full height in these mossy water-courses, without rising above the level of the surrounding surface. It was along this slippery ditch that a few persons seeking concealment from their enemies had proceeded to the hiding-place to which it led. The fact that a certain number of persons had concealed themselves somewhere in the locality, was discovered by a man of the name of Farquhar, who, though he did not know the exact spot which they had selected as their place of refuge, had yet noticed one of their party stealing cautiously in the dusk to a neighbouring house, to obtain provisions for his hungry companions. This man informed the commander of a company of troopers, who were either stationed in the district or incidentally passing along the line between the garrisons in Carsphairn and Ayrshire, that he had observed something suspicious, and intimated his readiness to accompany him, in the dusk of the evening, to the house at which he expected the man would call as usual. The commander of the party, whose name, it is said, was Darnley, consented, and led his troopers privately to the place. Accordingly, as was anticipated, one of the Covenanters in hiding was observed in the obscurity of the twilight approaching the house. He had come near without suspecting harm, but was soon made aware of his danger, by the whispering of voices and the appearance of men and horses at a short distance from him. He instantly retraced his steps and fled. Darnley and Farquhar pursued, and keeping on his track, came up to him as he reached the edge of the trench that conducted to the hiding-place. The Covenanter, whose name was James Douglas, stumbled, and Darnley fell with him into the deep hag. The noise drew the associates of Douglas from their concealment, and they came in a body to the place where the two men were lying struggling in the bottom of the rut. They rescued their associate, and led Darnley, as their prisoner, to their randezvous, and remonstrated with him on the impropriety of his conduct, pointing out the injustice and wickedness of the cause in which he was embarked, entreating him seriously to consider the danger in which his soul was placed, and exhorting him earnestly and affectionately to look to the Saviour for forgiveness. The kind treatment he received from them, and the good and salutary advices they gave him, made, it is said, a deep and lasting impression on his mind. In a short time he abandoned the cause of the persecutors, and embraced the principles of the Covenanters. He fought at the battle of Bothwell Bridge on the side of the Covenanters, and fell covered with wounds; and just before he expired, one of his former associates, who happened to pass the place where he lay, recognised him, and upbraided him with treachery in leaving the king's service, and connecting himself with rebels. With his dying breath, however, he bore testimony to the uprightness of his motives and to the goodness of that cause in which he was now a sufferer. " I do not regret," said he, " the step which I have taken; I die with a heart full of comfort, and in the faith of the blessed Redeemer of the world."

CHAPTER XVI.

Story of Alexander Brown.

ALEXANDER BROWN, the subject of the following sketch, is supposed to have been a native of the parish of Muirkirk, in which, during the heavy times of persecution, he rented a small farm, the name of which is not now known. He was cousin to John Brown of Priesthill, who, among the saintly names that graced the period in which he lived, was without all controversy one of the most illustrious. Their places of abode were contiguous, and sweet and refreshing were the hours of their hallowed intercourse when they talked of Zion's affliction and of the wailings of a bleeding Church, whose glory the haughty oppressor was trampling remorselessly in the dust. These holy men, however, encouraged themselves in the Lord their God, and sought communion with the saints in prayer and Christian fellowship. Brown and his cousin of Priesthill, whose story is told with unrivalled pathos in the "Scots Worthies," took sweet counsel together when travelling into the heart of the remotest solitudes to hear the Word of God preached by the gentle Renwick, or the good Cargill, and others of the faithful witnesses for "Scotland's covenanted cause." It is not known at what period of his life the subject of this narrative was brought to the knowledge of the truth, but certain it is that he was a true and devoted follower of the Saviour. In "killing times" he was "in perils oft, in weariness and painfulness, in watchings often, in hunger and thirst, in fastings often." But the shield of a divine protection was over him, and his deliverance in the most imminent dangers display the overruling care of Him who was the comfort and salvation of that scattered remnant whose blood flowed alike on the streets of the populous cities and on the sides of the desert mountains. Tradition has not named the year in

which the following incident, productive of important consequences to Alexander Brown, took place. Claverhouse and
his troopers were scouring the moorland districts in the
upper parts of the counties of Ayr and Lanark, which, from
the beginning of the "troublous times," had been the haunt
of many a houseless wanderer. He had been informed that
Brown, who had hitherto eluded his vigilance, was at home,
unapprehensive of danger, and therefore might easily be
caught. Claverhouse and his troopers were instantly in
motion. Brown was at a short distance from his house
when he descried the approach of the dragoons, and he was
fully aware of their design in visiting his lonely dwelling.
He knew that they saw him where he stood, and he found
that he could neither flee nor conceal himself. He had reason to believe, however, that he was not personally known
to his enemies, and hence he concluded that by employing
an innocent stratagem he might perchance escape detection.
Assuming, therefore, a cool and careless demeanour, he
walked deliberately toward the advancing troopers, as if his
business in the moor lay in the direction in which they were
approaching, and as if apparently anxious also to gratify his
curiosity by inspecting their military parade. This movement on the part of our worthy tended to lull suspicion, and
the coolness which he displayed so completely outwitted his
wily foes that they applied to him for information respecting the object of their search. "Know you if Alexander
Brown be within," asked the leader of the party. "He is
not at present within, Sir," replied Brown, with an air of
indifference, "he went out lately, and I have not seen him
return." "He *is* in the house," shouted a surly trooper,
"and you want to conceal the fact." "What I tell you is
the truth," retorted Brown with some degree of warmth, "I
know he is not within." This altercation was suddenly terminated by the stern authority of the commander, who imposed instant silence, and with a voice that awakened the
echoes of the glen, commanded the party to advance on the
cottage, and dashing the rowels into the sides of his black
war-steed; he was the first to draw bridle at Brown's door. In
a moment the soldiers were at work, and made, as usual, a
strict and unsparing search. Every place that could conceal a human being was closely inspected, but the object of
their search was not to be found. Claverhouse, enraged at
the disappointment, ordered his ruthless troopers to set fire
to the entire farm-steading, and to reduce the whole to a
heap of ashes. In a brief space the spiral flame was seen

darting through the roof of the heath-thatched cottage, like
the pointed tongue of the deadly serpent, when, thrust from
the envenomed jaws of the insidious reptile, it pierces with
a fatal sting the body of the unwary passenger. At length
the whole range of buildings was enveloped in lurid fire and
smoke, and presented in the heart of the solitary wild an
appearance similar to a ship on fire in the midst of the blue
and lonely waste of the ocean. What moved the Cavalier
to this alternative was the belief that the occupant of the
premises was lurking somewhere about the building, and he
was determined not to leave the place till he had accomplished his destruction. But though the dragoons showed
no favour to Brown, they had pity on his cattle, and drove
them all to the bent, that they might be reserved for their
own use afterwards. When the fire was raging along the
line of the houses, the soldiers, with their loaded muskets,
stood waiting for Brown, expecting every moment that he
would issue from the conflagration to seek safety in the open
field. In this, however, they were disappointed, and had the
mortification to see the little *onstead* reduced to a heap of
smoking ruins without having gained their object. Brown
witnessed from an eminence, to which he speedily betook
himself when the soldiers left him, the entire desolation of
his humble cot, and the spoiling of all his goods; but, like
David, when he looked on Ziklag in ashes, and found himself in danger of his life, he "encouraged himself in the
Lord his God," knowing that in heaven he had a better and
an enduring substance.

After this, Brown, despoiled of all his worldly substance,
but not yet bereft of his life, wandered for several months
from place to place, till his enemies had abandoned the
search as hopeless. When the noise made about him had
subsided, and when the storm for the time-being was hushed,
he engaged himself as a shepherd at Carmacoup, a few miles
above the ancient town of Douglas. How long he was suffered to remain unmolested in this retreat, we have no information; but another severe trial was awaiting him. There
were enemies, treacherous men, who, though not cased in
armour, were nevertheless ready, for a sum of money, the
wages of unrighteousness, to betray him to those who thirsted
for his blood. Claverhouse being apprized of his retreat,
marched with great secrecy and expedition to Carmacoup;
and the only notice which Brown had of his approach was
the array of his troop rushing along the heath towards the
house which he had left a few minutes before. Brown, who

had not forgotten the means of preservation which he had formerly employed with success when sought for by the enemy, prayed hastily for direction and help in the hour or his perplexity and peril, and then, turning from his path, threw himself in the way of the dragoons that were advancing at a quick pace. On their coming up to him they halted, and rested on their steeds, smoking with perspiration and white with foam, and fixed their searching eyes upon him. Being prepared for the encounter, however, he met their scrutinizing glances without the slightest apparent agitation, and answered their questions with a simplicity and a tact which forbade the entrance, even for a moment, of the slightest suspicion. After a short confabulation with the stranger respecting Alexander Brown, and the likelihood of his being found at Carmacoup, Claverhouse hastened away, followed by his soldiers with their long cloaks streaming in the wind. In a few moments the trampling of the cavalcade and the clashing of armour died on the ear of Brown, who was again favoured with a deliverance when within the very grasp of the foe. Being now left alone he fled over the moors and heights to a place called Hackshaw, about four miles to the north of Carmacoup, where he found a safe retreat in its wild ravines and deep morasses.

After lurking a few days in Hackshaw, he removed to the farm-house of Cleuchbrae. Cleuchbrae, in the parish of Lesmahagow, lies about two miles north of Hackshaw, and is situated on the west bank of the Nethan, which rises near Cumberhead—a place famed as the resort of the wanderers —and falls into the Clyde at Crossford. In many places the banks of this dark whirling stream are exceedingly romantic. The rocks on each side are rugged, and clothed with wood. At Cleuchbrae, this stream, near its junction with the Logan, runs in a deep and narrow ravine, the precipitous sides of which are decorated by the stately oak, the fragrant birch, and the tapering mountain-ash, which in summer waves its scented blossoms in the breeze, and in autumn is thickly studded with its gorgeous clusters of ruddy *rowans*, which furnish many a delicious repast to the crowds of sweet warblers which nestle among its leafy branches. Cleuchbrae, at the time to which our narrative refers, was tenanted by a worthy man of the name of Lean, whose door was always open to the lonely wanderer who, for Christ's sake, had left all that was dear to him on earth. Here Brown met with a cordial reception. Lean's family consisted of four daughters; and to one of these, in particular, his visit was especially

welcome. With the pious and hospitable family of Cleuchbrae Brown had lived for years in terms of the closest
friendship; but something stronger than mere friendship was
cherished by him toward one of the household, with whom
nothing but the precarious times in which they lived
prevented an honourable union. It was agreed on by the
family that, owing to the strict search that was now being
made for him, Brown should retire to some place near them
that afforded a more perfect concealment. Cleuchbrae was
a suspected house, and being in the vicinity of Shelly Hill
and Waterfoot, places which Claverhouse had often visited,
and where parties of his dragoons, for weeks, occasionally
resided, it was therefore deemed prudent that our wanderer
should leave the house. The next care was to find a hiding-
place, if possible, not far from the house; and, for this purpose, the steep and bosky sides of the Nethan were minutely
searched, if haply a secure retreat might be discovered among
its sheltering rocks; but no place suitable could be found.
What nature, however, had denied, labour procured. Brown,
assisted chiefly by his betrothed, excavated in the bank of the
stream, opposite to Cleuchbrae, a cave, among the mantling
bushes and thick underwood, which completely answered the
purpose of concealment. The operations necessary to accomplish the design were carried on with the utmost secrecy,
and for the most part in the night season. Brown quarried
the stones and loose earth from the place; and she who had
volunteered her services as a fellow-labourer, conveyed, under
the faint glimmering of the moon, through the trees, the rubbish to a distance, and disposed of it in such a manner that
nothing could lead to detection. At length, the little cell
was finished, and its entrance was so perfectly concealed by
the shrubs and pendent branches of the larger trees, as to
afford a high degree of security. In this asylum our worthy
remained for two whole years; and she who had been his
companion in labour, like a ministering angel, daily visited
his lonely abode with a supply of provisions, accompanied
with many an exhortation to maintain his constancy in that
cause in which he was called to suffer hardship.

In the dark nights he frequently visited the hearth of the
kindly family at Cleuchbrae, and, in case of a surprise by the
enemy, he had his way of escape ready through the window
of the apartment, which looked down upon his cave at a short
distance from the house. During his stay at Cleuchbrae,
however, no search was made for him, for none knew the
place of his retreat, except a few in whom implicit confidence

could be placed. One of these few was John Black of Red-shaw, in the parish of Douglas (a lineal descendant of whom is at present resident in Hazelside in the same parish—one who inherits, too, all the kindly feelings of his ancestor). Black had an interview with Brown, who had now been eighteen months in the concealment of the cave at Cleuch-brae, and expressed a wish that he should now leave his hiding-place and become his shepherd at Redshaw. Black, however, could not prevail with him to relinquish the place in which he had found so much security and peace, to expose himself again to the notice and fury of his enemies. After an interval of six months, his friend Black paid him another visit, and at last succeeded in drawing him from his retirement into active life, and with considerable regret he took his leave of Cleuchbrae. He was not long resident at Redshaw, however, before his troubles were renewed. Claverhouse was again in pursuit of him, and again he had nearly become the prey of the destroyer.

Early on a Sabbath morning, when he had gone out to the heath to inspect the state of his flocks, he observed a com-pany of dragoons on their way from Douglas sweeping over the hills before him, and rapidly advancing. His heart for a moment failed him, but his despondency was of short con-tinuance. He committed himself to the gracious care of Him whose providence had hitherto watched over him, and shielded him from the vengeance of his enemies. "Call upon me in the day of trouble; I will deliver thee, and thou shalt glorify me." None but those who have experienced it, can conceive the confidence and ease of mind which, in perilous circumstances, the fervent utterance of the heart in prayer imparts. It was impossible for Brown to escape by flight; the troopers were near, and their horses were fleet, and he therefore determined to have recourse to his former plan of outwitting or outbraving the enemy, when no other scheme of escape was practicable. Accordingly he summoned all his fortitude, and turning round in an apparently careless manner, whistled aloud on his dog, that was lagging at some distance behind. When the joyous animal came frisking to his feet, he threw his plaid with a jocund air over his shoul-ders, and, adjusting his blue bonnet on his head, began to chant in a lively strain one of our sweet Scottish airs—pro-bably to the words of a psalm adapted to his circumstances. The cheerful sound of the music attracted the notice of the dragoons, who conceived that no sober Covenanter could so profane the Sabbath as to employ on its hallowed hours, the merry voice of the songster. The dragoons came up; it was a critical moment for Brown—life or death hung upon it. When they came close to him, however, though they slackened their pace, they did not halt, and riding slowly past, one of the party exclaimed: "That, at least, is not Alexander Brown, else he would not be singing songs on the Sabbath-day." The propriety of the remark seemed to be felt by the company, and they marched on without taking further notice of him. When the troopers had passed him, and were fairly out of sight, Brown lost no time in seeking a place of immediate concealment; and this he found in a deep moss-hag in the neighbourhood. The dragoons arrived at Redshaw in search of him whom they left behind them on the moor. They examined every place without finding their object, and having ransacked the dwelling-house, they returned to Douglas. This was the last time that this good man was exposed to trouble from the enemy; for the Revolution, which took place soon after the occurrence now related, emancipated the nation at once from spiritual and civil bondage, and conferred on every man the perfect freedom of worshipping God according to the dictates of his own conscience.

Brown, when the danger was over, returned to sympathize with his kind friend at Redshaw, who, on his account, had sustained the spoiling of his goods, being reckoned a suspicious character when he harboured such men as Alexander Brown in his house. Tradition has not forgotten the fair maid of Cleuchbrae, who, shortly after this, and in more peaceful times, became the honoured wife of our worthy Covenanter, with whom she was already united both in affection and in principle. After their marriage they took up their residence at a place called Little Redshaw. They had a family, and both lived to a good old age. They died at Redshaw, and were interred in the ancient churchyard of St Bride, in Douglas.

The descendants of Alexander Brown and of Lean of Cleuchbrae are numerous, particularly in the parishes of Lesmahagow and Douglas. Two of the great-grandchildren of Alexander Brown are at present living in the town of Douglas, and are every way worthy of the honoured name of their ancestor.

CHAPTER XVII

James Gavin of Douglas—Capture in the Ravine.

THE romantic locality of Douglasdale, in the upper ward of Lanarkshire, teems with many a tale of thrilling interest. The Water of Douglas, a dark blue stream, as its name indicates, wends its course through the delightful valley to which it gives the appellation, and falls into the majestic Clyde. The strath through which the river flows was, in times long gone by, the scene of many a bloody conflict; and there many a leal-hearted patriot bravely lost his life in the earlier struggles for Scotland's independence, against the encroachments of her southern neighbours. Few places in the southwest of Scotland, perhaps, retain more of the traditions of the " olden times" than this district. The hills, and woods, and glens, and mosses, and ancient feudal towers, have all legends of their own, relative to times either more recent or more remote. Such recitals, it is true, are not confined to Douglasdale only; they are sown either more profusely or more sparingly over the breadth and length of Caledonia.

> " O wild, traditioned Scotland,
> Thy briery burns and braes
> Are full of pleasant memories,
> And tales of other days.
> Thy story-haunted waters
> In music gush along ;
> Thy mountain glens are tragedies—
> Thy heathy hills are song.
>   *   *   *   *
> Land of the Bruce and Wallace,
> Where patriot hearts have stood,
> And for their country and their faith
> Like water poured their blood ;
> Where wives and little children
> Were stedfast to the death,
> And graves of martyr warriors
> Are in the desert heath."

The ancient village of Douglas stands in the vicinity of the princely mansion of the lord of the manor, which, from the green lawn on which it is situated, rears its towers among the sturdy trees which, centuries ago, witnessed many a deed of high and chivalrous daring on the part of the warlike ancestors of the famous house of Douglas. The village must in feudal times have taken its rise from the castle, and must have been the spot on which the retainers of the bold chieftain constructed their huts. The Church of St Bride, partly in ruins, stands on a rising ground in the centre of the more ancient part of the village, in the midst of the field of graves, and is a pile of very great antiquity.

Few names have sounded longer and louder in the ears of Scotsmen than that of Douglas. It was a name which not unfrequently made the throne of the Scottish monarchs totter beneath them. Theobold the Fleming founded, after the Saxon times, the family of Douglas. To this individual, Arnald, abbot of Kelso, granted, in the year 1147 and afterwards, the lands of Douglasdale in Lanarkshire. His firstborn son, according to the practice of the times when landowners took the name of their lands, assumed the title of Douglas; and hence has sprung that illustrious line whose name, through the descent of successive generations, has gathered so much martial renown.

In the times of the Episcopal persecution in Scotland, the parish of Douglas, like that of Sanquhar, suffered less than might have been expected. The leniency of those in power prevented, in both places, the mischief which might otherwise have ensued. The hand of Providence in this circumstance appears very obvious; for the wild localities in Douglasdale, and in the upper parts of Nithsdale, became by this means an asylum to the wanderers, who found there, at certain seasons at least, less molestation.

One circumstance, which would seem to account for the quietude of Douglas at this period, was, that the Rev. Peter Reid, minister of the parish, accepted the Indulgence; at least his name is mentioned in the list of the indulged who were cited to appear before the council in 1677—the year of the death of the venerable John Semple, the indulged minister of Carsphairn, during whose incumbency that parish also was kept in a state of similar repose. It was in the parishes of the curates chiefly that the greatest distress prevailed. These hirelings acted the part of government spies and informers, and were the cause of indescribable affliction over the whole country.

Another circumstance which tended to shield the inhabitants of Douglasdale in those oppressive days, was the tolerance of the house of Douglas. That family, it is said, never manifested a persecuting spirit. The Marquis of Douglas, though occasionally instigated by the council to support them in their measures, permitted every man on his lands to worship God according to his conscience; and, instead of annoying the Covenanters, he petitioned for the pardon of some, and obtained a mitigation of the punishment of others. The conduct of this nobleman must have had great weight with the smaller proprietors in his neighbourhood, who received no encouragement, from his example, to display anything like the keenness of a persecuting temper. The intolerance of an unprincipled baron, and the ferocity of an ignorant and bigoted squire, wrought more havoc in the bosom of the peaceful families of the land than tongue can tell.

It is probable that the curate who succeeded Peter Reid in Douglas, was a man of a gentle disposition, or that at least his disposition was modified by the presiding influence of the marquis. The curates were often greatly irritated at the disrespect shown them by their parishioners, and the scanty attendance on their ministry; and they sometimes broke out with great vehemence against the people. The curate of Lesmahagow, when he was one day preaching to a very thin audience, exclaimed: " Black be my fa', but they are a' aff to the hill folk thegither. Sorrow gin I dinna tell, and they'll a' be shot or hangit by Yule." In those days the curate of a parish was either silent, or lodged information, according to circumstances; for his conduct as a time-server was generally regulated by the will or example of the more powerful in his locality.

Notwithstanding the general quietude of the parish of Douglas during the stirring times of persecution, there were certain individuals even there, the prominence of whose religious character was such as to preclude the possibility of their being allowed to remain unnoticed. John Haddoway, merchant in Douglas, and James White, a writer in the same place, together with two brothers of the name of Cleland (James and William), were especially, after the battle of Bothwell Bridge, taken notice of by the council. Two years prior to this, however, we find the same persons regarded with a suspicious eye by the vigilant oppressors of the time, and actually summoned before them. Wodrow, the historian, takes notice of this circumstance in the following words: " By a letter to the Marquis of Douglas, they (the council) acquaint him that John Haddoway, his chamberlain, and

James and William Cleland, sons of Thomas Cleland, his garner keeper, having been before the council, February 1677, for being at conventicles and other disorders; and some witnesses were examined, and the process delayed, and his lordship's bond taken to produce them when called; they being now to go on in that process, desire him to exhibit them on the 27th instant, according to his bond." It appears that these persons were acquitted at this time—probably through the influence of the marquis. It is obvious, however, that matters in the parish of Douglas began to assume an aspect not at all pleasurable to the ecclesiastical superiors of the period; for the council acquainted the marquis on the same occasion, " that being informed of the vacancy of the kirk of Douglas, and that the people of that parish live *disorderly*, they desire that he may plant that kirk with some regular or orthodox minister, and take advice of his Grace the Archbishop of Glasgow, to whom they have recommended the planting of it, if he (the marquis) does it not readily." The disorderly living of the people of Douglas, here referred to in a letter from the council, is easily understood; it refers to their nonconformity, and their frequenting of conventicles.

There resided in Douglas, at this time also, an eminent Christian of the name of James Wilson, with whom the venerable Peden used to associate, and who sometimes accompanied him in his wanderings. Janet Cleland, too, a mother in Israel, and probably a relation of the two Clelands already mentioned, lived there, and was the individual who dared to express her sympathy with Hackston of Rathillet, when he was conveyed by the troopers a prisoner through Douglas, after the skirmish at Airs-moss. " At Douglas," says he, " Janet Cleland was kind to me, and brought a surgeon to me, who did but little to my wounds, only he staunched the blood." We are not therefore to conclude that there were few or no worthies to be found in certain localities, simply because little mention is made of them; circumstances prevented their being dragged into notice, when otherwise they would have appeared a great host.

Among the few of the natives of the sweetly secluded vale of Douglas that suffered in these trying times, was James Gavin. His name and certain circumstances connected with his history, have been retained by tradition; and it would be a matter of regret if the memorial of so worthy a man were to perish. When the moors and the glens of Scotland were the hiding-places of the scattered remnant, this lowly man, in order to maintain a good conscience, and communion with his God, betook himself to the lonely caves and dark mantling bushes of the forest. Tradition had nearly left him out of mind, had not his great-great-granddaughter, Helen Gavin in Douglas, who fondly cherishes the name of her godly ancestor, produced from the stores of her memory the only lingering and veritable notices of one who reflects a credit on his descendants.

James Gavin was a native of the village of Douglas, but the year of his birth is unknown. What were the character and condition of his parents we cannot tell, but he himselr was a God-fearing man, and a consistent follower of the Saviour in whom he believed. The period of his life at which he connected himself with the cause of the covenants is not stated; but certain it is, when he did embark in the cause, he adhered to it with unflinching constancy till the end. Owing to his good sense and great piety, he acquired much influence in the village, and was at length regarded as a leading man among the brethren.

He was a tailor to trade, but his humble and honest occupation detracted nothing from his weight of character as an influential person. True worth is not embodied in wealth and worldly distinction, but in genuine godliness. At what particular period of his nonconformist profession he was first marked out by his foes we are not informed, nor how much he suffered prior to his capture by the cruel Claverhouse. It was reported that this active and merciless agent of the dominant faction was at the head of a company of his troopers ravaging the parts adjacent to Douglasdale, and shooting without remorse the helpless wanderers whom he met on the hills and deserts. The news of the approach of this redoubted persecutor put James Gavin upon his guard. He was aware that his name and principles were not unknown to the enemy, and that they were watching the earliest opportunity to apprehend him. In pursuing his vocation then, he made as little noise as possible, waiting till the threatened tempest should blow over. In those days it was much more customary than now, for persons exercising the handicraft of our worthy, to go from place to place pursuing their employment, in the different country houses where their services were required, and where they generally remained till their work was finished.

James Gavin, knowing that the dragoons were in the neighbourhood, and that they would make strict search wherever they came for suspected persons, deemed it prudent not to lodge in the houses where he plied his sedentary employment,

but sought a retreat elsewhere. He frequently took refuge
in any barn or other out-house to which he had access, and
as frequently had recourse to the thickets in the glen, and to
the cavities of the rocks, to hide himself from the eye of his
oppressors. This was his practice when, in times of imminent
peril, he happened to be located in the more rural parts, to
which the approach of the enemy might be expected. It is
easy to imagine the anxiety and discomfort of a situation such
as this; in suspense by day, and in hazard by night, the lives
of such persons hung in doubt before their eyes.

When Gavin wrought in the village, either in his own
house or in the houses of his neighbours, he generally withdrew in the dusk of the evening to the sheltered banks of
Earnsallach burn, and hid himself till the morning. In this
retreat he had peace; and though he was exposed to the
damps and colds of the dreary night, his heart was comforted
with the thought and with the experience that he was near
God, and that he was suffering not as an evil doer, but as a
follower of the Redeemer.

Earnsallach is a small mountain stream which issues from
the bleak moorlands behind, and falls into the Douglas Water
about three quarters of a mile above the village. This
streamlet, at one part of its course, forms a beautiful cascade,
which easily attracts the notice of the traveller as he wends
his way through the waste. And many are the sweet linns
that are to be met with among the unnoticed rills that pursue
their fairy course in the deep dells among the hills, and on
which no eye gazes but that of the watchful shepherd, as he
follows the wanderings of his fleecy charge on the mountains.
There are spots of beauty and of wild grandeur in the mountainous and heathy tracts of Scotland, of which those who
live in the more cultivated districts have no conception.

When the rivulet leaves the cascade over which it shoots
its foaming and rapid waters, it pursues its way through a
deep and narrow ravine, the sides of which are rendered sufficiently rugged with shattered and procumbent rocks. The
trees that grow on each margin, though neither majestic
nor picturesque, interweave their pendent branches with the
shrubs that spring from the fissures of the rocks beneath,
and cast a deep gloom over the torrent as it struggles along
its rough and noisy channel, and in the lonely sides of which
James Gavin spent many a watchful night.

In ancient times, the principal road which led from Douglas
to Sanquhar crossed Earnsallach burn about three hundred
yards below the linn, and passed along a desolate moor,

called the *Black Gait*—a name which it received from the dark and deep moss which it traverses. This place is not without its interest, nor its tales of bygone times. The hair-breadth escapes of Covenanters and troopers in this dangerous morass are not spoken of, but there is in its vicinity an old grey cairn, denominated " Bryce's Cross." Tradition affirms that this stony pile commemorates the murder of a travelling chapman, who lost his life ages ago, by the wicked hands of those who wished to possess his property. The people of a forgotten age reared this monument, not in approbation, but in detestation of the nefarious deed which was perpetrated on the moor. The view from this spot is extensive, and takes in a wide field of covenanting interest. The district on all sides was traversed by the feet of the worthies of the covenant, seeking hiding-places in the wilds, or gathering to the conventicles in the solitudes. But though the eye roams over a scene which in itself is cheerless and uninviting, there is nevertheless a moral interest in the landscape, when we attach to it the history of those who wandered, and suffered, and prayed in its deserts. Near this place are the green heights of Auchensauch (the field of willows), which in later times witnessed the renewal of those covenants for the maintenance of which our forefathers endured so much. The view from this elevation, on a fine summer day, when the sky is bright, is uncommonly fine, and of great extent.

The road by the " Black Gait" was the thoroughfare along which the dragoons used to pass in their raids between Douglas and Sanquhar. It happened, very early on a sum-mer morning, and long before the inhabitants of the moor-lands were awakened from their sleep, that a company of troopers passed this way on their march from the south to the Nether Fauldhouse—now the property of Mr James Thomson in Douglas. The Nether Fauldhouse is in the parish of Lesmahagow, and was, in the times of persecution, a kind of station or temporary garrison for the soldiers. From this place they issued forth in all directions to commit those deeds of rapine and cruelty in which they rioted. So notorious was the wickedness and profligacy of the troopers while they lay at this place, that it received the appellation of *Hell's Byke;* and by this name it is still known in the sur-rounding district. This circumstance is of itself sufficient to decide the character of those who were employed as the hireling agents of those unprincipled men who wielded the sword of persecution, and bathed it remorselessly in the best blood of the land. If this single station was a sort of pande-

monium, packed like a hive of hornets, and prepared to per-
petrate all manner of mischief, what must the larger garrisons
have been, where great numbers of men were convened and
permitted to act without moral restraint? These garrisons,
besides being sources of annoyance to the helpless peasantry,
must have been schools of crime, in which their inmates were
trained in all kinds of wickedness.

The cave in which James Gavin was lying in concealment
on the morning on which the troopers passed along the
"Black Gait," in their descent on Douglas, was near the
place at which they crossed Earnsallach burn. The noise of
the cavalcade, it would appear, had attracted the notice of
the little dog which Gavin kept as his companion in his
lonely hiding-place. This kindly animal, his faithful attendant, and his nightly guardian at the mouth of his cave, was
now to become the innocent cause of his detection, and the
means of a long train of afflictions to his master. The dog,
on hearing the sounds which escaped the ears of Gavin fast
asleep in the hole of the rock, ran in the direction whence
they proceeded, and, observing the soldiers advancing, barked
loudly and fiercely. The troopers halted, and fixed their
eyes on the little brisk assailant, to consider the matter for
a moment. "There is game in that glen," said the officer in
advance, "that same dog has a Whig not far from his tail."
The cautious and wily trooper, long exercised, no doubt, in
his vocation, had learned to read symptoms, and to draw forth
a meaning which would have escaped the sagacity of other
men; and he concluded from the circumstances, that some
wanderers were concealed in the ravine, and that the dog
had sprung from their side the moment the trampling of the
horses' feet caught his ear in the distance.

On this assumption, he commanded several of the men to
dismount, and to descend into the gulley, while the rest of
the troopers were stationed here and there at the different
points from which the persons in concealment might be expected to issue. The men on foot followed the dog as he
retired into the thicket, occasionally turning round and
barking at his pursuers. When they lost sight of him, they
were guided by the noise which he made, till at length they
approached the mouth of the little cave, where the kindly
animal had taken refuge by the side of his master, when he
licked his face and hands, as if to awake him from his sleep.
Gavin was soon raised from his slumbers, and made fully
sensible of his situation. The soldiers seized their victim,
and raised a shout of exultation, which announced to their

companions, who waited the result, the success of their mission. The helpless man, guarded by his captors, was brought from the recesses of the ravine, where he had spent many a lonely but happy hour, and stationed in the presence of the commander, who is said to have been Claverhouse. What were the feelings of our worthy now, when he was actually in the hands of those whom he so much dreaded, we cannot say. We are sure that he would not be forsaken in the hour of trial by Him in whom he trusted. The fear of trials at a distance is sometimes more oppressive than even the trials themselves when they have really come.

When he was brought before Claverhouse, who seems to have been more than ordinarily good-humoured that morning, the Cavalier, considering it to be an act of great clemency, said : " I will spare your life for the sport you have afforded us this morning;" and, pointing to a rough-looking dragoon, added with the same breath, " Crop off his ears with the *big shears.*" Gavin happened to have the implements of his trade along with him, and the trooper, at the bidding of his master, proceeded, as a matter of sport, to shear away the poor man's ears close by his head, till the warm blood came streaming into his neck and over his shoulders; and in this painful and pitiable plight he stood as an object of derision and merriment to the soldiers, who usually enjoyed as a high treat whatever was revolting to the feelings of ordinary men. The sufferings and indignity to which Gavin was at this time subjected he endured for conscience' sake; and his power of endurance was strengthened from the consideration that many of his brethren were suffering, with unshaken constancy, afflictions much more severe and trying. It is distressing to think on the savage cruelties inflicted by a brutal soldiery on the peasantry of Scotland, at a time when lawless power was rampant in the land, and when none durst reclaim but at the risk of their lives. Little did this honest man reck perhaps, when he retired to his covering in the evening, that he would be dragged from it in the early dawn, and used in the manner here described; but he was prepared by grace for whatever might befall him, and no trial, when it came, would be deemed strange.

When they had accomplished this deed of cruelty, the soldiers marched away with their bleeding victim to the place of their rendezvous. His fate after this was banishment, and he was transported, with others, to the Island of Barbadoes. In this exile he remained a living martyr to the principles of civil and religious liberty, till the Revolution broke his chains, and restored him to liberty, his country, and his family. His dwelling-house, which, during his banishment, had fallen into decay, was rebuilt by him, and stands in the village of Douglas till this day. It is a thatched tenement of a single story, and the emblems of the handicraft of honest James Gavin are to be seen carved on the stone above the door, with the date A.D. 1695. It cannot now be ascertained how long he lived after his return to his native place; but tradition affirms, that he enjoyed many years of peace and prosperity, and saw his children grow up around him. The descendants of this good man are numerous and respectable.

CHAPTER XVIII.

John Frazer of Carsphairn—Remarkable Deliverances.

THE wilds of Carsphairn, in the upper parts of Galloway, were, in the days of Prelatic persecution, the scene of much oppression and suffering. The labours of the good John Semple, minister of the parish, one of the holiest and most devoted men of his time, were uncommonly blessed for the conversion and edification of many souls. Under his ministry " the wilderness rejoiced and blossomed as the rose," and a race of men arose whose eminence in spiritual gifts and graces attracted general notice, and which made the worthy Mr Peden often say " that they had moyen at the court of heaven beyond many Christian professors of religion he knew."

The gatherings on sacramental occasions at Carsphairn were extraordinary; the people flocked from all parts of the surrounding country, and even from a great distance. At these seasons the Saviour was present, bearing testimony to the word of his own grace; and copious and sweet was the hallowed influence which came over many hearts. Mr Semple was minister in Carsphairn several years prior to the Restoration, at which period he was cast into prison, where he lay nine or ten months; and being afterwards dismissed by the council, he returned to his parish, where he continued, under the wing of the Indulgence, to preach the Gospel with great fervour and efficacy till the end of his life. After his death, which took place in 1677, in the seventy-second year of his age, no less than two garrisons were stationed in Carsphairn; by means of which, and the vengeful officiousness of Peter Pearson the curate, the Christian people, who were numerously scattered throughout the district, were greatly harassed and afflicted.

In the farm of the upper Holm of Dalquhairn, in the parish

of Carsphairn, lived John Frazer with his wife Marion Howatson.   John Frazer had for many precious years enjoyed the
ministry of Mr Semple; by means of which he had profited
much.   He was a man, it would appear, of eminent piety;
and this was enough to insure the hatred, and to bring upon
him the vengeance, of those whose oppressive measures were
chiefly directed against those whose worth rendered them in
any way conspicuous.

Canning, the laird of Muirdrogat, resided in the vicinity of
John Frazer, and, being an underling of the persecutors,
caused him no small trouble.   This Canning was originally
a Covenanter, but, having deserted his profession, he became
an infamous informer, and was made collector of the cess
and excise in Carsphairn.   He is mentioned by Wodrow in
the following words: "Robert Cannon of Mardrogat, who
once had a profession of zeal and seriousness, was singularly
useful to the soldiers in discovering the haunts and hiding-
places of the wanderers.   This man was at Pentland, but
was lately gained by the managers, and now turned profane
and wicked.   His lewdness, blasphemy, cursing, swearing,
cruelty, and dissimulation, were notour in that country; and,
as apostates generally are, he was very bloody.   He got
money at Edinburgh, and undertook to lead the soldiers to
Mr Richard Cameron."

When Canning and John Frazer were young men they
were very intimate, and sat in the same church, listening to
the sermons of their venerated pastor, Mr Semple.   Canning,
however, never displayed much seriousness, even in the days
of his greatest religious profession, so that, even during the
time of public worship, he caused his honest companion, John
Frazer, no small uneasiness, by means of his light and irre-
ligious manner.   While Frazer was hearkening with the
deepest attention to the blessed truths of the Gospel, Canning
was making signs to him, and using various means to withdraw his mind from the solemn subjects on which the man
of God dwelt with a holy earnestness and pathos, when he
urged on the immediate acceptance of his audience the great
salvation.   Everything tended to show that Canning's religion amounted to a mere formality, and that he had never
felt the transforming power of the Gospel on his heart.   It
was not so with his neighbour; he saw the truth, and felt its
power, and became a decided follower of the Saviour, and as
such exposed himself to no small degree of persecution.

John Frazer now found that Canning, his former acquaintance, was become his enemy, and that he sought on all occa-

sions to circumvent him. Woodrow, alluding to the general circumstances of Carsphairn and its vicinity at this time, says: " In the parish of Carsphairn, I find Inglis, with his men, persecuting violently in September. Parties were continually searching by night and day in that and the neighbouring parish of Dalry, for such who had been hearers of Mr Cameron. The soldiers were particularly set upon the finding out of *John Frazer* and John Clark, two pious, worthy countrymen, who, they alleged, had been very intimate with Mr Cameron. Frequently the soldiers missed them very narrowly; and those two, as well as many others, were trysted with very remarkable and providential deliverances from those who were hunting after their life."

John Frazer now found it necessary to be more especially upon his guard, and to withdraw occasionally from his home, when danger was apprehended. Muirdrogat, the informer, watched every opportunity to get him into his power, and uniformly sent the soldiers to his house when he thought there was any likelihood of his being at home. On every occasion, when any work was to be done on the farm which required Frazer's superintendence, the dragoons were sure to make their appearance. At one time, when he was directing the operations of his servants, who were employed in some work which needed his oversight, a company of horsemen was seen approaching. Frazer saw it would be in vain to betake himself to the fields, as in that case discovery and pursuit would be unavoidable; and, being at a loss what to do, he sought a place of concealment in the interior of the house. He had little expectation of securing himself from observation, and, therefore, in his perplexity, ran into a small closet, and crept into a bed which formed a part of its homely furniture. In order to prevent, as far as possible, the mischief which was thought likely to ensue, one of the domestics, with all celerity, heaped a quantity of wet turfs on the grate, which, as was common in those times, stood exactly in the middle of the kitchen, or chief apartment of the ancient farm-houses in Scotland. The powerful heat below quickly disengaged the moisture with which the new load of fuel was saturated, and filled the place with a dense blue smoke, which rolled its lazy volumes from the floor to the roof, and from the gable to the door, in cloudy masses, so impenetrable to the sight, that one human being could scarcely discern the face of another. The soldiers entered, but the murky atmosphere of the chamber prevented their seeing what was within. In the meantime, the master of the house, who had retreated into the adjoining closet, into which the smoke had also found its way, was enveloped in the bed-clothes, and lay in trembling anxiety awaiting the result. In the search, one of the soldiers entered the ante-chamber, and found Frazer in the concealment of the bed. The soldier supposed that he stumbled on the object in quest of whom they had come, and, in order to make the matter sure, he applied what he imagined would be a test of his character, and requested him to sing a certain song which he named—probably one of the profane songs which were common among the troopers. To this Frazer objected, and, instead of complying with the dragoon's request, he began to chant, in a low and solemn tone, an old and forgotten hymn, which commenced with the following lines:—

> " For all the babes in Bethlehem town
> King Herod sent and slew."

The dragoon interrupted him, and at the same time remarked, that he would certainly bring himself to an untimely end, if he persisted in his nonconformist practices. From whatever motive, however, it might proceed, the soldier did not injure him, nor did he inform the party of the discovery he had made; and while the uproarious troopers were searching all the places about the dwelling-house and out-buildings, Frazer remained safe in his concealment. The worthy man whom God had thus shielded, even in the presence of his enemies, watched his opportunity, and, leaving the house with all expedition, betook himself to the moorlands, with his shepherd's plaid thrown across his shoulders, and his dog trudging by his side.

At another time he experienced a deliverance equally providential. His restless enemies, bent on his destruction, having watched an opportunity, sent a company of dragoons to his house, with strict injunctions to seize his person. Accordingly, having set out at a convenient time, the troopers arrived at the upper Holm of Dalquhairn at an hour when they thought themselves secure of their object. The approach of the soldiers, it would appear, was not observed by any individual belonging to the household, so that the dwelling was invested before the inmates were aware of the circumstance. In order to secure their prey, the soldiers placed themselves at every door and window, so that none could possibly escape without their notice. It happened at the time that John Frazer was within, and his escape seemed to be impracticable. Finding it in vain to attempt to dart out at the door, he ran to a small window at the back part of the house, and sought to escape through it. At this window, however, a dragoon was stationed, and, when Fraser thrust his head and shoulders through the little opening, he was immediately confronted by the soldier, who happened to be alone on the spot. " So ho ! you are there, friend, are you ?— the very man, on the word of an honourable Cavalier," muttered the dragoon, as John dragged himself from the aperture, and stood before the burly sentinel. " I am in your power," said the worthy man. " Yes," replied the trooper, " but I feel, somehow or other, as if I were not inclined at present to use that power; nobody is witness to this interview—run to that covert, and hide yourself; do not flee to the hill, for your flight may perchance be seen; and though you were as light of foot as a roe, our fleet horses will outrun you." The covert to which the humane soldier pointed, was a dense willow bush, which grew on the margin of the burn, at the back of the dwelling-house, whose pliant and drooping branches, bending over the stream, kissed the bosom of its limpit waters as they were bidding adieu to the upland solitudes, and hastening away to accompany the kindred rills that were pursuing their course to the distant ocean. In this retreat among the willows by the gurgling brook, John kept himself till the search was ended and the party had withdrawn from the place ; the God in whose cause he was enduring hardships, having again disposed one of his enemies to show him favour at a moment when his safety was despaired of.

A good man who observes and acknowledges the hand of God in everything, decerns many a providential interference in his behalf, which greatly strengthens his faith, and affords many a theme of sweet musing on the gracious care and love of Him whose tender mercies are over all his works. Few men similarly situated had greater reason to exercise thankfulness for repeated deliverances in perilous circumstances, than John Frazer. The following incident is illustrative of this. Toward the close of a dreary winter day, he left his concealment in the cold and lonely moors, and plodded his way to his friendly home, to enjoy the genial heat of the blazing hearth, and the equally necessary refreshment of food. As the household lived in the constant fear of a visit from their marauding foes, who came as it best suited them, either by night or by day, it was judged prudent that John should sleep during the night in the barn. The reason for this precaution was, that the troopers on their arrival generally searched the dwelling-house before they proceeded to the office-houses. Accordingly, when the family retired to rest, the honest man, who was now like a stranger in his own dwelling, betook himself to the barn, where, among the dry straw piled around, a comfortable bed was prepared, furnished with abundance of soft and woolly blankets, of which there is generally a plentiful store in the houses of the moorland farmers. On this friendly couch John Frazer enjoyed for a few hours a sweet and refreshing sleep. About the middle of the night, however, the quietude of the cottage was interrupted, not by the " cock's shrill clarion," but by the arrival of the dragoons, who chose this season the better to secure their object.

It was agreed among the troopers that three of their number should station themselves at different places at a short distance from the house, in case that he after whom they had come should escape to the fields, while the rest should proceed to the domicile, and commence an unsparing search.

It happened that the ground was covered with snow, so that, when the cavalry approached, their arrival was not indicated by the usual noise of the horses' feet on the pavement. The first place they entered was the stable, where they sought provender and shelter for their horses. It was customary in many parts of Scotland for the male servants to sleep in the stable in the *loft* immediately above the stalls of their horses, where they found a dormitory more than commonly warm and comfortable during the long and cold winter nights. When the troopers had arranged matters according to their mind in the stable below, their next work was to awaken the young man who slept in the apartment above, on a bed which bestrode the joists, across which a few rude boards were placed to render the footing less dangerous. The youth, however, being in a profound sleep, did not answer at the repeated and loud calls of the men, and from his silence they drew the conclusion that there was a number of Covenanters concealed about the place, as on all former occasions he had answered at their first call. On this assumption, one of the party ran to call in the three troopers who were stationed at their different posts around the house, to assist in securing the persons who, they imagined, were concealed in the dark corners of the stable. By means of the noise and confusion made in the adjoining stable, John Frazer awoke, and, hastily drawing on a part of his clothes, saw from the barn door which he warily opened, a dragoon riding round to the stable. The true position of matters became instantly apparent, and, without further consideration, he fled from the place by a back door, and ran half-apparelled and barefooted through the deep and sinking snow, at his utmost speed, to the distance of no less than three miles, till he reached the house of a friend, where he obtained a shelter for the night.

When the soldiers had examined the stable, without finding what they expected, they proceeded to the dwelling-house, and, being equally unsuccessful there, they entered the barn. Having searched the various places which were calculated to afford concealment, they at last stumbled on the bed which, but a few minutes before, contained the person they were so anxiously seeking. Their chagrin and disappointment knew no bounds when they ascertained beyond a doubt that John Frazer, part of whose body clothes, which in the hurry of escape he had forgotten to put on, was lying on the bed from which he had so lately risen, had actually been in the place, and near them, but was now beyond their reach. They now saw the mistake they had committed in making so much noise in the stable, and in calling in the sentinels, who, if they had been allowed to remain on their stations, might have intercepted him in his flight; but Providence had planned his escape, and confounded the devices of his enemies.

In default, however, of the man whom they sought, the troopers seized on everything they found in the house. What they could not carry away, they destroyed on the spot, and departed determined to execute their schemes with greater caution the next time they had occasion to return.

At another critical moment John Frazer owed his deliverance to the following simple circumstances. In the landward parts of Scotland, more especially in former times, the farmhouses were the principal places of resort to the wandering poor, who sought from the hospitable inhabitants a morsel of bread and a night's lodging. This boon was scarcely ever denied, particularly by the people of the moorland districts, who considered it not only humane, but also an essential part of their religion, to befriend the needy. Owing to the considerable number of mendicants who sometimes met at the same place, seeking *quarters*, as they termed it, or a shelter for the night, there was generally a corner in the barn appropriated for their reception during the night, well furnished with soft hay and warm blankets. To this retreat they withdrew at a certain hour, after family worship, and after having been regaled with a good supper. But besides the barn, there was also, in some houses, a small untenanted apartment, frequently employed in the same way, and in which stood what was called " the poor man's bed," and which was seldom without an occupant.

One night when John Frazer had ventured to pay a visit to his home, at a time when he imagined there was but little risk in doing so, a company of soldiers, at the dead of night, rode hastily into the close or area before the door, with a view of surprising the family at an unusual hour. The house was instantly, like a beleaguered city, surrounded by the troopers, who were determined that on this occasion he should not escape

their hands. Frazer being fully alive to the danger of his
situation, abandoned all hopes of escape, and was prepared to
resign himself to the will of Providence, and to meet death in
the cause of his Redeemer with constancy and faith. Escape
was impossible, and to seek for concealment within appeared
hopeless. His wife, who was a pious and prudent woman, and
being greatly concerned about her husband's safety, was nearly
at her wit's end. In the moment of solicitude and peril, and
when there was no time to deliberate, she pointed to "the poor
man's bed," and urged him to run to it without delay. He did
so, and his wife following, covered him hastily with tattered
clothes, and an old rug. In this retreat he lay as if he had been
a mendicant, who had been admitted to a night's repose on the
lowly couch. The dragoons entered, and accomplished their
usual search without finding him. The soldiers having searched
the house so often, were acquainted with every part of it, and
knew "the poor man's bed," and the kind of people who occupied it. They saw, on looking into the apartment, an individual
in the bed; but it never once occurred to them that that individual was the man they were seeking, and they turned away
without disturbing the poor man in his resting-place. Providence in this way shielded this worthy man, his enemies supposing him to be one of those needy persons whom his charitable
hand had often relieved; and he was now, as the reward of his
benevolence, saved, under the impression that himself was one
of them.

After this, John Frazer was almost a constant exile from
his house, and remained for the most part in the moors and
remote solitudes in company with those who were subjected
to similar harassings. His heart, however, was in his home;
and the strong affection which he cherished for his family
often prompted him to visit those in whom he was so deeply
interested. One evening he left his retreat in the wilds,
and came to his house about midnight, and, having roused
the inmates from their slumbers, obtained admittance. In
the bosom of his happy family he forgot his sufferings and
his danger, and remained with them till the dawn. When
the day was fully ushered in, and the glorious sun had poured
on hill and moor a flood of splendour, gladdening the wilderness and its lonely tenants, Marion Howatson, anxious to enjoy the company of her husband another day, having looked
out afar on the waste, and seeing no appearance of the enemy,
prevailed with him to remain, in the fond hope that no harm
would befall him. The husband and the father complied with
the wishes of his family, and rejoiced in the prospect of a more
lengthened stay than he had anticipated. The day advanced,
and the sun had risen to his meridian height; nothing seemed

likely to interrupt the tranquillity of the family in the Holm of Dalquhairn, and John hoped that in the dusk of the evening he would be able to retire unperceived, and to withdraw in safety to his retreat in the desert.

But as the serenity of a morning which promises a bright and tranquil day sometimes proves deceitful, so the expectations of John Frazer and his wife ended in disappointment. Whether the troopers had received information from some wily spy, or had merely set out at a peradventure of their own accord, it is of little consequence to ascertain; but so it happened, that they arrived at the upper Holm of Dalquhairn as the family were comfortably seated round the dinner-table. Their arrival was sudden and unnoticed by any person, till they had actually surrounded the house.

John Frazer had hitherto succeeded in making his escape, but on this occasion it was otherwise. The troopers entered the house, and seized him where he sat. They bound him firmly with ropes, tying his arms behind his back. They next carried him to the stable, and cast him into one of the stalls, where they left him, and locked the door behind them. Having thus secured their prey, they proceeded to the dwelling-house, where they entertained themselves with a plentiful meal at the expense of him whose person they had so iniquitously imprisoned. It was a hilarious occasion to the troopers, who had at last succeeded in their object, and they regaled themselves with what liquors they found in the house, and continued carousing and boasting of their success till they exhibited no unequivocal symptoms of intoxication.

During the time of their rude and profane festivities, the worthy man, who was bound in the stable like a victim for the slaughter, was musing on the event which had befallen him, and on its probable consequences. His prayer was to the God of his life, who had hitherto delivered him, and who was able to deliver him still.

As the troopers remained long quaffing the stout brown ale, with which in those times the houses of the Scottish tenantry were plentifully supplied from their own malt, Frazer crept into a dark part of the stable, and rearing himself bolt upright, crushed himself into a corner, waiting till he should be dragged forth by his merciless foes. At length the soldiers rose from the festive board, and prepared to depart. They entered the stable reeling and staggering among the horses, and scarcely knowing what they were about. Having led their steeds into the open air, every one being occupied with his own concerns, and oblivious of all things else, they mounted and rode off in a noisy and disorderly manner, leaving behind, by a marvellous oversight, the prize which they chiefly valued. When the party had fairly left the place, and were seen scouring along the bent, Marion ran to the stable, and found her husband standing safe in the corner; and congratulating him on the wonderful deliverance, she instantly cut the cords that bound his hands and set him free.   Their gratitude to the Preserver of their life may easily be conceived, when they saw the prey taken from the mighty at the very moment when it was about to be devoured.

This worthy couple, however, suspected that the danger was not over; they knew that the troopers, whenever they should observe their mistake, would return armed with all the fury of disappointment, and that, being in a state of intoxication, they would wreak their vengeance on them without mercy.   Accordingly, John prepared for instant flight, and Marion, knowing that they would as little spare her as her husband, resolved for her own personal safety to accompany him, leaving the children, in the meantime, to the care of a servant.   Without losing time, therefore, they proceeded to the fields to seek, for a season, a hiding-place till the fury of their enemies had abated.

It was not long after they retired till the dragoons, as was anticipated, returned.   They had missed their prisoner when they were well advanced on their way, and, with blank astonishment at the circumstance, they turned and hastened back with winged speed to recover the prize.   When they arrived at the place, they found that Frazer had fled, and his wife along with him.   Their rage was excessive; and, knowing that it was in vain to search for the fugitives in the pathless deserts, they proceeded to work all the mischief they could within the dwelling-house, and having satisfied their revenge, as far as was practicable, they returned as they came.

The houseless pair now wandered on the hills in the vicinity of their home, and frequently visited their household in the absence of the enemy.   The mother's heart yearned over the helpless children, who were now bereaved of her affectionate care, and often did she steal them a visit at the imminent risk of her life.   A family can seldom be placed in a more painful situation than where parents and children are thus severed by the pitiless hand of persecution.   The mourning of the tender-hearted mother sitting in the lonely desert, and the wailings of the helpless children by the hearth, bespeak the endurance of affliction, under which human nature is ready to sink.

It was not long after this occurrence, however, till the welcome news of the Revolution sounded, like the silver trumpet of a hallowed jubilee, through the breadth and length of a wasted land.   The happy tidings that the arm of the oppressor was broken, and that the children of tribulation were now to walk forth out of the furnace, reached the dreary caves in the wilderness and the lowly cottages in the glens, and the gloomy prisons in the crowded city; and all hearts bounded with joyousness, and gratitude for a deliverance so signal and so opportune was expressed in loud acclamations of praise to Him who works deliverances in Jacob.

John Frazer and Marion Howatson returned from their wanderings, to seek, without the fear of further interruption from the enemy, a resting-place in their own house.   Great was the satisfaction expressed by the artless children when they understood that their father and mother were now to abide with them. Still their weeping, it is said, was at times excessive, when the painful suspicion obtruded itself that their parents might yet be obliged to flee from their home, and leave them as before.   So great was the occasional distress of the poor children on this point that the heart of their affectionate mother was often wrung with anguish at their unfeigned affliction, and it was with great difficulty that she succeeded in allaying their apprehensions, and in soothing their sorrows.

How long the worthy persons survived the days of their tribulation is not said.   There are, however, at present living one great-grandchild, and two great-great-grandchildren of these sufferers, and they fondly cherish the memory of their godly ancestors.

CHAPTER XIX.

Alexander Williamson—Gathering at Carsphairn—Incident.

THE Yochan is a beautiful stream which discharges itself into the River Nith, on the south side, exactly opposite the town of Sanquhar. Its banks are skirted with wood, close to the water's edge, presenting, on a small scale, a specimen of the extensive forests which, in remote ages, covered the greater part of the country. The bed of this river, composed for the most part of blue whinstone, is worn smooth and deep by the constant action of the current. The different stages of the river's progress, in its gradual sinking to its present level, are distinctly marked by the most unequivocal indica-tions on both sides of its course ; and the geologist, who seeks to extort from nature the knowledge of facts which no his-tory has recorded, may here find sufficient entertainment, and subjects enow of curious investigation, for many a long sum-mer's day. The stream, along the entire line of its track, which is only about eight or nine miles, is adorned with scenery charmingly picturesque, the beauties of which are seldom disclosed to any save the anglers and the shepherds, who are almost the only persons that visit its solitary banks. Its seclusion, its close retreats, and its woody coverts, ren-dered it an eligible place of resort to the persecuted remnant who sought safety in retiring as far as possible from the dwellings of men. The Yochan, near its source, where the deep and rugged glen through which it pours its waters rises toward the hills and the wilder parts of the district, was more especially frequented by the worthies of the covenant. It formed a kind of central meeting-place for the refugees of

Ayrshire, Nithsdale, and Galloway. From the green and sheltered spots on the high ridges of the mountains where they lay concealed, they could easily, without being discovered, discern at a great distance on all sides, if anything of a hostile nature was in motion. Glen-Harra Rig is particularly mentioned as being a place of this description — a beautiful green plot, far up the valley, from which an extensive view is obtained, and where the wanderers often assembled for social intercourse and the worship of God. It was in such places that, without restraint or fear of discovery, they could raise on high the loud voice of praise, the heavenly melody of which, coming from hearts alive to God, and wafted along on the gentle breeze, fell on the ears of the shepherds by the distant cairn, revealing to them a secret which, rather than disclose, they would submit to lose their lives.

There lived, in times of persecution, in a place called Cruffell, near the source of the Yochan, a man of the name of Alexander Williamson. This man was a Covenanter, and one who feared God with all his house. His principles forbade him to attend the ministrations of the curate; and this exposed him to the fierce displeasure of those who laboured to bring the entire community to one uniform mode of religious worship. Williamson associated chiefly with those who were of kindred sentiments with himself on ecclesiastical matters, and consorted with the pious men who occasionally withdrew to the upland wilds from the face of those who thirsted for their blood. His place of residence soon became noted among the wanderers, who uniformly courted the remotest retreats; and many a friendless but patient sufferer in the cause of truth and godliness, found a cordial welcome at his hearth, and a meal at his board, and a nightly shelter under his roof; and he was approved in his deed, and the blessing of him that was ready to perish came upon him. What a privilege is it to be made serviceable to Christ's people, and what an honour to be helpful with our sympathies and beneficence to those who are suffering for his sake! If, when his people are suffering in his cause, the Head complains from heaven: "Saul, Saul, why persecutest thou *me!*" may we not suppose that, when these sufferings are alleviated by the soothing hand of kindness, Christ is gratified, and looks down from heaven with an approving smile on those who have done this for *his* sake? It has been observed, that as those who have oppressed God's heritage have, in many instances, been scattered abroad, and their houses left desolate; so those who have befriended his cause, and maintained, in the face of scorn

and persecution, their adherence to the truth, have been preserved, and their offspring, for many generations, honoured
among men. The descendants of many of the worthies are to
this day known in the land; and so is the posterity of Alexander
Williamson.

In the family of our worthy there was an infant child that
had not yet been devoted to the Lord in baptism; and the
administration of this ordinance was greatly desiderated by
the pious head of the household. The sealing ordinances, as
they are called, were, in those days of the Church's tribulation, rarely enjoyed; and it was only at field-preachings, or
on the occasion of the casual visit of a banished minister, that
the sacrament of baptism could be observed. Cruffell, as
Williamson was familiarly denominated from the name of his
residence, had heard that there was to be a great gathering
in the wilds of Carsphairn, in which parish the godly John
Semple ministered with amazing success for many a year.
The news of this conventicle, to be held on an early day, spread
with rapidity far and wide; and a vast congregation from all
parts was anticipated. The distance between Cruffell and the
proposed place of meeting was not so great but that the
journey might, with considerable ease, be performed on the
Sabbath morning. It was agreed between Williamson and his
wife that the infant should be carried to Carsphairn for
baptism, while she should remain at home with the rest of
the children, who were too young to travel so far. Accordingly the appointed period arrived. It was a fine morning,
when the days were at the longest, and moss and moor were
dry as dust, and every track and footpath in the best trim for
pedestrians. Having suitably arrayed the child, and committed
him to a worthy female acquaintance, who, on this occasion,
was to act the part of a mother, the company departed, and
descended the rugged hills in the direction of the Water
of Ken, not far from its source. They were well acquainted
with every glen and moss, and hillock and brook, in the wild
uplands—

> " Where rivers, there but brooks,
> Dispart to different seas ; "

and they could track their way with perfect precision, where
others would lose themselves and wander in perpetual bewilderment. They entered on the beautiful pastoral valley of the
Ken, whose pellucid stream is fed by many a rill and tributary
from the bordering hills, having the magnificent Cairnsmuir
on their right, whose bold and apparently perpendicular front
rises to an enormous height, taking the precedency of all the

congregated mountains in the midst of which he stands. There are few tracks in the south-west of Scotland to perambulate which, on a bright summer's day, would more richly repay the true lover of scenery and the picturesque, than the upper strath of the Ken. Our little band passed along this sweetly sequestered vale in the stillness of the early Sabbath's morn, remembering the sanctity of the day, meditating on the grace of Him whose resurrection it commemorates, conversing on the absorbing matters of the Gospel salvation, and occasionally adverting to the trying times in which they lived, when the public ordinances of religion were observed by them at the risk of their lives. As they went on, and approached nearer and nearer the place of meeting, companies, dressed in their best apparel, were seen issuing from the narrow glens, and descending the steep hills on all sides, and mingling themselves with the living streams that were pouring along the more frequented roads that cross and recross, intersecting the country in every direction. The solitudes of Carsphairn had been fixed on for the meeting, because they were supposed to occupy the most central position for assembling the inhabitants of the higher parts of Galloway, Ayrshire, and Nithsdale; and probably also because that district was not at the time so much infested by the troopers. The hills in the neighbourhood of this place present a harsh and melancholy aspect; and so perfectly dreary in some parts is the scene as to produce an unusual depression of spirits in the spectator. The wilderness of Arabia Petræa, in which the Israelites wandered for the space of forty years, can hardly furnish anything in appearance more dismal than is to be witnessed in certain points of this locality.

When the people had convened, gathered from all parts of the west, like a great flock of sheep which the shepherd has collected to some grassy spot in the wilderness that they may repose for a while in good pasture, the worship of God commenced. The preacher stood on a temporary elevation, that he might be easily discernible from every corner of the field on which the company had spread themselves. Warders were stationed on the distant heights, and watchmen at the more common thoroughfares, and at the narrow outlets of the hills, all ready to give the preconcerted signal in case of danger. With these precautions, and reposing more especially on the guardianship of a gracious Providence, the assembly, with a feeling of confidence and security scarcely conceivable by us, raised, in the retreat of the desert, with one heart and one voice, " the loud acclaim of praise."

Those who have witnessed the field or tent-preachings on
sacramental occasions, which till the other year were common
in the higher localities of Ayrshire and Nithsdale, and which,
in one or two instances, are still in use, know well the effect
which the voice of a great multitude, singing in the open
air the high praises of our God, has on the mind. The effect
is deeply solemnizing. There is something awful, and yet
something delightfully soothing, like the swell and the cadence
of a full-toned trumpet heard from afar. And the effect is
greatly heightened when the worshipper fixes his eyes on the
roof and on the walls of that spacious temple in the midst
of which he stands—a temple built by God himself, and per-
fected with the garniture of his own hands. How poor is the
most elaborate and gorgeous structure reared by human skill
compared with this! Here the Divinity is plainly to be seen
in his own workmanship, and the spirit of devotion is both
enkindled and fed from the contemplation of the magnificent
operations of Him " who is wonderful in counsel and excellent
in working."

After the preliminary services of praise and supplication,
the minister proceeded to address the large assemblage that
had gathered round him. The minds of the people were
wound up to the highest pitch of attention and expectancy,
when the man of God rose up to speak to them on the solemn subjects of the Christian faith. The earnestness and
unction of his manner, together with a consideration of the
circumstances in which they were placed, produced a deep
impression on every heart. The preacher descanted at
considerable length on the character of the times, dwelling with particular emphasis on the suffering state of the
Church of God in the land — the bush burning, but not
consumed — the precious metal smelted down in the furnace, but not wasted away. It was not to be wondered
at, that, in those long-continued days of oppression, when
men's hearts were ready to fail them, the preachers of the
period should give vent to an imbittered eloquence in de-
picting their wrongs, especially when they thought on the
precious blood that had been so wantonly and profusely shed
on scaffolds and on fields—the blood of the best and bravest
hearts that the land could boast of. It was no wonder, nor
was it wrong, that a prominency should be given to these
considerations. But then there was a danger, in some cases,
of substituting this theme for the Gospel, or, at least, of leaving less room for the message of salvation. On the present
occasion, however, the servant of Christ, whose name tradition has not whispered, though he forgot not the engrossing

topic of the Church's affliction, failed not to announce "the glorious Gospel of the blessed God." He knew that this was the grand instrument of salvation—the blessed means, in the hand of the Holy Spirit, of bringing the soul into union with Jesus Christ, and of reconciling the heart to God; and therefore, with all faithfulness and fervency, as one who himself had experienced the power of the truth, did he urge on the crowds who were listening to his words the belief and acceptance of the doctrine of Christ. How sweet must it have been to hear in the lonely wilderness the beseeching voice of heavenly mercy inviting and encouraging sinners to come without delay or qualification to the common Saviour! Many a time of refreshing from the presence of the Lord, which no pen has recorded and no tradition has preserved, must have been experienced by God's people, when for his sake they retreated to the wilderness to keep pure and entire that mode of worshipping him which in their conscience they believed to be agreeable to his Word. A parting word of exhortation to stedfastness in the profession of the Gospel, and of encouragement to the faint-hearted in that dark and evil time, would doubtless be imparted by the messenger of Him who said to his ancient Church in affliction: " Be thou faithful unto death, and I will give thee a crown of life."

When the discourse was closed, the parents who had children to present for baptism stood forward in a row, each having his little babe in his arms. During the time that the ordinance was being administered, the audience silently prayed for the descent of the promised blessing on the parents and their offspring; and the servant of God, in an audible voice, besought the gracious influences of the Holy Spirit, the shedding down of which was symbolized by the pouring of water upon the body, and prayed that the children of every household that feared the Lord might be trained up to occupy the place of their fathers, and to fill the room of those who, through the violence of persecution, had been taken away from the earth. At length the services were concluded, and the parting benediction was pronounced. Still the multitude seemed loath to part—to quit, it might be for ever, that place which had been a Bethel to many, and they knew not where they would meet next; for the Word of the Lord was scarce in those days, and the heavenly manna which was gathered in the wilderness was gathered at the peril of their lives. The multitude at last broke up and separated, having taken many an affectionate farewell, and many a lingering look of him whom God had sent to them with the refreshing words of eternal life. It was a beautiful sight to see so great a crowd dispersing themselves in all directions, and repairing to their several homes; some toiling up the mountainous ascent in lengthened rows of single files, tracing the narrow footpaths formed by the sheep on the brow of the hills, others pursuing their course along the deep windings of the glens, and others traversing the broken surface of the dark and heather-tufted moss, and all departing in peace, no enemy having been allowed to come near them, God having blessed them with inward peace and outward tranquillity, "making them to lie down in green pastures, and leading them beside the still waters." The pious men who "led the flocks" of God "to the back side of the desert," denied themselves every comfort, and braved every danger for their sake; and they did not go without their reward.

> "At the risk of their lives with their flocks they would meet,
> In storm and in tempest, in rain and in sleet;
> Where the mist in the moor-glens lay darkest, 'twas there,
> In the thick cloud concealed, they assembled for prayer.

> "In cities the wells of salvation were sealed,
> More brightly to burst in the moor and the field;
> And the Spirit which fled from the dwellings of men,
> Like a manna-cloud rained round the camp in the glen."

In the residence of Alexander Williamson none were to be found on this Sabbath but his wife and the helpless children; for all had resorted to the conventicle at Carsphairn. It will not be out of keeping with the character of this pious household, to suppose that the worthy mother and her children were employed in a manner suitable to the sacredness of the day. It is not to be conceived that, as a woman professing godliness, she would be engaged in any other way than in reading the Holy Scriptures, and in endeavouring to impress the truth on the tender minds of her little ones, directing their thoughts to Jesus the Saviour, and praying with them for that heavenly influence which is necessary to regenerate and sanctify the soul, and in this way converting her solitary cottage into a church, where God's presence was enjoyed as well as in the midst of the public assembly. "And these words which I command thee this day shall be in thine heart, and thou shalt teach them diligently unto thy children; and shalt talk of them when thou sittest in thine house, and when thou walkest by the way, and when thou liest down, and when thou risest up." Mothers have much in their power in training their households either for good or for evil, and they are greatly responsible for the trust committed to them. What blessed effects would follow if mothers were to act a faithful part toward their children! "Train up a child in the way he should go, and when he is old he will not depart from it." If due instruction were imparted, and accompanied with fervent and believing prayer, the result would be truly gratifying. "In the morning sow thy seed, and in the evening withhold not thine hand; for thou knowest not whether shall prosper either this or that, or whether they both shall be alike good." If we use the means in faith, we may rest assured that the Lord will not restrain the blessing. "I will pour my Spirit upon thy seed, and my blessing upon thine offspring, and they shall spring up as among the grass, and as willows by the water courses; one shall say, I am the Lord's, and another shall call himself by the name of Jacob, and another shall subscribe with his hand unto the Lord, and surname himself by the name of Israel."

As this good woman was engaged in these religious exercises on God's holy rest, and not expecting that the quietude of her dwelling would be interrupted, all on a sudden she observed a party of horsemen coming up the glen. She guessed their purpose—she knew that they were in search of her husband. The cradle which had been occupied by the infant in the morning was standing empty on the floor, and it occurred to her that inquiry might be made respecting the absence of the babe, which might unhappily lead to the discovery of the errand on which her husband had gone. In haste she wrapped a bundle of clothes together, and, placing it in the cradle, threw over it a clean covering, and was rocking and humming a lullaby when the dragoons entered. "Where is your husband?" demanded the soldiers sternly. "He is not at home," replied she; "and I cannot tell where he may, at this moment, be." This answer did not satisfy the party, and they proceeded forthwith to examine every corner of the dwelling and out-houses. The search was minute. They investigated every place of supposable concealment. The beds within and underneath, the closets, the lofts, the peat-house, the stable, the barn, and the hay-stack —all were explored; but nothing could be found. When they saw that their exploration was in vain, they gave vent, as on all similar occasions, to profane and abusive language, and at last were obliged to depart without their object. There is one thing very obvious in this case—that the fear of Cruffell's wife must have been very great lest the troopers should happen to linger in idle sport about the place until the company returned from the meeting. It was no uncommon thing for the dragoons when they came to a house, especially in the more desert parts, to regale themselves plentifully at the expense of those to whom they paid their visit, consuming bread and meat and ale till they had gratified their appetite, and then destroyed the remainder. They scampered off, however, leaving the good woman and her children unharmed in the solitude of their mountain.

The heart of the mother and the wife swelled with grateful emotion, and on her knees she rendered thanks to the God of her life for the signal deliverance afforded. It is more especially in times of trial that the faith of the Lord's people is tested. It is easy to trust when danger is afar off; but when it comes near, and threatens to overwhelm us "in a moment suddenly," it tries our confidence to the uttermost. How sweet must it be to experience a deliverance as the consequence of faith, and to discern the hand of our heavenly Father stretched out for our defence because we trusted in him!

As the day began to close, the friends returned from the conventicle, and the sweet infant, now admitted as a member of the visible Church, was placed again on its mother's knee. The occurrences of the day were rehearsed, and Williamson was deeply impressed with the accident related by his wife. The sense of the danger which he had escaped on the one hand, and the spiritual benefit bestowed on himself and his friends on the other, bound him with a new tie of obligation to Him who is at once the guardian of the life and the saviour of the soul. The mercies which God secretly, and unobserved by us, works out for us, generally affect us more deeply. The kindness of God to Jacob in preserving, unknown to him, the life of Joseph, and in making him governor over all the land of Egypt, was perhaps regarded by the patriarch as a more truly disinterested display of divine care and goodness than any mercy of a merely temporal kind he had ever enjoyed. When the evening meal was served, the family assembled for the closing act of worship, on which occasion the grateful head of the family, with an increased confidence of faith, poured out his heart before the Lord, and rendered thanks for all that paternal care which had that day been experienced, and for all the rich communications of heavenly grace which had been conferred; then all retired to rest under the sheltering wings of Him who never slumbers nor sleeps.

We see from this incident that the way of duty is always the safest and the most comfortable. Had Williamson, on this Sabbath, remained at home, it is every way likely that

he would have lost his life, or been carried off a prisoner.
But he was found in God's way, and at the post of duty,
though that post was not without its danger, and God preserved both him and his household.   When the children of
Israel of old went up to the annual festivals at Jerusalem, it
was promised that no enemy should invade their dwellings
in their absence ; and, relying on this promise, they did what
God bade them, and they experienced the fulfilment of his
word.   Now, though we have no specific promise of this
kind, that the Lord will exercise a particular providence over
our households, when, at a distance from them, we are waiting on him in his ordinances, yet we have the general promise of the divine protection to keep us and ours in all our
ways when we trust in God: "Commit thy way unto the
Lord ; trust also in him, and he will bring it to pass."   There
is an anecdote told of two women who lived in the same
neighbourhood, but whose residence was at a considerable
distance from their usual place of worship.   As they were
sitting together one day in the church, one of them was
hastily called out, and the other being her neighbour followed her.   When she reached the door, it was announced to
her that one of her small children, whom she had left behind,
was burned to death by accident.   " It cannot be my child,"
replied the woman.   "Why may it not be your child?"
said her friend ; "does not the messenger from the very
place plainly declare that it is?"   "No matter," persisted
she, "it cannot be my child."   "It is foolish in you to speak
in that way; what ground have you for your assertion?"
"Well, then," answered she, "I will show you the ground
of my confidence in this case.   I committed my household
to the Lord before I left home, and besought him to keep
them from all harm when I was in the way of my duty—
worshipping in his house; and I had confidence in prayer
that he would grant what I requested.   I have done the
same for years past, and I have never yet found anything
wrong on my return, and I have as little reason to expect anything wrong to-day."   They reached their home, and what
was the fact?   It was the child of the other woman, her
companion, that had lost its life.   " In all thy ways acknowledge him, and he will direct thy paths."   Let us always do
our duty, and leave the event to God, and we shall find that
he will manage matters for us a thousand times better than
we could for ourselves.   Alexander Williamson, on the
Sabbath specified, went in the way of the Lord, and the Lord
blessed him in his going out and in his coming in.

Alexander Williamson died in 1709, and was buried in the churchyard of Sanquhar, where the rude *thrugh* stone still points out his resting-place. He was born in 1635, and lived throughout the whole of the troublous times. His wife, Marion Haining, reposes with him in the same grave.

It appears that this worthy had removed from Cruffell prior to his decease, and had taken up his residence at Burnfoot, where he died. The farm of Burnfoot is situated on the south side of the Nith, about a mile above the town of Sanquhar. The prospect from the farm-house is one of the most enchanting in the locality. On the north, the romantic scenery of the Crawick bursts with admirable effect on the view. The twin hills of Knockenhair and Carco, clad in velvet green, overlook the sweet vale beneath; while the bold front of Castle Robert height is seen in the background, peering over the intervening ridge, like a lion lifting his head from his lair, and peeping from his covert into the open space beyond. On the rising ground between, and on its very summit, grows a solitary tree, the last remnant of an ancient forest, whose form, painted on the soft blue sky, or on the curtains of the snowy mist, uniformly arrests the eye of the spectator, as it roams over the charming scene. To the east are to be seen the dark heights of Morton and Durisdeer frowning in the distance, while on the south the wooded slopes of Eliock ornament the skirts of the wilderness. The whole field of vision round and round presents a delightful aspect, and forms, on a large scale, one of those scenes in the survey of which the eye never tires. The site of Burnfoot, as a residence, was well selected by the ancient people, and it is now made still more eligible by the hand of the architect, and of the agriculturist.

CHAPTER XX.

Reeves of Cruffell—Kers of Scar—Hiding-places.

If we were left to form our estimate of the character of the persons to whom these sketches refer from the odium which their adversaries endeavoured to attach to their name, we would be ready to conclude that they were the vilest and most infamous of men, and that it was their crimes which exposed them to the severe treatment which they met with. Instead, however, of their being what their enemies alleged, they were in reality a class of the best and holiest men of whom the land could boast. The cause which they advocated, and in the support of which they suffered, was righteous. It was the cause of Christ; and it was to assert the prerogative of the Mediator as the sole Head of his own Church, to preserve the ordinances and institutions of grace in their simplicity, to exhibit the Gospel in its purity, and to transmit God's testimony, in its truth and evidence, to posterity. They suffered because their principles were too unyielding for the ecclesiastical despotism of the times, and because they would not compromise the truth, to gratify the caprice of a licentious monarch and a bigoted priesthood; and therefore they were stigmatized as wrong-headed zealots, who refused to yield obedience to the lawful powers. "But Wisdom is justified of her children." And though there are many, even now-a-days, who seem inclined to regard them as enthusiasts, whose religion consisted chiefly in wrangling about modes and forms, while essentials were misunderstood or overlooked, yet the veracious histories of the period in which they lived and suffered can attest how holily and unblamably they conducted themselves, "in the midst of a crooked and perverse generation." The religious doctrines which these men maintained are detailed in the Bible, and the perfect sincerity of their belief of these doctrines is evinced, not only by the purity of their lives, but also by the grievous sufferings which they voluntarily endured. The great proportion of these honoured men were persons in the humbler walks of life, and whose names, had it not been for the persecutions which they sustained, would never have been heard of.

> " They lived unknown,
> Till persecution dragged them into fame,
> And chased them up to heaven."

And now they are individuals whose names grace the annals of the Church of God in Scotland—who live embalmed in the memory of posterity, and who are had in remembrance before God. And let their memorial survive, and their ashes repose in peace, till the morning of that momentous day when He for whose name they were counted worthy to suffer reproach, and buffeting, and the spoiling of their goods, and death itself, shall publicly honour them as his faithful witnesses in a temporizing and a backsliding age. It is not they whom men honour, but they whom God honours, that are truly noble.

On one occasion, when Clavers and his men were scouring the west, they descended on the range of hills that stretch from Afton to the east. Reports had reached them that parties of the Covenanters were skulking among the hills, and they determined to search them out. No news were more gratifying to the Cavaliers of those days, than to hear of anything that might afford them employment in the way of their profession—in chasing and shooting those godly men who, for conscience' sake, had abandoned everything that was dear to them in this world. Nothing was too adventurous for the troopers, either on moss or on mountain, when once they were fairly engaged and warmed in the pursuit. And strange stories are told of these reckless and graceless men, in reference to their daring and hazardous feats. A number of the worthies, it would appear, had concealed themselves in a retreat near the source of the Afton; and Clavers, having been informed of the circumstance, marched with his troopers at his back to surprise them in their hiding-place. His approach, however, was observed; for in those days of peril men had a kind of presentiment of coming danger. They were constantly on the watch night and day, and rarely did anything of a suspicious nature escape their observation. Their senses of sight and hearing seemed to be sharpened and improved by incessant use, in circumstances in which their life depended on their vigorous exercise. Even in sleep they seemed to be watching, and at every interval in their broken slumbers they listened. They never felt themselves entirely secure, unless it were in the howling storm, or when the drifted snow had almost buried the lonely shieling that afforded them shelter.

In their raid the troopers had surprised at least one individual, whom they pursued across the mountains. The poor man fled for his life, and hasted over hill and hollow, straight in the direction of Cruffell. The horsemen were not able to follow him with the same speed as on even ground, for sometimes an impassable morass would all at once intercept their progress, when it was necessary to make a long sweep to the right, or to the left, to avoid it. At other times the deep rocky channel of the torrent forbade their advance, and again the abrupt face of an interposing mountain forced them to adopt a circuitous route. All these obstacles favoured the escape of the fugitive, who gained both breath and space, and was therefore enabled to preserve a safe distance in advance of his pursuers. In this way, he held on his successful flight till he passed what are called the *Reeres* of Cruffell. The reeves are folds erected by the shepherds, for the management of their sheep, at certain seasons of the year. It happened to be that season which, among shepherds, is called *clipping time*, when the fleece is carefully and neatly shorn from the back of the sheep. At this work of clipping there were no fewer than nine men busily employed within the folds of Cruffell, while a young lad was stationed at the opening for the purpose of assisting the shearers. At the moment when the poor man, who was fleeing for his life, passed the reeves, nobody observed him but the assistant shepherd at the door of the fold; for the others being seated in a bending posture, within the ring, could not so easily perceive what was passing without. In a short time the party in pursuit came up, and, approaching the reeves, asked the shepherds if they had seen the man of whom they were in quest. They declared they had not. This asseveration did not satisfy the stern and suspicious commander, and he proceeded to put them one by one to their oath. The men could honestly assert, and they could as honestly swear, in the presence of the great God, the Searcher of hearts, and the Judge of all the earth, that they had not seen the individual mentioned. But there was one who had seen him, and who could have put them on the track in which he had gone. It happened, however, that this one person was the only individual of the company of whom they took no notice, and to whom they put no questions; and he had no inclination to reveal gratuitously, a secret which neither bribery nor threatenings could otherwise have extorted. The party, therefore, having satisfied themselves that the man was not concealed about the folds, and that the shepherds knew nothing of him, yielded up the chase. We cannot sufficiently admire the many providential interferences in behalf of the Lord's people, in the day of their distress. Had the young man at the folds been interrogated, and forced to reveal what he had seen, there is every likelihood that the fugitive would have been overtaken, especially as his strength must have, by this time, been greatly exhausted.

In the meantime, the man pursued his way up the little glen through which runs the brook called Cruffell burn, and held his course for the valley of the Scar;—and so "the race is not to the swift, nor the battle to the strong," else this worthy man would have been overpowered. If David, on the day that the Lord delivered him from the hand of all his enemies, had occasion to say: " It is God that girdeth me with strength, and maketh my way perfect; he maketh my feet like *hinds'* feet, he setteth me upon my high places;" surely this same individual, who was chased like a roe on the mountains, but whose " feet and ankle bones received strength " to bear him away before the face of his pursuers, had as good reason to ascribe praise to God for the means of his deliverance. There is no doubt that the mouth of this pious man would be filled with grateful acknowledgments to God; while, on the other hand, the mouths of his persecutors would be full of bitter execrations.

It was within the vale of the Scar that this helpless wanderer found, for a season, a resting-place from the weariness of his flight, after a day of toil and solicitude. Tradition does not say at whose hearth he found a welcome, but the household that received him, admitted one who brought his blessing along with him. The romantic localities of the Scar were not unknown to the Covenanters, and its secluded glens were frequently occupied with the interdicted conventicle, even in the depth of winter, when the congregation sat contentedly on the cold snow, listening to the words of eternal life. These were times of peril and self-denial, when men followed Christ for his own sake. " If a man will come after me, let him take up his cross and follow me." The old people in the place had a tradition, that these devoted men, when they durst not meet in any house for social prayer—an exercise in which they greatly delighted—assembled in a hollow place at the foot of the Crag of Hallscar, where, without interruption, they could call on the name of the Lord, and, by mutual intercourse, strengthen one another's hands in the work of truth and righteousness. "They that feared the Lord spake often one to another; and the Lord hearkened, and heard it, and a book of remembrance was written before him for them that feared the Lord, and that thought upon his name. And they shall be mine, saith the Lord of hosts, in that day when I make up my jewels; and I will spare them, as a man spareth his own son that serveth him."—Mal. iii. 16, 17. When, therefore, our worthy descended into the valley for shelter, he came among friends, and met a people who espoused the cause in which he was suffering, and were, therefore, ready to afford him the succour which he needed.

The Scar was a place of refuge in the times of persecution to the two brothers of Ker of Kersland, a gentleman that suffered much in those trying days. He was a man of great worth and integrity, and submitted to imprisonment, and banishment, and the forfeiture of his property, that he might maintain a good conscience, and he at last died in a foreign land. The two brothers of Kersland, Archibald and Andrew, were embarked in the same cause with himself, and suffered accordingly. In seeking a place of retreat among the wilder parts of the south, they came into the secluded valley of the Scar, and there took up their abode. The place to which they first came was the Shiel, at that time a farm-house in the immediate neighbourhood of the stupendous rock called Glenquhargen Craig. Here they lived some years in the capacity of shepherds, not thinking themselves degraded in following any servile occupation to gain an honest livelihood. The circumstances in which they had been brought up were very different from this; yet they submitted with thankful hearts to the lot which Providence in the days of trial had assigned them. They were both young men, under twenty years of age, when they came to the south, under the pressure of the persecution to which they were exposed. Shortly after they came to the Shiel, their brother of Kersland spent a whole winter with them. This was after the burning of Glasgow jail, in which he happened to be confined at the time. "The well affected people of the town," says his biographer, "got long ladders, set the prisoners free, and Kersland among the rest, after he had been eight years in confinement. After the hurry was over, he inclined to surrender himself, but hearing from his lady of the archbishop's design against him, he retired and absconded during that winter." The winter alluded to was the one he lived with his brothers in the seclusion of Scar Water; the tradition respecting which circumstance is still fresh in the memory of their descendants. Conventicles were frequently kept in Scar Water, by means of the Kers, and other worthies who associated with them. The fugitives, then, who sought refuge in this retired valley, could not want friends who would gladly open their doors to receive them. The two Kers, by means of their good behaviour and industry, became persons of some consequence in the place of their retreat, and ultimately rose to great respectability. From being shepherds, they became farmers. Andrew rented the farm of Shiel, and Archibald that of Woodend, a few miles farther down the stream. This, however, must have been after the Revolution, as it is not likely that two men of their principles could, during the heat of the persecution, establish themselves as farmers in a district that was under so strict a supervision. Andrew died in the Shiel, it is supposed, about the year 1740, and his brother Archibald a good while prior to this date. When Andrew was buried in the churchyard of Penpont, the minister of the parish, who was present, said : " There lies the precious dust of one who was counted worthy to suffer for the cause of Christ." The descendants of the Kers are to be found in Sanquhar, Penpont, and Muirkirk.

It may not be without its interest, perhaps, to give here a brief description of some of the places in which the worthies secreted themselves. The dwelling-house of Glenglas, near the source of the Yochan, is said to have been partly constructed for the purpose of affording a hiding-place to the destitute Covenanters. At the one end it had a double gable, the one wall at the distance of a few feet from the other, leaving a considerable space between, extending the whole breadth of the building. This narrow apartment was without windows, unless it might be a small sky-light from the roof. The entrance to this asylum was not by a door, but by a small square aperture in the inner wall, called by the country people a *bole*. This opening was generally filled with the " big Ha' Bible," and other books commonly perused by the household. When instant danger was dreaded, or when it was known that the dragoons were *out*, this chamber was immediately resorted to by those who had reason to be apprehensive of their safety. The books in the *bole* were removed till the individual crept into the interior, and then they were carefully replaced, in such a way as to lead to no suspicion. Like the prophet's chamber in the wall, this place could admit "a bed, and a table, and a stool, and a candle-stick," and in the cold of winter it had a sufficiency of heat imparted to it by means of the large fire that blazed continually close by the inner wall.   In this situation, a person could easily have been secreted for days and weeks, had it been necessary, while his food was stealthily conveyed through the bole.   A more simple and perfect contrivance can scarcely be imagined, and one only wonders that it was not more frequently adopted where it was practicable.   In this way, the head of a family might have lived at home, in comparative security, even though closely watched by his enemies.

There is, in the midst of an extensive moor, about two miles to the west of Sanquhar, a romantic spot, called "Pamphy Linns," which is supposed to have been occasionally frequented in the troublous times of our witnessing ancestors.   It is a very striking scene; and so little indication is there of the existence of such a fairy nook, that no person in passing through the heathy tracts, in its close vicinity, could ever imagine that anything remarkable was to be met with.   And yet there is hidden below the general level of the mossy plain a spot of real enchantment; for some of the finest points of Scottish scenery, as a celebrated writer remarks, escape the eye of the passing traveller.   Two gurgling streamlets, that issue in crystal purity from the hills in the background, meet together, and, immediately above the point of their junction, they have worn their troubled channel to a great depth, and by the erosion of their waters have formed spacious cavities in the sandy rocks that rear themselves to a great height on each bank.   The semicircular bend of one of these cavities is, at its base, perhaps fifty or sixty feet; and the sweep of the arch, from the lowest part behind, along the roof of the cave to its opening above the stream, is in proportion; and to the eye of the spectator, crouching under the extreme part of the rocky recess, the rounded mouth of the cave, where it meets the sky, has the appearance of a majestic rainbow.   On the other part of the linn, where the torrent rushes down a craggy declivity of great height, the rocks are so fearfully excavated as to shoot far over head in a horizontal position, threatening an instantaneous fall, and apparently upheld by nothing but the hand of Omnipotence.   These gloomy excavations have been formed in ages long gone by, and in one place the rivulet seems to have been almost wholly arched over, forming an immense caldron of dark and deep waters, boiling and eddying in the profound beneath.   The superincumbent mass has

in some places, tumbled down, and is lying in scattered fragments, like the broken arches and colonnades of some magnificent temple. A place like this, even among the splendid
scenery of the mountains, could not pass without admiration;
but when it is met with in the heart of an uninteresting
moor, it is like an oasis in the desert. It does not appear,
however, that the Pamphy Linns—supposing them a resort of
the persecuted adherents of the covenant—were so much a
place of security from their enemies as of shelter from the
tempest. Every hole and crevice in the locality are dis-
coverable on the first inspection, so that no individual could
possibly effect a sufficient concealment; but then, as a place
of protection from the wind and the rain, to which these houseless wanderers were so often exposed, it would be eagerly
sought.

Among the curious hiding-places to which the worthies
resorted, the cave of Garrick Fell is not the least interesting. Garrick Fell is a hill in the parish of Closeburn in
Nithsdale, and lies to the east of the ancient parish of Durisdeer, famous for its Roman antiquities, and more famous still
as the scene of Christian martyrdom. The cave of Garrick
Fell was known to only a very few; and so complete is its
seclusion, that even now the shepherds who daily traverse
the locality in which it is situated, cannot discover its entrance. It is likely, however, that the rocks and loose stones
have of late fallen down, and closed the aperture, as a worthy
man, who died a few years ago, was well acquainted with it
in his younger days. It was in this cave, as tradition affirms,
that Peden occasionally concealed himself; and a story of
some interest is told of him connected with it. The house
of Gilchristland Shiel, in Closeburn, it appears, was frequently visited by this zealous and unwearied preacher.
Under its hospitable roof he many times rested and was refreshed, after his exhaustion and watchings among the mountains. The providence of that God who watches over all, and
especially over those who trust in him and do his work, furnished for his servants who, in those times of trial had left
all for his truth's sake, even in the remotest solitudes, a
friendly abode, in which the kindest treatment was experienced. These places of rest and entertainment, like the inns
which everywhere meet the wayfaring man, were more numerous than we are at first ready to imagine. Every glen, and
moor, and hill, and forest, had its hut, whose door was ever
open for the reception of those who were scattered abroad by
persecution. There is to be met with, in the pastoral dis-

tricts, a hospitality to which inhabitants of towns are in a great measure strangers. There is an honest kindness of heart unostentatiously displayed by the ruder occupants of the desert, which may well put to shame the more ceremonious politeness of the urbane part of the community. The hospitality of those days, however, was not simply that of a natural benevolence, or merely conventional custom—it was the hospitality of principle—it was beneficent treatment for Christ's sake; for they looked on the men who bespoke their sympathy as sufferers, especially in the cause of the Gospel.

Mr Peden, during his temporary residence at Gilchristland Shiel, was not idle; for as this pious household failed not to minister to him in temporal things, he did not fail to minister to them in spiritual things. To minister in the Gospel was his work and his delight, and for the truth's sake he endured the loss of all things, and subjected himself to hardships of every description. One day he was engaged in his spiritual vocation, expounding the Scriptures to the family, and probably to a few of the neighbours met with them. He enlarged on the precious truths of the Gospel, and his little audience were intent on the weighty matters presented to their notice, and were happy in listening to the joyful sound. They were assembled in a retreat where little danger was anticipated, and therefore, without much anxiety about their safety, they gave their minds entirely to the religious exercise in which they were employed. The apparent eagerness with which this little flock in the wilderness received the doctrine of Christ, filled the breast of the preacher with a heavenly satisfaction, and imparted a holier earnestness to his address. To the man whose great object is to win souls to Christ, nothing is more gladdening than to witness the truth taking effect on those to whom it is propounded. And in what blessed circumstances must that company of worshippers be, on whom the Spirit in his saving influences has descended, softening the heart, and uniting the soul to Christ, in a relation never to be dissolved!

As Mr Peden and his company were thus engaged, a sound like the wailing of an infant, and then like the soft bleating of a sheep, was heard not far from the house. Nobody took notice of it, nor was it necessary, as every one knew what it was. In a little the same sound was heard again, but in rather a stronger tone. No one stirred. At last the sound was heard, with startling violence, close at the door, and then louder still within the door, and so impatiently incessant, that the shepherd rose to drive away the

intruder that had come so unseasonably to disturb their
serious thoughts. It was a large sheep that, without any
apparent cause, sought, on a fine day, when the rest of the
flock were grazing tranquilly on the bent, shelter about the
door. The shepherd instantly turned it out to the heath,
and following it a short distance from the house, discovered,
to his surprise, a party of moss-troopers advancing in the
direction of his cottage. All within was consternation, and
the poor sheep, whose obtrusive bleatings were considered as
a special annoyance, was now regarded as a harbinger of
mercy, sent to warn them of their approaching danger.
Whatever cause may be assigned for the visit of the poor
animal on this occasion, it is obvious that Providence made
use of it as a means of rescue to the equally helpless sheep
of his fold, who were convened within. The Lord is never
at a loss for instruments when he has work to perform, or
deliverances to accomplish; "for all are his servants."

The meeting was instantly dispersed, and Mr Peden
hastened to the cave of Garrick Fell. The dragoons, disappointed in their object, returned without perpetrating any
act of violence, and the honest shepherd and his household
gave thanks to Him who had provided for them a feast of
good things in the wilderness, and who had not permitted the
enemy to mingle their blood with their sacrifice. Their
spiritual meal was sweet, and sweet also was the deliverance
vouchsafed. Meanwhile, the venerable servant of God
reached his cavern with safety, and there praised and honoured
Him who had added this one deliverance more to the many
formerly experienced. This cave, the roof of which was the
superincumbent mass of the mighty mountain, was capable
of accommodating with ease several persons at once. Its entrance, which was narrow, was concealed by a special provision of nature— a large bush of heather growing from the
turf on the upper part of the aperture, and spreading downwards like a thick veil, covered the upper half of the opening ; and the lower part was screened by a green bracken
bush, which, springing from the bottom, spread itself like a
feathery fan, till it met the pendent heather, and then the
two, like the folding-doors of an inner chamber, closed the
entrance in such a way that no individual in passing could
possibly recognise the existence of any such place, however
near he might approach it. What a slender barrier sometimes serves as a complete protection to those whom Providence would shield from harm ! Here the good man was
as safe in God's keeping as if he had been encompassed

by the impenetrable walls of the solid mountain; and his enemies might pass and repass full in his view, without the slightest suspicion on their part that he was actually within their reach. It is easy to conceive the state of mind with which Mr Peden must have looked through the heathery curtain which formed the door of his cell, on those who sought his life, as they marched in order immediately before his face, noticing their menacing aspect, hearing their angry words, and observing at leisure the deadly weapons which were prepared for his destruction. The feelings of a person in this situation must be somewhat akin to those of the man who, from his well-sheltered and comfortable chamber, contemplates the storm as it rages without. The cave of Garrick Fell might be cold and damp—still it was not cheerless, for God was there, and its occupant enjoyed both personal security and peace of mind. We need not be afraid of suffering for Christ's sake; for in proportion to our outward afflictions is our inward consolation : " As thy day is, so shall thy strength be." Some of those who outlived the long period of the Church's distress in Scotland, declared, in testimony of their Master's kindness to them in the days of their trial, that the happiest season of their life was the season of their persecution.

CHAPTER XXI.

THE village of New Cumnock is pleasantly situated on the banks of the Nith, a short way from its source, and about twelve miles to the west of Sanquhar. It stands at the head of a beautiful plain, through which the river pursues its serpentine course with many a graceful sweep, resembling, as has often been observed by travellers, the links of the Forth at Stirling, though on a much smaller scale. Each side of the stream below the village is walled in by a chain of mountains, extending many miles in an easterly direction. The range on the south side appears to be the eastern spur of the *Uxellum Montes* of Richard, which formed the line of demarcation between the ancient Novantes and the Damnii. The line of mountains on the north, commencing with the green-clad hill of Corsancone, is supposed to form the western extremity of Ettrick forest; and this supposition seems to receive countenance from the fact that the name Ettrick is occasionally to be met with in the chain—as Loch Ettrick, Ettrick Stane.

It appears that the district round New Cumnock was a field much frequented by our suffering ancestors. In their days it was in a much wilder state than it is now, and afforded in its woody coverts a comparatively safe retreat from their pursuers. The stream of the Afton issues from among the dusky mountains on the south, and mingles with the Nith near the village. The grandeur of its scenery is the boast of the people of the neighbourhood; and it was in its deep recesses, and among its rugged and inaccessible steeps, when the Church was driven to the wilderness, that many a faithful witness for God's truth, and for Christ's kingly supremacy, sought a refuge; and far from the dwellings of men, the hawk and the erne were their companions the cranberries gathered among the heather were occasionally their food, and the dark moss water their drink. "They wandered in the wilderness, in a solitary way; they found no city to dwell in; hungry and thirsty, their soul fainted in them; then they cried unto the Lord in their trouble, and he delivered them out of their distresses."

Lochbruin is situated on the east side of the Afton towards the mountains; and the hill in its immediate vicinity, bearing the same name, is, on the top, full of deep moss-hags, and presenting a most uninteresting appearance. To the south lies Cairnsmoor, a mountain of Alpine grandeur, at whose rocky base, in the farm of Knockengarroch, is a cave which in former times was resorted to by the wanderers, and where, on account of the difficulty of finding its entrance, they were lodged in almost complete security. In traversing the wilder parts of the country, and observing the many secret places that seem so entirely adapted to the purposes of concealment and refuge, one can scarcely help entertaining the idea that the great Author of nature, when he made the world, formed by anticipation these abodes of secrecy, that in after ages "the earth might help the woman," when, in times of persecution, she should be obliged to flee "into the wilderness, where she had a place prepared of God." And there is little reason to suppose, had it not been for those informers with whom the "camp of the saints" was infested, that ever their enemies would have discovered their retreats, especially in the more dreary and desolate localities. But the spirit of evil prompted them to the work of spoliation and death; and so accustomed were the dragoons to scour moss and hill, that it became to them an employment of great excitement, and they followed it with as keen a relish as ever sportsman followed his game. The pleasure, however, which they derived from this pastime was not without its abatements; for not a few of them occasionally lost their lives in various ways. Some plunged into the deep morass, in which man and horse sunk never to emerge; others were killed in falling down the rocky precipice; others were carried away by the roaring flood; while others, again, were shot by the oppressed party in self-defence.

Lochbruin was the residence of a devoted Covenanter of the name of Campbell, a good man, whose care was to live to God, and to follow Christ when his cause was tried. During the persecuting period a man's religion was tried to the uttermost, and his sincerity fairly put to the test by means of those afflictions to which he was subjected for the truth's

sake. A hypocrite had no inducement to connect himself
with a suffering remnant; because neither name nor profit
was to be reaped from the adoption of their profession. On
the contrary, scorn, and poverty, and death, were to be expected as the portion of all who identified themselves with
their cause. By the grace of Him whom they honoured,
however, these holy men were enabled to live above the
world, and to despise alike its favour and its frowns, for the
sake of Him whose credit and whose interests lay nearer
their hearts than all earthly considerations together. The
love of Christ constrained them, so that they counted not
their own lives dear unto them, that they might maintain
that faith which was once delivered unto the saints, and pro-
pagate that truth which had been intrusted to them. Their
maxim was, that they would rather suffer themselves, than
that the interests of true religion should suffer by them.

As the farmer of Lochbruin was one day at home, and enjoying himself in the midst of his family—a luxury which,
in those precarious times was but rarely tasted—and dreading
no immediate danger, a young man belonging to the household burst into his master's apartment with the information
that the dragoons were in sight. All was consternation. The
merciless enemy, that spared no age nor sex, was at hand;
and a happy and harmless family might in a few minutes
present an appalling scene of havoc and desolation. What
was to be done ? Every one knew that the interests of the
household depended on the safety of its master; and, therefore, instant flight or concealment was the first consideration.
Flight was determined on, as being the more preferable
alternative in the present circumstances; and Campbell
hastened to reach the height above his dwelling before the
troopers should get within shot of him. "To the Nypes,"
cried the commander of the party; "I see the old bird has
flown, and is soaring toward the highest eminence." The
Nypes is a lofty ridge that rises above Lochbruin; and it was
in this direction that Campbell was fleeing when first observed
by the soldiers. A vigorous pursuit commenced. The dragoons ascended the steep with all the speed their heavy
horses could make; and ere they reached the summit, that
spreads out into a wide mossy platform, Campbell was a good
way in advance, dashing through the long heather, and wad-
ing the smeary peat ground till his strength was nearly exhausted. His pursuers were gaining ground; and, seeing it
was in vain to contend, he resolved to conceal himself, if
possible, in the heath, and there to leave himself in the hand

of Providence. Having, therefore, reached a place in the moor, the inequality of which screened him from the view of the troopers, he plunged into a deep and narrow trench in the moss, the sides of which were skirted with thick bushy heather, which nearly covered the opening above. Here he lay flat on his back looking up to the sky, which was little more than visible through the shaggy coverlet that waved above him. The heavy tramp of the cavalcade approaching was distinctly heard, till at length a tremulous motion, imparted to the yielding turf, announced their immediate presence—then one spring, and another, and another, till the whole party leapt over; while he distinctly recognised the bright shoes on the feet of their horses, and the long scabbards dangling by their side. He lay with a palpitating heart till their sound died away in the distance, and then he ventured to look up, and saw his deliverance complete. The Lord, in whom this good man trusted, did not desert him in the evil day, but wrought for him a deliverance in the very presence of his foes, and hid him as in a grave till the storm rushed past, and left serenity behind. "Keep me as the apple of the eye; hide me under the shadow of thy wings from the wicked that oppress me, from my deadly enemies who compass me about." This humble man literally laid his body in the dust till his oppressors passed over him, without being permitted to trample on him; and then the Lord, the lifter up of his head, gave him once more his life for a prey. His enemies "compassed him in his steps, they set their eyes bowing down to the earth; but the Lord disappointed them, and delivered his soul from the wicked." We are ready to say, surely this man must have been very thankful for this wonderful rescue; and who can doubt it? These men knew well how to appreciate every providential interference in their behalf; but ought we not to be as thankful, nay, much more thankful, when we reflect that we live in times when we enjoy an exemption from all sufferings and hazard whatever on account of our religious sentiments? "The lines are fallen unto us in pleasant places; yea, we have a goodly heritage." We may profess what form of religion we choose, without the fear of being dragooned into the profession of an opposite form. This exemption is the precious inheritance which our excellent forefathers have handed down to us; and it is the fruit of their strivings, and perils, and sufferings unto the death; for it was not for themselves only that they strove, it was also for the benefit of succeeding generations, whose spiritual welfare was with them a matter of no inferior moment. Let us, then, maintain this liberty wherewith Christ has made us free, and transmit it to the race that is to come. Our religious privileges are highly to be estimated; and the best way in which we can show our estimation of them is by a cordial reception of the truth as it is in Jesus. All our wrangling about external privileges, valuable as these privileges may be, will not avail us, unless we become sincere believers in Christ; and the offer of salvation is made to every man in the Gospel, and happy is he who receives the offer. All, without exception, are warranted to accept of Heaven's greatest and richest boon—the Lord Jesus Christ; and all who accept it are saved. Many, in struggling for their civil and religious rights, have in the bustle lost their souls, because, in the din of the strife, they forgot the main thing; but the worthy men who, in a former age, contended valiantly for the truth, felt, at the same time, the saving power of that truth.

Not far from Lochbruin, on the west side of the Afton, lived William Good, another eminent Christian. This man was also a Covenanter, and an individual whose ruin was therefore determined on. His place of residence was Little Mark Lane, in the immediate vicinity of Dalegles or Daleccles, which literally signifies Kirkland, and which designation plainly intimates that there existed in this neighbourhood, in ancient times, a place of worship. The name is Celtic, and clearly shows that the worship of God was observed here long prior to the Saxon period. It appears from the earlier records of our country, that St Columba, who lived in the sixth century, was especially successful in spreading the Gospel throughout the west of Scotland, and that his preachers had there established themselves in many places, which to this day bear their name. This holy and devoted man was a native of Ireland, and of royal descent. " He was educated under St Caran, and other Irish bishops. After founding some monasteries in Ireland, zeal for the propagation of Christianity induced him to leave his country and pass over into Britain. The southern parts being converted, he came, as Bede informs us, to preach the Word of God in the provinces of the northern parts. He arrived at the time when Bridius, a most powerful king, reigned over the Picts, and in the ninth year of his reign, and converted that nation to the faith of Christ by his preaching and example. He was attended by twelve companions, and founded the monastery. or college, of Iona—a very different society from the later monkish institutions. For, although they had a certain rule

and might deem certain religious regulations necessary for
the preservation of order, their great design was, by communicating instruction, to train up others for the work of the
ministry. Those societies which sprung from them became
the seminaries of the Church of Scotland. They lived, says
Bede, after the example of the venerable fathers, by the
labour of their own hands." There is every likelihood, then,
that the church to which the lands of Dalegles belonged was
originally erected by the followers of Columba; and that the
true Gospel was preached among the ancient Celtic people
who inhabited this district, and who have left behind them,
in the name of the place, a memorial of their piety. One
dwells with pleasure on the reflection, that the rude people
of forgotten ages, who inhabited these upland wastes, were
visited with the message of grace, and were subdued and
sanctified by the pacific and purifying doctrines of the glorious Gospel.

William Good, and his wife, Anne Campbell, lived together as heirs of the grace of life, and were fellow-helpers
to the truth. Their lot had fallen on evil days, and therefore they did not expect to live without molestation; and
hence, they were thankful for any short interval of repose
with which Providence might be pleased to favour them.
They lived with death before their eyes; for every day
brought a report from some quarter that a faithful witness
for the truth had lost his life by the hand of the enemy; and,
therefore, they looked upon themselves more and more every
hour in the light of strangers and pilgrims in the earth.
Persons in this situation must experience an abstraction of
mind from earthly interests, and an approximation of soul
to that heaven to which they are journeying, which is but
seldom and faintly realized by those who are at ease, and who
inherit the peaceable days of Zion's prosperity. But they
who lived in times of persecution, and had tribulation in the
flesh, were not wretched on that account; for, just in proportion to their external troubles was their internal enjoyment of the peace of God. " I will not leave you comfort-
less: in the world ye shall have tribulation, but in me ye shall
have peace."

One day as William's wife, who was busy at her domestic
employment, happened accidentally to step to the door, she
observed in the distance a company of horsemen coming apparently straight to the house. She at once guessed their
errand, and instantly informed her husband, who was within.
She advised him to flee; but on considering the matter, this

was found to be impracticable, as the troopers were so near
He could not leave the house without being observed, and
there was no place of safety to which he could betake himself so near at hand as to be able to reach it before the dragoons came up. If concealment was to be attempted at all,
it must be somewhere within the house; and the hope of being
successful in this endeavour was but slender, considering the
smallness of the dwelling. There was no time, however, to delay; the enemy was at hand, and life was sweet. " But where
shall I abscond?" said he to his wife, whose concern for his
safety was extreme; " into what nook shall I creep ? I see
no corner that can afford a hiding-place." " The spence,
gudeman, the spence; run to the spence." The spence was
an apartment in the older farm-houses of the country districts, which was appropriated more especially to the use of
the family; and was of a somewhat genteeler description
than the kitchen, which was common to the servants. It
was to the spence, then, that honest William Good betook
himself, at the suggestion of his wife, as being the only likely
place in the domicile where he might remain undiscovered.
The spence, in the house of Little Mark Lane, had for some
time been converted into a lumber-closet, into which were
crowded articles of every kind that were unfit for use, or not
immediately required. Old chests, and barrels, and chairs,
and pots, were all huddled together. Among the trumpery
that occupied the apartment, then, William Good hid himself, like Saul of old, among the stuff; the one from his
friends, and the other from his foes. The door of the spence
opened on the kitchen, and the anxious wife placed before it
a ponderous stone trough which stood near, and this prevented the door from being easily opened, and, at the same
time, tended to lull suspicion. The walls of the kitchen,
round and round, were of a sooty black, japanned by the peat
smoke of a century; and the door of the ante-chamber being
of the same hue, the risk of discovery was less likely. Such
was the posture of affairs when the dragoons approached the
house. No sight was more appalling to the helpless peasantry
than that of a gruff-looking, swearing trooper, roughly clad,
sunk to the knees in large boots, with a grisly helmet on his
head, a coarse cloak hanging from his shoulders, and a huge,
cumbrous scabbard rattling on his heels. These, for the most
part, were men of blood, who rioted in human sufferings, and
to whom the wailings of humanity were merriment. A party
of such men now stood in the presence of the terror-stricken
Anne Campbell, whose fears were more for her husband's

safety than for her own. In the midst of her fears, however, she succeeded in maintaining an external composure before her enemies, lest any apparent trepidation on her part should beget a suspicion that the object of their search was within reach. It is wonderful to think how greatly the Lord's people are strengthened in the day of trial, and enabled " to gird up the loins of their mind." It was in the time of her greatest extremity, that the wife of John Brown of Priesthill exhibited the greatest moral heroism, to the astonishment and confusion of her deadly foes. The farm-house of Little Mark Lane underwent a strict and unsparing scrutiny; and barn, and stable, and cow-house, were all explored with as much keenness as if they expected to find some great and costly treasure, on the possession of which their future happiness was solely to depend. But though they sought, they found not. The sanctuary in which the master of the house had taken refuge was left inviolate. They never imagined that there was any such apartment within the premises; and their eyes were holden that they did not see it. It sometimes happens, that we experience a deliverance from danger when we least expect it, and that the evil which we dreaded is warded off in a very surprising manner. Almost every person may remember some incident in his history illustrative of this remark, and proving that "man's extremity is God's opportunity." The party left the abode of these good people whom God cared for, and sheltered by his power, under the impression that he of whom they were in quest was not there. When the danger was over, William left the place of his concealment, mixed again with his household, and received their gratulations on account of the narrow escape which he had made. Every one applauded Anne for the manner in which she had secreted her husband, and praised the contrivance to which the necessity of the case had so promptly given birth. If William had been seen at the door instead of his wife, his doom would have been sealed; as in that case the dragoons would have been quite certain of his being in the house, which they would not have quitted till they had found him. But the Providence that intended to deliver him ordered it otherwise, and hid him from the eyes of those who were bent on his destruction. It will surely not be deemed out of keeping with the character of this good man, to suppose that his gratitude on this occasion bore some proportion to the greatness of his deliverance; and that his prayer to the God of his life would be characterized with an increase of holy fervour, and of simplicity of confidence; and that his

future life would be more sincerely and entirely devoted to
the service of Him who had graciously saved him from a
violent and cruel death. A grandson of William Good died
in Sanquhar about eighteen years ago, at a very advanced
age ; and he was a son in every respect worthy of such an
ancestor.

CHAPTER XXII.

Alexander Gray of Cambusnethan Mains—James Gray.

In the catalogue of our Scottish martyrs, we are not to include those only who suffered death by the immediate hand of their persecutors. There were many who died martyrs, whose blood stained neither the heath nor the scaffold, but who lost their lives owing to the many hardships to which they were subjected for their adherence to the truth. Hunger, and cold, and fatigue, the buffetings of the storm, and exposure in damp and dreary caves, wore down the stoutest constitutions, and superinduced diseases which brought multitudes to a premature grave. The numbers who died by this means have not been accurately calculated, but they cannot be small; and many of them being strangers in the locality where they ended their days, must have been buried quietly in the moors and wastes by those who were brethren and sufferers in the same common cause. These worthies, as they belonged to the great cloud of witnesses who held the testimony of Christ in the day of Scotland's tribulation, deserve the honourable appellation of martyrs; for they were really such in every sense, excepting that of a military or public execution. The traditions respecting such individuals are not indeed so numerous as those respecting the witnesses who came to a more tragical end; but they are not the less valuable, nor less deserving of record. The present chapter shall be occupied with a few notices of two brothers of this class, of the name of Gray, whose worth of character and stedfastness of principle deserve remembrance.

Alexander Gray, the first of the brothers whom we shall notice, was born in the parish of Cambusnethan, where his parents long resided, and where he lived till the period of his death, which was near the close of the persecution. Tradition has preserved but few particulars of his life; but

these, scanty as they are, are fully decisive of the excellency
of his character as a man of sincere godliness. He was
warmly attached to the principles of civil and religious liberty,
for which the Covenanters so nobly and disinterestedly contended.

The district in which Alexander Gray lived had produced
many worthy Christians, and many leal-hearted patriots.
The upper and middle wards of Lanarkshire were famous for
the support of the covenants in the stirring times of the
second Charles; and many a brave heart poured forth its best
blood in behalf of a cause for the maintenance of which no
sacrifice was deemed too great.

Cambusnethan occupies a beautiful locality on the Clyde,
the vale of which, as a popular writer remarks, "is soft, sunny,
and fructiferous, and one of the finest pieces of country that
Scotland can boast of." Cambusnethan House is an elegant
mansion, and stands a few miles above the town of Hamilton,
and almost in the centre of a district of orchards and splendid
villas. It is second only to the princely castle of Mauldslee,
standing in a like position about two miles farther up the
river, in the parish of Carluke. It was near this latter place
that Gavin Hamilton resided, who suffered in 1666. Cambusnethan has been the scene of Christian martyrdom; for it
was here that Arthur Inglis was killed by the troopers, when
they found him sitting in the field reading the Word of God.
On the eastern boundary of this parish, and at the junction
of Clydesdale and Lothian, is the famous Darmeid Muir,
where many a conventicle was held by the worthies in those
suffering times; on which account, as Patrick Walker informs us, it got the name of the " Kirk of Darmeid." It is
a secluded spot, and surrounded by high moorlands; so that
a company of worshippers could remain long in its secrecy
without their being observed, and the marshes and mosses
contiguous to it would present an effectual barrier in the case
of pursuit by horsemen. In this place Richard Cameron, on
his return from Holland in 1680, held a fast with Cargill and
Douglas; and here they agreed to maintain more firmly the
standard of the Gospel, in the face of the abounding defection of the times. This led to the Sanquhar Declaration,
which was published in the midsummer of this year. In
1683 Mr Renwick commenced his ministerial work in Scotland on the same hallowed spot, " taking up," as his biographer
remarks, " the testimony of the standard of Christ where it
had fallen, at the removal of the former witnesses, Messrs
Cameron and Cargill."

The following is a tradition respecting a conventicle which met at Darngavel in Cambusnethan. When the assembly was engaged in worship, and raising aloft the voice of praise, the melody, wafted by the breeze, was heard at Blackhall, at the moment a trooper happened to call, in passing. The sound reached his ear, and excited his suspicion. The farmer, who was friendly to the Covenanters, and a man of humane disposition, made the following remark : " Whenever my neighbour of Darngavel shears one of his sheep, or taks aff ony twa o' his lambs, he sets the hale flock a-bleating." This seemed to satisfy the dragoon, who departed without making further inquiries.

It was in Cambusnethan Mains that Alexander Gray resided, in company with his brother James, who rented the farm. This house was a rendezvous to the Covenanters, who in that part of the country were obliged to wander from place to place; and many a desolate sojourner found here a friendly shelter and prompt assistance in the day of distress. The Mains of Cambusnethan was therefore a noted house— a house equally well known to the sufferers and to the dragoons; and many a visit was paid by the latter, with a view to apprehend those who had taken refuge under its roof. It is worthy of remark, that the troopers were in no instance successful in capturing any who resorted to the place. Gray and his friends, however, were frequently in danger, and the utmost caution and vigilance were necessary to avoid the snares that were laid for them.

The laird of Cambusnethan, like many others of his station in society at the time, sided with the ruling party, it is said, and countenanced the oppressors of the people of God. The same thing was done by the great majority of the gentry throughout Scotland, in order to retain their worldly possessions; so that the laird in this instance was not alone. Many of them complied more through necessity than inclination; and perhaps the laird of Cambusnethan was of this number. Those of them, however, who entered heartily into the cause of the persecutors, were a particular annoyance to the peasantry; and, co-operating with the curates, they wrought no small havoc in the Church. They acted the part of little tyrants in the different localities where they resided, and were equally dreaded with persons of greater influence. Often did the laird sally out with the full determination to seize Alexander Gray, dead or alive. If professing Christians would show but the tithe of that zeal in the service of God that the wicked manifest in the service

of Satan, what a different scene would soon present itself!
Believers in that case would be like a dew from the Lord in
the midst of the land, and the principles and practices of evil
would be so counteracted by them, that the kingdom of
darkness, in all its interests, would soon be weakened, and
come to nought.

The laird of Cambusnethan's wife, however, was a very
different person from himself; she was a Covenanter in principle, and one who feared the Lord. Her mind was deeply
imbued with religion, and she had great pleasure in spiritual
exercises. Her husband's conduct was a matter of sincere
grief to her, and her righteous soul was vexed from day to
day with his unrighteous ways. Her chief object was to
seek the kingdom of God, and his righteousness; and his
principal employment was to persecute the unoffending subjects of that kingdom. Lady Cambusnethan, as she was
courteously denominated by the country people, employed
all her efforts to counterplot the devices of her husband respecting the sufferers, and, through her instrumentality, they
were often warned of approaching danger. She made it her
endeavour to learn from the laird the names of the persons
for whose apprehension he might happen to be making preparations, and when she learned who they were against
whom evil was meditated, she instantly conveyed the necessary information, that they might forthwith provide for their
safety. It is not known how many worthy individuals this
good woman was the means of shielding from harm; but
she frequently succeeded in rendering abortive the measures
of her husband by imparting timely warning.

The household of Cambusnethan Mains were often indebted to the lady for their safety in the day when mischief
was plotted against them, and many a stealthy messenger
found their way to Alexander Gray and his friends. By
this means the designs of the persecutors were frustrated,
and they were obliged to return without accomplishing their
object.

It appears that, on every fitting occasion, the lady sought
to hold intercourse with those of the Covenanters who happened to be in the neighbourhood of her residence. It was
necessary, however, to attend to this in the most private
manner, lest the knowledge of the circumstance should bring
on her the displeasure of the laird, and expose the helpless
wanderers to a still more severe treatment. The society of
religious persons must have been highly valued by this pious
woman, inasmuch as it was seldom her lot to enjoy the ordi-

nances of religion in the connection which, in her conscience, she most approved of. On one occasion, when her husband was from home, the people in the vicinity agreed to call from his retreat one of the wandering ministers, who was concealed in the district, to hold a conventicle in the place. It was in the depth of winter, and the snow lay thick on the ground. This circumstance, however, did not prevent a goodly company from assembling; for in those days, when the Word of the Lord was scarce, people deemed it no hardship to meet even in the midst of the roaring tempest, to listen to the glad sound of the Gospel, preached by the honoured men who had renounced all for the truth's sake. On this occasion the congregation, having assembled in some retired spot, sat on the cold snow, while the form of the preacher, it is said, was but dimly seen through the smoky drift. The lady was one of the hearers on this inclement day, so eager was she to hear the Word of God. She was wrapped in a shepherd's plaid, and seated in the *beild* of a whin bush by the side of a " fail'dyke;" and though all was tempestuous and dreary without, yet all was serene within, and the peace of God comforted the hearts of those whose persons were exposed to the beating of the storm, while they followed their Redeemer in the way of their duty. It was doubtless in such circumstances that many caught their death—seated on the wet ground, or on the sinking snow, while they were exposed to the chilling sleet and drenching rain, as well as in the cold damp caves. The lady had, no doubt, enough ado to screen herself from the suspicion of enemies; for her husband had in his own house, and in the person of his wife, what, if known, would have proved his worldly ruin; and therefore his worthy spouse was obliged to conduct herself so as to excite no surmises. Her presence at the conventicle does not seem to have been known to any, save to a few trusty friends to whom the secret could with all safety be imparted. When the services were ended the people sought their several homes, and the preacher betook himself to his hiding-place, and in a brief space the drifting snow left no trace of their footsteps.

The family of Cambusnethan Mains, and particularly Alexander Gray, were under deep obligations to the gentlewoman. But, though she was a successful instrument in protecting this good man from the crafty designs of his enemies, she could not shield him from disease. For no fewer than twenty-one years his life had been in jeopardy; and yet, during that long period he had never swerved from his principles, nor in any instance yielded a compliance with the wishes of the oppressor, in order to gain a temporary release from his harassings. Nor is saying this to affirm anything peculiar to Alexander Gray, for the same thing may be asserted of almost all his brethren in those distressful times, when the faith and patience of the saints were tested to the utmost. For many weeks in succession he was obliged to absent himself from his own house, and to seek a lodging in dreary caverns, in unsheltered moors, or in the lonely mountain dells. In the time of a severe storm, when the cattle of the field and the fowls of the air draw near the abodes of men for shelter, the covert of an out-building or of a rude barn, with a corn-sheaf for his pillow, and the newly thrashen straw for his bed, was deemed by him to be no small luxury. We, in days of peace and domestic comfort, can form but little conception of the manner in which such men as Alexander Gray would appreciate the rude accommodation of a barn or a shieling, when the retreat of the dark moss-hag or the feathery covert of the brackens of the hill was their usual haunt.

The constitution of Alexander Gray was originally good, it is said to have been even robust. His was a manly and well-built frame, which promised to wear for many a long year. The treatment, however, to which it was subjected ultimately made inroads on it, and at length forced it entirely to give way. Hunger and cold, and fatigue and anxiety, may be sustained for a few days, or even for a few weeks, without much damage; but years of painful endurance in this way must tell another tale. Accordingly, after exposure to a severe winter, and to a chilling and inclement spring, the health of Gray began to decline, and the symptoms of some deeply-seated disease showed themselves. No medical aid could be procured, as no practitioner in the place could be trusted with the secret of his hiding-place. The enemies of these worthy men endeavoured to close up every avenue of human sympathy through which the outlettings of a brotherly kindness might perchance flow in their direction. In those days the men of the healing art, whose very office it is to alleviate the sufferings of humanity, were either so inhuman themselves, or so much under the control and supervision of the rulers of the time, that, in the case of a Covenanter suffering under a severe malady, and particularly needing their assistance, they could not be confided in. Our worthy was, therefore, wholly left to the secret help of friends, and to the care of Providence.

At the close of summer, therefore, Gray's case was considered hopeless, and his situation was very distressing. He was at the time lying in a cave, and at some distance from his house. The abode to which he was now confined, to avoid the detection of his enemies, was a most unsuitable place for a sickly man, the extremity of whose disease had brought him to the brink of the grave. As the cavern was distant from his dwelling-house—a circumstance which rendered attendance on the patient inconvenient—his brother James, who waited on him with all the assiduity of fraternal kindness, sought for him a resting-place near the house. This was in the midst of a field of standing corn, whose crowded stalks afforded a comfortable shelter from the winds on all sides. Here a bed was prepared, and all the attention shown him that his afflictive condition required; still the disease was not arrested, but the fever burned in his veins as formerly. In this exposed situation, the cold and damp atmosphere of night must have contributed materially to hasten on the crisis that was obviously at hand. When his affectionate brother saw that his life was drawing near its close, he resolved on removing him to the house, be the consequences what they might. He perceived that a discovery would make little difference to his brother, whom a few brief hours, or days at farthest, must bring to the house appointed for all living; and as for himself he was prepared to abide the consequences.

In conveying Alexander Gray into the house, the utmost secrecy was necessary. The danger of placing the dying man on his own bed was apparent to every one, because on the slightest search made by the enemy, a discovery would be made at once. There was in the house a dark lumber-closet unoccupied, and here a couch was spread as soft and comfortable as circumstances would allow; and into this place was the good man carried by his affectionate relations, who watched over him with unceasing kindness till he died.

During the time that Alexander Gray lay in the farm-house, the lady, who had heard of his illness, wished much to pay him a visit, both to show her respect for an honoured follower of the Saviour, and to receive his blessing before he died. Accordingly this Christian woman called at the Mains of Cambusnethan, her ostensible object being to see the condition of the dairy, the furniture of which, it had been reported, was kept by the " gudewife " in a very cleanly style; but her real object was to see the dying man. By this means her true errand, which was known to the family, was concealed from the servants, to whom it would have been imprudent to intrust the secret. The pious wish of the lady was not, however, gratified, as it was not possible to approach the bed of the dying saint without being seen by the servants. She returned so far without her errand, though not without the blessing of the good man, though she had not the pleasure of hearing it pronounced with his own lips. God's people, how different soever their stations in life may be, are nevertheless one in spirit, and they feel the indescribable bond of Christian attachment uniting their hearts together in the Lord. This Christian gentlewoman, though occupying a much higher standing in society than this suffering witness for Christ, considered herself on a level with him as a believer, and felt for him as a fellow-saint. She came to visit him in his affliction because he belonged to Christ, and to speak a word of comfort to him, and to hold fellowship with him in the Spirit; and she was doubtless blessed in her deed, and the favour of Him whose suffering servant she had come to see, would rest upon her. " Inasmuch as ye did it unto the least of these, my brethren, ye did it unto me." Alexander Gray died full of faith and patience, and in the comfortable views of the glory that was to be revealed. His life of wanderings and distress ended in peace, and he entered into the joy of his Lord. This worthy man was as much a martyr for civil and religious liberty, as if he had fallen by the bloody Clavers on the moor, or by the hand of the executioner on the scaffold. His life was really sacrificed in the cause, though it was not taken away by violence; and his name is retained among the honoured worthies who "loved not their lives unto the death."

James Gray, after the decease of his esteemed and beloved brother, felt his heart still more strongly attached to the cause which he had espoused. He was a man of true piety and of unbending principle. The suffering of the party with which he was connected, did not deter him from casting in his lot among them. He was on all occasions ready to assist the sufferers, whatever might be the distress in which he himself might be involved. When the Covenanters rose in the west; for self-defence in asserting their privileges, he was ready to unite with them. He was not, indeed, at the battle of Bothwell Bridge, but he was on his way to join his brethren there. Having understood that the sufferers were in arms, he made ready with all haste, and proceeded toward the place of their encampment. As he was marching onward, however, he was met by the fugitives from the battle-field, who informed him of the mournful fate of their companions.   To advance was needless, as the fate of the day was already decided, and he returned with a number of the fleeing party to his own house.   Their hearts were full of grief; and sorely did they lament the disastrous issue of the conflict.   The mystery of Providence in permitting their defeat they could not well understand; but, believing that the great Ruler of the world does all things well, they felt resigned to the divine disposal.   The time of their deliverance, however, was not yet come; but the principles which eventually wrought out their emancipation eight years afterwards, did from this period operate more energetically and widely on the public mind.

The family at Cambusnethan Mains courteously entertained the wanderers, and with an unsparing hand supplied their necessities.   The homely fare prepared for the daily use of the household was found inadequate to the wants of the company that had arrived, and hence all the female occupants were instantly employed in making suitable preparations. The empty bread-basket was soon replenished with *cakes*, hard and hot from the *girdel*, and creamy milk and fragrant butter, fresh from the well-kept dairy, were placed beside the ponderous *kebbock* on the hospitable board; and many a hungry and weary wight was, on that occasion, after thanks given to Him who fills all his creatures with plenteousness, refreshed and strengthened by the simple but healthful fare of which they partook.   " Use hospitality one to another, without grudging," is the injunction of Scripture; and it is an injunction which our persecuted forefathers did not treat with neglect, even though their compliance with it exposed them to the spoiling of their goods, and also to the loss of their lives.   The company at Cambusnethan Mains, after the kindly entertainment they had received, dispersed and sought safety in their various places of concealment.   James Gray was after this subjected to much trouble from his enemies, though they did not succeed in apprehending him. He was preserved during the trying times that followed; he saw the Revolution, and lived many years after it.   The descendants of James Gray are persons of honest reputation in the places where they live, and the character of their ancestor is worthy of their imitation.

The " bread roller," as it is called, which was so busily employed on that eventful day in the kitchen of Cambusnethan Mains in spreading out on the baking board the oaten cakes and the broad thin scones, "the wale o' Scotia's food,"

P

is still preserved, and is in the possession of a female descendant of the name of Gray, resident in Douglas, and great-
great-grandniece to Alexander Gray. It has been carefully
handed down as an heirloom in the family, and is kept as a
valuable relic of the olden time.

There is in the town of Douglas another memorial of covenanting days—the "meal-basin" of John Brown, the martyr
of Priesthill. It is a specimen of good workmanship, considering the times. It is made of plane-tree, and is capable of
containing at least two pecks of meal. It is in a state of
good preservation; and although the wood-worm has made
in it many perforations, it may yet, with tolerable care, be
kept for generations to come. It is interesting to hold in
one's hand the identical vessel which rested on the knees of
the saintly Priesthill, while his wife rained from her hand
the snow-white meal with which she thickened the porridge
that steamed over the fire of glowing peats piled endwise on
the hearth.

CHAPTER XXIII.

Curate of Kirkbride—Two Pious Families.

KIRKBRIDE is an old ruinous church among the mountains in the upper part of Nithsdale. The parish, which originally derived its name from the church, was, upwards of a hundred and thirty years ago, divided, and attached to the respective parishes of Durisdeer and Sanquhar. The church, the naked walls of which are still standing, is very small—not capable of containing perhaps above a hundred persons. It stands on a sloping side of a green mountain, and commands an extensive prospect to the south-east. The view is terminated by the dark blue mountain of Criffell, which overlooks the Solway Frith, and a large tract of the west coast of England. This part of the country was, in ancient times, for the most part clothed with a dense forest, especially in the straths and valleys, and round the bottoms of the mountains; and this is probably the reason why this church was built so far up on the breast of the hill, and above the upper limits of the forest. The scenery in the immediate locality of the ruin is very grand. The hills around are not clad with heather—they are covered with deep verdure. On the right there is a deep glen, called "The Lime Cleuch"—probably on account of the limestones which have occasionally been found in it. The sides of this glen are bold and precipitous, and the mountains at its upper extremity rise to a great height. On the left is the deep and darkly-wooded ravine through which the Enterkin pours its troubled stream, whose romantic or rather terrible *pass* among the Lowther Hills, is celebrated for the battle of the rescue which took place in the times of the covenant, and in which also Drumlanrig, of persecuting notoriety, intercepted, on his journey to Edinburgh, a party of Covenanters, on a Sabbath morning, on their way to a sacramental occasion in the low country, bu' whom he durst not attack in the narrow and dangerous defile, though he promised to hold a reckoning with them on another day. To the north of the venerable ruin lies the small but beautifully secluded valley of Strathquhairn, in the centre of which stands a solitary hut built of stone and turf, and which is not without incidents of its own. The lonely churchyard, overgrown with rank grass, contains a variety of tombstones which mark the resting-place of the ancient dead. Some of these monuments are of considerable antiquity, and bear inscriptions in characters so fantastic that few can decipher them. From the eastern gable of the building is still suspended the bell, the sound of which assembled the people of forgotten generations to the worship of God; its iron tongue is, however, now silent, save when an occasional preacher congregates among the graves the worthy inhabitants whose "fathers worshipped in this mountain."

It is not correctly known in what particular era this little place of worship was first erected, although tradition has its own tale respecting it. It is probable, however, that it has been reared since the Reformation, on the site of an older structure. The religious history of the place is not without interest. It is reported to have been the very first of the parishes, in the south-west of Scotland, the majority of whose population threw off the Papal yoke, and embraced the principles of the Reformers. The tradition is, that the reformed worshippers, who were not permitted to occupy the church, because the civil authorities had not yet declared the Protestant religion to be the religion of the land, met in the west corner of the churchyard, around an aged thorn tree, under which the preacher stood. The truth of this tradition seems to receive confirmation from the fact, that among the many persons and things annually excommunicated by the Pope, the ancient thorn tree in the burying-ground of Kirkbride is particularly denounced. This circumstance was attested by a literary gentleman, a licentiate of the Church of Scotland, a very worthy man, lately deceased, who, when in Rome with his pupil, heard the thing with his own ears; and the circumstance was to him the more interesting, that Kirkbride was not two miles distant from the place where he was born. The people always had this tradition, but its certainty was not before absolutely known.

It appears, then, that the doctrines of the Reformation were very acceptable to the secluded and simple-hearted people of this parish, and that the truth in its saving power had been very generally felt among them. The good effects of that great spiritual awakening which in those early times was experienced, continued for many generations. The most of the ancient families, however, who had for ages inhabited the *braes* of Kirkbride, have been dispersed, through means of the agricultural changes that have been introduced into the district. Still there is found, among their thinly-scattered population, the lingering spirit of their pious ancestors, and much worth is still resident in the lowly cottages. In the landward parts of the country there subsists more true religion than we are generally aware of; and there, like the exquisitely beautiful flowers which are occasionally to be met with in the desert, Christ has many a choice one unknown to the world, but whom he tends with special care, and rears with his gracious hand as precious plants soon to be transported to another soil.

The expulsion of the curate of Kirkbride—an affair both amusing and instructive—forms the principal incident relative to this place in times of Prelatic usurpation. The curate of Kirkbride, it would appear, was a person of a very different description from the curate of Sanquhar. Like many of his brethren, he seems to have been a bold and imperious character—one whose moral history was not what it should have been, and a preacher whose doctrine was not the doctrine of Christ. He pressed like a heavy and intolerable incubus on the parish; and the poor people who, in better times, had been accustomed to a purer doctrine, and to a milder treatment from their spiritual guides, felt the bitterness of the change. A hireling had been intruded among them, who cared not for the flock, but left them to wander on the mountains in the dark and cloudy day—a hireling whose voice the sheep knew not, and whom they could not follow, because he was a stranger, and they knew not the voice of strangers. In this situation, then, with no one to care for their souls, a spirit of ecclesiastical insubordination began to show itself. The little parish was agitated from end to end, and its rural quietude and Christian peacefulness were troubled. The cottagers met in companies in each others houses, and freely detailed their grievances. They lamented the circumstances in which they were placed, and expressed both anger and sorrow; but what more could they do? They might murmur and complain in secret, but they could not alter the complexion of the times. Their enemies were too numerous and powerful to be resisted, and the rod of oppression was wielded by a hand too potent for

any feeble arm among them to wrench it from its grasp
Their situation was not solitary. A moral desolation overspread the whole land, and wailing and distress were common
in every quarter. The spirit of the community was bowed
down to the dust under the load of an oppression which
men durst not attempt to throw off. Still the state of matters in the parish was not to be borne with, and something
must be done for their relief; and therefore these simple
people came to the conclusion, that if that detested branch of
Prelacy, the curate, were removed, all would be well. It
never entered their artless minds that their meditated outrage would be revenged, or that another equally bad, if not
worse, might perchance be returned in the room of him whose
fugitation they wished to effect. But who was to perform
this deed of high and chivalrous daring ? who was to be found
possessed of the hardihood to undertake the enterprise of
expelling the obnoxious incumbent for ever from the place
where his presence was so unbearably offensive ? Six individuals, it is said, undertook to rid the parish of the evil
complained of. The leader of this little band was a worthy
man of the name of Clark, some of whose lineal descendants
are at the present day resident in the neighbourhood. These
champions, then, having engaged valorously to assert the
inalienable rights of the small Christian community with
which they were more especially connected, equipped themselves in a manner befitting the onerous task which they had
undertaken to accomplish. Their design was preserved in
deep secrecy from the party whom they were going to assail,
that they might with the greater promptitude, and without
any obstruction, perform the deed. And faithfully and religiously was the secret kept on the part of those to whom it
was confided; for even here there were spies and informers
ready to communicate anything that looked suspicious in
word or deed.

The manse of Kirkbride was an unique specimen of the
rude masonry of the olden times. It was constructed chiefly
with a view of defending its inmates from the storms of
winter, to which, from its elevated situation, it was peculiarly
exposed. Not the least vestige of anything ornamental was
to be seen about its exterior; but then it had all the strength
of an ancient feudal castle. It walls were of great thickness,
and so firmly compacted, that, on being demolished a few
years ago, it was with much difficulty that they were overturned. Whatever it was prior to the Reformation, it is
obvious that after that period it was the residence of men

who, in point of sanctity and usefulness, had few compeers, and with whom its present occupant, the curate, was not once to be named. It was the remembrance of such men, who had been instrumental in conveying to many of the poor parishioners the knowledge of the truth, that alienated their minds from him who now professed to exercise among them the functions of a spiritual oversight.

In pursuance, then, of their grand purpose respecting the curate, Clark and his company presented themselves on the day appointed before the manse of Kirkbride. They arranged themselves in front of the house, and demanded an audience of the curate. The servant, who met them at the door, returned to inform her master that a party of six men wished to see him. "Who are they? and what do they want? If they are asking charity, tell them to go elsewhere." "They are not beggars, Sir," replied the maid; "they are tall, stout men, with bonnets on their heads, their hose drawn above their knees, and armed with large clubs." "Tell them that they can have no admittance here, and that they must be gone instantly." She returned with the message, and the men became clamorous, and threatened to force an entrance. The noise at the door roused the curate, who looked through the window and saw the men, and knew them to be his avowed enemies. He instantly learned their design, and perceived, from their determined looks, and from their warlike attitude, and the terrific brandishing of their ponderous clubs, that his life was in hazard. To defend himself was impossible, and the only means of safety was flight. During the altercation, then, between the assailants and the servant, he made his escape through a window unperceived. After a short delay, the men rushed into the house, and the maid, not knowing that her master was gone, was in a state of great consternation. The strictest search was made, but he could not be found. At last they observed him running at his utmost speed to reach the height above Strathquhairn. The man had been uncomfortable in his situation through the dislike of the people, and his life being sweeter to him than his curacy, he abandoned the one that he might retain the other. The elopement of the curate so far secured the object of the persons who, on this occasion, did him the honour of a visit, and Providence prevented them from inflicting any injury on his person; which they might probably have done if he had refused to vacate his place at their command. What became of this man afterwards is not known; but it is not unlikely that he would

soon be supplied with another situation of a similar description, considering that he would be regarded by his own party
in the light of an insulted and persecuted individual, who
richly deserved their sympathy and support. His departure,
however, must have afforded a subject of heartfelt gratulation to the poor people to whom his ministrations were so
unacceptable. People can derive no spiritual profit from the
services of a man who has been thrust in upon them by the
strong hand of power, reckless of the consequences of such an
ungracious intrusion. The inhabitants of Kirkbride, at this
period, by no means enjoyed a millennium; and there is
little likelihood, though the obnoxious incumbent was driven
from his occupancy, that the affairs of the parish would
undergo any amendment worth the mentioning till the more
auspicious times of the Revolution, when the Lord loosed
the bands of his enthralled Church, and turned her captivity
" like streams of water in the south." We who live in the
days of a happy religious liberty, when every man can sit
under his own vine, and under his own fig tree, without any
restriction, or any to make him afraid, should learn to value
our privileges, and to improve the breathing-time which God
has granted us. We cannot tell how soon the bright sky
above our heads may suffer an obscuration, nor are we sure
that days of trial do not await us. The great Head of the
Church may yet see fit to purge his floor by the sifting winds
of persecution, before he gather his wheat into his garner.

There is another anecdote which was current among the
older people of this district. There lived somewhere in this
parish, or immediately on its confines, two pious families, the
heads of which respectively had incurred the odium of the
Prelatic party. Their pertinacious nonconformity rendered
them so peculiarly offensive to the ecclesiastical supervisors
of the period, that injunctions were given to a number of
soldiers to embrace the first opportunity of apprehending
them. This military appointment soon became known to
the two honest Covenanters, who used every precaution to
keep themselves out of harm's way. They knew the vigilance of their enemies, and the artful methods which they
would employ to circumvent them. On this account they
were often obliged to withdraw from their own houses; and
the two companions in suffering took up their abode in the
woods, and at other times crept by stealth into the dwelling
of some friendly neighbour, who pitied and sheltered them in
their perilous circumstances. Every attempt on the part
of the soldiers to seize them at home proved abortive; and

so often were they thwarted in their purpose, that they resolved to abandon the project as utterly impracticable. It occurred, however, to the persons who professed to have a deeper interest in the matter than the hireling troopers, that if the husbands could not be captured, their wives at least might be caught. In those times of religious oppression, it was comparatively rare to witness helpless females arrested by the rough hand of persecuting violence; and when any incident of this description did take place, it was regarded as a display of uncommon barbarity. Hence the women, however religiously attached to the covenanting party, were generally, though not always, overlooked. In this instance, however, no leniency was shown, and the soldiers were instructed to lay hold of the wives in default of their husbands.

When this became known, these virtuous women found themselves in the same predicament as their husbands, and saw it necessary to provide for their safety in a similar manner. Their case, as females, however, was more distressing. They were less capable of enduring hardship, and their absence from home could be less easily dispensed with. It happened one day that the dragoons were out on the search, and the women having received information of the circumstance, betook themselves in company to the fields. There was in the vicinity of their abode a rising ground covered with tall broom, whose pliant and slender branches, loaded with lovely yellow blossoms, waved gracefully in the wind. It was in the very heart of this broomy hillock, and in the secrecy of its densest covert, that they concealed themselves. As they were sitting here, closely wrapt in their mantles, the soldiers were heard descending the brow immediately behind them. They had dismounted, and were leading their horses through the mazes and entanglements of the bushes, and in their progress they happened to advance almost in a direct line to the spot where the two timid daughters of the covenant were crouching in fearful apprehension. The horsemen came on jesting, and laughing, and switching the flowery broom, and at length approached so closely to the hiding-place of the matrons, that, as they passed them, their long military cloaks came trailing over the heads of the cowering fugitives, who felt as if a mountain were falling on them, and crept closer and closer to the ground, as if they would have sunk beneath its surface. The crisis, however, was over. The soldiers moved on, and the women remained undiscovered. Thus did the Lord preserve these feeble and helpless persons who trusted in him. What befell them and their husbands after this period is not said; but there is no doubt that the same God who had guided them hitherto, would continue to be their guide even unto death.

The paucity of anecdotes regarding the Covenanters who resided in Kirkbride is rather remarkable, considering the firm hold which, from an early period, the principles of the Reformation had of its inhabitants; and their spirited conduct respecting the curate shows that these principles had not been abandoned. The want of traditional incident, however, by no means proves that the good people who tenanted this locality had either swerved from their constancy or were overlooked by their enemies. The likelihood is, that the tales of interest respecting their persecuted ancestry have died out with the people of a former generation. This, at least, has been eminently the case in other places not far from the scene of this narrative, where, within the last few years, scores of instructive rehearsals respecting our covenanted worthies, which nobody thought it worth the while to arrest in their progress to oblivion, have departed irrecoverably with a few aged men lately deceased. But though names and occurrences are forgotten, principles live —principles which are indestructible, and principles which are destined to rectify and keep in order the whole framework of society, and finally to pervade the entire living mass of mankind throughout the world. The immediate benefit which resulted from the successful contendings of our forefathers was at first confined only to a single point of the geographical surface of the earth; but from that point, as from a centre, the truth has radiated, and shall ultimately spread abroad among all nations. The attempt to suppress the truth of God in Scotland by persecution was the very means, in the hand of Providence, of reviving that truth, and of diffusing it more widely around. The persecution which commenced in Jerusalem with the martyrdom of Stephen, was the occasion of the dissemination of the Gospel, not only throughout the land of Judea, but also throughout other countries. It was then that the waters of the sanctuary began to swell and rise like a mighty flood, dispersing themselves far and wide through all lands. Persecution opened the sluices through which issued, in copious floods, the streams of those sacred waters which had been pent up within the walls of the holy city, and then the full river of God flowed in majestic current far onward into the sterile regions of Heathenism, which it refreshed and fertilized, causing "the desert to rejoice and blossom as the rose." In our beloved land the claims of civil and religious liberty were neither so well understood nor so warmly appreciated as after the attempt made to suppress them. The rude blasts of persecuting violence, however, made that fair and stately tree under whose spacious boughs we now repose strike its roots deeper, and take a firmer hold of the soil; and now, like the tree which Nebuchadnezzar saw in vision, which "was strong, whose height reached unto heaven, and the sight thereof to all the earth; whose leaves were fair, and the fruit thereof much, and in which was meat for all; under which the beasts of the field dwelt, and upon whose branches the fowls of heaven had their habitation;" like this tree it shall be "in the midst of the earth," and it shall eventually overshadow all lands, and shall continue without decay unto the end.

CHAPTER XXIV.

James Harkness—Scene at Biggar—Curate of Moffat.

A WHILE after the commencement of the persecution in Scotland, James Harkness of Locherben, with a number of others, it is said, left his native country and took refuge in Ireland. It was in the Emerald Isle that they looked for that repose from the vexatious harassings of their persecutors which they could not find at home. In Ireland the refugees from the south and west of Scotland frequently found an asylum in the day of the Church's tribulation. It was to this country that the venerable Peden sometimes resorted, when he wished to retire from the *bluidy land,* as he termed Scotland, when the sword of persecution was bathed in the blood of the saints. James Harkness, however, did not feel himself at ease in Ireland; he began to view himself in the light of a deserter from the ranks of that noble band of confessors who were jeoparding their lives on the high places of the field, in maintaining the standard of Zion in the day of conflict. The loud wailings of his brethren in their native land were wafted across the seas, and his heart was stirred within him, for he felt himself identified with the afflicted remnant, and he hastened back to help to "support his fainting mother's head" in the day when her enemies were sorely incensed against her, and when they were passing over her prostrate body, and treading her down like the mire on the streets. He therefore embraced the first opportunity of returning to that scene of suffering and of conflict from which he had for self-preservation withdrawn. Some of his friends and acquaintances who had accompanied him to Ireland, remained in the land of their refuge, where, having, it is said, acquired possessions, they became permanently resident. James Harkness and his brother Thomas, however, returned to their native land, where the one suffered martyrdom, and the other acted a prominent part in the memorable rescue at Enterkin.

The notoriety which the two brothers acquired in the cause of the covenant, pointed them out to their enemies as individuals that were particularly obnoxious. James they denominated Harkness with the "long gun," and Thomas they styled Harkness with the "white hose." The importance of the two brothers, as leaders of the covenanting party, is sufficiently obvious from the fact, that Clavers frequently attempted, by means of his emissaries, to negotiate with James, with a view to gain him over to the ruling party, and promised him, as the price of his compliance, a captainship in the royal forces. Every lure of this description, however, was indignantly rejected by him, and he preferred suffering to worldly honour and emolument, when, by compliance, the claims of conscience must necessarily be disregarded. It was not to be expected that one who had suffered persecution for the truth's sake, would himself become a persecutor, and plot the ruin of that cause and of those friends he so ardently loved. But when the object of his enemies—which was, by means of solicitation and fair promises, to gain him to their party—failed, they were determined to seize him and his associates by force, and where they could not bend the will, to punish the person. As he and his friends were skulking among the wild mountains and solitary glens of Nithsdale, they were surprised by a party of dragoons, who hastily surrounded them, and took them prisoners. It was in vain to resist; they were in the firm grasp of the powerful foe, from which they could not extricate themselves. The commander of the party who apprehended them, was a man of a fiery and cruel disposition, and he used them with great harshness. It appears that prisoners were frequently treated in a very barbarous manner by the soldiers who conveyed them to their place of destination. They were permitted to act as they pleased, no superior authority offering to control them; and, indeed, the rigour exercised on their part, so far from giving offence, would be regarded with approbation by the officers. Of this rigour we have an example in the case of the good Cargill, whose feet Bonshaw tied below the horse's belly, in a way so hard and painful that the worthy man was obliged to remonstrate with him on his cruelty.

When they arrived at Edinburgh—to which place they were conveyed to be tried—they were put into a place of confinement, from which, before they were brought to trial they succeeded in making their escape. They then proceeded homewards with all the secrecy and despatch they could, and passing Biggar, where the leader of the party who conducted them to Edinburgh happened at the time to be resident, they resolved to visit him. Their design in waiting on him was to put in execution a project which they had devised for the purpose not of injuring, but of frightening, one who had caused them so much trouble and inconvenience. As they approached his house he observed them, and at once knew them to be the prisoners who were recently under his charge. He could not understand how they had possibly got free, and, dreading mischief from them, he hid himself. At the door they asked civilly for the captain, and said they wished to see him on particular business. His wife, who had been apprised of the character of her visitors, said he was not at home. Harkness began to fear lest their intention should be defeated, when a little boy standing near said: "I will show where my father is," and forthwith conducted them to the place of his concealment. They instantly dragged him out, as the soldiers used to do the Covenanters from their hiding-places, and appeared as if they were going to take his life. They imitated in all respects the manner in which the dragoons shot the wanderers in the fields. Having furnished themselves with a musket, probably from his own armory, they caused him to kneel down, while they tied a napkin over his eyes, and desired him to prepare for immediate death. The poor man, in the utmost trepidation, was obliged to submit. He bent on his knees, and, being blindfolded, he expected every moment when the fatal shot would be poured into his body. Harkness, after an ominous silence of a few seconds—a brief space, doubtless, of intense anxiety and agony to the helpless captain—fired, but fired aloft into the air. The innocuous shot went whizzing over the head of the horror-stricken man, who, though stunned with the loud and startling report, sustained no injury. Having then, by way of chastisement, succeeded in making him feel something of what the poor Covenanters felt when their ruthless foes shot them without trial or ceremony in the fields, they took the bandage from his eyes, and raised him up, almost powerless with terror, to his feet. The circumstance made a deep impression on his mind; he saw he was fully in the power of the men who had thus captured him, and that, notwithstanding, they had done him no harm. Surprise and gladness took the place of the fear of death and of the anguish of despair, in the grateful man's bosom. He confessed that the sparing of his life was owing to their Christian clemency, and to the merciful character of their religious principles. He freely admitted that the spirit with which they were actuated, was very different from that displayed towards them by the party to which he belonged, and that they had amply rewarded him good for evil. He was deeply affected by a sense of the favour shown him, at a time when he had nothing before him but a prospect of immediate death. Kindness, it is said, is the key to the human heart, and in this instance it was attended with the very best results. He avowed on the spot his conviction of the sinfulness of the cause in which he was engaged, and his determination to quit for ever a service in which he was too plainly fighting against God. What kindness he showed on this occasion to Harkness and his companions is not said, but it is affirmed that he became a new man. He inquired into the nature of the Gospel, and embraced with a cordial faith the doctrine of Christ; and all this resulted from the incident above narrated. The ways and means by which the Lord is sometimes pleased to direct the attention of sinners to the truth are surprising, and any means will do when he works. It is not said what incidents befell this individual owing to the change of his views on religious matters; but there can be no doubt that he was afterwards subjected to the same persecutions as those of the party with which he was now associated. Desertion from the ranks of the persecutors must have been visited with punishment peculiarly severe; but He who changed his heart could support him under all his trials, and enable him to hold fast his profession.

After this Harkness returned to the south, and kept himself in the retirement of his native mountains. The following anecdote is told of him; but whether the incident which it records took place prior to his being taken to Edinburgh, or after his return, is not said. A party of dragoons called on the knight of Closeburn, and requested his aid in apprehending James Harkness in his house at Locherben, as being a restless and indomitable Covenanter. The good knight was obliged to accompany them, and to guide them through the woods and uplands to the abode of Harkness. A great deal of rain had fallen about the time, and the morasses were full, and all the streams and rivulets overflowed their banks. But though this was the case, so anxious were the troopers to obtain their object, that no consideration could induce them to wait another opportunity. The assiduity which wicked men often display in the service of Satan should stimulate Christians to greater activity and perseverance in the good work of the Lord. It is lamentable to see the people of God so slothful in doing his will, when the adversaries of goodness are so zealous in promoting the interests of the evil one.

As the party proceeded on their way to Locherben, Harkness observed their approach. As they were not far from the house when he first saw them, he had no opportunity of making his escape; but necessity, it is said, is the mother of invention, and he adopted, on the spur of the moment, the following plan, with a view to elude, if possible, the observation of his enemies. It occurred to him that the only chance of escape was to attempt to act the part of the cowherd; and accordingly, having thrown around him a tattered plaid, and taken a staff in his hand, he was in the act of driving the cows to the bent when the party arrived. They never once imagined that the man of whom they were in quest would thus dare to present himself in the very presence of his foes, reckless of the consequences that might ensue. His apparently listless manner in driving the cattle before him slowly and heedlessly, tended to lull suspicion on the part of the dragoons, and hence they took no notice of him. It was the intention of Harkness, in case he should be accosted by any of the party, to pretend to be an insane sort of person, and in this way to imitate David, who "changed his behaviour before Achish, king of Gath, and feigned himself mad." One of the party having proposed to ride up, and put some questions to him, the knight, who well knew who he was, and who saw at once the purpose for which he had assumed this guise and occupation, remarked, that it was not worth their while to waste time with an old and insane man, from whom nothing satisfactory could be expiscated, and proposed that they should instantly enter the house. The trooper was by this means diverted from his purpose, and the whole company proceeded without delay to the dwelling-house. Having dismounted and entered the abode of our worthy, they began the search. During the time the soldiers were within, Harkness drove the cows with all haste over a rising ground, in the neighbourhood of the house, and then betook himself to flight, and succeeded in making his escape. The Providence that had hitherto protected him, shielded him on the present occasion also, and accomplished his deliverance. Their errand having proved fruitless, the worthy knight left the soldiers to find their way homeward through the woods and moors in the best manner they could, and enjoyed, in his own mind, the satisfaction of having contributed to save the life of a good man.

Another anecdote is told of him, relative to an incident that is said to have befallen about the termination of the persecuting period. The people of Moffat, like many of their neighbours in similar circumstances, were tired of the curate of the parish, and earnestly wished his removal. In order to accomplish this purpose, they applied to Harkness, who happened at the time to be residing in the neighbourhood, to assist them in the project. He acceded to their request, and having collected a number of trusty persons, went to the manse, and desired the incumbent to withdraw in a peaceable manner. The curate made a virtue of necessity, and departed, leaving the inhabitants to congratulate themselves on the removal of an incubus that pressed so heavily upon them. Great was the dissatisfaction throughout the country generally, on account of the intrusion of the curates, but no effectual redress could be obtained, and the partial expulsions which took place were attended with no lasting advantage.

The following account, which Wodrow gives of the curates, amply justifies the aversion of the people to their incumbency, and their anxious desire for their removal. " When the curates entered the pulpit," says the historian, " it was by an order from the bishop, without any call from, yea, contrary to the inclinations of, the people. Their personal character was black, and no wonder their entertainment was coarse and cold. In some places they were welcomed with tears in abundance, and entreaties to be gone; in others, with reasonings and arguments which confounded them; and some entertained with threats, affronts, and indignities, too many here to be repeated. The bell's tongue in some places was stolen away, that the parishioners might have an excuse for not coming to church. The doors of the churches in other places were barricaded, and they made to enter by the window literally. The laxer of the gentry easily engaged them to join in their drinking cabals, which, with all iniquity, did now fearfully abound, and sadly exposed them. And in some places, the people, fretted with the dismal change, gathered together, and violently opposed their settlement, and received them with showers of stones. This was not, indeed, the practice of the religious and more judicious; such irregularities were committed by the more ignorant vulgar; yet they were so many evidences of the regard which they were like to have from the body of their parish-

u

ioners. Such who were really serious mourned in secret, as
doves in the valleys, and from principle could never countenance them; and others dealt with them as hath been said.
The longer they continued, and the better they were known,
the more they were loathed for their dreadful immoralities."
Considering the character of these men, therefore, and the
nature of their doctrine, it is not to be wondered at, that
the people, in certain localities, should have attempted their
expulsion.

CHAPTER XXV.

William Smith—House Conventicle—Welch of Scar—Fell of Balmaclellan—Sir Thomas Kirkpatrick.

THE parish of Closeburn occupies a beautiful spot in the central basin of Nithsdale. The locality is sweetly diversified with wooded spaces, cultivated fields, and undulating heights. It has been long famed for its rural academy, within the walls of which many a literary character has received an early training. The illustrious Boston of Ettrick, who sometimes assisted the famous Mr Murray of Penpont on sacramental occasions, received at one time a call to this parish—a circumstance respecting which so much is detailed in the Memoirs of that distinguished man. In the immediate neighbourhood of Closeburn, and in the parish of Morton, stands the village of Thornhill, on a rising ground, occupying the centre point of the charming basin to which Closeburn gives the name. Thornhill itself, a pleasant village, commands a delightful view of the spacious valley with which it is surrounded; few inland districts, perhaps, can furnish, on a similar scale, a finer prospect. On the west, is seen the ducal castle of Drumlanrig, couching like a lion in the forest, with all the variegated scenery in the vicinity of that princely residence; on the north are the frowning hills of Morton, to the east of which lies the far-famed Crichope Linn; and farther on in the distance are seen the circling hills of Durisdeer, so green and gay as to seem the guardians of some enchanted fairy dell; and all around, on the south and southwest, the scene opens in all the richness of a high cultivation, and terminates in the extreme prospective with a long-extended ridge of mountains.

The Cairn of Closeburn is situated on the banks of a streamlet called the Ballachin Burn, and was, in the times of persecution, tenanted by a worthy man named William

Smith. At the head of this burn there is a linn which was selected as a place of concealment by the oppressed Covenanters. William Smith was frequently obliged to leave his own house and retire to the linn, from the keen vigilance of his enemies. He was a good man, and firmly attached to those principles which it was the object of the dominant party to suppress; and he chose to subject himself to every kind of hardship rather than violate his conscience by yielding in the smallest degree to the requisitions of those who sought to corrupt the truth of God, and to rob men of the sacred boon of liberty—that birthright gifted by God himself, and which none but base-minded men will repudiate. He who cares little for civil freedom will care as little for religious liberty; and he who will not contend for the one will as little contend for the other. God has committed to us the trust of freedom as citizens, to be preserved for the sake of our freedom as Christians; for the profession of true religion cannot be maintained without it: and he who surrenders this privilege to the caprice of a tyrant acts a recreant part, for which the sovereign Judge of all will call him to account. What a noble sight is it to see poor men, in low stations, contending for high principles, and maintaining an elevation of character which may well put to the blush the boasted pretensions of the polite and the great, who despise alike the poor man and his cause!

It appears that William Smith often spent whole nights in the linn, not daring to venture home, lest he should be apprehended by his enemies. The inconvenience of this must have been very great, as this place was his only shelter in all kinds of weather—the most inclement as well as the most mild. On one occasion his wife, who constantly visited him in his retreat, induced him to spend a night under his own roof; and she agreed to keep watch while he was asleep, and to rouse him on the first approach of danger. Accordingly, under the cloud of night, he stole to his dwelling, in the hope of obtaining, without interruption, one night's refreshing rest in his own warm bed. His affectionate wife, who must have been of a kindred spirit with himself, felt, no doubt, a peculiar satisfaction in witnessing her husband enjoying the calm repose of a sound sleep, after so much watching and fatigue. Like a guardian angel, she watched by his couch, occasionally performing her work in the house by the cheerful light of the fire, which was blazing on the hearth; and many a time, we may suppose, she stood still to listen if anything of a suspicious nature was approaching. As the night passed on, she would fancy that every advancing hour would lessen the probability of any unwelcome visit from those she most dreaded, and that her husband, refreshed and invigorated, would hie away in safety before the break of day, and reach his place of refuge undiscovered. At the dead of night, however, her pleasing reverie was disturbed by an ominous sound in the distance— her heart began to fail, and all her fears were realized, when the heavy trampling of horses was heard at the door. The first thing was to rouse her husband—which was the work of a moment. He sprang from his bed, fully alive to the danger of his situation, and according, no doubt, to preconcerted measures, made his escape by a window in the back part of the house. The tradition that he fled naked, and remained in this condition in the linn till his wife brought his clothes in the morning, is scarcely credible—at least, it is not at all likely; because, in his precarious circumstances, it is more feasible to suppose that all due precautions would be taken by Smith in this instance, and that he would sleep partly in his apparel, and be ready, with " the swiftness of arrowy haste," to dart away prepared for his cold lodgement in the linn. The husband having made his escape, the soldiers interrogated the wife respecting the reset of rebels in her house; and having satisfied themselves in reference to her declaration that nobody was within, they departed without further interference; but not without a sharp reproof from the mistress of the lowly dwelling, for the unmannerly disturbance they had caused in the quietude of the night. In the early morning she visited the linn, carrying food to her husband, whom she, no doubt, congratulated on the providential deliverance he had experienced. Is it an unlikely thing to suppose that these pious persons, before they parted at the linn, would offer up the united prayer of a cordial thankfulness to the Author of their mercies; and that, considering that the one of them, at least, had obtained a respite from death, they would feel toward each other the glow of a warmer and more elevated attachment?

On another occasion this good man experienced a deliverance no less remarkable. Claverhouse, having heard of a religious meeting that was to be held on a certain night at the Clanchrie of Closeburn, was proceeding with his troopers to the place, for the purpose of surprising the conventicle. In his way to the meeting-place, he had to pass through the glen, near the linn where Smith concealed himself. It was a clear moonlight night, and Smith was sitting alone by a bieldy bush, attempting to read a religious book—tradition says the Confession of Faith—by the help of the lunar rays. A devotional heart will seize every opportunity of holding communion with God, whether it be by night or by day, whether in the comfortable chamber or in the open air. The devout feelings of our worthy could not fail to be excited, when he cast a glance on the lofty firmament, bespangled with the myriads of brilliant stars, which proclaim the glory of Him who, by his power and his wisdom, garnished the heavens, and gave every shining orb a tongue to speak his praise. "O Lord, our Lord, how excellent is thy name in all the earth, who hast set thy glory above the heavens!" While the pious man was thus endeavouring to read the moonlit pages, and was meditating on things divine, the heavy tread of horses was heard approaching, and Claverhouse and his company stood before him. They were surprised at finding a man at this hour in such a seclusion, and engaged in such an occupation. It immediately occurred to Claverhouse that the man must be a Covenanter, and he charged him with the crime of reading the Bible, as a proof of the allegation. In those times it was enough to convict a man of rebellion, and to expose him to the punishment of death, if he was known to be one who was in the habit of reading the Word of God, and of regulating his conduct by its precepts. The dragoons, in passing along the highway, have been known to shoot at persons sitting in the fields with a book in their hand, on the supposition that they could not belong to their party, and were consequently disaffected persons. A painful instance of this we have in the case of Arthur Inglis, farmer in the Nether-town of Cambusnethan, who, on the day after the battle of Bothwell, "whilst looking after his cattle which were grazing on a field, set himself down on a fur, and was reading his Bible, when he was unfortunately seen by some soldiers passing on the highway; they immediately concluded him to be a Whig, and one of them discharged his piece at him, but without effect. The good man, conscious of no guilt, and probably not perceiving that the shot was directed at him, only looked about at them, and did not offer to move; the soldiers immediately came up to him, and without even asking a single question at him, struck him on the head with their swords, and killed him on the spot." This, as narrated by Wodrow, shows the fearful lengths to which the lawless soldiery in those times proceeded.

Smith affirmed that he was not reading the Bible, and in

the meantime cautiously dropped the book into the bush by the side of which he was sitting. Instead, however, of harming him in any way, Claverhouse deemed it better for the present to press him into his service, and to oblige him, as his pioneer, to conduct the party to the Clauchrie. It must have been a sore trial to Smith, to be thus forced to guide the enemy to a house in which they expected to capture a number of innocent persons who were engaged in the worship of God, and with whom he himself would doubtless have been, had he known that the meeting was to take place. Being compelled to proceed, he advanced with a heavy heart, meditating, no doubt, by what possible means he could make his elopement. As they were moving along, a black heavy cloud came sailing over the clear disc of the moon, and enveloped the party in thick darkness; and Smith, embracing the opportunity of the temporary obscuration, turned round unperceived, and secreted himself in the heart of a tall bush of broom. In his perplexity Providence thus unlocked a door by which he both obtained his own liberty and was delivered from the distressful predicament of being the leader of the enemy to the house of unsuspecting friends. "God is faithful, who will not suffer you to be tempted (tried) above what ye are able, but will with the temptation (trial) also make a way to escape, that ye may be able to bear it." The yearnings of this man's heart were known to God, and his silent and fervent prayer was not despised; and he who, but a few moments before, was indebted to the bright countenance of the moon, which shone full upon him, and by the aid of which his eye was able to scan here and there a word of grace, was now no less indebted for the hiding of the same countenance behind the sable curtain of the clouds; and thus it is that light and shade in the Christian life are equally blessed of God for the spiritual benefit of his people. Having missed their guide, the dragoons were in a great rage, and beat about among the bushes in strict search of the fugitive. So closely did they environ the bush in which he was concealed, that he sometimes felt as if the horses' feet were touching him. Finding, however, their search to be in vain, they became quite uproarious, and Claverhouse gave orders to shoot at random among the bushes. The cries of the soldiers, and the loud report of the fire-arms, alarmed the people at the Clauchrie, who, suspecting that the enemy was near, consulted their safety by a speedy retreat from the place. Smith kept his station in the bush, and, though the shots were flying thick, he remained uninjured. The enemy

at length retired without gaining their object, and proceeded
to the Clauchrie, where they found nobody, they themselves
having communicated due warning of their approach, and
afforded the meeting time to disperse. In this wonderful
way did Providence defeat the designs of the wicked; and
Smith, who deemed himself particularly unfortunate in
being obliged to conduct the troopers to the evening conventicle, was the cause, by means of his accidental escape, of
giving notice to the meeting before the threatened danger
fell upon them. Had Claverhouse not met with Smith,
there is every likelihood that the people at the Clauchrie
would have been surprised by the soldiers, and not a few,
perhaps, might have lost their lives. This circumstance, then,
which at the time this good man judged to be a great calamity, turned out in the end to be a great deliverance.

In the vicinity of Dalswinton, and contiguous to Closeburn,
was a certain house in which the pious Nonconformists of that
neighbourhood usually held their meetings for prayer. This
house was situated on a rising ground, from which a view of
a considerable extent was obtained. When the meetings
were convened in the day-time, watches were stationed on
the top of the house, to give opportune and prompt warning,
in case of the approach of the enemy, by whom visits were
paid at the most unexpected seasons. Below the floor of the
house there was a secret recess, capable of holding about a
dozen of persons at a time, the mouth of which was closed
with a flat stone. This place was a convenient and safe retreat when at any time those under hiding were surprised
by the dragoons. It happened one night, when a number of
pious persons were met for the purpose of religious conversation and prayer, that a company of troopers suddenly surrounded the dwelling. The arrival of the soldiers threw all
into confusion, and there was no opportunity of effecting a
retreat to the receptacle below, for the intruders were on the
floor of the apartment before the inmates were aware. There
was in the ash-pit beneath the grate—which, at that time, in
all probability stood in the centre of the room—a great quantity of peat ashes of a light dusty nature, and easily put in
motion. When the soldiers were crowding into the place,
and all was in commotion, a young woman belonging to the
household lifted a large water-pitcher, and hastily dashed its
contents among the ashes and on the fire-place. In an instant, a dense and suffocating cloud of dust and smoke filled
the chamber, the effect of which was as startling and con-
founding to the dragoons as if a bombshell had exploded

among their feet. In the uproar, while the soldiers were rubbing their scalded eyes, and coughing, and stamping, and groping with their hands, not being able to distinguish friend from foe, the entire party, with the exception of one individual, made their escape. This individual was a young man, who was wounded by a musket-shot, and seized on the spot. He bled profusely, but the wound was not mortal, and he was afterwards conveyed to Edinburgh, where, it is said, he was tried and executed. Tradition has not preserved his name, otherwise we might be able to recognise him among the sufferers whose tale is recorded by the historian. The very high esteem in which this young person was held by his pious friends and neighbours, was displayed by them in a very extraordinary way. A number of females assembled on the spot where he was wounded, and, in order to testify their regard for him, they stained their snow-white handkerchiefs in his crimson blood, and preserved them as precious memorials of one who was held in universal admiration. This incident is a proof of the powerful attachment which the friends of religion in those days cherished for one another. They lived in times of common peril, and persecution operated as a tie which bound them in closer union, and which quickened the pulse of Christian sympathy, and sent it with a fuller throb throughout the suffering body of the faithful. The spirit of a heavenly kindness is the spirit of a genuine Christianity, and the love of the brethren is the distinguishing badge of true discipleship: "By this shall all men know that ye are my disciples, if ye love one another."

In the parish of Irongray, a few miles from Dumfries, there lived, in the times of the sufferings of the Church of Christ in Scotland, a Mr Welch, laird of Scar, who was much harassed for his nonconformity by those who, in those days, swayed the rod of oppression in the land. Irongray was the scene of the ministerial labours of the famous John Welch, grandson of " the incomparable John Welch of Ayr," whoso ministry, in the times immediately after the Reformation, was attended with eminent success in the west of Scotland, and which made the good Mr Dickson, minister of Irvine, frequently say, " that the grape gleanings at Ayr, in Mr Welch's time, were far above the vintage at Irvine in his own time." The secret of this holy man's success in the Gospel seems to have been his fervent and incessant prayers; for it is recorded of him, " that a distressing languor pervaded his frame, together with a great weakness in his knees, *caused by his continual kneeling at prayer; in consequence of*

which, though he was able to move them, and to walk, the
flesh of them became hard and insensible, like a horn." And
no wonder, when we consider that he often spent whole
nights in prayer, in the church of Ayr. His grandson in
Irongray was in every respect worthy of so illustrious an ancestor. The laird of Scar, here referred to, was in all likelihood a branch of the same family, as the Welches were descended from the house of Collieston in Irongray; and if so,
he appears to have inherited the religious independence which
characterized his pious kindred. Mr Welch of Scar, then,
was an individual on whom his enemies were determined to
lay their hands on the very first opportunity; and, accordingly, a party of soldiers was one day sent to his house, for
the purpose of apprehending him. The worthy man happened
to be accompanying his servant, who was ploughing in a field
in the vicinity of his residence, when the dragoons made their
appearance. Mr Welch intimated his suspicions to his servant, and his fears respecting the possibility of escape. The
servant, who seems to have been an intrepid man, and one
who was more solicitous about his master's safety than his
own, proposed instantly to unyoke the horses, and that Mr
Welch should ride home, as if he were the servant, and in
no fear of meeting with the dragoons; while he, on the other
hand, should flee toward the hill, in the full view of the
soldiers, as if he were the person in quest of whom they
had come. The proposal was acceded to by the laird, who
proceeded leisurely homewards with the horses, while the
ploughman betook himself with all speed to the neighbouring
height. The scene was witnessed by the troopers, who, con-
cluding that the fugitive was the man they sought, instantly
set out in pursuit. M'Lauchrie, for that was the servant's
name, pursued his way through the underwood, and along
the by-paths on the slope of the hill, till he reached the summit, where he was concealed in a dense mist, which was
hovering on the top of the rising ground. In this way both
master and servant escaped; for the soldiers, having missed
their object, rode off without visiting the dwelling-house,
thinking it needless to search the nest when the bird was
flown. A good man like Mr Welch could not fail to reward
the generous conduct of his servant, who, by this stratagem,
delivered him from those who sought his life. He accordingly repaid him with a favourable lease of the farm of Glenkill, on his own estate, in which place the M'Lauchries continued to reside till a very recent period. Men are seldom
losers by self-denial and disinterested behaviour; they have

the approbation of their own minds, the approbation of their
fellow-men, and, what is infinitely more, the approbation of
God. This man, whose desire it was to serve his master, a
man whom he loved, and loved in all probability because he
was one of Christ's people, and for whose safety he was prepared to make no small sacrifice, was afterwards rewarded
with a comfortable settlement in life, which was not only enjoyed by him to the end of his days, but also by his posterity
after him for several generations. What became of Mr Welch
afterwards, or how he succeeded in eluding the vigilance of
his enemies, is not said; but it appears that his house was
frequently ransacked and plundered by the soldiers who came
in search of him, and who on one occasion, when they could
find nothing else, carried off the domestic fowls, declaring
they would not leave on the premises of Scar so much as a
crowing cock. This godly man, however, who was actuated
by the spirit of a true follower of Christ, and had counted
the cost of following such a Master in the days of peril and
of plunder, would no doubt take joyfully the spoiling of his
goods for the sake of Him " who, though he was rich, yet for
our sakes became poor, that we through his poverty might
be made rich."

In addition to the incidents now mentioned relative to the
providential deliverances experienced by the people of God
in the time of the Church's affliction, another anecdote may
here be given. The parish of Balmaclellan, in Galloway,
contiguous to Dalry, was frequently infested by the troopers,
who went everywhere in search of the Nonconformists. The
minister of Balmaclellan, whose name was Thomas Warner,
would not submit to Prelacy, and was therefore one of those
ejected by the act of council at Glasgow in 1662. He was
not the only preacher who in that part of the country remained firm to the Presbyterian interest; for his immediate
neighbours, John Semple of Carsphairn, John M'Michan of
Dalry, and John Cant of Kells, were equally devoted to the
same cause, and were subjected to the same treatment. It
may easily be conceived that the united labours of these good
men, in these four contiguous parishes, would have a mighty
influence on the population in that inland district, and that
a goodly host of pious persons would be reared under their
ministry, to bear testimony to the truth in the day of trial.
This fully accounts for the often-repeated visits of the soldiers, who were sent in frequent detachments to this locality.
And it is worthy of remark, that the number of witnesses in
Scotland was fully as great in many of the landward parts

as in the populous towns; and these not merely collected in
the desert by flight from persecution, but were actually bred
there, and nurtured by the words of truth and sound doctrine,
through the instrumentality of the holy men whom the Head
of the Church had placed in these retired situations, as we
find that the greatest men, both in point of talent and of
sanctity, have not uncommonly been so located. It happened,
on one occasion, that a conventicle was to be held at the
Fell, in the parish of Balmaclellan. The news of this intended gathering had spread abroad, although with as much
caution as possible, lest tidings thereof should reach the ears
of the enemy; and tidings did reach their ears, by means
of some of those informers who were numerously scattered
over the country. A company of dragoons was therefore
despatched from a neighbouring station, who were enjoined
to disperse the meeting, and, as usual, to seize the ringleaders.
This party, on their way to the conventicle, which, it appears,
was kept in the night season, lost their road, and meeting
with a shepherd on the way, they compelled him to conduct
them to the Fell. The shepherd consented, knowing that in
the dark he could easily make his escape, or, if he chose, lead
them into a snare, which would prevent their intended mischief. The shepherd marched foremost as the leader of the
party, who intrusted themselves entirely to his guidance.
On their way to the place there was a marshy piece of
ground, straight into the heart of which it was the intention
of the shepherd to conduct them. Accordingly, having
reached its margin, their guide directed them to follow, and
to keep as near him as possible. He pushed forward on the
soft and sinking surface, while they hilariously followed,
neither seeing nor suspecting any mischance, till the whole
company plunged to the saddle-girths in the deep quagmire,
from which a speedy extrication was impossible. In this
predicament the shepherd left them, uttering imprecations
and threats of vengeance, while he proceeded with all haste
to the Fell, to warn the meeting of their danger. The statement of the shepherd was readily believed, and the conventicle was forthwith broken up. Thus did the great Shepherd
cast the shield of a special protection over these few sheep
in the wilderness, just at the time when the wolves were
about to enter the fold to waste and destroy.

But the shepherds and humble peasantry were not the
only instruments in shielding from harm the Covenanters,
who were, generally speaking, of their own standing in
society. Those who moved in a higher circle were some-

times employed by Providence in the same work. A party of troopers were one day sent to the mansion of Sir Thomas Kirkpatrick of Closeburn, for the purpose of demanding his assistance in searching for Whigs in his woods. It appears that the woods and heights, and linns and cottages of Closeburn, furnished shelter to many a wanderer, and afforded more ample scope to the strolling soldiery, who spread themselves abroad in quest of those who sought to maintain the privilege of worshipping God according to the dictates of their own conscience. The Rev. William Black of Closeburn, who was opposed to Prelatic usurpation, and therefore outed in the sixty-two, would, no doubt, have been the means of diffusing throughout the parish the spirit of nonconformity, and, what is more, the spirit of true Christianity. Sir Thomas was obliged to comply with the demand, and accompanied the soldiers into the woods. In proceeding to the different localities which were supposed to be resorted to as hiding-places by the Covenanters, Sir Thomas pursued the nearer route, by the narrow footpaths that led through the woods, while the horsemen were obliged to take the more circuitous roads. In winding his way among the thick trees, Sir Thomas came upon a man fast asleep by the side of the path before him. The man was obviously one of the individuals whom the soldiers had come to seek; but the gentleman in whose way Providence had thus placed him had too much humanity to publish his discovery. Near the place where this person was reposing on his grassy bed, under the guardianship of Him who never slumbers nor sleeps, was a quantity of newly-cut brackens, which Sir Thomas turned over with his staff to cover the sleeping man from the prying eyes of the troopers. The action was observed by one of the horsemen, who cried out that the guide was doing something suspicious; but before any of the party got time to dismount, and to investigate the matter, Sir Thomas turned round, and in an indignant tone asked if he could not be permitted to turn over the loose brackens and withered leaves of the forest without their permission; and so the matter ended, and the man remained undiscovered. This anecdote shows the power which the military at that time assumed, and the insolence of the soldiery towards even those who were their superiors. Gentlemen and commoners were treated alike by the lawless troopers who were let loose on an oppressed country.

CHAPTER XXVI.

Fergussons of Threerigs—Craigdarroch - Wilson of Croglin—
John Gillespie.

THE small estate of Threerigs, in the parish of Glencairn, was, in the times of persecution, possessed by a worthy gentleman of the name of Fergusson, who died a few years prior to the Revolution. This gentleman was related to the laird of Craigdarroch, mentioned in a former chapter. He had two sons, Alexander and William—the former of whom was the heir of Threerigs. The two sons were Nonconformists, and ardently attached to the principles of civil and religious liberty. But though they approved themselves the warm friends of the oppressed, and abetted the suffering followers of Christ to the utmost of their power, it does not appear that they were taken notice of before the year 1684. The house of Caitloch, in Glencairn, seems to have been a place of frequent resort to the Covenanters in those troublous times. It was to this place that the Rev. John Blackadder of Troqueer, near Dumfries, fled for refuge when he was ejected from his parish. One day Alexander Fergusson, the eldest son of the laird of Threerigs, paid a visit to Caitloch, for the purpose of meeting with any of the suffering party who might happen to be there in concealment; and during his stay at this place, a company of troopers reached the neighbouring village of Minihive, on their way to Caitloch and the parts adjacent, in search of Nonconformists. The pleasant village of Minihive lies in the midst of a sweet opening among the hills by which it is surrounded, and commands a delightful variety of scenery. In the immediate vicinity of this secluded village stands the ruin of the identical house in which was born Renwick, the last of the martyrs, to whose memory a handsome monument is erected near the spot. It was to Minihive that one of the sons of Mr Blackadder, a boy of ten years of age, fled naked in the night season, when the dragoons were plundering his father's house at a short distance from the village. " I ran," he says, " the length of half-a-mile in the dark night, naked to the shirt. I got to a neighbouring toune called the Brig-end of Minihive, where, thinking to creep into some house to save my life, I found all the doors shut, and the people sleeping; upon which I went to the cross of the toune, and got up to the uppermost step of it, and there I sat me down and fell fast asleep till the morning. Between five and six a door opens, and an old woman comes out, and seeing a white thing on the cross, comes near it, and when she found it was a little boy, cries out, ' Jesus, save us ! what art thou ?' With that I awoke, and answered her : I am Mr Blackadder's son. ' Oh, my puir bairn, what brought thee here ?' I an-swers : There is a hantle of fearful men with red coats has burnt all our house; my breether, and my sister, and all the family. ' O puir thing,' says she, ' come in and lie down in my warm bed;' which I did, and it was the sweetest bed I ever met with."

Mr James Brotherstones, minister of the parish of Glen-cairn, in which Minihive is situated, was ejected at the Restoration. He was, consequently, one of those who re-mained firm to his principles, both doctrinally and ecclesi-astically; and not a few of his parishioners followed his ex-ample, and some of them obtained the crown of martyrdom; of whom it is unnecessary to take notice here, as they have already obtained an honourable niche in the page of the historian.

When the dragoons left Minihive, the first place to which they proceeded was Caitloch; and having, it would appear, arrived rather unexpectedly, they seized a number of persons, among whom was Alexander Fergusson. This little band of captives was conducted to Minihive to undergo an exami-nation before the authorities. Fergusson had in his pocket a number of musket balls, which he scattered unnoticed among the thick grass by the way-side, that he might divest himself of everything which, in the view of his enemies, might be deemed suspicious. It happened that the laird of Craigdar-roch was among the examinators when the prisoners were introduced; and seeing the son of his friend of Threerigs among the rebels, he was deeply distressed at the circum-stance. He was fully aware that the slightest evidence of his being a Covenanter would insure the ruin of the fine young man who stood before him, and perhaps the ruin of the whole family. Craigdarroch did not seem to recognise him as a kinsman, nor did Fergusson take any notice of the laird. They knew that anything like a mutual recognition would be viewed in an unfavourable light. Meanwhile Craigdarroch was endeavouring to devise some means for the rescue of his friend; and the plan which he formed was successful. He was sitting apparently at his ease, and casting a careless look at the prisoners, when all on a sudden, as if caught by surprise, he raised his voice in a loud and indignant tone, and addressing Fergusson as if he had been his shepherd, exclaimed : " Sandy, what business have you here ? how came you to leave my sheep on the hill without my permission ? what right have you to go strolling from house to house, exposing yourself to danger in gratifying your taste for silly gossiping ? Begone, Sir, begone instantly, and attend more carefully to your flock, else you may expect a quick dismissal from my service." On his being accosted in this authoritative manner by his friend, Fergusson took the hint. and stole away, as if ashamed, under the weight of the reproach which had been thus sharply administered. In this way the young laird of Threerigs escaped the danger which was pending over him; and he retired without interruption, and without a question being asked at him. Some time after this occurrence Craigdarroch met him, and congratulated him on his seasonable deliverance; at the same time remarking, that great caution was to be observed by him in his future movements. " I am," said he, " as warmly attached to the cause as you are; for it is the cause of liberty and religion. I have been successful in effecting your rescue by very simple means on this occasion; but should you happen again to be apprehended and brought before these men, it will not be in my power to deliver you a second time. Information has been lodged against you as a suspected person, and no means will avail to save you should you now fall into the hands of your enemies : therefore, my young friend, look to yourself." It appears that the family of Threerigs showed very great kindness to the persecuted Covenanters. There was a wood on the estate, in the thickets of which numbers of the sufferers were concealed, and fed by the family; and the knowledge of this circumstance eventually proved their ruin.

The caution given by Craigdarroch was not without reason; nor were his apprehensions for his friend's safety groundless. It soon became publicly known that Alexander and his brother had fully espoused the covenanting interest; and the violent party took up the matter, and resolved to bring the malcontents to punishment. Accordingly, they were summoned before the superintendents of the district; but not choosing to appear, they were declared rebels. Their cattle and their goods were seized, their house pillaged, and their estate transferred to their neighbour, the laird of Glencrosh. Being thus reduced to the greatest straits, and destitute of all things but a good conscience and a good cause, they were obliged to retire with the rest of the wanderers to the wilds and mountains for safety. They had lost, for Christ's sake, everything they valued on earth but their lives; and now to preserve them in an honest and Christian manner was their chief care. The privations to which they were subjected, and the trials they endured in common with their Christian friends, with whom they were now obliged to wander from place to place, were neither few nor small. It furnishes us with an eminent proof of the power of the Gospel on the heart, when we witness two young persons, in comparative affluence, in comfortable circumstances, and with the prospect of rising in the world, voluntarily renouncing all, that they might " hold fast the profession of their faith without wavering." Nothing tests a man's religious sincerity more perfectly than the call to the entire renunciation of self and the world for the truth's sake. It was this which put the character of Moses to the proof, as a believer in the God of his fathers, when he might have enjoyed the highest honours in the land of Egypt; but he " refused to be called the son of Pharaoh's daughter, choosing rather to suffer affliction with the people of God, than to enjoy the pleasures of sin for a season, esteeming the reproach of Christ greater riches than the treasures of Egypt; for he had respect to the recompense of reward."

Alexander Fergusson, though exposed to manifold hardships during the few years that remained of the persecution from the time of his open avowal of his profession, nevertheless escaped the merciless hands of his persecutors, and lived many years after the Revolution, though he did not regain the possession of his estate. The fate of his brother William, however, was somewhat harder. His name is found in Wodrow's list of those who, in 1684, were declared fugitives : " William Fergusson, son to the deceased William Fergusson of Threerigs." He was on one occasion, when wandering in the parish of Tynron, hotly pursued by a company of dragoons, who observed him lurking near the road along which they were travelling. He fled to the base of a

huge rock called Craigturrach, with a view to ascend the
rugged precipice. One of the troopers having dismounted,
followed him, and fired upon him as he was climbing the
giddy eminence. Having missed his aim, however, he flew
to the rock, and mounting its beetling front with nimble
hands and feet, reached the summit in equal time with the
fugitive. The merciless trooper, on nearing him, struck him
a furious blow with his pistol, and overpowered him. He
then brought him a prisoner to the party at the bottom of
the hill, who gave him up to the proper authorities, by whom
he was banished to America, from which exile he never returned. It must have been painful to these pious and affectionate brothers, to be thus separated by the rude hand of
persecuting violence. They were all that was dear to each
other on earth; they were sufferers in the same common
cause of goodness; they had an interest in the same heaven,
where all their hopes and wishes centred; and there, in that
land of peace, when all their toils and wanderings on earth
should terminate, they expected to rest together. How sweet
is the idea of rest to the weary! and how surpassingly sweet
is the thought of the heavenly rest to God's weary heritage!
The Church of Christ may, in times of tribulation, be like a
solitary bark tossed on the tumultuous billows of a troubled
sea, and every moment ready apparently to be engulfed in
the raging flood; but still she sinks not; for though she
seems to descend to the depths below, anon she is seen heav-
ing on the crest of the wave. An invisible hand upholds
her—the Lord is in the ship; and though he appear to be
asleep when "the heathen rage, and the people imagine a
vain thing, when the kings of the earth set themselves, and
the rulers take counsel together, against the Lord and against
his Christ," yet he will rise up in the greatness of his might,
and rebuke the winds and the waves, and there shall be a
great calm. Heaven, however, is the only haven of repose to which the Church of God can look, and where she
is to expect a quietude without interruption and without
end.

Fergusson of Craigdarroch, though he did not go the full
length of his kinsmen of Threerigs in the avowal of his principles, was always friendly to the Covenanters; and when it
was in his power, he uniformly shielded them from the vengeance of their enemies. It was his custom, it is said, to
ride almost every day to some part of the district in which
he resided, to gather what information he could respecting
the situation of the persecuted, and then to lay his plans for

their defence accordingly. He always rode armed, according to the custom of the times, that he might be prepared for any emergency. One day, as he was proceeding into the country on horseback, he met, near Maxwelltown, a small party of Whigs in full flight before a party of dragoons. There was in their way a gate called Etone Ligget, through which the fugitives had passed; and the troopers, as they approached this place, were encountered by Craigdarroch, who kept them in check for a time, till the objects of their pursuit were out of danger. Having gained his purpose, he turned his swift steed, and crossing the River Cairn at a place called the Gaps Mill, escaped. The dragoons being strangers in the neighbourhood, did not know who their opponent was, and the circumstance was not discovered. The action was a daring one, both as it subjected him to great personal risk at the time, and as it exposed him, had he been recognised, to the full vengeance of the ruling party. This anecdote bears a strong resemblance to the one told of the same gentleman in a former chapter, and the probability is, that they both refer to the same incident. The fact, however, is illustrative of the good-will which this worthy man bore to the oppressed cause of freedom and religion, and of his readiness, when circumstances permitted, to render those who suffered in this cause effective assistance.

Some of the descendants of the Fergussons of Threerigs, who lost all their worldly property for their conscientious adherence to the cause of the covenant, are at present living in the neighbourhood of Sanquhar and Drumlanrig; and though moving in the humbler walks of life, reflect no discredit on their pious ancestry.

Wilson of Croglin, in the parish of Tynron, was a man of a kindred spirit with Craigdarroch. He never openly avowed his attachment to the covenanting cause; but he cherished a strong sympathy with the sufferers, and endeavoured, without risk to himself, to serve them to the utmost of his power. He was a justice of the peace, and was therefore well acquainted with the designs of the party with which he was connected. His leniency to the sufferers was apparent from the methods he adopted to screen them from their enemies. The Nonconformists in the parish of Tynron were kept in a condition of comparative safety under his sheltering wings. In the fugitive roll given by Wodrow, there are several persons named who belonged to that parish, and some of them Croglin's own tenants, who were denounced as rebels, or guilty of reset; and yet it is believed that not one of them was brought to trouble, owing, it is said, to the good management of Croglin. It was the practice of this benevolent man to communicate, in a way as private and efficient as possible, any knowledge he possessed of the designs of the persecutors respecting the sufferers. It was his custom, when he returned from the meetings which were held in the district, to walk into the kitchen at a certain hour of the night, when the domestics had retired to rest, and there, like the man in the wood of Eliock, to convey, by way of soliloquy, to what in the cottages of Scotland is called the *crook*, or iron chain which is suspended in the inside of the chimney, any information that might be of importance to the Covenanters. Having stationed himself before the fire-place, and touching the *crook* with the end of his staff, he addressed it by the name of *Hog ma Drog*, a kind of soubriquet which he employed to save appearances, and said: "Though we must not tell the secrets of our counsel to any mortal creature, yet, as thou art neither flesh nor blood, I may tell thee, *Hog ma Drog;*" and then patting on the pendent chain gently with his staff, uttered what he wished to communicate respecting the projected movements of the enemy. During his speech to the *crook*, a male servant was, by agreement, uniformly concealed in a retired corner, where he could hear distinctly every word spoken by his master. This man, a trusty servant, carried, without loss of time, the news to the parties immediately concerned, who were by this means enabled to avoid the mischief plotted by their enemies. Such men as Fergusson and Croglin were of inestimable service to the oppressed remnant; they stood between the two parties, and while they ostensibly belonged to the one party, they in heart and in principle belonged to the other. This medium sort of party was made use of by Providence to restrain the persecutors, on the one hand, or at least to counteract their devices; and, on the other hand, to shield the persecuted, and frequently, no doubt, to regulate their procedure. These persons were held in high esteem by the Nonconformists, even though they did not go the whole length of their views, nor assume that decided and fearless stand which they themselves had done. There are some men who want the moral courage to proceed the full length to which their principles would naturally conduct them— their love of ease, their fear of reproach, their concern for their personal safety, and their solicitude about their worldly interests, all combine to modify their views, and to persuade them to adopt that more cautious policy which will be at-

tended with less risk to themselves.   How far such conduct
receives the divine approbation, is another question.   It is
obvious, that a firm and honest mind will stoutly follow the
line of duty, reckless of all anticipated results, and will leave
consequences entirely with Him whose commands, apart
from every prudential consideration, must be promptly
obeyed.   When conscience and duty call, we are not to sit
down to make the previous calculation how far a compliance
with the call will either injure or promote our worldly interests, and then to shape our procedure accordingly.   No;
with the simplicity of little children, we must just do what
God bids us, indifferent to all that may befall us, knowing
that he will make all things work together for good to them
that love him.   In those persecuting times, however, the
want of decision on the part of not a few arose, probably,
from a partial ignorance of the nature and bearings of the
great principles for which the Covenanters contended; and
this being the case, the importance of their cause would not be
felt with that pressure of conviction which would thrust them
forward into the ranks of those who were disinterestedly
sacrificing their all for the sake of the truth.   They deserve
to be remembered with *gratitude,* who in any way assisted
our oppressed forefathers when they were persecuted for
righteousness' sake; but they deserve to be remembered
with *honour,* who, " for conscience towards God, endured
grief, suffering wrongfully."

In addition to these anecdotes, the story of John Gillespie
may here be given.   This man lived at a place called the
" Water Meetings," in Crawford Moor.   Even in this wild
district a garrison was stationed in 1684, for the purpose of
suppressing the conventicles that were being held in that
remote wilderness.   The Rev. Gilbert Hamilton of Crawford
was a Nonconformist, and it is likely that his ministry was
attended with so much success as to be the means of rearing
not a few witnesses for the cause of the Reformation.   Garrisons were at the time become very common in the south
and west, though they became still more so a few years
afterwards.   Two were placed in Carsphairn, and one at
Caitloch, besides the one just mentioned.   These were intended not only to keep their respective localities in order,
but also to hem in the south and north of Nithsdale.   They
were supplied with a certain number of foot and horse, ready
at all times to sally forth at a moment's warning; so that
much of Scotland was, as Wodrow remarks, as if it had been
a country conquered by the enemy.   The country people

were greatly harassed by the soldiers passing between the
garrisons, and many of the murders in the open fields were
perpetrated by these strolling parties; and this probably, as
we have before remarked, may account for the graves that
are to be seen in the moors and on the mountains, of which
no person in the present day knows anything further, than
that they are reported to be the graves of Covenanters.   In
these deserts many a martyr probably sleeps in his shroud,
unknown alike to history and to tradition.   These garrisons
were, for the most part, the head-quarters of a licensed banditti, who lived in a great measure on the plunder of the
peaceful inhabitants.

John Gillespie was not a Covenanter; but then he was not
a Malignant.   He could feel for suffering humanity, and was
ready to embody his sympathy in deeds.   One cold winter
evening, when the storm was descending on the moorlands,
and the drifting snow was beginning to be piled in heaps by
the eddying winds, our shepherd was busily engaged in gathering his flock to a place of safety on the waste.   On such
occasions the occupation of a shepherd is anything but a
sinecure; he has to face the roaring of the tempest and
the suffocating drift, when others are snugly seated by the
blazing hearth, luxuriating in the comfortable feeling of
a complete security from the raging of the blast without.
In the hilly districts the storms of winter sometimes visit the
desert rather unexpectedly.   The heavy flakes of snow begin to fall through the still and oppressed atmosphere, then
the wind rises in fitful gusts, and at length blows with terrific fury, pouring the light drift in smoky streams along the
heath, till flocks, and cottages, and all, are occasionally
buried beneath the powdery heap.   It was when one of
these blasts was beginning to rise, a little before the evening
dusk, that John Gillespie observed two men, apparently
fugitives, take refuge under the sheltering brow of a deep
moss-hag.   It was his conviction that they courted this retreat, as much as a hiding-place from their pursuers as a
covert from the storm.   He did not, however, approach
them, fearing lest strolling parties from the neighbouring
garrison might be at hand, who might bring him into trouble
if they chanced to see him holding intercourse with the wanderers.   When he came home, and had laid aside his snow-
clad plaid, and was stretching his shivering limbs on the
hearth before a blazing pile of peats, that expelled the winter's cold from the homely apartment, he informed his wife
of what he had seen in the moss.   " Why, then, did you not

bring them home with you?" said she; "the storm is gathering apace, and the men must perish ere the morning." "I
durst not venture near them," replied he, "nor speak to
them, for fear of the dragoons, who, I suspect, were pursuing
them." "The troopers will not continue long out on such a
night," answered she; "and, with your leave, I will go and
fetch them to the house." The danger in this case was lest,
on the morrow, a search should be made in the cottage, and
lest ensnaring questions should be put to the shepherd respecting the fugitives. To obviate this difficulty it was
agreed, that if the men should be brought to the house,
Gillespie should not see them, nor converse with them, but
should retire by himself to some private place in the cottage
till they should go to rest; and that they should depart in
the early morning. Gillespie's wife then hastened to the
moor, and brought the two men from their cold retreat in
the moss. They accepted the shelter of the shepherd's
dwelling with grateful hearts, and could not but observe the
conduct of a kind Providence in leading them by the hand
to a comfortable habitation. They were kindly entertained
in the lowly dwelling; and having returned thanks to the
Preserver of their lives, and sought a blessing on those whose
hearts the Lord had disposed to show them kindness in the
day of their distress, they retired to rest, and left the storm
to spend its fury on the waste. On the morrow they arose
with the dawn; and having engaged in the worship of God
with the shepherd's household, he himself abiding in concealment, they departed from the hospitable hut to seek a
retreat at a greater distance from danger.

It was not long after they had departed, however, till a
party of dragoons arrived at Gillespie's house in search of
the men who, on the preceding evening, had taken refuge in
the moss. The leader of the company is said to have been a
Captain Stewart, who asked the shepherd if he had seen or
conversed with the men of whom they were in quest. He
acknowledged that he saw two men such as they described,
wandering in the moss in the dusk when the snow was beginning to fall, but that he went not near them, nor had any
intercourse with them, and that he knew not where they
were. All this the shepherd could honestly affirm; and as
he was known to be no Covenanter, he had no doubt that his
statements would be received. In looking about the dwelling, however, the commander observed a large Bible lying
open, as if it had been recently perused. This excited suspicion, and he concluded that Gillespie was now become a

Religionist; and this single circumstance, as he imagined, amply justified him in making him his prisoner. It was certainly a melancholy state of things, when the mere perusal of the Word of God was deemed enough to attach to a man the character of a rebel. The suppression of true religion seemed as much the object of the persecutors as the suppression of Presbyterianism. They were a class of men who hated the very semblance of godliness, and who would have rejoiced to see the land overspread with irreligion and profanity. They were, for the most part, wicked men themselves, and therefore they could not tolerate in others the existence of that which operated as a severe and incessant condemnation of their own ungodliness.

Honest John Gillespie was made prisoner, and tried on no other charge than the finding of an open Bible in his house. The trial, however, issued in his favour; for, however unreasonable the men who sat in judgment in such causes might be, there were frequently cases brought before them which even irrationality itself had not the effrontery to condemn. The shepherd was dismissed, and he returned to his quiet occupation in the moorlands, and was left to his own prudence how to conduct himself with respect to the suffering wanderers.

On this occasion he was put to some trouble, but Providence prevented him from suffering unjustly. He had shielded two of the homeless followers of Christ on the night of the storm, and the Lord shielded him in turn from the storm of persecuting rage which was about to burst on his defenceless head, and he was permitted to revisit his habitation in peace. How he acted afterwards—whether he left the Prelatic Church and joined the suffering party—is not known; but it is not improbable that the incident which befell him tended to rouse him to reflection, and to balance in his mind the claims of the respective parties; in which case it is not difficult to see in what direction his convictions would lean. It would be gratifying, no doubt, to ascertain the subsequent history of many such, the incidents of whose life tradition has preserved; and there can be little question that the result, in most cases, would be very pleasing. In writing a full and even-handed history of the Church of God, it would be necessary to take up religion as it existed in the cottages, and not merely to delineate the character and proceedings of eminent men and Church courts. Our ecclesiastical notices hitherto may be compared to the geographical sketches which a traveller professes to

give of a country, and in which he describes chiefly its pro
minent features and lofty mountains and the storms which
play around their summits, while he leaves out of its topography the lowly valleys, the fertile plains, the lovely glens,
and the peaceful hamlets. Justice, therefore, has not yet
been done to the religious history of our land in reference to
the times that are past, and probably cannot now be done,
as the memorials of the piety that has existed in the humble
walks of life have not been retained, and materials enow
cannot now be gathered, from which to construct a regular
narrative. The statistics of religion in every Church, congregation, and household of those who fear God, have yet to
be made out, before a satisfactory estimate can be taken of
the amount of real godliness in the land.

CHAPTER XXVII.

South Mains.

The farm-house of South Mains, in the vicinity of Sanquhar, stands on an elevated sand-bank, at the base of which flows Nith's " fair flood," and the greater part of whose gravelly heap has, in the lapse of ages, been washed away by the stream. From this house, directly across the river, the eye rests on the beautiful lands which were once the possession of Ross of Ryehill—a family which, in ancient times, was of great note in this part of Nithsdale.

South Mains borders on the richly-wooded lands of Eliock, which, as was remarked in a former chapter, were possessed by Dalziel of Carnwath, who kept a small troop of dragoons at Eliock House. There was in Dalziel's household a male servant who favoured the Covenanters, and who took every occasion of being serviceable to them. As he waited constantly on his master, he had ample opportunities of knowing the plans which were frequently concerted at the festive board respecting the sufferers. When the party became hilarious at their wine, their designs were freely unfolded, without the slightest suspicion that any one was listening who was likely to communicate that information which would ultimately defeat their measures. It was the care of this man, however, to notice everything that was said or whispered respecting the persons whom it was his wish to shield from the premeditated vengeance of their enemies; but whether this was done from a well-principled sympathy with their cause, or merely from a sympathy with their sufferings as unoffending persons, is not said. There is a little streamlet, called the Carple Burn, which takes its rise in the dark moorlands on the south, and gurgles through the pleasure-grounds of Eliock, till it discharges itself into the Nith. The banks of this sweet rivulet are in some places

deeply shaded with wood, and must, in former times, have
furnished a tolerably secure retreat as a place of concealment.
On the margin of the brook there grew a large tree, which
wreathed " its fantastic roots " among the stones and shelving
rocks which overhung its channel.   At the root of this tree
there was a hollow place sufficiently roomy to contain at
least one person without his being readily observed.   This
place, it would appear, was, when any of the Covenanters
were in the neighbourhood, at a certain time of the day,
uniformly occupied by one of their number.   It was not,
however, so much for the purpose of concealment that this
little cell was resorted to, as for the purpose of receiving information from the domestic servant respecting the projected
movements of the dragoons.   It had been agreed on between this friendly man and the suffering party that he
should, at a stated hour, come to the tree, and that when he
had anything of importance to communicate, he should address the tree, and tell *it* what he intended should be heard
by the man beneath.   The reason of this method of procedure was, that the servants were, in all probability, either
laid under the obligation of an oath, or strictly enjoined,
under the penalty of the severest punishment, not to divulge
anything that they heard or knew of the intended proceedings of their masters respecting the persecuted.   The severity
of the persecutors was well known to their domestics, who,
though they were of their own party, and in their pay, could
not but observe the relentless tyranny and cruelty exercised
toward a class of pious and harmless men.   The fear of their
vengeance, therefore, would operate as a powerful restraint
in preventing their menials from holding the most distant
intercourse with the intercommuned party.   It appears,
therefore, that this method was adopted by the servant for
the purpose of more successfully evading any ensnaring
questions that might be put to him.   He spoke to the tree—he
accosted no man; and in addressing his discourse to a deaf
tree, he might think that he was not responsible, if, perchance, his speech should be heard by a listening ear.   Even
in this, however, there was danger; for among the thickets
there might be more listening ears than one, and ears that
were wide open to every suspicious whisper; so that no
soliloquy in the grove, however apparently incidental and
undesigned, would, if it partook of the nature of a divulgence
of secrets, be permitted to pass with impunity.   The conduct
of this man seems to have been very disinterested, when he
exposed himself to no small hazard in his honest endeavours

to convey warning to those over whose innocent heads imminent danger was pending; but the blessing of him who was ready to perish would come upon him. One day this servant understood, from the discourse to which, owing to his official situation in the family, he was permitted to listen, that the dragoons were, on a time specified, to visit certain localities in the neighbourhood, where he knew a certain number of Covenanters were in concealment at the moment. He felt concerned for their safety, and longed for the arrival of the usual hour at which he was accustomed to visit the tree. When the time came, he proceeded with all speed and secrecy to the appointed place, stationed himself near the root of the tree, under the hollow trunk of which he perceived that there lay in silence and concealment one of the party in whose welfare he was interested. Having stood, as may be supposed, for a while in an apparently careless and idle manner, like a person who had arrived at the spot by mere accident; and having, by cautious observation and attentive listening, satisfied himself that nothing suspicious was near, he began, in a low but audible voice, to address the tree : " O fair and stately tree, many a time have I stationed myself in meditative mood, under your wide-spreading boughs and mantling foliage, to listen to the murmuring of the gentle stream, and to hear the delicious music poured from the throats of the charming songsters that fill thy leafy branches. I have come this evening to taste anew these rich enjoyments; because it may hap that to-morrow by this time I shall be elsewhere, as I shall be called to follow my master, with his band of troopers, to pursue some of those unhappy Covenanters, who are understood to be lurking in some place not far from hence. And so adieu, my favourite tree; and may you stand unscathed by the winds of heaven, and untouched by the woodman's axe, till I visit you again." In some such cautious way did this trusty man convey the information intended for him who occupied the cavity underneath, and then withdrew without taking the slightest notice of him. When the servant retired, the man crept from his hiding-place, and stole away unperceived to his companions. He informed them of the designs of the enemy, and they resolved on an immediate escape; and before the dawn they left their lurking-place. In attempting a somewhat dubious flight, they came to South Mains at an early hour, and were admitted by the master of the house to the shelter of his dwelling. Though tradition says little regarding this man yet the circumstance of his having received under his roof a company of men whose "names were cast out as evil," and his having done this at the greatest risk to himself, would indicate the existence both of religion and of humanity in his breast. Nor is it likely that the men would have ventured to his abode, and intrusted their secret to his keeping, if they had not known him to be one who favoured their cause. The name of the worthy farmer of South Mains was William Hair; but though many such are unknown to us, they are had in remembrance with Him who has said : " Whosoever shall give you a cup of water in my name, because ye belong to Christ, verily I say unto you, he shall not lose his reward."

In the house of South Mains the wanderers were kindly treated. A plentiful breakfast was set before them, of which they partook with grateful hearts; and the more so, as their hunger was generally appeased by a precarious meal; for when one repast was received, they often could not tell where the next was to come from. As they were partaking of the hospitable entertainment which was so seasonably and amply provided for them, a few dragoons from Eliock were observed approaching the house. Their first impression was, that their flight had been discovered, and that the troopers came to apprehend them in the farm-house. The honest farmer, who plainly foresaw the mischief that would befall both himself and his guests if their retreat should be found out, hastily conducted them to the barn, and concealed them among the corn sheaves in the mow. In a few moments the soldiers arrived, and demanded an interview with the farmer. With a considerable degree of trepidation, which he attempted to hide the best way he could, the worthy farmer appeared before them at the door. " We have come," said they, " to buy corn for our horses." This announcement restored the good man to something like his usual composure, and he led them to the barn to examine the heaps of grain which lay on the floor. When the dragoons entered, the handful who were concealed among the sheaves at the extremity of the barn were filled with apprehension, and naturally imagined that all was over. Their fears, however, were partially allayed when they heard that the errand on which the troopers were come was corn, and not fugitives. They lay, nevertheless, in breathless anxiety, lest any incident should discover their retreat; and it was not till the men had finally retired that their solicitude was fully removed. The soldiers departed peaceably, and the men remained unnoticed. Their situation, however, was precarious; for had one of the dragoons dragged but a single sheaf of corn from the mow to cast it to his horse—a circumstance which might easily have occurred—their hiding-place might have been revealed. These good men sometimes experienced deliverances in very unlikely circumstances; while in circumstances as unlikely they were at other times discovered and captured by their enemies.

CHAPTER XXVIII.

James Nivison of Closeburn Mill—Wonderful Escapes.

The farm of Closeburn Mill was, in the times of persecution, tenanted by James Nivison, a man of a saintly character and of unbending integrity. His house was an occasional resort to the wanderers that frequented the district. The curate of Closeburn had no good-will to this worthy man, and he sought every opportunity to injure him. James refused to attend his church—a circumstance which gave unpardonable offence to that Prelatic underling—and he failed not to lodge information against him, as being a disaffected and disloyal person. He had one friend in the parish, however, in the person of Sir Thomas Kirkpatrick, whose lenity to the sufferers that crept into the woods and glens near him was displayed on various occasions. When the worthy knight learned the determination of the curate respecting James Nivison, and knowing the vindictive disposition of the man, he entreated James to yield so far as to consent to enter the church, though it were only to go in by the one door and out by the other. With this, however, he would by no means comply; alleging that it would be a compromise of his principles to yield even this apparently trifling matter. The knight could not but admire the firmness and honesty of purpose displayed by this virtuous man, in a case in which he deemed his conscience concerned. Anxious, however, to protect his tenant, he made another proposal, and assured him, if he would come only to the "kirk-stile," it might still be in his power to save him; but Nivison continued firm in his determination, and even went so far as to declare, that if the turning of a straw, in obedience to the unprincipled rulers of the time, would save him from trouble, he would not comply. He was resolved to follow what he conceived to be the plain line of his duty, and to preserve a good conscience, whatever might betide. This decision of mind, which some may probably be inclined to call obstinacy, did not lessen him in the estimation of the laird of Closeburn, who determined, since he could make no more of it, to communicate to his honest tenant whatever he knew of the designs of the enemy respecting him, and by this means to afford him opportune warning of the danger that threatened him.

Sir Thomas had a domestic servant, whose leanings towards the Covenanters were no secret to his master, and him he instructed to understand the import of certain signs, by which, when he could not hold conversation with him, he wished to communicate the designs formed against the Covenanters who at the time might happen to be lurking in the neighbourhood, and especially against his friend James Nivison. When, therefore, any proposal was made to Sir Thomas to lend assistance to the persecutors in searching the woods and linns on his estate for persons under hiding, information of the circumstance was instantly communicated, by means of the servant, to Nivison, and others concerned. In this way much mischief was prevented, and the purposes of the enemy in many instances defeated. When these occasional warnings were given to Nivision, he had one place of resort to which he generally fled, and this was the darkly wooded sides of Crichope Linn. Crichope Linn is, perhaps, one of the most striking scenes of the kind in the south of Scotland, and the caverns in its precipitous banks are well calculated to afford a concealment, which few who know the danger of the attempt will care to invade.

One day, however, the dragoons came upon James without warning, and on his first view of their approach he saw that they were too near the house to admit of his making an escape to the woods. In his perplexity he ran into the mill, crying he was now in the power of his enemies, as the soldiers were just at hand. "Not so fast," replied the miller; "doff your coat, and here is mine in exchange." The miller having hastily arrayed his master in his dusty coat, next took a mealy sack, and powdered him all over from head to foot, and left him busily engaged in his own occupation. The soldiers who saw him enter the mill soon followed in the pursuit. Having entered the lower apartment, they examined every corner with the closest scrutiny; they next ascended the upper story in quest of him who, they were certain, was somewhere within. This place they searched with equal care, and with equal want of success. It never

GLEANINGS AMONG THE MOUNTAINS.

occurred to them that the man who was working at the mill
was the individual whom they were seeking, and therefore
they paid no attention to him. When they found that all
their efforts to find the fugitive were fruitless, and probably
supposing that he had left the building by some way unknown to them, they were about to retire, when one of the
party, looking in the miller's face, exclaimed : " Here he is !
—the very man we have been seeking !" On hearing this,
James, who seemed to the soldiers to be entirely absorbed
in his employment, turned round, and, with a dauntless
countenance and apparent surprise at the affirmation, said,
with a firm and deliberate tone : " I think the *devil* seems to
be in these men." Such an expression, they thought, could
never proceed from the mouth of a *douce* Covenanter, and
therefore they interfered no further, believing, at the same
time, that his habiliments indicated the presence of an entirely different person from him of whom they were in quest.
What James said was true; they were actuated by the spirit
of evil in promoting the interests of Satan, to whose service
they seemed to have sold themselves; and when these worthless men heard any one use the name of their master in conversation, they thought they recognised in him a fellow-ser-
vant. On the present occasion they left the mill without
having accomplished their purpose.

The expedients to which the persecuted Covenanters were
often obliged to resort to save themselves were various,
sometimes even amusing, and very generally successful. A
story, somewhat akin to this of James Nivison in the mill, is
told of three men of Auchengrouch. They had been wandering among the moors, and having spied in the distance a
company of dragoons coming along the bent, they betook
themselves to Auchengrouch House. Having made known
their circumstances to the family, the question was, how or
where they were to conceal themselves, in case the troopers
should call. It was proposed by the mistress of the house,
that they should instantly array themselves in female apparel, to try if by this means they could elude the observation of the soldiers. The proposal was agreed to, and the
three men were speedily decked in women's clothes. The
troopers came leisurely along the heath, and at length arrived at Auchengrouch. The men in female guise were
busily employed, as if they had been domestic servants, and
the gudewife was occasionally raising her voice in a loud and
imperious manner, giving her orders to one in this way and
to another in that, when the dragoons dismounted. " You

s

seem to be rather noisy this morning, good woman," said the
commander of the party, as he drew near to enter the
dwelling. "It may be I have reason," replied she; "my
servants must obey my orders, as your soldiers must obey
yours, and when they fail they must abide reproof." In this
way she succeeded in diverting the attention of the troopers;
and the men in disguise, we may suppose, like persons
ashamed when found in a fault, would naturally avert their
faces from the soldiers, and steal from their presence as
quickly as possible. It is obvious, that the slightest scrutiny
on the part of the dragoons would have discovered the
stratagem, and therefore it was their object to avoid this
scrutiny. No discovery was made, and with grateful hearts
they saw the soldiers again on the moor at a distance from
the house.

James Nivison, notwithstanding the hints which he occasionally received to provide for his safety, was often surprised by the visits of the soldiers who came in quest of him.
One day, when he was least expecting it, a party of troopers
approached his house; and he, having no other place to flee
to, darted through a window in a back part of his cottage,
and sought refuge in the garden. The little plot of herbs
was at this time in its most luxuriant state, and the large
stocks of green *kail*—a vegetable indispensable in the gardens of the Scottish peasantry—meeting at the tops in lengthened rows, formed a long vaulted cavity so large as to admit,
underneath the broad and verdant *blades,* the body of a full-
grown man without being perceived. It was into one of
these deep furrows, and beneath the green arch, that James
Nivison crept, that in this earthly bed he might lie secure
from the prying eyes of the soldiers. The dragoons arrived,
and proceeded to the search as formerly; and, as formerly,
were unsuccessful. Having questioned his family respecting
his place of concealment without expiscating anything satisfactory, they departed, expressing their determination to
repeat their visits till they found him. Had the dragoons
entered the garden with the slightest suspicion of his being
concealed within its precincts, there is little doubt that
he would have been discovered. It is wonderful to think
how narrowly those good men sometimes escaped, when
almost the turning of a straw would have revealed their
retreat. Wodrow gives a striking instance of this in the
case of Maxwell of Moncrief, who happened to be in Edinburgh at the time when Mitchell made the attempt on the
life of the Archbishop. When the search was being made

for the persons who had committed the outrage, Maxwell, fearing lest he should be apprehended among the crowd, sought refuge in the inn where he had stabled his horse. " He had no place in town," says the historian, " he could flee to; but he came to Moffat his stabler's house, and begged his landlord to hide him. Moffat told him very coldly that he had no place to put him in, and very indifferently pointed to a large empty meal-tub standing in a public drinking-room, adding, if he pleased he should cover him with it. No other shift offering, it was done, and in a few minutes the constable and his men came in to search the house, and were soon satisfied, expecting no prey there. They sat down in that very room with the meal-barrel at the end of their table, and called for some ale. While sitting, they fell a talking about the unsuccessfulness of their search. One of them says, ' I am sure there are many Whigs in town;' another of them rapped violently on the head of the meal-tub under which Moncrief was hidden, swearing : 'It may be there is one under *that;*' and so it passed as a jest, and they were permitted to do no more. Quickly they left the room, and fell to their work in other houses; and the gentleman came out, having tasted of the bitterness of death almost."

Many similar instances might be mentioned of deliverances equally providential. A party of dragoons on the border was chasing the fugitives of a scattered conventicle, and was pursuing a worthy woman of some note among the Covenanters, of the name of Janet Gass. They came to the house where she had concealed herself in a large empty chest; and, on entering, they asked if a person of the name of Margaret Glass lived here; they were told that no person of that name resided in the house, nor was even known in the neighbourhood. The evasion turned on the mistake of the name mentioned by the dragoons, and the poor woman eluded their search.

In those trying times, when men were driven to their wit's end, many expedients, consistent with honourable principle and a good conscience, were resorted to in order to preserve the precious life. It is not in our power, however, to justify every expedient, nor to applaud every plan adopted in their extremity by the honest sufferers of that period, for the purpose of escaping the harassings of their restless oppressors. John Campbell of Lochengarach, in Ayrshire, was the object of persecuting malignity to the curate of the parish in which he resided. John, or some one for him, sent one day a card to the curate, requesting an interest in his prayers as a person at the point of death. The curate concluded that John was near his end, if not actually dead, and accordingly deleted his name from the list of those he was in the habit of distressing. It is true that honest John might justly be considered, by himself and his friends, as being every day at the point of death, because his life was constantly exposed to the wanton cruelty of an unbridled soldiery; but then this was obviously not the sense in which the matter was in- tended to be understood by the curate.

James Nivison now saw that there was to be no peace nor safety for him in his own house; and that, therefore, it would be necessary for him to resort to some place of more per- manent security among the woods and lonely caves of the hills, and to associate with other wanderers who frequented the deserts and dreary glens far from the abodes of men. His life hung in doubt every day before his eyes; and there- fore he deemed it better to retire to the solitudes than to be teased with incessant anxiety and uncertainty. He com- municated his intention to his wife, and showed her the necessity now imposed on him of leaving her and the sweet babe behind him for a season, under the more especial pro tection of Providence, seeing his presence was the occasion of so much disquietude to the household. " And, my dear wife," says he, " comfort yourself, since it is stern necessity that forces us to a temporary separation. God will be with us both—with me in the wilderness, and with you in this house, in which, though solitary, you shall not be alone. In removing for a season, I will thereby provide both for your safety and my own."

But the wife of James Nivison was, in a moral sense, a heroine, and she was not to be deterred from following the fortunes of her husband, from the consideration that she must lodge in the cold damp cavern, or in the dark forest, exposed to unwonted hunger and fatigue. The thought that she was to be with her husband compensated for all, and she was resolved to follow him, and to suffer with him in the same common cause. No remonstrance, on the part of her husband, could induce her to remain behind him. " I will accompany you," said she firmly, " I will accompany you; and if the archers should hit you, I will be present to staunch your wounds, and to bind up your bleeding head; in what- ever danger you may be, I will be at your side, your affec- tionate wife in life or in death." How valuable are virtuous love and genuine Christian attachment! Many waters can- not quench love, neither can the floods drown it. Thus James

Nivison and his wife, too happy in each other's affection to complain of hardship, and happier still in the love of their Saviour, left their home to wander they knew not whither, but safe under the guidance of Him who never leaves nor forsakes his own people, and more especially when they are suffering for his sake.

Their first place of retreat was the woods and caves of Crichope Linn. The mother carried the babe, the companion of their sufferings and their wanderings. The tender infant, exposed to hardship in common with its parents for Christ's sake, could ill endure the cold and other inconveniences to which the household was now subjected. To protect the child, however, from the keen and inclement air, James employed part of his time in preparing a portable cradle, of pliant twigs cut from the willow bushes that grew in the linns and by the sides of the mountain stream. In this little basket was the infant, wrapped in a warm blanket, deposited and rocked asleep, while the soft lullaby, chanted by the affectionate mother, filled with a sweet plaintive music the dark recesses of the cave, the sound of which, wafted stealthily on the fitful breeze, was carried adown the gloomy ravine, and died away among the distant woods. When they removed from cave to cave, the wicker bed was carried with them, and was found to be of great use for the accommodation of the babe, over whom the hearts of the parents yearned with the fondest solicitude.

This pious and devoted pair, with their offspring, were shielded, during the years of persecution that remained, from the malice of their foes. They left their all on earth for Christ's sake, and, by the kindness of the people in the moorlands, they were never suffered to want, God providing for them in the day when they could not provide for themselves. What were the varied incidents which during their wanderings befell them, tradition does not say; but they outlived the reign of oppression, and at last, with glad hearts, returned to their home, from which they had formerly departed in sadness. This worthy man met with his death in the following manner: While he was working among some horses before his own door, one of them struck him violently on the breast, and killed him on the spot. Thus was he, who had weathered many a storm, and escaped the perils of a protracted persecution, killed by accident before his own house, in circumstances in which no danger was apprehended. When the worthy knight of Closeburn was informed of his death, he exclaimed: " Now has God, who sustained this good man in all his tribulations, taken him to heaven by a stun and gentle surprise." "Be ye also ready, for in such an hour as ye think not, the Son of Man cometh." James Nivison died in 1704, and was buried in the ancient church-yard of Dalgarnock, in the parish of Closeburn.

CHAPTER XXIX

Patrick Laing.

PATRICK LAING was born at Blagannoch, in the year 1641. He was educated by his worthy father in the principles of the Reformation, and his mind seems to have been early embued with religion. His father was subjected to many hardships on account of his adherence to the cause of civil and religious liberty, being frequently spoiled of all his goods, and otherwise exposed to the fury of the oppressor. Patrick lost his mother when he was very young, and after her decease the affections of the father seemed to concentrate wholly on the son. In process of time, however, his father took another wife, by whom he had a numerous family; and Patrick, not finding himself very agreeably situated, resolved to embrace the first favourable opportunity of leaving the place of his nativity. He was now in his eighteenth year, and of a hale and vigorous constitution; and he determined to avail himself of a more stirring occupation than that of a simple and retired shepherd. Accordingly, he directed his attention to the army, and enlisted in the Scots Greys. In this situation he behaved with great propriety, and recommended himself by his dexterity in the sword exercise to his officers, who cherished for him a great esteem, and regarded him as one of the best and bravest soldiers in their troop. Patrick, though in the king's service, was still a Covenanter; for he had enlisted in the army prior to the Restoration, and at a time when the country had not the slightest suspicion that the recall of Charles would be attended by any of those consequences to the Church in Scotland which actually ensued. Though he was a trooper, therefore, he nevertheless cherished all those reforming and covenanting principles in which he had been so sedulously educated, and he lamented that it was his hap to appear as the opponent of a cause

which was so dear to his heart. A short time after his connection with the army, he was sent to Ireland, where he
remained for some time, and where, as he frequently said,
he uniformly experienced the greatest kindness. It was not
long, however, till, Charles having renounced the covenants,
and turned persecutor, the company to which Laing belonged
was recalled to England; and it being known that many of
the party were Covenanters, they were detained in the south,
lest, being sent into Scotland, they should leave the ranks,
when they found they were to be employed in warring against
their brethren who conscientiously adhered to the cause of
the covenants. Laing, when he saw the real posture of
affairs, continued in the army with great reluctance, and
often deliberated with himself how he would act in case of
being despatched, with his fellow-soldiers, to harass those
who were suffering for the truth's sake.

An anecdote, of rather an amusing description, is told of
him respecting an encounter which he had with an Italian
bully during the time that his regiment lay in London. The
Italian had visited England for the purpose of challenging
the bravest of her sons to a single combat. No one dared
to accept the challenge, till Patrick, hearing of the circumstance, offered to enter the lists with the vaunting foreigner.
The affair, it seems, made a great noise, and interested not a
few in the higher and more influential circles. The Italian
was said to be invincible, and was a man of gigantic stature,
and had killed or otherwise disabled all who had dared to
oppose him. On the day appointed the combatants met.
The Italian appeared on the one end of the stage vapouring
and towering in his height, decorated with the cross and
with three shining stars, and otherwise accoutred in a manner befitting the character he had assumed. On the other
end stood Patrick, a tall, *buirdly* man, with a martial aspect
and a dauntless breast. His features were strong and coarse,
and his eyes had a remarkable and perplexing squint. The
Italian, like the Philistine of Gath who cursed David by his
gods, defied his antagonist in the name of the Pope and of
all the saints. Laing, whose blood as a Reformer was stirred
at the bare mention of the fooleries and abominations of
Popery, advanced with a manly stride to meet his braggart
foe. As he stepped forward, the Italian, who had not before
seen him, was puzzled at his dubious stare, and, terror-struck
at his whole appearance, sprang from the stage, crying that
it was a fiend and not a man who had met him, and left
Patrick the conqueror without having drawn a sword in the

strife. This incident acquired him great renown. His mere appearance had put to flight a man who had regularly challenged perhaps the greater part of Europe. The Lord Mayor of London, it is said, bestowed on him some substantial gifts, and his officers became so enamoured of him, that they procured his advancement in the army, at a time when he fondly expected his discharge. The above incident is attributed by some to a man of the name of Douglas, a kinsman of Patrick Laing, and from the same place.

During his residence in England, the persecution was raging in Scotland, and the sufferers were fleeing in every direction for their lives. To escape the incessant harassings of the enemy, a party of the Covenanters had fled over the Border, and sought refuge in the northern parts of England. The report of this circumstance reached the authorities; and Patrick Laing, whose regiment, it appears, happened at the time to be stationed in the same neighbourhood, was sent with a company to apprehend them. This was precisely the trial which he had all along feared might befall him, and now he was called to endure it. To disobey the orders of his superior was as much as his life was worth, and to lend himself as an instrument in persecuting the people of God was what his conscience would not permit. He was not prepared to desert the service, nor was he ready to give a positive refusal to the command of his officers. Accordingly he marched with his little troop in search of the reputed rebels, but contrived so to conduct matters as to allow the party apprehended to escape with great advantage to themselves, and the soldiers returned without accomplishing their errand. It was whispered that the affair was mismanaged, and that the blame rested with Laing. He was accordingly committed to prison, and, being tried, was sentenced to banishment. Every worthy person, and every brave man, lamented his fate, and none expressed for him a warmer sympathy than his own officers. His friends petitioned in his behalf, and a certain English nobleman, who, on account of the affair with the Italian, felt interested in him, exerted himself in his favour, and used every means to accomplish his deliverance. When the day appointed for his transportation arrived, he was still detained in custody, and day after day passed in dreary succession, till the poor prisoner expected to end his life in his cell. Through confinement and disease he was reduced to a mere skeleton, and was at last released from the prison-house in an apparently dying condition. He was then permitted to retire to his native country; and accordingly, whenever his

strength permitted, he moved slowly northward, and, after
many a tedious step, arrived among the heath-clad mountains of his nativity. It was long before he recovered his
full strength, having been so much wasted by disease, and
so much exhausted by his long and fatiguing journey. He
brought with him a sum of money, which in those days was
reckoned a little fortune, namely, about thirty pounds, which
he had received in gifts from his well-wishers; and with this
money it was his intention to settle himself in some occupation, by which to earn an honest livelihood. Having been
brought up among the mountains, he still loved the wild
solitudes; and hence he resolved to plant himself in some
moorland glen, as the occupant of a little farm, to follow, as
in the days of his early youth, the bleating flocks in the peace
and retirement of the wilderness. His heart, alienated from
military occupations, clung with fondness to the scenes of
his childhood; and finding, no doubt, that the life of a soldier was not the most favourable to the growth of piety, he
eagerly sought a place of seclusion in the desert. His wishes
at length were gratified, and he found a place of retreat
among the wild Glenkens of Galloway. Here he located
himself, in the hope of finding, for a season at least, that
tranquillity which his heart so much desired. Permanent repose he knew he could not find; for the persecution
of the party to which he was conscientiously attached was
nothing abated, and he laid his account to meet with trouble
in common with his brethren. A man like Patrick Laing
could not remain long in obscurity; and Grierson of Lag
soon learned that a stranger had settled within the district
over which he exercised a superintendence. It was found
that the stranger did not attend the curate, and that he professed covenanting principles, and that, consequently, he was
an individual whose movements it was necessary to watch.
In those times it did not require much to bring a man into
suspicion, and very little served as an occasion of violent
proceedings. It was not long, therefore, before our worthy
began to meet with annoyance from the adverse party, and
he soon found that no rest was to be expected even in this
retired situation. The occasions on which he was sought
after were numerous, and equally numerous were his escapes
from the hands of his enemies. In order to facilitate his
flight from his pursuers, he kept a fleet pony in constant
readiness, which, being accustomed to scour hills and mosses,
often carried him with great speed out of the way of the
heavy troopers, who were less calculated to traverse the

rugged surface of the wilderness. The circumstances connected with one of his many escapes have been preserved by tradition in the line of his kindred. He was on one occasion returning home, leading his pony, that carried a load of meal thrown across its yielding back, when he observed a party of dragoons approaching. He knew the certain consequences that would ensue if he walked on till he met them, and therefore, without a moment's hesitation, he tumbled the load on the ground, and, vaulting the nimble animal, sped for safety along the heath. The troopers, observing the movement, instantly commenced the pursuit. Patrick, seeing the horsemen following him, with all speed hastened to reach the bottom of a precipice called the Lorg Craig. The dragoons perceiving his intention, divided into different parties, pursuing separate routes, with a view, if possible, to circumvent him, and intercept his progress to the Craig. He reached the rock, however, before the soldiers came up, and having scrambled to the middle of the precipice, and standing still for a moment to breathe, the troopers approached the base. He was fully aware that they would leave their horses and climb after him, and he now regretted that he had with him no weapon of defence, in case he should be closely attacked. There was now no way of escape left for him but to mount, if possible, to the top of the rock; and the danger with which this was attended was to be preferred to the danger of being exposed to the firing of the musketry. He made the attempt, and succeeded; and when he reached the highest part, where he stood in security, he gave three loud cheers in mockery of his pursuers, who, he knew, durst not follow his dangerous track.

On account of the incessant harassings to which he was now subjected, he saw it was in vain to continue longer in the place. His life was in perpetual jeopardy, his cattle were taken away, he was spoiled of his goods, and himself declared an outlaw. Having left the Glenkens, he resorted, with other wanderers, to the higher and wilder parts of the country. He had come to his native land for repose, but he found no rest for the sole of his foot, for he was connected with a cause the maintaining of which demanded many a sacrifice. He knew this; for he had counted the cost, and was prepared to endure whatever the Saviour, in whom he trusted, called him to suffer for the truth's sake. In his wanderings he chose for his hiding-place the darkly-wooded retreats of the Yochan, and found hospitable entertainment in the houses of the pious people who here and there inhabited its banks.

The farm-house of Bar, near the lower extremity of this romantic stream, is particularly mentioned as having been a place of resort to this good man; and the worthy tenant used frequently to remark, that in worldly things he was more than ordinarily prosperous since the time that he opened his door to Patrick Laing, as a sufferer in the cause of Christ; and there can be no doubt that the Lord blesses those who protect and assist his people for his sake. In Cleuchfoot also, a farm about a mile to the west of Sanquhar, which lies on the southern slope of a lofty and green-clad hill which stretches its base to the margin of the Nith, he found a home; and its kindly tenant, John Hair, often contended with the *gudeman* of Bar which should have him more frequently as an inmate. His company was courted, doubtless, for the excellence of his character, and for his godly and edifying conversation; for, as the word of the Lord was scarce in those days, intercourse with religious people was eagerly sought and highly prized. Patrick could, no doubt, also tell of wars and hairbreadth escapes, and striking incidents, and strange scenes, which would excite the wonderment and interest of the simple and secluded people among whom he now sojourned. Cleuchfoot was a more public place than Bar, lying on the line of the great thoroughfare to Ayrshire, along which parties of soldiers were constantly passing and repassing, and hence his seclusion here may at first sight seem less complete; but then there was in the immediate vicinity of the house a dense thicket, into the heart of which he could plunge at any time, on the slightest warning, besides two deep ravines, formed by the rushing of the mountain torrents, in whose dark and bosky sides he could secrete himself from the most prying eye, and remain in perfect security. In this way did he dispose of himself, wandering secretly from place to place till the Revolution—an event which, though it brought relief to others, made, on the whole, but little alteration in his circumstances, at least for a while.

It appears that at this time a goodly number of soldiers was required for the protection of some of our foreign settlements, and inquisition was made for the best and most likely men to be sent abroad on this errand. Grierson of Lag, who since the happy Revolution had little to do in the way of persecuting the people of God, was appointed to enlist, or otherwise impress into the service, what men he could find in Galloway and Nithsdale. He had his eye particularly on Patrick Laing, whom he hated as a Covenanter, but admired as a soldier, and he resolved to employ every means to get him into his power. This intention was known to Laing, who found it as necessary now to keep himself in concealment as during the period of the persecution. Lag had reported that Patrick was a deserter, and in this way he obtained authority to apprehend him; and, with all the restlessness and cruelty of the persecutor, he exerted himself to seize his person. One of the last attempts made by Lag to get hold of him, was when he was one day quietly angling in the silvery stream of the Yochan. He saw at some distance three men slowly advancing up the river, and apparently occupied as he was. He began, however, to entertain suspicions of their design, and thought it best to consult his safety in due time. In order, therefore, to test their purpose, while at the same time he would gain some advantage by the movement, he withdrew from the stream, and ascended with all haste the brow of the mountain. No sooner was this perceived by the men, than they commenced a vigorous pursuit, and by this means fairly revealed their purpose. The tract along which he fled was a steep ridge, having on either side a streamlet purling far below. The three pursuers separated; one ascended the ridge behind him, and the other two took each a parallel rivulet, so that unless he should get out to the high lands before all the three, it would be impossible for him to escape. His strength was now fast failing, and his pursuers were gaining ground at every step, and the hope of getting away from them became every moment more faint. In his perplexity he discovered before him a hollow space of spratty ground, in which he resolved to hide himself, and abide the will of Providence. When he reached the place, he plunged to the waist in mud, and in all probability the miry slough would have become his grave, if he had not promptly extricated himself. As he was struggling to free himself from the sinking ground, he observed on one side a place scooped out by the little brook beneath the bank, into which he crept from the view of the men, who were just at hand. When they came to the place, they had no suspicion that the object of their pursuit was hiding below the vaulted turf, and they passed on with all haste in quest of him. He remained in his concealment till the day passed away, and in the dusk of the evening he returned. His deliverance was unexpected, but He in whom he trusted protected him, and heard his prayer in the day of his distress.

After this, to avoid further annoyance, he removed to the north of Scotland, where lived one of his old officers, a pious man, whom he wished to visit. How long he remained in this quarter is not known, but here he was at least free from anxiety. Shortly after his return to the south, a meeting of the Society people was held at Cairntable, in the neighbourhood of Muirkirk, at which he was present. The procedure of that convention, whatever it was, did not please him, and from that period he withdrew from their connection.

After this he was allowed to remain undisturbed to the end of his days. He died at the house of Cleuchfoot, at the advanced age of eighty-five years. His dust lies in the old churchyard of Kirkconnel, without a stone to mark his resting-place. His sword was in the possession of a man of the name of Hair, in Sanquhar, a descendant of the family of Cleuchfoot, lately deceased. Thus the wanderings of this good man, after a long and honoured pilgrimage, terminated. His name is revered by the posterity of his kindred, and his pious example is the object of their imitation.

CHAPTER XXX.

Friarminion—James Glendinning—Cargill at Covington Mill.

THE farm of Friarminion lies midway between Sanquhar and Muirkirk, and in the very heart of the dreariest solitudes in that part of the country. It borders on the wilds of Hind-bottom and Blagannoch, and other desert places, where the weary and oppressed people of God often met in large conventicles to hear the Gospel. The ancient house of Friar-minion stood on the margin of a mossy streamlet, at the base of Mount Stewart on the west; and many a man of God, and many a friend of the covenant, found a shelter at its hospitable hearth. It seems, indeed, to have been a central point in the wilderness for the congregating of the sufferers, when any matter of importance was under consideration. It was in this lonely place that, in 1686, the general meeting of the societies was held, for the purpose of deliberating on the propriety of hearing other suffering ministers besides Mr Renwick. Few localities were better adapted, or furnished greater facilities, for the gatherings of the persecuted. It occupied a midland situation, and it afforded the ready means of escape, either to the mountains or into mosses, when danger was near.

It was a fine summer day, and a party of the sufferers, in their wanderings in the desert mountains, drew near Friar-minion, and took refuge in a sheep-fold, in search of repose after their fatigue. The fold into which they entered stood on the slope of a green hill, at a considerable distance from the dwelling-house. From this spot a good view is obtained of the dale land beneath; and the weary outcasts within could easily ascertain, by peering over the turfen wall, if any of their enemies were in the immediate neighbourhood. Entertaining no suspicion, therefore, and being much in need of rest, they laid themselves down to sleep, under the watchful

288 TRADITIONS OF THE COVENANTERS, OR,

care of Him who never fails to be the guardian of those who put their trust in him. As they lay in this situation, they were roused from their slumbers by the loud and pitiful bleating of a sheep at the door of the fold. The bleating of a sheep was no uncommon occurrence, and in other circumstances could never have excited the least attention; but by persons in their situation, the most apparently trifling incident was seldom disregarded, as they lived under the incessant apprehension of approaching danger, and could not tell how suddenly, nor from what quarter, their vigilant enemies might come upon them. On hearing the sound, some of the party rose to their feet, and looking over the wall of their dormitory, found that the bleating of the ewe was to them as much a voice of warning as a similar occurrence was to Mr Peden and his friends in Gilchristland Shiel; for a company of dragoons were actually approaching. They appeared to have come from the Wellwood heights, in the bosom of which lies the delightful vale alluded to in the "Cameronian's Dream:"—

" And Wellwood's sweet valley breathed music and gladness,
The fresh meadow blooms hung in beauty and redness,
Its daughters were happy to hail the returning,
And drink the delights of July's sweet morning."

The party within the fold started to their feet and prepared for flight, well knowing that if the dragoons came upon them where they lay, the place of their retreat would speedily be converted into a slaughter-house. They were fully aware that their flight would be observed; but they thought it better to risk pursuit on the hills, than to venture a concealment in the fold, where, if they should be found, their fate would be inevitable. Having, therefore, determined on making their escape, they issued from the fold, and fled towards the hill. The mountain, though steep, could easily be traversed by the cavalry, but beyond this, there stretched a tract of dark moss, into which the horsemen could not penetrate. To this they directed their course, as being a sure retreat from the troopers, if they should happen to pursue them. In their company were two men of the name of Clark, probably from Auchengrouch, who, being notorious Nonconformists, were particularly obnoxious to the Prelatic faction. One of these men, when the party were toiling up the ascent, was seized with sickness, and could not continue his flight. It was now dreaded that the dragoons, if they chanced to perceive them, and chose to follow, would easily make them their prey, as they could not abandon their sickly companion. Two of the stoutest men in the company, however, took hold of him, and helped him forward with all the haste they could make. At length they reached the moss, where they concealed themselves among its deep hags and tall heather, and in this way escaped the hands of their enemies. It is not said whether the dragoons pursued them, nor is any mention made of the hairbreadth escapes of the fugitives from the firing of the troopers. The anecdote is not characterized by any striking incident, and is produced simply as introductory to a story of a somewhat more stirring nature, the scene of whose incident is nearly conterminous to the locality described.

James Glendinning rented a sheep-farm in the vicinity of Cairntable, a high mountain to the east of Muirkirk. He was a young man of great bodily strength, of a powerful and reflective mind, and of a generous disposition. He married an amiable young woman, the daughter of a small proprietor somewhere in the neighbourhood. They were Episcopalians, and attended the ministry of the curate of Muirkirk. His wife, who seems to have been a woman of considerable shrewdness, often conversed with him on the position of affairs in the trying times of persecution; and it was frequently observed by them, that there must certainly be something more than common in the case of the Covenanters, who took joyfully the spoiling of their goods, and who submitted to death itself, rather than renounce their principles. Their godly and inoffensive lives, and the great privations to which they were subjected, called forth the sympathy of Glendinning and his wife in their behalf, and they frequently opened their door with an hospitable welcome to those whom they deemed worthy but injured men. It happened on one occasion, that Glendinning, having gone to the metropolis with a flock of sheep for sale, witnessed the death of one of the martyrs in the Grassmarket. The scene was novel and striking, and his attention was powerfully arrested. He heard the martyr's dying *confession*— not of any crime of which he had been guilty, and for which he was now called to suffer, but of his faith in that Redeemer who on earth had shed his precious blood for the remission of sins—and in that short confession he probably heard more of the Gospel than he had heard during his whole lifetime before. He heard the martyr's dying *testimony*, emitted against the prevailing errors of the time, and in favour of that truth in behalf of which a standard had been lifted up; and from this he must have learned more of the nature of that cause in which the Cove-

T

nanters were embarked than had ever entered into his mind
to conceive. That maligned cause he now perceived to be
the cause of God, and a cause worthy of all the contendings
and sufferings of the dishonoured remnant that walked with
God, and was " faithful with the saints." He heard the
martyr's last *prayer*—a prayer which breathed of heaven, and
which was expressive of the deepest penitence, and yet full of
confidence and delight in God—a prayer which uttered good-
will to all men, and in which forgiveness was sought, even
for those who were about to imbrue their hands in his blood.
He witnessed " the martyr's heroic grappling with *death*,"
and the serenity and joy with which he surveyed the appalling apparatus of a public execution, and noticed the myste-
rious exultation which he seemed to feel the moment before
he was launched into eternity. All this he witnessed with
an absorption of mind, the effect of which was overwhelming
and decisive. A new light shone into his mind; he felt himself the subject of emotions and determinations to which he
had formerly been a total stranger ; and he left the spot to
which, while he witnessed this solemn and affecting spectacle,
he was unconsciously rivetted, with a heart which God had
touched, and into which the elementary principles of saving
truth had entered. "The blood of the martyrs is the seed
of the Church"—a seed sown in many hearts, and which has
been abundantly productive. The enemies of the truth were
greatly outwitted by means of the public executions of the
Covenanters ; for, instead of deterring men from embracing
their views, these exhibitions were an effective means of
disseminating their principles, and of leading to inquiry respecting the reason of their sufferings—the uniform result of
which, in every honest mind, was favourable to the cause of
the oppressed. Their enemies, indeed, seemed ultimately to
be aware of this fact ; and hence, to prevent the effect which
the speeches and the prayers of the sufferers on the scaffold
had a tendency to produce on the multitude, recourse was
had to the beating of drums to drown the voice of the speaker.
The shootings which took place on the mountains and in the
moors, no doubt, attracted sympathy in the different localities
where they occurred ; but the executions, which were witnessed in the crowded streets of a populous city, produced
an effect on hundreds at once, and left impressions which
were never effaced.

On Glendinning's return to his home, he detailed to his
wife the various occurrences that he had witnessed in his
journey, and especially the scene of martyrdom in Edinburgh.

He made known the change that had taken place in his sentiments and feelings, and his determination to follow, for the future, the cause of the persecuted. He departed from his house with a heart inclined to pity those who were subjected to unrighteous sufferings, though he did not understand the principles on which they acted and endured hardship; but he returned a new man, and with a heart not only well-disposed to the persecuted, but one with them, and with a soul in unison with theirs, not simply on public grounds, but in the faith of Christ the common Saviour, to whom it was now his intention to devote himself, and his household, and his all. To all this he found a ready response in the breast of his wife, whose soul was knit to his, and to whose superior judgment she was always prepared to bow; at the same time, she failed not to warn him of the difficulties which, on taking this step, he was likely to meet with, and the distress which in all probability, would be brought on his household. They were fully aware of the spirit with which the party to which they hitherto belonged was actuated, and they had no reason to count on a dispensation in their favour, or that in their case the rigour of persecution would in any degree be abated; on the contrary, they had ground to suspect that their treatment would be even more severe than that of others. "Let us, my dear wife," said Glendinning, "commit the matter wholly to the God in whom we trust, and with whose cause we are now identified; the Saviour in whom we believe will not forsake us in the day of trial." He then brought a Bible from the shelf, and placing it on the table, said : " There is one duty which among many others we have heretofore neglected, —I mean family worship; it is my intention, therefore, to perform that duty this evening." This service, by which a formal acknowledgment of God is made by a household, is now a-days fallen into lamentable disuse among professing Christians. It is a duty, however, which no one who has any regard for the divine honour, and regard for personal responsibility, or any concern for the spiritual welfare of a family, can possibly omit. The religion of that household in which God is not worshipped, is either extinct or greatly on the wane. They who refuse to engage in this simple and pleasant exercise, dishonour the Christian profession, and give no evidence that they have any part in Christ. Who can tell how much of the disorder, and unhappiness, and poverty, which prevail in many a household, may be owing to the neglect of this duty ? While, on the other hand, the harmony and prosperity with which other families are blessed, may, through the divine favour, be mainly attributed to the conscientious and Christian performance of this duty.

Glendinning having with his household engaged in the worship of God, rose from his knees, and, walking across the floor, uncovered the cradle in which lay their infant child, and, lifting the babe in his arms, placed him gently on his mother's knee, and in a firm and solemn tone, said: " I commit you, my dear wife, and this sweet babe, to the fatherly care of the great Shepherd of Israel, whom we have this evening avouched to be our God. As for me, I am resolved to live and to die adhering to that cause which we have now espoused ; and if my days shall be cut short by the violence of persecution, God, the God under whose shadow we have taken shelter, will be to you a husband and to this child a father." It is easy to conceive the feelings of the loving husband and the tender wife on this occasion; but God comforted them by his grace, and fortified their hearts by his promise, under the forebodings of evil to come : " Fear not, for I am with thee; be not dismayed, for I am thy God. I will strengthen thee, yea, I will help thee, yea, I will uphold thee with the right hand of my righteousness."

James Glendinning having now taken this decided step, made no secret of his change of principles, but on every occasion, when duty called, prudently and honestly avowed his sentiments. The rumour that Glendinning had now become a Covenanter soon spread abroad. The report reached the ear of the authorities, and it was decided that he should forthwith be treated as a malcontent; and Claverhouse, who was at that time harassing the west, despatched one Morton with a small troop to apprehend him. Information of the circumstance having been communicated to Glendinning, he, at the earnest entreaty of his wife, reluctantly withdrew from his house on the night in which they had reason seriously to expect a visit from the dragoons. Accordingly, as was anticipated, Morton with his party arrived under the cloud of night at the house, and entering in a body, expected to pounce at once upon their prey The object of their search, however, was not within, and therefore in their rage and disappointment, they vowed all manner of vengeance on the defenceless and terror-stricken woman. Morton observing the cradle on the floor, turned down the clothes, and rudely seized the sleeping babe by the tiny arm, and held him up naked and screaming before his mother's face, while in his right hand he grasped the keen and glittering blade, fiercely swearing that in one instant he would hew the sprawling brat in pieces, unless she revealed her husband's hiding-place. By this time Glendinning, who had removed to no great distance, had cautiously approached the house, with all the yearning solicitude of a husband and a parent to ascertain, if possible, what the ruthless foe was doing within; and looking through a small window in the back part of the house, he witnessed the appalling scene described. All his manhood was roused in a moment, and without the calculation or the fear of consequences, he turned round to the entrance and rushed into the interior with his drawn sword. " Hold, ye murderers !" vociferated he, as he sprang to the rescue of his child : " hold, ye savage murderers !—back ! back ! or I will sever your heads from your bodies." He tore his darling child from Morton's grasp, and aimed a furious blow at his head. The stroke fell upon a dragoon who had interfered, who was stunned by it and driven backwards; and a second blow laid another trooper bleeding on the floor. Morton retreated to the entry, over-awed by the terrific aspect of Glendinning, who was like a towering giant armed with the might of twenty men; and suspecting that others were at hand to aid him in the conflict—for he did not think it credible that one man durst venture alone, and without immediate support, into the midst of an armed band of troopers—he withdrew, and having recalled his men, speedily left the place. After the departure of the soldiers, Glendinning soothed his wife and child the best way he could. They had met with a hard beginning, but it was not unexpected. The God in whom they trusted had preserved their lives, and for this their hearts swelled with gratitude; and the trying incident, instead of causing them to swerve from their purpose, confirmed them the more in their good resolutions, and led them to a firmer trust in the Saviour, and to a closer dependence on the God of their life. " Because he hath set his love upon me, therefore will I deliver him ; I will set him on high, because he hath known my name." Glendinning and his wife now plainly saw that there was no rest nor safety for them in their native land, and they resolved to emigrate to Holland, which was an asylum to the persecuted people of God in this country. He was, it is said, a well-educated man, had a good address, and was endued with great martial heroism; and, through the kindness of some friends and gentlemen, he was introduced to the Prince of Orange, who promoted him to an honourable post in his army. His behaviour amply justified the good opinion which the Prince and others had been led to

form of him. He returned at the Revolution an officer in
the Prince's army, and fought at the battle of Killiecrankie,
where Claverhouse fell, and where he witnessed the death of
his former antagonist, Morton. Thus did God preserve and
prosper this worthy man, who, for the sake of the truth, was
willing to abandon all he possessed on earth, and even his
own life. " Them that honour me I will honour."

The locality in which these incidents occurred calls to
mind the good Cargill, who, at Hindbottom, in the neighbouring wilds, preached the Gospel to the children of the
desert. He was a man remarkable for the holiness of his
life. He was unwearied in his Master's service, preaching
in season and out of season, and was favoured with much
success in his ministry. He lived very near God, and in the
blessed enjoyment of the assurance of his salvation for thirty
years, and ended his course by an honourable martyrdom.
He frequently resided at Covington Mill, the place where,
after much searching for him, he was finally seized by Irvine
of Bonshaw, who, when he apprehended him, exclaimed in
ecstasy, " O! blessed Bonshaw, and blessed be the day that
ever I was born, that hast found such a prize—a prize of 5000
merks, for apprehending of him this morning." Andrew
Fisher of Covington Mill, it would appear, was one of those
who opened his door to the suffering servants of Christ in the
day when their enemies forbade, on the penalty of death, or
the confiscation of property, any to receive them into their
houses, or to minister to their necessities. On one occasion,
during his stay at the house of this good man, his enemies
visited the place in quest of him. On his perceiving their
approach he retired from the dwelling-house, and Andrew
Fisher concealed him in the under part of the adjacent kiln.
The place into which he crept was deeply covered with the
ashes of the material which had been burnt for the purpose
of drying the corn spread on the floor above. The walls and
the roof were thickly coated with a dusty and sooty substance,
which was easily shaken off by the gentlest touch, or blown
into a cloud by the slightest breath. The height of the
apartment might allow a man to stand upright, if his feet
were buried so deep in the ashes as to reach the floor below.
In this seclusion he placed himself exactly under one of the
broad beams which, in those simple times, when modern
improvements were unknown, supported the cross-spars on
which was spread the straw, which prevented the grain from
falling through into the cavity beneath. When the search
in the house was completed, the soldiers proceeded to the

kiln to make investigation there. When they came to the place, instead of entering the kiln *logie* or fire-place below, a pit of darkness and dust, they went to the kiln-head or upper apartment, where the corn is spread out for drying. Having examined every corner, and tossed about the straw which lay on the floor, they thrust their long sharp swords down between the narrow spars on each side of the broad beam under which Mr Cargill was crouching, with a view to ascertain what was beneath. He saw the clear blade of the deadly weapon close at his shoulder or at his breast, as he happened to turn himself under the beam; and he could easily have grasped it and snapped it in two; but then, such an incident would have revealed the secret which he had no desire to disclose. In this uncomfortable situation he continued praying in his heart, and looking up to God for protection, till the soldiers, having abandoned the search, left the place. When the risk of detection was over, he emerged from his sooty cell, having sustained no injury further than the inconvenience of a disagreeable posture and soiled garments. Better it is, however, to have one's raiment sullied in such circumstances, than to have the character sullied by foul compliances, as was too frequently the case in those days of trial, when many took offence at the cross of Christ, and went back and walked no more with him.

> " Though ye have lien among the pots,
>   Like doves ye shall appear,
> Whose wings with silver, and with gold
>   Whose feathers covered are."

Mr Cargill, along with his friend, escaped on this occasion, and was preserved for a greater length of time for the work which he had yet to perform. He delighted to frequent the desert, both because there he had an opportunity of preaching the Gospel with less interruption, and because there, in the wilds, was many a hallowed spot that was very dear to him as the scene of Christian martyrdom. The recollections of the sufferings of their brethren in the solitudes bound the Covenanters as with a charm to the wilderness; and the Saviour, near his people in affliction, seems to have retired with them. "Surely," said Mr Renwick, "if God could be tied to a spot, it would, methinks, be to the moors of Scotland; the mosses and the mountains of the west are flowered with martyrs."

CHAPTER XXXI.

Lady Greenhill—the Confession—the Charter-chest—the Door—
the Plaid.

The barbarity of those whose work it was to oppress and
destroy our worthy forefathers, for their attachment to the
cause of truth, seems to have increased as the persecuting
period advanced towards its termination. The wicked men
who were engaged in deeds of cruelty became more hardened
and more dexterous in the perpetration of crime; and Satan,
knowing that his time was but short, exerted himself with
greater energy and fury, and excited in the breasts of his
agents a spirit of uncommon ferocity. Individuals who,
during the earlier part of the persecution, were allowed to
remain in comparative quiet, were, during the latter years,
subjected to the same treatment as others. Neither the
bloom of maiden innocence and beauty, nor the wailings of
helpless childhood, nor the entreaties of the widowed mother
could prevail with those whose hearts were dead to every
soft emotion and every generous feeling. The delicacy of
sex yielded no protection to the pious maiden, and the
domestic privacy afforded no shelter to the worthy matron
in those days of tribulation and misrule.

Mrs Renton, the subject of the following traditionary
notices, was born in the parish of Douglas, and descended
of a worthy family of the name of Summerville, in the same
place. She was, at the time tradition brings her into view,
a widow. She had been married to the proprietor of a small
estate called Greenhill, in the parish of Wiston. The mansion-house of the manor was situated at a short distance from
the base of Tinto, the vicinity of which was the scene of
much persecuting violence.

Respecting the religious character of Mrs Renton's husband tradition has said nothing. She herself, however, was

a woman of real piety, and her abode was the ready asylum of the houseless wanderer, who had voluntarily left all for Christ's sake. Lady Greenhill, as she was familiarly denominated, according to the custom of the times, was regarded as an influential person in the district where she resided, and her example was therefore considered as the more pernicious. It was known that she was guilty of reset and harbour, as well as of being attached in principle to the cause of the Covenanters, and hence the ruling party determined, if possible, to bring her to another way of thinking. In the district in which she lived, the lady was not solitary in her nonconformist practices. The parts about Tinto were often visited by the *outed* ministers, and especially by the good Cargill, whose administrations in that neighbourhood were attended with uncommon success; and consequently, many in these places were reared up to bear witness to the truth in the day of defection. Patrick Walker says, that Mr Cargill had great delight in coming to Clydesdale, because here he had the greatest liberty in preaching and praying; and several other ministers, he adds, at that time did the same There were many "solid and serious Christians" in the places round Tinto, whose houses afforded a retreat to the sufferers, and Greenhill was one of them. On this account, says the same writer, the persecution raged very hotly in the upper ward of Lanarkshire, and particularly in the vicinity of Tinto, during what he terms the "two slaughter years of 1684 and 1685." It was very probably about this time that Greenhill was so often the scene of danger.

One day in the busy season of harvest, Claverhouse and his troopers suddenly made their appearance before Greenhill. The labours of the field at this period require the assistance of every hand, and few refuse to lend their aid in securing the yellow treasures which the ripening autumn has presented to the husbandman. Harvest is the most hilarious time of the year. It is the season which crowns the hopes of the agriculturist, and fills his heart with gladness. It is the season when the swains pour forth from the cottages, in joyous mood, to assail with the gleaming sickle the spacious corn fields, waving their golden produce in the rustling breeze. In that more homely age to which this sketch refers, the household of the laird and the family of the cotter took their places side by side on the harvest *rig*, and plied with buoyant spirits and willing hands the labours of the field. When Clavers arrived at Greenhill, he found none of the domestics within, and the reapers had just finished their mid-day repast, and were again in the field—

> " Swelling the lusty sheaves,
> While through their cheerful band the rural talk,
> The rural scandal, and the rural jest,
> Flew harmless."

Lady Greenhill that day occupied the place of a servant within doors, preparing the meals for the reapers at their stated hours, while all the inmates were sent to assist in the pleasant toil of *shearing*. The lady belonged to a class of housewives of which there is now, in the same rank of life, scarcely a remnant to be found. No portion of her time was spent in trifling, useless pursuits, and idle visits. By her the harpsichord was not struck for the purpose of killing a vacant hour, nor was the toilet made an altar on which to offer sacrifice to her personal vanity. The object of this truly virtuous lady was to imitate the apostolic injunction to women professing godliness: "Whose adorning, let it not be that outward adorning of plaiting the hair, and of wearing of gold, or of putting on of apparel; but let it be in the hidden man of the heart, in that which is not corruptible, even the ornament of a meek and quiet spirit, which, in the sight of God, is of great price; for, in this manner, in the old time, the holy women also who trusted in God adorned themselves." There is a gaiety, and a frivolity, and a worldly affectation among some religious professors, which plainly indicate what manner of spirit they are of; and hence, as an excellent writer remarks, "were Christ and his apostles now upon earth, in their plain and lowly form, it is much to be feared that they would be thought hardly good company enough for many of the present race of genteel and modish professors of religion."

The lady of Greenhill was a grave and prudent woman, and did not think it beneath her to engage, when necessity required, in menial occupations; she had too much good sense and true moral dignity to be ashamed of this. In this respect she resembled the virtuous woman, whose character is finely drawn by the pen of inspiration: "She seeketh wool and flax, and worketh willingly with her hands; she girdeth her loins with strength, and strengtheneth her arms. She layeth her hands to the spindle, and her hands hold the distaff; she stretcheth out her hand to the poor, yea, she reaches forth her hands to the needy. She openeth her mouth with wisdom, and in her tongue is the law of kindness; she looketh well to the ways of her household, and eateth not the bread of idleness."

The troopers, as has been stated, arrived at Greenhill immediately after the departure of the reapers to the harvest-field; and nobody was left within but the lady, who was busily employed in her domestic duties. The trampling of the feet of the horses, and then a loud thundering at the door announced the arrival of a party of visitors by no means welcome. Being taken by surprise, she was for a moment in perplexity whether to seek a place of concealment, or to open the door to the intruders. Finding, however, that it would be in vain to attempt to secrete herself within the house, she resolved, as the only alternative, to meet them at the door. Accordingly, having roused herself to the resolution, and having put up a mental prayer to the Preserver of her life, she unbarred the door, and admitted the bustling troopers. " Is Lady Greenhill within?" vociferated the commander of the party. " I am Lady Greenhill," was her cool and ready answer. " If," replied Clavers, " you were the lady, you would not so readily acknowledge it." Claverhouse had never seen her before, and consequently could not recognise her; and the servile dress in which she was then habited tended to lull suspicion, and not one of the party ever dreamed that she was any other than one of the lady's female servants. Claverhouse, thinking that the supposed servant wished to amuse herself by attempting to practise a harmless deception on the gallant troopers, in passing herself off as the lady of the mansion, pushed his way into the interior, and entered the parlour, expecting to find Mrs Renton seated at her ease, and, without more ado, to make her his prisoner on the spot. The commander, not having found her, as he anticipated, asked again, in a firmer and more impatient tone, where the lady was. The lady observing that she was not recognised, began to think that under this disguise she might probably escape detection, if she could act her part so as not to weaken the impression that she was really a household servant. Accordingly, when the question was again asked by the Cavalier, she replied: " I am all that you will get for Lady Greenhill to-day." On this the troopers were enraged, and with deep oaths declared that the lady was certainly within, and that they would not leave the place till they found her. They proceeded instantly to the search, and the house was ransacked from cellar to garret. The lady all the while preserved her incognito, acted well her part, and sustained the character of an active and industrious Scottish maiden. The noisy and mischievous dragoons were racing about, and rambling through every apartment of the dwelling-house; and the lady, safe in the disguise of a servant, and apparently entirely at her ease, was occupied in the toils of the kitchen, and intent only on her work. The soldiers having accomplished their eager search without success, were greatly chagrined at their disappointment, and vented their rage in blasphemous language. Finding it in vain to pursue their object any farther, they began to make preparations for their departure. Having regaled themselves with what food and liquor they could find, and having in revenge destroyed what they could not consume, they despatched the supposed servant to fetch a man from the field, to conduct them through the pass of Howgate Mouth, on their way to Lanark.

Howgate Mouth is a deep and rugged defile, which intersects the western declivity of Tinto. In the days of our forefathers it was rather a dangerous pass, especially to those on horseback; and hence the necessity of a guide for the safe conduct of travellers. That necessity happily does not now exist, as a good thoroughfare has been made through it. The dragoons moved along the defile, following the track of their cautious guide, who led them down with all the precision he could. As they were passing onward, they began to interrogate the man concerning the lady, and endeavoured to expiscate some information respecting her retreat. "Yon," said he, "was the lady that *cried* me frae the craft; everybody is on the rig the day but hersel'." On this the commander of the party imagined that the man was wishing to impose on him in the same way as the supposed female servant in the house; and not being disposed to receive any further jests on the subject, he drew his sword, and demanded a distinct reply to his question, respecting the hiding-place of his mistress. The man could give no other answer than he had already given; and he continued firmly to assert that the female they met in the house was the identical person of whom they were in quest. His asseverations, however, were not credited by the soldiers; and they proceeded to belabour him with the broad side of their drawn swords, declaring that if he persisted in concealing the truth, he should do so at the expense of aching bones. On every repetition of the blows which the dragoons, by way of amusement to themselves, so liberally applied to his back and shoulders, his reply was uniformly the same—"Yon was just the lady though." At last, having sufficiently chastised his obstinacy, as they thought, and having got beyond the dangers of the pass, they dismissed him to tell his tale of woe to the merry reapers; but whether the cudgelling he had received rendered him unable to wield the sickle for the remainder of the day, tradition does not say.

On this occasion, the worthy lady escaped in a way she did not expect. She could not tell a lie when interrogated by her enemies; and He who desires truth in the inward parts, was pleased to shield her from discovery.

After the incident which has just now been narrated, the lady saw the necessity of adopting precautionary means, in case of a subsequent attack; and, accordingly, she prepared a hiding-place, to which, in the hour of danger, she might retreat. The dragoons, as was anticipated, were not long in paying Greenhill another visit, for the purpose of apprehending its mistress. Notice of their approach was intimated to the lady, who instantly fled to her concealment. The soldiers, in their usually disorderly and unmannerly way, entered the house, and commenced a strict search. They continued in their work of mischief and impertinence, till an incident occurred which put a stop to their proceedings for that day. The lady's little daughter, a girl of ten years of age, happened to follow the soldiers to a room which was subjected to a very minute search. In this apartment there happened to be a certain piece of furniture in the form of a handsome little chest. One of the dragoons, on observing it, exclaimed: Here is the lady's charter-chest; let us examine its contents, and we may perchance find something that will reward our morning's toil. On his opening the lid of this chest, the little girl, who stood immediately behind the plundering dragoon, pushed him forward, and pressed the lid upon his hand. The dishonoured trooper, finding his mistake, raised himself from his position, and, red with rage and disappointment, turned round upon the girl, who rushed impetuously from the chamber. The soldier stormed, and swore, and drew his sword to pursue. "Hold, sirrah," exclaimed the officer in command, amused at the mortification of his gallant trooper, "hold, and at your peril venture to touch a hair of her head; I like the spunk of the girl, and for the present I will permit the old fox to abide in her concealment, for the sport which the young one has afforded us." No further search was made, and the party instantly left the place.

Some time after this, the worthy matron of Greenhill was again assailed in her castle, by her old enemies the troopers. One evening, when the rays of the setting sun were gilding the summit of the lofty Tinto, and when the shadows of the that a company of troopers were rapidly approaching. There was not a moment for deliberation; the lady fled from the house, and concealed herself in an adjoining building. The house of Greenhill was an erection of feudal times, and was sufficiently strong to afford protection against the roving bands of rival barons. Connected with the mansion-house was a large court, formed by ranges of office-houses; and it was here that, in the olden times, the cattle were driven for security, when there was any apprehension of the Annandale and other border thieves being abroad. Claverhouse sent his troopers into every apartment of the dwelling-house, and they failed not to accomplish a most unsparing search; but, after all their pains, they were unsuccessful—the lady was not to be found. This additional disappointment enraged Claverhouse excessively. The extent of devastation committed within the house on this occasion is not mentioned; but we are informed that, on their departure, they conceived the scheme of barricading the building in such a way, as that neither ingress nor egress might be effected. He commanded his powerful and vengeful dragoons to secure every window and door, in the firmest manner, exclaiming, that since it was the lady's pleasure to *go out*, it was his that she should not *go in*. The injunction was instantly obeyed, and every door and aperture were closed and fastened, and the keys carried off by the doughty troopers. By this means it was believed that no small degree of annoyance and trouble would be given to the good lady and her domestics, while the soldiers departed pleased with the thought, that they had at least wrought some mischief in keeping with their lawless occupation.

On the withdrawment of the soldiers, the lady issued from her concealment, and, in company with the servants, who had now assembled in the court, found the house in the situation described. An attempt to gain admittance at doors and windows was made, but without success. At last the lady, when trial had been made at the different doors without being able to effect an entrance, observing one that had not been attempted, laid her fingers on the handle, and immediately the door swung back upon its hinges, to the astonishment of the domestics, some of whom asserted that it was as firmly locked and barred as the others, and insinuated that a special Providence had interposed to remove the obstacles which their united efforts could not otherwise have been able to accomplish. The lady, however, entertained no such notions; she saw at once that the leaving of the door unlocked was an oversight on the part of the dragoons, and that Providence

had no doubt ordered it so; but she had no belief of anything miraculous in the case.   The gratitude of this good
woman, on account of this seasonable deliverance, may easily
be conceived; and, in reference to the event of that evening,
as being a token of the divine kindness to herself and her
household, she could lay her head on her pillow, and say—

> " Our soul's escaped as a bird
>   Out of the fowler's snare ;
>   The snare asunder broken is,
>   And we escaped are."

And in the morning, after the protection and sweet repose of
the night, she could unite with the Psalmist again, and sing
with a glad heart—

> " I laid me down and slept, I waked,
>   For God sustained me ;
>   I will not fear though thousands ten
>   Set round against me be."

There is in the life of this good woman another incident
worthy of recording, which veritable tradition has preserved.
One day when she happened to be in the field among the
cattle, that were grazing peacefully on the flowery lea, she
observed a company of troopers sweeping along the base of
Tinto, and advancing in the direction of Greenhill. She was
irresolute for a moment; to return to the house without
attracting their notice was impossible, and the open fields
afforded no hiding-place.   On the descent of the troopers,
however, into a hollow, which for a little concealed her from
their view, she hastily snatched the plaid from the shoulders
of the girl that tended the cows, and having wrapped it round
herself, as if she were the person whose employment was to
watch the cattle, she sat down on the grass to wait the result.
The cavalcade came on apace, and, without seeming to take
notice of her, rode hastily past at a short distance from the
place where she was sitting.   She turned her head warily
round, and, with a palpitating heart, saw the party dismount
at Greenhill.   During their stay in the house, her anxiety
was intense, but her solicitude was even greater when she
saw them preparing to depart.   " Am I discovered !" said
she to herself; " has any of my household been compelled to
point me out to the enemy ? and is my time now come when
I shall be captured sitting here defenceless in the field ?   To
thee, O thou Preserver of my life, thou God of my salvation,
I resign myself; help me to glorify thee, whether it be by
life or by death."   While these busy cogitations occupied
her mind, she observed, to her inexpressible relief, the

troopers, with their commander in advance, wheel round and
ride off in an opposite direction. They soon disappeared,
and she returned to the house with a heart swelling with
grateful emotions to Him who had so wonderfully shielded
her in the hour of peril; and this was the last time she was
disturbed by the marauding persecutors. We are not, however, to suppose that these few incidents were all that befell
this pious woman from first to last; there were doubtless
many other trials to which she was subjected by the enemy,
which tradition has not retained.

Lady Greenhill lived many years after the persecution.
She maintained a godly, and useful, and consistent life, and
at last closed her eyes in peace, in hope of eternal life,
through that Saviour in whose cause she had been honoured
to suffer not a little.   Her ashes repose in the ancient churchyard of St Bride's, of Douglas.

Lady Greenhill preserved an unshaken attachment to her
principles, in those troublous times in which her lot was cast;
and this is more than can be affirmed of some of her immediate neighbours, in the same rank of life. The lady of St
John's Kirk was what is termed a "high professor," and
seemed to be inalienably attached to the principles of the
Covenanters and to the truths of the Gospel. She frequently
entertained the persecuted servants of Christ in the day of
their distress, and followed the Gospel to the fields at her
own peril; and yet this individual, notwithstanding all her
high and imposing pretensions, was guilty of foul defection,
and even went the length of persecuting those with whom
she formerly associated—so faithless is the human heart, and
so deceitful sometimes are the fairest appearances, and the
most promising professions.   Walker mentions this woman's
abandonment of her principles, and says, that "she turned
so far out of the way, that she became a persecutor, and
would not suffer any to dwell on her lands that would not
hear the curates, and take the oath of abjuration."   The
example of this woman, who lived only a few miles from the
residence of Lady Greenhill, had no influence on her in
causing her to swerve from her constancy.   We have need of
grace to enable us to cleave to the Lord with full purpose of
heart; for, without his upholding arm, we would soon give
way, and make shipwreck of faith and a good conscience.

These traditionary facts, relative to the lady of Greenhill,
have been communicated by Mrs Wilson of Douglas, a great-
granddaughter of the lady, and granddaughter of the little
girl who defeated the dragoon so magnanimously, in the affair

of the charter-chest. The grandmother lived to the great age of ninety-two, and Mrs Wilson has herself attained the honourable age of eighty-one. When she speaks of her persecuted ancestors her age seems to be forgotten, and she appears to be carried back to the days of her youth, when with intense interest she used to listen to the incidents recited by her grandmother, who witnessed what she so feelingly narrated. " The righteous shall be had in everlasting remembrance."

CHAPTER XXXII.

James Gourlay of Cambusnethan—John Mathison.

JAMES GOURLAY belonged originally to the Carse of Gowrie, from which place he removed to Cambusnethan, and occupied the farm of Overtown, situated on the southern boundary of that parish. Nothing further is known of him till the battle of Bothwell Bridge, at which he was present, and rendered to the covenanting party what assistance was in his power. On the disastrous issue of that conflict, Gourlay with the rest sought safety in flight. He directed his steps towards a wood in the neighbourhood, in which he hoped to find concealment. As he ran to the thicket, he found in his way many of the bodies of his associates who had fallen in battle, and over which he stepped with caution as he scoured the slippery field that was dyed with the blood of many of the best and bravest of Scotland's sons. In his flight he was intercepted by a lofty wall that crossed his path, and over which it was his intention to spring. This, however, he found to be impracticable; and as his enemies were in eager pursuit, death or capture seemed inevitable. In the urgency of the moment, however, and when time for deliberation there was none, he pulled from his pocket a large clasp-knife, the blade of which he thrust into a chink of the wall, and then placing his foot on the projecting haft, he reached the coping, and lighted without injury on the other side. When he was in the act of passing over the wall, and was for a moment resting on its summit, the bullets, it is said, from the muskets of his pursuers rattled against the stones and went whizzing past his ears. In an instant, however, he was out of danger, and was concealed among the thickets of the wood.

In the history of an ancient battle, which was fought in a forest, it is recorded that "the wood devoured more people that day than the sword devoured;" but on this day the woods afforded a shelter to many from the fierce fury and vengeful sword of their enemies. James Gourlay, however halted not till he reached the banks of the Clyde, and observing a deep and smooth-flowing part of the majestic river, which was overshadowed by the pliant branches of the trees and shrubs that grew so thickly on its margin, the thought occurred to him, that the best mode of concealment would be to plunge into the stream, and there to stand to the neck in the water under the mantling of the bushes. Accordingly he waded into the pool, and sought an asylum in the deep waters, where he continued till the darkness of the night afforded an opportunity of escape.

It is not said in what place he found refuge for the night; but if he ventured home he could not long remain in obscurity, for parties of dragoons, as history informs us, were scouring that part of the country in search of the Bothwell fugitives on the day after the battle, when Arthur Inglis of Nethertown, his neighbour, fell the victim of their wanton and reckless cruelty. He escaped, however, on the present occasion, with his life; but the affair of Bothwell left him a memento, for his station, during so many hours, in the cold river after the heat of battle, induced a pulmonary affection, which, though it did not shorten his days, afflicted him through life.

There is, in the immediate vicinity of Overtown, a romantic ravine of nearly two miles in length. This ravine, called the Garrion-gill, is deep and bosky, with a sweet rivulet flowing along its rocky bed in the bottom. It forms the southern limit of Cambusnethan, bounding on the parish of Carluke. It is generally believed that this was a retreat of the worthies of Clydesdale during the times of persecution. There is towards the middle of the dell a precipitous and towering projection, with an ancient ruin on the summit. It bears the name of Castle Hill, and was evidently a place of security in feudal times. On both sides of this glen are huge masses of rock, that have obviously undergone the action of fire. The burnt appearance of the rocks is, in the popular opinion, the effect of some powerful conflagration from the brushwood and the protruding seams of coal having been set on fire, for the purpose of scorching the Covenanters from their hiding-places in the dark sides of the ravine. Geologists, however, might probably find another cause for these appearances; but, be it as it may, it is certain that James Gourlay and others often hid themselves in this place, in the gloomy hollows of the rocks that were thickly shaded with the leafy branches of the mantling trees.

The house of James Gourlay was at different times beset by his enemies. On one occasion they made an assault at midnight, and thundering at the door, demanded instant admission. Gourlay sprang from his bed, and having hastily donned his garments, answered his assailants from within, that being fully in their power, he would instantly open the door. Having committed himself to the care of the God in whom he trusted, and summoning all his courage according to the emergency, he quietly unbolted the door on the back part of the dwelling. He was aware that every door and window were guarded by the troopers, but he was determined to make one bold effort for his life. Accordingly, having opened the door with as little noise as possible, he darted in the darkness through the midst of the guards, overthrowing one and pushing aside another, till he found his way to the edge of the ravine, adown which he glided in safety, and escaped their hands.

On another occasion he was seized by the troopers, and conveyed as their prisoner toward Hamilton. When the party had forded the Clyde, which in those days had no bridge at the place, they halted at a house by the way-side, and having locked up their horses and their prisoner in the same place, they went either to regale themselves in a small ale-house, or in pursuit of some other person. During their absence, which was rather long continued, it occurred to Gourlay that now was the time to attempt his escape. With this idea he mounted one of the horses, and having placed his feet on the animal's back, he reached the joists above, and, with all the expedition possible, tore an opening in the thatch, through which he made his way to the roof, from which he descended unnoticed, and hasted to the river, which he forded, and hid himself among the bushes, and thus eluded the grasp of his foes.

From the defeat at Bothwell till the Revolution—a period of about nine years—James Gourlay sustained many hardships, and was exposed to much danger. He had a place in the Garrion-gill, at a short distance from his own house, to which he retired in more hazardous times. His wife, Mary Weir, a virtuous woman, and a crown to her husband, prepared a thick woollen covering for him, when, by day or night, he had occasion to "lodge solitary in the woods." It is said that this good woman, in the absence of her husband, occasionally laboured in the field for the support of her household, with a sucking infant bound in a plaid on her back

The days of persecution, however, ceased at length, and James Gourlay was permitted to return to his house in peace. There lived in Garrion-haugh, a person who, in order to save himself, had taken the test, and who, for his officiousness in informing against the friends of the covenant, had acquired the nickname of *Beadle*. This individual, a low, sneaking, and time-serving character, came to Gourlay when times were changed, and professed a great deal of kindness. He held out his hand in token of friendship, but honest James Gourlay thrust it away with indignity, and seizing him by the collar, pushed him out of the apartment where they had happened to meet; after which occurrence he was no more troubled with the hollow pretensions of friendship from so worthless a man.

James Gourlay lived many years after the persecution, and having approached the age of threescore and ten, he was brought to his grave in peace; and his ashes, with those of his honoured spouse, repose in the old churchyard of Cambusnethan. The hallowed spot is marked by an antiquated grave-stone, the inscription on which is partially obliterated. It retains the names of the deceased, and the date 1714.

The descendants of this worthy man are numerous in the neighbourhood of Cambusnethan, especially two families of Gourlay and Gibb.

The preceding account of James Gourlay was communicated by his great grandson, a member of the Secession congregation in Cambusnethan, who in his youth resided with his grandfather, William Gourlay, eldest son of James Gourlay the Covenanter. He is now on the border of fourscore years, but he remembers, with the freshness of youthful impression, the events and incidents narrated to him by his ancestor.

James Gourlay is mentioned by Wodrow. " I find," says the historian, " March 14th, James Forrest, younger, John Collin, *James Gourlay*, &c., were before the committee for public affairs; and, as they say in their joint testimony before me, the chancellor, after a long speech aggravating their rebellious principles, reset, &c., declared to them that they were banished to West Flanders, never to return, on pain of death."

That James Gourlay here mentioned is the same with the subject of the foregoing sketch is more than probable, when we consider that his name is coupled with that of James Forrest, who belonged to Cambusnethan; for we find, in another part of the historian, the following statement : " James

Forrest, in Oldyards, in the parish of Cambusnethan, and his son, with his nephew, Robert Gourlay, were seized by a party of soldiers. After some time's imprisonment, they were banished to West Flanders." Robert Gourlay was, in all likelihood, a relation of James Gourlay, unless we suppose that Robert has been written by mistake for James; but this supposition is not likely, as tradition says nothing about the banishment of James—an incident which would not readily have been forgotten.

As a sequel to this brief account of James Gourlay, we may here give the story of John Mathison. John Mathison rented the farm of Rosehill in Closeburn, in Nithsdale; but his adherence to the cause of the covenant exposed him to many hardships and much suffering in woods and caves, to which he was obliged to resort for safety. He is expressly mentioned by Wodrow in connection with other three cove- nanting brethren, who in 1684 were sentenced to be trans- ported to the plantations. He is probably the same person mentioned by Patrick Walker, under the title of Captain John Mathison, the frequent companion of the venerable Peden in his wanderings in Nithsdale.

Rosehill, in Closeburn, was a farm on the estate of Sir Thomas Kirkpatrick, a gentleman who manifested no small degree of sympathy with the oppressed peasantry of Scot- land. In the farm of Baraby, in the neighbourhood, lived an individual who unblushingly followed the occupation of an informer; and this person having learnt that John Mathi- son, and a few of his companions, were concealed in a cave on the farm of Kirkpatrick, in the same parish, called on Sir Thomas, and requested him to send a messenger to the com- mander of a company of dragoons who were at this time located at the house of Ballagan, in Marburn. Sir Thomas despised both the character and the occupation of the man who addressed him, refused to comply with his request, and desired him to become his own messenger, and to execute his own behests. The informer, seeing it needless to per- sist, set out with all expedition to Ballagan to fetch the soldiers necessary to assist him in apprehending the wan- derers.

Sir Thomas, on perceiving that the traitor had executed his purpose, and brought the dragoons from the distance of several miles, instantly despatched a servant to give warning to the persons concealed in the cave. This act of kindness, however, was too tardy to render any effective assistance to those in concealment, for the dragoons came in sight of the cave just as the Covenanters were in the act of making their escape. As the troopers were now very near, and as the ground over which the men were attempting to flee was marshy, they made but little speed. When the informer saw that they were entangled in the boggy field, he advised the dragoons to dismount and pursue on foot, while he held the horses. They did so, and soon caught the fugitives, who perceived that it was needless to flee, as they were now fully within the musket-shot of their enemies.

They were taken to Edinburgh, where they received the sentence of banishment, and were forthwith transported to the Island of New Jersey. When they reached their place of destination, they were committed to the oversight of a hard task-master, who treated them with great inhumanity, so that the ill usage to which they were subjected caused the death of some of them. From this place, however, they were removed, and put to the service of another master, whose wife showed them no small sympathy. This woman was a heathen, and for the kindness she manifested to the sufferers, they laboured to impart to her the knowledge of the gospel. For this purpose they embraced every opportunity, and improved every incident that befell—one of which tradition has retained. It was the custom of the exiles to convene every Lord's-day for prayer and fellowship, and their meeting-place was for the most part in the woods. It happened one Sabbath, during a great thunder-storm, that the lightning fell on a neighbouring building and destroyed it. When the few worshippers came home from their place in the woods, they found their mistress in considerable concern respecting the occurrence. Mathison endeavoured to impress her mind with the fear of God, and showed that the same accident might have befallen her, and more especially as she had been busily employed about her worldly affairs on the day of hallowed rest. The exhortation to which the incident gave rise was not lost on the poor woman, for she expressed her determination to abstain henceforth from all secular labour on that sacred day; and there is every reason to believe that her mind eventually became savingly influenced by the truth of God.

When the news of their release arrived, Mathison and his friends met to thank their mistress for the kindness she had shown them in the land of their banishment. They prayed with her, and besought that every blessing, temporal and spiritual, might be bestowed on her, and that all the kindness they had received from her might be amply rewarded.

On this occasion she appeared to be suitably affected, and expressed herself in a Christian manner. She said that the reward she looked for was the blessing of that God and Saviour the knowledge of whom they had taught her. It was a consolation to them to think, that their afflictions in banishment were compensated by the bringing of one soul to that Saviour in whose cause they suffered the loss of all things.

When John Mathison came home from his banishment, he was accompanied with one Thomas Smith, belonging to the village of Penpont, who had been apprehended with him by the soldiers at the time they fled from the cave.

The circumstances connected with his return to his family are somewhat interesting. It was in the time of harvest, when Mathison, after several years' exile, visited once more his beloved home. The peaceful fields were waving with their yellow produce, and the merry bands of reapers were busy gathering in the golden stores of autumn. No strolling parties of dragoons were interrupting the labours of the husbandmen, nor scattering the helpless peasantry over the face of the country; the wayfaring man was no longer intercepted on his journey, nor teazed with ensnaring questions on the part of an insolent soldiery. All was peace, for the arm of the oppressor was broken, and the blood-stained sword of persecution was returned to its scabbard. Men, conscious of liberty, seemed to tread the earth with a firmer step, and to breathe a freer air. John Mathison drew near his dwelling with a throbbing heart, not knowing what might have befallen his family in his absence. When he entered the house, he found his beloved wife busily preparing dinner for the reapers in the field. He did not at first make himself known, being desirous that his wife should herself make the discovery. She did not, however, recognise him; for the climate, and the hardships to which he had been subjected, had made a considerable alteration on his countenance. The mistress of Rosehill imagined that he was a wayfaring man, who had turned aside to rest for a moment under her roof, and she proceeded to exercise that hospitality for which the peasantry of Scotland have been so much distinguished. A table was instantly set before him, on which were placed refreshments suitable to a person in his situation; and this probably she did the more promptly, as she might be considering at the moment how her poor husband was faring in a foreign land. Having discharged this duty, she proceeded to carry to the harvest field a portion for the reapers; and

when she rose to depart, the stranger rose too, and followed
her. His heart was full; he had seen his wife in life and in
good health, and he now felt a pressing solicitude to see his
children, and to know how it fared with them. She observed
him tracing her steps at a respectful distance, and was
somewhat offended at the pertinacity of the stranger, remarking that she believed he wanted a second dinner, not
appearing to be satisfied with what he had received in the
house. This drew the notice of the reapers to the intruder,
and every one stared at the man who had thus unceremoniously presented himself on the *rig*. One of his sons, a
young man, on whose memory the lineaments of his father's
visage were deeply imprinted, stared with surprise, and
hastily whispered to his mother, " If my father be alive, this
is certainly he." She turned round, and gazing wistfully for
a moment in the stranger's face, exclaimed, " My husband !"
and ran to his embrace. The delightful recognition of the
long-lost husband and father put an end, for the time being,
to the labours of the field, and the whole party returned
with gratulations and gladness to the house. The remainder
of the day was spent in listening to the tale of John Mathison, and in rendering grateful acknowledgments to the Preserver of his life.

John Mathison lived several years after his return from
banishment, and maintained to his death the same honoured
character of a devoted Christian. His ashes lie in the churchyard of Closeburn. A stone was erected by his children, on
which were engraven the names of the persons who were
banished with him, and also the name of the individual at
whose instance they were apprehended. This monument,
however, was one night demolished by the informer, whose
infamy he considered it was designed to perpetuate, in connection with the honourable mention of the worthies. The
traitor, however, was obliged to replace the stone by another,
but he omitted the original inscription. The date on the
grave-stone is 17—.

Such is a brief sketch of John Mathison, as transmitted
orally by his descendants. There is, however, a pretty large
account of his sufferings and wanderings written by himself,
and is at present in the possession of a family in Galloway,
but it is questionable if it can be recovered.

Many such accounts, composed by individual sufferers in
those trying times, are doubtless in existence in not a few of
the households in the country, where they are kept as precious memorials of an ancestry who loved not their lives

unto the death. Could these be drawn from their obscurity, and submitted to a slight revision, they might, in a published form, be very instructive, and would probably in some points cast additional light on certain portions of the history of the distressing period in which they lived. It is these notices of individual sufferers that we now chiefly desiderate, and not so much the acts of council and royal proclamations which swell the volume of Wodrow. This volume of " Traditions" contains nearly twice the amount of *materiel* respecting the sufferers that is to be found in the historian of the persecuting times. Of this the " Banner of the Covenant," recently published, is a proof; for that small volume contains almost the whole that is published in that history, on this particular subject, and something more gathered from other quarters.

CHAPTER XXXIII.

Newton-Stewart—Escape from the Conventicle—Mr Renwick—
Incident at the Cottage in the Ravine.

THERE are comparatively few of the more prominent characters who suffered in the persecuting times, whose history
has excited greater sympathy in the breasts of posterity than
that of the youthful and gentle Renwick. His character
during his public life was greatly maligned, not only by his
persecutors, who daily thirsted for his blood, but also by a
numerous party among those who professed to abet the common cause he so strenuously laboured to support. It was
his lot to fall on evil times, and evil tongues and reproach
had wellnigh broken his heart. His labours in maintaining
the standard of Zion, and, as Mr Peden expresses it, "in
holding up his fainting mother's head" in the day when few
of her sons durst venture openly to render her assistance,
were almost incredible. He was incessant in his preaching
on the wild morasses or desert mountains, and in remote and
lowly cottages, where he was attended sometimes by few,
and at other times by great multitudes; and sweet and
solemn were the seasons of divine refreshment which, like
a dew from the Lord, came upon the hearts of those who
had met by the fountains of salvation that were opened in
the wilderness.

His life, written by Alexander Shiels, is excellent; but
then, it is chiefly a defence of his public character. The
great desideratum, which we now-a-days would like to see
supplied, is a minute account of his private history—of his
wanderings, his escapes, the effects of his ministry, and the
providential incidents which befell him. This, however, at
this distance of time, it is impossible to supply. In the days
of his biographer there existed ample materials for such a
history, which to posterity would now be invaluable. There
is scarcely an anecdote given by the writer of his life, of the

description we would now like to see, though there are general statements made, which show that his history was an eventful one, and fraught with unrecorded incidents of a very stirring nature.

In prosecuting his Master's work with that ardour and devotedness for which he was so much distinguished, as the compiler of his brief but chequered life tells us, he found no rest " but in the remotest recesses in the wilderness, exposed to the cold blasts of winter storms in the open fields, or in some shepherd's summer-shiel in the mountain, used in summer, but lying waste in winter—which yet were the best chambers he could find, where he made some fire of sticks or heath, and got meat with much difficulty out of places at a great distance, mostly from children, who durst not let their parents know of it. Here he, and they that were with him, did sometimes remain several days and nights, not daring to look out, both for hazard of being seen, and for the boisterousness of the storm." In another place his biographer remarks, that he and his companions " were made to lie many nights and days in crowding numbers in caves and holes under ground, without room to sit or stand, without air, without refreshment or hope of relief, save what was had from Heaven; the murdering pursuers sometimes coming over and by the mouth of the hole, while they were at their duty, praying or praising, undiscovered; and when forced from thence, he hath often been compelled, wet and cold, hungry and weary, in great hazard, to run barefooted many miles together for another subterraneous shelter."

The following traditional incident is said to have befallen when he was on one occasion preaching in the wilder parts of Galloway. It was known that a conventicle was to be held by him among the desert mountains, in a place the name of which is not given; and to this place the leader of a party of dragoons repaired with his men, for the purpose of surprising the meeting, and of seizing the preacher. Mr Renwick and his friends, by certain precautionary measures, were made aware of their danger, and fled. In the eager pursuit, the commander of the troopers shot far ahead of his party, in the hope of capturing by his single arm the helpless minister, on whose head a price had been set. Mr Renwick, however, succeeded in eluding the pursuit, in wending his way through the broken mosses and bosky glens, and came in the dusk of the evening to Newton-Stewart, and found lodgings in an inn, in which on former occasions he had found a resting-place. After a tedious and fruitless chase through moor and wild, the leader of the troopers arrived at the same place, and sought a retreat for the night in the same inn. It appears to have been in the winter season when this occurrence took place; for the commander of the party, feeling the dark and lonely hours of the evening hang heavy on his hand, called the landlord, and asked if he could introduce to him any intelligent acquaintance of his, with whom he might spend an hour agreeably in his apartment. The landlord retired, and communicated the request to Mr Renwick, and whatever might have been his reasons for the part which on this occasion he acted, Mr Renwick, it is asserted, agreed to spend the evening in the company of the trooper. His habiliments would, no doubt, be of a description that would induce no suspicion of his character as a Nonconformist minister; for in those days of peril and necessity, there would be little distinction between the plain peasant and the preacher, in regard to clothing. It is highly probable that the soldier was a man of no great discernment; and hence Mr Renwick succeeded in managing the interview without being discovered by the person in whose presence he was, and without his being suspected by others who might happen to frequent the inn. The evening passed agreeably and without incident, and they parted with many expressions of high satisfaction and good-will on the part of the officer, who retired to sleep with the intention of resuming his search in the morning.

When all was quiet in the inn, however, and when sleep had closed the eyes of its inmates, Mr Renwick took leave of the landlord, and withdrew in the darkness and stillness of the night to the upland solitudes, in which to seek a cave, in whose cold and damp retreat he might hide himself from the vigilance of his pursuers.

When the morning came, and the soldiers were preparing to march, the commander asked for the intelligent stranger who had afforded him so much gratification on the preceding evening. The landlord said that he had left the house long before the dawn, and was now far off among the hills to seek a hiding-place. "A hiding-place!" exclaimed the leader. "Yes, a hiding-place," replied the innkeeper; "this gentle youth, and inoffensive as you have witnessed him to be, is no other than the identical James Renwick after whom you have been pursuing." "James Renwick! impossible!— a man so harmless, so discreet, and so well informed; if he is James Renwick, I for one, at least, will pursue his track no longer."

The officer, accordingly, marched away with his dragoons, and searched the wilderness no farther for one of whom he had now formed so favourable an opinion. It was probably with the full concurrence of Mr Renwick that the master of the inn divulged the secret when danger was no longer to be apprehended, and done, in all likelihood, with a view to show the troopers that the Covenanters were not the men that their enemies affirmed they were—wild, and fanatical, and ferocious; and by this means, if possible, to leave a good impression on the mind of those who, without cause, were seeking their destruction.

The following tradition is akin to this, if not another version of the same anecdote. The report having spread of a meeting to be held somewhere in the deserts, a party of troopers was sent to disperse the conventiclers. On the night prior to the day of the meeting, the soldiers took up their lodgings in a house not far from the appointed place. It happened that the minister who was to officiate was in the house at the time when the dragoons arrived. The commander of the party not being aware of the circumstance, asked the master of the house if there was any person within with whom he might beguile the evening in conversation. He replied, that perhaps he might be able to find an individual of the description he wished, and that, at least, he would do his endeavour to entertain him in the best way he could. The circumstance having been made known to the preacher, he, on reflection, agreed to become the companion of the dragoon for the evening, and having disguised himself in such a way as to preclude all likelihood of a discovery, was ushered into the apartment. The soldier was highly entertained with the conversation of his new associate, and mentioned that his design in coming to the place was, if possible, to apprehend the preacher who was to hold the conventicle on the morrow. "I think," said the stranger, giving a significant nod with his head, "I can possibly help you in that pinch." "Indeed!" replied the officer, "that will be good service." "Keep yourself easy," answered the minister, "and do not whisper the matter to any one, and I here plight my honest word, that I will put his hand in yours by to-morrow at such an hour."

The morrow came, but the stranger, with whom the officer wished again to confer on the chief point of the preceding evening's discourse, was nowhere to be found. Not knowing how the thing might turn out, the commander with his troopers marched toward the place of the conventicle. When they came near the assembly, the preacher was proceeding with his discourse; and as the soldiers advanced on the outskirts of the congregation, he commanded the party to stand still and hear the word of the Lord. His manner struck the dragoons with awe, and they halted. In a brief space the leader recognised his evening companion, and remembered his promise; and being astounded at the peculiarity of the circumstances, waited the event. During the progress of the discourse, the great and solemn truths of the Gospel made a deep and evident impression on the mind of the officer, and he stood listening with absorbing interest till the services were closed, and then the preacher descended from his station, and went straight to the place where the dragoons stood, and, according to his promise, put his hand in the hand of their commander. This he did, it is said, with perfect impunity; for the soldier, whose mind was now changed, refused to seize his person, and having drawn off his party, allowed the congregation to withdraw in peace.

This anecdote may appear to some to be destitute of probability, considering the hazard of the attempt on the part of the minister, and the folly of persisting in holding the conventicle when the troopers were so near. But there is every likelihood that the dragoons were on this occasion very few in number—perhaps not exceeding half-a-dozen; and the preacher, whoever he was, being aware that the numbers who would meet with the conventicle, fully prepared to defend both themselves and him, might be six times that number, saw but little risk in pursuing the method he chose to adopt. Tradition says that the officer, whose name has not been preserved, renounced his former connection, and cast in his lot with the suffering people of God, having undergone a decided change by grace.

The following anecdote of Mr Renwick will be read, perhaps, with some degree of interest: In his wanderings in the wilder parts of Galloway, to elude the vigilance of his enemies, he came to Balmaclellan, and agreed with some of the serious people there to hold a conventicle in a solitary place among the mountains. The news of the projected meeting was circulated with all possible secrecy, and on the day appointed a great assembly convened from all parts of the surrounding district. The morning was lowering, and heavy showers were falling on the distant heights, swelling the mountain streamlets, as they descended with impetuosity into the valleys. Notwithstanding the caution, however, with which the intelligence had been communicated, the enemy received information, and came upon tne congregation just as they were going to commence worship. On the approach of the troopers, the people fled in all directions; and Mr Renwick, accompanied by John M'Millan and David Ferguson, fled towards the winding Ken. It was the design of Mr Renwick to escape to the house of a friend, in the parish of Penningham, and there to conceal himself for a season. The place where they attempted to ford the stream was at a considerable distance above the village of Dalry. The river was greatly swollen by the heavy rains that had fallen among the hills during the morning; and before they entered into its turbid waters, they agreed to engage in prayer among the thick bushes that grew on its margin. When they rose from their knees, and were about to step into the dark rolling tide, they observed, to their amazement, a party of dragoons landing on the opposite bank. They had reached the place in pursuit during the time the three men were at prayer, and without noticing them, or hearing their voice, they rushed into the ford, in haste to cross before the waters became deeper. This occurrence seemed to the party to be a providential interference in their favour, for it was at the moment they were employed in devotion that their enemies arrived and missed them; and there is every likelihood, had they not lingered for a space to implore the divine protection, that they would have been toiling in the midst of the stream at the very time the horsemen reached the place. John M'Millan, from whose lips this tradition has been transmitted to posterity, used to say that he was never so much impressed, either before or after, with anything he ever heard, as by the remarks made by Mr Renwick on this occasion; and that, moreover, they were the means of directing his attention more particularly to providential occurrences during the after period of his life.

As his two friends were to accompany Mr Renwick no farther than the ford, they resolved not to leave him till they should see him in safety on the other side. As the current was powerful, they resorted to the following means to assist him in crossing: They provided themselves with the long branches of the mountain ash, which were grasped by the three at equal distances, so that if one should be carried off his feet by the strength of the current, the others, standing firm, should accomplish his rescue. Mr Renwick entered the stream first, and the three proceeded in a line as steadily as they could, till he reached the bank in safety; the other two then returned to the place they left. No sooner, however, had they stepped from the channel of the river, than the flood descended with great violence, covering the banks on both sides, and sweeping every obstacle before it. Such an occurrence is not unfrequent in the upland districts, where the thunder-clouds discharge themselves with great impetuosity among the hills.

Mr Renwick, now alone on the south side of the stream began to seek a place of shelter in which to pass the night, which was now fast approaching. He entered the mouth of a narrow glen, along which he proceeded in quest of a resting-place, and having found a hollow under a projecting rock, he crept into it and fell fast asleep. After a short repose he awoke, and, ruminating on his uncomfortable couch, he heard distinctly the sound of singing at no great distance. The idea naturally occurred to him that there might be other fugitives in the ravine besides himself, who, seeking refuge from their foes, were engaged in the midnight hour, like Paul and Silas, in singing praises to God in their hiding-place. He rose to search them out, and, following the sound through the thickets of the underwood, discovered a light proceeding from a hut at a short distance before him. He advanced with cautious step, and in the full expectation of finding a company of friends, with whom he should spend the remaining hours of the night in security and comfort. The night was very dark, and his footing along the narrow pass precarious, at the bottom of which the foaming streamlet, which leapt from linn to linn as it dashed over its rugged bed, was the only object which was visible, and by it he attempted to guide his way. At length he reached the house, and stood still to listen, but, to his disappointment, the sounds which he heard were those of mirth and revelry. It was a shepherd's cot, and a party had convened within for the purpose of jollity and drinking.

Mr Renwick hesitated for a moment whether to seek admission or to retreat to his hiding-place; but being drenched in rain, and shivering with cold, he resolved to attempt an entrance. He knocked at the door, which was immediately opened, and he was forthwith conducted into the midst of the apartment. The master of the cottage, whose name was James M'Culloch, a rude, blustering person, and no friend to the Covenanters, received the stranger graciously on this hilarious evening. He advanced him to a seat near to a rousing fire of peats, and ordered a repast to be immediately set before him. The demeanour of Mr Renwick formed a complete contrast to that of the party among whom he was now placed, and seemed to excite some suspicion on the part of

M'Culloch, who now and then muttered something about rebels and conventicles, and so forth. M'Culloch's wife, however, was a woman of a different description; she was humane, seriously disposed, and a friend to the sufferers. She had some guess of the party to whom the stranger belonged; and, dreading a disclosure in the progress of the evening, she hurried Mr Renwick to bed in an adjoining apartment.

As she conducted him to his dormitory, she requested him to be on his guard before her husband, who had no warm side to the persecuted people, informing him at the same time, that he was in perfect safety under her roof during the night. She made a comfortable fire in the little chamber, before which she suspended his dripping clothes, that they might be ready for him in the morning. Mr Renwick having committed himself to the guardianship of Him who watches over all, crept under the soft and warm bed-clothes, and slept soundly till the early morning. Awaking about the break of day, and groping about the obscure apartment for his clothes, he could not find them. Uneasy suspicions began to arise in his mind, and he dreaded some mishap, when the mistress of the cottage entered, and informed him that his garments having been so very wet, she had not succeeded in getting them sufficiently dried; but that she had brought part of her husband's apparel, which she requested him to put on for a few hours. Mr Renwick complied, and the circumstance was the means of saving his life. M'Culloch had gone out before Mr Renwick rose, to drive his sheep from the low grounds, which were flooded with the rain that had descended so copiously during the night. After the devotions of the morning, in which M'Culloch's wife cordially joined, he walked out to the fields to breathe the early refreshing air. Previously to his leaving the house, he had thrown over his shoulders a shepherd's plaid, which action being observed by one of the dogs that lay near the fire, the sagacious animal rose and followed him. Mr Renwick ascended a gentle eminence near the dwelling, and, as he stood on its summit, his attention was directed, by the barking of the dog, to a company of dragoons that were newly come in sight, and were very near. Mr Renwick, forgetting that he was now attired in a shepherd's dress, expected to be instantly seized. The troopers rode up to him, and asked if he was the master of the cottage; he replied he was not, and informed them where he was to be found. After some further conversation about rebels and fugitives, they concluded that there would be none on this side of the river, as the stream had been so greatly swollen since the dispersion of the conventicle ; and accordingly they departed without further inquiry.

When the soldiers were gone, Mr Renwick returned with all speed to the house ; and having put on his own clothes, and breakfasted, he set out without delay for Penningham. Thus Providence delivered, within a few hours, this helpless man twice from imminent danger by the simplest means, and preserved him for further service in the cause of Christ.

John M'Millan and David Ferguson, who returned to the north bank of the Ken, after they parted from Mr Renwick, were hastening along the margin of the river, when they were met by a company of horsemen. They turned to flee ; David Ferguson concealed himself under a brow by the water's edge, and John M'Millan retreated to a thicket at a short distance from the place. The soldiers, observing the flight of M'Millan, pursued him, but he escaped. Ferguson, however, was never more heard of ; it is supposed that he was swept away by the strength of the stream, and found a watery grave ; and thus he died a martyr though not by the immediate hand of his persecutors.

CHAPTER XXXIV.

Andrew Hamilton of Drumclog—George Henry.

ANDREW HAMILTON of Drumclog was a noted Covenanter, and took a prominent part in the memorable transactions that preceded the Revolution. The descendants of this worthy man retain the following traditions respecting him :—
    After the disastrous conflict at Bothwell Bridge, the severities of the persecution were greatly heightened. The infamous Claverhouse, with his troopers, scoured the country in all directions, for the purpose of apprehending the insurgents, and of bereaving them of their life. This cruel-hearted Cavalier rioted in the murder of the helpless people of God, who were crushed to the dust under the mad despotism of vindictive rulers. He was their legalized slaughter-man, the ready executioner of their will, and he delighted in acts of savageness from which common humanity recoils.

> " Then, worthy of his master, came
>   The despot's champion—*bloody Graham ;*
>   He stained for aye a warrior's sword,
>   And led a fierce. though fawning horde,
>   The human bloodhounds of the earth,
>   To hunt the peasant from his hearth.
>   Tyrants ! could not misfortune teach
>   That man has rights beyond your reach ?
>   Thought ye the torture and the stake
>   Could that intrepid spirit break.
>   Which even in woman's breast withstood
>   The terrors of the fire and flood ? "

The troopers were frequently sent out to apprehend the laird of Drumclog, where they might perchance find him. On one occasion the soldiers, who had been sent in quest of him, were so near the house before he was aware of their approach, that he found it impossible to flee from the place without being discovered. In his perplexity he ran into the adjoining cow-house, and crept underneath a heap of straw, which lay in a corner. This mode of concealment was frequently adopted by the sufferers in similar circumstances, and in many instances with unexpected success. On the arrival of the dragoons, two of them dismounted to search the buildings, and the rest guarded the various outlets. One proceeded to the dwelling-house, and the other to the office-houses, and commenced an unsparing search. The trooper who entered the place where Hamilton was concealed, began to turn over the straw that lay on the floor, and was gradually nearing the corner where the object of his search nestled. When Hamilton heard the trooper tossing about the rustling straw, he concluded that all was over, and every moment expected when the soldier should stumble upon him. In this situation we may easily conceive his feelings, and something of the intense mental anxiety to which he must have been the prey. His ruthless enemies, with the instruments of death in their hands, were within a few feet of him, and the next thrust of the deadly sword among the loose litter might pierce his heart. In a few minutes his suspense was at an end; for the dragoon discovered him buried beneath the straw. The worthy man, now in the power of the foe, resigned himself to the divine will, expecting either to be shot before his own door, or to be carried away a prisoner But, to his astonishment, the dragoon, instead of seizing him, or of giving the least intimation of the discovery he had made, said to him in a kindly whisper : " Lie still—hide yourself better under the straw—I will not discover you." This unlooked-for incident was justly regarded by this good man as a special interposition of Providence in his behalf, at the very instant when he was entirely in the hands of his enemies. He afterwards often expressed to the family the grateful sense which he entertained of the goodness of God to him on that emergency. And it was perhaps in answer to his prayer, made in his lowly hiding-place, that He who has the hearts of all men in his hand gave him favour in the presence of one who had come with the avowed purpose of seeking his life, and from whose grasp it was impossible to escape.

When the generous dragoon was leaving the apartment, he met the other trooper, who had accomplished an unsuccessful search in the dwelling-house, exactly in the door-way. In order to prevent his entrance, and the consequences that might ensue, he exclaimed : " The rebel has escaped us—he must be somewhere in the immediate neighbourhood; haste,

let no time be lost, lest he get beyond our reach." On this
the party instantly rode off in the eager pursuit, and the
laird remained unscathed. The conduct of the dragoon in
this case, furnishes an instance, among others, either that
there were friends occasionally to be met with among the
troopers, or, at least, men in whose breasts the kindly sympathies of humanity were not wholly extinguished.

But though the worthy laird of Drumclog was preserved
during the persecuting period, and got his life for a prey, he
was nevertheless despoiled of much of his worldly property.
The times of persecution were not only times of murder,
they were also times of plunder. The robbing of men of
their lives, and the enriching of themselves with their property, was a principal work of the lawless men who ruled in
the councils of that dark and bloody period. Claverhouse
carried off all the cattle that were on his farm, with the exception of a few sheep which were grazing on the moor of
Hawburn. The laird of Hawburn was inimical to the Covenanters, and did many things in the way of lodging information against them, for the purpose of ingratiating himself
with the ruling party. There are some men so despicably
mean that they will submit to anything, however debasing,
for the purpose of promoting their own interests at the expense of their neighbours. Such men, however, generally
overshoot themselves, and Providence sometimes rewards
them with the reverse of that on which they calculated.

Hawburn gave notice to the dragoons that Hamilton had
a number of sheep on the moor, which at any convenient
time they might make their booty. He had a flock of his
own on the same moor; and lest the troopers should be inclined to be somewhat indiscriminate in their levy, he accompanied them to the place, and pointed out those that belonged to his neighbour, and saved his own. In this way
did the laird of Hawburn treat his virtuous acquaintance,
who sought not his hurt, but lived peaceably by him.

Some time after the persecution was ended, honest Andrew
Hamilton meeting Hawburn incidentally, took the liberty,
now when men could speak with safety, to address him in
the following style : " It was a very unfriendly and unjust
action on your part, knowing, as you did, that the dragoons
had robbed me of all my cattle, to inform them of the few
sheep which were left me on the moor. You thought to
promote your own interests by taking part with the enemies
of religion and liberty against those who are the friends of
both; and no doubt, in consequence of this, you are in better

worldly circumstances than I am. You have lost nothing;
I have lost all my property, except the land. Yet it is not
unlikely, reasoning from the principles of the divine government—though I am no prophet who say so—that the means
you have taken to preserve your property may, in the end,
prove your destruction. The Drumclog may remain in my
family, while the Hawburn may go from yours."

What impression these statements made at the time is not
said; but the fact has turned out that the Drumclog is still
in the family of Hamilton, while the Hawburn has long since
passed to other hands. It is also worthy of notice, that the
present proprietor of Drumclog has lately purchased the
moor from which his ancestor's sheep were, at the instigation
of Hawburn, driven away by Claverhouse, so that it now
forms a portion of the lands of Drumclog. This certainly
shows something like a divine retribution even in the present
life; and though it may be dangerous for short-sighted and
partial-judging creatures like us to draw in every case our
own conclusions from providential incidents, lest we do so
with an incautious and erring conjecture, yet there are some
events from which the deduction is so plain that we cannot
avoid the conclusion : " Behold the righteous shall be recom-
pensed in the earth; much more the wicked and the sinner."

In addition to the preceding, the following anecdotes are
worthy of notice:—

George Henry, and his wife, Agnes Campbell, lived in
Markland, in the parish of Sorn, not far from the resting-
place of the worthies who fell at Airsmoss. This worthy
couple were Covenanters, and befriended the sufferers who
occasionally resorted to their dwelling for shelter. On one
occasion, a company of wanderers, who happened to arrive at
Markland, were hospitably entertained in an apartment called
the " chamber "—a place attached to the dwelling house.
During the time the party were convened in the chamber, a
company of dragoons arrived unexpectedly before the house.
Agnes ran to meet them, requested them to dismount, led
them into the kitchen, and speedily engaged them in eating
and drinking. When they were busy regaling themselves
in the kitchen of Markland, George Henry, solicitous about
the safety of his friends in the chamber, conveyed them
unobserved from the place, and aided their escape from the
presence of their enemies.

Agnes Campbell had two brothers of the same of Cook,
who, with her husband, were engaged in the skirmish at
Airsmoss. During the time of the conflict, Agnes was in

great distress respecting the issue. When she observed the victorious enemy moving from the field, she hastened to the scene to seek her relations, and to administer what assistance she could to the wounded. When she approached the battle-field, the chief objects of her solicitude were not to be found —neither her husband nor her brothers were anywhere to be seen; and whether they had secured their safety by flight, or were captured by the foe, she was utterly uncertain. In recounting the slain, however, she found the body of Richard Cameron, of whom it is said, that "he lived praying and preaching, and died praying and fighting." She spread her cloak over the bleeding corpse of the martyr, more honoured by her than his fellows who lay slaughtered around him; and having surveyed with a heavy heart the gory field, on which so many of the worthies had fallen in their contendings for the truth, she returned solitary to her home. Her hus-band, of whose fate she was entirely ignorant, had fled into the heart of the dark moss, which was impassable to the heavy horses of the dragoons, and hid himself till the enemy was out of sight; and, when the danger was over, he returned to his own house, and relieved by his presence the anxiety of his wife.

The place where the skirmish was fought is a green spot close by the edge of the moss. The Covenanters had posted themselves as near the moss as possible, that into it they might effect a retreat in case of a discomfiture. The fatal scene was on the east end of Airsmoss, and not far from the farm-house of Boghead, from which some of the Cove-nanters, it is said, issued on the morning of the conflict. A tolerably handsome monument is now erected on the field, to perpetuate the memory of the nine brave men who fell there in the support of their country's liberties. It is a con-spicuous object in the desolate moorland, not far from the road between Cumnock and Muirkirk. In that lonely wil-derness repose the ashes of the "martyr warriors," whose principles of religious and civil freedom will yet prevail, and will ere long arise in giant might, and crush the power of the oppressor and the bigot.

CHAPTER XXXV.

Muirhead of Monkton—Cotters of Carmacoup.

THE Rev. Mr Muirhead, the subject of the following sketch, is said to have lived in Monkton, in Ayrshire. Robert Maxwell was minister of Monkton at the Restoration, when he was ejected for his nonconformity, and confined to his parish. If Mr Muirhead was minister of this place, as it is said he was, it must have been at a period considerably later, and he must have been introduced under the wing of the Indulgence. This good man, as tradition says, was deprived of his charge, because he harboured for a week in his house a pious outlawed preacher. But though he was forbidden by the law to preach, he kept conventicles in his own house, which were frequented by the serious people in the neighbourhood. His practice, in this respect, however, was peculiarly offensive to the ruling party, who forthwith proceeded to apprehend him. There was, in the vicinity of his residence, a secluded spot in the corner of a field, to which he was in the habit of retiring for secret devotion. This place was encircled with tall broom, and densely guarded by the prickly whins. In the heart of these bushes he found a sanctuary and a place of retreat, in which he spent many a hallowed hour. It happened one evening, when a party of soldiers came to his house, for the purpose of apprehending him, that he had retired to his asylum among the bushes to conclude the day with prayer, and continued longer in the exercise than usual. Little did the worthy man suspect that, during the brief space of his retirement, his enemies were actually within his house in quest of him. They had arrived almost at the moment he disappeared among the broom, and continued searching with the utmost eagerness till within a few minutes of his return, when, having been unsuccessful, they left the place. When Mr Muirhead entered, he found all within in a state of confusion, and was anxious to know the cause. Of this he was not long ignorant, and was both astonished and delighted to find that Providence had shielded him in a manner so unforeseen.

It was now obvious to this worthy servant of Christ, that his ruin was plotted by his enemies, and that he must instantly provide for his safety. His own house could afford him no security, as his foes might invade it at any hour, either by day or night, and therefore another place of refuge was immediately sought for. It was considered that, as his retreat among the bushes in the field was known to none but to his household, it might be adopted as a suitable hiding-place, to which he might for a season resort. Accordingly preparations were made, with all due celerity and secrecy, to render the place as comfortable as possible. Blankets were furnished in abundance, and spread on the grassy floor, as a couch on which to repose by night, and on which to sit by day, in the concealment of the bushes. There was, however, among the few friends who were attached to Mr Muirhead, and who regularly attended the meetings held for prayer and conference, one, like Judas among the little family of the disciples, who was determined to betray the venerable man to his enemies on the first opportunity. Mr Muirhead continued to meet with the little conventicle on every fitting occasion. On a certain day on which the meeting was to take place, the saintly man, having crept from his hiding-place, was walking in a retired corner of the field, to avoid observation, when he was noticed by a man at some distance. This individual was one of his warmest friends, who had at the same time a near relation in great affliction, and at the point of death. He accordingly walked up to Mr Muirhead, and requested him to accompany him to the sick-chamber of his kinsman. With this invitation he promptly complied, and proceeded with all speed to the house of the dying man. As they were passing on, they observed a company of horsemen advancing in the direction of the village, of the design of whose visit Mr Muirhead had no doubt. Having reached the house where his assistance was required, he spent the evening with the afflicted person, knowing that it was in vain to return to the meeting, as it must have been dispersed by the soldiers.

During the absence of Mr Muirhead, the friends met according to appointment, and as they were waiting the arrival of the minister to conduct their devotions, a party of horsemen rode up to the door. The troopers dismounted

and burst into the apartment, expecting to seize Mr Muirhead, without much trouble, in the midst of the company.
The little conventicle was thrown into confusion and dismay,
expecting to be severely handled by the rude and unmannerly dragoons. They demanded Mr Muirhead as their
prisoner in the king's name, but every one was ready to
affirm that he was not present. This assertion, however,
was not so easily to be credited by the soldiers, who, on
seeing a venerable-looking old man in the assembly, instantly
concluded that he was the individual sought for, and him
they seized and bound on the spot. Having thus, as they
opined, secured their prey, they dispersed the meeting, and
marched away with their captive. They had not gone far,
however, when, having discovered their mistake, they dismissed the poor man with what they considered suitable
admonitions.

In the meantime Mrs Muirhead was in great distress about
her husband. He had not appeared at the meeting at the
time appointed—he was not to be found in his hiding-place
—no person had seen him; and she concluded that he had
fallen into the hands of the enemy. She spent a perplexed
and wakeful night, bewailing the fate of her honoured husband, and her own helpless condition; but by-and-by, to
her delight and surprise, her husband, having returned from
the cottage, presented himself in the apartment. Her heart
swelled with gratitude to the Preserver of their lives. Mr
Muirhead explained the reason of his absence; and she
informed him of the visit and behaviour of the dragoons, and
at the same time expressed her suspicions of treachery on
the part of an individual belonging to the meeting. Mr
Muirhead was unwilling to admit the idea that any one of
their professed friends could be so base as to act in such a
manner. "I am nevertheless of the opinion," said she, "that
there is a traitor among us, who, for the sake of worldly
advantage, has engaged to work our ruin; and that traitor I
believe to be John Guthrie. I observed him yesterday
smiling to the leader of the troopers, and talking to him in
a very familiar way; which, if he had been a true-hearted
friend, I do not think he would have done."

In a short time this same individual called on Mr Muirhead, and congratulated him on his happy escape from the
dragoons, and requested him to call another meeting of the
friends that night, as it was not likely that they would be
disturbed by a visit from the soldiers so soon after the
occurrence of the preceding evening. Mr Muirhead, who

was unwilling to entertain suspicions of John Guthrie, said that he was engaged to spend the evening with Thomas M'Murtrie, the sick man, and that therefore he would defer the meeting till another time.

Accordingly, Mr Muirhead met in the evening with a few friends in M'Murtrie's house, where he engaged in religious exercises by the bed of the dying Christian. The devotions of the party, however, were unexpectedly interrupted by the sudden intrusion of John Guthrie, attended by Captain Grierson, and a company of soldiers. Mr Muirhead was, at the moment of their entrance, on his knees at prayer, and Grierson without ceremony, made him his prisoner on the spot. The scene was truly affecting: the venerable saint was forcibly raised from his kneeling posture; the house was filled with weeping and consternation; and the afflicted man, now very near the end of his pilgrimage, gave signs in the midst of the tumult that all within his breast was peace.

Grierson committed the prisoner to the care of two of his troopers, with special charges to prevent his escape. It was the intention of the commander, it is said, to carry his cap-tive to Dumfries, to which place he was bound on matters of importance. On their way they had occasion to pass through a wood, where the following incident occurred: It was clear moonlight, and the soldiers were able to march with nearly as much precision as in the open day. As they were threading their way among the trees, a number of per-sons were seen running to and fro, in apparent confusion and flight. Grierson instantly concluded that they were a com-pany of Covenanters, whom the soldiers, passing through the wood, had incidentally disturbed in their concealment. The command was given to pursue, and to fire on the fugitives. The two men who guarded Mr Muirhead hastily tied him to a tree, and speedily followed their comrades in the pursuit. The loud report of fire-arms was heard at frequent intervals in the gloomy retreats of the forest, and Mr Muirhead, reflect-ing for a moment on the possibility of extricating himself, found that he was but loosely attached to the tree, and so he easily succeeded in untying the cords. Having disengaged himself from his bonds, he darted away among the thickets, in the direction of his home. As he was wending his way through the underwood, he was observed by one of the sol-diers, who, taking his aim in the glimmering moonlight, fired and wounded him on the knee, which instantly staid his flight. He was seized the second time; and when Grierson had routed the party in the wood, he commanded two of his

strongest men to carry him on their shoulders to the place
where the horses were stationed. In passing through the
wood, Grierson observed some persons skulking among the
trees, and, fearing lest a shot should reach him from among
the bushes, he ordered his men to march at full speed. The
two dragoons who were carrying the prisoner, being impeded
with their burden, were unable to proceed with the requisite
celerity, and Grierson became impatient. It happened, that
in passing through the wood they had to cross a stream; and
when they arrived at the ford it occurred to the leader of
the party that the most expeditious way of disposing of their
incumbrance would be to throw the worthy man into the
water. Accordingly, when the two men were in the midst
of the torrent, and scarcely able to keep their footing under
the weight of their burden, he commanded them to cast the
rebel into the pool, and leave him to his fate. To this command the soldiers, hardened as they were, hesitated to yield
obedience; upon which, when Grierson observed it, he came
behind, and, with one forcible and remorseless push, plunged
him into the deepest part of the river, where he sank to the
bottom, and was no more heard of. In this way was a godly
and inoffensive man treated by a base and truculent persecutor, in whose breast a feeling of compassion had no place.
Mr Muirhead owed his death to the cowardice as well as
to the cruelty of his enemies. He died a martyr, and has a
name among the worthies "who loved not their lives unto
the death," and his memorial deserves to be rescued from
oblivion, and to be kept in perpetual remembrance.

Carmacoup, the scene of the following traditionary notice,
is situated in the beautiful vale of Douglasdale, a few miles
to the westward of the ancient town of Douglas. Soon after
the Saxons and Flemings found their way into the upper
ward of Lanarkshire, a stronghold was reared on the site on
which the mansion-house of Carmacoup now stands. This
place received its name, in all probability, from Cormac, an
ancient proprietor of the lands, and was called Cormac's Hope
and in later times pronounced Carmacoup. A few fragments
of the original stronghold remain, and are attached to the
present modern building. Some of the aged people in the
locality still speak of the ruins of the massive walls and
vaults of the olden structure, which they had seen in their
younger days. A few years ago an earthen mound, of considerable magnitude, which was encircled at its base by a
low stone wall, stood on the east side of the dwelling. This
remnant of antiquity furnished ample evidence that, in the

earlier Saxon times, the lairds of Carmacoup possessed baronial power in its full extent. On this moat the baron sat in judgment, and gave sentence either according to the nature of the case, or his own caprice. The feudal stronghold at Carmacoup, however, is now superseded by a building more in accordance with the peaceful times in which we live. Early mention is made of the place; and in Home's History of the House of Douglas, it is recorded that "the lands of Carmackhope, with Glaspen, Hartwood, Lennox, and Leholm," were in 1259 " disposed by William, the fifth Earl of Douglas, to Hugh Douglas, his son and heir, on his marriage to Marjory Abernethy, sister to Hugh, Lord Abernethy." In after times, however, the lands of Carmacoup ceased to belong to the house of Douglas, having been bestowed on some faithful and intrepid follower of the chief of Douglasdale.   The Douglases were princely in their acknowledgment of valuable services; and of this the munificent gift of Hazelside, with other lands, to the trusty and heroic Dickson, is a proof. The lands of Carmacoup, after having passed, in the lapse of a few ages, from one family to another, are now inherited in entail by the present proprietor.

In the heavy times of persecution, a despotic act was passed by the Privy Council, by which every heritor and landholder were made responsible for those who lived on their grounds, and were subjected to heavy fines and imprisonment if they failed to lodge due information against all who entertained covenanting principles. The laird of Carmacoup, after the passing of this act, became solicitous about his own safety, on account of the number of cotters who resided on his lands, and whose religious principles he had good reason to believe were more in accordance with those of the Covenanters than with the mind of those who issued this intolerant and unrighteous edict. Not a few of the cotters had imbibed the opinions of the persecuted party; for the hills of Carmacoup, and the retreats of its woods and streams, were frequented by the wanderers; and the ravines and caves around Cairntable afforded shelter to many a helpless Covenanter in the dark and troubled day. In this way the cotters had frequent opportunities of intercourse with the sufferers, and this had led them to examine and to adopt their principles.

At this time there was a goodly number of cottages on the lands of Carmacoup, and the greater part of them was not far from the base of Cairntable, a dark height, which rears its frowning head in the midst of the desert moorlands. In ancient times the house of Douglas had a stronghold in the vicinity of this mountain, and at that period the population in this wild and bleak district was surprisingly great. The hamlets and clusters of cottages in this locality had their origin from the castle or stronghold on the skirts of the mountain, to which the Douglases occasionally resorted in time of danger, and there set their enemies at defiance. "Little knows King Henry the skirts of Cairntable," said the Earl of Angus; "I can keep myself there from all his English host."

The tale of the poor cotters is touching. All of them, with a few exceptions, had received notice to quit their habitations, and remove from the lands at the first term. Tradition says that "thirty chimneys ceased to smoke on Whitsunday at noon, on the fair lands of Carmacoup." At a meeting which had been held a few days prior to their removal, the cottagers agreed to convene on the morning of the day of their departure, at a place called the Bottoms, near the foot of Cairntable, where they purposed to engage in devotional exercises before they separated to seek other residences. The eventful morning came; it was clear and beautiful—the sun rose in a cloudless sky. The lark was carolling his song high in the air; the lambs were gambolling on the grassy knolls; and the curlew, with his loudest scream, was sweeping over their heads in rapid gyrations, as they moved slowly and mournfully to the place of meeting. It was a solemn assembly; sorrow was depicted on every countenance—a sleepless night was passed by all—the eyes of some were red with weeping, and the warm tears bedewed many a fair cheek—the father contemplated with a yearning heart his helpless family, and the mother stood sobbing with her smiling babe cradled on her arm.

When all were convened, they formed themselves into a circle on the bent; and a venerable father being placed, by universal consent, in the middle of the ring, they began the devotional exercises by singing a psalm. The aged man read a portion of Scripture adapted to their circumstances, and then, kneeling down on the brown heath, poured forth a prayer full of holy fervour and childlike confidence in God, and committed the helpless and destitute company of worshippers to the particular care of that Saviour, for attachment to whose cause they were now called to suffer hardships, and to submit to banishment from their native place. It was interesting to see a company of honest peasants, who had not now a place in the world which they could call their home, invoking Him who, when on earth, had not where to lay his head. The spirits of the party were refreshed by means of this heavenly communion, and by means of the Christian converse they had together; and having girded up the loins of their minds, they were prepared to follow the leadings of Providence, and to submit in all things to the disposal of their heavenly Father. When they arose to separate, it is said that the aged saint stood up in the midst of the company, and, with a loud and firm voice, pronounced the following prayer : " May He who was with the patriarchs in their wanderings, even the God of Abraham, of Isaac, and of Jacob, go with us ! Amen."

The attachment which the inhabitants of the hilly districts and of the deserts cherish for the homes of their fathers is remarkable; and we may easily conceive with what reluctance this little band of witnesses would leave their native moorlands. They would, no doubt, cast " many a longing, lingering, look behind " to the lowly cottages in which they had been reared, to the rugged mountains and the dark heath which they had traversed from their infancy, and to the kindly neighbours with whom they had lived in friendly intercourse, and whose faces, in all likelihood, they would never more see on earth.

Tradition has retained no further notice of these simple-hearted occupants of the wilderness. Not even a single name has been transmitted to posterity, and the history of their after-wanderings cannot now be ascertained; but it is not at all improbable that the blood of some of them stained the purple heath, or streamed on the scaffold. Such, then, is the story of the flitting of the Covenanters, the cotters of Carmacoup.

CHAPTER XXXVI.

Andrew Forsyth of Kirkowan.

THE annals of our nation can furnish no period so dismal, and so deeply stained with crime, as that which is denominated *"the persecuting period."* Some of the years of this lawless time were styled, by way of eminence, " the killing-time," or " the slaughter years," on account of the vast number of murders that were committed by the soldiers in the fields; for wherever they found a man whom they suspected to be a religious character, but who, in their style, was designated a rebel, they, without trial, and frequently without warning, shot him dead on the spot. The south and west of Scotland was converted into a spacious hunting-field, on the wide arena of which the blood of God's saints was made to run like water. The Cavaliers of those days engaged with heart and hand in the ungodly crusade against their country's liberties, and were guilty of acts of cruelty at the bare recital of which we feel a cold shuddering creep over our frame. The heart bleeds painfully when we think on the hardships to which our virtuous ancestors were subjected, in following what they conceived to be the plain line of their duty, and in maintaining their privileges as Christians, and their rights as citizens. They dared not, as the poet says—

> " They dared not, in the face of day,
> To worship God, nor even at the dead of night,
> Save when the wintry storm raved fierce,
> And thunder-peals compelled the men of blood
> To crouch within their dens ; then dauntlessly
> The scattered few would meet in some deep dell,
> By rocks o'er-canopied, to hear the voice,
> Their faithful pastor's voice, who, by the glare
> Of sheeted light'ning, ope'd the Sacred Book,
> And words of comfort spoke."

They counted themselves particularly privileged when they were allowed to hold even one Sabbath-day, from morning

Y

till night, without being scattered by the savage troopers, whom the spirit of a bigoted and intolerant age had let loose on the unoffending peasantry of Scotland. These troopers traversed the country in every direction for the purpose of hunting down, under the sanction of tyrannical authority, the peaceful subjects who simply claimed the common birth-right of every man—the privilege of worshipping God according to the dictates of their own conscience.

They "suffered," says Bishop Burnet, "extremities that tongue cannot describe, and of which the heart cannot conceive, from the dismal circumstances of hunger, nakedness, and the severity of the climate, lying in damp caves, and in hollow clefts of the naked rocks, without shelter, covering, fire, or food. None durst harbour, entertain, relieve, or even speak to them, upon the pain of death. Many, for venturing to receive them, were forced to fly to them, and several were put to death for no other offence. Fathers were persecuted for supplying their children, and children for nourishing their parents; husbands for harbouring their wives, and wives for cherishing their husbands. The ties and the obligations of nature were no defence, but it was made death to perform natural duties, and many suffered death for acts of piety and charity in cases where human nature could not bear the thoughts of suffering it. To such an extent was the rage of the persecutors carried."

"Thus," as the Rev. Mr Gilmour remarks in his "Voice of Warning" to the inhabitants of Greenock, "thus, according to the hitherto unquestioned, and we believe unquestionable, testimony of this learned, and pious, and impartial historian, a mere profession of religion exposed our forefathers to proscription and ruin, but it brings honour and reputation to their sons. For them to be men of piety and prayer was to fix them to the stake and the scaffold, while it fixes our personal worth, and stamps us with the public approbation. For them to meet upon the Sabbath-day was to put their lives in jeopardy, and to peril all that was dear to them; while the same principles and practice are esteemed reputable by the great mass of society at the present day. We are not exposed to civil proscription, because we exercise the right of private judgment in matters of religion—we are in no fear of military executions, because we maintain the principles of the Reformation—we are not threatened with the displeasure of an earthly sovereign, because we advocate the Mediator's universal supremacy in opposition to everything like Erastian usurpation and unscriptural magisterial power

—we have no fear of the stake, or the tree, or the scaffold, because we openly avow our attachment to civil and religious liberty—*we* have no necessity for planting sentinels on the surrounding hills to warn us of a cruel, mercenary, and unprincipled soldiery, because we take the liberty of worshipping the God of our fathers. These days of ecclesiastical domination, and of arbitrary political power, are no more. Tyrants and tyranny are equally an abomination in our land."

Our ancestors were eminent alike for their patriotism and their Christianity, and having been so, they have transmitted to us the invaluable boon of freedom, civil and religious. The tree of liberty, that fair and stately tree that was planted by the hands of a still more remote ancestry, our fathers in the late persecution watered with their blood, and it has grown, and spread its branches far and wide; and now underneath its goodly boughs it affords a spacious shelter from the scorching heat of persecution, and from the storms of tyrannical misrule. We may think that, with all our advantages, we have many things to complain of; and so perhaps we have, but then the causes of our complaints are not once to be named with those of our forefathers. We enjoy the full protection of the three great privileges for which all civil government is instituted, namely, that of life, liberty, and property; and no citizen who enjoys this can say that he is hardly dealt with. But these our persecuted ancestors did not enjoy; they were plundered of every one of them, and their names cast out as evil.

Andrew Forsyth, the subject of the following interesting anecdotes, belonged to the parish of Kirkowan in Galloway. His father was a respectable farmer, whose property consisted chiefly in sheep, which he reared on the dark heathy mountains. Galloway was, in those times, famous for the goodly number of adherents to the cause of the covenants, who lived in its glens and moorlands. The ministry of Samuel Rutherford in Anwoth, of Peden in Glenluce, of Semple of Carsphairn, and of Werner of Balmaclellan, brought forth a host of witnesses for the truth, who grew up in the solitudes at first unnoticed, but who afterwards created a great deal of annoyance to the rulers of the period, to whom religion and Presbyterianism were alike offensive. Galloway formed a considerable section of that spacious field which Mr Renwick cultivated, and many a day did he spend in its wilds, preaching the Gospel, and watering God's weary heritage in its lonely deserts. Many and striking were the in-

cidents which befell this youthful servant of Christ in his
journeyings through this rugged territory. The witnesses
who, by the ministrations of these forementioned eminent
men, had been called into the field, were, after the removal
of these labourers in the vineyard, kept together by Mr Renwick, and emboldened by his example and his exhortations
to maintain the standard of the Gospel on the mountains
and the moors of their native district. And bravely did they
maintain it; for the men of Galloway were " giants in those
days"—true and intrepid defenders of the cause for which so
many of them cheerfully sacrificed their lives.

Andrew Forsyth was at first no Covenanter; he regarded
the Nonconformists as a class of fanatics, and as an association of rebels, of which it was the duty of their country to
rid itself as soon as possible. But though he cherished a
decided aversion to their principles, he was never known to
aid in persecuting them, nor in lodging in any instance information against them. It was his occupation to drive his
father's sheep to market, and in this way he acquired the
name of the "Galloway drover." His father, it would appear,
was of a different mind respecting the persecuted people,
though he never fully adopted their views, and was never
considered as belonging to their society. He was, on the
whole, a kindly man, and often harboured the wanderers as
they came his way, seeking a retreat among the hills.
Andrew often remonstrated on the impropriety of his extending hospitality to a set of people whose principles, as he
thought, ought to be strenuously opposed. The old man
tried to reason with his son, but in vain. A conventicle had
been dispersed in the neighbourhood of Newton-Stewart, and
three men in their flight came to Forsyth's house for refuge,
one of whom was the preacher. They had been harboured
here for some days, when Andrew was absent at the market.
On his arrival he was much displeased on finding that his
father had been so incautious as to shelter the fugitives, and
he pointed out to him the extreme hazard to which the
household was exposed on account of his imprudence. His
father replied, that the appearance of the men was such that
he could not find it in his heart to put them away, and he
was sure that they would make the same favourable impression on him if he once saw them. Accordingly, through
solicitation, Andrew at last consented that they should be
brought into what is called the *spence*, or family apartment,
that by means of a brief interview he might for once judge
for himself, having no doubt but that his unfavourable opi

nion of the party with which they were connected would be confirmed. When the men came in, Andrew was struck with their grave and pious aspect, and he felt considerably embarrassed. The demeanour of the youngest of the three especially arrested his attention. His countenance was fair, and suffused with a sweet placidity; his voice was soft and plaintive; his conversation cheerful, and full of heavenliness. No man could look on him without loving him. The gentleness of his manners, his contentment with his lot, and his fervent gratitude for the least attention shown him, deeply impressed Andrew's heart, and put to flight, in a few brief minutes, a whole host of prejudices which had been for a long time collecting and festering in his breast. Can such a meek, and harmless, and saintly-looking man, be a rebel? thought Andrew. There was nothing wild, fanatical, or ferocious about the men; they were quiet, modest, timid, and fearful of giving offence, and in every point entirely the reverse of what Andrew had depicted to himself of the class to which they belonged. But when he heard Mr Renwick pray—for he it was whose youthful aspect and Christian bearing had so peculiarly struck him—a change came over his sentiments, and before they parted for the night Andrew felt himself another man.

It was not till some months after this that Andrew determined to unite himself to the persecuted people. It was in the end of autumn that he set out to the north with a drove of his father's sheep to dispose of them in the market, and in his slow and weary progress he reached Glenlee, a place on the banks of the Deuch, a stream which flows through the parish of Carsphairn. As he lay here with his flock, he heard in the moorlands, at some distance, a sweet and heavenly sound wafted on the gentle breeze, now swelling full on the ear, and again dying away into a faint melody. He rose to seek the party, for he was convinced that a company of worshippers were concealed in the heath; and being guided by the sound, he came to the edge of a deep moss-hag, in the seclusion of which he found a handful of persons engaged in devotional exercises. He listened, and was edified, and was more and more convinced, from the contentment and happiness which they seemed to experience amidst all their privations and their perils, that God was with them, and that their cause was righteous. He discovered himself to the company, and desired to hear from them a full statement of their principles, in which he wished to be more perfectly indoctrinated. From what he witnessed, and heard, and felt on this occasion, he came to the full determination to become one of the witnessing remnant, and to follow his honest convictions, regardless of all consequences.

When Andrew returned from the market, he communicated his resolution to his father; but instead of gaining, as he expected, the old man's concurrence, he met with a severe reprimand. The truth is, Andrew's father had by this time become a suspected person, and whispers were loud and frequent of his having harboured the intercommuned. The laird on whose lands he resided had given him to understand, that unless he desisted from these practices, he must submit to a speedy and unceremonious ejection. This roused his fears, and he began to calculate his worldly interests; and not being altogether persuaded of the justness of the principles of the persons whom, contrary to the existing laws, he had dared to entertain, he deemed it expedient to withdraw his countenance from them, lest he should be brought into trouble, and probably to ruin. He, therefore, raised very serious objections to his son's proposal, and showed the danger to which this step would expose not only him, but all his father's household. Such considerations prevented many from joining the persecuted people, whose leanings might otherwise have disposed them to unite with them. Andrew listened to his father's remonstrances with all the respect which a child owes to a parent, and felt fully inclined to obey him in everything but what regarded the conscience. The laird had threatened to eject the father, and now the father in turn threatened to eject the son, unless he resiled from his determination. Andrew was sorely pained at the resolution expressed by his father respecting his banishment; for he loved his father with a strong affection, and this affection was increased by the gracious principle that had now taken possession of his heart. His resolution, however, was taken, and it was a matter of principle and of conscience, and whatever might be the result, he was determined to obey God rather than man. But then, Andrew could not bear to witness the ruin of his father's house, nor could he endure the thought of bringing down his honoured head with sorrow to the grave; and therefore he resolved to withdraw from under the domestic roof, and to remove to a distance, that no injury might, on his account, come upon his kindred. These were times when a man's profession of religion obliged him to forsake father and mother, sisters and brothers, wife and children, and houses and lands, that he might retain a good conscience and an honest reputation

In pursuance of his determination, then, Andrew cast himself on Providence, and betook himself to the wilds. It was, however, his design to obtain the situation of a shepherd in some moorland farm, where he might live in obscurity, and cherish the views he had recently adopted. In his progress northward among the mountains, he came to Glenlee, in the vicinity of which he formerly met with the worshippers in the moss-hag, and having made himself known to the tenant, he engaged to become his shepherd. The farmer of Glenlee was a Covenanter, a man of decided principle, and with him Andrew enjoyed every advantage, both in reference to instruction, and example, and encouragement. Here he could vent the free expression of his sentiments without offence or fear of discovery, as the family were all of one opinion on these matters. During his stay at Glenlee, Andrew made great proficiency in his knowledge, in utterance, and in zeal, so that in a short time the shepherd was spoken of in the district, and his fame began to spread abroad. In this lay his chief danger. The curate of Carsphairn, who appears to have been the incumbent who succeeded Peter Pearson, whose tragic end has already been detailed, heard of the shepherd of Glenlee, and sent him notice that certain offensive reports were circulated respecting him. It is probable that this curate, remembering the fate of his predecessor, did not wish to proceed to extreme measures, lest the hand of retribution should reach him in his turn; for, doubtless, the incidents of this nature which might occasionally befall, tended to teach some men moderation in their dealings with the Nonconformists. The curate advised him to escape, as he could not be answerable for the consequences, should the military become acquainted with the circumstance.

After this, Andrew was in daily expectation of meeting with trials from the persecuting party, and it was not long till a company of troopers were sent to apprehend him. The day on which the soldiers were sent in quest of him, he happened to be absent, having gone to a place called Fingland, a short distance from his residence. On his return he encountered the troopers in the moor. He guessed their errand, but found it impossible to escape. He resolved, therefore, to accost them in such a way as was likely to prevent suspicion. Accordingly, when he met them, he assumed a great deal of frankness, and asked if they were in quest of the drover. Being answered in the affirmative, he seemed to take an interest in the matter, and informed them that he saw him a short time ago at Fingland, and entreated them not to lose a moment, but to gallop to the place with all speed. The horsemen, without making further inquiries, hurried on, in the expectation of finding him before he had time to escape. When he parted from them, he retired to a place of concealment till they left the neighbourhood. He now found that he must either depart from Glenlee, or act with greater caution. He was unwilling to leave so excellent a family, and hence he thought on some plan by which he might secure himself, and yet remain in the place. Accordingly, he sought out a retreat in the heart of a solitary moss, where he formed for himself a chamber in the soft peat ground, the entrance to which was overhung with shaggy heath and the green crawberry bushes. Here he could repose in perfect concealment, and without the least risk of discovery. To this retirement he betook himself when danger was apprehended; and many a time were the soldiers scouring the bent in quest of him, when he was snugly hid in his mossy bed. As the visits of the military to Glenlee were now frequent, he was under the necessity of spending the greater part of his time among the hills, not daring to venture home till night. One day, in his absence, the soldiers came to Glenlee, with the intention of apprehending the drover. The farmer and his wife were strictly questioned respecting him, but no satisfactory information being obtained, they, in their madness, bound the honest couple with ropes to the stakes in the cow-house, and then left them. When Andrew came home in the evening he found the house empty, and everything in a state of confusion. Dreading that some mischief had befallen the inmates, he was greatly concerned, and on making search he found his master and mistress bound beside the cattle. On inquiry he found that this had befallen them on his account, and therefore he came to the resolution of leaving Glenlee, that the family might not henceforth be exposed to further molestation for his sake.

As the soldiers had been so recently at the place, Andrew thought that there would be no risk in remaining in the house during the night, and then to take his departure at the early dawn. The little company drew round the hearth, and commenced the devotional exercises of the evening. In this exercise they engaged with sorrowful hearts, for they knew that it was the last time, at least for a season, and perhaps for ever, that they would meet all together in the domestic group, for worship in the house of Glenlee. When prayer was ended, and when they were conversing on various topics before they retired to rest, the trampling of a multitude of horses was heard at the door. The hasty approach of the enemy precluded all possibility of escape; and Andrew, afraid to expose the worthy people of the house to danger a second time on his account, resolved to sit by the fire, and to abide the consequences. When the soldiers rushed into the apartment, Andrew rose up and asked what they wanted. "We want," said they, "the Galloway drover; and you are the man we suppose." "I am not a drover," said he, "but a shepherd." "No matter, you are our prisoner." Andrew was instantly overpowered and bound on the spot. He was placed on horseback behind one of the troopers, and his feet tied below the horse's belly with a straw rope, which was twisted for the occasion. The night was dark, and the track extremely rugged, and Andrew suffered greatly from the springing and plunging of the heavy horse in the morasses. The pain occasioned by the tight binding of his ancles was frequently very great, but then the cause of his uneasiness was ultimately the means of his release. Owing to the violent motions of the animal in leaping the mossy furrows, the straw rope gave way, and the prisoner's feet were disengaged. The horse on which Andrew and the trooper were placed was, owing probably to the double weight which he carried, thrown considerably into the rear. At last the animal lost his footing on the uneven ground, and fell prone in the moss, and the two riders were violently precipitated on the bent. The soldier was stunned by the fall, and lay in a state of insensibility. The murkiness of the night prevented the others from readily seeing what had befallen. Andrew sprung to his feet, and seeing his opportunity, flew along the heath, and was in a few seconds beyond their reach. He escaped to a glen on the Water of Deuch, where he remained during the night. The soldiers halted to ascertain the nature of the occurrence, and were beyond measure chagrined at the accidental release of their captive, whom they could not find in all the moor. They proceeded to their garrison, knowing it was in vain to return to Glenlee to seek him a second time. In the morning, Andrew called on his worthy friends to inform them of his escape, and to tell them that he intended to retire to Fingland in the meantime, and to keep himself in as much secrecy as possible. The worthy couple were delighted beyond measure on finding Andrew safe, for they had mourned all night on his account, knowing that either death or banishment would be his lot. But Providence had rescued him, and they mingled their cordial greetings on account of the deliverance, and they thanked God and took courage.

At Fingland, which is about a mile from Glenlee, Andrew found a retreat, but not a retreat without molestation. Some time after this Mr Renwick held a conventicle at this place, on which occasion a number of children were baptized. Information of the meeting had been communicated to one of the garrisons in Carsphairn—for even this upland parish was supplied with two—and a party of soldiers were sent to disperse the worshippers. The services were ended just as the dragoons came up, and Andrew fled to his seclusion in the moss. Two of the horsemen pursued, and when they were within musket-shot, they fired and wounded him severely in the left arm. He escaped, however, to his cavern, where he continued alone in a very weakly and distressed condition, and must have died had not Providence sent him relief. It was a misty day, and a drove of sheep, coming across the wilderness, had lost the direct path and come in a body into the moss where the wounded man was secreted. He heard the bleating of the sheep, and, moving aside his heathery curtain, shouted as loudly as his strength would permit, and the two shepherds who conducted the flock were attracted to his cavern. He made known his situation, and the men administered what relief they could, and supplied him with part of the provisions which they carried with them. He recovered, by this means, a little strength, and was at length, with much difficulty, enabled to find his way to Fingland. It was long before he fully regained his vigour, but he strove to keep himself out of the way of the enemy—a thing which was not easily done by a man confined through weakness to one spot, and more especially as there were constantly strolling parties of troopers passing between Cumnock and Carsphairn along the line in which Andrew had his places of concealment.

When he recovered sufficient strength to move about, he left the higher parts, and came down to the glens of Afton, where he met with friends; but, as Claverhouse was scouring these parts, he was still obliged to hide himself in the dens and caves of the earth. He was, accordingly, reduced to a state of great destitution, and at one time he was forced to subsist for some days on the eggs of the wild fowls, which he found in considerable abundance in the lowly nests among the bushy heather and in the tufted bent. As he was one day wandering solitary and pensive on the hill, he met with the shepherd of Montquharow, to whom he made himself known. The man took him to his house, a place which had never been suspected, and not hitherto visited by the soldiers, and here he continued in comparative safety and comfort. In this place he might have remained for a considerable time in concealment, but having heard of a conventicle that was to be held near the head of the Water of Deuch, he left his retreat to assemble with the worshippers. On his return he was pursued by a party of soldiers; but he escaped from them by ascending the steep sides of the hills, and, pursuing his course to the east of Montquharow, descended on the banks of the Scar. When he reached this secluded valley he laid himself down on the bent, and fell asleep. As he lay here he was found by a shepherd of the name of Ker, who was himself a Covenanter. He was taken to his house and kindly entertained, and here he resided till the Revolution. After this he returned to Kirkowan, where he lived for many a long year, and having reached an advanced age, he died in peace. His descendants are still resident in that district, and maintain a respectability of character worthy of their honoured ancestor.

CHAPTER XXXVII.

Gordons of Earlston—Story of the White Flag.

THE sufferers in the cause of civil and religious liberty, in the times of Charles II. and his brother James, were, for the most part, individuals in the lowly walks of life. This circumstance reflects an unspeakable credit on the thinking and virtuous peasantry of Scotland. They were men of religious habits, and well acquainted with the fundamental principles of Christianity. The doctrines of the Gospel they understood and believed. They experienced the power of true religion deeply on the heart, and by the precepts of the Bible they regulated their conduct. They clung firmly to the great principles of the Reformation; and when the day of trial came, the day on which their adversaries sought to sever them from these principles, they were found to be identified with them; and the destruction of these principles was the destruction of their lives.

But the honest portion of the peasantry was not alone in this attachment. Not a few of the gentlemen of the country aided and abetted the same cause; and here, among this class of persons, the trial to be sustained was even greater than among the inferior ranks. They were persons more conspicuous in their station, and therefore the more easily observed by their enemies; and they were individuals who, on account of their worldly possessions, were called to make a greater sacrifice. Their wealth was an object of cupidity to their persecutors, who sought only a pretext to despoil them of all they possessed. The indiscriminate plunder of the property of those who were known to incline to covenanting principles, operated as a most powerful check on others of their class who might otherwise be disposed to maintain the same cause. Such individuals found it no easy matter to make the sacrifice which their more independent and conscientious brethren had the manliness to do; and therefore, instead of standing honestly forward in the defence of the right, they meanly subjected themselves to the yoke of their rulers, and became the truckling minions of a base faction. These country lairds, in connection with the curates, were the cause of unspeakable distress throughout the land; and they became the more violent in persecuting, in proportion as they wished to screen themselves, and to impress their rulers with the notion of their loyalty.

There were some, however, who yielded not, and on whose minds the conviction of the truth had taken too firm a hold to allow them to act a recreant part. These gentlemen hesitated not to sacrifice property, and ease, and honour, and even life itself, for what they considered it their obvious duty to maintain at whatever cost. Such persons proved a special blessing in the localities where they resided. They harboured the field-preachers, they encouraged conventicles, they ministered to the wants of the wanderers, and, by a good example, they stimulated the contending remnant to stedfastness in their profession.

Of this class of gentlemen were the Gordons of Earlston, in Galloway, to whom the following anecdotes refer.

The ancient house of Earlston stands on the banks of the silvery Ken, at a short distance above the village of Dalry. It is thickly surrounded with woods, which cover the base of the southerly slope of the rising ground, near the foot of which it rears its dark and time-worn turrets. To a stranger passing along the opposite bank of the river, from which a full view of the fair lands of Earlston is obtained, few objects more dreary than the ancient pile, looming in the bosom of the forest, can be contemplated. The solitary yew tree, tho dusky holly, and the enormous oak, recall the times and scenes that have long since departed, and left the stately tower now tenantless in the lonely woods. One can scarcely conceive of a prison-house, to be confined in which would, on account of its deep dreariness, sooner break the heart than this.

These reflections, however, naturally occur to a stranger only; for when the name and the history of the place are known, the whole train of dismal cogitations is dissipated in a moment, and a bright sunshine gilds the entire scene. These are the lands, and this the house, of the illustrious Gordons of Earlston—illustrious for their piety and their patriotism, and who occupy no obscure niche in their country's history.

This ancient family entertained, at an early period, the disciples and the doctrines of Wickliff. They got possession of a New Testament in the vulgar tongue, which they read in meetings convened in the wood of Airds, in the vicinity of Earlston. In those times of Popish bigotry it was a high offence to read the Holy Scriptures, and an offence which was readily visited with the anathemas of the Church. These early conventicles in the woods of Earlston were kept with the greatest secrecy, and we may easily suppose were attended with the divine blessing. On how many hearts of those congregated in the stillness of the forest, to hear the Word of God, a sacred influence descended, we cannot at this distance tell; but we know this, that the truth of God, which at that time took a saving hold of the minds of some of the house of Earlston, remained in that family for generations after, and yielded fruit to the glory and praise of God.

William Gordon suffered no little affliction in the times of persecution. After having endured a long train of hardships for his stedfast adherence to the principles of the Reformation, he was killed, subsequently to the disaster of Bothwell, by a party of English dragoons who were in quest of the fugitives; and he left behind him an honoured name.

His son, Alexander Gordon, was no less noted as a Covenanter. He was present at the battle of Bothwell Bridge, and narrowly escaped the hands of the enemy, by means of one of his own tenants, who, seeing him as he rode through Hamilton, advised him to dismount and to conceal himself. He accordingly complied with the suggestion, entered a house, arrayed himself in female apparel, and betook himself to the rocking of a cradle in which an infant lay asleep, and by this means escaped. He continued under hiding for several years after this, till, going to Holland in the year 1683, he was caught on the last day of May, or the first of June, and committed to prison. He was accused, without the least foundation, of a plot against the king's life. But though the very reverse of proof was led on this point, he was nevertheless sentenced to be beheaded at the Cross of Edinburgh, on the 28th of September following. Whether his judges were convinced of the iniquity of his sentence we cannot say; but he was reprieved from time to time, although continued in close confinement, in different places, till the Revolution, which opened the doors of his prison-house and set him free. His excellent lady, Janet Hamilton, daughter of Sir Thomas Hamilton of Preston, was his constant companion in all his tribulations. " Her character has been eulogized by the impartial historian of the Church of Scotland (Wodrow); and her religious meditations in the solitary dungeon of the Bass have been republished, under the title of ' Lady Earlston's Soliloquies.' "

After the battle of Bothwell, till his apprehension in 1683, he was obliged to keep himself in close concealment. He underwent a variety of hardships in his attempts to elude the vigilance of his enemies, hiding himself in woods and caves, and into the privacy of his own house, During his father's time the house of Earlston was made a garrison for Bannatyne and his troopers, so that the worthy man, being expelled from his own dwelling, constructed for himself a hiding-place in the deep and impenetrable thickets in the vicinity of the mansion-house, in which, on many occasions, he found a secure retreat. It does not appear that the resort was ever discovered by the enemy during the years of careful search that was made for the obnoxious members of that household. The existence of such a place was rumoured by tradition among the people of the neighbourhood, who, to this day, fondly cherish the memory of the Gordons of the house of Earlston; but no person could tell where it was. Its discovery, however, was made of late years by an inhabitant of the village of Dalry, who was one day searching the woods not far from the castle. It is a small narrow building, in the heart of the thickest and most impervious underwood, which, even at the present time, when the forest is much less dense than it must formerly have been, is almost undiscoverable. Here, in this secrecy, did the worthy William Gordon, and his son Alexander, the companion of his sufferings, often hide themselves in the day of peril; and this was the oratory in which many fervent supplications were addressed to the throne of grace by these sufferers for conscience' sake.

Alexander Gordon was a person much more obnoxious to the ruling party than even his father. His concern in the affair of Bothwell stigmatized him as a rebel; and this, independently of any charge of treason against the king's person, was enough to instigate his enemies against him. Accordingly he was incessantly sought after, both on his own lands and elsewhere. The strolling parties of the military, who were traversing every part of Galloway, had a watchful eye on Gordon as a leading and influential person in that part of the country. The house of Earlston, when it did not happen to be occupied by a garrison, was frequently subjected to a sudden and unsparing search. On one of these occasions,

when the military were on their way to the castle, a man
from the village of Dalry, who sympathized with Gordon in
his perilous condition, hastened by the nearest path through
the woods to warn him of his danger, as the dragoons were
just at hand. On receiving this notice, Alexander hastily
arrayed himself in the clothes of a working man, and was
busily employed in cleaving wood, with the assistance of a
female servant, in the court of the castle, when the soldiers
appeared. Part of their company was stationed before the
gate, and the others entered the house. The commander
asked the wood-cleavers if Earlston was within, and on receiving an answer in the negative, the officer commanded
Gordon to throw down his axe and assist him in the search.
He complied with an air of indifference, as if it were the
same thing to him whether he was employed in splitting firewood, or in searching for fugitives. He conducted him
through every apartment, and seemed to enter as heartily
into the matter as the soldiers themselves. No one for a
moment suspected the guide, whom, when they found their
search to be fruitless, they questioned respecting his master's
hiding-place in the woods. On this point, however, they
found no satisfaction; for Gordon not being the person whom
they took him to be, referred in his answers to another *master*
than him whom they sought. His Master, he said, had no
hiding-place that he knew of: and he was certain that if he
understood that any person whatever was seeking him, he
would show himself in a very brief space. The man, however, did not comprehend the allusion; and thinking the
supposed servant to be an open, candid man, they left the
place, disappointed at not having accomplished their object.
But Earlston's time was not yet come; and he was shielded
for the present, even though the eyes of his foes were upon
him, and who, if they had been at a little pains, might easily
have seen through the disguise.

At another time this worthy man made an equally narrow
escape. He had withdrawn from his concealment in the
woods, to spend a short time, if possible, without molestation,
in the castle. The hiding-places in the fields were extremely
disagreeable—cold, damp, and dreary; and, therefore, even a
single night's lodging in a warm comfortable house was no
small luxury. There grew, and still grows, close to the side
of the avenue that leads to the castle, an enormous oak, that
has weathered the storms of ages. Into this tree, which
spreads its goodly boughs far on every side, affording underneath a spacious shade, Earlston had the means of climb-

ing when danger was near. Among its leafy branches he found a place of perfect security, and could look down from his elevation through the thick foliage, and observe what was going on beneath, while none suspected that he was perched so snugly above their heads. A party of troopers visited the castle with the usual design of apprehending the obnoxious proprietor. On the news of their approach, he ran to the tree, and seizing the rope, by which he swung himself to the first branch, which is about ten feet from the ground, he hid himself among the mantling branches. Having placed himself aloft in the heart of the tree, he remained in perfect safety till the men left the place. In those trying times every conceivable mode of concealment was resorted to, and plans adopted, from the necessity of the case, which would never enter into our minds. "Necessity is the mother of invention;' and in their times the truth of this adage was fully verified.

The name of Gordon is still warmly cherished in the localities of the Ken. Their godly example produced a mighty effect on their own dependents more immediately, and on those of the humble walks of life more generally. The good which might be done by those in the higher circles, were their conduct such as becomes the Gospel, is incalculable; for their example is readily imitated by the ranks below them. The responsibility of such persons, therefore, is great—just as their influence is great for good or ill. The Gordons have left behind them an honoured name as sufferers in the cause of truth; while not a few families, in similar circumstances, who adopted a different plan of procedure in those afflictive days, are either forgotten or remembered without respect.

The family to whom the following anecdote has a reference, pursued a course very different from that of the Gordons. Dalyell of Glenae coincided with the measures of the ruling party, and lent himself to the work of persecution, either from inclination or to please those in authority. This man was empowered by the council, 1677, in common with several noblemen and gentlemen throughout the country, with an ample commission to suppress conventicles. The particular locality assigned to Dalyell was Dumfries-shire; and we may easily conceive that he did not fail to execute his commission.

It happened on one occasion that this gentleman was passing through Gavin Moor, accompanied, it is said, by a single attendant—a body servant. Gavin Moor is a wild district in the parish of Closeburn, and was often resorted to in the times of the covenant by the wanderers, who found a retreat in its

z

solitudes. As he was proceeding along the waste, wending his
way towards his own residence, on the Water of Æ, he came
upon a man fast asleep among the brackens, or the long grass,
close by the footpath. The horse on which Dalyell rode
started, and snorted so loudly that the man awoke, and,
springing to his feet, found himself in the presence of an
enemy. Dalyell recognised him as a fugitive who had sought
concealment in the moor. On his being commanded to surrender himself a prisoner, the man stood on the defensive.
Dalyell, unwilling to brook the insult, sprang from his steed,
and seizing his ponderous glaive, advanced on the Covenanter,
not doubting that he would speedily settle the matter by his
single arm. In the braggart style of a swaggering dragoon,
he exclaimed that he would either make him his captive, or
lay his body lifeless on the heath. But he reckoned without
his host; for the Covenanter was a powerful man, and one
whose arm could wield a sword as dexterously as his vaunting opponent; and this the assailant soon found to his cost.
A man who is obliged to stand up suddenly in defence of his
life, finds himself inspired with a determination, and armed
with a courage, of which, in his calmer moments, he might
think himself incapable. At first the contest seemed to
be equal, and the issue doubtful; but the Covenanter, at a
happy moment, with a brawny arm and a skilful movement,
twirled the sword from Dalyell's right hand, and bending
forward, lifted the glittering blade from the ground, and encountered the foe with his own weapon. Dalyell, outwitted
by this movement, and fully aware of his danger, implored
mercy at the hand of the man whose hostility he had un-
righteously provoked. The victorious combatant, having no
desire to take the life of his persecutor, said that he would
spare him on one condition. "I will accede to any condition," said Dalyell, "you may see fit to propose." "The
condition is a very simple one," replied the Covenanter, "and
one that imposes no hard exaction; it is merely this—that
when in pursuit of any of the Covenanters, or when you
come to surprise any conventicle, you see a white flag elevated on a staff, you cease from the pursuit, and refuse to
invade the conventicle." This seemed to Dalyell a trifling
imposition when laid in balance with his life; and he agreel
to the condition without remonstrance.

On the truce being thus concluded, the brave and humane
Covenanter repaired to the hiding-places of his friends to
communicate the intelligence. The news of the rencontre,
and the terms to which Dalyell had acceded, were published

far and wide among the friends, that any party, when attacked by this commander, might know to exhibit the flag, and thereby escape the threatened mischief. This circumstance, however, was not contemplated by Dalyell at the time; he imagined that this Covenanter only was likely to employ the signal agreed on, and that he, in all likelihood, would be rarely met with. The plan, however, was turned to a general use, and was found productive of much good.

The success of the scheme was soon tested. A conventicle was held at Mitchelslacks, in Closeburn, at which our heroic Covenanter happened to be present. A detachment of soldiers was sent to surprise the meeting, and the commander of the party happened to be Dalyell himself. When the troopers were in sight, a white handkerchief tied to the end of a shepherd's crook was seen streaming in the wind. The signal was presented at a peradventure, for the worshippers did not know whether Dalyell might be with the soldiers or not; but the attempt was made to prove the matter, and the result was favourable; for the commander, when he saw the meeting disperse, withheld his men from running on the people, and marched off in another direction. It is not likely that the secret of the signal was ever made known by Dalyell to any of his own party, as this might have been detrimental to him, and the circumstances in which the agreement was made would not have excused him in the jealous eyes of the faction to which he belonged; nor is it likely that the matter was ever divulged by the Covenanter, beyond the circle of friends who lived within the locality over which Dalyell's power extended. Things in those days were worked with great caution, because much, either for good or ill, depended on judicious management.

Often was this commander defeated in his designs by the display of the white flag; for though the individual to whom the promise was made did not happen to be present, others instructed in the secret did it for him. So frequently was Dalyell encountered with the handkerchief, that, in the irritation of his spirit, he bitterly expressed his disappointment, and declared that the Covenanter to whom he plighted his faith was like the devil, so fleet and variable in his movements, that he was to be found in every place where a conventicle was kept—not knowing that the secret was communicated to others whose interests it equally served. It is affirmed that in no one instance did Dalyell ever infringe his promise, but kept it most religiously in every case. Though he was a persecutor, he was honourable in this matter: and

imitated the conduct of the man who had his life completely
in his power, but spared him with a generous clemency. It
was never the intention of the Covenanters to shed blood,
nor to lift the arm of resistance against the righteously constituted authorities of the land—they were men driven to
desperation by a wicked misrule; and if, on any occasion
blood was shed by them in self-defence, are they, therefore,
to be stigmatized as rebels ?

CHAPTER XXXVIII.

Roger Gordon of Largmore.

ROGER GORDON of Largmore, in the parish of Kells in Gallo-way, was probably the son of John Gordon of the same place, who died of his wounds after the battle of Pentland. "John Gordon (of Largmore)," says Wodrow, "was very sore wounded, and lost much blood, through this and his lying in the fields some nights after the engagement. When he came home to his own house, after a few days he died, and escaped the fury of his persecutors, who were resolved to carry him to Edinburgh in a litter."

Roger Gordon, it would appear, was at the battle of Both-well Bridge, from which he escaped unhurt. He proceeded in company with a few others southward, travelling by night and hiding by day. In their cautious progress they reached the village of Minihive, where they were kindly entertained and kept in concealment till the dusk of the evening, when they departed. On leaving the village, they went in the direction of Castlefairn Water. It was a beautiful moonlight night, by which means their way was made almost as plain as if it had been noonday. They moved on in silence, each oc-cupied with his own reflections, and all deeply impressed with a sense of the kindness of Providence in preserving them from the dangers to which, in those perilous times, they were constantly exposed. In their track they were frequently startled by the sudden rising of the coveys of wild-fowl which had cowered down in the lonely heath to doze till the dawn of day, but whose repose had been interrupted by the feet of wanderers. Many a time were their breasts, by this means, filled with alarm; for being accustomed to hasty sur-prisals from the enemy, even the timid fowls of the desert, rising on their whirring wings, stunned them for a moment.

As they were moving on in friendly communings, the

trampling of horses' feet was heard in the distance, and a company of troopers was seen advancing at a hasty pace. They had not come in quest of the wanderers, of whom they knew nothing—they were on a different errand. A conventicle had, on that night, convened at a place called Craggy Mains, and the troopers, having received information of the circumstance, were on their way to disperse it. The friends instantly betook themselves to flight, upon which, when the soldiers observed it, they pursued. The ruggedness of the ground, however, and the partial obscurity of the bewildering mist which now and then enveloped them, as it came trailing along the moor, prevented their enemies from following them with sufficient speed to overtake them. When the fugitives perceived that the horsemen were losing ground they took courage, and wended their way through moss and moor with all celerity, with the view of reaching the house of Knockalloch, on Craigdarrach Water. At this place there dwelt a friend whose door was always open to the wanderers who were forced to seek in the desert a hiding-place from their enemies. When they reached the house they were received with a cordial welcome, and were hospitably entertained by the kind inmates. In this abode they fondly hoped that they had got beyond the reach of their pursuers, who they did not think would follow them so far, traversing a path that was so uncertain and dangerous. They were soon seated at the comfortable board near a blazing fire of peats, and thankfully enjoyed their meal after much fasting and fatigue. They recounted the perils of their flight, and the disasters of the conflict of Bothwell, to the sympathizing inhabitants of the cottage of Knockalloch, who listened with the deepest interest to the minutest incidents of the recital. When they had satisfied the inquiries of their friends, and were about to retire to rest, the thundering of the feet of a number of horses was heard in the immediate vicinity of the house. It was the arrival of the troopers, who had pertinaciously followed their prey through the trackless wild, and had actually reached Knockalloch. The unsuspecting party within were thrown into consternation at the unlooked-for incident, and the poor wanderers now concluded that they were fully in the hands of their enemies.

There was in the house of Knockalloch a dairy of a rather peculiar construction; it was a small apartment behind a bed toward the back part of the house, and regularly furnished with wooden shelves for the reception of the clean milk *boyns,* and the lusty cheeses with which the *gudewife* stored the receptacles. Beneath the floor of this little chamber was a cellar of some depth, dark and damp, the descent into which was through a small trap-door on the floor. This underground apartment was peculiarly adapted to the purposes of concealment, for when the trap-door was closed, and any article of furniture placed upon it, no stranger was likely to suspect that there was any cavity below.

When the dragoons rode hastily into the close or space before the house, the mistress hastened to the dairy with the fugitives, while the husband met the soldiers at the door. The bustling troopers speedily dismounted, and entered the dwelling in the eager hope of instantly finding the objects of their pursuit. Contrary to their expectations, however, no person was to be seen within; but, as usual, they proceeded to examine every corner. In their careful search they stumbled into the dairy, to see what might perchance be found behind the bed. Here, also, they were disappointed— nobody was to be seen—and they had no suspicion that there was another apartment below their feet. But though they were unsuccessful in their main object, they were in no small degree gratified with the sight of the creamy milk and sleek cheeses which were so invitingly placed before them, and they commanded the mistress to furnish them with a repast of the best fare which her house could afford. With this the good woman gladly complied, from the thankful consideration that the friends were undiscovered, and in safe keeping in the cellar. When the party had refreshed themselves to their satisfaction they left the place; but not without expressing pretty loudly their disappointment at losing the fugitives, and at being led away from the conventicle.

On another occasion Roger Gordon made a narrow escape from the devouring sword of a leader of a party of dragoons, when in the wilds. He was proceeding, with a number of others, men and women, among whom was his own wife, to a conventicle which was to be held in a desert place in the neighbourhood of Minigaff. The little company, in pursuing the most secluded route to the place of meeting, passed along the bottom of a narrow and deep ravine, whose precipitous sides were rough with bold and projecting rocks, half buried among the trees and shrubs, that were calculated to afford a secure retreat to the wanderers who sought a hiding-place from their persecutors. In a retirement of this description the sufferers could have kept themselves hid for days and weeks in spite of the most vigilant search, did not spies, who knew almost every lurking-place, conduct their enemies to these hidden chambers in the crevices of the rocks and the mantling of the underwood.

When the little band emerged from the dark ravine, and had reached the heathy ground above, where the space is open and the view extended on all sides, they were unex-pectedly encountered by a company of soldiers on foot, who happened to be crossing the moor at this place. Companies of the military were to be met with everywhere, and as fre-quently on the deserts as on the public highways; for it was in the solitudes that the persons of whom they were in quest concealed themselves. The number of the male part of the Covenanters was, on this occasion, equal to the number of the soldiers, and a conflict instantly ensued. The Covenanters had neither swords nor fire-arms with which to protect them-selves, but with the weapons which they had, consisting of sticks and clubs, they made a stout resistance. Roger Gor-don, who was a strong and sturdy man, assailed the leader of the party with great bravery; and so stiff and dubious was the contest, and so full of interest to both parties, that the other combatants, forgetting their own strife, stood mute and mo-tionless viewing the terrific onslaught on the issue of which so much depended. At length Roger Gordon, having broken the sword of his opponent, struck him with the ponderous club on the arm, which instantly fell powerless by his side. He then seized him in his arms and flung him with vehemence on the ground, the stunning effect of which was so great that the man appeared to be killed. When Gordon's friends per-ceived the result of the conflict, they raised a shout of tri-umph, which resounded through the moorland, and fell on the ears of the distant shepherds as they tended peacefully their flocks on the waste. Roger's wife, who, during the struggle, manifested the greatest solicitude for the fate of her honoured husband, and who stood weeping and praying in her heart for his safety, when she saw him the conqueror and unscathed, sprung to his arms and mixed her tears with the heavy drops of perspiration which fell from his manly brow, and blessed the God of their life for the deliverance he had wrought. The friends then went on their way, and left the soldiers to assist their disabled commander. They reached the conventicle without further interruption, and engaged with their brethren who, in equal peril with themselves, had met to worship in the wilderness.

After this Roger was more severely persecuted than for-merly. Every skirmish which befell between the troopers and the Covenanters, however incidental was certain, in the result, to heighten the fury of the dominant party within the particular locality. Great distress was by this means experienced by many a helpless family, on whom the enemy thought fit to wreak their vengeance. The house of our worthy, after the disaster in the moor, was frequently visited by the troopers, who never departed without perpetrating some act of mischief. He seldom or never visited his family by day, on account of the vigilance of his adversaries, and it was only under the cloud of night that he durst occasionally venture to his own hearth. One evening, after long wanderings and hidings in the mountains, he entered his dwelling in hopes of being permitted to spend one night without interruption. His expectations, however, were blasted; for in a short time after his arrival a company of dragoons rode up to the door. He hastily doffed part of his apparel, and speedily arrayed himself in the coarser and more tattered clothes of the farm servant, and went to meet the visitors. He held the horses while they dismounted, and then led the animals to the stable, the soldiers in the dark supposing that he was the servant. During the time that he was in the stable, assisted by one of the dragoons in foddering the horses, the rest of the party were busily employed in searching the house. In the darkness and confusion, having seized a pitcher for the apparent purpose of fetching water to the horses, he embraced the opportunity of making his retreat from the place in the obscurity of the night. He then repaired, with all convenient speed, to his accustomed hiding-place in one of the lofty ranges of the Galloway mountains, called the *Mill* or *Meaul ae.* A place of greater solitude than this can scarcely be found, and a retreat which, in the night season, it was impossible for the troopers to find. Here, in the heart of the desert, and in the crevices of the frowning rocks, this man of God had to seek a shelter from the face of his angry foes; but he was safe in nature's concealment and the hiding-place of Jehovah's protection.

When the soldiers found that they were out-witted, their indignation knew no bounds; but then they could not help themselves, for they could not guess to what place he had fled, nor could they search the fields in the darkness of the night. They vowed, as usual, their determination to renew the search, and to continue it till they found him, when ample vengeance would be inflicted on his hapless person.

On another occasion, Roger and a companion in tribulation were concealed in a retreat in the wilds, and, dreading no harm, felt comparatively at ease. Their place of conceal-

ment, unfortunately, had, unknown to them, been discovered
by an informer or some unfriendly neighbour, who forthwith
proceeded to conduct a party of military to the spot. It happened, however, that the approach of the enemy was discovered by them in time to afford them opportunity to escape.
In their flight they were observed by the horsemen, who rode
at their utmost speed to overtake them. Fortunately, in the
wilds there were many things calculated to facilitate the
flight of the fugitives, and many things that retarded the pursuit of the horsemen. The two wanderers, seeing it necessary
to quicken their pace, ran down the shaggy slope of a steep
hill, in the direction of a deep and narrow ravine, in the side
of which was a dark cavern scooped out under the shelving
rocks, that shot procumbent over the yawning trench beneath. To this cave our worthies bent their steps with the
speed of men fleeing for their lives, and they succeeded in
descending to the depths below before their pursuers got
within reach of them. Scarcely had they mastered the precarious descent, and placed themselves, breathless and exhausted, within the rocky chamber, than an incident occurred
which appalled both the pursuers and the fugitives. The
ravine in which the wanderers had taken refuge was deep
and strait, and originally formed by the sudden rushing of
the waters from the mountains after a heavy thunder-storm,
or by the hasty melting of the snows in winter. To a spectator, on approaching this *gullie*, no appearance of the bed of
a water course was perceptible on the plain of the moorland
before him. The opposite edges of the ravine seemed, at a
short distance, to meet and to form a uniform surface, and
it was not till the traveller was almost on the very brink of
the descent that he could suspect such an opening in the
ground to exist at the place. The dragoons, who were now
pushing along at full speed in the direction of the fugitives,
had no suspicion of the perilous cleft which yawned across
their path, and they raced heedlessly along the heathy turf.
One of their number, keener in the pursuit than his fellows,
was careering considerably in the advance of his party, and
came with precipitancy to the very edge of the gulf. It was
too late to rein his impetuous steed, and the horse and his
rider tumbled into the chasm, and were dashed to pieces in
the bottom, the crimson tide of life dyeing the limpid waters
of the brook as it gurgled along its rugged channel. The
place where the trooper fell was exactly before the mouth of
the recess in which the friends had taken refuge. They were
horrified at the terrific incident, and could not but notice the

hand of God in the circumstance—their lives being preserved, while one of their adversaries, in seeking to destroy them, had come to an end so fearful and so distressing. The Lord some- times takes the wicked in their own snare, while those whom they would oppress are permitted to escape. Doubtless the great body of the troopers who had engaged in this unrigh- teous warfare little knew what they did—they obeyed the orders of their masters without any inquiry into the nature of the service in which they were engaged; but then, they were for the most part brutish and wicked men, who de- lighted in those acts of cruelty to which their savage leaders conducted them. Their ignorance, however, did not excuse them before God, and not unfrequently was his displeasure manifested against them for their deeds of profligacy and murder.

The painful catastrophe which befell the dragoon put an end to further pursuit for that day. A few of the party de- scended into the ravine and brought out the dead body of their comrade, and forthwith left the place, carrying with them also the harness of the war-horse, whose carcass they left among the stones of the brook.

It was no trivial part of the afflictions of these good men, that they were often obliged to retire to a distance from their families, who might fare ill in their absence, while they themselves were exposed to hunger and cold in the inhos- pitable caves and dens of the earth. For weeks together Roger Gordon was never under his own roof, but was forced to abide in the clefts of the rock, or under the projecting brow of a moss-hag, or among the brackens in the dell, or in the brushwood in the glens; and had it not been that these men were supported with the peace of God within, and with the conviction that they were suffering in a good cause, they must have sunk under the weight of their oppression, and ceased any longer to contend. At one time, when Roger paid a visit to his own house, a company of soldiers appeared in the immediate vicinity of the place ere the inmates were aware. He was in the act of passing out at the one end of the close as the troopers were entering at the other. He was instantly made prisoner, under the suspicion that he was the person they were seeking. They happened to ask him if he was the laird of Largmore, when he replied: " I am the laird of Glenmont" this Glenmont being a hill within his own estate. The answer staggered them, and thinking that they were mistaken, they let him go, and proceeded forthwith to search the house. When he found that he was free, he instantly withdrew and fled again to his concealment in the wilds.

This good man survived the times of persecution, and enjoyed many happy days of peace and prosperity. He presented the parish of Kells with a large new bell for the church in the year 1714, and a pair of communion cups, which are still preserved. In the gable of the church there is a stone with an inscription to his memory.

CHAPTER XXXIX.

John M'Clement.

JOHN M'CLEMENT was a native of the parish of Barr, in Ayrshire, and having married, he removed to the neighbourhood of New Galloway. During his residence in this place he was brought to the knowledge of the truth, and became an associate of the serious people, who often met for prayer in the district. His wife, however, was a person of a different description, and from her he received no small opposition on account of his frequenting conventicles and private meetings for religious conference. She loved her husband, and was an affectionate mother; but she was a stranger to the power of religion, and could see no good reason why people should expose themselves to hardships for their adherence to the Gospel. She failed not to remonstrate with her husband on the alleged impropriety of his conduct in exposing his household to the merciless treatment of the dragoons, when they might otherwise live in safety in attending the ministry of the curate. John easily sympathized with his wife, knowing that she did not see in the same light as he did, and that what was a matter of conscience to him, was to her a thing of mere indifference. He sustained with the utmost patience the opposition he met with, and at the same time laboured assiduously to impart to her the knowledge of Christ. He loved her tenderly, and her soul's welfare was to him a matter of unspeakable solicitude.

They had a little girl whose name was Janet, and who seemed, from the religious conversations she had heard, to be deeply impressed with her father's sentiments. This child, about twelve years of age, stole, whenever an opportunity presented itself, to the field-preachings which her father was in the habit of attending; and on these occasions salutary impressions were made on her youthful heart, and she was at length brought to the knowledge of that Saviour

in whom her father trusted. Her conduct in this respect,
however, was peculiarly offensive to her mother, who used
her with more than ordinary harshness when at any time
she ventured to a conventicle. The child, however, having
imbibed the spirit of the Gospel, uniformly displayed the
greatest meekness under the severe treatment she received
from her parent. She never allowed an angry feeling to
arise in her bosom, nor an improper word to escape her lips.
Her temper and demeanour made an impression on her
mother, who one day said to John: "I think Janet's disposition is of late much more sweet and kindly than it used to
be; she seems to be the most affectionate and obliging of all
our children." "My dear Mary," replied John, "the change
you perceive in Janet is the result of the grace of God, which
changes the heart, and makes us new creatures; and this grace
she has received in hearing the Gospel preached in the fields."
This remark greatly displeased Mary, who, in her usual style,
entreated her husband not to bring ruin on the family, by
instilling into his children his strange notions, and inducing
them to follow his example.

After this, Mary, though she could not prevent John from
attending the interdicted conventicles, was determined to
exercise her authority over her young daughter, and to
restrain more effectually than heretofore her propensity for
field-preachings.

Several years after this, a conventicle was announced to
be held at Carsphairn, and on the day appointed a great
company assembled. Janet M'Clement had found her way
to the gathering, expecting to meet with her father, who was
from home—probably under hiding. Among the people,
accordingly, she found her honoured parent, with whom she
expected to unite in the sweet fellowship of the saints; but
her expectations were defeated, for the meeting was hastily
dispersed by the soldiers, and the helpless flock of Christ
was scattered and pursued in every direction. In the confusion, John M'Clement was separated from his daughter, and
fled into a neighbouring morass, where he succeeded in concealing himself till the danger was past. Janet, having
missed her father, pursued her way homeward over a mossy
and uneven ground of many miles' extent, and the poor girl,
on the point of expiring, through fatigue and hunger, reached
her home when the day was far spent. On entering the
house her mother met her with a severe reprimand, which
she received with a becoming submission, and without answering again. Her exertions, however, in her flight had so

completely overpowered her gentle frame, that she was seized with a severe fever, which in a short period ended her days. During her illness her mother was deeply affected with two things—her daughter's meekness and her own unkindness. When she reflected on these, and considered the prayers and the exhortations of her husband by the couch of her dying child, she felt a relenting of heart to which she had formerly been a total stranger. A new light began to dawn upon her mind, and the conduct of her husband and of her daughter was presented to her in a very different aspect. One day she said to Janet: "I fear, my dear child, that I have been too harsh to you; my treatment of you has not been such as became a mother, when I imagined that you might expose us to danger in following your father's ministers. You were always pleasant to me, but your kindness and gentleness have been more especially noticeable since you began to accompany your father to the outed preachers; and now I am afraid I shall lose you, and my heart will pain me after you are gone." "My dear mother," replied Janet, "I am indeed very ill, and I do not think I shall recover; but my heart is full of peace, and my trust is in the Saviour. Death is not a pleasant prospect, and especially to a young person. I have now reached the age of womanhood, and life was opening before me; but it is the will of my Saviour that I should bid an adieu to all, and I am willing to depart, and I long to enter into his rest. But, my dear mother, I am anxious on your account, and it would greatly lighten the affliction of my dying bed to see you turning to the Saviour, and seeking his face with all your heart."

Janet never rose from her bed; but ere she departed to her rest she had the satisfaction of seeing a blessed change wrought on her mother. She died in the spring of the year prior to the Revolution, at the early age of twenty.

After this John enjoyed the peculiar pleasure of seeing Mary walking in the steps of their departed child. It was now her practice to accompany her husband to those religious meetings of which she formerly so much disapproved.

The following incidents which befell John M'Clement are worthy of notice. On one occasion a meeting was convened at Fingland, in Carsphairn, at which John happened to be present. During the time the friends were engaged in religious exercises, a party of horsemen arrived at the place, and dispersed the assembly. John, among others, made his escape from the house and fled, but was closely pursued by the troopers. As he descended toward the Water of Ken,

and the pursuers rapidly gaining ground upon him, he came
to a small sheep-fold, within which were confined a ewe and
a lamb, while a shepherd's plaid was spread like a curtain
over the entrance into the enclosure, to prevent their escape.
When the fugitive arrived at the fold, where, owing to the
inequality of the ground, or some other intervening object,
he was concealed from the view of the dragoons, he seized
the plaid, threw it across his shoulders, and having caught
the ewe by the horns, led her to the outside of the fold, and
just as the troopers came up he was in the act of putting the
lamb to suck.   The soldiers asked him if he saw a man running past him in the line of their pursuit.   "I did not," he
replied, "notice any person pass me here; but if you are in
chase after a fugitive, I would advise you to ride in the direction of the Holm Glen, as being as likely a place as any I
could think of to which he would betake himself." The
horsemen followed his counsel; and John having replaced
the ewe and the lamb in the fold, and restored the plaid,
hastened from the spot to seek concealment at a distance.

At another time, when John and his wife were returning
from a conventicle across the moors, and had nearly reached
their dwelling, they observed two troopers following them in
the distance.   They quickened their pace, and reached the
house before the soldiers arrived.   John, by the advice of
Mary, hid himself in the little garden among the tall and bushy
kail-stocks.   The dragoons arrived and made inquiries, and
Mary attempted to satisfy them in the best manner she could.
She entertained them in the house, while one of the children
held the horses at the door.   She succeeded in saving appearances, and in evading the questions which were asked respecting her husband.   The soldiers departed pleased with their
reception; and John, leaving his retreat in the garden, entered
his house with a grateful heart.

The last time John was harassed by the dragoons was
when he was returning from a conventicle in Carsphairn.
He was pursued by a number of troopers for several miles.
He fled at his utmost speed; but his enemies were fast gaining ground, and must certainly have overtaken him, had he
not resorted to the following stratagem.   In his flight he
happened to evade for a few minutes the view of his pursuers, either by turning round a knoll, or in passing through
a hollow place.   He came upon a sheep newly dead, lying on
the heath, when he instantly doffed his coat, and seizing the
sheep by the legs, threw it across his shoulders, and advanced,
as if he had been the shepherd bringing home the carcass, in

the direction in which the soldiers were approaching. He met his enemies in the face, moving tardily along with his burden, as if he had been unconscious of their presence. The troopers, who had not the slightest suspicion that he was the person of whom they were in quest, asked him if he observed a man crossing the moor before them. "I did," replied John; "but he made a short turn in the hollow there, and has taken a different route; ride straight along the height in the direction of Minigaff, and lose no time." The troopers took his advice, and scoured over the bent in quest of their object. When the party was out of sight, John threw down his burden, went back for his coat, and escaped in safety to his house. This worthy man evaded all the perils of the persecution, and died at an advanced age in the neighbourhood of New Galloway. His descendants occupied the farm of Star, in the parish of Barr, within the last forty years.

CHAPTER XL.

Bell of Whiteside—Clark of Drumcloyer.

Mr Bell was the proprietor of the estate of Whiteside, in the parish of Anwoth, in Galloway, the scene of the early ministry of the famous Samuel Rutherford.   He was the son of the heiress of Whiteside, who, after his father's death, was married to the Viscount of Kenmuir.   Mr Bell was a man of uncommon piety, and possessed of great prudence and intelligence.   No gentleman in the district in which he lived was more highly esteemed for his religion; and his good sense procured the respect of persons of every class.   He was implicated in the affair of Bothwell, and being a landed proprietor, he was exactly one of those against whom the persecutors wished to find a pretext.   Immediately after Bothwell his house was pillaged, and all the best of his horses carried off.   Claverhouse made Whiteside a garrison for his troopers, where he lay for several weeks, till all the provisions were consumed, and the meadows eaten up by the horses.   When he was, through necessity, obliged to leave the place, he took away everything that was valuable, tore the very timber from the building, and destroyed the plantations.   He drove away the whole stock of sheep and all the horses, and at the same time gifted the entire crop to the curate, who greedily and dishonourably received it.

For several years after Bothwell, Mr Bell was forced occasionally to wander and hide in remote places, when he durst not venture to reside in his own house.   " Many were the straits," says Wodrow, " that this excellent gentleman was put to, in his wanderings, those four or five years which I must pass."   The following anecdotes respecting this worthy man are in circulation in the district.

One day when he was at home, and suspecting no harm, a company of soldiers appeared near the house.   It happened at the time that a female servant was employed in assorting a quantity of crockery, and it instantly occurred to her that Mr Bell should disguise himself, and take in his hand a basket filled with the earthenware, and walk slowly away, and appear as if he were a dealer in that article, proceeding to the next house to dispose of what he had to sell. The stratagem succeeded, and he passed the soldiers without discovery, and escaped.

At another time, this good man was surprised in his own house by the unexpected arrival of a troop of horsemen in quest of him. He fled into a retired apartment, and hid himself in a large oak chest which stood in a corner. The more immediate danger in this case was, lest he should die of suffocation. To prevent this, however, one of his attendants, in closing down the lid, took care to insert a piece of cloth, so as to leave an opening for the circulation of air. The soldiers examined every chamber, and groped into every nook, sparing no place whatever in the close search which they plied with all diligence and exactitude. They entered the place in which Mr Bell was concealed, in a very uproarious manner, tossing about the furniture, and prying into every place of supposable retreat. The good man lay with a beating heart, expecting every moment the covering of his hiding place would be lifted up, and himself dragged forth to a military execution. But though the old chest stood in their way, the men never seemed to notice it, because the likelihood of its interior containing the person of him whom they were so eagerly seeking never once entered their mind. They passed and re-passed the ancient piece of furniture, and probably sat down on it, as happened in cases somewhat similar, and yet it never occurred to them to lift the lid to see what was within; for though they might not expect to find the man, they might find some articles of clothing, or what else might perchance suit their cupidity, property being sometimes as acceptable to them as persons. It was therefore the more wonderful that the chest was left unheeded, and unsubjected to their greedy scrutiny. At length Mr Bell heard, to his great relief, the company leave the apartment, and retire from the place. He considered this deliverance as a special interference of Providence, and often afterwards mentioned the circumstance with heartfelt gratitude.

Owing to the incessant harassings to which this good man was subjected, and the uncertainty of a single night's security in his own house, he was obliged to seek a hiding-place in the fields. He found a cave in a retired spot, within his own lands, in which he secreted himself in time of danger. The enemy knew that he had a retreat somewhere in the vicinity, and were desirous of finding it. Its discovery, however, was not so easily accomplished, and therefore they had recourse to deception in order to gain their object. They engaged a spy to watch the movements of the household, and to notice if any person carried food in the evening dusk, or in the early morning, to any solitary place among the woods or glens in the neighbourhood. This scheme was successful, and the individual to whom the business was intrusted, followed stealthily in the steps of a person belonging to the family, who seemed, in as guarded a manner as possible, to be conveying provisions to Mr Bell in his cave. The informer, rejoicing in his success, hastened to give information, and to receive the promised reward.

Next day a company of troopers was conducted to the place, in the confident expectation of seizing on the worthy man in the secrecy of his retreat. It happened, however, that on their approach Mr Bell was not in the cave, but in a field adjoining, and from the place where he stood he observed the horsemen rapidly advancing. He instantly removed from the spot and fled. He was seen by the soldiers, and a vigorous pursuit commenced. He ascended a hill in the neighbourhood, in the direction of a field of moss, in which a number of people were digging peats. When the workers saw Mr Bell hastening at his utmost speed across the moss, they soon conjectured the cause. When he approached them, one of the men, eager to save him, cried: " Make haste, Mr Bell, throw off your coat, and take this spade and dig in the hag with me." Mr Bell instantly saw the propriety of the advice, and, without the hesitation of a moment, he did as he was bidden. In a brief space the dragoons appeared on the edge of the moss in hot pursuit. The labourers, aware of what was coming, were plying their work, and apparently unconscious of the presence of the soldiers. The commander of the party, however, with a loud voice, summoned their attention, and asked if they saw a man pass that way. One of the workers answered that a short time ago they saw a man wending his way across the moor, in the direction in which they were marching. On hearing this, the soldiers continued their pursuit, and Mr Bell was left undiscovered in the midst of the peat-makers.

This good man, however, did not always thus escape. He came to a hasty and a bloody end, by the hand of the infamous Lagg, by whose means he gained the martyr's crown,

The account of his death, and the circumstances which led to it, may here be given in the words of Wodrow: " Sir Robert Grierson of Lagg, with some of Claverhouse and Strachan's dragoons, probably upon some information about Mr Bell of Whiteside, came into the parish of Tongland, in the stewartry of Galloway, and there, upon the hill of Kirkconnel, surprised him, and David Halliday, portioner of Mayfield, Andrew M'Robert, James Clement, and Robert Lennox of Irelington, and most barbarously killed them on the spot, without so much as allowing them to pray, though earnestly desired, and, as several accounts before me bear, after they had surrendered themselves, and he had promised them quarter. And it is a frequent remark in many papers before me, that that bloody and unnatural man used, whenever he seized people in the fields, immediately to despatch them, without allowing them time to recommend themselves to the Lord. In this case, Mr Bell, whom Lagg knew well enough, earnestly desired but a quarter of an hour to prepare for death; but the other peremptorily refused it, cursing and swearing, ' What the devil, have you not had time enough to prepare since Bothwell?' and so immediately shot him with the rest, and would not suffer their bodies to be buried. A little after this barbarous murder, the Viscount of Kenmuir, Claverhouse, and Lagg, happened to meet at Kirkcudbright, where Kenmuir challenged Lagg for his cruelty to one whom he knew to be a gentleman, and so nearly related to him, and particularly, that he would not allow his dead body to be buried. Lagg answered with an oath, ' Take him if you will, and salt him in your beef-barrel.' Whereupon the Viscount drew upon him, and would have run him through, if Claverhouse had not interposed and parted them. Dreadful were the acts of wickedness done by the soldiers at this time, and Lagg was as deep as any."

Thus died Mr Bell, a gentleman of great respectability—a warm-hearted patriot, and a true Christian. His death happened in February 1685—one of those slaughter years which have been emphatically denominated " the killing time." He is buried in the churchyard of Anwoth, and his resting-place is pointed out by a stone with a suitable inscription.

The following anecdotes refer to John Clark of Drumcloyer, in the parish of Irongray. This good man was often eagerly sought for, and keenly pursued by the soldiers. One day, when the troopers came in search of him, he observed them from the house, and fled. His flight was perceived, and they followed. He entered a field in which his servant was following the plough; and being for a short space out of the sight of his pursuers, he was induced by the ploughman to take his place, while he, in his master's guise, should continue the flight.   When the troopers advanced to the edge of the field, they beheld the man running at his full speed, and the supposed servant quietly guiding the plough in the lengthened furrow, and whistling in chorus with the cheerful lark, carolling high in the air above his head.   The troopers staid not to interrogate him, but hastened eagerly forward to seize the object of their pursuit.

There was a cave in the rocks underneath the bridge that crosses the Scar, a streamlet that lay in the way of the fugitive.   When the stream happened to be full, there was no access to the cave except by seizing the branches of the trees and bushes that grew in the crevices of the rocks, and by this means descending to the mouth of the gloomy recess.   When the water was fordable, any person might find the cave, and enter it with ease; but when it was swollen to overflowing, an entrance was impossible, save by the means described, and then few durst try the experiment, for life was endangered by the attempt.   On this occasion the stream happened to be in full flood, rolling its foaming and muddy waters with impetuous current under the sounding arch, and past the mouth of the cavern.   When the man came to the place, he swung himself down the face of the precipice by the tough and pliant branches, and safely reached the hiding-place.   As he stood beneath the rugged roof of the dripping cavity, the troopers approached, and the feet of the horses were heard passing in thundering haste along the bridge above him, and anon the sound died away in the distance. It was not long, however, till the party returned; for, when they had proceeded a certain way along the road without seeing the fugitive before them, they concluded that he must have disappeared among the thickets about the bridge.   The trampling of horses, and the mingling of many voices, announced to the man in his hiding-place that his foes were collected at the bridge.   The loud report of their muskets, the rustling of the bullets among the leafy branches, and the rattling of the shot against the rocks, convinced him that the suspicions of the soldiers were that he was hidden somewhere among the bushes, and that they were determined to explore his retreat.   He, however, felt perfectly at ease, for he knew that their efforts would be all in vain.   The cave, even supposing they knew it, could not be entered below, and if they should attempt to descend the precipice as he had done, it was amply in his power to push them one by one into the roaring flood beneath; for in his position one man could master a hundred. On this account he remained perfectly unmoved, and allowed them to spend their powder, and their ball, and their oaths, at their pleasure; for all were innocuous as it respected him; and therefore, in the security of his stronghold, he set the entire party at defiance. When the soldiers had wearied themselves in their fruitless efforts, they left the place, and the man withdrew from his concealment at his own convenience. His disinterested conduct saved his master, and Providence preserved himself, and so both were shielded from the fury of the oppressor. This servant greatly loved his master, and was willing to peril his own life for his sake; and for the sake of that greater Master whom they both loved. " We ought to lay down our lives for the brethren." He acted well, and he had his reward; for he experienced an inward satisfaction on account of what he had done. He had the approbation of all good men; and, what is infinitely greater, he had the approbation of God. Had the dragoons overtaken him, his doom was certain—he would have been shot on the spot; but yet, with this fearful risk before him, he ventured to take his master's place, if perchance he might be the means of his deliverance; and he was successful—the Lord blessed his generous effort. He was, it is said, a powerful man, and perhaps, " swift as the roes upon the mountains;" and therefore, he might fear the less, and feel more confident in his undertaking.

After this, John Clark and a number of his friends, who had met at a conventicle, narrowly escaped being captured by the troopers. The meeting was appointed to be held in a remote place among the hills, and information had been circulated among the friends with the usual secrecy. It happened, notwithstanding, as was not uncommon in such cases, that an individual who appeared to be a friend, but who was in reality a traitor, had communicated with the enemy on the subject of the projected meeting; and the troopers being apprised, were in readiness at the time specified. When the day came, the worshippers congregated in the lone waste, on a spot most suitable to the purpose. They sat down on the edge of what is called the Braiky Moss, into the heart of which, in the event of a surprisal from the enemy, they could easily retreat and save themselves. Such precautions were generally taken when the assemblies of God's people met in the wilderness. Long experience had taught them many a salutary lesson, and hence they generally chose a place near the side of an intricate morass, or at the base of a steep mountain, or on the edge of a deep ravine; and many a time did such positions save them, for the troopers could climb neither the abrupt face of the height, nor plunge into the precipitous glenlet, nor wade the sinking moss, while the people on foot could, with comparative facility, evade the pursuit of their foes.

On this occasion, the little conventicle had no suspicion that the military had received information of their meeting, and though precautions were taken, yet no interruption was anticipated. Shortly after worship was commenced, however, the dragoons made their appearance, and the direction in which they seemed to proceed plainly indicated that they were guided by one who knew the place, and that they were led on for the purpose of attacking the worshippers. When the announcement of the circumstance was made, the assembly rose to flee. John Clark saw the confusion, and perceiving the danger which might ensue if the company should be scattered along the heath, he requested them to keep in a body, and to enter the moss together, with the view of eluding their pursuers. They, accordingly, complied with his advice, and followed the guidance of those who knew the intricacies of the morass, and who could conduct them, by a secure footing, to a place of safety. The little company, like a flock of sheep driven together by a furious dog, were collected among the dark moss-hags, a timid group, cowering before the fury of their adversaries, and looking for shelter to Him who alone can shield in the day of calamity. The horsemen rushed impetuously onward to the edge of the moss, and not sufficiently anticipating the consequences, as they saw the worshippers, with an apparently firm footing, advancing on the uneven surface of the peat ground, they urged forward, eagerly intent on reaching the little party before them. Their miscalculations, however, became speedily apparent, when the heavy horses plunged to the belly in the swampy moss one after another, and rider after rider was thrown from over the head of his charger, as if falling prostrate on the battle-field. The terror of the conventiclers was now supplanted by the sense of the ridiculous, and they could not help, even in their precarious circumstances, enjoying the sport which the vanquished troopers now afforded them. They taunted their magnanimous assailants with the failure of their enterprise, and invited them to advance to the onslaught. But the crest-fallen soldiers, tossed from their sprawling steeds, struggling to extricate themselves, and covered ingloriously with the smeary moss, had something else to think of Their own lives were in jeopardy, and their chief care was, if possible, to regain the firm ground. The discomfiture in the moss afforded ample time to the friends to pass over to the other side, where it was impracticable for the horsemen to follow them; but though they durst not pursue, they cried, and their cries were threats of vengeance. Their menaces, however, were unheeded, and the worshippers retired and sought their several homes in peace, and with hearts full of gratitude to the Preserver of their lives.

CHAPTER XLI.

Lochgoin—James Howie—John Howie.

THERE is, perhaps, no place in the west of Scotland, the bare mention of whose name recalls so many associations of covenanting interest as Lochgoin. Situated in the very heart of the moors of Fenwick, in Ayrshire, it afforded an asylum to the wanderers who, expelled from their homes for their adherence to the cause of religion, sought a refuge in the wilds and solitudes of their native land. The farm-house of Lochgoin occupies an elevated situation in the bleak moorland, and commands a prospect of great extent over many miles of heath and moss that were traversed by the feet of many a lonely sufferer in the dark times of persecution. In the far distance, the eye roams in the direction of Drumclog, the memorable scene of the defeat of the redoubted Claverhouse, by a company of Covenanters who met in the wilderness to worship God. And farther on appear the dusky heights and trackless wastes around Muirkirk, in the bosom of which was shed the blood of many an honoured martyr; the most illustrious of whom, perhaps, was the saintly Priesthill, who fell before his own door, by the hand of one of the most reckless and remorseless men who at that time acted a part so dastardly and so impious in the scene of Scotland's tragedy. The parish of Fenwick, of which Lochgoin forms a point so celebrated, abounded, in the times of Prelatic oppression, with many a trusty Covenanter and leal-hearted patriot. A goodly company of Christian men were reared under the ministry of the famous William Guthrie, who was the first incumbent of this parish, and whose labours in the Gospel were attended with a success so great, that his little glebe was studded with houses built by those who wished to enjoy the preaching of a man whose ministrations were attended with so much power from on high. He was one of the worthies who suffered in those times, although his life was not taken away by violence; for he was permitted to die in his own bed. The church in which he preached the everlasting Gospel, to the conversion and edification of so many souls, still stands ; and the pulpit from which he addressed great crowds, in strains so sweet and heavenly, still occupies its place. In the churchyard are the graves of several martyrs, whose hallowed dust, there at rest, awaits the quickening of the general resurrection.

In the house of Lochgoin are sundry relics of the covenanting times, to see which, and to visit the residence of the renowned author of the "Scots Worthies," hundreds of strangers annually come from afar. Among the curiosities at Lochgoin, are—the flag of the covenant, which waved on the standard of the men of Fenwick ; the drum, the sound of which convened the party, and which they followed to the field of conflict; the rusty sword of the brave Captain Paton, one of the leading patriots in the west, together with his Bible, a little dingy volume, well thumbed and worn with constant perusal—the identical volume which he handed down to his wife from the scaffold, the moment before he was turned over by the executioner, when he ended his life as an honoured witness to the truth, and sealed his testimony with his blood, and of whom it has been said, that "he lived a hero, and died a martyr."

Lochgoin possesses a well furnished library, containing many volumes of antiquity and of interest; and also some beautiful manuscripts of large notes of sermons preached by some of the worthies who held conventicles in that desert. The family of Lochgoin has subsisted on the spot for about seven hundred years, and came originally as refugees from some of the Waldensian or Piedmontese valleys, in the times of some of the early continental persecutions. No fewer than nine-and-twenty persons of the name of John Howie, or Hoy, have occupied the place in their successive generations. The father of the present occupant was the compiler of the "Scots Worthies;" and the bower in the little garden in the front of the house, is still pointed out as the place where, on the fine days of summer, he used to sit in retirement, and arrange and write the materials of that work which has earned for him so much renown, and which has found a place in almost every cottage in Scotland. This worthy man, besides other works, wrote a history of his own religious experience, in a small volume, and which affords the fullest evidence that he was a man who lived with God, and walked in the steps of a pious ancestry.

Doubtless many an incident of thrilling interest happened at Lochgoin, in the days of Scotland's troubles, which has not found a place in the notices of the times, and which tradition has failed to keep in mind. The worthy man who rented Lochgoin in the days of Zion's affliction was James Howie, who, along with his son John, endured numerous hardships, and sustained heavy losses, for their adherence to Scotland's testimony. Twelve times was their house plundered, and once were all their cattle driven away, and themselves forced to flee into the moors for shelter. A few of the more striking traditionary incidents respecting the venerable James Howie, who was great-grandfather to the writer of the " Scots Worthies," are given in the end of the volume of Memoirs of that author. As, however, this publication is now little known beyond the locality where he lived, the incidents are in danger of passing into oblivion. I shall here take the opportunity of presenting them anew, reserving to myself the liberty of stating them in my own words.

James Howie, to whom chiefly the following notices refer, was not a native of Lochgoin. He belonged to the Mearns branch of the family, but he was married to Isabel, eldest daughter of John Howie, with whom he resided after his marriage at Lochgoin. The old man, the father-in-law, who was infirm, and much afflicted with asthma, had one night a dream of rather a striking nature. After the disaster at Pentland, a number of those concerned in that rising sought refuge in the wilds in the vicinity of Lochgoin: and the residence of the Howies became, in a manner, their head-quarters. It was the place in the lonely waste to which they resorted for prayer and social intercourse; and the humble roof often sheltered many a hungry and weary wanderer. One night, when a number of the refugees met in his house, the aged man dreamed that he was at the Cross of Kilmarnock, and distinctly heard General Dalziel give orders to a party of his dragoons to repair to Lochgoin to search for the reputed rebels who had been at Pentland. When the soldiers were about to depart, as he thought, they seized on him, and compelled him to act as their guide to Lochgoin, the which, as it was situated in the heart of the moors, was by no means easy of access, especially to horsemen. When the party had advanced about two miles on their way, he imagined that one of the soldiers used him rudely, on which he awoke, and found it was a dream. In a little he fell asleep again, and dreamed that he met with the troopers a second time, whom he accompanied on their march till they came to a stream which they had to pass, when one of the sturdy dragoons seized him by the shoulders and pushed him forcibly into the torrent till it reached his knees, and the sudden chill of the cold water broke his slumbers; and he began to be a little thoughtful. He fell asleep for the third time, and once more met with the soldiers, and went along with them, till they came to the bottom of the rising ground on which his dwelling stood, when, being maltreated by them as formerly, he started from his bed, and cried to the persons in concealment to look out on the moor and see if danger was approaching. One of the company ran to the little turfen eminence that was reared a few yards from the house, for the purpose of observation—and which stands till this day—and saw, to his astonishment, in the grey of the morning, the muskets and points of the bayonets of a party of military just at hand. He hastened back to make the announcement, and the company within instantly made their escape, and hid themselves in the hollow of a brook behind a moss, which afforded them a retreat from the vigilance of their enemies. The worthy old man, whose dream was the means of saving the fugitives, hastily left his bed, and wrapping his cloak about him, went out and stationed himself at the end of the house. When the party advanced, John was leaning against the wall, and apparently panting for breath. The troopers, astonished at seeing a man in this position at so early an hour, cried out, taking the divine name in a profane manner, " What have we here?" " It is e'en an aged man," said John, " infirm and breathless, who is under the necessity, at this unseasonable hour, of leaving his bed to seek relief in the open air. The smoke of the fire which, on account of the cold, he is obliged to keep burning in the hearth, is like to stifle him by reason of this cough." This statement seemed to the dragoons to account naturally enough for the existence of the fire which they found blazing within, and lulled their suspicions of its having been kept burning for the accommodation of the party who had just fled from the apartment. The soldiers, when they had searched the dwelling and found nobody, enter-tained themselves with what provisions they could find, and in the early morning returned to Kilmarnock. Thus the dream of the good old man, however it may be accounted for, was the means employed by Providence of saving a handful of helpless men, who, in the time of their peril, sought refuge under his hospitable roof.

But though the house of Lochgoin was often visited by the

soldiers, this did not prevent the frequent keeping of the conventicles there. On another occasion we find Captain Paton, John Kirkland, George Woodburn, with James Howie, and two other persons whose names are not mentioned, convened at Lochgoin for the purpose of spending the night in prayer. The night happened to be very stormy, and the friends considering the circumstance as contributing to their security, thought it probable that they might be permitted to spend their time without interruption. They prayed and conversed together, and when the morning dawned they went by turns to look from the rising ground in the vicinity of the dwelling, lest the enemy should, even on such a stormy night, venture abroad. By this time the persecutors had learned that the most likely occasions on which to find the wanderers within doors, was during tempestuous weather; and with this idea a party was commissioned on the same evening to visit Lochgoin. Accordingly, a company of soldiers came unawares to the spot, conducted, it would appear, by one Sergeant Rae, who, having stationed the men without, boldly entered the house, thinking to secure those within without any interruption. As he advanced, in the bustling way of a trooper, along the inner passage, Isabel Howie met him, and seizing him by the shoulders, pushed him backwards, till she thrust him without the door, where he fell with violence, and his musket flew out of his hand. He instantly regained his feet, and ran to the west end of the house for the purpose of calling in his soldiers. In the meantime the persons in hiding, who were now sufficiently aware of their situation, made their escape by the cow-house, which was attached to the dwelling on the east end. When Rae observed this, he fired, while John Kirkland, one of the fugitives, turned, and discharged his musket at the assailant, and then fled with the rest. Kirkland's shot had very nearly proved fatal, for it passed so close to the sergeant's head, as to carry away the pendant knot of hair from the one side. The soldiers always found it a dangerous matter to engage with the Covenanters, however few in numbers; and therefore they were for the most part wary in their advances, especially in the dark. As the party in flight proceeded over the bent, a Highland sergeant, whose name is not mentioned, pursued with great eagerness and impetuosity, in the full expectation of seizing some of them. John Kirkland, who saw the danger in which their worthy leader, Captain Paton, was placed—who, being old and breathless, was not able to run, so as to secure his safety by flight—stood still for the purpose of retarding the pursuers until the captain should escape. When the enemy was within a short distance of them, John Kirkland and his friends discharged their pieces, and the Highland sergeant fell, shot with a ball through the thigh. As he lay sprawling on the heath, his companions came up, who, thinking that it was one of the fugitives that had fallen, cried out that they had now gotten one of the dogs, as they termed them; but they soon found that it was their own Highland sergeant who had received the injury; and so little friendship is there among the wicked, that one of them, on learning the circumstance, exclaimed that he wished the ball had passed through his heart! By this time the fleeing party had gained ground, and in a brief space they got beyond the view of their pursuers; but it was not till they had fled three or four miles that they got fairly out of their reach.

James Howie and his son John went out at another door, and took a different direction, and escaped. Next day the dragoons visited Lochgoin, and drove all the cattle from the farm to Dean Castle, and shut them up in a close at the end of the building, where they were kept for eight days. The calves which they left behind, and which they found inconvenient to take along with them, were fed with milk by the friendly neighbours till the cows were brought back. Sir William Muir of Rowallan sent fodder to the cattle during the time they were retained at the castle, and at last bought the whole from Captain Inglis for 600 merks, and restored them to Lochgoin by what was then called steelbow, so that the troopers when they revisited Lochgoin had no power to touch them. Before the Revolution, James Howie had them all relieved in a private way, and Rowallan paid.

After the incident which befell the magnanimous dragoon at the door of the house of Lochgoin, Isabel Howie never deemed herself safe. She was obliged to retire from the place, and to seek shelter in the moors; and many a cold night she spent in the moss-hags, with a baby at her breast. But she was suffering for Religion's sake; and not unfrequently were the doors of hospitable neighbours opened for her reception. In this precarious way she lived till the fury of her enemies abated.

Some time after this, in the month of November, the troopers visited Lochgoin, and staid all night in the house. They kindled large fires, emptied the barrels of all the beef which had been laid up for the use of the family during the winter, boiled large quantities of it, and having consumed as much as they could, they carried off the remainder. In

searching the house they found a new Bible, which they denominated a Whig book, and consigned it to the flames. In
the confusion, two little boys had crept cowering into a corner,
and while the soldiers were voraciously devouring the meat,
one of them, more humane than the rest, proposed to give
them a morsel, but the others rudely repelled the proposal,
using their master's name by way of an oath; and so the
poor trembling children got nothing.

One morning, a little before sunrise, the dragoons were
approaching Lochgoin, which having been observed by Mrs
Howie, she awoke her son John, and informed him of the
circumstance; accordingly he speedily arose, donned his
clothes, and fled. He had not retreated many yards from
the house, when the troopers, having arrived at the place,
observed him. They discharged their muskets once and
again in full volley after him; but being swift of foot he got
beyond their reach. In his flight, and before he was aware,
he came upon his father, who was also running for his life;
and John, fearing lest he should bring the troopers upon his
aged parent, who could not flee so fast, took another direction, for the purpose of decoying the soldiers from the old
man's track. In changing his route, he came to the dry
channel of a streamlet, which had worn its course far beneath its mossy bank; and into this excavation he speedily
crept, taking the precaution to drag after him a heathery
turf, for the purpose of concealing the mouth of the cavity.
The place where he lay used to be frequented by otters when
the stream was full; but being at that time quite dry, he
found it a very convenient lurking-place. The troopers came
straight to the spot in search of the fugitive; their feet
thundered on the turf above him, and he plainly heard their
oaths and execrations. Some of them asserted that he was
in the place below where they stood, and others vociferated
that he was not so much of a wild beast as to bury himself
alive. During the discussion, and before they had time to
proceed to the search, they observed his father on the heath
at some distance, and instantly they set out in full chase
after him; he was saved, however, by getting beyond a rising
ground, where they lost sight of him. In their disappointment at the loss of James Howie, they caught a shepherd lad
who was tending his flock at no great distance from them,
and interrogated him, on his oath, " if he had seen a black
dog with white hose and shoes on his feet." He replied that
he did not see a *black dog* in the guise in which they described
him. This the shepherd could honestly affirm, for he was

not obliged to understand their figurative expressions; and besides, James Howie had by this time thrown off his black coat, and his hose and shoes, for the purpose of aiding him in his flight.   It was considered as rather a remarkable circumstance that the troopers themselves did not at this moment observe Howie, who was not more than a quarter of a mile distant from them, running bare-footed and begirt with a brown vest.   But though they lost the track of the fugitive, they noticed another shepherd following his sheep on the waste, and pursued him.   The shepherd, however, was a nimble person, and though they followed him for several miles, they lost him; and, in the meantime, James Howie effected his escape.   When the troopers had wearied themselves in traversing the moor, they returned to Lochgoin and plundered the house of everything valuable; for these men were robbers as well as persecutors.

Lochgoin, as has already been observed, was a place of common resort to the wanderers who in those times were, for conscience' sake, driven from their homes.   Ministers and gentlemen, as well as those in the humbler walks of life, found Lochgoin an asylum in the hour of their distress.   Mr Renwick on one occasion visited this friendly mansion in his wanderings through the deserts.   His shoes were worn to tatters, and James Howie, who loved him for his Master's sake, not only entertained him hospitably, but furnished him with a pair of new shoes, to fit him for his sojournings in the wilderness.   A cup of cold water given to a disciple shall not lose its reward; and James Howie was blessed in his deed. Mr Shiels and the lairds of Kersland and Kinloch frequented this house, and spent many an hour of spiritual intercourse with its inmates.

James Howie refused to attend the curate in the church of Fenwick, and to pay the cess which was imposed on the subjects for the purpose of suppressing the Gospel in the fields; and, consequently, he and his son John were placed on the fugitive roll, and treated as outlaws.   He survived the Revolution, and died 1691.   His son John reached the great age of ninety-one, and breathed his last in 1755. Their ashes repose in the same grave in the churchyard of Fenwick.

James Howie never became a member of the Revolution Church; because it was not based on the principles of the Second Reformation.   Mr Fowlis, the first minister of Fenwick after the Revolution, held many a conversation with him on the subject, but could bring him to no accommodation; nor were the conversations which even Mr Shiels held with him attended with a different result.

Near the end of his days he drew up a testimony, after the form of those in the "Cloud of Witnesses," in which he expresses his adherence to the work of reformation, and strongly testifies against the defections of the times.

A few days previous to his death his mind was greatly clouded, and he was distressed with fears respecting his interest in the Saviour. He told his sons, that if he died in this state of spiritual darkness, they were to destroy his testimony; but that if he should experience a deliverance, they were to preserve it. The desired relief, however, was granted; and he enjoyed much of the Saviour's presence before his departure. Sitting on a couch near the fire, with his wife and children about him, this man of God prayed three times with a heavenly earnestness, which must have been greatly edifying to all present; and at the termination of the first prayer he cried out, "He is come," alluding to the gracious presence of the Saviour, who had condescended to visit his servant with the light of his countenance—to loose his bonds, and to fill his heart with joy. At the close of the second prayer, which was only about half-an-hour before he expired, he cried again, "He is come." He removed from the world with the high praises of the Redeemer in his mouth, celebrating the free grace of God that had such respect to poor sinners, of whom he deemed himself chief.

This godly man left a sweet savour behind him. He was an honest witness for Jesus Christ, suffering many hardships in his cause; and when he came to his end, he experienced the same consolations which filled the hearts of the blessed martyrs on the field and on the scaffold.

CHAPTER XLII.

Grierson of Lagg—John Dempster of Dalry

EVERY Scotsman has heard of the notorious Lagg, of persecuting memory. In his wanton cruelties and savage manners
he was second to none in the period in which he lived—not
even to Claverhouse himself. His fame, it is true, was of a
more local description than that of some others of the Cavaliers of his time; but the terror of his name was equally great
within the district over which he presided. The upper parts
of Galloway were assigned to this daring champion of Prelatic
usurpation, as the locality within which he was licensed to
roam at pleasure, committing havoc where he saw fit on the
unoffending people of God, who sought only to be permitted
to worship him according to the dictates of their own conscience, and agreeably to his Word. His residence, when in
Galloway was Garryhorn, in the parish of Carsphairn; in
which district, as Wodrow informs us, there were no fewer
than two garrisons stationed, for the purpose of keeping the
peasantry in subjection. This fact is a proof that there existed even in that wild part of the country a goodly host of
witnesses for the truth, in order to suppress whom their
enemies saw it necessary to employ measures of no common
severity. If Lagg was another Claverhouse, Peter Pearson
the curate was another Sharp. This man lay as a grievous
incubus on the parish of Carsphairn; and his vigilance in
detecting the Nonconformists, and in communicating information to Lagg and others, contributed to the violent death
he met with in his own house—the circumstances connected
with which have been narrated in a former chapter.

The house of Garryhorn was the head quarters of Lagg in
Carsphairn. The bed on which he slept is still preserved,
and is strongly panelled with boards of black oak, overlap-
ping each other like tiles on the roof of a house. There was

formerly at the foot of this bed a sort of kennel, in which he kept a number of dogs, which were employed both in hunting and in scenting out the hiding-places of the wanderers. This nuisance, however, has long since been removed, and the chamber is now the comfortable dormitory of the worthy shepherd of the farm, who occupies in peace the identical bed of the redoubted persecutor. Lagg lived after the Revolution, and long after he had nothing to do in the way of persecution. He lived a dreaded and a hated object by the virtuous peasantry who had suffered so much at his hands. After his power of doing mischief was taken from him, he became an object of great curiosity to many, so that a sight of the persecutor was eagerly sought by those who had heard so much of him. Among others who were solicitous to obtain a view of this once terrible man, was the servant of Colonel Vance of Barnbarroch, in the vicinity of Wigton. His master being on a visit to Lagg, the young man made known to him his wish. The Colonel told him that he would find occasion to call him into the room sometime during the evening. When he was called, and had placed himself in his master's presence, Lagg turned himself round in his chair and thundered out, " Ony Whigs in Galloway noo, lad ? " The attitude, and the countenance, and the voice, made an impression which remained with the lad till his latest day.

Lagg, whose hands were deeply imbrued in the blood of his countrymen, was the murderer of the worthy man some of the incidents of whose life form the subject of the present chapter.

John Dempster, the Covenanter, lived at Garryyard, in the parish of Dalry, in Galloway. He followed the occupation of a tailor, and was one of the patriots who fought at Bothwell Bridge. Being a noted Nonconformist, a strict search was frequently made for him in the district where he resided. So intent were his enemies on his apprehension, that he was obliged to leave his house, and to seek an abode in the woods and caves of the neighbourhood. He selected a hiding-place in the rugged sides of the Black Water, a stream which empties itself into the silvery Ken a few miles above the village of Dalry. The cave of the rock in which he lodged was the place where, in the summer months, he plied his trade, while his wife conveyed to him his food by stealth.

On one occasion his wife, in the evening dusk, had brought him a supply of provisions, and having learned that the enemy was not in the neighbourhood, she persuaded him to leave his retreat, and to seek shelter for one night under his own roof. The worthy man was induced to visit his household, in the hope that he might be permitted to remain for a few hours in his own lowly hut without interruption, and then to return in the morning to his rocky cell. The night, accordingly, was spent without the intrusion of the military, and John, after the morning's repast, and after the accustomed family devotions, was preparing to return to his hiding-place by the purling brook. It was a fine morning; and his wife, whose solicitude for her husband's welfare was incessant, went to the front of the house to ascertain if the space within the field of her vision was clear of the wandering troopers, who were frequently abroad at all seasons seeking to surprise the helpless and unwary. As she cast her anxious eye afar over the landscape, she noticed a band of dragoons marching at their utmost speed in the direction of the house. The unwelcome tidings were communicated to John, who lost not a moment in making his escape. As he was running at his full stretch, having thrown off his shoes to facilitate his flight, he was observed by the horsemen, who pursued him hotly, and fired several times without effect.

John fled in the direction of Earndarrock Wood, a thicket about the distance of half a mile from his house. Between him and the wood there lay a moss or space of boggy ground, to which, when the dragoons approached, their progress was suddenly arrested. One of their number, however, found his way round by the end of the morass, and spurring furiously his war-steed, came up to John as he was attempting to scramble over the dyke that surrounded the wood. He had no weapons of defence; but remembering that he had with him the large scissors which were employed in cutting the good broad cloth, he drew them from his pocket, and just when the horse had neared him so close that he felt his head rubbing and pressing on his shoulder, he drove, with the force of desperation, the sharp-pointed instrument into the animal's forehead. The violent stroke made the horse rear and spring to the one side, so that his rider, who had uplifted his sword to strike, was cast impetuously on the ground. This overthrow afforded John time to dart into the wood before the party reached the spot. The troopers, leaving their horses at the edge of the wood, pursued him on foot to the brink of a deep ravine, adown the rugged sides of which he made his way with all possible haste. His pursuers, finding it inconvenient to descend after him, employed themselves in tumbling large fragments of rock after him; but John escaped unhurt, and having reached the opposite side of the ravine, concealed himself among the bushes.

His wife witnessed the pursuit, from the door of her house, with intense anxiety. It is impossible to describe her feelings at the moment she saw the dragoon reach him, before he succeeded in entering the wood. When, however, she observed the fall of the trooper, and perceived her husband running into the thicket, her hopes revived. Her fears, however, were renewed, when she saw the party dismount and dive into the wood, hunting among the trees, and yelling like bloodhounds after their prey.

In a short time they emerged from the plantation, and returned to the house, where the afflicted wife and children were lamenting the loss of the husband and the father. The disappointed troopers declared that they had killed the rebel in the ravine, and had left his mangled body among the underwood. They enjoyed a malignant satisfaction in lacerating the good woman's feelings to the uttermost, who had no difficulty in believing their assertions respecting the murder. Such incidents were of daily occurrence, and the death of John was considered as nothing new nor incredible. The soldiers, on witnessing the excessive affliction of the family, wrought all manner of mischief, eating and drinking at their will, and destroying what they could not use.

When the troopers were gone, the household gave vent, without restraint, to sincere and uncontrollable sorrow. "Come, my children," said the mother, "let us go into the wood and seek the bleeding body of your father, who has fallen an honoured witness for Jesus Christ by the hands of these cruel men." The sun was now advancing to his meridian height; and the family, a weeping company, was preparing to go to traverse the wood in every direction. The dragoons were now out of sight, and it might be supposed that nothing was to be dreaded from them, as they had declared they had now perpetrated the murder they had so long sought to accomplish. When the mother, with her children, was on the eve of departure, a new thought struck her in a moment, and she stood still and considered. "My dear children," said she, "it has even now occurred to me that this account of your father's death by the dragoons is probably, after all, a mere fabrication of their own, to serve a purpose. Perhaps your father yet lives, and is in safety in some undiscovered hiding-place in the ravine; and the object of these unprincipled men may be to send us in search of him whom they could not find, and then to trace our steps and capture him. No trust can be put in the statements of these men; and perchance there is a snare laid to entrap us." It was exactly as the honest woman opined; the troopers invented the story for the purpose of imposing on the simple-hearted cottagers, that through their means they might the more easily accomplish their purpose.

Still it was a matter of uncertainty; and the surmises of the mother, though amounting to a high probability, were not fully satisfactory, and the afflicted household earnestly longed for the shadows of the evening. John, in his cavern, was greatly solicitous about his family. He knew that the soldiers would be chagrined and exasperated at the disappointment they had met with, and that, therefore, they might vent their fury on his helpless wife and children. He durst not move from his retreat so long as the light of day continued, lest his enemies should be lying in wait in the skirts of the wood, ready to shoot or apprehend him on his first appearance. With impatient look he watched the progress of the descending sun, that under the cloud of night he might steal cautiously to his cottage to see how matters stood there, and to impart the joyful intelligence of his safety. As the distressed inmates of the cottage were making preparation for an instant departure to the wood, the sound of footsteps was heard at the door, and the object of their solicitude stood before them. The surprise and the gladness of the household were indescribable; the affectionate wife fainted in her husband's arms, being overpowered by the strength of her emotions, and the children were bathed in tears of joy. The state of matters was fully rehearsed on both sides, and the liveliest gratitude was expressed to the great Preserver of life by this pious company.

As John's place of concealment within the precincts of the wood was now known to the enemy, it was obvious that they would not cease to frequent the spot till they finally succeeded in their object; and, therefore, it was agreed that he should seek a place of shelter in another quarter. There was an intimate friend of his, a sufferer under hiding, who had a cave in a hill above New Galloway, and to this man our worthy resolved to pay a visit. He accordingly left his family for a season—went in quest of his friend—found him in his hiding-place, and was warmly received by him.

He had not long remained here till he received information that a strict search was to be made on the mountain by the soldiers, who, it was supposed, were conducted by a spy who seemed to have some notion of the hiding-place. On the reception of this friendly caution, John and his friend left the cave to seek concealment elsewhere. As they were traversing the hill they observed a company of troopers who guided by an informer, were coming directly to the cavern which they had just abandoned. They now plainly perceived that the warning they had received was not without ground, and that their only security lay in the speed of their flight. The dragoons, who by this time had them fully in their view, commenced a vigorous pursuit. The fugitives directed their course towards Loch Ken, a beautiful sheet of water which stretches along the valley, in the line of the River Ken, below New Galloway. They next turned in the direction of Balmaclellan, and were about to ascend the little eminence that leads to the village, when they perceived that they were out of their enemies' view; and seizing the advantage, they turned to a linn in the Garple Glen, at a short distance from the place where they were, in which they had formerly found shelter, and which had been a place of retreat to many a wanderer in those fearful times. They reached the cave in safety; and the troopers arrived at Balmaclellan, where they searched every house in which they supposed the men might have taken refuge, but without success, and they were obliged to return to their quarters without their prey.

The place in which the cave was situated was a deep rugged recess, in the retirement of which the Gospel had often been preached by the outed ministers. The Rev. Mr Verner, the ejected minister of Balmaclellan, on one occasion preached to a small audience in this place, and baptized, it is said, no fewer than six-and-thirty children at one time. The baptismal water was contained in the hollow basin of a rock; from which circumstance the spot received the name of "The Holy Linn," which it retains till this day. Mr Verner was one of those excellent men who maintained the standard of truth in a degenerate age, and who was subjected to many privations in his Master's cause. It is said that he accounted the union of his daughter in marriage with the curate of the parish as one of the greatest trials which befell him in those troublous times. Nor is this to be wondered at; for John Row, the curate, if he it was to whom she was united, was a very bad man, and one who in the end apostatized to Popery. Mr Verner was again minister of Balmaclellan after the Revolution.

We come now to the incidents which led to the martyrdom of John Dempster, by the cruel hands of the infamous Lagg. On one occasion, when he was returning in the evening twilight from his place of concealment, he was met by a party of Lagg's men on Knockgree Hill, as they were returning to their garrison in the vicinity of the persecutor's residence. John descended the mountain closely pursued by his enemies, and crossed the Water of Deuch. The gloom of the evening, however, and the dark heath over which he was fleeing, perplexed his enemies, and in their bewilderment they lost his track. They rode round and round, backward and forward, in expectation of stumbling upon him in some lurking-place, but were disappointed, and obliged to abandon the search. John sped to the lofty mountain of Craighit, where he found shelter for the night among the crevices of the rocks. Craighit was not a proper place for persons in John's condition, as it was full in the view of Lagg Castle; and had it not been that he was greatly fatigued and overpowered, and perhaps sickly, he never would have allowed the light of day to dawn on him in this situation. Next morning Lagg was at the head of his troopers for the purpose of searching for wanderers in the neighbourhood. He had his eye on Craighit, and thinking that he saw an object in the distance, he brought his telescope to assist his vision, and by this means he obtained a distinct view of John cowering behind a rock on the hill. On this welcome discovery he instantly divided his men into two companies—the one made a circuit to the south, and the other to the west, with a view to circumvent the fugitive. John saw their movements, and instantly left his last place of shelter on earth. The scene of the pursuit was in full view of the people of Carsphairn, who looked on with absorbing interest, and with deep sorrow, to see the worthy man pursued like a partridge on the mountain. He left Craighit, crossed the Garry Burn, and hastened to reach the Bow Hill, with the intention of sliding down the back part of it into Loch Doon, if perchance he might there find another hiding-place.

The dragoons were pursuing with the utmost eagerness, and as hilariously as if they had been in keen chase after the furtive reynard. Lagg stood below in sight of his men, where he had a full view of all that was passing on the hill; and when, owing to the inequalities of the ground, the soldiers lost sight of the object of their pursuit, he made signs to them, and pointed out the direction in which they were to follow. When John reached the Bow Hill, he became fully aware of his situation, and saw that it was impossible to escape, as his pursuers were just at hand. He gained the height, however, and ran along it to a considerable distance to a point called the Meaul Hill. Here the dragoons in two divisions met and closed him in. He was now entirely in the power of his ferocious enemies, who exulted in their success as joyously as if they had seized the richest prize. The poor captive, panting and exhausted, was allowed no time to kneel on the heath in prayer, nor to commit his soul formally to Him in whose presence he was about to appear as a sufferer in His cause. But though this favour was not granted, he was not unprepared. He had sought the Saviour before, and he had found him, and now he was ready when called on to die in defence of his truth. His capture and death were almost instantaneous, for the merciless troopers shot him dead on the spot.

Thus fell a good man who had endured many hardships, and braved many storms of persecution, for a number of years. He died an honoured witness for Christ, and sincerely lamented by the worthy people of the district in which he was known.

There is to be seen on the solitary mountain a rude stone which marks the place where he fell, and under which, in all likelihood, his ashes repose; as it was common in those times to bury the mangled body of the martyrs in the identical spot where their blood was shed. " The mosses and the moors of Scotland are flowered with martyrs."

CHAPTER XLIII.

Lagg at Airdoch--Glen of Dunscore—M'Caig of Milton--Incident.

THE estate of Airdoch, in the parish of Dalry, in Galloway, was, in the time of the persecution, possessed by Major Robert Stewart, a staunch adherent to the cause of liberty. His son Robert was, along with three of his companions, killed by Claverhouse at the Water of Dee, in 1684. He was a youth of rare godliness, and sustained a character so unimpeachable that his very enemies applauded him; and even Claverhouse, after he had shot him, was forced to exclaim : " Stewart's soul now sings in heaven !" The death of this young gentleman left a sting in the breast of the persecutor similar to that he experienced a few months after this, when he shot, with his own hand, John Brown of Priesthill on the bent before his door. The murderers of the holy men who testified in behalf of truth during this trying period, had sometimes a difficult task to smother their convictions of the innocency of their victims, whom their wanton cruelty laid bleeding at their feet. Their character, when contrasted with the excellency of those whom they despoiled of their lives, frequently appeared even to themselves so hideous, that they could scarcely bear the sight; and so pained sometimes were they with the acute sense of their baseness, that the feeling was past endurance ; but they succeeded in tearing the arrow of conviction from their hearts, and the rankling wound soon closed, and their conscience gave them little annoyance— they drowned reflection in deep carousals, and hardened one another in wickedness. The troopers, it would appear, from a conviction of their impieties, verily believed that the punishment of hell would be their inevitable portion, as their conversation plainly testified. No words were more frequently in their mouths than the " devil, hell, and damnation." When any of their number died, they had no hesitation in asserting

that they were gone down to perdition, and as little hesitation in affirming that they themselves would follow to the
pit of misery in their turn.   Instances from the histories of
the period might be adduced in proof of these statements.
The following, from "Naphtali," may here be given: "In
the town of Kirkcudbright, when one Captain Fin, a horseman, died, one of his companions coming to see him, and
finding him dead, came near, and rudely gripping the dead
man, used this horrid expression: 'What, devil! art thou
dead, man? and did not tell me before, that I might have
sent a letter to hell with thee (to such a comrade of his as
he named, who had lately died before), to take up my winter
quarters.'"   Such was the style of these men in speaking of
the other world, and in looking forward to their condition in
a future state.   They lived in entire forgetfulness of God,
and spent their days in riotous blasphemy, and they had
nothing before them but "a fearful looking for of judgment
and fiery indignation to devour them."   These men were the
fit agents of hell in doing the work of Satan, in killing the
saints of God, and in making havoc of all that was good in
the land.

Airdoch, like many of the smaller mansion-houses in those
times, had a court-yard before it, surrounded by a high wall
A strong gate closed the entrance, which was also defended
by a powerful watch-dog, which failed not to give faithful
warning on the approach of strangers.   On one occasion,
Lagg, with a company of troopers, paid a visit to Airdoch,
for the purpose of apprehending some of the obnoxious inmates.   The party, in their usual rude and blustering style,
broke open the gate without ceremony, and rushed uproari-
ously into the court.   The family within observed the approach of the military, and were thrown into confusion.   The
faithful watch-dog considered his province invaded by a
company of persons who had no right to intrude themselves,
and he became quite outrageous, and attacked with desperate
energy whatever came in his way.   Troopers, and swords,
and muskets, he recked not—he was set for the defence of
the dwelling, and he was determined to wage war with all
indiscriminately.   Lagg seemed to be both amused and angry
with the animal, and he exclaimed, in his rough way: "Do
you see what sort of lap-dogs these Whigs keep!"   On this
the dog flew at the commander, who probably was attempting to chastise him with his whip, and seizing him by his
military cloak, pulled him so furiously, that he dragged him,
with all his warlike accoutrements, in one fell dash on the

ground. Here the haughty Cavalier lay ingloriously under
the feet of the dog, which stood over him, and would have
torn his heart out of his body had not the dragoons inter
fered. But even they were not at first competent to the release of their valorous chieftain; for the dog pertinaciously
refused to let go his victim. They durst not touch him, lest
he should turn on them with equal fury—they durst not strike
him with their swords, lest they should wound their master—
they durst not fire, lest the shot should miss its aim, and pass
through the body of him whom they wished to succour. Probably the soldiers enjoyed the sport not a little, and they had,
perhaps, no objections to see a man humbled whom it was
impossible they could respect ; and as there is no real friendship among wicked men, they might have no serious misgiv-
ing at witnessing the discomfiture of one whose cruelty, as it
extended so largely to others, could not fail in occasionally
reaching themselves. How the dog was disengaged, it is not
easy to say; but when Lagg rose to his feet, he mounted his
horse, and left the scene of his ignominious defeat.

The treatment which Lagg received from the dog in the
close of Airdoch was very different from what the honest
farmer of Lochenkit received from his dog on his return from
a long banishment in the time of the persecution. After his
release he hastened home to visit his family, of whose circumstances, during his long absence, he was entirely ignorant.
He drew near his house with a palpitating heart, and knocking at the door, his wife made her appearance. He asked
if she could entertain a stranger for a night. She replied,
that she was but a poor widow, whose husband had many
years ago been torn from her by the rude hand of violence,
and that she was not fond of receiving into her lonely dwelling persons with whom she was not acquainted. In the
meantime his favourite dog, now worn out with age, scented
his old master, and springing from the hearth, bounded to
the door, and leapt, in his former fondling manner, on his
breast and shoulders, and displayed, by every freak and
gesture, his intimate acquaintance with the stranger, and
the excess of his joy at the meeting. The gudewife was
astonished at the circumstance, and looking at the dog and
then at the man, she exclaimed: " My husband ! " Providence
had sent him back, after a long separation, having protected
him in a thousand perils, to visit his home and to bless his
household. The posterity of this worthy man, whose name
was Grier, are to this day resident in the district, and by
them the anecdote has been retained.

Lagg and Claverhouse were intimate friends, companions
in wickedness, who delighted in debauchery and profanity,
in pillaging and in bloodshed. Two characters more fitted
for the work in which they were engaged could scarcely
have been found. Galloway, Nithsdale, and Annandale, was
the wide field over which they roamed, committing all kinds
of wickedness, and perpetrating the most unrestrained acts
of injustice, rapine, and cruelty. The district appointed them
by the council was considered by them as their appropriate
kingdom, within the limits of which they might do as they
pleased, without the fear of being called to account, and without the least regard to the remonstrances of the peasantry.
The names of these two men were terrible to the people,
and their coming to any place was considered as a circumstance much more to be dreaded than the visitation of a
pestilence; and men fled at the very report of them as from
an invading army, and hid themselves in the mountain deserts
and in the caves and holes of the earth. The distress of the
people in certain localities is scarcely conceivable; and this
distress was owing simply to the lawless ravages of these
unprincipled Cavaliers, who rioted in mischief, and enriched
themselves by the spoliation of their countrymen. It would
be saying too little merely to affirm that the council winked
at the villanies perpetrated by the troopers throughout the
land, for their procedure was positively sanctioned by that
infamous court. The members of the council plotted mischief
in the secrecy of their chambers, or in the hours of their
disgraceful carousals, and what they plotted they commissioned their emissaries to execute. Wicked as the council
were, their agents were equally so; and if the leading actors
in this crusade were bad men, their subordinate instruments
were still worse—the subalterns in the army imitated their
commanders, and even outstripped them in proficiency in
vice, and in all degradation of conduct and character.

The names of Lagg and Claverhouse are to this day almost
as familiar in the cottages of the south of Scotland as in the
times in which they lived; and this shows the dreadful notoriety as persecutors to which these men had attained. Not
only were they and the rest of their order feared by the
Nonconformists—they were equally dreaded by those of their
own party. The farmers and little lairds, of whatever religious profession, were, in common with others, frequently
subjected to their pillagings and unceremonious intrusions,
whenever it served their purpose. These two companions
in sin emboldened each other in their wickedness, and pro-

ceeded from bad to worse, till they reached such proficiency in iniquity as to leave far behind them many of their competitors in the career of crime. No deed of ruffianism was too daring for these men, and no atrocity too revolting and fierce. Their names have been transmitted with indelible infamy to posterity. It will be long before the south of, Scotland forget that such men shed profusely, and without remorse, the blood of a pious ancestry, whose only fault was " non-compliance with a wicked time."

In their ramblings through the country they brought terror and ruin to many a hearth, dragging the parents from the children, and the children from the parents. These associates in crime came one day, in their raids, to a place called the Glen of Dunscore, for the purpose of visiting a family who was suspected of harbouring the outcasts, to see what might be acquired by way of pillage; for they were mean men, and guilty of low acts of theft, infinitely beneath the dignity of gentlemen—gentlemen! that title never befitted them. It was on a fine day in harvest, and all belonging to the house were in the field, gathering the yellow treasures of autumn. The field, it would appear, in which the reapers were employed, was not in sight of the troopers, otherwise it is likely they would have visited it first, for the purpose of apprehending those whom they wished to secure, or at least to interrogate them respecting the wanderers. When they arrived at the house, no person was within but a little girl of ten or twelve years of age. Claverhouse was artful, and could easily assume a great deal of apparent gentleness of manner, and by this means he could throw unsuspecting people off their guard, and expiscate all he wished to know; but Lagg was blustering and imperious, and attempted to gain his object by frowns and threatenings. He accosted the child, and asked some questions respecting the sort of people that frequented the house, and if she ever carried food to people in the fields—to which questions no satisfactory answers were returned, further than that she carried porridge to the herd-boy, when he could not leave the cows in the fields; and that as to the night lodgers she knew nothing, because she went early to bed, and slept soundly till the morning. Lagg considered this as an evasion, and began to storm at the child, and threatened to shoot her on the spot. On this she burst into tears, and cried vehemently. "You have spoiled the play entirely," said Claverhouse; " she will now say anything, be it right or wrong, to save her life." When they were gone, the girl ran to the harvest-field to tell what had happened. The reapers were alarmed, and dreading a second visit from the party, betook themselves to their hiding-places. The chief place of resort in cases of alarm, was an old kiln at the end of the barn, which had been fitted up for the reception of a number of persons at a time, and was considered as a place of great safety by the family. Here they concealed themselves till they thought all danger was over. In such painful and precarious circumstances were our ancestors placed!—they could not pursue their occupations in the house nor in the field with safety, because strolling military bands, like plundering and murdering banditti, had spread themselves over the whole land.

But Claverhouse had, in the south, other companions in iniquity besides Lagg. Lowrie of Maxwelltown was one of his associates, a person whom Wodrow denominates "a bloodthirsty man." The small lairds who abetted the measures of the persecuting party, for the purpose of securing their lands, were the means of immense annoyance and distress in their own localities. They acted like little tyrants, and laboured strenuously to ingratiate themselves with those in power, for the sake of worldly advantage. The *lairds*, and the *curates*, and the *dragoons*, were the three grand instruments of mischief in the landward parts; so that the oppression of the country was very great.

The Milton of Tynron was at this time possessed by a worthy man of the name of M'Caig. His leanings toward the covenanting cause were well known, and being a small proprietor, something was to be had by the voracious plunderers in case of his conviction. Claverhouse and Lowrie agreed to surprise the dwelling of this honest man, and to make him their captive. They accordingly approached the place in as stealthy a manner as possible, lest the object of their search should by any means elude them. When they came to the house, M'Caig was concealed in a garret. The stair by which the ascent was made to this place was in a decayed and crazy state, and could be ventured on only by those who were thoroughly acquainted with its condition. A full-grown person leaning his entire weight on it, would have brought the whole to the floor with a crash, to the endangering of life and limb. When Claverhouse had accomplished a strict search in the under part of the house, he proposed to ascend the garret to ascertain what could be found there. He approached the foot of the ladder, for the purpose of making a nimble flight to the attics, when Mrs M'Caig cried that the steps would give way. This to the Cavalier seemed to intimate that there was somewhat in the loft she did not wish to be discovered, and therefore he was more bent on attempting the ascent. He placed his foot firmly on the lowest step, and then on the next, and so on, till the frail framework began to creak, and to exhibit symptoms of instantly giving way. Lowrie cried, and Claverhouse clung to his dubious position on the ascent, fearing to move either up or down lest he should be precipitated, with the fragments of the ladder to the floor. At length he succeeded in cautiously reaching the ground, leaving the garret and its contents unmolested. When they found the ascent impracticable, they drew their swords, and reaching upwards with the full length of the arm, inserted the sharp points between the open spaces of the boards, through which they thrust their glittering blades, if peradventure they might by this means discover M'Caig concealed on the floor above. And they were right in their conjectures, and almost unerring in probing the very spot where he lay, for the point of one of the swords grazed his knees, piercing his clothes through and through without wounding him. Had the sword been thrust upward a few inches onward in the same line, it would have entered his bowels or some other vital part, and the wound might have proved mortal; and, at any rate, the dripping of the blood through the crevices must have revealed the secret of his hiding-place, and then his capture was certain. Having, however, failed in their attempt, the men of blood withdrew, and M'Caig, at his own convenience, descended from his retreat.

The name of Lagg, when anything suggests itself respecting him, cannot easily be passed by. He was one day advancing with his troopers in the neighbourhood of Auldgirth Bridge, which spans the Nith about eight miles above the town of Dumfries. It was, we say, in the neighbourhood of where the bridge now stands; for it existed not in those days, when men in peril had to pass the flooded streams without such aids. The scenery around this spot is enchanting. The lands of Blackwood, a finely cultivated estate, stretching along the banks of the Nith, and the pleasant mansion-house situated not far from the margin of the stream, are the admiration and delight of every traveller who passes this sweet vale. In the days of Lagg, there were none of the improvements now visible in this lovely locality; still the natural scenery was fine, and could not fail to arrest the attention of even the uncultivated troopers. Lagg was descending a road, through what is called the Crainey Wood, leading with him a helpless prisoner. The circumstance became known, and a friend of the captive bent on his rescue, concealed himself in the wood by the side of the highway, with the full determination even to peril his own life in attempting to effect the deliverance of his friend. Accordingly, when the party came directly opposite to the place where the man had secreted himself, he sprang with a shout from the thicket, and demanded the release of the captive. Lagg, probably having but few men with him, was taken by surprise, and thinking that in all likelihood a company of men were concealed in the underwood, and prepared to fire from the secrecy of their ambuscade, if he should happen to manifest the least resistance, complied, and delivered the prisoner to the assailant. His fears prevailed, and his courage fell before the valorous bearing of the Covenanter, who generously endangered his own life to save his friend.

CHAPTER XLIV.

John Willison of Crawford—Conventicle at Normangill—M'Cron of Carsphairn.

JOHN WILLISON was tenant of Glengeith, in the ancient parish of Crawford, in the upper ward of Lanarkshire. The aspect of this parish is very wild. Vast tracts of moorland and dark heathy mountains constitute its general appearance. In ancient times its glens and straths were thickly covered with wood. The sterility of its surface, however, is largely compensated by the richness of its minerals. The valuable veins of lead which are imbedded in its rugged hills have been for ages past a source of wealth to the proprietors. In the streams and rills of this upland waste, gold in no small quantities has been found. The localities contiguous to Crawford on the south were equally rich in gold, and hence they were termed by the ancients, " God's treasure-house in Scotland." The four principal streams, compared by them to the four rivers in Eden, in which the golden particles were chiefly found, were Glengonar, Short Cleuch, Mennock, and Wanlock. The gold found in Glengonar was of a pale colour; that found in Short Cleuch was red; the gold of Mennock was rough; and that got in Wanlock is not characterized. In the time of Queen Elizabeth, and James VI. of Scotland, hundreds of men were occasionally employed in collecting this precious metal; and when its quality was tested, it was found to vary from no less than £76,000 to £136,000 per ton. The gold-gathering, however, is not now practised, excepting on a very small scale, by a few lead miners, merely for amusement.

The place of John Willison's residence was in the moorlands—retreats where much of the piety and worth of our native land in times of religious oppression sought refuge. The parish of Crawford was favoured with the valuable ministrations of the Rev. Gilbert Hamilton, who, under the wing of the Indulgence, preached the Gospel to the children of the desert. Many a genuine Christian, it would appear, was reared under his ministry; for after his removal it was found necessary to establish a garrison in this wild locality. The establishment of a garrison was always the indication of the existence of a numerous race of Nonconformists in the neighbourhood. It says much for the faithfulness and success of the incumbents in the respective parishes of Carsphairn and Crawford, that in these secluded districts the persecutors were obliged to locate a military force to overawe the peasantry. Many a holy man had, in those times of distress, his home in the glens and wilds of Crawford, where communion was held with God and with his saints. The deserts toward the source of the Clyde were a wide field, which was painfully traversed by the feet of many a lonely wanderer who fled to the moors and uplands from the face of the destroyer.

Not far from the residence of John Willison are to be seen the traces of a magnificent Roman encampment; this is at Gadenica on Little Clyde, an ancient Celtic town that for ages was lost to antiquarian research, but of which the site has now been discovered. The Damnii, a British tribe that spread from the shores of the Western Seas, and filled the glens and straths of Upper Clydesdale, had here a stronghold, and a well-peopled town. No stranger, in surveying the bleak scene, would ever imagine that Roman hosts and Celtic clans once filled this wilderness with a busy population, where now only a single farm-steading, or a solitary shepherd's hut, is to be seen.

John Willison was a man of excellent character, and warmly devoted to the interests of the suffering party. He endured much hardship in the maintenance of his principles as a Covenanter; and seldom durst he, after the establishment of the garrison in the parish, sleep a night in his own house. He resorted to hiding-places among the hills, where he concealed himself from the vigilance of his enemies. His own precarious situation taught him to exercise a deeeper sympathy with his fellow-sufferers, who, like himself, were forced to flee from their dwellings. His door was ever open to admit the wanderers who sought refuge in the deserts in his vicinity. In order to accommodate with greater security those who occasionally visited his house for shelter, he built, close to the back of the cow-house, a small room, into which he made an entrance from the inside through the wall, close by the cow-stalls, and this aperture he covered

with a plaid. This apartment, which was named the Shunam-
mite's chamber, was furnished with a bed, a table, and a few
chairs, and was altogether a very comfortable hiding-place,
and afforded a tolerable degree of security. In this asylum
the good Cargill often found a retreat, in which he spent many
a solitary but pleasant hour. But others besides Cargill found
refuge here. Particular mention is made of one Kent, said
to be a preacher, who frequently concealed himself within it.
He seems to have been a person in some measure known to
the soldiers, who on one occasion came to apprehend him in
Willison's house. Kent, who had been lingering for some
days about the place, frequently employed himself in angling
in the rivulets. One day, having habited himself in the
smearing clothes of his worthy host, he withdrew to a neighbouring stream to amuse and refresh himself in wiling the
silvery trout from its limpid waters. He was in the very
heart of the wilderness—far removed from human habitations; but, retired as was the place, he could not elude the
troopers, who found their way to glen, moss, and mountain, in
their raids, traversing the locality in every direction. Accordingly, a strolling party of horsemen encountered Kent as
he was bending over the stream, apparently absorbed in his
occupation. His disguise saved him from instant capture,
and perhaps from instant death. The party had no suspicion that he was the man they were seeking, and were moving past without accosting him, when one cried out: "That
fellow there has got a set of Kent's teeth in his mouth." It
would appear from this that there was something peculiar
about his teeth, and that they were regarded as the well-
known mark of the man. "My teeth!" replied Kent, "what
is there about my teeth more than another man's?" The
sharpness of his manner, and his undaunted bearing, lulled
suspicion, and one of the party exclaimed: "If this were Kent,
instead of fishing here, he would be praying and sighing beside the brook." The remark seemed appropriate, and the
dragoons, jeering and jesting, marched on without taking
further notice of him.

The soldiers proceeded to Glengeith, in quest of Willison.
The honest man, however, was not within when they arrived
—he was in his retreat among the hills. They accomplished,
however, their usual search, thrusting their sharp-pointed
swords and daggers into the bed-clothes, and underneath the
bed, exploring every nook and corner where there was the
least likelihood of concealment. When they saw that their
efforts were fruitless, they wrought, in their uproarious way,

all manner of mischief, by way of amusement to themselves. In their madness they seized a basket full of clothes and placed it deliberately on the fire, where in a moment it was in a blaze. The mistress of the house, who was at this time near the hour of her confinement, was in great distress, and remonstrated with the men on the impropriety of their con duct. Her remonstrances, however, only tended to excite them to acts of greater folly and outrage, and they threatened, in angry tones, to place her by the blazing basket on the fire. "I have no doubt," said she, "but your wickedness would prompt you to the perpetration of such an act, did not the providence of God restrain you; but without his divine permission you cannot touch a hair of my head." The roistering troopers having wearied themselves with their pranks of mischief, left the place in quest of other adventures.

John Willison, though greatly harassed in those troublous times, escaped the hands of his enemies, and lived a number of years after the Revolution. His dust lies in the old churchyard of Crawford.

He had two daughters, Janet and Bessy, who maintained the principles and walked in the steps of their parents. The following anecdote is told of Janet, in reference to the expulsion of the curate of Crawford. This man, like the curate of Kirkbride, in Nithsdale, lay as a heavy incubus on the parish, of which the people were determined to rid themselves as soon as practicable.

Accordingly, a number of stout men, it is said, having arrayed themselves in women's apparel, presented themselves one Sabbath in the church of Crawford, when the offensive curate was officiating, and requested him to leave the place. As he did not appear to be very hasty in obeying the summons, the party proceeded to drag him from his station; and Janet Willison, seizing him firmly by the arm, drew him from the pulpit, the door of which she shut behind him, expressing at the same time a sincere wish that no other Prelatic incumbent might ever again address an audience from that place. Janet was a heroine who shrunk neither from suffering nor from acting in the cause she had warmly and conscientiously espoused.

> "Tyrants !
> Thought ye the torture and the stake
> Could that intrepid spirit break,
> That even in *woman's* breast withstood
> The terrors of the fire and flood ?"

If Janet was courageous in the cause, Bessy displayed a spirit no less manly. It was in the dead of winter, as the story tells, and the moorlands were broadly sheeted with snow, when Bessy one day set out to join a conventicle which was to meet somewhere in the neighbouring solitudes. On passing the end of Bodsberry Hill she encountered a company of dragoons, who suddenly arrested her progress. They accosted her in very coarse and unseemly language, and employed certain epithets that roused the soul of the virtuous Bessy. As the vulgar troopers continued to taunt and rail, she administered a reproof so spirited and so caustic that her doughty assailants shrunk under the merited castigation, and retired discomfited from her presence, leaving her to plod her way to the conventicle without molestation. The exact spot where this conventicle met is not mentioned, but it must have been in one of the most sequestered nooks of the wilderness. The desert was the place where the insulted standard of the Gospel was reared, and held aloft in the firm grasp of that noble band of witnesses who were prepared to barter even their lives in its defence. And bravely did they guard the sacred trust, and baffle, in the end, the wicked devices of their craven-hearted persecutors.

> "———— In solitudes like these
> Thy persecuted children, Scotia, foiled
> A tyrant and a bigot's bloody laws.
> There, leaning on his spear,
> The lyart veteran heard the Word of God,
> By Cameron thundered, or by Renwick poured
> In gentle streams; then rose the long, the loud
> Acclaim of praise. The wheeling plover ceased
> His plaint, the solitary place was glad,
> And on the distant cairn the watcher's ear
> Caught doubtfully at times the breeze-borne note."

It was from a descendant of this worthy family, an old lady of nearly ninety years, that the preceding notices were received.

The farm of Normangill is in the parish of Crawford, a wild and secluded part of the country. It was in the year 1683 that, as tradition affirms, a conventicle was held in this place. The moorlands of Crawford were a wide field of resort to the persecuted wanderers, and many a time was God's weary heritage refreshed, as they sat by the wells of salvation which were opened in this desert. The company of God's hidden ones referred to had met for worship in the obscurity of the night: that company was small, amounting to fourteen persons only. A notice of this meeting, however, had beforehand been conveyed to the military, who lost no time in marching to the spot, to surprise the worshippers. By the time the soldiers arrived at Crawford, the night had

set in, and gradually become so very dark, that they could
not proceed to the meeting-place without a guide. Having,
therefore, pressed into their service a person to conduct them
through the trackless moor to the house where the assembly
had convened, they advanced with more security, eagerly
intent on their mission of evil. The man whom they had
compelled to become their conductor bore no good will to the
business, and began to revolve in his mind by what means
he might defeat the designs of the enemy. The darkness
was favourable to any plan he might see fit to adopt, and,
knowing the locality well, he led them by a circuitous route
to protract the time as much as possible. Aware, however,
that it would be attended with great hazard to himself if he
should lead the troopers away from the place altogether, he
resolved that when they came near the house he would
endeavour to make a noise so great as to alarm the people,
and to admonish them of approaching danger. There happened to be in the neighbourhood of the farm-house in which
the conventicle was held, a steep and rugged scar that overhung a brawling streamlet; and the guide, supposing that he
was in the vicinity of this precipice, began to sound the alarm
to the soldiers at the utmost pitch of his voice. This he did
repeatedly, and with increasing vehemence, as they drew
near their destination. The stratagem had the desired
effect, and the watchman that was on the alert hastily conveyed the intelligence to the worshippers. On this announcement the meeting instantly broke up, and in the darkness of
the night left the place unobserved. When the soldiers, led
by their wary guide, arrived at the place, they found no person but the mistress of the house and her children. After
having interrogated her to no purpose, and having searched
the place in vain, they resolved, owing to the murky state of
the night, to remain in the house till the morning. They
made themselves merry, eating and drinking what they could
find, and next day, when they departed, they did so, it is said,
like robbers, carrying many valuable articles along with them.

The little company withdrew to a place called Winter
Cleuch, on the farm of Nunnery, in the same parish. The
shepherd who occupied this cottage, being himself one of the
party, entertained them hospitably, and kept them in concealment till the search in the neighbourhood was over. The
minister, who formed one of the number (his name is not
given, but he must have been Mr Renwick), continued to
preach in the shepherd's lonely dwelling, to which several of
the serious people in the vicinity secretly resorted.

The retreat, however, was at length discovered. There was a person in Crawford who, for "filthy lucre's sake," was ready at any time to give information respecting the wanderers. This man learned that the conventicle of Normangill had taken refuge in the shepherd's cottage, and lost no time in imparting the knowledge of the fact to those to whom the information would be acceptable. Tradition says that he hastened to Douglas to fetch troopers for the purpose of apprehending the rebels; and here we cannot help noticing the accuracy of tradition in detailing circumstances for which itself cannot account. It is well known that there was a garrison stationed at Crawford, and we may be ready to ask, Why not bring the soldiers from their nearest quarters? but in looking into the history of the period, we find that the garrison at Crawford was not appointed till 1684, whereas the incidents here related are said to have occurred in 1683. The general correctness of tradition, and, in fact, its minute accuracy in multitudes of instances, is amazing, and shows how firm a hold these anecdotes have taken of the popular mind, and with how much truth, even in trivial circumstances, they have been transmitted to us. They are generally short, and this, as D'Israeli remarks, has insured both their permanence and their fidelity. Few except those who have paid some attention to it, can believe how trustworthy historical tradition is, and how safely in the main it may be relied on. The justness of this remark, were it necessary, might easily be made apparent in not a few instances, as regards the traditions respecting our suffering ancestors.

The informer, accompanied by a party of dragoons, reached Crawford when the night was far advanced. Having rested there for some time, they proceeded on their way to Winter Cleuch, with the intention of reaching it by the dawn of day. The morning happened to be cold and inclement, and the mist was trailing its snowy drapery along the dark brows of the hills. Every object was magnified far beyond its just dimensions, and appearances were mistaken for realities. It happened that the worthy shepherd, the covering of whose house required certain repairs, had prepared on the bent, in the immediate vicinity of his hut, a quantity of turfs which he had piled up in little heaps in regular rows on the heath. In the obscurity of the morning, and by means of the mistiness of the atmosphere, the turfy pillars presented the appearance of a numerous body of tall and *buirdly* men in a martial attitude, waiting to assail the advancing troopers.

At the moment the soldiers arrived, the shepherd's wife,

who had gone incidentally to the door, was, to her utter consternation, sternly confronted by them.   The poor woman, in
despair, concluded all was lost, and was about to hasten to
the interior to announce the approach of the dreaded foe.
The commander of the party ordered her to stand, for his
suspicious eye had caught a glance of the heaps of turf on
the rising ground, and he supposed it was a band of Covenanters prepared for a vigorous onslaught. " Who are these,"
he eagerly asked, " whom I see standing before us on the hill
there so early in the morning?"   The terror-stricken woman,
not apprehending what was passing in the mind of the leader,
nor guessing at his suspicions, replied: "They are *dasses o'
divots*, Sir."   The magnanimous trooper, not comprehending
what was meant, never having heard the expression before
perhaps, exclaimed, " Dassie Davie! Dassie Davie ! who the
plague can this Dassie Davie be, with all this army at his
back this morning?   I plainly perceive," said he, turning an
anxious look on his own handful of troopers, and retreating
apace—" I plainly perceive that we are betrayed.   This pretended informer, who has led us a long night's dance, has
been employed by his party to bring us within the reach of
a numerous force, for the purpose of destroying us."   He
then ordered his men to retreat, and to save themselves by
a timely flight from the face of the warriors on the eminence,
who seemed to keep their ground with unflinching obstinacy.
By this illusion Providence shielded the helpless people in
the hut, at the very moment when their enemies were at the
door.   Had they been an hour later in arriving, the clearer
light of the morning would have revealed the secret, and the
troopers would have done their work.

   In connection with this, the following incident may here be
narrated.   There lived in the parish of Carsphairn, at a place
called Half-Mark, in the vicinity of Garryhorn, the residence
of the notorious Lagg, a person of the name of M'Roy.   This
man was a Covenanter, and was in reality what he professed
to be, a holy and upright character.   He was a peaceable and
unobtrusive man, and one who took great delight in reading
the Scriptures and in prayer.   It happened one Sabbath
morning that this good man, having driven his cows to the
fields to graze, sat down on the turf, and having taken from
the corner of his plaid the Sacred Volume, began to peruse
its blessed contents as an exercise suitable at all times, but
more especially on the holy Sabbath.   Lagg and his men, it
would appear, were early abroad on the same morning, but
for a very different purpose—their object was, not to worship

God and to keep his Sabbath, but, if possible, to suppress his worship, and to desecrate the hours of holy rest. They sallied out to seek their own pleasure on the Lord's-day, and with a view to discover any small conventicle of worshippers in the moors, whom they might, as it best suited their caprice, either capture or kill. In their raid they came upon M'Roy devoutly studying the Word of God. The poor man had found his salvation in this Word, and now he was poring over it with a believing and a grateful heart, and enjoying more true satisfaction by far, in the possession of this treasure, than the men of the world can experience in all their riches and in all their fair and spacious inheritances. "The kingdom of heaven is like unto a treasure hid in a field; the which when a man hath found he hideth, and for joy thereof goeth and selleth all that he hath, and buyeth that field."

This lowly and heavenly-minded man was, in spirit, holding converse with his God, when Lagg and his troopers came suddenly upon him. The good man was taken by surprise, but, by the grace of Him in whom he believed, he was ready for whatever event might befall. The ruthless persecutor asked, in a rough and imperious tone, what book he was reading? The pious man, looking up in his face, meekly replied: "It is the Bible." And who can tell how much He, who knew what was coming upon his faithful witness, had fortified his heart for his hour of trial, by means of the consolations of that Gospel on which he was meditating at the very moment when his deadly foes presented themselves before him? The reading of the Bible was a sin not to be forgiven by Lagg, who, like the rest of his brotherhood employed in the same work of wickedness with himself, regarded it as a symptom of disloyalty that merited its appropriate punishment. When the honest man made the confession that it was the Word of God he was reading, Lagg instantly exclaimed, that his cows must forthwith find another herd, as his life, as a rebel, was now forfeited. M'Roy no sooner heard the sentence of death pronounced, than Lagg, without ceremony and without compunction, shot him dead on the spot. The summons was indeed hasty, and he was called, at a time and in a place he did not expect, "to seal" his testimony with his blood; but he was not unprepared to enter that rest in heaven, of which the Sabbath he had begun to keep holy on earth was a figure. His murderers left his bleeding body on the heath, and went onward, prepared to act a similar tragedy in the case of the next suspected person with whom they might happen to meet.

CHAPTER XLV

Thomas M'Haffie—Clark of Brandleys.

IF the charge of ignorance and fanaticism has been brought against the honest supporters of the cause of the covenants, it can be very easily repelled. That they were ignorant men, and persons stimulated only by enthusiastic principles, no one who is acquainted with their history can for a moment admit. They were men of good information, and well instructed in the nature of the principles on account of which they suffered. Theirs was no blind attachment to a mere theory of which they had no proper understanding; for they well knew the grounds on which they stood, and the tenets in support of which they were prepared to risk life, and property, and all. They furnished their persecutors with sufficient reasons for the part which they acted in opposing their wishes, and often so confounded their opponents in argument that they had not a word to say; and this was done, not merely by the more learned of the party—gentlemen and ministers—but frequently also by the illiterate peasants, who were dragged from the plough or the workshop, or from following the flocks on the heath. Let any one read the account of their examinations before the Privy Council, or the statement of their principles given in the "Cloud of Witnesses," and say if they were uninstructed persons or men of weak minds, who could not give a reason of the hope that was in them. In fact, they understood the principles of civil and religious privilege much better than their oppressors; for, not to speak of the poor ignorant dragoons, or of their equally ignorant but more barbarous commanders, who were merely soldiers of fortune, fighting for their daily bread against the liberties of the subject, their judges on the bench appeared, many of them, to be pitiably ignorant men, not even understanding the broad principles of legislation, nor the theory of the social compact.

Education, it is true, was not so common among the people then as it is now; but the want of it is by no means apparent among the covenanting peasantry of Scotland, who shone as lights in a dark and troubled time. The instructions which they received from their ministers were of the most substantial kind, and served to illuminate and guide them through the intricate paths which they had to tread, when perplexities and snares were on every side. They were well versed in all the leading points both of privilege and doctrine. They contended for the supremacy of the Lord Jesus Christ in his Church—a prerogative which the ruler of the nation impiously sought to arrogate to himself. They protested against tyranny in the State, and Erastianism in the Church, and against all the Popish tendencies of the measures adopted by the Government of the day. They bore witness against the breach of those vows under which the covenanting obligations laid the whole nation. But it was not merely in these things in which they were instructed; they were equally well acquainted with the grand and peculiar doctrines of the Gospel. The method of a sinner's acceptance with God was well known and appreciated by them; for this topic received a special prominence in the discourses of their preachers; and this accounts for the amazing success of their ministry. And not only were they well trained in all the leading doctrines of the Gospel—they were equally versed in the precepts of Christianity, and taught to maintain that holiness without which no man shall see the Lord. Religious books were in those days both rare and expensive; and, therefore, they resorted chiefly to the Bible for information; and by this means they were nurtured on the plain Word of God to an extent unequalled perhaps in our own times. To affirm of the Covenanters that they were an illiterate horde of enthusiasts and bigots, who were ignorant of even the simplest elements of religious truth, or of civil and ecclesiastical matters, is an untruth and a gratuitous slander.

We cannot turn to a single anecdote or historical statement respecting these illustrious men, without noticing the excellent use which they made of the Scriptures. They were " the men of their counsel," as David expresses it; and by their constant reading of the Bible they acquired more understanding than all their rulers. The Word of God was their constant companion; and wherever they reposed, in the caves, or among the brown heath, or on the green hill-side, they had recourse to the oracles of truth for strength and comfort in their manifold perils. Great indeed was the power and

sweetness of this Word to them—they read every portion of
it as if it had been spoken to them immediately by the mouth
of God—it was the pasture on which they fed, and it was
pleasant to their taste.   In illustration of this, we may produce the following anecdote of Thomas M'Haffie, of the
parish of Straiton, in Carrick.   He was one day proceeding
to a meeting near Maybole, but was observed and pursued
by a company of troopers, who probably had been advertised
of the projected conventicle.   He fled back to a very wild
retreat called the Star, in the upper part of Ayrshire, where
it borders on Galloway.   The desolation of this region is
extreme, being a territory entirely covered with rocks and
stones without end.   To this rugged seclusion, M'Haffie,
who was joined by two of his covenanting friends, repaired,
and in this place of refuge, altogether inaccessible to horsemen, the three fugitives deemed themselves safe.   When
they had rested a little, and saw that their enemies had
retreated from the pursuit, M'Haffie drew from his pocket
the Bible, the constant companion of his wanderings, and
proposed that they should refresh themselves by reading
some portions of that blessed book.   He began, tradition
says, by reading the two following verses of the 102d Psalm
" For He hath looked down from the height of his sanctuary; from heaven did the Lord behold the earth; to hear
the groaning of the prisoner; to loose those that are
appointed to death."   They were well acquainted with those
passages of Holy Writ that had a special reference to God's
Church in affliction, and they were the means of fortifying
their hearts in the day of general defection.   Other parts of
Scripture are referred to, on which our three worthies dwelt
in sweet meditation, which it is unnecessary to specify.   The
prayer, it is said, which, in the midst of this lonely wilderness of rocks, he offered up, was of the most powerful and
melting description; and the Lord heard the groanings of the
prisoners, and imparted to them the foretastes of the heavenly
blessedness.

This good man, however, did not always so escape the ven
geance of his enemies; for he ultimately fell into their hands,
and obtained the martyr's crown.   On the morning of the
day on which he was shot, he was concealed in a glen on the
farm of Linfairn, in the parish of Straiton.   At this time he
was very unwell and weakly, owing to exposure in the cold
damp caves in which he was forced to hide himself from his
foes.   In this sickly condition he heard the approach of the
soldiers, and rose from his resting-place to flee for his life

He reached the house of a friend, but he no sooner entered than he threw himself on a bed, being feverish and exhausted. Captain Bruce, who commanded the party, arrived at the house, and made M'Haffie an easy prey. He ordered his men to drag him from his couch, which they instantly did, and having led him out to the field, they, without ceremony, shot him dead on the spot. This murder was committed in the depth of winter 1685. A rude stone on the farm of Linfairn marks the identical spot where he fell. He was interred in the churchyard of Straiton, and the following is part of the inscription on his tombstone:—

> "Though I was sick, and like to die,
> Yet bloody Bruce did murder me;
> 'Cause I adhered, in my station,
> To our covenanted Reformation."

Wodrow notices the death of this worthy man in the following words: "Sometime in this month (January), Thomas M'Hassie (M'Haffie), son to John M'Hassie, in the Largs, in the parish of Straiton, in Carrick, was despatched quickly. This good man was lying in his house very ill of a fever. Captain Bruce and a party of soldiers coming into the house, put questions to him, which he refusing to answer, and declining to take the abjuration oath, they took him out of his bed to the high road near by, and without any further process, or any crimes I can hear of laid to his charge, shot him immediately."

The following detached anecdotes may here find a place. The first relates to Clark of Brandleys, who is, doubtless, of the family of Auchengrouch. Brandleys is situated in the moor to the east of Sanquhar Town Common, and not far from the mouth of the wild Glendyne. It is in the heart of a pastoral district, which stretches along the base of the brown hills on the north, and is sweetly retired in the bosom of the moorland. The Clarks had spread themselves widely over this locality; for besides the original family in Auchengrouch, there was a branch in Glenim, a branch in Leadhills, and one in Brandleys. The Clark who resided in this latter place occupied the farm after the Revolution. It was when times of turbulence were reduced to quietness, and when men enjoyed once more the blessings of civil and religious liberty, that Clark of Brandleys was driving northward a flock of lambs for sale. The shepherds in those days were provided with a tall crook or *kent*, as it was called, which they used in assisting them to overleap the ditches on the moss, and the torrents on the mountain-side, and which was also occasionally needed to drag from the lairy moors a helpless sheep which was unable to extricate itself. With this patriarchal implement in his hand, Clark was slowly driving before him his bleating charge. The roads in those days were miserably bad, and, owing to this circumstance, he was much retarded in his progress, and in order to reach the market in time, was obliged to proceed on the Lord's-day. When he had advanced to the neighbourhood of Carnwath, and was passing, in the stillness of the Sabbath, a farm residence, the master of the dwelling, who happened at the time to be in the field, observed the man driving the flock of lambs, and in his zeal against this act of Sabbath desecration, accosted Clark in a style of the bitterest reproof. Clark eyed his man for a moment, and recognised him. He knew him to be a disbanded trooper, and one of the party who had been engaged in the slaughter of Daniel M'Michael at Dalveen. The remembrance of the circumstance, connected with this hypocritical display of affected zeal for the sanctity of the Sabbath, roused his manly indignation. He left his flock for a moment, and stepping forward, looked sternly in the man's face, and exclaimed: " You ruthless villain, was it not you who, with the rest of your companions, poured the murderous shot into the body of the good Daniel M'Michael, when the green heights of Dalveen reproved, in startling echoes, the wicked deed, and with a voice of thunder spoke back to your guilty conscience ? Do you, who shed without remorse, on the moors and mountains, the best blood of Scotland's sons, now take upon you the saintly task of reproving me for what you conceive to be the sin of Sabbath-breaking ?" With this Clark seized with both hands the ponderous crook, and laid on the person of his assailant a lusty stroke, which brought him to the ground. Our hero then moved on with his charge, leaving the prostrate farmer to rise at his leisure

CHAPTER XLVI.

Luke Fraser and his Companions—Incidents.

GLENMEAD is a very wild locality in the mountainous parts of Closeburn, in Nithsdale. It was, in the days of persecution, tenanted by Luke Fraser, a man of great worth, and of unbounded hospitality to the suffering party, who resorted to his house as a hiding-place. Its situation among the hills rendered it an eligible retreat to those who sought a refuge from their raging persecutors; but Luke's house was not only a mansion of hospitality, it was also a place of worship, for many a little conventicle was held within its walls. The ejected preachers and the intercommuned wanderers soon became acquainted with such a place as Glenmead, where they found a shelter and a friendly welcome. Luke Fraser sometimes entertained a goodly number of persons at once in his house; for he never thought it a hardship to share his substance with those who were driven to the wilderness as outcasts for Christ's sake. There was, on his grounds, a cave in a solitary and secret place, to which, in seasons of more than ordinary peril, he conducted the persons of whom the persecutors were in quest.

Among the numerous wanderers who occasionally resorted to Fraser's house, the following are particularly mentioned : John Fraser, his brother; John Clark of Glenhead, in Carsphairn; and John Panter of Ballagan, in Durisdeer.

The story of John Fraser has already been given in a former chapter, so that it is unnecessary to state any thing further concerning him here.

John Clark of Carsphairn is mentioned by Wodrow as a sufferer in connection with John Fraser. It is probable that he is the John Clark who was a frequent companion of Mr Peden, in his wanderings in the wilds of Galloway. He

D d

is mentioned by Patrick Walker in the following passage :
" About this time he (Mr Peden) and John Clark, who ordinarily was called ' Little John,' were in a cave in Galloway,
and had wanted meet and drink for a long time. He said :
' John, better be thrust through with the sword, than pine
away with hunger. The earth, and the fulness thereof,
belongs to my Master, and I have a right to as much of it
as will keep me from fainting in his service. Go to such a
house, and tell them plainly that I have wanted meat so
long, and they will give it willingly.' John did as he was
desired, and the people readily supplied him with food."

This John Clark was narrowly watched by Canning of
Muirdrogat, the informer, who was at all due pains to lodge
information against the honest man, which caused him much
distress, and obliged him to wander many a weary foot in
the desert wilds. In his wanderings he attached himself to
Mr Peden and the few that occasionally consorted with him,
and met, no doubt, with many an incident and many a wonderful preservation in company with this devoted servant of
Christ. Clark, and his friend John Fraser, frequently took
refuge in Straquhanah Cave, in the upper part of the valley
of the Ken. In this romantic locality, the grandeur of whose
scenery is the admiration and delight of the few travellers
who occasionally pass that way, did our two worthies conceal themselves, that they might be near their families.
Towards the source of the Ken there is a hollow place
called the " Whig Holes," a secure retreat on the side of the
mountain of Altry, where, in the covenanting times, the
assemblies of God's people frequently convened for divine
worship. The place is far up on the breast of the hill, and
affords a seclusion so perfect, that no company of troopers
travelling in the plains below could even see the place, far
less discern who were in it. A rising ground, like a green
wall, stands in front, concealing immediately behind it a
deep basin, while the mountain shoots aloft to a great height,
and beneath descends precipitously to the brink of the Ken
It is said, that when a conventicle happened to be held here,
a warder was placed on each side of the basin, where an extensive view is obtained in the direction of Carsphairn on
the one hand, and on the other, a full prospect toward the
source of the river. The line along this sweetly secluded
stream was the route of the military between Sanquhar and
Carsphairn ; and hence, more than ordinary precautions were
required on the part of the Covenanters, when at any time
they happened to meet on the hill. The " Whig Holes "

was selected not only as a place of security, but also as a centrical spot for the people of the upper parts of Nithsdale and the higher parts of Galloway; and many a time has the hallowed sound of praise ascended from the steep sides of the lofty Altry, heaven being witness to the sufferings and the constancy of that remnant, who held fast their testimony and their faith in the dark day of defection and relentless persecution. The shepherds in the vicinity of this place are proud to point out the spot to the passing traveller, where the people of the desert congregated, at the risk of their lives, to maintain the standard of the Gospel among the lonely mountains.

On one occasion, when John Fraser and John Clark were in concealment in the cave, information was conveyed, by means of a spy, to Lagg in Carsphairn, who instantly sent a company of troopers to apprehend them. The approach of the soldiers, however, was observed, and the two friends fled for their lives. They escaped in the following way : As they were hastening over moor and meadow, they crossed a field in which a man was mowing, and laying in lusty swathes the dewy grass, and as their pursuers were not immediately in sight, they hid themselves beneath the long rows of the newly cut grass, and waited the result. The horsemen came on apace and entered the field, and not dreaming that the fugitives were cowering so near them, they passed on without even speaking to the mower, in hasty pursuit of those who, they thought, were still in flight before them. They remained in concealment till the danger was over, and they left the neighbourhood, changing their place of retreat to the wilds of Closeburn, and sought refuge in the house of Luke Fraser of Glenmead.

The third of the individuals already mentioned, was John Panter of Ballagan. Ballagan is in the parish of Durisdeer, on the south side of the Nith, and situated at the head of the valley of Marburn. This vale stretches southward to the woods of Drumlanrig, where it terminates in a lovely basin clothed with trees, and intersected by the mountain streamlets. Ballagan, it would appear, was anciently a feudal strength. The name signifies the "hamlet in the hollow." Part of the old stronghold was in existence within the memory of the elder people living, but is now entirely demolished. Panter of Ballagan was either tenant or proprietor of the place in the persecuting times; and a detachment of dragoons was occasionally stationed at his house, on account of his nonconformity. The wife of John Panter seems to have been a mother in Israel, and one who testified firmly against the defections of the time. We find the following mention made of her by Wodrow: " Elizabeth Glendinning, spouse to John Panter, in Ballagan, of the parish of Durisdeer, for noncompliance, and not hearing the established ministers, was imprisoned for some time, and sent to Edinburgh, where she died in prison." This happened in the year 1685—the "killing time."

The three forementioned persons, with others whose names are not given, having convened in the house of Luke Fraser, were, along with himself, apprehended by a party of dragoons, and conveyed to Edinburgh. When they were brought to the city, it was found that all the jails were filled, and that no room could be afforded for the reception of additional prisoners. But though there was no accommodation in the common prison-houses, the poor captives were not allowed to go free. A neighbouring house was employed as a temporary prison, in the garret rooms of which the seven men from Closeburn were confined. It would seem that some of their number had been either followed at the time, or soon after, by their wives and other friends, who brought victuals, which were handed to the prisoners by the keepers; but no permission was granted to their relatives to see them.

One of the wives, who possessed a great deal of shrewdness, planned, while on the spot, a scheme by which the friends in confinement might perchance accomplish their escape With her eye she calculated the height of the building, and then hastening home, bought a rope of sufficient thickness to sustain the weight of a man; and this she coiled as neatly and closely together as possible, and placed it in the heart of a quantity of curds, which she speedily formed into the shape of an ordinary-sized cheese. When it was sufficiently pressed and hardened, she placed it on her back, and proceeded with all expedition to Edinburgh, and found means to convey it into the hands of her husband. The cheese was deemed a great boon by the poor sufferers, who received any gift of this description with much thankfulness. On making the first incision into the soft *kebbuck*, they were astonished to find the interior crammed with a coil of ropes. The design became instantly apparent, and they were more gratified to think that they had now the means of escape, than if the cheese had been solid food.

Their projected escape now occupied their minds, and as the nights were long and dark, they expected to accomplish their purpose without detection. Having ascertained the strength of the rope, and found that it would easily bear the weight of any single person at a time, their next object was to make a place of egress through the roof of the house. As the place in which they were confined was close to the roofing, they easily removed a part of the covering, and formed an aperture sufficiently large through which to pass to the outside. Having thus with the utmost caution cleared the way, and made all things ready for their departure, they waited with anxiety till a proper hour of the night, when they found all in dead silence on the street below. When the end of the rope was fixed to a secure place, probably to the foot of a couple in the roof, or to some part of the furniture in the chamber, they began their perilous descent, one by one, while the husband of the good woman who brought the cheese, being the strongest and heaviest of the party, remained till the last, lest the slender rope should give way under his weight. It was agreed that, on his descent, the others who had reached the street in safety should stand round the foot of the rope, which it was thought might become somewhat weakened by the constant tension, and that, if it should break by his weight, they might be ready to prevent as much as possible the injury he was likely to sustain, by falling on the hard pavement. The descent was successfully accomplished by every one of the party till it came to the turn of the last individual, who had resolved to remain behind till he saw all his companions at liberty. When his full weight was fairly attached to the rope, and when he had descended a considerable way, it began to yield, and in a moment it was snapped asunder. The worthy man was precipitated into the midst of his companions, who, by stretching out their arms to seize him, partially broke his fall. He fell, however, with a violence so great that, though he was not killed, he was unable to walk a single step. The whole party then hastened from the spot, carrying with them their disabled companion. They stole out of the city in the quietest manner they could, and sought a place in a cottage in the vicinity, where they left in charge their friend, while they betook themselves to a greater distance.

When the day dawned it was found that the prisoners in the garret had escaped, and a strict search was instantly made for them. Soldiers and others were sent out in every direction, to make the closest scrutiny in the houses and cottages in the neighbourhood of the town. The fugitives, however, were by this time far beyond their reach, and were pursuing their route toward their native mountains. The hapless individual, nevertheless, who had received so serious an injury in his fall, did not so escape; he was found by the emissaries in the place where his friends had left him, and was instantly carried to prison. He was condemned by the council, and, it is said, was executed on the same day.

The six persons who escaped travelled by night, and kept themselves in hiding by day. They were sometimes very nearly discovered by the enemy, but always succeeded in eluding their vigilance. They came at last to Lesmahagow, a place famous in those days for witnesses and confessors. In this place they were courteously received by the friends of the cause, who promptly supplied their wants, and furnished them with arms for self-defence. After leaving Lesmahagow, the troopers having obtained notice of their movements, pursued them closely, till they reached the wilds of Crawford Moor, where greater opportunities of concealment were afforded them. They kept their route on the east side of the Lowther Hills, till they approached the stupendous height that overlooks the famous pass of Enterkin. They proceeded into the pass, and having reached the place where Harkness and the black M'Michael rescued the prisoners in 1684—a circumstance which made so much noise at the time, and caused so much distress in the upper parts of Nithsdale —they saw advancing on the path straight before them a small company of soldiers conveying two prisoners bound with cords, either to the garrison in Crawford Moor or to Edinburgh. The friends placed themselves in the attitude of defence in the narrow pass, with the determination to rescue the prisoners. As the dragoons advanced, and as the parties came nearer each other, Luke Fraser perceived that the leader of the troopers was the identical person who guarded him and his friends to Edinburgh. The position occupied by the covenanting party was as favourable as could well be desired for the purpose of accomplishing their design. They stood on the rising ground above the soldiers, and it required comparatively little exertion to arrest their progress. Fraser demanded the dragoons to set free the prisoners; adding, at the same time, that he and his companions were the individuals whom, only a few days ago, he had conducted as prisoners to Edinburgh, and that, having accomplished their own deliverance, they were prepared to dispute the passage with him, and were resolved to liberate the captives. The commander, reflecting on the situation in which he was placed, although the numbers on both sides were equal, saw the impracticability of maintaining anything like an advantageous dispute with his opponents, and felt inclined to accede to the proposal. The path was so narrow, and the descent beneath so steep, that a vigorous and simultaneous onset on the part of the Covenanters must have precipitated the whole party into the yawning gulf below. The commander began to propose conditions, but Luke Fraser replied, that no conditions could for a moment be listened to—the immediate release of the prisoners was what they required, and if this was not granted, they would proceed instantly to accomplish their rescue. The trooper was obliged to comply, and the two prisoners were set at liberty. Their deliverance was wrought in a place where others of their brethren in similar circumstances had been rescued from the hands of their enemies, and it was accomplished at a time when, perhaps, they least expected it. It not unfrequently happens that we are extricated from perilous circumstances at a moment when there is not the slightest appearance of a favourable interference.

It is said that the Covenanters who, on this occasion, had succeeded in the rescue of their two brethren, finding that the soldiers were entirely in their power, proceeded to make a further demand. They required the leader of the party to make a promise, some say an oath, that he should never, from that day onward, lend himself as the agent of the persecuting faction. To this the man demurred, considering that, as they had obtained the prisoners, they had all that they ought reasonably to require. The patriots, however, were determined to extort a promise, and expressed their resolution, that if it was not granted they would, without ceremony, hurl the entire party over the steep into the stream below. The commander, it is said, seeing the danger of his situation, promised, over an open Bible, to do in this case as he was required; after which he was permitted to pass peaceably along. Whether the trooper kept his promise or not we cannot say, but these few Covenanters did what they could to withdraw him from the work of bloodshed in which he had been engaged. It is likely the man would consider his word no longer binding when he had fairly got beyond the reach of his assailants.

CHAPTER XLVII.

George Hepburn—Incidents.

OUR suffering ancestors not only overcame their enemies in argument, and by their unflinching constancy unto the death, but they frequently overcame them by the power of their doctrine and their holy example. They overcame, for they often made converts of their opponents, and brought their persecutors to the acknowledgment of the truth. We have read of a persecutor becoming a preacher of that Gospel which he thought to destroy; we have read of an Infidel, who sat down to study the Bible for the avowed purpose of writing its refutation, becoming a convert to its truths, and who, instead of writing against it, wrote in its defence; and we have not a few instances in the late persecution in Scotland, of individuals actively employed in bearing down the Gospel, the standard of which had been so conspicuously and successfully reared in the fields, who were converted by the truths they were hired to suppress, and who joyfully suffered affliction in maintenance of these truths, in common with their brethren who were subjected to persecutions. Such converts, indeed, were, if possible, much more severely handled than others, because they were viewed as traitors to the cause they had formerly espoused, and as persons who had been in possession of certain secrets which it was not convenient should be divulged. But the power of the truth constrained them, and they were prepared to endure any hardship rather than renounce their convictions and return to their former connections. The following anecdote relates to a person of this description, who, by the grace of God, was turned from darkness unto light.

George Hepburn was a native of Sorn, in Ayrshire—the birth-place of the venerable Peden. He lived in a place called Blackside, about two miles above the village. His father, a worthy Covenanter, fell at the battle of Pentland, and the loss appeared so serious in the eyes of George, who was but a boy, that from that time he entertained an inveterate prejudice against the cause of the covenant. When he grew to manhood he enlisted himself on the side of the persecutors, deeming them more innocent in the matter of his father's death than the Covenanters. He assumed the infamous occupation of an informer, and was assiduous in searching out the helpless people who were dispersed in their hiding-places over the face of the country. He made it his business to attend conventicles and private meetings in disguise, and then to pounce upon his prey at a convenient season. On one occasion as he was returning from Hamilton, and having crossed the Clyde near Bothwell, he advanced along the northern bank of the stream in quest of adventures, and came, either incidentally or by design, on a conventicle which had convened in a solitary place, just as worship had commenced. The evening was cold and inclement, and the falling snow was beginning to drift among the trees under whose covert the party had assembled. Hepburn cowered down to avoid detection, behind a dyke, where he could observe and mark the persons before him, especially the preacher. He listened to the words of the text from which the man of God intended to discourse to the people : " Blessed are ye when men shall revile you, and persecute you, and shall say all manner of evil against you falsely, for my sake. Rejoice and be exceeding glad : for great is your reward in heaven." These words, as he afterwards used to remark, went to his heart like an arrow shot by a skilful hand. Smitten by the sword of the Spirit, the poor persecutor sat trembling behind the fence, and as he gazed occasionally on the audience, he fancied he saw peace depicted on every countenance as far as he could discern through the whirling snow that was now driven by the eddying winds. The contrast between the situation of the conventiclers and his own seemed to be very great—they had peace, but he was wretched. His first intention, on perceiving the meeting, was to trace the footsteps of the preacher as he retired from the spot, with a view to lodge due information, and to receive the promised reward; but other thoughts now occupied his mind. He felt himself a sinner, a lost sinner, and his sins appeared to be specially aggravated on account of the virulent opposition he had manifested toward the persecuted remnant. His spirit was oppressed with solicitude, and agitated with anxious forebodings. When the meeting broke up the storm seemed to be at its height, and till it should abate he crept in among the thick underwood, and lay in sad rumination on the state of his soul. His mental affliction was very great, and he exclaimed, almost involuntarily : "God be merciful to me, a sinner."

As he lay under the shelter of the friendly bush, he thought he heard the whispering of voices at no great distance, and he drew near to listen. As he was straining his ears to catch the sound, he heard one of the persons, who, like himself had plunged into the thicket during the bitterest of the blast, say to the other : " I am much mistaken if I did not see Hepburn the informer skulking behind the dyke; and if it be as I suspect, the soldiers will be scouring the neighbourhood to-morrow." " It is marvellous to me," said the other, " that the son of so worthy a man should turn out so ill, and he the son, too, of many prayers : his father was a godly man, and sealed an honourable testimony with his blood." George hearkened to their discourse, and if his heart was oppressed before, it was doubly so now, and deeply did he regret the step he took when he first engaged to become an informer to the curate of Sorn. His first thought was to reveal himself to them, and to make known his perplexities; but then he feared they would not credit his statements; and judging of them by his own previous disposition, he imagined that they might perhaps vent their fury on him, and perchance kill him. The opinion he had formed of their probable vengeful temper was soon altered, when he heard the prayer which, in the solitude of the bush, and in the howling of the tempest, they addressed to Heaven, and when in that prayer special supplications were presented to the God of all grace in his behalf. He perceived that they were men of a forgiving spirit, whose Christian and kindly dispositions led them to seek the salvation of his soul, and his heart melted as he listened to the outpourings of such a godlike benevolence.

When the storm abated, the men prepared to withdraw from the covert, and to seek a boat by which to cross the Clyde on their way home. Hepburn perceived that they were going in the same direction as himself, and he followed them in the dark, with the design, if possible, to cross with them undiscovered. He succeeded in his purpose, and reached the opposite bank of the river without being known. As they went in company, they asked him if he had been at the conventicle. He said he had; but he did not appear to be very communicative. The men supposed that his silence

was the result of caution, and they told him that he need not
fear them, as they were persons of the same way of thinking
with himself. Their kindly manner induced him to make
himself known; he plainly declared to them he was Hepburn
the spy, informed them of the change which his sentiments
had undergone, and declared his resolution for the future.
At this the worthy men were utterly astonished, and experienced a sort of uneasy feeling at being in the presence o₁
so notorious a character; of whom, notwithstanding all his
professions of penitence, they stood in doubt. As, however,
they were under no apprehensions of immediate danger,
they began to converse with him as a person under serious
concern, and laid before him the nature of the Gospel in the
most impressive manner they could, in the sincere desire and
hope that he might believe and be saved. Their discourses
deepened his convictions, and for a while increased his distress; but in process of time it pleased the God of all grace to
open his heart to understand the truth, and to bring him to
the faith of Jesus Christ. This was a brand plucked out of
the burning, and in his case the Saviour showed his readiness
to save even the chief of sinners. O how much it illustrates
the riches of free grace, when sinners of the most infamous
character are in such a manner translated into the family of
God's dear Son! In the Gospel God offers to sinners indiscriminately the pardon of their sins; for with him there are
no exceptions made, and no comparisons instituted between
great and little sins, with a view to cancel the less in preference to the greater; for great and small have nothing to do
in the case of the pardon of sin. No man is pardoned
simply because his sins are fewer and less aggravated than
the sins of others; and no man is rejected because his sins are
greater than the sins of others. In pardoning our sins, our
gracious God makes no requisition after anything good or
worthy in us to authorize him to confer on us the boon o₁
forgiveness. No; this donation of his divine charity is entirely free and unrestricted: no gift of his is more gratuitous than this—it is without money and without price. Tho
pardon is bounded by no limitations whatever; for where
there exists a sin to be forgiven, there is a pardon to be
found with God. Who is a God like unto thee, that par-
doneth iniquity? who is like unto thee in grace and truth?
and whose salvation is like unto thine, O Lord! The grace
of forgiveness manifested toward sinners through Jesus
Christ is grace so transcendental in its nature, as to overwhelm with astonishment even those spirits of light that have

for ages inherited the beatitudes of heaven: " Which things the angels desire to look into."

Hepburn, who had hitherto been employed in the service of the curate of Sorn, in the way of gathering information respecting the Nonconformists, had not visited the manse for a long time, and the incumbent, astonished at the circumstance, determined to call on him to see what was the matter. It was in the month of April, a busy month with the shepherds, and as the curate advanced along the heath, he found George actively engaged among the ewes; and when interrogated respecting his long absence, he had the ready and resonable excuse of being incessantly employed among his fleecy charge; and it was well for him that he had that excuse, for the curate had begun to suspect him, and his suspicions would have been confirmed, if he had looked on the book which was lying on the bent, and which George had been anxiously perusing when the curate came in sight—the book was the Bible, the uniform index, as it was deemed, of a man's nonconforming propensities. The curate was said to be a Highlandman, an illiterate and boorish sort of a person, who knew little about his office, and cared not for the souls of his parishioners. Having strictly enjoined George to be more punctual in his visits for the time to come, he left him without making any discovery.

Hepburn had now come to the full determination of openly and avowedly attaching himself to the cause of the persecuted, and he longed for another opportunity of hearing the Gospel at a conventicle. He was fully aware that the party which he had for so long a time opposed would not be ready to trust him, especially as many informers, under a pretence of a change of sentiments, had insinuated themselves into their meetings, both private and public, for the express purpose of discovering and betraying them to the enemy. He resolved, however, to use every means to make his sincerity apparent. It was not long till the projected meeting of a conventicle was circulated among the friends, and he rejoiced in the prospect. The day came, and George took his place openly among the people. His appearance created no small uneasiness to those who knew him; but William Steel of Lesmahagow, one of the three who spent the night in the moss-hag with John Brown of Priesthill, a short time prior to his martyrdom, on observing him, rose from his place among the crowd, and seizing him by the hand, welcomed him to the assembly of God's people, trusting that he was still in the same mind in which he appeared to be on the night they crossed the Clyde in company. This interview inspired the people with confidence, and they regarded him as one converted to the faith of Christ. After the services, he introduced him to the minister, and to a number of the friends, as a sheep that wandered from the fold, but who was now returned to the Shepherd and Bishop of souls, as the son of an honoured witness for Christ, now determined to walk in his father's footsteps.

The fact that George had withdrawn from the Prelatic party was now made public, and the infuriated curate used every means to get him into his power. His master being obliged to dismiss him from his residence in Blackside, he was forced to retire into concealment; so that he who once compelled others to hide, was himself made a wanderer for his adherence to the principles he had formerly persecuted. The sincerity of his profession was fully tested by the willing manner in which he submitted to the afflictions of a persecuted lot.

One night before he left Blackside, a party of troopers surrounded the house for the purpose of apprehending him. The family were all in bed, and sound asleep, when the trampling of horses, and a loud knocking, was heard at the door. George, who for some time past had been apprehensive of his safety, was the first to hear the disturbance. Fully aware of their errand, he sprang from his bed, and having arrayed himself as hastily as possible, was the first to open the door. The night was dark, and he hoped he might be able to escape. On opening the door to admit the uproarious visitants, he was asked if George Hepburn was within, when he promptly replied that he was. The soldiers rushed into the house, in the certain prospect of seizing their prey, and when all was in confusion, George made his escape, and fled from the place. This was the first attack made by his enemies, and he was successful in eluding their grasp.

George was now a wanderer, concealing himself in mountains and in thickets, and consorting with those who were forced to betake themselves to the dens and caves of the earth. One of the places to which he resorted was Wellwood, in the parish of Muirkirk, a frequent retreat in those times of oppression, and celebrated in the following lines of Hislop the poet .—

" And Wellwood's sweet valley breathed music and gladness :
The fresh meadow blooms hung in beauty and redness;
Its daughters were happy to hail the returning,
And drink the delights of July's sweet morning."

At Wellwood he found a safe and comfortable abode for a few months; but the curate of Sorn having discovered his hiding-place, determined to employ every means for his apprehension. It happened on a clear moonlight night that a company of dragoons arrived at Wellwood, with the intention of seizing Hepburn. He was in bed, as were the whole family; and when his danger was perceived, every one became solicitous about his safety. The bright shining of the moon, sailing in silvery majesty along the dusky vault of the nocturnal sky, was unfavourable to his escape; for the watchful troopers were stationed around the dwelling to prevent his elopement. There happened at the time to be a large quantity of wool piled in sacks at the one end of the house, and among these George, in his perplexity, resolved to attempt a concealment. Accordingly, he crept in among the wool sacks, and ensconced himself in a soft hiding-place from the vigilance of the soldiers. The dwelling was searched in every corner without success; and the troopers coming to the place where the wool lay, instead of tearing it down, thrust their long swords between and into the heart of the sacks, if perchance they might probe any lurking fugitive among the wool. Their swords, however, did not reach the place where Hepburn lay; and they withdrew, thinking any further search unnecessary. This was the second time that this recent convert escaped his enemies, and Providence afforded him respite, that his faith in the Gospel, and his confidence in his profession, might become stronger.

During the short time which, after this, he remained at Wellwood, he was under the necessity of leaving the house at night, and of seeking a hiding-place on the banks of the Ayr. Here he found a cave to which he resorted every night, for the space, it is said, of six months. At length, having become tired of this precarious way of living, he determined to leave the district. Accordingly, he removed to the higher parts of Galloway, where he expected to meet with less annoyance; but in this he was disappointed. On his way to Galloway he called at the house of a true friend to the cause —Mr Campbell of Lochbruin. He was not at home, the soldiers having been in pursuit of him on a previous part of the day, and he had taken refuge among the dark and frowning heights on the romantic Water of Afton. Hepburn was prevailed on by the hospitable wife of William Campbell to spend the night in their house, as she expected her husband home in the evening. During the night the soldiers again visited the place, in the hope of finding Campbell, and they unhappily

seized on Hepburn. He was now in the firm grasp of his
foes, who bound him tightly, and placed him on horseback
behind one of the troopers, and having twisted a rope of hay,
they attached him to the horseman, and rode off. In crossing a deep ravine, however, called Carcaw Burn, the rope
gave way, and he slid from behind the dragoon and lighted
safely on his feet, and being favoured by the obscurity of
the night, he made his escape, and left the soldiers to grope
their way after him in the best manner they could.

Having obtained this unexpected deliverance, he proceeded, according to his intention, to Galloway.   As he
advanced into the country, he fell in with Mr Renwick, to
whom he now attached himself, and became his companion
in travail. Many a time he listened to the glorious Gospel
preached by this interesting youth, and great was the spiritual
benefit he derived from his ministrations. In company with
Mr Renwick, he frequently made narrow escapes from the
military in the houses where they lodged.

Hepburn survived the persecution many years. He retired into Nithsdale, where he settled, and died, it is said, in
1728. He is probably the person who hid in a cave nearly
opposite the village of Kirkconnell, a few miles above the
town of Sanquhar. The old people have a tradition of a
person of the name of Hepburn, who concealed himself in
the fore-mentioned place, but can state nothing definite
concerning him.

CHAPTER XLVIII.

James Muirhead—Mrs Hewatson—John Ferguson of Wee Woodhead.

THE town of Dumfries is situated on the fair stream of the Nith, and occupies a place in the heart of one of the sweetest localities in the south of Scotland. This place, not unknown in Scottish history, was, in times of persecution, the scene of Christian martyrdom, and several of the witnesses for Christ's crown and covenant have their resting-place in its ancient burying-ground. The inhabitants of Dumfries had their own share of the troubles which befell the country in the stirring times of the royal brothers. The worthy men who moved in this emporium of the south, and in its immediate vicinity, felt, like their brethren in other places, the strong arm of oppression in the days when the honest inhabitants of the land were called to endure hardships for conscience' sake. One of the individuals who, belonging to this place, was in his day honoured to bear witness to the truth, and to suffer in its behalf, was James Muirhead, a bailie of the town. He was a man, it is said, of strict integrity in all his transactions, of great religious seriousness, and of uncommon placidity of mind. His brethren in the magistracy generally looked up to him with much deference; for he was a man universally esteemed. When he was in office, he laboured assiduously to screen the Nonconformists; and it was owing to his great efforts in this way that he was suspected of favouring the persecuted party. The justness of their principles, the holiness of their lives, and their constancy in suffering, had, it would appear, been operating for a good while deeply on his mind, and leading him gradually to the adoption of their views. At length the obvious interest which he manifested in behalf of the Covenanters led to his expulsion from office, and this being considered as a public stigma, he became generally regarded as an obnoxious person. When matters were brought to this pass, he saw it was now needless to conceal his principles, and perceiving the danger in which he was placed, found it necessary to secure his safety by flight. To this his friends urged him, for they saw the storm that was coming, and they were anxious to hide him from its fury. He left the town in great secrecy, and pursued his way to Tinwald, where, in a friend's house, he found a retreat in quietude. In this concealment he remained for a good while, hoping, no doubt, that the tempest would soon pass away, and that he might in due time be forgotten; but his enemies were on the watch, for they considered him as an individual who ought not to pass with impunity. His retreat was at length discovered, and a party of soldiers were sent in as cautious a manner as possible to apprehend him. Accordingly, in an unexpected hour, they arrived at the place where he lodged. Their coming was so hasty, that all about the house was thrown into confusion. The great anxiety of the inmates was about the concealment of the refugee, and for doing this effectually no time was afforded, as the troopers were just at the door. There stood in the kitchen a wooden seat in the form of a sofa, called a *lang settle*—a piece of furniture common in those times. Underneath this seat the gudewife directed Muirhead to creep with all despatch, while she hastily covered him with a bundle of old clothes. The soldiers entered, and began the usual search, but though they explored every place, they never thought of looking below the lang settle, although they passed and repassed it, and probably sat down upon it. The troopers departed, and our worthy escaped.

His place of concealment in Tinwald being thus discovered, he found it necessary to seek another retreat. He now resolved to join the company of the wanderers who were lurking in the hilly parts of Kirkmahoe. This circumstance imparted much satisfaction to the sufferers in that district, whose hands were strengthened by the accession of so worthy a person to their number. In these secluded parts he and his associates continued for some time, till they were discovered. This occasioned their removal to another part of the locality; for these worthies had no fixed place of abode, but were driven about "like a ball in a wide country." At last, when he and a number of his friends in affliction were hiding in the neighbourhood of Carberrie Hill, on the west side of the Nith, opposite Dumfries, they were caught by the enemy, who exulted in their success in having at length apprehended a

man who had been for so long a period the object of their
search. The troopers, it is said, used the party with great
cruelty, and vented their rage in a very barbarous manner.
Every indignity was employed; for they considered Muirhead
a capital offender. His capture happened in the year 1684.
His sufferings and death are incidentally mentioned by Wodrow, in speaking of the harassings of Mr William M'Millan
of Caldow, in the parish of Balmaclellan, in Galloway: "On
the 22d of November, he (Mr M'Millan) with upwards of
eighty others, men, women, and some children, were carried
to Moffat kirk, where they lay that night under great extremity of cold, being wet through, and most of them being
in the hazard of drowning in the waters under the cloud of
night, before they could reach that station. Next day, being
Sabbath, the soldiers' travelling day, they were carried
twenty-four miles to Peebles, under a guard of three troops
of dragoons, commanded by Captain Clelland. There several
of the prisoners were sorely beat and cruelly mocked by the
barbarous soldiers, and all of these in hazard of their lives by
crossing the water in a violent *spate.* Upon the 24th, they
were carried to Leith Tolbooth, and reproached bitterly as
hey went through Edinburgh. There they were so thronged
that they could scarce stand together, and had no convenience so much as to ease nature. Here *James Muirhead,*
late bailie of Dumfries, through the terrible fatigue, fell
into a severe distemper; and such was the barbarity of this
time, that neither surgeon nor physician was allowed him,
and he died in Leith Tolbooth a little after their arrival."
Thus died among the hands of his barbarous foes this good
man, and though he was not publicly executed on the scaffold,
nor privately shot on the moorlands, yet he obtained the martyr's crown.

The following tradition relates to a worthy woman in the
same county. The farm of Laight is situated in the beautiful valley of the Scar, in the parish of Tynron. It was in
the times of the persecution occupied by Thomas Hewatson,
in whose household was the fear of the Lord, and whose wife
was, in common with himself, firmly attached to the cause of
the covenants. The house of Laight, which stands on a rising ground, on the west bank of the pleasant stream which
winds its way through the valley, was frequently visited, in
the days of ecclesiastical oppression, by rude troopers, who
were commissioned to seize the obnoxious inmates. Mrs
Hewatson, to whom the following anecdotes refer, was a
woman whose rare worth and firm religious principles gained

for her a name too celebrated for her to remain unnoticed
by the Prelatic superintendents of the locality in which she
resided.   Thomas Hewatson was obliged to escape to some
hiding-place in the moor, or in the thickets of the glens,
leaving behind him his wife and children, who were at all
times exposed to the rapacious visitations of the ruffian soldiery.   It was in the incidental absence of both parents one
day that the dragoons happened to visit the place in quest of
them.   The troopers gathered the children around them, and
questioned them very particularly respecting their father and
their mother; but they could elicit nothing satisfactory.   The
men, however, were determined not to pass over the matter
in this way, and they proceeded to bring the children to compliance.   They led them out to the field, and plainly informed
them that they would instantly shoot them if they did not
give the requisite information.   They forthwith blindfolded
them, preparatory to the dreadful act, but the children remained inflexible; and though the dragoons did not shoot as
they threatened, yet the terror into which they were thrown
resulted in a severe fever, which brought them to the very
brink of the grave.

Mrs Hewatson, after the flight of her husband, found it
necessary to make her escape also.   One day she observed a
party of soldiers coming in the direction of the Laight, and
she was well aware that she was the person of whom they
were in quest.   She hastily left the house, descended the
bank which led to the Scar, and having crossed the stream,
plunged into the heart of the woods and thickets, which
afforded a dense concealment to fugitives.   In her flight she
reached a little cottage, which stood at the upper extremity
of a pleasant green lawn, at the foot of a steep height, not
far from the house of Auchenbenzie.   In this hut she sought
refuge from her pursuers, and received a cordial welcome.
Agitated and out of breath, she placed herself on a seat, and
having scattered her long flowing hair over her face and
shoulders, she seized a little child, placed it on her knee, and
was chanting a plaintive lullaby over the infant when the
soldiers entered.   They inquired at the master of the cottage, whose name was Black, if he saw the woman of whom
they were in pursuit.   He replied that he did, and that he
had no doubt, if she was continuing her course with the same
speed as when he first observed her, that by this time she
would be a considerable distance from the place.   On hearing this the troopers, who had no time to lose, set off in full
race after the poor woman, as if they had routed and were

pursuing the forces of a whole kingdom. They missed their
object, however; and having to encounter in their progress
what was literally a forest of tall bushy broom, and thickets
of entangling underwood, they were forced to retrace their
steps, and to retreat without their errand to their garrison.
This worthy woman was thus shielded by Providence, and
spared to be the mother of a numerous progeny. The Hewat-
sons are still resident in the locality, and from one of the
lineal descendants the preceding anecdote has been received.

The following traditions have been preserved respecting
John Ferguson of Wee Woodhead, in the upland parish of
Carsphairn, whose mountain glens and wild retreats concealed
many of the worthies, whom it was the work of the oppressors of those times to exterminate. Few districts in the west
caused the persecutors more trouble than Carsphairn; for few
places contained more worthy men, and men more staunch in
their adherence to their country's liberties. John Ferguson,
along with the patriots of Carsphairn and its vicinity, assisted
at the battle of Pentland, the first gathering to which took its
rise in the village of Dalry, contiguous to Carsphairn. This
being the case, a more than ordinary number of the friends
of religious liberty was drawn from that locality. John Ferguson was mounted on a small but nimble pony, which carried him, in company with his brethren, to the scene of conflict. It is well known how this conflict terminated. It was
lamentably disastrous to the patriots, who were routed by
that cruel persecutor, Dalziel of Binns, and upwards of fifty
of their number were left on the field. In the discomfiture,
John Ferguson fled with the rest, on his pony, but not being
able to keep up with his companions, he was about to dismount, and flee on foot, when at the moment a large black
war-steed came snorting to his side. This happened to be
a cavalry horse belonging to the dragoons, which had lost his
rider in the battle, and having scampered off from the field
in the midst of the confusion and the shouting, came galloping after the fugitives. John grasped his flowing mane, and
in an instant was in the saddle, and darting forward with the
speed of an arrow, got beyond the reach of his pursuers.
This occurrence was regarded by this honest man as in an
especial manner providential; for otherwise he must have
been left behind, and in all likelihood overtaken by the
enemy. How far the troopers pursued the routed Covenanters in the direction in which the men of Carsphairn were
fleeing is not said, or whether they were successful in capturing any by the way; but Ferguson being mounted on his

fleet and spirited charger, soon got beyond the reach of the foe, who had not the same interest in pursuing as he had in fleeing. In his way he crossed the Clyde by a circuitous route, to avoid the centre of Nithsdale, which was the straight road to his home, but which was more populous, and more frequented by the military. When he reached the river, and when his horse was drinking of the cooling stream, the little pony, which he never expected to see again, stood by his side. It had followed him unperceived, and being without its rider, came the more swiftly along. He now pursued his way cautiously through the moorlands, and along the by-paths, till he reached Carsphairn, and with a grateful heart acknowledged that Providence had not only shielded him in the battle, but had also furnished him with the means of escape at the moment prompt assistance was needed.

After this, John Ferguson was obliged to conduct himself with great caution, and to live as quietly in his retreat as possible. Little is known of him for a number of years after this; and living in the parish of an indulged minister, he was, on that account, less liable to disturbance; for the venerable John Semple was the last man in the district who would have ventured to hurt a hair of his head. His heart beat in too close a unison with the patriotic men who contended so nobly for their country's weal, to act in the slightest degree to their prejudice. It was not till after his decease that Carsphairn became the scene of so much oppression.

Whether John Ferguson was at Bothwell, tradition does not say; but it is not at all unlikely that he was. Wodrow makes mention of one John Ferguson, against whom the council instituted proceedings for being at Bothwell. His residence, to be sure, was Enterkin Mains, a place at no great distance from Carsphairn, and where it is not improbable that John Ferguson may at one time have lived.

It was after Claverhouse came on the field, however, and that was the year prior to Bothwell, that John Ferguson was more particularly taken notice of by the persecutors. Attempts were now made to seize him, either in the fields or in his own house. Owing to the wary manner in which John now lived, and the secrecy he observed in his hiding-places, it was found to be no easy matter to apprehend him. To accomplish his capture, therefore, two men, in the guise of friends, were hired by the enemy to circumvent him. Having arrayed themselves in a garb calculated to excite the least suspicion, they met him one day on the hill, as he

was keeping his sheep, and asked him if he knew where
John Ferguson lived. They spoke, doubtless, in such a style
as to induce the belief that they were two wanderers belonging to the friendless remnant, who were seeking the house of
a friend, in which they might meet with a kindly reception
in the day of peril and privation. It was an easy thing for
these men to assume the demeanour of friends to the persecuted cause, and even to assert that they themselves were
suffering afflictions for the Gospel's sake, that in this way
they might the more easily accomplish their purpose. The
address of the men awakened suspicions in John's breast,
and this put him instantly on his guard. Happily for him,
however, the men did not know him, and having come from
another place, they were simply inquiring the way to his
house, in the expectation of seizing him there. "If you
want John Ferguson," said he, "I can conduct you to his
house : you will find him a very friendly man, and ready to
assist, as far as may be in his power, those who need. The
way to his house may not be so easily found by you through
the trackless moor, but I will guide you, as I happen to be
going that way." When they arrived at the hut, John desired the men to turn round by the footpath which led to
the door in the front of the house, while he attempted to
rouse the inmates by crying through the window in the back
part of the building. The window to which he approached
had a few panes of glass in the upper part, while it opened
by a board below. As the men were slowly moving round
to the door, John hastily opened the board in the little window, and calling on his wife, informed her that the men before the door were spies, or rather soldiers in the guise of
friends come to apprehend him—that he had brought them
to the house without their knowing who he was—that she
was to entertain them in the best manner she could, without
letting her suspicions appear—that he would escape, and that
she would know the reason of his absence. John's intention
in accompanying the spies to his house was, no doubt, twofold;—the one, to inform his wife of his circumstances; and
the other, to procure a little of what was necessary in point
of food and clothing. Having also informed her of the precise place where he meant to conceal himself, he could depart with an easier mind. Having thus briefly communicated
with his wife, he instantly retired and fled to the mountains.
The men entered, and were not long in showing to what party
they belonged; for having asked for the husband, and finding
that his presence in the house was denied, they were resolved

not to depart till they had fully satisfied themselves with regard to the truth of the assertion. They accordingly proceeded to make a strict search, and behaved in a very insolent manner. Whether they at last suspected that the shepherd who conducted them to the house was the man they were seeking, is not said; but they departed greatly disappointed, and John regarded this deliverance with a grateful heart.

The next escape which this worthy man made was much more wonderful. The farm of Wee Woodhead borders at one point on what is called the Lane of Carsphairn. This streamlet, which is in some places very deep, forms many beautiful windings in its course, and the flat spaces in the bosom of its curvatures afford excellent meadow ground, from which the hay is carefully gathered in its season. As he was one day busily employed in making hay on the meadow, close by the side of the Lane, he observed, at no great distance from him, a company of troopers advancing straight to the place where he was. It happened that, exactly at the spot where he was working on the margin of the stream, there was a dark and deep pool thickly overshadowed by a cluster of willow bushes, bending their palmy branches down on the surface of the waters. It occurred to John that there was no way of escape but by plunging into the pool, and concealing himself under the water. He instantly crept into the heart of the willows, and having thrown his rake and his bonnet into the rivulet, he grasped the branches of the thicket, and let himself down at his full length, close under the bank of the stream, keeping his head above the waters, under the dense mantling of the bushes. Here he placed himself, holding firmly by the roots of the shrubs, and waited the arrival of the soldiers. In a brief space they were on the spot, and seeing the bonnet and rake floating on the pool, they concluded that he must be under the water. They searched with care all about the willows, and probed with their swords among the long grass which generally gathers thick around the roots of underwood growing by the brink of streams. Nothing, however, was to be discovered; and when they had looked and sought in vain, they came naturally enough to the conclusion that he was drowned in the attempt to conceal himself, and that in this way he had spared them the savage satisfaction of shooting him in the hay field. He distinctly heard their oaths and their threatenings respecting himself, and with much pleasure heard them express their conviction that he was drowned in the pool. They retired, and at his own convenience he withdrew from his watery hiding-place, but not without sincere acknowledgments to the Preserver of his life.

The meadow by the Lane is to this day connected with the name of John Ferguson. These traditions have been preserved in his family with pious care, and were communicated by a lineal descendant.

CHAPTER XLIX.

John Colvin of Dormont. *

IN gleaning the wide field of covenanting interest, we have hitherto found but little in Annandale; and yet many a worthy person resided in this district, and many a faithful adherent to the cause in support of which our forefathers struggled so manfully and so constitutionally. The blood of the martyrs was shed in this locality, as well as in other parts of the land. The famous James Welwood of Tundergarth reared under his ministry many a godly person, who flinched not in the day when Zion's troubles came thick upon her, like the heavy hailstones which descend from the bosom of the ominous cloud that lowers fearfully over the earth. The savour of Mr Welwood's piety was retained for many years after his decease. The letter which, in 1655, he wrote to a brother minister, shows the stedfastness of his spirit in the midst of the Church's distress, and the almost prophetic forecastings which he had of the still greater tribulations which were to come. Mr Welwood laboured assiduously for the salvation of souls; for his heart was in his Master's work, and he lived very near him in heavenly fellowship. As a proof of the uncommon spirituality of this good man, we may adduce the following anecdote given by Patrick Walker: "The night in which his wife died he spent in prayer and meditation in his garden. The next morning one of his elders coming to visit him, lamented his great loss and want of rest, but he replied : 'I declare I have not all this night had one thought of the death of my wife, I have been so taken up in meditating on heavenly things. I have this night been on the banks of Ulai, plucking an apple here and there.' "

His son, John Welwood, suffered much in those trying times, preaching the Gospel in the fields, and wandering from place to place. He died in Perth, 1679, in the thirtieth year of his age. "When drawing near his end, in conversation with some friends, he used frequently to communicate his own exercise and experience; and with regard to the assurance he had of his own interest in Christ he said : ' I have no more doubt of my interest in Christ than if I were in heaven already.' At another time he said : ' Although I have been for some weeks without sensible, comforting presence, yet I have not the least doubt of my interest in Christ. I have ofttimes endeavoured to pick a hole in my interest, but cannot get it done.' The morning he died, when he observed the light of day, he said : ' Now eternal light, and no more night and darkness to me;' and that night he exchanged a weakly body, a wicked world, and a weary life, for an immortal crown in that heavenly inheritance which is prepared and reserved for such as him."

Annandale then produced great men and illustrious witnesses for Jesus Christ. The vale of the Annan, when seen from the rising ground on the east of Torthorwald heights, presents a splendid scene. Beneath lies "Marjory o' the mony lochs," and the ancient castle of the Bruce, mouldering among the stately trees on the margin of the glassy lake whose silvery waves, rippling before the southern breeze, murmur in the ear many a tale of the feudal times, connected with the grey ruins that still appear in solitary grandeur. The whole valley, stretching from south to north, where it terminates at the base of the frowning heights between it and the wilds of Tweedsmuir, furnishes a diversity of scenery so enchanting that few localities in the south of Scotland can equal it. The wilder parts on either side of this fair strath afforded places of retreat to the worthies of the covenant, who, in that part of the country, were subjected, like their brethren elsewhere, to the rude treatment of the times.

It was at Dormont, in Annandale, that John Colvin and his youthful wife Sarah Gibson lived. They belonged to the covenanting party, and were sore harassed on account of their stedfast adherence to their principles. The house of John Colvin was ever open to the wanderers, to whom he afforded a ready shelter in the day of their distress. At length John became so noted for his hospitality to the intercommuned sufferers, that the persecutors deemed it necessary to suppress the obnoxious household.

In those perilous times men were put to many shifts, and were obliged to resort to many devices, to secure themselves in the moment of danger, when it came unexpectedly upon them. Accordingly, there was in the cottage of Dormont a rather ingenious place of concealment. The beds, which were constructed of wood, in the form of oblong boxes, and neatly roofed in above, were movable at pleasure, although they had all the appearance of fixtures. Between the boards of the beds and the wall was an empty space, into which an entrance was made by shifting the back parts of the beds, and closing them in such a way as no suspicion could possibly be entertained. The space behind was occupied as a hiding-place by the fugitives who occasionally resorted to Colvin's house; and many a time were persons concealed in this seclusion, and fed by the Christian kindness of the man who entertained them at the risk of his own life.

One day John Colvin and his wife were thrown into great consternation by the following incidental circumstance : A party of troopers, who, it appears, had been out on a hunting excursion, happened to call at Dormont on their way home, though not for the purpose of searching the place, which, probably at the time of the occurrence of this incident, had not been regarded as peculiarly a place of retreat to the refugees. At the moment the horsemen rode up to the door, there were no fewer than eight of the covenanting party seated at dinner in the house. The soldiers, without dismounting, cried lustily for food to their hungry dogs, that were weary and exhausted with the chase. Sarah hastily lifted the food from the board at which the men had been partaking, while they were doubtless, by this time, making their retreat to the hiding-place, and carried it out to the dogs. She next brought a basket of good oaten cakes or thick bannocks, and therewith fed the horses from her own hand. This prompt display of hospitality called forth the commendations of the party, who were exceedingly gratified by the attention shown them, and they departed without entering the house.

But the visits of the dragoons to the cottage at Dormont were not always incidental. John Colvin and his wife became more than merely suspected persons—they were looked on as flagrant rebels, and as individuals who had even forfeited their lives by harbouring the obnoxious party, who gave the rulers so much annoyance, and on whose extermination they were bent. A company of horsemen were one day sent to Dormont to seize both the husband and his wife, for the purpose of inflicting on them such a punishment as might deter others from following their practices. When they came to the place, Colvin was not at home, and Sarah, having observed their approach, fled from the house to seek

a place of concealment. She was a young woman of low
stature, and of rather a swarthy complexion. In her retreat
from the house the soldiers observed her, and judging by
her hurried movements that she was one of those of whom
they were in quest, they quickened their pace, in order to
overtake her. It was the depth of winter, and the keen frost
had crusted with thick and smooth ice the streams and the
pools, and the hilarious youth of both sexes were jocundly
employed in the healthful exercise of sliding on the glassy
surface of the frozen lakes. As the young wife fled from her
pursuers, she encountered a company of boys and girls amusing themselves on the ice that covered a sheet of water in
her track. She instantly made her situation known to them,
in full confidence of obtaining their sympathy. It was immediately suggested that, as they were not in sight of the
troopers, Sarah should throw her hair loose over her face and
shoulders, and follow in the row of the sliders as they proceeded one after another, in fleet and heedless movement,
from one extremity of the pool to the other. The suggestion
was speedily acted on, and Sarah possessing a sufficiently
girlish appearance to prevent her from being distinguished
from her companions, mingled in the youthful sport, and was
careering along the slippery surface when a party of the
soldiers, detached from the rest that turned aside to the house,
came up. They looked at the merry group on the ice, and
passed by in the chase without taking any notice of the individuals that might be there, and without asking any questions
respecting the fugitive. In this way Sarah escaped, and remained at a distance from the house till the troopers departed.
In those times the slightest incident not unfrequently occasioned the concealment of the wanderers. Sometimes when
escape was deemed impossible, a trifling occurrence was the
means of a complete deliverance, and of a deliverance so
striking, that in it the hand of Providence was plainly visible.
    The next time the military visited the cottage of Dormont,
they chose the evening, after the darkness had set in. This
plan was adopted the better to prevent their approach from
being noticed before they were just at the place. When the
trampling of the feet of the horses was heard at the door,
John, who justly suspected the character of the visitants, retired into the space behind the beds. Sarah was found on
the floor when the men entered, busily employed with the
affairs of her household. She seized her infant in her arms,
and looked on with astonishment, as the blustering troopers
rushed into the apartment, prepared to lay waste both life

and property in the execution of their purpose. The husband was the person whom they chiefly wanted, and they dealt with Sarah to reveal his hiding-place. When they could not by any solicitation induce her to make the discovery they wished, they proceeded to acts of violence, and cruelly mal-treated the helpless woman. Sarah cried, and the infant screamed, and all was in turmoil and peril together. John, in his hiding-place, heard the tumult; and perceiving that the lives of his wife and child were in imminent danger, his whole nature was stirred within him, and though his house had been filled with demons instead of men, the circumstance could not have appalled him, nor quashed the vehemence of his spirit, when he considered the situation of those who were dearest to him on earth. Accordingly, he sprang from his retreat, and with all the energy of his strength seized the ruffian trooper who had laid his rude grasp on her neck, and was pushing her violently to and fro on the floor of the apart-ment. "Stay, villain, and quit your hold!" cried John with terrific voice; " cease, miscreant, or you lie dead at my feet !" The soldier stood with astonishment, and was overawed by the majestic and awful bearing of his assailant. A scuffle instantly ensued, in which Sarah and the infant were knocked to the ground. In the confusion she rose and fled to the door, crying in desperation, and at the utmost pitch of her voice, for help; and Providence had help at hand, otherwise there is no saying what mischievous consequences might have resulted. It happened at the moment that Sarah ran to the door, that a company of wanderers were approaching the house in the dark, to seek shelter under this hospitable roof for a night. Her cries informed them of the true state of matters within, and at the same time inspired them with a courage that was not to be overawed either by selfish fears or by the power of the enemy. A virtuous household was in distress, a household that feared God, a household that was suffering in his cause, and a household that had often shielded them or their brethren in the day of their peril; and, there-fore, no consideration was to interfere in preventing them from effecting its rescue. One man is worth ten when his nature is roused, and his fortitude elevated to its proper height. The dragoons had bound John, and were in the act of dragging him out, when a shout, uttered with the energy of thunder was heard at the door—the shout of a company of assailants rushing to the onslaught. The uproar within ceased for a moment. The shouting without continued, and anon there was the rustling of men entering the house in the dark, with menacing voices. The thing could be no mistake; the soldiers plainly perceived that now they were attacked in their turn, and that the men were Covenanters, brave, determined, and ready to sell their lives in the honourable defence of the injured. That blood would be shed they had no doubt, and how to escape in the confusion was now the sole care of each individual. The darkness concealed the real number of the Covenanters; and the dragoons, who in perilous circumstances were generally cowards, wished to evade, if possible, a conflict in which it was likely they would suffer defeat. The soldiers stole, as best they might, to the door; and the assailants from without not wishing to injure them if they could succeed in removing them from the place and in saving the family, allowed them to depart; which they did with all convenient speed. John Colvin had often sheltered the wanderers, and now Providence made use of them, in their turn, to shelter him. On this night they came to his dwelling, seeking a hiding-place; and they came like special messengers sent to accomplish his rescue when he was in the very hands of his foes. Thus was he rewarded for his kindness to those who were enduring privations for the sake of truth and a good conscience. " Truly there is a reward to the righteous."

The last incident which befell John Colvin and his wife is the following : It happened on a fine summer morning that a company of dragoons sallied forth into the moorlands, on their wonted mission of evil, to seek out, and drag to punishment, the unoffending people hiding in the lonely retreats of the wilderness. The company of troopers, which appears to have been large, separated into two parties, to proceed by different routes, when, having accomplished their respective circuits, they were to meet in a certain place, and return to their garrison together. One division struck off into the moors, and the other went in the direction of Dormont. John Colvin was hiding in the desert, when his wife at home was visited by the soldiers. She had just laid her babe asleep in the cradle, and was seated with the Bible open on her knee meditating on the blessed word of truth, when the trusty dog which lay at her feet began to growl and bark at the approach of some person in the distance. She rose to see what was the matter, and to her surprise she saw the party riding toward the house. She instinctively fled from the door, to conceal herself in a thicket at a short distance from the house. It now occurred to her that she had left the infant in the cradle on the floor; but it was too late to think of returning, as the horsemen were just at hand. Her concern for herself was absorbed in her care for the child, and she prayed for its protection, and trusted that the soldiers would either not notice it, or if they did, that they would not disturb it. When the soldiers entered, they could find nobody; but one of them on perceiving the infant asleep in the cradle, affirmed that the nurse could not be far off, and that, if they set the babe a-crying, the mother would soon make her appearance. Accordingly, the child was lifted from his couch, and rudely awakened by the surly trooper, who held it in his arms. When he opened his little eyes, and gazed on the strange and gruff face of the soldier, he screamed dreadfully, and looked about for his mother; but no mother was there, and then he screamed still louder. The men expected every moment that the mother would spring to the assistance of the babe; but no mother appeared, and it was plain she was not within. The soldier proceeded to the open air, that the cries might reach the parent, if she was anywhere within hearing; and he carried him round the house, if perchance she might come to his assistance. She heard what was going on, and her heart was pierced by the cries of her sweet infant; but what could she do? If she appeared, her capture was certain, and the safety of the child in nowise secured. Her brain was bewildered; she could save neither herself nor her babe, and she remained in concealment, hoping that the soldiers would tire, and return him again to his cradle, and depart.

The troopers, finding their scheme was unsuccessful, removed from the place; but then they carried the child with them; and the mother, in her inexpressible bewilderment and grief, beheld the party advancing over the waste, with their little captive stolen from her arms.

In the meantime, John, who had been wandering and hiding in the wilds, was wending his way through the moorlands, to visit his home; for his heart yearned over his wife and child, and he longed to see how they fared. As he was hastening onward, he encountered the first division of the horsemen, with whom was the commander. John was not personally known to any of the party, but the officer requested his assistance in guiding them from place to place. He had no good-will to be found in their company, but to avoid suspicion, he complied. Indeed, there was no alternative; for in those imperious times the will of the military was a law. There was no fear, however, that he would guide them to the prejudice of any of his brethren who might happen to be in the locality.

The party from Dormont, carrying the infant, joined their commander in the moor. The child was still crying bitterly; for its wailings had not softened the hearts of the troopers, and they carried it with them in a sort of cruel triumph. When the officer saw the plight of the poor babe, he was much displeased with the conduct of the men, and deemed it an act of inhumanity in them thus to carry off a poor help-less infant, which could be of no manner of service to them. His heart melted when he heard its infantile cries; for he was probably a parent himself, and had sweet babes at home, and the heart of a parent knows well how to feel for the woes of children, even though they be strangers. Happily John Colvin did not recognise the child; for his features were swollen with crying, and his face fouled and disfigured with tears. Had he been near enough to discern his own child, the discovery must have proved fatal. The commander, whose heart was moved to compassion, ordered the dragoon to hasten back to the place from which he had brought the babe, and to leave him where he found him. The man did as he was bidden, and deposited his captive again in the cradle, and not seeing the mother, nor any person about the place, he rode back with all speed to his troop. In this way was the poor infant preserved, who might otherwise have found his bed in the cold moss-hag.

During the absence of the child, Sarah's heart was wrung with anguish. She blamed herself as his murderer—she re-garded her cowardice as excessively criminal—and considered that she ought rather to have lost her own life than exposed the life of her babe. She issued from the heart of the thicket, and stared wildly in the direction of the moor where the party had carried the child. She at length perceived a horseman returning, and riding rapidly toward the house; and not knowing his final purpose, she concealed herself in the space behind the beds, and was there when the soldier entered with the sobbing babe, and laid him where he found him; and now her fears were disappointed, and her prayers answered. She clasped the infant to her bosom, and fondled and caressed him, while the tears of maternal affection came showering warm on his little face. He was now at rest on his mother's breast, and her heart overflowed with thank-fulness.

In the evening John reached his home, after a day of no little fatigue, in following the troopers in their capricious movements in the moors and glens. The little family were glad to meet again, after a season of no common solicitude and peril to every member of it. John recounted the things that had befallen him during his absence in his hidings in the deserts, and more particularly the incidents that had occurred in the preceding part of the day; and especially, how he was moved by the condition of a poor infant, whom the soldiers had brought from some cottage in the moor-lands. When he mentioned the child, Sarah burst into tears; and holding up the babe in her hands—"That," said she, "is the child you saw with the soldier—your own child, who was stolen from the cradle, when I was concealed in the heart of the thicket;" and then she related the occurrences of the day. John took the boy in his arms, and blessed God for the deliverance, and said he felt especially grateful that he did not recognise him at the time, as in that case a discovery must inevitably have been made, to the ruin of the entire household.

This worthy couple survived the persecution, and were enabled to maintain their fidelity during the trying times that passed over them. They were blessed with additional children, and their descendants exist at the present day. The preceding anecdotes were communicated by a great grand-daughter, Sarah Millar, in Dunscore, who received them from her mother, Margaret Colvin; and Margaret heard them from the mouth of Sarah Gibson, the person to whom, along with her husband, the traditions refer.

CHAPTER L.

Curate of Closeburn—Samuel Clark.

" Truth is stranger than fiction," is a saying that has been a thousand times verified. The occurrences in real life are sometimes so wonderful, so striking, so intricate, and yet so admirable in their development, that in reading the detail of them, we are apt to slide into the notion that the whole has been ingeniously conjectured by the writer, and presented in an artificial, and yet apparently simple manner, for the purpose of producing effect. Things have actually fallen out in human affairs so romantic in their nature, that no novelist, in the warmest moments of his imaginings, could ever scheme the like; and hence writers of this class generally depend more on real incidents than on their own inventions, to impart a vivid colouring and gairishness to their ideal productions. The incidents which befell during the persecuting period, and the interferences on behalf of the sufferers, are many of them so passing strange, and so apparently improbable, that were it not for the statements of veracious history, we might be inclined to regard the whole as an imaginative picture. The notices, also, of those times that have been transmitted to us by tradition are full of diversity and interest, and are altogether too distinctive in their character for mere invention; so that, in traversing the wide field of persecuting activity, and gathering in its thousands of incidents, we will scarcely find two or three of them that are exactly alike. That the incidents have a kindred relation is just what might be expected, since a similar agency was uniformly employed on the side of the persecutors, and seeing that, on the side of the persecuted, it was as uniformly men of the same principles that suffered, while all of them resorted to the same or similar means for deliverance.

The parish of Closeburn, which has been frequently mentioned in these Traditions, contained a goodly sprinkling of the worthies who were subjected to trial in the days of Prelatic oppression. The curate of this parish was a determined opponent of the Nonconformists, and he plotted and wrought against them with all assiduity. His persecuting propensities were, it is true, modified by the leniency of the lord of the manor, whom, for selfish purposes, he did not choose to offend. On every favourable opportunity, however, he exerted himself in opposing and vexing all who showed the least reluctance to attend his ministry. The dislike of the more serious people to this man was great, and the knowledge of this fact irritated him the more, and prompted him to the adoption of more stringent measures, with a view to humble them, and to bring them to compliance. The withdrawment of many of the parishioners from the church was therefore to be visited with his displeasure in such a way as would prove a warning to others. He knew that he had much in his power, and that a single word conveyed to the military would bring a host of troopers on the parish, who would deal with the poor people as it best pleased them. He knew that there was a goodly number of children in the parish who were not baptized, because the parents refused to receive that ordinance from the hands of an Episcopalian; and therefore, to bring the matter more distinctly to the test, he intimated one Sabbath from the pulpit, that all the unbaptized children must be presented within the walls of that church on a given day, and there and then be baptized by himself, else information should be instantly lodged against them as Nonconformists and rebels. This announcement caused great distress in the district, and every cottage in which was a child unbaptized was filled with concern. The disposition of the incumbent was well known, and it was not expected that he would resile from his determination, and therefore they must either comply or expect the worst. This tyrannical measure filled the minds of the poor people with perplexity, and they could not well determine how to act. Their convictions led them to one conclusion, and their fears prompted them to another; so that, between a sense of duty and a dread of suffering, they were at their wits' end.

Among the recusants in the parish of Closeburn at this time was one Peter Stranger, a devout man, and a warm friend to the persecuted people. Peter and the curate could never agree; for their principles were as wide as the poles asunder. Peter was a farmer, and a person of some influence in the place, and he among the rest had a child unbaptized. The curate's mandate was regarded by Peter with horror, and he deemed it a stretch of insupportable tyranny to which he would by no means submit. But man is an inconstant creature, and liable to be powerfully wrought upon either by interest or by fear. Peter, notwithstanding his inward reluctance and loud remonstrances, sorrowfully submitted, along with a number more in his situation, to come to the church on the day appointed. It was a day of grief to the worthy people, and a day of exultation to their enemies, who doubtless ridiculed their want of firmness, notwithstanding their boasted professions. The curate himself must have been especially gratified, when he perceived that his influence was such as to overmaster the most scrupulous of his parishioners, and to bring them to a compliance with his wishes. Little cared he for the pain he inflicted on these simple-hearted people, whom he thought thus to ensnare; but "the triumphing of the wicked is short," and a visitation of a very awful nature prevented this man from carrying his purpose into effect. The people were standing in groups in the churchyard, and the bell was emitting its solemn tones, to warn the worshippers that the hour for assembling within the hallowed fane was come. The curate made his appearance, advancing slowly on his way to the church, congratulating himself, no doubt, on the success of his scheme, and rejoicing in the prospect of gaining a public and signal victory over the refractory portion of his parishioners. His earthly course, however, was near its close; for just as he stepped within the kirkyard, he fell down, and in a moment expired, upon the grassy graves over which he was treading. The circumstance created unspeakable alarm among the people, who rushed out of the church on the report of the astounding visitation. The curate was dead, the congregation dispersed, and the desponding company, who had so far yielded compliance, retired, eased of an insupportable pressure that lay on their minds. The death of such a man would, no doubt, be a matter rather of gratulation than of grief to the oppressed people, over whom he ruled with a rod of iron.

This occurrence happened near the termination of the persecution; for he was, it is said, the last curate that was in Closeburn. It would be too much to affirm that the curate's death is to be viewed as a special judgment from Heaven; for both good and bad men have died in a similar manner.

We are often rash in our conclusions, and are as ready to decide amiss as to judge righteously, and therefore we ought to be very cautious. The event, however, was very striking, and its language to the people might perchance be a sermon much more impressive than any that the curate would that day, if spared, have delivered.

It is related that the worthy Peter Stranger, who survived the troublous times, was, when he died, buried exactly at the curate's feet. They were opposed to each other during their lifetime, but they were scarcely divided in their death, being placed near each other in the grave, where

> "In peace the ashes mix
> Of those who once were foes."

After Peter's burial a certain rustic wag, on perceiving the contiguity of the graves, inscribed on his tombstone the following doggerel rhyme:—

> " Peter Stranger, strangely placed
>   At the auld curate's feet,
> And surely they that placed him there
>   Were very indiscreet;
> For prelates and for Prelacy
>   He held as mortal foes,
> Nor did he spare to clip their wings
>   Whene'er occasion rose."

The subsequent traditions relate to Samuel Clark of New Luce, in Galloway. He sat under the ministry of Mr Peden, a man who was the instrument of great good to many souls in that part of the country. Samuel Clark profited much by Mr Peden, and grew in grace under his ministrations. He used frequently to mention the great advantage he derived from the prayers of this eminently holy man; for it is to be remembered that the worthies of that age were men of prayer, and it is to this circumstance chiefly that we are to attribute the uncommon success of their ministry. They lived near God, in communion with him; for the more they were persecuted the nearer they drew to the Rock of their safety. Samuel Clark cherished an uncommon respect for Mr Peden, and well might he, for he was the means of much spiritual benefit to him; and those who have been instrumental in leading us to the Saviour, and in fostering in our hearts the principles of the divine life, can never be forgotten by us as long as we live. He accompanied him in his wanderings in the dreary parts of the country, and especially among the wilds of Galloway; in which district both of them had an especial interest. Many a time did they pray and commune together in the deserts and in the caves of the earth, and God was with them, and filled their hearts with peace; for though their lot was cast in suffering times, they were not on that account unhappy. They only are unhappy whose minds are ill at ease—not they whose confidence the Lord is, and on whom the light of his countenance shines.

In those days of peril, Samuel Clark made several narrow escapes from the enemy. On one occasion, on the dispersion of a conventicle, when sundry of the worshippers were seized, Samuel fled, and wandering in the wilder parts, came to a friend's house, where he resided for a while. At length, however, the soldiers visited this place also, and he was obliged to flee again. He ran in the direction of the lofty Cairnsmoor, from the summit of which the greater part of Galloway can be seen. As he fled along the heathy and rugged sides of the mountain, with the troopers in pursuit, he crept in among the tall heather to hide himself. The horsemen advanced, spreading themselves along the face of the height, that they might not miss his track. The main body of the pursuers passed the spot without noticing him, till the last of the party, a single man, slower in his move- ments than the rest, happened to light on the identical spot where Clark lay concealed. The soldier's eye caught the legs of the man protruding beyond the heathery covert, and, guessing the secret, smote him gently on the feet, and said: " Creep farther into the bush, for your limbs are seen." The humanity of this trooper forbade him to com- municate the discovery, and riding after his companions, he allowed the fugitive to escape.

At another time Clark had been at a meeting at a place called Irelington, when the troopers came upon the assembly, and dispersed the worshippers. He fled, and the horsemen followed. At length, wearied out with fatigue and want of food, he sat down under the covert of a tall whin bush, and taking off his bonnet, he addressed the great Preserver of his life in the following strain: " O Thou who didst shield thy servant Peden in the day of his distress, when he called upon thee, and didst throw over him and me, Thy unworthy follower, the misty covering which hid us from the face of our pursuers, hide me now, in the hollow of Thine hand, from mine enemies, who are hunting for my life." The soldiers came up, but they missed his hiding-place, having passed by on the other side of the bush; and his prayer was answered. " In my distress I called upon the Lord, and cried unto my

God; he heard my voice out of his temple, and my cry came before him, even into his ears."

The last notice we have of this honest man is connected with a very wonderful deliverance he had from a violent death. He had heard that old Mr Peden was at Sorn, his native place, and he longed to see his esteemed and venerated minister, with whom he had often taken such sweet counsel. Accordingly, he set out from his residence among the wilds of Galloway, northward, to the abode of his friend. The journey was attended with great danger; but his heart was set on the adventure, perilous as it was. The ardour of true Christian affection is not easily subdued, and indeed the more it is opposed the stronger does it become. As he approached the place of his destination, he encountered a company of Claverhouse's troopers, who seized him on suspicion as a rebel, and carried him off as their captive. It appears to have been towards the evening, for they lodged during the night in the kirk of Sorn, with the plain intimation that he was to be executed without fail in the morning. In this prisonhouse he was kept during the lonely hours of the night; and we can easily imagine the manner in which he would be exercised in the house of prayer, having the immediate prospect of death before him. Many of his brethren enjoyed no such privilege; they were shot where they were found, with the shortest warning, and without permission even to pray. The hours of the night would be sedulously occupied in fervent supplication to Him "who was able to save him from death," or to sustain him with constancy to meet it as a witness for Jesus Christ in the day of general defection and of scorn. At length the morning dawned, and Clark expected it to be his last day on earth. But Providence had ordered it otherwise. A great tumult was heard outside of the church in the early morning; men were running to and fro in much confusion, and the soldiers were calling in haste to their fellows; but in a little the hubbub ceased, and all without was as still as the lonely graves that surrounded the solitary church. The report had reached the village that a conventicle was to be held in the moors at some distance, and all the military were hastily marched off to the place. The prisoner began to look about him, and seeing no soldiers guarding the church, he bethought himself of the propriety of attempting his escape; and he stole out either by a door or window, and fled with all speed into the mossy retreats in the neighbourhood, and completely eluded his enemies, who, in the confusion, seemed to have forgotten him

TRADITIONS OF THE COVENANTERS; OR,

He went in quest of Mr Peden, and found him in a place
near Muirkirk. Mr Peden delighted to wander in the wilds,
not only to visit the cottages of the pious peasantry, but also
the graves of the martyrs. It was interesting to see the
devout old man, near the termination of his pilgrimage, sitting by the grave of Cameron, in the wilds of Airsmoss, and
while he thought on the sufferings of the scattered remnant,
and on the happiness of those who had got "honestly off the
stage," lifting up his eyes and his hands to heaven, and
exclaiming, " O to be wi' Ritchie !"

The two friends were happy at meeting, and they spent
their time in religious converse and prayer. Having accomplished his object, he returned to the Galloway mountains,
and never again had the pleasure of an interview with his
beloved minister, who probably died shortly after this.
Clark was often pursued among the hills, but he evaded his
foes, hiding in the glens and caves of this sterile region. He
survived the persecuting period many a long year, and at
last died in peace in 1730.

NOTE.

Note A, p. 2.

As so many references are made in the preceding pages to the town of Sanquhar and its neighbourhood, as being the central point of a wide locality, within which many of our worthy forefathers, in the time of the Church's affliction during the reign of the royal brothers, sought refuge and endured much, it may not be out of place, perhaps, to present the reader with a few notices of this ancient burgh. The details that may be given, however, will doubtless be interesting chiefly to the inhabitants of the place.

The name *Sanquhar* is Celtic, and literally signifies the *Old Fort*, and plainly indicates that there existed here, during the British times, a place of strength, a fortification of an ancient date even in those remote ages. The Scoto-Irish, who settled in this locality, called the place *Sean-caer*, or Sean-chaer. In 1296, the name of this place was written Senechar. In the charters of Robert I. and of David II. this name was commonly spelt Senechar and Sanchar, and in after times Sanquhair and Sanquhar, after the manner of the Scoto-Saxon orthography.

The particular site of the " old fort" from which Sanquhar derives its name, is in all likelihood the beautiful green eminence on the little farm of Broomfield, in the immediate vicinity of the town. This spot bears the obvious marks of an ancient British fortification, of which no tradition whatever has been preserved. It has been surrounded with a deep trench, the vestiges of which are distinctly visible at the base of the knoll on the summit of which the fortification was reared. No remains of the foundation of anything like a stone building have hitherto been discovered, although the hillock on one side has been deeply trenched on by digging—a circumstance confirmatory of its having been an ancient British strength, as the people of those times almost uniformly constructed their fortifications of wood, all traces of which have long since perished. The ruinous castle at the other extremity of the town belongs to the Saxon period, a comparatively modern date, and there is no evidence that it stands on the site of a more ancient fortress, which may be supposed to have given its name to the place. It is therefore every way probable that the forgotten fort on the north-west has been the remote origin both of the town and its name.

On the north of this low hill fort, at the distance of a few yards, was the famed well of St Bride, a monkish fountain, which sent forth its limpid waters from the sunny slope of a verdant bank. In the days of Romish superstition this sacred well was doubtless visited by many a devotee who had faith in the virtue of its consecrated waters, and many a holy requiem would be chanted by the saintly pilgrims, as they reclined by the gurgling spring under the shade of the scented hawthorn, or the palmy willow that loves to guard the fountains and the brooks. Whether any miracle was ever wrought at this well, by the influence of its presiding saint, tradition does not say; its fame, however, has long since died away, and now at last its waters are dried up, by means of the mining excavations which have been carried on around it; and the identical spot from which welled the stream so hallowed in the eyes of former generations, will, ere long, be entirely unknown.

The old church of Sanquhar, which was lately demolished to make room for the present structure, which occupies its site, was a building of great antiquity. Tradition says it was coeval with the High Church of Glasgow, and was reared by the same architect. From some sculptured stones that were found in its walls, it is obvious that it must have been very ancient, whether its date be what tradition has assigned it or not. There were originally several altars in this church, one of which was known by the name of the altar of the *haly bluid.* "Sir John Logan, vicar of Colven, granted certain lands and rents of houses within the burgh of Dumfries, for the support of a chaplain to celebrate divine service at the altar *sacri cruoris domini,* in the church of Sanchar. This was confirmed by the king in November, 1539. The patronage of the church of Sanquhar was an appendage to the barony, which was acquired by the family of Crichton. In the fifteenth century, the rectory of Sanquhar was constituted a prebend of the cathedral church of Glasgow, with the consent of the patron, whose right still continued. The benefice was usually conferred on a younger son or other relative of the family. Mr Ninian Crichton was patron of Sanchar in 1494, and Mr William Crichton was rector during the reign of James V. In Bagimont's Roll, the rectory of Sanchar, then a prebend of the chapter of Glasgow, was taxed at £10. After the Reformation the patronage was continued with Lord Sanchar till 1630, when it was sold, with the barony, to Sir William Douglas of Drumlanrig." If a conjecture may be hazarded, we may suppose that the church at the west end of Sanchar took its rise in the Celtic times, and was built in the neighbourhood of the fortification; and that the church at its east end, of which nothing now remains, originated with the family of Ross, on whose lands it was reared.

There was recently discovered in the gardens adjoining the wall of the church-yard, the foundation of an ancient structure, deep in the soil, and running nearly in a line with the south side of the church. The thickness of this wall is about four feet, and the stones are strongly cemented with mortar, and in the heart of it were found carved stones of a still older edifice. There can be little doubt that this foundation points out the site of the ancient monastic buildings connected with the church of Sanquhar. This supposition seems to receive confirmation from the fact that this wall, at its eastern extremity, turns at a right angle pointing towards the church, to which, in all likelihood, it was formerly joined.

"Between six and seven hundred years ago," says the author of the "Caledonia," "Godrey de Ross obtained from Richard Moreville, the constable of Scotland, the lands of Stewarton, wherein he was succeeded by his son James de Ross, who granted some lands in this manner to the monks of Paisley. Such were the progenitors of the Rosses of Hawkhill, of Ross of *Sanquhar* in Nithsdale, and other families." The manner in which our Saxon and Norman ancestors, in colonizing the country, settled themselves in their different localities, was the following: A baron obtained a grant of lands, on which he sat down with his followers, and built a castle, and a church, and a mill, and a brew-house, and in this way founded a hamlet, which, according to the custom of the times, was denominated the *ton*, or town of the baron. It was in this manner that many of the inland towns and villages in Scotland sprang up. The retainers of the baron built their huts, which were generally constructed of turfs or of twigs, near his castle, for the sake of mutual defence; and as the importance and strength of a baron consisted chiefly in the number of his vassals, every encouragement would be given to settlers, so that in a short time the hamlet, growing up under the walls of the castle, would increase into a town. The circumstance, also, of the barons always connecting a church with a castle, accounts for the great number of places throughout the landward parts of the country to which the name of chapel is attached, though there may not now be the least vestige either of the church or of the castle remaining. Many of these baronial chapels, in all probability, became, in process of time, parish churches; and this accounts both for the irregular distribution of many of the parish churches, and for the inconvenience of their situation.

In the vicinity of Ryehill, the seat of the ancient Rosses of Sanquhar, is a small but beautiful green moat, the meeting-place of the feudal barons, who held their courts for judicial purposes in the open air; and many a hapless wight, convicted of capital offences, was, in those precarious times, with little ceremony and brief warning, suspended on the gallows-tree, in the presence of the folk-mote or public assembly of the people, who were convened to witness his monitory execution. But to the "lovers of hoar antiquity," perhaps, the monuments and relics of ancient buildings will be chiefly interesting. The author of the "Statistical Account of the Parish of Sanquhar," published in 1793, says, "A stone was found some time ago with the following inscription: 'Here lies the good Sir John Ross of Ryehill; here lies the good, good Sir John Ross of Ryehill; here also lies the good, good, good Sir John Ross of Ryehill.' Near the residence of the Rosses there seems to have been a large pile of building, perhaps the hospital of Senewar, a religious foundation, though this cannot be ascertained. Several of the stones, of a Gothic figure, are built into the walls and windows of houses where this edifice once stood. There is also a large font, or rock basin. Human bones have been found in digging and ploughing up the field in which it stands, and a key of an enormous size was found not above twenty years ago, much consumed with rust, and is now lost."

The remarkable simplicity of the inscription on the tomb-stone indicates its great antiquity, while the spot where it was found points out the identical locality of the church and church-yard. The place where the religious fabric stood is known to the inhabitants by the name of the King's Scar, which rises abruptly from the edge of the river, and which, along with a slender streamlet, which purls past the deserted field of graves, receives the epithet of royalty—not, as has been supposed, from the visit of a prince, but from its having been the residence of an original character, who, upwards of a hundred years ago, had located himself on the pleasant field by the margin of the rill, and who for some particular cause had acquired the soubriquet of *king*. The castle of Sanquhar, to the west of Ryehill, whose mouldering walls are yet magnificent in their ruins, existed prior to the age of Edward I., in whose reign it was, in common with the whole line of castles from Carlisle to Ayr, in the possession of the English. Its recapture by Sir William Douglas of Douglasdale is recorded to have been by the following stratagem. One of the retainers of Douglas, of the name of Dickson, bribed the carman who drove firewood to the castle from the neighbouring forest, and having exchanged clothes with him, came early in the morning with a car-load of fuel, and demanded admittance. The gates were readily opened, and when he entered the inner portal, which leads to the enclosure within the castle walls, he speedily cut the traces, and left the car with its burden jammed immovable in the entrance. Sir William and his men then scrambled over the wood, and sprang into the area, and, following Dickson, entered the castle, which was kept by Beauford, the commander of the southern forces, and put the entire garrison to the sword, with the exception of one man, who, escaping through a postern, fled to Enoch Castle, in Durisdeer. The famous Knight of Douglasdale, now master of the stronghold, was in his turn attacked by the English, and sustained a siege of a fortnight's duration, till news reached the ears of the assailants that brave Sir William Wallace was on his way from Crawford Moor to the relief of the garrison. The English then abandoned the siege, and, moving in a body southward, collected the forces from the different strengths on the route, and sustained a signal defeat by the army of the Scottish patriot, on the plains of Dalswinton, with the loss of several hundred men. But those days of feudal restlessness and peril are now past, and, in our times of civilization and of peace, we can listen to the stirring incidents of a romantic and adventurous age with feelings of a comfortable security; and we have only to contrast the condition of our times with the situation of our ancestors, to learn the value of our social and political privileges. A beautiful little tale, founded on the above incidents, appeared in the " Glasgow University Album for 1836."

The castle of Sanquhar was doubtless built by the family of the Rosses, and though the precise date of its foundation cannot now be ascertained, yet it cannot well be less than six hundred years, since we find it in full state in the days of the illustrious but ill-fated champion of Scotland's liberties, nearly five hundred and fifty years ago. It was in all likelihood the first Saxon stronghold of any consequence that was reared in the locality. It was originally surrounded by a deep fosse on the north side, which at the western point communicated with the River Nith, which at that time flowed immediately under its southern wall.

Deeds of darkness, such as were common in old feudal fortresses, were perpetrated also in this. About fifty years ago, when clearing the floor of one of the murky vaults, there was discovered the mouth of a well or deep pit, and in digging down among the rubbish with which it was filled, a large coffin was found, constructed of the coarsest materials, and which contained the skeleton of a tall, strong man, without the head, obviously the carcass of one whose life had been taken away by violence, and which had been plunged into the well, and covered up, to prevent discovery. On the north side of the building was an oblong mound, or earthen dyke, which, when removed, was found to be full of human bones, and which was probably the burying-place of the ancient warriors who fell before its walls. Crichton *Peel*, as this venerable ruin is called, from Crichton, who married the heiress of Sanquhar, the last of the line of the Rosses, is still the boast of the people of the neighbourhood, who feel themselves connected with it by many interesting associations.

Sanquhar appears to have consisted originally of two small villages, occupying respectively the upper and lower ends of the present town The town-house, erected about a hundred years ago, stands near the western extremity, and is, considering its antiquity, a substantial and even elegant structure. It was reared on the site of a former edifice, appropriated to the same use, the appearance of which was fresh in the remembrance of some of the aged people of the last generation, who described it as having been a building of the height of two stories, and thatched with heather. There were other two houses of some note within the burgh—the one belonging to Lord Sanquhar, and the other to the Earl of Carnwath: the former, a dark, suspicious-looking edifice, something like the dreaded house of Major Weir in the West Bow of Edinburgh, is long since entirely demolished; and the latter, now dwindled into a second rate building, is still standing. The ancient Cross, at the base of which the *Declarations* of Cameron and of Renwick were published, stood near the centre of the town, but has long since been removed.

Sanquhar, like many other places similarly situated, is not without its tales of legendary interest. The story of the apparition of Abraham Crichton, which made so much noise in the middle of the last century, not only in the south, but in the city of Edinburgh itself, where its merits were publicly discussed, and which was deemed worthy of a niche in the literary periodical published by Thomas Ruddiman, was firmly believed by the older people in this place; but, like all other stories of the same description, it eventually vanished into smoke, the particulars of which are too puerile and absurd to admit of recital. The smiling village of Crawick Mill, which belongs to this burgh, was once proverbial for its witchcraft throughout the south and west; an art which is now happily neither believed in nor practised. This little hamlet is now celebrated for its carpet manufactories, and its industrious population.

Most places are ambitious for the honour of having given birth to some illustrious character; and Sanquhar, not to mention other individuals of name and respectability that have sprung from it, can point to itself as the birth-place of the late celebrated Dr Andrew Thomson of S¹ George's, Edinburgh.

It appears that from a remote period, Sanquhar has been favoured with a sound Gospel ministry—probably from the time of the Refor mation till the present day. At the Restoration, John Carmichael, who was at the time minister of Sanquhar and Kirkconnel, was ejected for his nonconformity and attachment to the principles of the Reformation; and since the termination of the reign of Prelatic usurpation in 1688, the parish has been supplied with a succession of worthy ministers in the Establishment. The Secession Church has had a congregation in this place for nearly a hundred years, and which now enjoys the ministrations of the fifth ordained pastor. The first of the series, a young man of the name of Ballantine, was ordained in the time of the Erskines, and is still mentioned as having been a youth of great piety and promise, but was removed in the flower of his days, and just as his early graces and endowments were beginning to expand themselves. He was buried in the church-yard of Sanquhar, and the following epitaph, said to be composed by Ralph Erskine, is engraven on his tombstone:—

This sacred herald, whose sweet mouth
Spread Gospel truth abroad,
Like Timothy, was but a youth,
And yet a man of God.

Soon did the young and ready scribe
A friend for Christ appear,
And was among the associate tribe
A covenanted seer.

He for the Reformation cause
Contending for renown,
Among that noted number was
The first that gained the crown.

His zealous soul with hasty pace
Did mortal life despise,
To feed the lambs around the place
Where now his body lies.

There is also in the town another congregation of the same denomination, of little more than twenty years' standing. The Baptists have a small association here; and the Reformed Presbytery have a preaching place, which is occasionally occupied.

The locality is well supplied with the means of grace; and the inhabitants seem, on the whole, to avail themselves of their religious advantages, and also to profit by them, at least if we may judge from the manner in which the different places of worship are attended. The people generally come well out to hear the Gospel, and there is to be witnessed on the Sabbath-days, at the dismission of the various congregations, the animating spectacle of the streets of the little burgh literally crowded with retiring worshippers.

ADDITIONAL NOTES.

———◆———

It has been suggested to the writer of these traditions that it might be of some importance to add a few notes, verifying the sources from which they have been drawn. He has, accordingly, complied with the hint, and has appended a few brief remarks, explanatory of the circumstances in which the mass of this traditionary lore was brought together.

CHAP. 1.—The anecdotes contained in the preceding chapter, with the exception of the little incident recorded at the end, were received from Robert Laing, shepherd, in Glenmuirshaw, in the upper parts of Kyle : he had resided for many years in the upland deserts, and was well versed in the tales and traditions current in the wild locality in the midst of which he wonned. He was an intimate friend of James Hislop, the poet, commonly called "The Muirkirk Shepherd," who composed the thrilling poem entitled "The Cameronian's Dream," an effusion that will keep its place for generations to come. Robert could never mention Hislop's name without the tear starting into his eye ; they were kindred spirits, both in poetic utterances and in traditionary lore. Robert was a man of high moral standing ; he was a truly religious person, and one of whom it is affirmed that he was never known to tell a lie.

He was a specimen of the brotherhood of shepherds in the covenanting days. He was a son of the devout David Laing, of Blagannoch, denominated the patriarch of the desert. It was these few traditionary notices which we first received from Robert Laing that originally gave the impulse to the collecting of these same traditions which compose this volume, and which probably never might have been given, had it not been for this pious shepherd. Robert has been for some years in his grave.

The last traditionary anecdote given in this chapter was received from a venerable man of the name of Purdie. He was a surgeon in the town of Sanquhar, where he had resided for about sixty years, and died in 1832, a very aged man. He came originally from Calder, where he was born not very long after the decease of the famous Patrick Walker, who lived through the persecuting times, being only a very youth when these troublous days commenced. He was the author of the sketches of Peden, Renwick, Cameron, Wellwood, and Cargill. Mr Purdie often spoke of Walker, for his parents were intimate with him, and had many anecdotes respecting him. He used to tell the anecdote of the quoits or penny-stone with great zest, and many things of the curate who saved the men on that occasion, whose name was Kirkwood.

Other traditions in this volume were communicated by him, and which will be noticed in their order. We have often wished that Sir Walter Scott had seen the doctor, for he was quite an original in his way. He traversed all the country round and round in the way of his profession for many a painful year, and was carried on the back of a sturdy mule in all his peregrinations o'er moor and mountain.

CHAP. 2.—The story of Pedenin Glendyne, was communicated by the venerable Doctor Purdie, whose memory was stored with such traditions, which he gathered from the very aged people of the locality, with whom he was familiar in his youth, and who lived only one generation later than the persons to whom the traditions refer. In this light the most of the traditions in this volume may be regarded as almost equal to veritable history.

The anecdotes relating to Castle Gilmour and Auchentagart were given by Mr John Ker, who farmed the eastern slope of what once formed a part of the Sanquhar town common. His house stood at the bottom of what is now supposed to have been an ancient Celtic battlefield. John was an intelligent and most worthy Christian man, who warmly cherished both the patriotism and the godliness of our persecuted forefathers. He received the anecdotes from the old persons who resided in the locality, and who again had them exactly as they were familiarly rehearsed before the peasants' hearth, generation after generation, without deviation of tale or circumstance.

The story of the venerable matron of Elliock was well known in the district, and her house stood on the face of the bleak moorland on the slope of the hill.

The traditions of the woman of Ingleston and of the laird of Craigdarroch, need no comment, they are so universally known in the district.

CHAP. 3.—The story of the conventicle in the moss of Blagannoch was given by Robert Laing, uncle to the Robert Laing already mentioned. He was an ingenious person, and withal a poet. His mind was stored with old traditionary lore, which he communicated with great facility. He was brother to the patriarch of the desert, and a lineal descendant of the family of Laing that had subsisted on the spot, generation after generation, for about four hundred years. Robert was a well-known character, and many curious anecdotes are told of him. He was well known to the writer of these sketches; he died a number of years ago.

CHAP. 4—The M'Michaels mentioned in this chapter are both of them historical personages; they are noticed in Wodrow. The one, James, who was termed the black M'Michael, killed the curate of Carsphairn, as mentioned by the historian; the other, Daniel, who was shot at the mouth of the pass of Dalveen by Dalziel of Kirkmichael, as related by the same historian.

The legend of Morton Castle was given in full detail by Alexander Fergusson, who resided in the holm of Drumlanrig. Sandy, as he was familiarly called, was full of anecdote and old incident. He had been in the army, and was a great musician; he was by trade a weaver. He was a remarkably facetious person, and his abode being in the vicinity of Drumlanrig Castle, the ducal family frequently paid him a visit. He stood high in the favour of his Grace of Buccleuch, who conferred on him a suitable pension, in acknowledgment of which, Sandy annually presented him with a fine walking-stick, formed and polished by his pocket-knife. Sandy was an honourable man, and was unwilling to accept of the Duke's gratuity so long as he, even in his old age, could earn a shilling for himself. None thought it below them to enter Sandy's domicile, however humble and sparingly furnished, for it was no small treat to spend an hour in intercourse with him. He was a descendant of the Fergussons of Threerigs, who suffered much in the times of persecution; their history is given in the twenty-sixth chapter of this volume.

On one occasion when the Duke, on his annual visit to Drumlanrig, entered, according to his wont, the cottage of Sandy to inquire after the worthy man and hear the news, Sandy addressed him in a somewhat lugubrious tone, "I hae nae staff for ye the year, my lord." "Indeed, Sandy, and how comes that?" "Oo, ye see, y'er grace, the woodman wadna let me gang in amang the hazels and cut a bit ryse, and sae I am stir disappointit." "Well, Sandy," replied his lordship, "from henceforth I grant you liberty to go anywhere among my woods to cut a staff, or what may suit you." And accordingly Sandy used the privilege. It is now long since Sandy died, at nearly the age of ninety years. He was a man much esteemed by all, and it was with much regret that we parted with him.

It was Sandy who communicated to the writer of this the account of the rescue at Enterkin pass, as detailed in the beginning of this chapter. It differs from the account as given by some of the historians of that period, and it would appear to have been a totally different rescue. It has long appeared to the compiler of these notices that there were more rescues than one in that dangerous pass; and this is just what might be expected, considering that this was one of the chief thoroughfares from the middle ward of Nithsdale to Edinburgh, along which the dragoons were in the habit of conducting, on special occasions, their prisoners to the capital. We regard Sandy's account, which he gathered from the old people in his youth, as tantamount to a proof of this. The breastwork is still to be seen on the opposite slope from which the men fired.

CHAP. 5.—The traditions of which this chapter is composed were communicated by Mr Alexander M'Millan, who was orginally a miner in the village of Wanlockhead, and latterly a schoolmaster at Menackbridge, in the parish of Sanquhar. Sandy, as he was familiarly named, was a person of sound judgment, and well instructed in various branches. Though at first a humble lead miner, he rose above his fellows, and by dint of self-application he soon secured for himself a praiseworthy standing. He was judicious, clear-sighted, and had withal a strong taste for covenanting lore. He was extensively acquainted throughout the middle and upper parts of Nithsdale. He made it his endeavour to collect all the floating traditions of the persecuting times wherever he went. He was most painstaking and assiduous in gathering and sifting every traditionary tale that came in his way; nothing was taken on trust, so far as diligent investigation could go. His extensive acquaintance with the families all around the wide district gave him ample opportunity of acquiring the most satisfactory information. He traversed the parishes of Closeburn, Kirkmahoe, Penpont, Keir, Morton, Minihive, Durisdeer, and Sanquhar, gathering everywhere, as the bee gathers the sweets from the opening flowers.

He had an excellent memory, and had the power of writing down with facility what he heard, and what his memory contained.

He was a truly Christian man, and possessed of a devout and ardent spirit, and deeply imbued with the principles of the Covenanters, for the which he would have rejoiced to suffer any day in the Grassmarket.

Sandy was one of the most extensive contributors to this volume of the Covenanters, and though he made no pretensions to anything like composition, yet he expressed himself clearly and unmistakably. The compiler was under no small obligation to Sandy, and he was one for whom he had a strong regard as a really religious man, and a member of his congregation. He emigrated to the western world, where he died.

CHAP. 6.—The contents of this chapter were communicated by a lineal descendant of the famous Andrew Clark of Auchengrouch, in the moors of Sanquhar. Andrew had nine sons, all devoted to the covenanting interest, and of whom one died a martyr in Edinburgh, as given in the traditions. Andrew lived near the mouth of the famous Glendyne, that remarkable defile in the mountains a little to the east of the town of Sanquhar, the hiding place of the venerable Peden. At Auchengrouch there was lately found a silver spoon with the initials A. C. carved on it. He has several descendants in this locality, who cherish his memory, and who hold the traditions of their ancestor.

CHAP. 7.—The first two traditions in this chapter were communicated by the truthful Robert Laing, of Glenmuirshaw, and latterly of Lady-

2 a

burn, in the same wild solitude, "lengthened and deep," and who con·sequently lived not far from the place where the two Richards resided.

The story of William Moffat was contributed by Mr Alexander Brown, bookseller and grocer in Sanquhar, who received it from a shepherd, familiarly denominated Wattie Wight, who lived in the wilds between Elvanfoot and Moffat. Wattie was well acquainted with the traditions current in that lonely district, and he was a man of good talent and Christian probity.

Mr Brown was a truly pious man, and he traversed the moors and glens of the more solitary parts of the country with books and other articles stowed into a little cart which carried both him and his goods, as he was partially lame of foot. He was a man well-known and highly esteemed, and always received a cordial welcome from the people of the moorlands, at whose hearths he both heard and retailed many things. His sojournings now are over, and he has slept a number of years in his quiet grave in the lone churchyard of Crawford or Leadhills.

CHAP. 8.—The incidents contained in this chapter were gathered by Alexander M'Millan, already mentioned. He was well acquainted with all the places above named, and no less so with some of the descendants of the worthies here noticed. The information was therefore derived from the most trustworthy sources.

CHAP. 9.—The names Harkness and Clark are still common in Middle Nithsdale—the joint testimony of the three men mentioned in this chapter, and who were executed in Edinburgh, is here copied from Wodrow.

The tradition of The Babe of Tweedhope-foot, whose name was Welsh, was given by Mr Ramage, a worthy man, who lived on the Clyde, near Abington, and who was well acquainted with the districts of Upper Tweeddale.

CHAP. 10.—The contents of this chapter were contributed by Mr John Johnston, of Benston, near Cumnock, where he still resides. He is now a man far advanced in life, a regularly educated man, and of strict integrity and truthfulness. He has kept a school for many years in Benston. He is thoroughly acquainted with the localities in the upper parts of Nithsdale, and the higher districts of Ayrshire. A vast quantity of the material composing these traditions was collected by him in all the places around his residence. He knew all the farmers, and shepherds, and householders scattered throughout the moorlands and wild places of the uplands, where boundaries of Galloway and Ayrshire meet, and in whose seclusions, as Wodrow the historian remarks, the covenanting witnesses concealed themselves; and it is worthy of remark, that in these solitudes there still linger a greater number of the descendants of the worthies who suffered in those trying times, than in almost any other locality. On this account, Mr Johnston had a rich field before him, and faithfully and painfully did he glean it.

Mr Johnston is a native of the parish of Sanquhar. His father, an extensive farmer, was at one time provost of the burgh of Sanquhar, and Mr Johnston himself was a bailie of the same. The nobleman on whose lands Mr Johnston resides, took special notice of him, and granted him several privileges, which his worthy character seemed to claim at his hand. A better hand than Mr Johnston could scarcely be desired for the purpose for which the writer of these pages needed him. He is a strong advocate of the temperance cause, and his lectures on that subject, in various parts of the country, were for a series of years greatly appreciated.

CHAP. 11.—The story of Thomas Brown of Auchlochan was transmitted from Lesmahagow by a most worthy man, a descendant of the family. Few places within the wide field of covenanting interest were more renowned than the district around Lesmahagow, and the traditions concerning its worthies are numerous.

The tradition respecting honest John Gill was from a granddaughter of the same family, and from whom the writer of these traditions is descended, who was familiar with the story from his boyhood.

CHAP. 12.—The traditions in this chapter were given by Mr Johnston above-mentioned. We may here notice a somewhat curious incident. Of the vast number of traditions which were collected from all quarters of the spacious field of persecuting violence, in the south-west of Scotland, and other places far beyond, not one was ever objected to on the supposed score of untruthfulness but one, and this has a reference to the Hugh Hutcheson noticed in the above chapter. A certain lady who, it seems, did not deem her descent from a covenanting ancestry to be a matter peculiarly honourable, said one day to the writer of these sketches, in a somewhat tart and petulant tone, "You state in your book of the Covenanters that Hugh Hutcheson, of Daljig, in Ayrshire, was an ancestor of mine. Now, I venture to affirm that there never was such a person as Hugh Hutcheson on the farm of Daljig, as you mention, and therefore the whole story is a fabrication." The writer of this was consequently taken aback, and wist not well what to say considering that —perhaps there might possibly be some mistake. A communication was instantly despatched to Mr Johnston, from whom the tradition had been received, informing him of the circumstance, and expressing sorrow if any inaccuracy had been committed. Mr Johnston was somewhat put about, although he knew the veritable source from which the story had been obtained, and he determined to probe the matter to the bottom. Accordingly, he set out one day to Dumfries House, the residence of the Marquis of Bute, near Cumnock, of whose estate in that part of Ayrshire the farm of Daljig is a portion. He told his tale to the factor or chamberlain, and requested a sight of the rental-books of the estate as far back as the year 1685. This was readily granted, and there was found, as Mr Johnston affirms, "Hugh Hutcheson, tenant in Daljig, in the year 1685." This was the very year that was wanted, and thus the tradition was verified —at least as far as the name, and place, and date were concerned—and so the matter was put to rest.

Inaccuracies there may be, and this in the transmission through sundry generations, is what is to be expected more or less, but only in minor details; but even in these, when comparing several concurrent testimonies in reference to the same story, we find the divergency so slight as not to be worth the mentioning.

CHAP. 13.—The contents of this chapter are from our trustworthy and able friend, Mr Johnston, who continues the story of Hugh Hutcheson.

CHAP. 14.—The story of John Paterson of Penyvenie, is from Mr Johnston, and obtained by him from a veritable source. This will plainly appear from the following incident:—When the story first appeared in print, a gentleman of the name of Paterson called one day on Mr Johnston, and bluntly put the following question:—"Where did the compiler of these traditions get the story of John Paterson of Penyvenie?" This coming so soon after the unceremonious denial by the lady respecting Hugh Hutcheson somewhat disconcerted our friend, thinking that, perhaps, the gentleman was going to meet the story with a similar denial, and he replied firmly, "It was from me that the author got the tradition, and I got it from a reliable quarter." "Well, then," said the gentleman, "I have to say that I have heard my aged grandmother rehearse the identical tradition twenty times without the slightest variation." Mr Johnston was relieved, and probably related the anecdote of the lady and Hugh Hutcheson. The gentleman was connected with the Patersons, and gloried in the relationship.

CHAP. 15.—The traditions here narrated are also from Mr Johnston, and are all equally reliable.

CHAP. 16.—The interesting narrative given in this chapter was communicated by Mr Brown, merchant in Douglas, Lanarkshire. The subject of the tradition was an ancestor of his own. a great-grandfather, for whose memory he cherished the warmest regard. The tradition came down in the line of the family, and was regarded as a precious heirloom, as Mr Brown was a great-grandchild, and was in every respect worthy of his honoured ancestor. He was one of the founders of the congregation that was formed in Douglas, in connection with what was termed the Burgher denomination ; and as an ornament to the Christian profession he exerted himself in promoting the interests of religion in the district. We knew him well.

Douglasdale was famous in the persecuting times. Mr Peden often visited the district, and many a witness was found among its populace who maintained the truth in the times of defection. The tales of the persecuted were long preserved and widely circulated in that sweet vale.

CHAP. 17.—The contents of this chapter were contributed by the Rev. John Jamieson, Douglas, Lanarkshire. He was a person fully competent to judge of the relevancy of a tradition, and he well knew the veritable sources from which he drew them—his mind being full of antiquarian lore, was ready to lay hold of any ancient story that might happen to descend in a straight line from the covenanting days. He has wonned in Douglas for upwards of forty years, and is therefore well acquainted with the history and character of almost all the families in the wide locality in which the wanderers of the covenant sojourned for many a weary year. His contributions to this volume are therefore of no small value.

We learn from an old manuscript, dated 1691, that James Gavin, after his return from Barbadoes, had several children baptized in the following order :— A son, 2nd of November 1694 ; a daughter, 1698 ; and a son in 1700. His wife's name was Helen Dickson. He had a relative of the name of William Gavin, perhaps a brother, who lived in Cleuchbrae, a small farmhouse at the mouth of the gorge of Earnsallach, and this may account for his being in hiding there when Claverhouse caught him. The house of Cleuchbrae was swept away many years ago.

James Gavin's house, which he built in Douglas after his return from banishment, is a structure that may yet stand for generations to come. It has shared a better fate than the lonely hut of the "godly carrier" of Priesthill, near Muirkirk, which is now cleared to its foundations, and is no more to be seen in its place on the solitary heath.

CHAP. 18.—The incidents composing this chapter were furnished by the painstaking Alexander Macmillan. He received them from the lineal descendants of the persons referred to, of whom three remained at the time—namely, one great grandchild, and two great-great-grandchildren.

CHAP. 19.—It is to Mary Wilson, the wife of the venerable Adam Good, who lived with her husband on the banks of the romantic Afton, a stream that flows into the river Nith at the village of New Cumnock, in Ayrshire, that we owe the contents of this chapter. Mary, who survived her worthy husband many a year, was full of the traditionary lore of the district in which she so long resided ; and she could detail with accuracy the thrilling incidents relative to the persecuted people who took refuge among the glens and thickets around the place of her residence. She was a woman of a good mind, and of a decidedly pious disposition. The Afton and its vicinity were places of resort to the houseless wanderers, who, for conscience' sake, left all behind them, and betook themselves to the wilds, and hence the traditions of their sufferings were permanent in that locality where Mary lived.

The line of the Afton was the great route of the soldiers between Carsphairn and the Water of Ken, in Galloway, to the higher parts of Ayrshire, and hence visits from the military were very common in that district, and on this account many painful occurrences befell.

CHAP. 20—The first part of this chapter is from the Mary Wilson above-mentioned. The middle part of it is from Mrs Osburn, Sanquhar, a lineal descendant of the Kers here mentioned, and with whose history she was fully acquainted. The latter parts are from two persons worthy of all credit, Robert Braidfoot, dyker, a truly religious and intelligent man, and Alexander M'Millan.

CHAP. 21.—This chapter is from Mary Wilson, and as her husband, Adam Good, was a grandson of the William Good here mentioned, it may not be improper to state here a few things concerning him. He was a member of what is now called the North United Presbyterian congregation of Sanquhar. He was a truly devout man, and of a very venerable aspect, being a person of a sedate turn of mind, and an exact expression in his look and demeanour of an old Scottish Covenanter. He was far advanced in life when we knew him, but we esteemed him as a father for his kindliness and homeliness of manners. As a shepherd, he lived much in the wilds, and was familiar with the stories of the covenanting times, which in his younger days were fresh in the popular mind. He was only one generation removed from the persecuting era. He was a person of great truthfulness and probity.

CHAP. 22.—This chapter is from the Rev. John Jamieson of Douglas, and narrated with all the truthfulness and accuracy peculiar to him.

CHAP. 23.—The curious story of the curate of Kirkbride, in Nithsdale, was told to the writer, with all its circumstances, by the late George Howat, nailer, in Sanquhar, an elder of the North United Presbyterian congregation in that town. He was a man of uncommon sagacity and penetration—of a clear head and a devout heart. The expulsion of the curate here mentioned must have been at the end of the persecution, instead of the beginning, as related in the tradition. After the Revolution, the great body of the curates retained their situations by a professed submission to presbytery, and were all admitted by the General Assembly. There were, however, some who were so obnoxious to the people, that their longer incumbency could not be tolerated, and hence the people in some of the parishes rose in a body, and forcibly expelled, with little ceremony, the intruders, whose presence was so hateful to them as the keenest instigators of the persecution. Patrick Walker, who mentions sundry cases of expulsion, and who was present at some of them, such as Dumfries, Peebles, Traquair, and other places, says that all was done in decency, and no violence was offered to any person. This, however, might not be the case in every instance, and so the parishioners of Kirkbride might, in what Walker terms the interregnum, feel themselves justified in expressing their sentiments somewhat roughly. The custom of the times, then, guarantees the truth of the tradition.

The tradition of the two pious families in the end of the chapter is from the venerable Dr Purdie.

CHAP. 24.—Communicated by Alexander M'Millan.

CHAP. 25.—This, in all its details, by Alexander M'Millan.

CHAP. 26.—This from Alexander Fergusson of Drumlanrig Holm, a descendant of the family of Threerigs, already mentioned. Sandy retained pertinaciously the traditions of his ancestry, and only one generation or so stept in between him and them. The accuracy of Sandy was great, and he sometimes wrote out traditions in full, and recited them word for word with great animation.

CHAP. 27.—A popular tradition, well known in Sanquhar and its vicinity. George Hair, a worthy man, and who died in advanced age many years ago, was connected with the family mentioned in this chapter. He may have been a lineal descendant, but of this we are not sure. The Hair were at one time numerous about Sanquhar, and not a few of them reside in the locality still. George had in his possession an old sword, handed down from the covenanting times, which he kept with peculiar sacredness. We have seen the implement, but what is now become of it we are not aware. It belonged originally to Patrick Laing of Blagannoch, whose story follows in the twenty-ninth chapter.

CHAP. 28.—Communicated by Alexander M'Millan, well acquainted with district around Closeburn Mill. The heights of Closeburn were much resorted to by the persecuted people of the middle district of Nithsdale.

CHAP. 29.—The narrator of this interesting story was Robert Laing of Thornhill, whom we have formerly noticed. Robert was descended of the same family, and felt peculiarly proud of his connection with the renowned Patrick Laing, at once the patriot and the Christian.

CHAP. 30.—Of the traditions given in this chapter, the first was from Robert Laing, the shepherd in Glenmuirshaw, already noticed; the second from a descendant of Andrew Clark in Auchengronch, in the moors of Sanquhar; and the third from an intelligent and pious shepherd of the name of James Scott of Fingland, in the wilds between Sanquhar and Muirkirk.

CHAP. 31.—This chapter, in all its interesting and accurate details, was communicated by the Rev. John Jamieson of Douglas.

CHAP. 32.—The story of James Gourlay is from the Rev. Andrew Scott, of the United Presbyterian Church, Cambusnethan, where he has ministered in the gospel for upwards of fifty years. He was thoroughly conversant with the whole traditionary details.

CHAP. 33.—The contents of this chapter were communicated by Bailie Johnston of Benston, already mentioned.

CHAP. 34.—For the story of Andrew Hamilton of Drumclog, we have the authority of the Rev. Dr Meikle of Beith, who has ministered there for between fifty and sixty years, and who is well known in the Churches as an author. Hamilton of Drumclog was an ancestor.

CHAP. 35.—The first tradition here is from Bailie Johnston of Benston, and the second from the Rev. John Jamieson of Douglas.

CHAP. 36.—The remarkably interesting story of Andrew Forsyth is from Bailie Johnston, whose accuracy of detail is so characteristic of him.

CHAP. 37.—The Gordons of Earlston are historical persons. The discovery of the hiding-place in the woods of Airds was incidentally made by Quintin Forester of Dalry. The information otherwise was given, so far as we can remember, by Mr James M'Queen, an aged Christian man in the village of Dalry, who cherished warmly the memory of the martyrs of Galloway.

The story of the white flag was from our indefatigable friend Alexander M'Millan.

CHAP. 38.—The contents of this chapter were from William Laing, a shepherd in Carsphairn. He was a son of Robert Laing of Thornhill. William was an ardent admirer of the heroes of the Covenant, and gathered among the wilds of Carsphairn the floating traditions of those "killing times," and rehearsed them with great zest. Carsphairn being the parish of the famous John Semple. a great host of worthies were reared under his ministry, the memorial of whose sufferings in that locality is warmly cherished and firmly retained by the older inhabitants. Garryhorn, in Carsphairn, being the seat of Lag, of persecuting memory, on this account, much suffering was inflicted by him throughout that wild district, and more especially when we reflect that two garrisons were stationed in that parish.

CHAP. 39.—The touching story of John M'Clement was contributed by Lilie Johnston.

CHAP. 40.—Bell of Whiteside is a historical character, around which these traditions cluster.

CHAP. 41.—The stories of the Howies of Lochgoin are from personal investigation, on a visit to the seat of the ancient family of Howie, by the writer many years ago. Lochgoin is a most interesting spot, and situated afar in the desert, and which was consequently a favourable place of resort to the wanderers of the Covenant.

CHAP. 42.—From William Laing, the shepherd at Garryhorn, in Carsphairn.

CHAP. 43.—Contributed by Alexander M'Millan.

CHAP. 44.—The first of the anecdotes composing this chapter were taken by the writer from the mouth of a venerable Christian lady, who was a descendant of the Willisons here mentioned. Mrs Proudfoot, the name of the lady, lived latterly at a place called Whitehill, in the vicinity of Sanquhar. She was a rare Christian woman, a mother in Israel, one among a thousand. The memory of her suffering ancestors was very dea to her. She lived to about the age of ninety years. Her death-bed experience was of the most edifying description. Considering her extreme age, and the long time since she died, it is probable that she received the traditions here given from persons who were acquainted with the sufferers themselves. The other two were communicated by Alexander M'Millan and William Laing respectively.

CHAP. 45.—The story of M'Haffie here given was from Bailie Johnston, and the other, Clark of Brandleys, was from a lineal descendant of the Clarks of Auchengrouch.

CHAP. 46.—This chapter is from Alexander M'Millan.

CHAP. 47.—The particulars in this chapter were collected by Bailie Johnston, who was fully acquainted with the traditions current in the defile of the Afton, and in the wild uplands of Ayrshire and Nithsdale, in the immediate vicinity of which he has resided for the most part of his life.

CHAP. 48.—The first of the anecdotes in this chapter is partially related by Wodrow. The second is well known in the valley of the Scar, and the third was communicated by the lineal descendants of the worthy to whom it refers.

CHAP. 49.—As is stated at the end of this chapter, "the preceding anecdotes were communicated by a great-granddaughter, Sarah Millar, in Dunscore, who received them from her mother, Margaret Colvin, and Margaret had them from the mouth of Sarah Gibson, the person to whom, along with her husband, the traditions refer."

CHAP. 50.—These traditions, regarding the curate of Closeburn and Samuel Clark of Galloway, were all popularly known in the localities where the two persons respectively resided; they have been gleaned by truthful persons familiar with the facts here narrated.

In addition to the notes which have now been appended to these traditions, a few remarks may, in conclusion, be made.

And here it is to be noticed, that the people among whom the traditions mainly circulated lived from generation to generation in the same locali-

ties, without almost any intermixture of strangers till within the last half
century or so.   On this account the old stories relative to the covenanting
times were kept entire among the original population, Now, however,
the case is different, for the inhabitants in the rural districts are gradually
removed from their ancient settlements, and a single glen, which we could
name, which two generations ago contained nearly five hundred people,
can now scarcely number fifty persons, and this is a mere specimen; hence,
had these traditions not been collected at the very time they were, they
could not have been gathered now ; the present generation furnishes no
host of traditionary men such as wonned among us a few years ago.

Another thing to be noticed is, that these anecdotes and traditions are
in keeping with the character of the times to which they refer.   In reading them we seem to be pursuing a series of incidents belonging to authen-
tic history.   There is nothing extravagant, nothing out of the way in their
details; they seem to be sober truth, and even more so than many things
related in the accredited page of history itself.   There are, to be sure,
wonderful interferences ; but then this is exactly what was to be expected
in answer to the prayers of godly men suffering in the blessed cause of the
Redeemer ; but there is nothing which lays claim to the miraculous.

And it may farther be noticed that the compiler of these traditions gives
them honestly as he received them.   He adds nothing to them, and
takes nothing from them.   It is true they were all re-written from the
papers handed in to him.   They were thrown into his own words, and
underwent a kind of translation, so that the composition is entirely his
own, with the exception of one or two communications from clerical
friends, and even these, in some instances, required a gentle alteration in
the wording.   The collectors of these traditions were generally persons
who were unaccustomed to write, and hence the necessity of a literary
revision ; but though this was the case, the literal meaning of every
sentence is strictly and religiously adhered to.

The writer, however, reserved to himself the liberty of gathering in
collateral circumstances, either from history or otherwise, for the purpose
of elucidation, or as confirmatory of the veritableness of a particular
tradition.   His extensive knowledge of the whole district in which he has
resided for upwards of forty years, and his acquaintance with its entire
topography in hill and dale and moorland, has enabled him to depict as
he saw necessary any particular scene on the wide and wild field of that
martyrland which he has so often traversed.   He has searched out the
hiding places of these saintly wanderers of the Covenant among the bushy
ravines, and in the deep glens in the bosom of the lonely hills.   He has
visited spots where the martyrs fell in the bleak and solitary wilds, and
he has contemplated the ruined huts that erst were the abodes of God-
fearing families, who bore witness to the truth in those dreary times, when
the best blood of the land flowed warm on the purple heath.   In his composing these traditions, therefore, he has made use of things borrowed
from all this, if not for the purpose of embellishment, at least for the purpose of entertainment and instruction.

The compiler has not the slightest doubt in his own mind that every one
of these traditions is true, only they are given merely as traditions, and,
accordingly, every reader is at liberty to estimate them simply as the
matter appears to himself.

R. S.

SANQUHAR, January, 1867.

www.ingramcontent.com/pod-product-compliance
Lightning Source LLC
Chambersburg PA
CBHW031814270326
41932CB00008B/415